The Gospel of
Sri Ramakrishna

VOLUME-I

THE GOSPEL OF SRI RAMAKRISHNA

VOLUME I

Original in Bengali
By
MAHENDRANATH GUPTA (M)
(A Direct Disciple of Sri Ramakrishna)

TRANSLATION BY

SWAMI NIKHILANANDA

Sri Ramakrishna Math
MYLAPORE MADRAS 600 004

Published by
ⓒThe President
Sri Ramakrishna Math
Mylapore, Madras-600 004

ISBN 81-7120-109-1

Printed in India at
Sri Ramakrishna Math Press
Mylapore, Madras-600 004

FOREWORD

IN THE HISTORY of the arts genius is a thing of very rare occurrence. Rarer still, however, are the competent reporters and recorders of that genius. The world has had many hundreds of admirable poets and philosophers; but of these hundreds only a very few have had the fortune to attract a Boswell or an Eckermann.

When we leave the field of art for that of spiritual religion, the scarcity of competent reporters becomes even more strongly marked. Of the day-to-day life of the great theocentric saints and contemplatives we know, in the great majority of cases, nothing whatever. Many, it is true, have recorded their doctrines in writing, and a few, such as St Augustine, Suso and St Teresa, have left us autobiographies of the greatest value. But all doctrinal writing is in some measure formal and impersonal, while the autobiographer tends to omit what he regards as trifling matters and suffers from the further disadvantage of being unable to say how he strikes other people and in what way he affects their lives. Moreover, most saints have left neither writings nor self-portraits, and for a knowledge of their lives, their characters and their teachings, we are forced to rely upon the records made by their disciples who, in most cases, have proved themselves singularly incompetent as reporters and biographers. Hence the special interest attaching to this enormously detailed account of the daily life and conversations of Sri Ramakrishna.

"M", as the author modestly styles himself, was peculiarly qualified for his task. To a reverent love for his master, to a deep and experiential knowledge of that master's teaching, he added a prodigious memory for the small happenings of each day and a happy gift for recording them in an interesting and realistic way. Making good use of his natural gifts and of the circumstances in which he found himself, "M" produced a book unique, so far as my knowledge goes, in the literature of hagiography. No other saint has had so able and indefatigable a Boswell. Never have the small events of a contemplative's daily life been described with such a wealth of intimate detail. Never have the casual and unstudied utterances of a great religious teacher been set down with so minute a fidelity. To Western readers, it is true, this fidelity and this wealth of detail are sometimes a trifle disconcerting; for the social, religious and intellectual frames of reference within which Sri Ramakrishna did his thinking and expressed his feelings were entirely Indian. But after the first few surprises and bewilderments, we begin to find something peculiarly stimulating and instructive about the very strangeness and, to our eyes, the eccentricity of the man revealed to us in "M's" narrative. What a scholastic philosopher would call the "accidents" of Ramakrishna's life were intensely Hindu and therefore, so far as we in the West are concerned, unfamiliar and hard to understand; its "essence", however, was intensely mystical and therefore universal. To read through these conversations in which mystical doctrine alternates with an unfamiliar kind of humour, and where discussions of the oddest aspects of Hindu mythology give place to the most profound and subtle utterances about the nature of Ultimate Reality, is in itself a liberal education in humility, tolerance and suspense of judgment. We must be grateful to the translator for his excellent version of a book so curious and delightful as a biographical document, so precious, at the same time, for what it teaches us of the life of the spirit.

ALDOUS HUXLEY

PREFACE

The Gospel of Sri Ramakrishna is the English translation of the *Sri Sri Ramakrishna Kathāmrita*, the conversations of Sri Ramakrishna with his disciples, devotees, and visitors, recorded by Mahendranath Gupta, who wrote the book under the pseudonym of "M." The conversations in Bengali fill five volumes, the first of which was published in 1897 and the last shortly after M.'s death in 1932. Sri Ramakrishna Math, Madras, has published in two volumes an English translation of selected chapters from the monumental Bengali work. I have consulted these while preparing my translation.

M., one of the intimate disciples of Sri Ramakrishna, was present during all the conversations recorded in the main body of the book and noted them down in his diary. They therefore have the value of almost stenographic records. In Appendix A are given several conversations which took place in the absence of M., but of which he received a first-hand record from persons concerned. The conversations will bring before the reader's mind an intimate picture of the Master's eventful life from March 1882 to April 24, 1886, only a few months before his passing away. During this period he came in contact chiefly with English-educated Bengalis; from among them he selected his disciples and the bearers of his message, and with them he shared his rich spiritual experiences.

I have made a literal translation, omitting only a few pages of no particular interest to English-speaking readers. Often literary grace has been sacrificed for the sake of literal translation. No translation can do full justice to the original. This difficulty is all the more felt in the present work, whose contents are of a deep mystical nature and describe the inner experiences of a great seer. Human language is an altogether inadequate vehicle to express supersensuous perception. Sri Ramakrishna was almost illiterate. He never clothed his thoughts in formal language. His words sought to convey his direct realization of Truth. His conversation was in a village patois. Therein lies its charm. In order to explain to his listeners an abstruse philosophy, he, like Christ before him, used with telling effect homely parables and illustrations, culled from his observation of the daily life around him.

The reader will find mentioned in this work many visions and experiences that fall outside the ken of physical science and even psychology. With the development of modern knowledge the border line between the natural and the supernatural is ever shifting its position. Genuine mystical experiences are not as suspect now as they were half a century ago. The words of Sri Ramakrishna have already exerted a tremendous influence in the land of his birth. Savants of Europe have found in his words the ring of universal truth.

But these words were not the product of intellectual cogitation; they were rooted in direct experience. Hence, to students of religion, psychology, and physical science, these experiences of the Master are of immense value for the understanding of religious phenomena in general. No doubt Sri Rama-krishna was a Hindu of the Hindus; yet his experiences transcended the limits of the dogmas and creeds of Hinduism. Mystics of religions other than Hinduism will find in Sri Ramakrishna's experiences a corroboration of the experiences of their own prophets and seers. And this is very important today for the resuscitation of religious values. The sceptical reader may pass by the supernatural experiences; he will yet find in the book enough mate-rial to provoke his serious thought and solve many of his spiritual problems.

There are repetitions of teachings and parables in the book. I have kept them purposely. They have their charm and usefulness, repeated as they were in different settings. Repetition is unavoidable in a work of this kind. In the first place, different seekers come to a religious teacher with questions of more or less identical nature; hence the answers will be of more or less identical pattern. Besides, religious teachers of all times and climes have tried, by means of repetition, to hammer truths into the stony soil of the recalcitrant human mind. Finally, repetition does not seem tedious if the ideas repeated are dear to a man's heart.

I have thought it necessary to write a rather lengthy Introduction to the book. In it I have given the biography of the Master, descriptions of people who came in contact with him, short explanations of several systems of Indian religious thought intimately connected with Sri Ramakrishna's life, and other relevant matters which, I hope, will enable the reader better to understand and appreciate the unusual contents of this book. It is particu-larly important that the Western reader, unacquainted with Hindu religious thought, should first read carefully the introductory chapter, in order that he may fully enjoy these conversations. Many Indian terms and names have been retained in the book for want of suitable English equivalents. Their meaning is given either in the Glossary or in the foot-notes. The Glossary also gives explanations of a number of expressions unfamiliar to Western readers. The diacritical marks are explained under Notes on Pronunciation.

In the Introduction I have drawn much material from the *Life of Sri Ramakrishna*, published by the Advaita Ashrama, Mayavati, India. I have also consulted the excellent article on Sri Ramakrishna by Swami Nirveda-nanda, in the second volume of the *Cultural Heritage of India*.

The book contains many songs sung either by the Master or by the devotees. These form an important feature of the spiritual tradition of Bengal and were for the most part written by men of mystical experience. For giving the songs their present form I am grateful to Mr. John Moffitt, Jr.

In the preparation of this manuscript I have received ungrudging help from several friends. Miss Margaret Woodrow Wilson and Mr. Joseph Campbell have worked hard in editing my translation. Mrs. Elizabeth David-son has typed, more than once, the entire manuscript and rendered other valuable help. Mr. Aldous Huxley has laid me under a debt of gratitude by writing the Foreword. I sincerely thank them all.

In the spiritual firmament Sri Ramakrishna is a waxing crescent. Within one hundred years of his birth and fifty years of his death his message has spread across land and sea. Romain Rolland has described him as the fulfilment of the spiritual aspirations of the three hundred millions of Hindus for the last two thousand years. Mahatma Gandhi has written: "His life enables us to see God face to face. . . . Ramakrishna was a living embodiment of godliness." He is being recognized as a compeer of Krishna, Buddha, and Christ.

The life and teachings of Sri Ramakrishna have redirected the thoughts of the denationalized Hindus to the spiritual ideals of their forefathers. During the latter part of the nineteenth century his was the time-honoured role of the Saviour of the Eternal Religion of the Hindus. His teachings played an important part in liberalizing the minds of orthodox pundits and hermits. Even now he is the silent force that is moulding the spiritual destiny of India. His great disciple, Swami Vivekananda, was the first Hindu missionary to preach the message of Indian culture to the enlightened minds of Europe and America. The full consequence of Swami Vivekananda's work is still in the womb of the future.

May this translation of the first book of its kind in the religious history of the world, being the record of the direct words of a prophet, help stricken humanity to come nearer to the Eternal Verity of life and remove dissension and quarrel from among the different faiths! May it enable seekers of Truth to grasp the subtle laws of the supersensuous realm, and unfold before man's restricted vision the spiritual foundation of the universe, the unity of existence, and the divinity of the soul!

NIKHILANANDA

New York
Sri Ramakrishna's Birthday
February 1942

NOTES ON THE PRONUNCIATION OF
TRANSLITERATED SANSKRIT AND
VERNACULAR WORDS

a	has the sound of			o in *come*.
ā	"	"	"	" *a* in *far*.
e, ē	"	"	"	" *e* in *bed*.[1]
i	"	"	"	" *i* in *kin*.
ī	"	"	"	" *ee* in *feel*.
o	"	"	"	" *o* in *note*.
u	"	"	"	" *u* in *full*.

ai, ay	has the sound of			*oy* in *boy*.
ch	"	"	"	" *ch* in *church*.
ḍ	"	"	"	" hard *d* in English.
g	"	"	"	" *g* in *god*.
jn	"	"	"	" hard *gy* in English.[2]
ś	"	"	"	" *sh* in English.

sh may be pronounced as in English.

t and d are soft as in French.

Other consonants appearing in the transliterations are pronounced as in English.

Diacritical marks have generally not been used in proper names belonging to recent times or in modern and well-known geographical names.

Sri Ramakrishna is pronounced in Bengal as Śrī Rāmkrishna.

[1] Final *e* in proper names is mute.

[2] Jnāna is pronounced as *gyāna*.

PREFACE TO THE SEVENTH EDITION

The 7th edition of the *Gospel of Sri Ramakrishna* is being published in two volumes for the convenience of readers. It is thought that it will be more handy in the present form, and in these days of high cost of books, the intending purchasers will find it convenient to buy it in two parts.

It has been brought to our notice that many superficial readers of the Gospel have been taken aback by the strong criticism of what is called 'Woman and Gold' by the Great Master. The correction is given in the explanatory foot-note on page 82. But to highlight the explanation, we are referring to it again in this Preface. "Woman and Gold" is the English translation for *Kaminikanchana*, which is an idiomatic expression that will convey to an Indian mind only the meaning of 'lust and lucre' or 'sexuality and greed'. It does not imply any disrespect for woman but only a criticism of man's sexually oriented outlook on her. To make the matter clear and bring the idea into greater prominence, we quote below the foot-note on page 82 of the book mentioned above:

> "The term "woman and gold", which has been used throughout in a collective sense, occurs again and again in the teachings of Sri Ramakrishna to designate the chief impediments to spiritual progress. This favourite expression of the Master, *"Kamini Kanchan"*, has often been misconstrued. By it he meant only "lust and greed", the baneful influence of which retards the aspirant's spiritual growth. He used the word *"kamini"*, or "woman", as a concrete term for the sex instinct when addressing his men devotees. He advised women, on the other hand, to shun 'man'. *"Kanchan"*, or "gold", symbolizes greed, which is the other obstacle to spiritual life."

Sri Ramakrishna never taught his disciples to hate any woman, or womanhood in general. This can be seen clearly by going through all his teachings under this head and judging them collectively. The Master looked on all women as so many images of the Divine Mother of the Universe. He paid the highest homage to womanhood by accepting a woman as his guide while practising the very profound spiritual disciplines of Tantra. His wife, known and revered as the Holy Mother, was his constant companion and first disciple. At the end of his spiritual practice, he literally worshipped his wife as the embodiment of the Goddess Kali, the Divine Mother. After his passing away the Holy Mother became the spiritual guide not only of a large number of householders, but also of many monastic members of the Ramakrishna Order.

Publisher

The recorder of the Gospel

MAHENDRANATH GUPTA

In the life of the great Saviours and Prophets of the world it is often found that they are accompanied by souls of high spiritual potency who play a conspicuous part in the furtherance of their Master's mission. They become so integral a part of the life and work of these great ones that posterity can think of them only in mutual association. Such is the case with Sri Ramakrishna and M., whose diary has come to be known to the world as the *Gospel of Sri Ramakrishna* in English and as *Sri Ramakrishna Kathamrita* in the original Bengali version.

Sri Mahendra Nath Gupta*, familiary known to the readers of the Gospel by his pen name M., and to the devotees as Master Mahashay, was born on the 14th of July, 1854 as the son of Madhusudan Gupta, an officer of the Calcutta High Court, and his wife, Swarnamayi Devi. He had a brilliant scholastic career at Hare School and the Presidency College at Calcutta. The range of his studies included the best that both occidental and oriental learning had to offer. English literature, history, economics, western philosophy and law on the one hand, and Sanskrit literature and grammar, Darsanas, Puranas, Smritis, Jainism, Buddhism, astrology and Ayurveda on the other — were the subjects in which he attained considerable proficiency.

He was an educationist all his life both in a spiritual and in a secular sense. After he passed out of College, he took up work as headmaster in a number of schools in succession —

* In the body of the *Gospel* he also appears under the assumed names of Mani, Mohini Mohun and Master (meaning school teacher). He is familiarly referred to in the circle of Sri Ramakrishna's devotees as Master Mahashay. Readers who want to know in greater detail about M. and his teachings may read the book ' *M* '—*the Apostle and the Evangelist* by Swami Nityatmananda. It is in five parts and records the conversations of M. in his later years with devotees, more or less on the lines of the Gospel.

Narail High School, City School, Ripon College School, Metro-
politan School, Aryan School, Oriental School, Oriental Seminary
and Model School. The causes of his migration from school to
school were that he could not get on with some of the manage-
ments on grounds of principles and that often his spiritual mood
drew him away to places of pilgrimage for long periods. He
worked with some of the most noted public men of the time like
Iswar Chandra Vidyasagar and Surendranath Banerjee. The
latter appointed him as a professor in the City and Ripon Colleges
where he taught subjects like English, philosophy, history and
economics. In his later days he took over the Morton School,
and he spent his time in the staircase room of the third floor of
it, administering the school and preaching the message of the
Master. He was much respected in educational circles where
he was usually referred to as Rector Mahashay. A teacher who
had worked under him writes thus in warm appreciation of his
teaching methods : " Only when I worked with him in school
could I appreciate what a great educationist he was. He would
come down to the level of his students when teaching, though he
himself was so learned, so talented. Ordinarily teachers confine
their instruction to what is given in books without much thought
as to whether the student can accept it or not. But M., would
first of all gauge how much the student could take in and by
what means. He would employ aids to teaching like maps,
pictures and diagrams, so that his students could learn by seeing.
Thirty years ago (from 1953) when the question of imparting
education through the medium of the mother tongue was being
discussed, M. had already employed Bengali as the medium of
instruction in the Morton School." [1]

Imparting secular education was, however, only his
profession ; his main concern was with the spiritual regeneration
of man — a calling for which Destiny seems to have chosen him.
From his childhood he was deeply pious, and he used to be moved
very much by Sadhus, temples and Durga Puja celebrations.
The piety and eloquence of the great Brahmo leader of the times,
Keshab Chander Sen, elicited a powerful response from the

1. *M — The Apostle and the Evangelist* by Swami Nityatmananda Part I. P. 15.

impressionable mind of Mahendra Nath, as it did in the case of many an idealistic young man of Calcutta, and prepared him to receive the great Light that was to dawn on him with the coming of Sri Ramakrishna into his life.

This epoch-making event of his life came about in a very strange way. M. belonged to a joint family with several collateral members. Some ten years after he began his career as an educationist, bitter quarrels broke out among the members of the family, driving the sensitive M. to despair and utter despondency. He lost all interest in life and left home one night to go into the wide world with the idea of ending his life. At dead of night he took rest in his sister's house at Baranagar, and in the morning, accompanied by a nephew Siddheswar, he wandered from one garden to another in Calcutta until Siddheswar brought him to the Temple Garden of Dakshineswar where Sri Ramakrishna was then living. After spending some time in the beautiful rose gardens there, he was directed to the room of the Paramahamsa, where the eventful meeting of the Master and the disciple took place on a blessed evening (the exact date is not on record) on a Sunday in March 1882. As regards what took place on the occasion, the reader is referred to the opening section of the first chapter of the *Gospel*.

The Master, who divined the mood of desperation in M, his resolve to take leave of this ' play-field of deception ', put new faith and hope into him by his gracious words of assurance : " God forbid ! Why should you take leave of this world ? Do you not feel blessed by discovering your Guru ? By His grace, what is beyond all imagination or dreams can be easily achieved ! " At these words the clouds of despair moved away from the horizon of M.'s mind, and the sunshine of a new hope revealed to him fresh vistas of meaning in life. Referring to this phase of his life, M. used to say, " Behold ! where is the resolve to end life, and where, the discovery of God ! That is, sorrow should be looked upon as a friend of man. God is all good."[2]

After this re-settlement, M's life revolved around the Master, though he continued his professional work as an educationist.

2. *Ibid* P. 33.

During all holidays, including Sundays, he spent his time at Dakshineswar in the Master's company, and at times extended his stay to several days.

It did not take much time for M. to become very intimate with the Master, or for the Master to recognise in this disciple a divinely commissioned partner in the fulfilment of his spiritual mission. When M. was reading out the Chaitanya Bhagavata, the Master discovered that he had been, in a previous birth, a disciple and companion of the great Vaishnava Teacher, Sri Chaitanya Mahaprabhu, and the Master even saw him ' with his naked eye' participating in the ecstatic mass-singing of the Lord's name under the leadership of that Divine personality. So the Master told M, " You are my own, of the same substance — as the father and the son," indicating thereby that M. was one of the chosen few and a part and parcel of his Divine mission.

There was an urge in M. to abandon the household life and become a Sannyasin. When he communicated this idea to the Master, he forbade him saying, " Mother has told me that you have to do a little of Her work — you will have to teach Bhagavata, the word of God to humanity. The Mother keeps a Bhagavata Pandit with a bondage in the world ! " [3]

An appropriate allusion indeed ! Bhagavata, the great scripture that has given the word of Sri Krishna to mankind, was composed by the Sage Vyasa under similar circumstances. When caught up in a mood of depression like that of M, Vyasa was advised by the sage Narada that he would gain peace of mind only on composing a work exclusively devoted to the depiction of the Lord's glorious attributes and His teachings on Knowledge and Devotion, and the result was that the world got from Vyasa the invaluable gift of the Bhagavata Purana depicting the life and teachings of Sri Krishna. From the mental depression of the modern Vyasa, the world has obtained the Kathamrita — the *Gospel of Sri Ramakrishna.*

Sri Ramakrishna was a teacher for both the Orders of mankind, Sannyasins and householders. His own life offered an ideal example for both, and he left behind disciples who followed the

3. *Ibid* P. 36.

highest traditions he had set in respect of both these ways of life. M., along with Nag Mahashay, exemplified how a householder can rise to the highest level of sagehood. M. was married to Nikunja Devi, a distant relative of Keshab Chander Sen, even when he was reading at College, and he had four children, two sons and two daughters. The responsibility of the family, no doubt, made him dependent on his professional income, but the great devotee that he was, he never compromised with ideals and principles for this reason. Once when he was working as the headmaster in a school managed by the great Vidyasagar, the results of the school at the public examination happened to be rather poor, and Vidyasagar attributed it to M's pre-occupation with the Master and his consequent failure to attend adequately to the school work. M. at once resigned his post without any thought of the morrow. Within a fortnight the family was in poverty, and M. was one day pacing up and down the verandah of his house, musing how he would feed his children the next day. Just then a man came with a letter addressed to 'Mahendra Babu', and on opening it, M. found that it was a letter from his friend Sri Surendra Nath Banerjee, asking whether he would like to take up a professorship in the Ripon College. In this way three or four times he gave up the job that gave him the wherewithal to support the family, either for upholding principles or for practising spiritual Sadhanas in holy places, without any consideration of the possible dire worldly consequences ; but he was always able to get over these difficulties somehow, and the interests of his family never suffered. In spite of his disregard for worldly goods, he was, towards the latter part of his life, in a fairly flourishing condition as the proprietor of the Morton School which he developed into a noted educational institution in the city. The Lord has said in the Bhagavad Gita that in the case of those who think of nothing except Him, He Himself would take up all their material and spiritual responsibilities. M. was an example of the truth of the Lord's promise.

Though his children received proper attention from him, his real family, both during the Master's life-time and after, consisted of saints, devotees, Sannyasins and spiritual aspirants,

ii

His life exemplifies the Master's teaching that an ideal house-holder must be like a good maid-servant of a family, loving and caring properly for the children of the house, but knowing always that her real home and children are elsewhere. During the Master's life-time he spent all his Sundays and other holidays with him and his devotees, and besides listening to the holy talks and devotional music, practised meditation both on the Personal and the Impersonal aspects of God under the direct guidance of the Master. In the pages of the Gospel the reader gets a picture of M.'s spiritual relationship with the Master — how from a hazy belief in the Impersonal God of the Brahmos, he was step by step brought to accept both Personality and Impersonality as the two aspects of the same Non-dual Being, how he was con-vinced of the manifestation of that Being as Gods, Goddesses and as Incarnations, and how he was established in a life that was both of a Jnani and of a Bhakta. This Jnani-Bhakta out-look and way of living became so dominant a feature of his life that Swami Raghavananda, who was very closely associated with him during his last six years, remarks : " Among those who lived with M. in latter days, some felt that he always lived in this constant and conscious union with God even with open eyes (i.e., even in waking consciousness)." [4]

Besides undergoing spiritual disciplines at the feet of the Master, M. used to go to holy places during the Master's life-time itself and afterwards too as a part of his Sadhana. He was one of the earliest of the disciples to visit Kamarpukur, the birth-place of the Master, in the latter's life-time itself ; for he wished to practise contemplation on the Master's early life in its true original setting. His experience there is described as follows by Swami Nityatmananda : " By the grace of the Master, he saw the entire Kamarpukur as a holy place bathed in an effulgent Light. Trees and creepers, beasts and birds and men — all were made of effulgence. So he prostrated to all on the road. He saw a tom cat, which appeared to him luminous with the Light of Con-sciousness. Immediately he fell to the ground and saluted it " [5]

4. Swami Raghavananda's article on M. in *Prabuddha Bharata* vol. XXXVII. P. 442.
5. *M — The Apostle and the Evangelist* by Swami Nityatmananda vol. 1 P. 40.

He had similar experience in Dakshineswar also. At the instance of the Master he also visited Puri, and in the words of Swami Nityatmananda, "with indomitable courage, M. embraced the image of Jagannath out of season."[6]

The life of Sadhana and holy association that he started on at the feet of the Master, he continued all through his life. He has for this reason been most appropriately described as a Grihastha-Sannyasi (householder-Sannyasin). Though he was forbidden by the Master to become a Sannyasin, his reverence for the Sannyasa ideal was whole-hearted and was without any reservation. So after Sri Ramakrishna's passing away, while several of the Master's householder devotees considered the young Sannyasin disciples of the Master as inexperienced and inconsequential, M. stood by them with the firm faith that the Master's life and message were going to be perpetuated only through them. Swami Vivekananda wrote from America in a letter to the inmates of the Math : " When Sri Thakur (Master) left the body, every one gave us up as a few unripe urchins. But M. and a few others did not leave us in the lurch. We cannot repay our debt to them."[7]

M. spent his weekends and holidays with the monastic brethren who, after the Master's demise, had formed themselves into an Order with a Math at Baranagore, and participated in the intense life of devotion and meditation that they followed. At other times he would retire to Dakshineswar or some garden in the city and spend several days in spiritual practice taking simple self-cooked food. In order to feel that he was one with all mankind he often used to go out of his home at dead of night, and like a wandering Sannyasin, sleep with the waifs on some open verandah or footpath on the road.

After the Master's demise, M. went on pilgrimage several times. He visited Banaras, Vrindavan, Ayodhya and other places. At Banaras he visited the famous Trailinga Swami and fed him with sweets, and he had long conversations with Swami

---

6. The idea is this : according to the rules of the temple the worshippers could touch the mage only in certain months of the year. M., overpowered by devotion, broke these rules in the complete forgetfulness of spiritual absorption and touched the Deity during the forbidden time.

7. Swami Raghavananda's article on M. in *Prabuddha Bharata* vol. XXX P. 442.

Bhaskarananda, one of the noted saintly and scholarly Sannyasins of the time.   In 1912 he went with the Holy Mother to Banaras, and spent about a year in the company of Sannyasins at Banaras, Vrindavan, Hardwar, Hrishikesh and Swargashram.   But he returned to Calcutta, as that city offered him the unique opportunity of associating himself with the places hallowed by the Master in his life-time.   Afterwards he does not seem to have gone to any far-off place, but stayed on in his room in the Morton School carrying on his spiritual ministry, speaking on the Master and his teachings to the large number of people who flocked to him after having read his famous *Kathamrita* known to English readers as *The Gospel of Sri Ramakrishna.*

This brings us to the circumstances that led to the writing and publication of this monumental work, which has made M. one of the immortals in hagiographic literature.   While many educated people heard Sri Ramakrishna's talks, it was given to this illustrious personage alone to leave a graphic and exact account of them for posterity, with details like date, hour, place, names and particulars about participants.   Humanity owes this great book to the ingrained habit of diary-keeping with which M. was endowed. Even as a boy of about thirteen, while he was a student in the 3rd class of the Hare School, he was in the habit of keeping a diary.   " Today on rising," he wrote in his diary, " I greeted my father and mother, prostrating on the ground before them " [8]. At another place he wrote, " Today, while on my way to school, I visited, as usual, the temples of Kali, the Mother at Tharitharia, and of Mother Sitala, and paid my obeisance to them."   About twenty-five years after, when he met the Great Master in the spring of 1882, it was the same instinct of a born diary-writer that made him begin his book, ' unique in the literature of hagiography ', with the memorable words : " When hearing the name of Hari or Rama once, you shed tears and your hair stands on end, then you may know for certain that you do not have to perform devotions such as Sandhya any more."

In addition to this instinct for diary-keeping, M. had great endowments contributing to success in this line.   Writes Swami

---

8. Swami Nityatmananda's ' *M — The Apostle and the Evangelist* ' Part I. P 29.

Nityatmananda who lived in close association with M., in his book entitled *M-The Apostle and Evangelist* : " M.'s prodigious memory combined with his extraordinary power of imagination completely annihilated the distance of time and place for him. Even after the lapse of half a century he could always visualise vividly, scenes from the life of Sri Ramakrishna. Superb too was his power to portray pictures by words."

Besides the prompting of his inherent instinct, the main inducement for M. to keep this diary of his experiences at Dakshineswar was his desire to provide himself with a means for living in holy company at all times. Being a school teacher, he could be with the Master only on Sundays and other holidays, and it was on his diary that he depended for ' holy company ' on other days. The devotional scriptures like the Bhagavata say that holy company is the first and most important means for the generation and growth of devotion. For, in such company man could hear talks on spiritual matters and listen to the glorification of Divine attributes, charged with the fervour and conviction emanating from the hearts of great lovers of God. Such company is therefore the one certain means through which Sraddha (Faith), Rati (attachment to God) and Bhakti (loving devotion) are generated. The diary of his visits to Dakshineswar provided M. with material for re-living, through reading and contemplation, the holy company he had had earlier, even on days when he was not able to visit Dakshineswar. The wealth of details and the vivid description of men and things in the midst of which the sublime conversations are set, provide excellent material to re-live those experiences for any one with imaginative powers. It was observed by M.'s disciples and admirers that in later life also whenever he was free or alone, he would be pouring over his diary, transporting himself on the wings of imagination to the glorious days he spent at the feet of the Master.

During the Master's life-time M. does not seem to have revealed the contents of his diary to any one. There is an unconfirmed tradition that when the Master saw him taking notes, he expressed apprehension at the possibility of his utilising these to publicise him like Keshab Sen ; for the Great Master was so

full of the spirit of renunciation and humility that he disliked
being lionised. It must be for this reason that no one knew
about this precious diary of M. for a decade until he brought
out selections from it as a pamphlet in English in 1897 with the
Holy Mother's blessings and permission. The Holy Mother,
being very much pleased to hear parts of the diary read to her
in Bengali, wrote to M. : " When I heard the *Kathamrita*,
(Bengali name of the book) I felt as if it was he, the Master, who
was saying all that." [9]

The two pamphlets in English entitled the *Gospel of Sri
Ramakrishna* appeared in October and November 1897. They
drew the spontaneous acclamation of Swami Vivekananda, who
wrote on 24th November of that year from Dehra Dun to M. :
" Many many thanks for your second leaflet. It is indeed wonderful. The move is quite original, and never was the life of a Great
Teacher brought before the public untarnished by the writer's
mind, as you are doing. The language also is beyond all praise, —
so fresh, so pointed, and withal so plain and easy. I cannot
express in adequate terms how I have enjoyed them. I am really
in a transport when I read them. Strange, isn't it ? Our Teacher
and Lord was so original, and each one of us will have to be
original or nothing. I now understand why none of us attempted
His life before. It has been reserved for you, this great work.
He is with you evidently." [10]

And Swamiji added a post script to the letter : " Socratic
dialogues are Plato all over — you are entirely hidden. Moreover, the dramatic part is infinitely beautiful. Everybody likes
it — here or in the West." Indeed, in order to be unknown,
Mahendranath had used the pen-name M., under which the book
has been appearing till now. But so great a book cannot remain
obscure for long, nor can its author remain unrecognised by the
large public in these modern times. M. and his book came to be
widely known very soon and to meet the growing demand, a
full-sized book, Vol. I of the *Gospel*, translated by the author
himself, was published in 1907 by the Brahmavadin Office, Madras.

9. *Ibid* Part I. P 37.
10. *Vedanta Kesari* Vol. XIX P. 141. Also given in the first edition of the *Gospel* published
from Ramakrishna Math, Madras in 1911.

A second edition of it, revised by the author, was brought out by the Ramakrishna Math, Madras in December 1911, and subsequently a second part, containing new chapters from the original Bengali, was published by the same Math in 1922. The full English translation of the *Gospel* by Swami Nikhilananda appeared first in 1942.

In Bengali the book is published in five volumes, the first part having appeared in 1902 and the others in 1905, 1907, 1910 and 1932 respectively.

It looks as if M. was brought to the world by the Great Master to record his words and transmit them to posterity. Swami Sivananda, a direct disciple of the Master and the second President of the Ramakrishna Math and Mission, says on this topic : " Whenever there was an interesting talk, the Master would call Master Mahashay if he was not in the room, and then draw his attention to the holy words spoken. We did not know then why the Master did so. Now we can realise that this action of the Master had an important significance, for it was reserved for Master Mahashay to give to the world at large the sayings of the Master."[11] Thanks to M., we get, unlike in the case of the great teachers of the past, a faithful record with date, time, exact report of conversations, description of concerned men and places, references to contemporary events and personalities and a hundred other details for the last four years of the Master's life (1882-'86), so that no one can doubt the historicity of the Master and his teachings at any time in the future.

M. was in every respect a true missionary of Sri Ramakrishna right from his first acquaintance with him in 1882. As a school teacher, it was a practice with him to direct to the Master such of his students as had a true spiritual disposition. Though himself prohibited by the Master to take to monastic life, he encouraged all spiritually inclined young men he came across in his later life to join the monastic Order. Swami Vijnanananda, a direct Sannyasin disciple of the Master and a President of the Ramakrishna Order, once remarked to M. : " By enquiry I have come to the conclusion that eighty percent and more of the

11. *Vedanta Kesari* Vol. XIX P 141.

Sannyasins have embraced the monastic life after reading the *Kathamrita* and coming in contact with you." [12]

In 1905 he retired from the active life of a Professor and devoted his remaining twenty-seven years exclusively to the preaching of the life and message of the Great Master. He bought the Morton Institution from its original proprietors and shifted it to a commodious four-storeyed house at 50 Amherst Street, where it flourished under his management as one of the most efficient educational institutions in Calcutta. He generally occupied a staircase room at the top of it, cooking his own meal which consisted only of milk and rice without variation, and attended to all his personal needs himself. His dress also was the simplest possible. It was his conviction that limitation of personal wants to the minimum is an important aid to holy living. About one hour in the morning he would spend in inspecting the classes of the school, and then retire to his staircase room to pour over his diary and live in the divine atmosphere of the earthly days of the Great Master, unless devotees and admirers had already gathered in his room seeking his holy company.

In appearance, M. looked a Vedic Rishi. Tall and stately in bearing, he had a strong and well-built body, an unusually broad chest, high forehead and arms extending to the knees. His complexion was fair and his prominent eyes were always tinged with the expression of the divine love that filled his heart. Adorned with a silvery beard that flowed luxuriantly down his chest, and a shining face radiating the serenity and gravity of holiness, M. was as imposing and majestic as he was handsome and engaging in appearance. Humorous, sweet-tongued and eloquent when situations required, this great Maharishi of our age lived only to sing the glory of Sri Ramakrishna day and night. Though a very well versed scholar in the Upanishads, Gita and the philosophies of the East and the West, all his discussions and teachings found their culmination in the life and the message of Sri Ramakrishna, in which he found the real explanation and illustration of all the scriptures. Both consciously and uncon-

---

12. *M — The Apostle and the Evangelist* by Swami Nityatmananda Part I, P 37.

sciously, he was the teacher of the *Kathamrita* — the nectarine words of the Great Master.

Though a much-sought-after spiritual guide, an educationist of repute, and a contemporary and close associate of illustrious personages like Sri Ramakrishna, Swami Vivekananda, Keshab Chander Sen and Iswar Chander Vidyasagar, he was always moved by the noble humanity of a lover of God, which consists in respecting the personalities of all as receptacles of the Divine Spirit. So he taught without the consciousness of a teacher, and no bar of superiority stood in the way of his doing the humblest service to his students and devotees. " He was a commission of love," writes his close devotee, Swami Raghavananda, " and yet his soft and sweet words would pierce the stoniest heart, make the worldly-minded weep and repent and turn Godwards."[13]

As time went on and the number of devotees increased, the staircase room and terrace of the 3rd floor of the Morton Institution became a veritable Naimisaranya of modern times, resounding during all hours of the day, and sometimes of night, too, with the word of God coming from the Rishi-like face of M. addressed to the eager God-seekers sitting around. To the devotees who helped him in preparing the text of the *Gospel,* he would dictate the conversations of the Master in a meditative mood, referring now and then to his diary. At times in the stillness of midnight he would awaken a nearby devotee and tell him : " Let us listen to the words of the Master in the depths of the night as he explains the truth of the Pranava."[14] Swami Raghavananda, an intimate devotee of M., writes as follows about these devotional sittings : " In the sweet and warm months of April and May, sitting under the canopy of heaven on the roof-garden of 50 Amherst Street, surrounded by shrubs and plants, himself sitting in their midst like a Rishi of old, the stars and planets in their courses beckoning us to things infinite and sublime, he would speak to us of the mysteries of God and His love and of the yearning that would rise in the human heart to solve the Eternal Riddle, as exemplified in the life of his Master.

13. *Prabuddha Bharata* Vol. XXXVII P 499.
14. *Vedanta Kesari* XIX P. 142.

The mind, melting under the influence of his soft sweet words of light, would almost transcend the frontiers of limited existence and dare to peep into the infinite. He himself would take the influence of the setting and say, 'What a blessed privilege it is to sit in such a setting (pointing to the starry heavens), in the company of the devotees discoursing on God and His love !' These unforgettable scenes will long remain imprinted on the minds of his hearers." [15]

About twenty-seven years of his life he spent in this way in the heart of the great city of Calcutta, radiating the Master's thoughts and ideals to countless devotees who flocked to him, and to still larger numbers who read his *Kathamrita*, the last part of which he had completed before June 1932 and given to the press. And miraculously, as it were, his end also came immediately after he had completed his life's mission. About three months earlier he had come to stay at his home at 13/2 Gurdasprasad Chaudhuary Lane at Thakur Bari, where the Holy Mother had herself installed the Master and where His regular worship was being conducted for the previous 40 years. The night of 3rd June being the Phalaharini Kali Pooja day, M. had sent his devotees who used to keep company with him, to attend the special worship at Belur Math at night. After attending the service at the home shrine, he went through the proof of the *Kathamrita* for an hour. Suddenly he got a severe attack of neuralgic pain, from which he had been suffering now and then of late. Before 6˙a.m. in the early hours of the 4th June 1932, he passed away, fully conscious and chanting : 'Gurudeva-Ma, Kole toole na-o ! O Master ! O Mother ! Take me in your arms !'

Sri Ramakrishna Math,
Madras,
March 1974.   **SWAMI TAPASYANANDA**

15. *Prabuddha Bharata* Vol XXXVII P 497.

CONTENTS

planes of the mind — Indescribability of highest plane — The "wicked
I" — The "servant I" — The "ego of a devotee" — Path of bhakti is
easy — Premā-bhakti — Purity of heart — God's grace is the ultimate
help — Vision of Divine Mother — God's nature like that of a child —
Two ways of God-realization — Constant practice urged.

Master's attitude toward the wicked — Paths of knowledge and devo-
tion — God's name destroys sin — Mystery of God's ways — God-vision
through pure love — Guru and Ishta — Life of worldliness — Master's
love for Rakhal — Adhar's first visit — Much reasoning condemned —
Master's birthday celebration — Warning to monks — Incarnation of
God — Master's different spiritual moods — Efficacy of earnest japa —
Dogmatism condemned — Parable of the elephant and the blind men —
Illustration of the ocean and the ice — Rakhal's inborn spiritual nature
— Parable of the homā bird — Renunciation, false and true — Nature
of the ever-perfect — Master's experiences in samādhi.

Narendra's music — True renunciation — Study of scriptures for the
beginner — Trailanga Swami and Bhaskarananda — The seer of God
transcends good and evil — Seeing God in everything — Characteristics
of divine love — Indications of God-realization — Efficacy of japa and
prayer — Parable of the two friends — Zeal for the Lord destroys
sin — Traits of bound souls — Two classes of perfect souls — The ever-
perfect — Worldly people lack perseverance — Master consoles a
bereaved father — Difficulty of overcoming vanity — Different manifestations of divine power — Free will and God's will.

Master's visit to Brāhmo festival — Love and prayer — How to lead a
householder's life — Why there is evil in the world — The need of a
guru — Personal God and formless Deity — God's true nature cannot
be described — The three gunas — Parable of the three robbers — Why
temples are holy — How to spiritualize the passions — Responsibility for
sins — Brāhmo worship — Religious quarrels condemned — Single-
minded devotion — Spiritual inspiration comes from God — Ramchandra
Dutta — Story of Harischandra — Story of Uddhava — Characteristics
of divine love — Parable of the three friends.

Master's attitude toward young disciples — His yearning for Narendra — Reminiscences of his God-intoxicated state — Reassurance to the
devotees — Parable of the tigress — Parable of the false ascetic — The
world is a dream — Parable of the farmer — Law of karma — Different
kinds of samādhi — Paths of love and knowledge — Master's exhortation
to a devotee to go forward — Reminiscences of boyhood — Earnestness
in spiritual life extolled — Different manifestations of God — Traits of
a true devotee — Seven planes of the Vedas — Advice to householders
— Problem of good and evil — Result of yoga through bhakti — Different classes of men.

Contents

Contents

INTRODUCTION

INTRODUCTION

By Swami Nikhilananda

SRI RAMAKRISHNA, the God-man of modern India, was born at Kāmārpukur. This village in the Hooghly District preserved during the last century the idyllic simplicity of the rural areas of Bengal. Situated far from the railway, it was untouched by the glamour of the city. It contained rice-fields, tall palms, royal banyans, a few lakes, and two cremation grounds. South of the village a stream took its leisurely course. A mango orchard dedicated by a neighbouring zemindar to the public use was frequented by the boys for their noonday sports. A highway passed through the village to the great temple of Jagannāth at Puri, and the villagers, most of whom were farmers and craftsmen, entertained many passing holy men and pilgrims. The dull round of the rural life was broken by lively festivals, the observance of sacred days, religious singing, and other innocent pleasures.

About his parents Sri Ramakrishna once said: "My mother was the personification of rectitude and gentleness. She did not know much about the ways of the world; innocent of the art of concealment, she would say what was in her mind. People loved her for her open-heartedness. My father, an orthodox brāhmin, never accepted gifts from the śudras. He spent much of his time in worship and meditation, and in repeating God's name and chanting His glories. Whenever in his daily prayers he invoked the Goddess Gāyatri, his chest flushed and tears rolled down his cheeks. He spent his leisure hours making garlands for the Family Deity, Raghuvir."

Khudiram Chattopadhyaya and Chandra Devi, the parents of Sri Ramakrishna, were married in 1799. At that time Khudiram was living in his ancestral village of Dereypore, not far from Kāmārpukur. Their first son, Ramkumar, was born in 1805, and their first daughter, Katyayani, in 1810. In 1814 Khudiram was ordered by his landlord to bear false witness in court against a neighbour. When he refused to do so, the landlord brought a false case against him and deprived him of his ancestral property. Thus dispossessed, he arrived, at the invitation of another landlord, in the quiet village of Kāmārpukur, where he was given a dwelling and about an acre of fertile land. The crops from this little property were enough to meet his family's simple needs. Here he lived in simplicity, dignity, and contentment.

Ten years after his coming to Kāmārpukur, Khudiram made a pilgrimage on foot to Rāmeśwar, at the southern extremity of India. Two years later was born his second son, whom he named Rameswar. Again in 1835, at the age of sixty, he made a pilgrimage, this time to Gayā. Here, from ancient times, Hindus have come from the four corners of India to discharge their

3

duties to their departed ancestors by offering them food and drink at the sacred footprint of the Lord Vishnu. At this holy place Khudiram had a dream in which the Lord Vishnu promised to be born as his son. And Chandra Devi, too, in front of the Śiva temple at Kāmārpukur, had a vision indicating the birth of a divine child. Upon his return the husband found that she had conceived.

It was on February 18, 1836, that the child, to be known afterwards as Ramakrishna, was born. In memory of the dream at Gayā he was given the name of Gadadhar, the "Bearer of the Mace", an epithet of Vishnu. Three years later a little sister was born.

BOYHOOD

Gadadhar grew up into a healthy and restless boy, full of fun and sweet mischief. He was intelligent and precocious and endowed with a prodigious memory. On his father's lap he learnt by heart the names of his ancestors and the hymns to the gods and goddesses, and at the village school he was taught to read and write. But his greatest delight was to listen to recitations of stories from Hindu mythology and the epics. These he would afterwards recount from memory, to the great joy of the villagers. Painting he enjoyed; the art of moulding images of the gods and goddesses he learnt from the potters. But arithmetic was his great aversion.

At the age of six or seven Gadadhar had his first experience of spiritual ecstasy. One day in June or July, when he was walking along a narrow path between paddy-fields, eating the puffed rice that he carried in a basket, he looked up at the sky and saw a beautiful, dark thunder-cloud. As it spread, rapidly enveloping the whole sky, a flight of snow-white cranes passed in front of it. The beauty of the contrast overwhelmed the boy. He fell to the ground, unconscious, and the puffed rice went in all directions. Some villagers found him and carried him home in their arms. Gadadhar said later that in that state he had experienced an indescribable joy.

Gadadhar was seven years old when his father died. This incident profoundly affected him. For the first time the boy realized that life on earth was impermanent. Unobserved by others, he began to slip into the mango orchard or into one of the cremation grounds, and he spent hours absorbed in his own thoughts. He also became more helpful to his mother in the discharge of her household duties. He gave more attention to reading and hearing the religious stories recorded in the Purānas. And he became interested in the wandering monks and pious pilgrims who would stop at Kāmārpukur on their way to Puri. These holy men, the custodians of India's spiritual heritage and the living witnesses of the ideal of renunciation of the world and all-absorbing love of God, entertained the little boy with stories from the Hindu epics, stories of saints and prophets, and also stories of their own adventures. He, on his part, fetched their water and fuel and served them in various ways. Meanwhile, he was observing their meditation and worship.

At the age of nine Gadadhar was invested with the sacred thread. This ceremony conferred upon him the privileges of his brāhmin lineage, including the worship of the Family Deity, Raghuvir, and imposed upon him the many strict disciplines of a brāhmin's life. During the ceremony of investiture he shocked his relatives by accepting a meal cooked by his nurse, a śudra woman. His father would never have dreamt of doing such a thing. But in a playful mood Gadadhar had once promised this woman that he would eat her food, and now he fulfilled his plighted word. The woman had piety and religious sincerity, and these were more important to the boy than the conventions of society.

Gadadhar was now permitted to worship Raghuvir. Thus began his first training in meditation. He so gave his heart and soul to the worship that the stone image very soon appeared to him as the living Lord of the Universe. His tendency to lose himself in contemplation was first noticed at this time. Behind his boyish light-heartedness was seen a deepening of his spiritual nature.

About this time, on the Śivarātri night, consecrated to the worship of Śiva, a dramatic performance was arranged. The principal actor, who was to play the part of Śiva, suddenly fell ill, and Gadadhar was persuaded to act in his place. While friends were dressing him for the role of Śiva— smearing his body with ashes, matting his locks, placing a trident in his hand and a string of rudrāksha beads around his neck—the boy appeared to become absent-minded. He approached the stage with slow and measured step, supported by his friends. He looked the living image of Śiva. The audience loudly applauded what it took to be his skill as an actor, but it was soon discovered that he was really lost in meditation. His countenance was radiant and tears flowed from his eyes. He was lost to the outer world. The effect of this scene on the audience was tremendous. The people felt blessed as by a vision of Śiva Himself. The performance had to be stopped, and the boy's mood lasted till the following morning.

Gadadhar himself now organized a dramatic company with his young friends. The stage was set in the mango orchard. The themes were selected from the stories of the *Rāmāyana* and the *Mahābhārata*. Gadadhar knew by heart almost all the roles, having heard them from professional actors. His favourite theme was the Vrindāvan episode of Krishna's life, depicting those exquisite love-stories of Krishna and the milkmaids and the cowherd boys. Gadadhar would play the parts of Rādhā or Krishna and would often lose himself in the character he was portraying. His natural feminine grace heightened the dramatic effect. The mango orchard would ring with the loud kirtan of the boys. Lost in song and merry-making, Gadadhar became indifferent to the routine of school.

In 1849 Ramkumar, the eldest son, went to Calcutta to improve the financial condition of the family.

Gadadhar was on the threshold of youth. He had become the pet of the women of the village. They loved to hear him talk, sing, or recite from the holy books. They enjoyed his knack of imitating voices. Their woman's instinct recognized the innate purity and guilelessness of this boy of clear skin, flowing hair, beaming eyes, smiling face, and inexhaustible fun. The pious elderly women looked upon him as Gopāla, the Baby Krishna, and the

younger ones saw in him the youthful Krishna of Vrindāvan. He himself
so idealized the love of the gopis for Krishna that he sometimes yearned to
be born as a woman, if he must be born again, in order to be able to love
Sri Krishna with all his heart and soul.

COMING TO CALCUTTA

At the age of sixteen Gadadhar was summoned to Calcutta by his elder
brother Ramkumar, who wished assistance in his priestly duties. Ramkumar
had opened a Sanskrit academy to supplement his income, and it was his
intention gradually to turn his younger brother's mind to education. Gadadhar applied himself heart and soul to his new duty as family priest to a
number of Calcutta families. His worship was very different from that of
the professional priests. He spent hours decorating the images and singing
hymns and devotional songs; he performed with love the other duties of his
office. People were impressed with his ardour. But to his studies he paid
scant attention.

Ramkumar did not at first oppose the ways of his temperamental brother.
He wanted Gadadhar to become used to the conditions of city life. But one
day he decided to warn the boy about his indifference to the world. After
all, in the near future Gadadhar must, as a householder, earn his livelihood
through the performance of his brāhminical duties; and these required a
thorough knowledge of Hindu law, astrology, and kindred subjects. He
gently admonished Gadadhar and asked him to pay more attention to his
studies. But the boy replied spiritedly: "Brother, what shall I do with a mere
bread-winning education? I would rather acquire that wisdom which will
illumine my heart and give me satisfaction for ever."

BREAD-WINNING EDUCATION

The anguish of the inner soul of India found expression through these
passionate words of the young Gadadhar. For what did his unsophisticated
eyes see around him in Calcutta, at that time the metropolis of India and
the centre of modern culture and learning? Greed and lust held sway in
the higher levels of society, and the occasional religious practices were merely
outer forms from which the soul had long ago departed. Gadadhar had never
seen anything like this at Kāmārpukur among the simple and pious villagers.
The sādhus and wandering monks whom he had served in his boyhood had
revealed to him an altogether different India. He had been impressed by
their devotion and purity, their self-control and renunciation. He had learnt
from them and from his own intuition that the ideal of life as taught by
the ancient sages of India was the realization of God.

When Ramkumar reprimanded Gadadhar for neglecting a "bread-winning education", the inner voice of the boy reminded him that the legacy of
his ancestors—the legacy of Rāmā, Krishna, Buddha, Śankara, Rāmānuja,
Chaitanya—was not worldly security but the Knowledge of God. And these
noble sages were the true representatives of Hindu society. Each of them
was seated, as it were, on the crest of the wave that followed each successive
trough in the tumultuous course of Indian national life. All demonstrated

that the life current of India is spirituality. This truth was revealed to Gadadhar through that inner vision which scans past and future in one sweep, unobstructed by the barriers of time and space. But he was unaware of the history of the profound change that had taken place in the land of his birth during the previous one hundred years.

Hindu society during the eighteenth century had been passing through a period of decadence. It was the twilight of the Mussalmān rule. There were anarchy and confusion in all spheres. Superstitious practices dominated the religious life of the people. Rites and rituals passed for the essence of spirituality. Greedy priests became the custodians of heaven. True philosophy was supplanted by dogmatic opinions. The pundits took delight in vain polemics.

In 1757 English traders laid the foundation of British rule in India. Gradually the Government was systematized and lawlessness suppressed. The Hindus were much impressed by the military power and political acumen of the new rulers. In the wake of the merchants came the English educators, and social reformers, and Christian missionaries—all bearing a culture completely alien to the Hindu mind. In different parts of the country educational institutions were set up and Christian churches established. Hindu young men were offered the heady wine of the Western culture of the late eighteenth and early nineteenth centuries, and they drank it to the very dregs.

The first effect of the draught on the educated Hindus was a complete effacement from their minds of the time-honoured beliefs and traditions of Hindu society. They came to believe that there was no transcendental Truth. The world perceived by the senses was all that existed. God and religion were illusions of the untutored mind. True knowledge could be derived only from the analysis of nature. So atheism and agnosticism became the fashion of the day. The youth of India, taught in English schools, took malicious delight in openly breaking the customs and traditions of their society. They would do away with the caste-system and remove the discriminatory laws about food. Social reform, the spread of secular education, widow remarriage, abolition of early marriage—they considered these the panacea for the degenerate condition of Hindu society.

The Christian missionaries gave the finishing touch to the process of transformation. They ridiculed as relics of a barbarous age the images and rituals of the Hindu religion. They tried to persuade India that the teachings of her saints and seers were the cause of her downfall, that her Vedas, Purānas, and other scriptures were filled with superstition. Christianity, they maintained, had given the white races position and power in this world and assurance of happiness in the next; therefore Christianity was the best of all religions. Many intelligent young Hindus became converted. The man in the street was confused. The majority of the educated grew materialistic in their mental outlook. Everyone living near Calcutta or the other strongholds of Western culture, even those who attempted to cling to the orthodox traditions of Hindu society, became infected by the new uncertainties and the new beliefs.

But the soul of India was to be resuscitated through a spiritual awakening. We hear the first call of this renascence in the spirited retort of the young Gadadhar: "Brother, what shall I do with a mere bread-winning education?"

Ramkumar could hardly understand the import of his young brother's reply. He described in bright colours the happy and easy life of scholars in Calcutta society. But Gadadhar intuitively felt that the scholars, to use one of his own vivid illustrations, were like so many vultures, soaring high on the wings of their uninspired intellect, with their eyes fixed on the charnel-pit of greed and lust. So he stood firm and Ramkumar had to give way.

KĀLI TEMPLE AT DAKSHINESWAR

At that time there lived in Calcutta a rich widow named Rāni Rasmani, belonging to the śudra caste, and known far and wide not only for her business ability, courage, and intelligence, but also for her largeness of heart, piety, and devotion to God. She was assisted in the management of her vast property by her son-in-law Mathur Mohan.

In 1847 the Rāni purchased twenty acres of land at Dakshineswar, a village about four miles north of Calcutta. Here she created a temple garden and constructed several temples. Her Ishta, or Chosen Ideal, was the Divine Mother, Kāli.

The temple garden stands directly on the east bank of the Ganges. The northern section of the land and a portion to the east contain an orchard, flower gardens, and two small reservoirs. The southern section is paved with brick and mortar. The visitor arriving by boat ascends the steps of an imposing bathing-ghāt which leads to the chāndni, a roofed terrace, on either side of which stand in a row six temples of Śiva. East of the terrace and the Śiva temples is a large court, paved, rectangular in shape, and running north and south. Two temples stand in the centre of this court, the larger one, to the south and facing south, being dedicated to Kāli, and the smaller one, facing the Ganges, to Rādhākānta, that is, Krishna, the Consort of Rādhā. Nine domes with spires surmount the temple of Kāli, and before it stands the spacious nātmandir, or music hall, the terrace of which is supported by stately pillars. At the northwest and southwest corners of the temple compound are two nahabats, or music towers, from which music flows at different times of day, especially at sunup, noon, and sundown, when the worship is performed in the temples. Three sides of the paved courtyard—all except the west—are lined with rooms set apart for kitchens, store-rooms, dining-rooms, and quarters for the temple staff and guests. The chamber in the northwest angle, just beyond the last of the Śiva temples, is of special interest to us; for here Sri Ramakrishna was to spend a considerable part of his life. To the west of this chamber is a semicircular porch overlooking the river. In front of the porch runs a foot-path, north and south, and beyond the path is a large garden and, below the garden, the Ganges. The orchard to the north of the buildings contains the Panchavati, the banyan, and the bel-tree, associated with Sri Ramakrishna's spiritual practices. Outside and to the north of the temple compound proper is the kuthi, or bungalow, used by members of Rāni Rasmani's family visiting the garden. And north of the temple garden, separated from it by a high wall, is a powder-magazine belonging to the British Government.

ŚIVA

In the twelve Śiva temples are installed the emblems of the Great God of renunciation in His various aspects, worshipped daily with proper rites. Śiva requires few articles of worship. White flowers and bel-leaves and a little Ganges water offered with devotion are enough to satisfy the benign Deity and win from Him the boon of liberation.

RĀDHĀKĀNTA

The temple of Rādhākānta, also known as the temple of Vishnu, contains the images of Rādhā and Krishna, the symbol of union with God through ecstatic love. The two images stand on a pedestal facing the west. The floor is paved with marble. From the ceiling of the porch hang chandeliers protected from dust by coverings of red cloth. Canvas screens shield the images from the rays of the setting sun. Close to the threshold of the inner shrine is a small brass cup containing holy water. Devoted visitors reverently drink a few drops from the vessel.

KĀLI

The main temple is dedicated to Kāli, the Divine Mother, here worshipped as Bhavatārini, the Saviour of the Universe. The floor of this temple also is paved with marble. The basalt image of the Mother, dressed in gorgeous gold brocade, stands on a white marble image of the prostrate body of Her Divine Consort, Śiva, the symbol of the Absolute. On the feet of the Goddess are, among other ornaments, anklets of gold. Her arms are decked with jewelled ornaments of gold. She wears necklaces of gold and pearls, a golden garland of human heads, and a girdle of human arms. She wears a golden crown, golden ear-rings, and a golden nose-ring with a pearl-drop. She has four arms. The lower left hand holds a severed human head and the upper grips a blood-stained sabre. One right hand offers boons to Her children; the other allays their fear. The majesty of Her posture can hardly be described. It combines the terror of destruction with the reassurance of motherly tenderness. For She is the Cosmic Power, the totality of the universe, a glorious harmony of the pairs of opposites. She deals out death, as She creates and preserves. She has three eyes, the third being the symbol of Divine Wisdom; they strike dismay into the wicked, yet pour out affection for Her devotees.

The whole symbolic world is represented in the temple garden—the Trinity of the Nature Mother (Kāli), the Absolute (Śiva), and Love (Rādhākānta), the Arch spanning heaven and earth. The terrific Goddess of the Tantra, the soul-enthralling Flute-Player of the *Bhāgavata*, and the Self-absorbed Absolute of the Vedas live together, creating the greatest synthesis of religions. All aspects of Reality are represented there. But of this divine household, Kāli is the pivot, the sovereign Mistress. She is Prakriti, the Procreatrix, Nature, the Destroyer, the Creator. Nay, She is something greater and deeper still for those who have eyes to see. She is the

Universal Mother, "my Mother" as Ramakrishna would say, the All-powerful, who reveals Herself to Her children under different aspects and Divine Incarnations, the Visible God, who leads the elect to the Invisible Reality; and if it so pleases Her, She takes away the last trace of ego from created beings and merges it in the consciousness of the Absolute, the undifferentiated God. Through Her grace "the finite ego loses itself in the illimitable Ego—Ātman—Brahman".[1]

Rāni Rasmani spent a fortune for the construction of the temple garden and another fortune for its dedication ceremony, which took place on May 31, 1855.

Sri Ramakrishna—henceforth we shall call Gadadhar by this familiar name[2]—came to the temple garden with his elder brother Ramkumar, who was appointed priest of the Kāli temple. Sri Ramakrishna did not at first approve of Ramkumar's working for the śudra Rasmani. The example of their orthodox father was still fresh in Sri Ramakrishna's mind. He objected also to the eating of the cooked offerings of the temple, since, according to orthodox Hindu custom, such food can be offered to the Deity only in the house of a brāhmin. But the holy atmosphere of the temple grounds, the solitude of the surrounding wood, the loving care of his brother, the respect shown him by Rāni Rasmani and Mathur Babu, the living presence of the Goddess Kāli in the temple, and, above all, the proximity of the sacred Ganges, which Sri Ramakrishna always held in the highest respect, gradually overcame his disapproval, and he began to feel at home.

Within a very short time Sri Ramakrishna attracted the notice of Mathur Babu, who was impressed by the young man's religious fervour and wanted him to participate in the worship in the Kāli temple. But Sri Ramakrishna loved his freedom and was indifferent to any worldly career. The profession of the priesthood in a temple founded by a rich woman did not appeal to his mind. Further, he hesitated to take upon himself the responsibility for the ornaments and jewelry of the temple. Mathur had to wait for a suitable occasion.

At this time there came to Dakshineswar a youth of sixteen, destined to play an important role in Sri Ramakrishna's life. Hriday, a distant nephew[3] of Sri Ramakrishna, hailed from Sihore, a village not far from Kāmārpukur, and had been his boyhood friend. Clever, exceptionally energetic, and endowed with great presence of mind, he moved, as will be seen later, like a shadow about his uncle and was always ready to help him, even at the sacrifice of his personal comfort. He was destined to be a mute witness of many of the spiritual experiences of Sri Ramakrishna and the caretaker of his body during the stormy days of his spiritual practice. Hriday came to Dakshineswar in search of a job, and Sri Ramakrishna was glad to see him.

[1] Romain Rolland, *Prophets of the New India*, p. 11.
[2] No definite information is available as to the origin of this name. Most probably it was given by Mathur Babu, as Ramlal, Sri Ramakrishna's nephew, has said, quoting the authority of his uncle himself.
[3] Hriday's mother was the daughter of Sri Ramakrishna's aunt (Khudiram's sister). Such a degree of relationship is termed in Bengal that of a "distant nephew".

Unable to resist the persuasion of Mathur Babu, Sri Ramakrishna at last entered the temple service, on condition that Hriday should be asked to assist him. His first duty was to dress and decorate the image of Kāli.

One day the priest of the Rādhākānta temple accidentally dropped the image of Krishna on the floor, breaking one of its legs. The pundits advised the Rāni to install a new image, since the worship of an image with a broken limb was against the scriptural injunctions. But the Rāni was fond of the image, and she asked Sri Ramakrishna's opinion. In an abstracted mood, he said: "This solution is ridiculous. If a son-in-law of the Rāni broke his leg, would she discard him and put another in his place? Wouldn't she rather arrange for his treatment? Why should she not do the same thing in this case too? Let the image be repaired and worshipped as before." It was a simple, straightforward solution and was accepted by the Rāni. Sri Ramakrishna himself mended the break. The priest was dismissed for his carelessness, and at Mathur Babu's earnest request Sri Ramakrishna accepted the office of priest in the Rādhākānta temple.

SRI RAMAKRISHNA AS A PRIEST

Born in an orthodox brāhmin family, Sri Ramakrishna knew the formalities of worship, its rites and rituals. The innumerable gods and goddesses of the Hindu religion are the human aspects of the indescribable and incomprehensible Spirit, as conceived by the finite human mind. They understand and appreciate human love and emotion, help men to realize their secular and spiritual ideals, and ultimately enable men to attain liberation from the miseries of phenomenal life. The Source of light, intelligence, wisdom, and strength is the One alone from whom comes the fulfilment of desire. Yet, as long as a man is bound by his human limitations, he cannot but worship God through human forms. He must use human symbols. Therefore Hinduism asks the devotees to look on God as the ideal father, the ideal mother, the ideal husband, the ideal son, or the ideal friend. But the name ultimately leads to the Nameless, the form to the Formless, the word to the Silence, the emotion to the serene realization of Peace in Existence-Knowledge-Bliss Absolute. The gods gradually merge in the one God. But until that realization is achieved, the devotee cannot dissociate human factors from his worship. Therefore the Deity is bathed and clothed and decked with ornaments. He is fed and put to sleep. He is propitiated with hymns, songs, and prayers. And there are appropriate rites connected with all these functions. For instance, to secure for himself external purity, the priest bathes himself in holy water and puts on a holy cloth. He purifies the mind and the sense-organs by appropriate meditations. He fortifies the place of worship against evil forces by drawing around it circles of fire and water. He awakens the different spiritual centres of the body and invokes the Supreme Spirit in his heart. Then he transfers the Supreme Spirit to the image before him and worships the image, regarding it no longer as clay or stone, but as the embodiment of Spirit, throbbing with Life and Consciousness. After the worship the Supreme Spirit is recalled from the image to Its true sanctuary, the heart of the priest. The real devotee knows the absurdity of worshipping the Transcendental Reality with material articles—clothing That which pervades the whole universe and the beyond, putting on a pedestal That which cannot be limited by space, feeding That which is disembodied and incorporeal, singing before That whose glory the music of the spheres tries vainly to proclaim. But through these rites the devotee aspires to go ultimately beyond rites and rituals, forms and names, words and praise, and to realize God as the All-pervading Consciousness.

Hindu priests are thoroughly acquainted with the rites of worship, but few of them are aware of their underlying significance. They move their hands and limbs mechanically, in obedience to the letter of the scriptures, and repeat the holy mantras like parrots. But from the very beginning the inner meaning of these rites was revealed to Sri Ramakrishna. As he sat facing the image, a strange transformation came over his mind. While going through the prescribed ceremonies, he would actually find himself encircled by a wall of fire protecting him and the place of worship from unspiritual vibrations, or he would feel the rising of the mystic Kundalini through the different centres of the body. The glow on his face, his deep absorption, and the intense atmosphere of the temple impressed everyone who saw him worship the Deity.

Ramkumar wanted Sri Ramakrishna to learn the intricate rituals of the worship of Kāli. To become a priest of Kāli one must undergo a special form of initiation from a qualified guru, and for Sri Ramakrishna a suitable brāhmin was found. But no sooner did the brāhmin speak the holy word in his ear than Sri Ramakrishna, overwhelmed with emotion, uttered a loud cry and plunged into deep concentration.

Mathur begged Sri Ramakrishna to take charge of the worship in the Kāli temple. The young priest pleaded his incompetence and his ignorance of the scriptures. Mathur insisted that devotion and sincerity would more than compensate for any lack of formal knowledge and make the Divine Mother manifest Herself through the image. In the end, Sri Ramakrishna had to yield to Mathur's request. He became the priest of Kāli.

In 1856 Ramkumar breathed his last. Sri Ramakrishna had already witnessed more than one death in the family. He had come to realize how impermanent is life on earth. The more he was convinced of the transitory nature of worldly things, the more eager he became to realize God, the Fountain of Immortality.

THE FIRST VISION OF KĀLI

And, indeed, he soon discovered what a strange Goddess he had chosen to serve. He became gradually enmeshed in the web of Her all-pervading presence. To the ignorant She is, to be sure, the image of destruction; but he found in Her the benign, all-loving Mother. Her neck is encircled with a garland of heads, and Her waist with a girdle of human arms, and two of Her hands hold weapons of death, and Her eyes dart a glance of fire; but, strangely enough, Ramakrishna felt in Her breath the soothing touch of tender love and saw in Her the Seed of Immortality. She stands on the bosom of Her Consort, Śiva; it is because She is the Śakti, the Power, inseparable from the Absolute. She is surrounded by jackals and other unholy creatures, the denizens of the cremation ground. But is not the Ultimate Reality above holiness and unholiness? She appears to be reeling under the spell of wine. But who would create this mad world unless under the influence of a divine drunkenness? She is the highest symbol of all the forces of nature, the synthesis of their antinomies, the Ultimate Divine in the form of woman. She now became to Sri Ramakrishna the only Reality, and the world became an unsubstantial shadow. Into Her worship he poured his soul. Before him She stood as the transparent portal to the shrine of Ineffable Reality.

The worship in the temple intensified Sri Ramakrishna's yearning for a living vision of the Mother of the Universe. He began to spend in meditation the time not actually employed in the temple service; and for this purpose he selected an extremely solitary place. A deep jungle, thick with underbrush and prickly plants, lay to the north of the temples. Used at one time as a burial ground, it was shunned by people even during the day-time for fear of ghosts. There Sri Ramakrishna began to spend the whole night in meditation, returning to his room only in the morning with eyes swollen as though from much weeping. While meditating, he would lay aside his cloth and his brāhminical thread. Explaining this strange conduct, he once said to Hriday: "Don't you know that when one thinks of God one should be freed from all ties? From our very birth we have the eight fetters of hatred, shame, lineage, pride of good conduct, fear, secretiveness, caste, and grief. The sacred thread reminds me that I am a brāhmin and therefore superior to all. When calling on the Mother one has to set aside all such ideas." Hriday thought his uncle was becoming insane.

As his love for God deepened, he began either to forget or to drop the formalities of worship. Sitting before the image, he would spend hours singing the devotional songs of great devotees of the Mother, such as Kamalākānta and Rāmprasād. Those rhapsodical songs, describing the direct vision of God, only intensified Sri Ramakrishna's longing. He felt the pangs of a child separated from its mother. Sometimes, in agony, he would rub his face against the ground and weep so bitterly that people, thinking he had lost his earthly mother, would sympathize with him in his grief. Sometimes, in moments of scepticism, he would cry: "Art Thou true, Mother, or is it all fiction—mere poetry without any reality? If Thou dost exist, why do I not see Thee? Is religion a mere fantasy and art Thou only a figment of man's imagination?" Sometimes he would sit on the prayer carpet for two hours like an inert object. He began to behave in an abnormal manner, most of the time unconscious of the world. He almost gave up food; and sleep left him altogether.

But he did not have to wait very long. He has thus described his first vision of the Mother: "I felt as if my heart were being squeezed like a wet towel. I was overpowered with a great restlessness and a fear that it might not be my lot to realize Her in this life. I could not bear the separation from Her any longer. Life seemed to be not worth living. Suddenly my glance fell on the sword that was kept in the Mother's temple. I determined to put an end to my life. When I jumped up like a madman and seized it, suddenly the blessed Mother revealed Herself. The buildings with their different parts, the temple, and everything else vanished from my sight, leaving no trace whatsoever, and in their stead I saw a limitless, infinite, effulgent Ocean of Consciousness. As far as the eye could see, the shining billows were madly rushing at me from all sides with a terrific noise, to swallow me up! I was panting for breath. I was caught in the rush and collapsed, unconscious. What was happening in the outside world I did not know; but within me there was a steady flow of undiluted bliss, altogether new, and I felt the presence of the Divine Mother." On his lips when he regained consciousness of the world was the word "Mother".

GOD-INTOXICATED STATE

Yet this was only a foretaste of the intense experiences to come. The first glimpse of the Divine Mother made him the more eager for Her uninterrupted vision. He wanted to see Her both in meditation and with eyes open. But the Mother began to play a teasing game of hide-and-seek with him, intensifying both his joy and his suffering. Weeping bitterly during the moments of separation from Her, he would pass into a trance and then find Her standing before him, smiling, talking, consoling, bidding him be of good cheer, and instructing him. During this period of spiritual practice he had many uncommon experiences. When he sat to meditate, he would hear strange clicking sounds in the joints of his legs, as if someone were locking them up, one after the other, to keep him motionless; and at the conclusion of his meditation he would again hear the same sounds, this time unlocking them and leaving him free to move about. He would see flashes like a swarm of fire-flies floating before his eyes, or a sea of deep mist around him, with luminous waves of molten silver. Again, from a sea of translucent mist he would behold the Mother rising, first Her feet, then Her waist, body, face, and head, finally Her whole person; he would feel Her breath and hear Her voice. Worshipping in the temple, sometimes he would become exalted, sometimes he would remain motionless as stone, sometimes he would almost collapse from excessive emotion. Many of his actions, contrary to all tradition, seemed sacrilegious to the people. He would take a flower and touch it to his own head, body, and feet, and then offer it to the Goddess. Or, like a drunkard, he would reel to the throne of the Mother, touch Her chin by way of showing his affection for Her, and sing, talk, joke, laugh, and dance. Or he would take a morsel of food from the plate and hold it to Her mouth, begging Her to eat it, and would not be satisfied till he was convinced that She had really eaten. After the Mother had been put to sleep at night, from his own room he would hear Her ascending to the upper storey of the temple with the light steps of a happy girl, Her anklets jingling. Then he would discover Her standing with flowing hair, Her black form silhouetted against the sky of the night, looking at the Ganges or at the distant lights of Calcutta.

Naturally the temple officials took him for an insane person. His worldly well-wishers brought him to skilled physicians; but no medicine could cure his malady. Many a time he doubted his sanity himself. For he had been sailing across an uncharted sea, with no earthly guide to direct him. His only haven of security was the Divine Mother Herself. To Her he would pray: "I do not know what these things are. I am ignorant of mantras and the scriptures. Teach me, Mother, how to realize Thee. Who else can help me? Art Thou not my only refuge and guide?" And the sustaining presence of the Mother never failed him in his distress or doubt. Even those who criticized his conduct were greatly impressed with his purity, guilelessness, truthfulness, integrity, and holiness. They felt an uplifting influence in his presence.

It is said that samādhi, or trance, no more than opens the portal of the spiritual realm. Sri Ramakrishna felt an unquenchable desire to enjoy God in various ways. For his meditation he built a place in the northern wooded section of the temple garden. With Hriday's help he planted there five sacred trees. The spot, known as the Panchavati, became the scene of many of his visions.

As his spiritual mood deepened he more and more felt himself to be a child of the Divine Mother. He learnt to surrender himself completely to Her will and let Her direct him.

"O Mother," he would constantly pray, "I have taken refuge in Thee. Teach me what to do and what to say. Thy will is paramount everywhere and is for the good of Thy children. Merge my will in Thy will and make me Thy instrument."

His visions became deeper and more intimate. He no longer had to meditate to behold the Divine Mother. Even while retaining consciousness of the outer world, he would see Her as tangibly as the temples, the trees, the river, and the men around him.

On a certain occasion Mathur Babu stealthily entered the temple to watch the worship. He was profoundly moved by the young priest's devotion and sincerity. He realized that Sri Ramakrishna had transformed the stone image into the living Goddess.

Sri Ramakrishna one day fed a cat with the food that was to be offered to Kāli. This was too much for the manager of the temple garden, who considered himself responsible for the proper conduct of the worship. He reported Sri Ramakrishna's insane behaviour to Mathur Babu.

Sri Ramakrishna has described the incident: "The Divine Mother revealed to me in the Kāli temple that it was She who had become everything. She showed me that everything was full of Consciousness. The image was Consciousness, the altar was Consciousness, the water-vessels were Consciousness, the door-sill was Consciousness, the marble floor was Consciousness—all was Consciousness. I found everything inside the room soaked, as it were, in Bliss—the Bliss of God. I saw a wicked man in front of the Kāli temple; but in him also I saw the power of the Divine Mother vibrating. That was why I fed a cat with the food that was to be offered to the Divine Mother. I clearly perceived that all this was the Divine Mother—even the cat. The manager of the temple garden wrote to Mathur Babu saying that

I was feeding the cat with the offering intended for the Divine Mother. But Mathur Babu had insight into the state of my mind. He wrote back to the manager: 'Let him do whatever he likes. You must not say anything to him.'"

One of the painful ailments from which Sri Ramakrishna suffered at this time was a burning sensation in his body, and he was cured by a strange vision. During worship in the temple, following the scriptural injunctions, he would imagine the presence of the "sinner" in himself and the destruction of this "sinner". One day he was meditating in the Panchavati, when he saw come out of him a red-eyed man of black complexion, reeling like a drunkard. Soon there emerged from him another person, of serene countenance, wearing the ochre cloth of a sannyāsi and carrying in his hand a trident. The second person attacked the first and killed him with the trident. Thereafter Sri Ramakrishna was free of his pain.

About this time he began to worship God by assuming the attitude of a servant toward his master. He imitated the mood of Hanumān, the monkey chieftain of the Rāmāyana, the ideal servant of Rāma and traditional model for this self-effacing form of devotion. When he meditated on Hanumān his movements and his way of life began to resemble those of a monkey. His eyes became restless. He lived on fruits and roots. With his cloth tied around his waist, a portion of it hanging in the form of a tail, he jumped from place to place instead of walking. And after a short while he was blessed with a vision of Sītā, the divine consort of Rāma, who entered his body and disappeared there with the words, "I bequeath to you my smile."

Mathur had faith in the sincerity of Sri Ramakrishna's spiritual zeal, but began now to doubt his sanity. He had watched him jumping about like a monkey. One day, when Rāni Rasmani was listening to Sri Ramakrishna's singing in the temple, the young priest abruptly turned and slapped her. Apparently listening to his song, she had actually been thinking of a lawsuit. She accepted the punishment as though the Divine Mother Herself had imposed it; but Mathur was distressed. He begged Sri Ramakrishna to keep his feelings under control and to heed the conventions of society. God Himself, he argued, follows laws. God never permitted, for instance, flowers of two colours to grow on the same stalk. The following day Sri Ramakrishna presented Mathur Babu with two hibiscus flowers growing on the same stalk, one red and one white.

Mathur and Rāni Rasmani began to ascribe the mental ailment of Sri Ramakrishna in part, at least, to his observance of rigid continence. Thinking that a natural life would relax the tension of his nerves, they engineered a plan with two women of ill fame. But as soon as the women entered his room, Sri Ramakrishna beheld in them the manifestation of the Divine Mother of the Universe and went into samādhi uttering Her name.

HALADHARI

In 1858 there came to Dakshineswar a cousin of Sri Ramakrishna, Haladhari by name, who was to remain there about eight years. On account of Sri Ramakrishna's indifferent health, Mathur appointed this man to the

office of priest in the Kāli temple. He was a complex character, versed in
the letter of the scriptures, but hardly aware of their spirit. He loved to
participate in hair-splitting theological discussions and, by the measure of
his own erudition, he proceeded to gauge Sri Ramakrishna. An orthodox
brāhmin, he thoroughly disapproved of his cousin's unorthodox actions, but
he was not unimpressed by Sri Ramakrishna's purity of life, ecstatic love
of God, and yearning for realization.

One day Haladhari upset Sri Ramakrishna with the statement that God
is incomprehensible to the human mind. Sri Ramakrishna has described the
great moment of doubt when he wondered whether his visions had really
misled him: "With sobs I prayed to the Mother, 'Canst Thou have the heart
to deceive me like this because I am a fool?' A stream of tears flowed from
my eyes. Shortly afterwards I saw a volume of mist rising from the floor
and filling the space before me. In the midst of it there appeared a face
with flowing beard, calm, highly expressive, and fair. Fixing its gaze steadily
upon me, it said solemnly, 'Remain in bhāvamukha, on the threshold of
relative consciousness.' This it repeated three times and then it gently disappeared in the mist, which itself dissolved. This vision reassured me."

A garbled report of Sri Ramakrishna's failing health, indifference to
worldly life, and various abnormal activities reached Kāmārpukur and filled
the heart of his poor mother with anguish. At her repeated request he returned to his village for a change of air. But his boyhood friends did not
interest him any more. A divine fever was consuming him. He spent a great
part of the day and night in one of the cremation grounds, in meditation.
The place reminded him of the impermanence of the human body, of human
hopes and achievements. It also reminded him of Kāli, the Goddess of
destruction.

MARRIAGE AND AFTER

But in a few months his health showed improvement, and he recovered
to some extent his natural buoyancy of spirit. His happy mother was encouraged to think it might be a good time to arrange his marriage. The boy was
now twenty-three years old. A wife would bring him back to earth. And she
was delighted when her son welcomed her suggestion. Perhaps he saw in it
the finger of God.

Saradamani, a little girl of five, lived in the neighbouring village of
Jayrāmbāti. Even at this age she had been praying to God to make her character as stainless and fragrant as the white tuberose. Looking at the full
moon, she would say: "O God, there are dark spots even on the moon. But
make my character spotless." It was she who was selected as the bride for
Sri Ramakrishna.

The marriage ceremony was duly performed. Such early marriage in India
is in the nature of a betrothal, the marriage being consummated when the
girl attains puberty. But in this case the marriage remained for ever uncon-
summated. Sri Ramakrishna lived at Kāmārpukur about a year and a half
and then returned to Dakshineswar.

Hardly had he crossed the threshold of the Kāli temple when he found himself again in the whirlwind. His madness reappeared tenfold. The same meditation and prayer, the same ecstatic moods, the same burning sensation, the same weeping, the same sleeplessness, the same indifference to the body and the outside world, the same divine delirium. He subjected himself to fresh disciplines in order to eradicate greed and lust, the two great impediments to spiritual progress. With a rupee in one hand and some earth in the other, he would reflect on the comparative value of these two for the realization of God, and finding them equally worthless he would toss them, with equal indifference, into the Ganges. Women he regarded as the manifestations of the Divine Mother. Never even in a dream did he feel the impulses of lust. And to root out of his mind the idea of caste superiority, he cleaned a pariah's house with his long and neglected hair. When he would sit in meditation, birds would perch on his head and peck in his hair for grains of food. Snakes would crawl over his body, and neither would be aware of the other. Sleep left him altogether. Day and night, visions flitted before him. He saw the sannyāsi who had previously killed the "sinner" in him again coming out of his body, threatening him with the trident, and ordering him to concentrate on God. Or the same sannyāsi would visit distant places, following a luminous path, and bring him reports of what was happening there. Sri Ramakrishna used to say later that in the case of an advanced devotee the mind itself becomes the guru, living and moving like an embodied being.

Rāni Rasmani, the foundress of the temple garden, passed away in 1861. After her death her son-in-law Mathur became the sole executor of the estate. He placed himself and his resources at the disposal of Sri Ramakrishna and began to look after his physical comfort. Sri Ramakrishna later spoke of him as one of his five "suppliers of stores" appointed by the Divine Mother. Whenever a desire arose in his mind, Mathur fulfilled it without hesitation.

THE BRĀHMANI

There came to Dakshineswar at this time a brāhmin woman who was to play an important part in Sri Ramakrishna's spiritual unfoldment. Born in East Bengal, she was an adept in the Tāntrik and Vaishnava methods of worship. She was slightly over fifty years of age, handsome, and garbed in the orange robe of a nun. Her sole possessions were a few books and two pieces of wearing-cloth.

Sri Ramakrishna welcomed the visitor with great respect, described to her his experiences and visions, and told her of people's belief that these were symptoms of madness. She listened to him attentively and said: "My son, everyone in this world is mad. Some are mad for money, some for creature comforts, some for name and fame; and you are mad for God." She assured him that he was passing through the almost unknown spiritual experience described in the scriptures as mahābhāva, the most exalted rapture of divine love. She told him that this extreme exaltation had been described as manifesting itself through nineteen physical symptoms, including the shedding of tears, a tremor of the body, horripilation, perspiration, and a burning sensation. The Bhakti scriptures, she declared, had recorded only two instances of the experience, namely, those of Sri Rādhā and Sri Chaitanya.

Very soon a tender relationship sprang up between Sri Ramakrishna and the Brāhmani, she looking upon him as the Baby Krishna, and he upon her as mother. Day after day she watched his ecstasy during the kirtan and meditation, his samādhi, his mad yearning; and she recognized in him a power to transmit spirituality to others. She came to the conclusion that such things were not possible for an ordinary devotee, not even for a highly developed soul. Only an Incarnation of God was capable of such spiritual manifestations. She proclaimed openly that Sri Ramakrishna, like Sri Chaitanya, was an Incarnation of God.

When Sri Ramakrishna told Mathur what the Brāhmani had said about him, Mathur shook his head in doubt. He was reluctant to accept him as an Incarnation of God, an Avatār comparable to Rāma, Krishna, Buddha, and Chaitanya, though he admitted Sri Ramakrishna's extraordinary spirituality. Whereupon the Brāhmani asked Mathur to arrange a conference of scholars who should discuss the matter with her. He agreed to the proposal and the meeting was arranged. It was to be held in the nātmandir in front of the Kāli temple.

Two famous pundits of the time were invited: Vaishnavcharan, the leader of the Vaishnava society, and Gauri. The first to arrive was Vaishnavcharan, with a distinguished company of scholars and devotees. The Brāhmani, like a proud mother, proclaimed her view before him and supported it with quotations from the scriptures. As the pundits discussed the deep theological question, Sri Ramakrishna, perfectly indifferent to everything happening around him, sat in their midst like a child, immersed in his own thoughts, sometimes smiling, sometimes chewing a pinch of spices from a pouch, or again saying to Vaishnavcharan with a nudge: "Look here. Sometimes I feel like this, too." Presently Vaishnavcharan arose to declare himself in total agreement with the view of the Brāhmani. He declared that Sri Ramakrishna had undoubtedly experienced mahābhāva and that this was the certain sign of the rare manifestation of God in a man. The people assembled there, especially the officers of the temple garden, were struck dumb. Sri Ramakrishna said to Mathur, like a boy: "Just fancy, he too says so! Well, I am glad to learn that after all it is not a disease."

When, a few days later, Pundit Gauri arrived, another meeting was held, and he agreed with the view of the Brāhmani and Vaishnavcharan. To Sri Ramakrishna's remark that Vaishnavcharan had declared him to be an Avatār, Gauri replied: "Is that all he has to say about you? Then he has said very little. I am fully convinced that you are that Mine of Spiritual Power, only a small fraction of which descends on earth, from time to time, in the form of an Incarnation."

"Ah!" said Sri Ramakrishna with a smile, "you seem to have quite outbid Vaishnavcharan in this matter. What have you found in me that makes you entertai. such an idea?"

Gauri said: "I feel it in my heart and I have the scriptures on my side. I am ready to prove it to anyone who challenges me."

"Well," Sri Ramakrishna said, "it is you who say so; but, believe me, I know nothing about it."

Thus the insane priest was by verdict of the great scholars of the day proclaimed a Divine Incarnation. His visions were not the result of an over-heated brain; they had precedent in spiritual history. And how did the proclamation affect Sri Ramakrishna himself? He remained the simple child of the Mother that he had been since the first day of his life. Years later, when two of his householder disciples openly spoke of him as a Divine Incarnation and the matter was reported to him, he said with a touch of sarcasm: "Do they think they will enhance my glory that way? One of them is an actor on the stage and the other a physician. What do they know about Incarnations? Why, years ago pundits like Gauri and Vaishnavcharan declared me to be an Avatār. They were great scholars and knew what they said. But that did not make any change in my mind."

Sri Ramakrishna was a learner all his life. He often used to quote a proverb to his disciples: "Friend, the more I live the more I learn." When the excitement created by the Brāhmani's declaration was over, he set him-self to the task of practising spiritual disciplines according to the traditional methods laid down in the Tantra and Vaishnava scriptures. Hitherto he had pursued his spiritual ideal according to the promptings of his own mind and heart. Now he accepted the Brāhmani as his guru and set foot on the tradi-tional highways.

TANTRA

According to the Tantra, the Ultimate Reality is Chit, or Consciousness, which is identical with Sat, or Being, and with Ānanda, or Bliss. This Ultimate Reality, Satchidānanda, Existence-Knowledge-Bliss Absolute, is identical with the Reality preached in the Vedas. And man is identical with this Reality; but under the influence of māyā, or illusion, he has for-gotten his true nature. He takes to be real a merely apparent world of subject and object, and this error is the cause of his bondage and suffering. The goal of spiritual discipline is the rediscovery of his true identity with the divine Reality.

For the achievement of this goal the Vedānta prescribes an austere nega-tive method of discrimination and renunciation, which can be followed by only a few individuals endowed with sharp intelligence and unshakable will-power. But Tantra takes into consideration the natural weakness of human beings, their lower appetites, and their love for the concrete. It combines philosophy with rituals, meditation with ceremonies, renunciation with enjoyment. The underlying purpose is gradually to train the aspirant to meditate on his identity with the Ultimate.

The average man wishes to enjoy the material objects of the world. Tantra bids him enjoy these, but at the same time discover in them the presence of God. Mystical rites are prescribed by which, slowly, the sense-objects become spiritualized and sense attraction is transformed into a love of God. So the very "bonds" of man are turned into "releasers". The very poison that kills is transmuted into the elixir of life. Outward renunciation is not necessary. Thus the aim of Tantra is to sublimate bhoga, or enjoyment, into yoga, or union with Consciousness. For, according to this philosophy, the world with all its manifestations is nothing but the sport of Śiva and Śakti, the Absolute and Its inscrutable Power.

The disciplines of Tantra are graded to suit aspirants of all degrees. Exercises are prescribed for people with "animal", "heroic", and "divine" outlooks. Certain of the rites require the presence of members of the opposite sex. Here the aspirant learns to look on woman as the embodiment of the Goddess Kāli, the Mother of the Universe. The very basis of Tantra is the Motherhood of God and the glorification of woman. Every part of a woman's body is to be regarded as incarnate Divinity. But the rites are extremely dangerous. The help of a qualified guru is absolutely necessary. An unwary devotee may lose his foothold and fall into a pit of depravity.

According to the Tantra, Śakti is the active creative force in the universe. Śiva, the Absolute, is a more or less passive principle. Further, Śakti is as inseparable from Śiva as fire's power to burn is from fire itself. Śakti, the Creative Power, contains in Its womb the universe, and therefore is the Divine Mother. All women are Her symbols. Kāli is one of Her several forms. The meditation on Kāli, the Creative Power, is the central discipline of the Tantra. While meditating, the aspirant at first regards himself as one with the Absolute and then thinks that out of that Impersonal Consciousness emerge two entities, namely, his own self and the living form of the Goddess. He then projects the Goddess into the tangible image before him and worships it as the Divine Mother.

Sri Ramakrishna set himself to the task of practising the disciplines of Tantra; and at the bidding of the Divine Mother Herself he accepted the Brāhmani as his guru. He performed profound and delicate ceremonies in the Panchavati and under the bel-tree at the northern extremity of the temple compound. He practised all the disciplines of the sixty-four principal Tantra books, and it took him never more than three days to achieve the result promised in any one of them. After the observance of a few preliminary rites, he would be overwhelmed with a strange divine fervour and would go into samādhi, where his mind would dwell in exaltation. Evil ceased to exist for him. The word "carnal" lost its meaning. The whole world and everything in it appeared as the līlā, the sport, of Śiva and Śakti. He beheld everywhere manifest the power and beauty of the Mother; the whole world, animate and inanimate, appeared to him as pervaded with Chit, Consciousness, and with Ānanda, Bliss.

He saw in a vision the Ultimate Cause of the universe as a huge luminous triangle giving birth every moment to an infinite number of worlds. He heard the Anāhata Śabda, the great sound Om, of which the innumerable sounds of the universe are only so many echoes. He acquired the eight supernatural powers of yoga, which make a man almost omnipotent, and these he spurned as of no value whatsoever to the Spirit. He had a vision of the divine Māyā, the inscrutable Power of God, by which the universe is created and sustained, and into which it is finally absorbed. In this vision he saw a woman of exquisite beauty, about to become a mother, emerging from the Ganges and slowly approaching the Panchavati. Presently she gave birth to a child and began to nurse it tenderly. A moment later she assumed a terrible aspect, seized the child with her grim jaws, and crushed it. Swallowing it, she re-entered the waters of the Ganges.

But the most remarkable experience during this period was the awakening of the Kundalini Śakti, the "Serpent Power". He actually saw the Power, at first lying asleep at the bottom of the spinal column, then waking up and ascending along the mystic Sushumnā canal and through its six centres, or lotuses, to the Sahasrāra, the thousand-petalled lotus in the top of the head. He further saw that as the Kundalini went upward the different lotuses bloomed. And this phenomenon was accompanied by visions and trances. Later on he described to his disciples and devotees the various movements of the Kundalini: the fishlike, birdlike, monkeylike, and so on. The awakening of the Kundalini is the beginning of spiritual consciousness, and its union with Śiva in the Sahasrāra, ending in samādhi, is the consummation of the Tāntrik disciplines.

About this time it was revealed to him that in a short while many devotees would seek his guidance.

VAISHNAVA DISCIPLINES

After completing the Tāntrik sādhanā Sri Ramakrishna followed the Brāhmani in the disciplines of Vaishnavism. The Vaishnavas are worshippers of Vishnu, the "All-pervading", the Supreme God, who is also known as Hari and Nārāyana. Of Vishnu's various Incarnations the two with the largest number of followers are Rāma and Krishna.

Vaishnavism is exclusively a religion of bhakti. Bhakti is intense love of God, attachment to Him alone; it is of the nature of bliss and bestows upon the lover immortality and liberation. God, according to Vaishnavism, cannot be realized through logic or reason; and, without bhakti, all penances, austerities and rites are futile. Man cannot realize God by self-exertion alone. For the vision of God His grace is absolutely necessary, and this grace is felt by the pure of heart. The mind is to be purified through bhakti. The pure mind then remains for ever immersed in the ecstasy of God-vision. It is the cultivation of this divine love that is the chief concern of the Vaishnava religion.

There are three kinds of formal devotion: tāmasic, rājasic, and sāttvic. If a person, while showing devotion to God, is actuated by malevolence, arrogance, jealousy, or anger, then his devotion is tāmasic, since it is influenced by tamas, the quality of inertia. If he worships God from a desire for fame or wealth, or from any other worldly ambition, then his devotion is rājasic, since it is influenced by rajas, the quality of activity. But if a person loves God without any thought of material gain, if he performs his duties to please God alone and maintains toward all created beings the attitude of friendship, then his devotion is called sāttvic, since it is influenced by sattva, the quality of harmony. But the highest devotion transcends the three gunas, or qualities, being a spontaneous, uninterrupted inclination of the mind toward God, the Inner Soul of all beings; and it wells up in the heart of a true devotee as soon as he hears the name of God or mention of God's attributes. A devotee possessed of this love would not accept the happiness of heaven if it were offered him. His one desire is to love God under all conditions—in pleasure and pain, life and death, honour and dishonour, prosperity and adversity.

There are two stages of bhakti. The first is known as vaidhi-bhakti, or love of God qualified by scriptural injunctions. For the devotees of this stage are prescribed regular and methodical worship, hymns, prayers, the repetition of God's name, and the chanting of His glories. This lower bhakti in course of time matures into parā-bhakti, or supreme devotion, known also as prema, the most intense form of divine love. Divine love is an end in itself. It exists potentially in all human hearts, but in the case of bound creatures it is misdirected to earthly objects.

To develop the devotee's love for God, Vaishnavism humanizes God. God is to be regarded as the devotee's Parent, Master, Friend, Child, Husband, or Sweetheart, each succeeding relationship representing an intensification of love. These bhāvas, or attitudes toward God, are known as śānta, dāsya, sakhya, vātsalya, and madhur. The rishis of the Vedas, Hanumān, the cowherd boys of Vrindāvan, Rāma's mother Kausalyā, and Rādhikā, Krishna's sweetheart, exhibited, respectively, the most perfect examples of these forms. In the ascending scale the glories of God are gradually forgotten and the devotee realizes more and more the intimacy of divine communion. Finally he regards himself as the mistress of his Beloved, and no artificial barrier remains to separate him from his Ideal. No social or moral obligation can bind to the earth his soaring spirit. He experiences perfect union with the Godhead. Unlike the Vedāntist, who strives to transcend all varieties of the subject-object relationship, a devotee of the Vaishnava path wishes to retain both his own individuality and the personality of God. To him God is not an intangible Absolute, but the Purushottama, the Supreme Person.

While practising the discipline of the madhur bhāva, the male devotee often regards himself as a woman, in order to develop the most intense form of love for Sri Krishna, the only purusha, or man, in the universe. This assumption of the attitude of the opposite sex has a deep psychological significance. It is a matter of common experience that an idea may be cultivated to such an intense degree that every idea alien to it is driven from the mind. This peculiarity of the mind may be utilized for the subjugation of the lower desires and the development of the spiritual nature. Now, the idea which is the basis of all desires and passions in a man is the conviction of his indissoluble association with a male body. If he can inoculate himself thoroughly with the idea that he is a woman, he can get rid of the desires peculiar to his male body. Again, the idea that he is a woman may in turn be made to give way to another higher idea, namely, that he is neither man nor woman, but the Impersonal Spirit. The Impersonal Spirit alone can enjoy real communion with the Impersonal God. Hence the highest realization of the Vaishnava draws close to the transcendental experience of the Vedāntist.

A beautiful expression of the Vaishnava worship of God through love is to be found in the Vrindāvan episode of the *Bhāgavata*. The gopis, or milk-maids, of Vrindāvan regarded the six-year-old Krishna as their Beloved. They sought no personal gain or happiness from this love. They surrendered to Krishna their bodies, minds, and souls. Of all the gopis, Rādhikā, or Rādhā, because of her intense love for Him, was the closest to Krishna. She manifested mahābhāva and was united with her Beloved. This union represents, through sensuous language, a supersensuous experience.

Sri Chaitanya, also known as Gaurānga, Gorā, or Nimāi, born in Bengal in 1485 and regarded as an Incarnation of God, is a great prophet of the Vaishnava religion. Chaitanya declared the chanting of God's name to be the most efficacious spiritual discipline for the Kaliyuga.

Sri Ramakrishna, as the monkey Hanumān, had already worshipped God as his Master. Through his devotion to Kāli he had worshipped God as his Mother. He was now to take up the other relationships prescribed by the Vaishnava scriptures.

RĀMLĀLĀ

About the year 1864 there came to Dakshineswar a wandering Vaishnava monk, Jatadhari, whose Ideal Deity was Rāma. He always carried with him a small metal image of the Deity, which he called by the endearing name of Rāmlālā, the Boy Rāma. Toward this little image he displayed the tender affection of Kausalyā for her divine Son, Rāma. As a result of lifelong spiritual practice he had actually found in the metal image the presence of his Ideal. Rāmlālā was no longer for him a metal image, but the living God. He devoted himself to nursing Rāma, feeding Rāma, playing with Rāma, taking Rāma for a walk, and bathing Rāma. And he found that the image responded to his love.

Sri Ramakrishna, much impressed with his devotion, requested Jatadhari to spend a few days at Dakshineswar. Soon Rāmlālā became the favourite companion of Sri Ramakrishna too. Later on he described to the devotees how the little image would dance gracefully before him, jump on his back, insist on being taken in his arms, run to the fields in the sun, pluck flowers from the bushes, and play pranks like a naughty boy. A very sweet rela-tionship sprang up between him and Rāmlālā, for whom he felt the love of a mother.

One day Jatadhari requested Sri Ramakrishna to keep the image and bade him adieu with tearful eyes. He declared that Rāmlālā had fulfilled his innermost prayer and that he now had no more need of formal worship. A few days later Sri Ramakrishna was blessed through Rāmlālā with a vision of Rāmachandra, whereby he realized that the Rāma of the *Rāmāyana*, the son of Daśaratha, pervades the whole universe as Spirit and Consciousness; that He is its Creator, Sustainer, and Destroyer; that, in still another aspect, He is the transcendental Brahman, without form, attribute, or name.

While worshipping Rāmlālā as the Divine Child, Sri Ramakrishna's heart became filled with motherly tenderness, and he began to regard himself as a woman. His speech and gestures changed. He began to move freely with the ladies of Mathur's family, who now looked upon him as one of their own sex. During this time he worshipped the Divine Mother as Her companion or handmaid.

IN COMMUNION WITH THE DIVINE BELOVED

Sri Ramakrishna now devoted himself to scaling the most inaccessible and dizzy heights of dualistic worship, namely, the complete union with Sri Krishna as the Beloved of the heart. He regarded himself as one of the gopis of Vrindāvan, mad with longing for her divine Sweetheart. At his request Mathur provided him with woman's dress and jewelry. In this love-pursuit, food and drink were forgotten. Day and night he wept bitterly. The yearning turned into a mad frenzy; for the divine Krishna began to play with him the old tricks He had played with the gopis. He would tease and taunt, now and then revealing Himself, but always keeping at a distance. Sri Ramakrishna's anguish brought on a return of the old physical symptoms: the burning sensation, an oozing of blood through the pores, a loosening of the joints, and the stopping of physiological functions.

The Vaishnava scriptures advise one to propitiate Rādhā and obtain her grace in order to realize Sri Krishna. So the tortured devotee now turned his prayer to her. Within a short time he enjoyed her blessed vision. He saw and felt the figure of Rādhā disappearing into his own body.

He said later on: "It is impossible to describe the heavenly beauty and sweetness of Rādhā. Her very appearance showed that she had completely forgotten herself in her passionate attachment to Krishna. Her complexion was a light yellow."

Now one with Rādhā, he manifested the great ecstatic love, the mahā-bhāva, which had found in her its fullest expression. Later Sri Ramakrishna said: "The manifestation in the same individual of the nineteen different kinds of emotion for God is called, in the books on bhakti, mahābhāva. An ordinary man takes a whole lifetime to express even a single one of these. But in this body [meaning himself] there has been a complete manifestation of all nineteen."

The love of Rādhā is the precursor of the resplendent vision of Sri Krishna, and Sri Ramakrishna soon experienced that vision. The enchanting form of Krishna appeared to him and merged in his person. He became Krishna; he totally forgot his own individuality and the world; he saw Krishna in himself and in the universe. Thus he attained to the fulfilment of the worship of the Personal God. He drank from the fountain of Immortal Bliss. The agony of his heart vanished forever. He realized Amrita, Immortality, beyond the shadow of death.

One day, listening to a recitation of the *Bhāgavata* on the verandah of the Rādhākānta temple, he fell into a divine mood and saw the enchanting form of Krishna. He perceived the luminous rays issuing from Krishna's Lotus Feet in the form of a stout rope, which touched first the *Bhāgavata* and then his own chest, connecting all three—God, the scripture, and the devotee. "After this vision", he used to say, "I came to realize that Bhagavān, Bhakta, and *Bhāgavata*—God, Devotee, and Scripture—are in reality one and the same."

VEDĀNTA

The Brāhmani was the enthusiastic teacher and astonished beholder of Sri Ramakrishna in his spiritual progress. She became proud of the achievements of her unique pupil. But the pupil himself was not permitted to rest; his destiny beckoned him forward. His Divine Mother would allow him no respite till he had left behind the entire realm of duality with its visions, experiences, and ecstatic dreams. But for the new ascent the old tender guides would not suffice. The Brāhmani, on whom he had depended for three years, saw her son escape from her to follow the command of a teacher with masculine strength, a sterner mien, a gnarled physique, and a virile voice. The new guru was a wandering monk, the sturdy Totapuri, whom Sri Ramakrishna learnt to address affectionately as Nangtā, the "Naked One", because of his total renunciation of all earthly objects and attachments, including even a piece of wearing cloth.

Totapuri was the bearer of a philosophy new to Sri Ramakrishna, the non-dualistic Vedānta philosophy, whose conclusions Totapuri had experienced in his own life. This ancient Hindu system designates the Ultimate Reality as Brahman, also described as Satchidānanda, Existence-Knowledge-Bliss Absolute. Brahman is the only Real Existence. In It there is no time, no space, no causality, no multiplicity. But through māyā, Its inscrutable Power, time, space, and causality are created and the One appears to break into the many. The eternal Spirit appears as a manifold of individuals endowed with form and subject to the conditions of time. The Immortal becomes a victim of birth and death. The Changeless undergoes change. The sinless Pure Soul, hypnotized by Its own māyā, experiences the joys of heaven and the pains of hell. But these experiences based on the duality of the subject-object relationship are unreal. Even the vision of a Personal God is, ultimately speaking, as illusory as the experience of any other object. Man attains his liberation, therefore, by piercing the veil of māyā and rediscovering his total identity with Brahman. Knowing himself to be one with the Universal Spirit, he realizes ineffable Peace. Only then does he go beyond the fiction of birth and death; only then does he become immortal. And this is the ultimate goal of all religions—to dehypnotize the soul now hypnotized by its own ignorance.

The path of the Vedāntic discipline is the path of negation, "neti", in which, by stern determination, all that is unreal is both negated and renounced. It is the path of jnāna, knowledge, the direct method of realizing the Absolute. After the negation of everything relative, including the discriminating ego itself, the aspirant merges in the One without a Second, in the bliss of nirvikalpa samādhi, where subject and object are alike dissolved. The soul goes beyond the realm of thought. The domain of duality is transcended. Māyā is left behind with all its changes and modifications. The Real Man towers above the delusions of creation, preservation, and destruction. An avalanche of indescribable Bliss sweeps away all relative ideas of pain and pleasure, good and evil. There shines in the heart the glory of the Eternal Brahman, Existence-Knowledge-Bliss Absolute. Knower, knowledge, and known are dissolved in the Ocean of one eternal Consciousness; love, lover, and beloved merge in the unbounded Sea of supreme Felicity; birth, growth, and death vanish in infinite Existence. All doubts and misgivings are quelled for ever; the oscillations of the mind are stopped; the momentum of past actions is exhausted. Breaking down the ridge-pole of the tabernacle in which the soul has made its abode for untold ages, stilling the body, calming the mind, drowning the ego, the sweet joy of Brahman wells up in that superconscious state. Space disappears into nothingness, time is swallowed in eternity, and causation becomes a dream of the past. Only Existence is. Ah! Who can describe what the soul then feels in its communion with the Self?

Even when man descends from this dizzy height, he is devoid of ideas of "I" and "mine"; he looks on the body as a mere shadow, an outer sheath encasing the soul. He does not dwell on the past, takes no thought for the future, and looks with indifference on the present. He surveys everything in the world with an eye of equality; he is no longer touched by the infinite variety of phenomena; he no longer reacts to pleasure and pain. He remains unmoved whether he—that is to say, his body—is worshipped by the good or tormented by the wicked; for he realizes that it is the one Brahman that manifests Itself through everything. The impact of such an experience devastates the body and mind. Consciousness becomes blasted, as it were, with an excess of Light. In the Vedānta books it is said that after the experience of nirvikalpa samādhi the body drops off like a dry leaf. Only those who are born with a special mission for the world can return from this height to the valleys of normal life. They live and move in the world for the welfare of mankind. They are invested with a supreme spiritual power. A divine glory shines through them.

TOTAPURI

Totapuri arrived at the Dakshineswar temple garden toward the end of 1864. Perhaps born in the Punjab, he was the head of a monastery in that province of India and claimed leadership of seven hundred sannyāsis. Trained from early youth in the disciplines of the Advaita Vedānta, he looked upon the world as an illusion. The gods and goddesses of the dualistic worship were to him mere fantasies of the deluded mind. Prayers, ceremonies, rites, and rituals had nothing to do with true religion, and about these he was utterly indifferent. Exercising self-exertion and unshakable will-power, he had liberated himself from attachment to the sense-objects of the relative universe. For forty years he had practised austere discipline on the bank of the sacred Narmadā and had finally realized his identity with the Absolute. Thenceforward he roamed in the world as an unfettered soul, a lion free from the cage. Clad in a loin-cloth, he spent his days under the canopy of the sky alike in storm and sunshine, feeding his body on the slender pittance of alms. He had been visiting the estuary of the Ganges. On his return journey along the bank of the sacred river, led by the inscrutable Divine Will, he stopped at Dakshineswar.

Totapuri, discovering at once that Sri Ramakrishna was prepared to be a student of Vedānta, asked to initiate him into its mysteries. With the permission of the Divine Mother, Sri Ramakrishna agreed to the proposal. But Totapuri explained that only a sannyāsi could receive the teaching of Vedānta. Sri Ramakrishna agreed to renounce the world, but with the stipulation that the ceremony of his initiation into the monastic order be performed in secret, to spare the feelings of his old mother, who had been living with him at Dakshineswar.

On the appointed day, in the small hours of the morning, a fire was lighted in the Panchavati. Totapuri and Sri Ramakrishna sat before it. The flame played on their faces. "Ramakrishna was a small brown man with a short beard and beautiful eyes, long dark eyes, full of light, obliquely set and slightly veiled, never very wide open, but seeing half-closed a great distance both outwardly and inwardly. His mouth was open over his white teeth in a bewitching smile, at once affectionate and mischievous. Of medium height, he was thin to emaciation and extremely delicate. His temperament was high-strung, for he was supersensitive to all the winds of joy and sorrow, both moral and physical. He was indeed a living reflection of all that happened before the mirror of his eyes, a two-sided mirror, turned both out and in."[4] Facing him, the other rose like a rock. He was very tall and robust, a sturdy and tough oak. His constitution and mind were of iron. He was the strong leader of men.

In the burning flame before him Sri Ramakrishna performed the rituals of destroying his attachment to relatives, friends, body, mind, sense-organs, ego, and the world. The leaping flame swallowed it all, making the initiate free and pure. The sacred thread and the tuft of hair were consigned to the fire, completing his severance from caste, sex, and society. Last of all he burnt in that fire, with all that is holy as his witness, his desire for enjoyment here and hereafter. He uttered the sacred mantras giving assurance of safety and fearlessness to all beings, who were only manifestations of his own Self. The rites completed, the disciple received from the guru the loincloth and ochre robe, the emblems of his new life.

The teacher and the disciple repaired to the meditation room near by. Totapuri began to impart to Sri Ramakrishna the great truths of Vedānta.

"Brahman", he said, "is the only Reality, ever pure, ever illumined, ever free, beyond the limits of time, space, and causation. Though apparently divided by names and forms through the inscrutable power of māyā, that enchantress who makes the impossible possible, Brahman is really One and undivided. When a seeker merges in the beatitude of samādhi, he does not perceive time and space or name and form, the offspring of māyā. Whatever is within the domain of māyā is unreal. Give it up. Destroy the prison-house of name and form and rush out of it with the strength of a lion. Dive deep in search of the Self and realize It through samādhi. You will find the world of name and form vanishing into void, and the puny ego dissolving in Brahman-Consciousness. You will realize your identity with Brahman, Existence-Knowledge-Bliss Absolute." Quoting the Upanishad, Totapuri said: "That knowledge is shallow by which one sees or hears or knows

---

[4] Romain Rolland, *Prophets of the New India*, pp. 38-9.

another. What is shallow is worthless and can never give real felicity. But the Knowledge by which one does not see another or hear another or know another, which is beyond duality, is great, and through such Knowledge one attains the Infinite Bliss. How can the mind and senses grasp That which shines in the heart of all as the Eternal Subject?"

Totapuri asked the disciple to withdraw his mind from all objects of the relative world, including the gods and goddesses, and to concentrate on the Absolute. But the task was not easy even for Sri Ramakrishna. He found it impossible to take his mind beyond Kāli, the Divine Mother of the Universe. "After the initiation", Sri Ramakrishna once said, describing the event, "Nangtā began to teach me the various conclusions of the Advaita Vedānta and asked me to withdraw the mind completely from all objects and dive deep into the Ātman. But in spite of all my attempts I could not altogether cross the realm of name and form and bring my mind to the unconditioned state. I had no difficulty in taking the mind from all the objects of the world. But the radiant and too familiar figure of the Blissful Mother, the Embodiment of the essence of Pure Consciousness, appeared before me as a living reality. Her bewitching smile prevented me from passing into the Great Beyond. Again and again I tried, but She stood in my way every time. In despair I said to Nangtā: 'It is hopeless. I cannot raise my mind to the unconditioned state and come face to face with Ātman.' He grew excited and sharply said: 'What? You can't do it? But you have to.' He cast his eyes around. Finding a piece of glass he took it up and stuck it between my eyebrows. 'Concentrate the mind on this point!' he thundered. Then with stern determination I again sat to meditate. As soon as the gracious form of the Divine Mother appeared before me, I used my discrimination as a sword and with it clove Her in two. The last barrier fell. My spirit at once soared beyond the relative plane and I lost myself in samādhi."

Sri Ramakrishna remained completely absorbed in samādhi for three days. "Is it really true?" Totapuri cried out in astonishment. "Is it possible that he has attained in a single day what it took me forty years of strenuous practice to achieve? Great God! It is nothing short of a miracle!" With the help of Totapuri, Sri Ramakrishna's mind finally came down to the relative plane.

Totapuri, a monk of the most orthodox type, never stayed at a place more than three days. But he remained at Dakshineswar eleven months. He too had something to learn.

Totapuri had no idea of the struggles of ordinary men in the toils of passion and desire. Having maintained all through life the guilelessness of a child, he laughed at the idea of a man's being led astray by the senses. He was convinced that the world was māyā and had only to be denounced to vanish for ever. A born non-dualist, he had no faith in a Personal God. He did not believe in the terrible aspect of Kāli, much less in Her benign aspect. Music and the chanting of God's holy name were to him only so much nonsense. He ridiculed the spending of emotion on the worship of a Personal God.

KĀLI AND MĀYĀ

Sri Ramakrishna, on the other hand, though fully aware, like his guru, that the world is an illusory appearance, instead of slighting māyā, like an orthodox monist, acknowledged its power in the relative life. He was all love and reverence for māyā, perceiving in it a mysterious and majestic expression of Divinity. To him māyā itself was God, for everything was God. It was one of the faces of Brahman. What he had realized on the heights of the transcendental plane, he also found here below, everywhere about him, under the mysterious garb of names and forms. And this garb was a perfectly transparent sheath, through which he recognized the glory of the Divine Immanence. Māyā, the mighty weaver of the garb, is none other than Kāli, the Divine Mother. She is the primordial Divine Energy, Śakti, and She can no more be distinguished from the Supreme Brahman than can the power of burning be distinguished from fire. She projects the world and again withdraws it. She spins it as the spider spins its web. She is the Mother of the Universe, identical with the Brahman of Vedānta, and with the Ātman of Yoga. As eternal Lawgiver, She makes and unmakes laws; it is by Her imperious will that karma yields its fruit. She ensnares men with illusion and again releases them from bondage with a look of Her benign eyes. She is the supreme Mistress of the cosmic play, and all objects, animate and inanimate, dance by Her will. Even those who realize the Absolute in nirvikalpa samādhi are under Her jurisdiction as long as they still live on the relative plane.

Thus, after nirvikalpa samādhi, Sri Ramakrishna realized māyā in an altogether new role. The binding aspect of Kāli vanished from before his vision. She no longer obscured his understanding. The world became the glorious manifestation of the Divine Mother. Māyā became Brahman. The Transcendental Itself broke through the Immanent. Sri Ramakrishna discovered that māyā operates in the relative world in two ways, and he termed these "avidyāmāyā" and "vidyāmāyā". Avidyāmāyā represents the dark forces of creation: sensuous desires, evil passions, greed, lust, cruelty, and so on. It sustains the world system on the lower planes. It is responsible for the round of man's birth and death. It must be fought and vanquished. But vidyāmāyā is the higher force of creation: the spiritual virtues, the enlightening qualities, kindness, purity, love, devotion. Vidyāmāyā elevates man to the higher planes of consciousness. With the help of vidyāmāyā the devotee rids himself of avidyāmāyā; he then becomes māyātita, free of māyā. The two aspects of māyā are the two forces of creation, the two powers of Kāli; and She stands beyond them both. She is like the effulgent sun, bringing into existence and shining through and standing behind the clouds of different colours and shapes, conjuring up wonderful forms in the blue autumn heaven.

The Divine Mother asked Sri Ramakrishna not to be lost in the featureless Absolute but to remain in bhāvamukha, on the threshold of relative consciousness, the border line between the Absolute and the Relative. He was to keep himself at the "sixth centre" of Tantra, from which he could

see not only the glory of the seventh, but also the divine manifestations of
the Kundalini in the lower centres. He gently oscillated back and forth
across the dividing line. Ecstatic devotion to the Divine Mother alternated
with serene absorption in the Ocean of Absolute Unity. He thus bridged the
gulf between the Personal and the Impersonal, the immanent and the
transcendent aspects of Reality. This is a unique experience in the recorded
spiritual history of the world.

TOTAPURI'S LESSON

From Sri Ramakrishna Totapuri had to learn the significance of Kāli, the
Great Fact of the relative world, and of māyā, Her indescribable Power.

One day, when guru and disciple were engaged in an animated discussion
about Vedānta, a servant of the temple garden came there and took a coal
from the sacred fire that had been lighted by the great ascetic. He wanted
it to light his tobacco. Totapuri flew into a rage and was about to beat the
man. Sri Ramakrishna rocked with laughter. "What a shame!" he cried.
"You are explaining to me the reality of Brahman and the illusoriness of
the world; yet now you have so far forgotten yourself as to be about to beat
a man in a fit of passion. The power of māyā is indeed inscrutable!" Totapuri
was embarrassed.

About this time Totapuri was suddenly laid up with a severe attack of
dysentery. On account of this miserable illness he found it impossible to
meditate. One night the pain became excruciating. He could no longer
concentrate on Brahman. The body stood in the way. He became incensed
with its demands. A free soul, he did not at all care for the body. So he
determined to drown it in the Ganges. Thereupon he walked into the river.
But, lo! He walks to the other bank.[5] Is there not enough water in the
Ganges? Standing dumbfounded on the other bank he looks back across
the water. The trees, the temples, the houses, are silhouetted against the
sky. Suddenly, in one dazzling moment, he sees on all sides the presence of
the Divine Mother. She is in everything; She is everything. She is in the
water; She is on land. She is the body; She is the mind. She is pain; She is
comfort. She is knowledge; She is ignorance. She is life; She is death. She
is everything that one sees, hears, or imagines. She turns "yea" into "nay",
and "nay" into "yea". Without Her grace no embodied being can go beyond
Her realm. Man has no free will. He is not even free to die. Yet, again,
beyond the body and mind She resides in Her Transcendental, Absolute
aspect. She is the Brahman that Totapuri had been worshipping all his life.

Totapuri returned to Dakshineswar and spent the remaining hours of the
night meditating on the Divine Mother. In the morning he went to the
Kāli temple with Sri Ramakrishna and prostrated himself before the image
of the Mother. He now realized why he had spent eleven months at
Dakshineswar. Bidding farewell to the disciple, he continued on his way,
enlightened.

Sri Ramakrishna later described the significance of Totapuri's lessons:

[5] This version of the incident is taken from the biography of Sri Ramakrishna by
Swami Saradananda, one of the Master's direct disciples.

"When I think of the Supreme Being as inactive—neither creating nor preserving nor destroying—, I call Him Brahman or Purusha, the Impersonal God. When I think of Him as active—creating, preserving, and destroying—, I call Him Śakti or Māyā or Prakriti, the Personal God. But the distinction between them does not mean a difference. The Personal and the Impersonal are the same thing, like milk and its whiteness, the diamond and its lustre, the snake and its wriggling motion. It is impossible to conceive of the one without the other. The Divine Mother and Brahman are one."

After the departure of Totapuri, Sri Ramakrishna remained for six months in a state of absolute identity with Brahman. "For six months at a stretch", he said, "I remained in that state from which ordinary men can never return; generally the body falls off, after three weeks, like a sere leaf. I was not conscious of day and night. Flies would enter my mouth and nostrils just as they do a dead body's, but I did not feel them. My hair became matted with dust."

His body would not have survived but for the kindly attention of a monk who happened to be at Dakshineswar at that time and who somehow realized that for the good of humanity Sri Ramakrishna's body must be preserved. He tried various means, even physical violence, to recall the fleeing soul to the prison-house of the body, and during the resultant fleeting moments of consciousness he would push a few morsels of food down Sri Ramakrishna's throat. Presently Sri Ramakrishna received the command of the Divine Mother to remain on the threshold of relative consciousness. Soon thereafter he was afflicted with a serious attack of dysentery. Day and night the pain tortured him, and his mind gradually came down to the physical plane.

COMPANY OF HOLY MEN AND DEVOTEES

From now on Sri Ramakrishna began to seek the company of devotees and holy men. He had gone through the storm and stress of spiritual disciplines and visions. Now he realized an inner calmness and appeared to others as a normal person. But he could not bear the company of worldly people or listen to their talk. Fortunately the holy atmosphere of Dakshineswar and the liberality of Mathur attracted monks and holy men from all parts of the country. Sādhus of all denominations—monists and dualists, Vaishnavas and Vedāntists, Śaktas and worshippers of Rāma—flocked there in ever increasing numbers. Ascetics and visionaries came to seek Sri Ramakrishna's advice. Vaishnavas had come during the period of his Vaishnava sādhanā, and Tāntriks when he practised the disciplines of Tantra. Vedāntists began to arrive after the departure of Totapuri. In the room of Sri Ramakrishna, who was then in bed with dysentery, the Vedāntists engaged in scriptural discussions, and, forgetting his own physical suffering, he solved their doubts by referring directly to his own experiences. Many of the visitors were genuine spiritual souls, the unseen pillars of Hinduism, and their spiritual lives were quickened in no small measure by the sage of Dakshineswar. Sri Ramakrishna in turn learnt from them anecdotes concerning the ways and the conduct of holy men, which he subsequently narrated to his devotees and disciples. At his request Mathur provided him with large stores of food-stuffs, clothes, and so forth, for distribution among the wandering monks.

Sri Ramakrishna had not read books, yet he possessed an encyclopedic knowledge of religions and religious philosophies. This he acquired from his contacts with innumerable holy men and scholars. He had a unique power of assimilation; through meditation he made this knowledge a part of his being. Once, when he was asked by a disciple about the source of his seemingly inexhaustible knowledge, he replied: "I have not read; but I have heard the learned. I have made a garland of their knowledge, wearing it round my neck, and I have given it as an offering at the feet of the Mother."

Sri Ramakrishna used to say that when the flower blooms the bees come to it for honey of their own accord. Now many souls began to visit Dakshineswar to satisfy their spiritual hunger. He, the devotee and aspirant, became the Master. Gauri, the great scholar who had been one of the first to proclaim Sri Ramakrishna an Incarnation of God, paid the Master a visit in 1870 and with the Master's blessings renounced the world. Narayan Shastri, another great pundit, who had mastered the six systems of Hindu philosophy and had been offered a lucrative post by the Mahārājā of Jaipur, met the Master and recognized in him one who had realized in life those ideals which he himself had encountered merely in books. Sri Ramakrishna initiated Narayan Shastri, at his earnest request, into the life of sannyās. Pundit Padmalochan, the court pundit of the Mahārājā of Burdwan, well known for his scholarship in both the Vedānta and the Nyāya systems of philosophy, accepted the Master as an Incarnation of God. Krishnakishore, a Vedāntist scholar, became devoted to the Master. And there arrived Viswanath Upadhyaya, who was to become a favourite devotee; Sri Ramakrishna always addressed him as "Captain". He was a high officer of the King of Nepal and had received the title of Colonel in recognition of his merit. A scholar of the *Gītā*, the *Bhāgavata*, and the Vedānta philosophy, he daily performed the worship of his Chosen Deity with great devotion. "I have read the Vedas and the other scriptures", he said. "I have also met a good many monks and devotees in different places. But it is in Sri Ramakrishna's presence that my spiritual yearnings have been fulfilled. To me he seems to be the embodiment of the truths of the scriptures."

The Knowledge of Brahman in nirvikalpa samādhi had convinced Sri Ramakrishna that the gods of the different religions are but so many readings of the Absolute, and that the Ultimate Reality could never be expressed by human tongue. He understood that all religions lead their devotees by differing paths to one and the same goal. Now he became eager to explore some of the alien religions; for with him understanding meant actual experience.

ISLĀM

Toward the end of 1866 he began to practise the disciplines of Islām. Under the direction of his Mussalmān guru he abandoned himself to his new sādhanā. He dressed as a Mussalmān and repeated the name of Āllāh.

His prayers took the form of the Islāmic devotions. He forgot the Hindu gods and goddesses—even Kāli—and gave up visiting the temples. He took up his residence outside the temple precincts. After three days he saw the vision of a radiant figure, perhaps Mohammed. This figure gently approached him and finally lost himself in Sri Ramakrishna. Thus he realized the Mussalmān God. Thence he passed into communion with Brahman. The mighty river of Islām also led him back to the Ocean of the Absolute.

CHRISTIANITY

Eight years later, some time in November 1874, Sri Ramakrishna was seized with an irresistible desire to learn the truth of the Christian religion. He began to listen to readings from the Bible, by Sambhu Charan Mallick, a gentleman of Calcutta and a devotee of the Master. Sri Ramakrishna became fascinated by the life and teachings of Jesus. One day he was seated in the parlour of Jadu Mallick's garden house[6] at Dakshineswar, when his eyes became fixed on a painting of the Madonna and Child. Intently watching it, he became gradually overwhelmed with divine emotion. The figures in the picture took on life, and the rays of light emanating from them entered his soul. The effect of this experience was stronger than that of the vision of Mohammed. In dismay he cried out, "O Mother! What are You doing to me?" And, breaking through the barriers of creed and religion, he entered a new realm of ecstasy. Christ possessed his soul. For three days he did not set foot in the Kāli temple. On the fourth day, in the afternoon, as he was walking in the Panchavati, he saw coming toward him a person with beautiful large eyes, serene countenance, and fair skin. As the two faced each other, a voice rang out in the depths of Sri Ramakrishna's soul: "Behold the Christ, who shed His heart's blood for the redemption of the world, who suffered a sea of anguish for love of men. It is He, the Master Yogi, who is in eternal union with God. It is Jesus, Love Incarnate." The Son of Man embraced the Son of the Divine Mother and merged in him. Sri Ramakrishna realized his identity with Christ, as he had already realized his identity with Kāli, Rāma, Hanumān, Rādhā, Krishna, Brahman, and Mohammed. The Master went into samādhi and communed with the Brahman with attributes. Thus he experienced the truth that Christianity, too, was a path leading to God-Consciousness. Till the last moment of his life he believed that Christ was an Incarnation of God. But Christ, for him, was not the only Incarnation; there were others—Buddha, for instance, and Krishna.

ATTITUDE TOWARD DIFFERENT RELIGIONS

Sri Ramakrishna accepted the divinity of Buddha and used to point out the similarity of his teachings to those of the Upanishads. He also showed great respect for the Tirthankaras, who founded Jainism, and for the ten Gurus of Śikhism. But he did not speak of them as Divine Incarnations. He was heard to say that the Gurus of Śikhism were the reincarnations of King

---

[6] This expression is used throughout to translate the Bengali word denoting a rich man's country house set in a garden.

Janaka of ancient India. He kept in his room at Dakshineswar a small statue of Tirthankara Mahāvira and a picture of Christ, before which incense was burnt morning and evening.

Without being formally initiated into their doctrines, Sri Ramakrishna thus realized the ideals of religions other than Hinduism. He did not need to follow any doctrine. All barriers were removed by his overwhelming love of God. So he became a Master who could speak with authority regarding the ideas and ideals of the various religions of the world. "I have practised", said he, "all religions—Hinduism, Islām, Christianity—and I have also followed the paths of the different Hindu sects. I have found that it is the same God toward whom all are directing their steps, though along different paths. You must try all beliefs and traverse all the different ways once. Wherever I look, I see men quarrelling in the name of religion—Hindus, Mohammedans, Brāhmos, Vaishnavas, and the rest. But they never reflect that He who is called Krishna is also called Śiva, and bears the name of the Primal Energy, Jesus, and Āllāh as well—the same Rāma with a thousand names. A lake has several ghāts. At one the Hindus take water in pitchers and call it 'jal'; at another the Mussalmāns take water in leather bags and call it 'pāni'. At a third the Christians call it 'water'. Can we imagine that it is not 'jal', but only 'pāni' or 'water'? How ridiculous! The substance is One under different names, and everyone is seeking the same substance; only climate, temperament, and name create differences. Let each man follow his own path. If he sincerely and ardently wishes to know God, peace be unto him! He will surely realize Him."

In 1867 Sri Ramakrishna returned to Kāmārpukur to recuperate from the effect of his austerities. The peaceful countryside, the simple and artless companions of his boyhood, and the pure air did him much good. The villagers were happy to get back their playful, frank, witty, kind-hearted, and truthful Gadadhar, though they did not fail to notice the great change that had come over him during his years in Calcutta. His wife, Sarada Devi, now fourteen years old, soon arrived at Kāmārpukur. Her spiritual development was much beyond her age and she was able to understand immediately her husband's state of mind. She became eager to learn from him about God and to live with him as his attendant. The Master accepted her cheerfully both as his disciple and as his spiritual companion. Referring to the experiences of these few days, she once said: "I used to feel always as if a pitcher full of bliss were placed in my heart. The joy was indescribable."

PILGRIMAGE

On January 27, 1868, Mathur Babu with a party of some one hundred and twenty-five persons set out on a pilgrimage to the sacred places of northern India. At Vaidyanath in Behar, when the Master saw the inhabitants of a village reduced by poverty and starvation to mere skeletons, he requested his rich patron to feed the people and give each a piece of cloth. Mathur demurred at the added expense. The Master declared bitterly that he would not go on to Benares, but would live with the poor and share their miseries. He actually left Mathur and sat down with the villagers.

Whereupon Mathur had to yield. On another occasion, two years later, Sri Ramakrishna showed a similar sentiment for the poor and needy. He accompanied Mathur on a tour to one of the latter's estates at the time of the collection of rents. For two years the harvests had failed and the tenants were in a state of extreme poverty. The Master asked Mathur to remit their rents, distribute help to them, and in addition give the hungry people a sumptuous feast. When Mathur grumbled, the Master said: "You are only the steward of the Divine Mother. They are the Mother's tenants. You must spend the Mother's money. When they are suffering, how can you refuse to help them? You must help them." Again Mathur had to give in. Sri Ramakrishna's sympathy for the poor sprang from his perception of God in all created beings. His sentiment was not that of the humanist or philanthropist. To him the service of man was the same as the worship of God.

The party entered holy Benares by boat along the Ganges. When Sri Ramakrishna's eyes fell on this city of Śiva, where had accumulated for ages the devotion and piety of countless worshippers, he saw it to be made of gold, as the scriptures declare. He was visibly moved. During his stay in the city he treated every particle of its earth with utmost respect. At the Manikarnikā Ghāt, the great cremation ground of the city, he actually saw Śiva, with ash-covered body and tawny matted hair, serenely approaching each funeral pyre and breathing into the ears of the corpses the mantra of liberation; and then the Divine Mother removing from the dead their bonds. Thus he realized the significance of the scriptural statement that anyone dying in Benares attains salvation through the grace of Śiva. He paid a visit to Trailanga Swami, the celebrated monk, whom he later declared to be a real paramahamsa, a veritable image of Śiva.

Sri Ramakrishna visited Allāhābād, at the confluence of the Ganges and the Jamunā, and then proceeded to Vrindāvan and Mathurā, hallowed by the legends, songs, and dramas about Krishna and the gopis. Here he had numerous visions and his heart overflowed with divine emotion. He wept and said: "O Krishna! Everything here is as it was in the olden days. You alone are absent." He visited the great woman saint, Gangāmāyi, regarded by Vaishnava devotees as the reincarnation of an intimate attendant of Rādhā. She was sixty years old and had frequent trances. She spoke of Sri Ramakrishna as an incarnation of Rādhā. With great difficulty he was persuaded to leave her.

On the return journey Mathur wanted to visit Gayā, but Sri Ramakrishna declined to go. He recalled his father's vision at Gayā before his own birth and felt that in the temple of Vishnu he would become permanently absorbed in God. Mathur, honouring the Master's wish, returned with his party to Calcutta.

From Vrindāvan the Master had brought a handful of dust. Part of this he scattered in the Panchavati; the rest he buried in the little hut where he had practised meditation. "Now this place", he said, "is as sacred as Vrindāvan."

In 1870 the Master went on a pilgrimage to Nadiā, the birth-place of Sri Chaitanya. As the boat by which he travelled approached the sand-bank close to Nadiā, Sri Ramakrishna had a vision of the "two brothers", Sri Chaitanya and his companion Nityānanda, "bright as molten gold" and with haloes, rushing to greet him with uplifted hands. "There they come! There they come!" he cried. They entered his body and he went into a deep trance.

RELATION WITH HIS WIFE

In 1872 Sarada Devi paid her first visit to her husband at Dakshineswar. Four years earlier she had seen him at Kāmārpukur and had tasted the bliss of his divine company. Since then she had become even more gentle, tender, introspective, serious, and unselfish. She had heard many rumours about her husband's insanity. People had shown her pity in her misfortune. The more she thought, the more she felt that her duty was to be with him, giving him, in whatever measure she could, a wife's devoted service. She was now eighteen years old. Accompanied by her father, she arrived at Dakshineswar, having come on foot the distance of eighty miles. She had had an attack of fever on the way. When she arrived at the temple garden the Master said sorrowfully: "Ah! You have come too late. My Mathur is no longer here to look after you." Mathur had passed away the previous year.

The Master took up the duty of instructing his young wife, and this included everything from housekeeping to the Knowledge of Brahman. He taught her how to trim a lamp, how to behave toward people according to their differing temperaments, and how to conduct herself before visitors. He instructed her in the mysteries of spiritual life—prayer, meditation, japa, deep contemplation, and samādhi. The first lesson that Sarada Devi received was: "God is everybody's Beloved, just as the moon is dear to every child. Everyone has the same right to pray to Him. Out of His grace He reveals Himself to all who call upon Him. You too will see Him if you but pray to Him."

Totapuri, coming to know of the Master's marriage, had once remarked: "What does it matter? He alone is firmly established in the Knowledge of Brahman who can adhere to his spirit of discrimination and renunciation even while living with his wife. He alone has attained the supreme illumination who can look on man and woman alike as Brahman. A man with the idea of sex may be a good aspirant, but he is still far from the goal." Sri Ramakrishna and his wife lived together at Dakshineswar, but their minds always soared above the worldly plane. A few months after Sarada Devi's arrival Sri Ramakrishna arranged, on an auspicious day, a special worship of Kāli, the Divine Mother. Instead of an image of the Deity, he placed on the seat the living image, Sarada Devi herself. The worshipper and the worshipped went into deep samādhi and in the transcendental plane their souls were united. After several hours Sri Ramakrishna came down again to the relative plane, sang a hymn to the Great Goddess, and surrendered, at the feet of the living image, himself, his rosary, and the fruit of his life-long sādhanā. This is known in Tantra as the Shoraśi Pujā, the "Adoration of Woman". Sri Ramakrishna realized the significance of the great statement of the Upanishad: "O Lord, Thou art the woman, Thou art the man: Thou art the boy, Thou art the girl; Thou art the old, tottering on their crutches. Thou pervadest the universe in its multiple forms."

By his marriage Sri Ramakrishna admitted the great value of marriage in man's spiritual evolution, and by adhering to his monastic vows he demonstrated the imperative necessity of self-control, purity, and continence, in the realization of God. By his unique spiritual relationship with his wife he proved that husband and wife can live together as spiritual companions. Thus his life is a synthesis of the ways of life of the householder and the monk.

THE "EGO" OF THE MASTER

In the nirvikalpa samādhi Sri Ramakrishna had realized that Brahman alone is real and the world illusory. By keeping his mind six months on the plane of the non-dual Brahman, he had attained to the state of the vijnāni, the knower of Truth in a special and very rich sense, who sees Brahman not only in himself and in the transcendental Absolute, but in everything of the world. In this state of vijnāna, sometimes, bereft of body-consciousness, he would regard himself as one with Brahman; sometimes, conscious of the dual world, he would regard himself as God's devotee, servant, or child. In order to enable the Master to work for the welfare of humanity, the Divine Mother had kept in him a trace of ego, which he described—according to his mood—as the "ego of Knowledge", the "ego of Devotion", the "ego of a child", or the "ego of a servant". In any case this ego of the Master, consumed by the fire of the Knowledge of Brahman, was an appearance only, like a burnt string. He often referred to this ego as the "ripe ego" in contrast with the ego of the bound soul, which he described as the "unripe" or "green" ego. The ego of the bound soul identifies itself with the body, relatives, possessions, and the world; but the "ripe ego", illumined by Divine Knowledge, knows the body, relatives, possessions, and the world to be unreal and establishes a relationship of love with God alone. Through this "ripe ego" Sri Ramakrishna dealt with the world and his wife. One day, while stroking his feet, Sarada Devi asked the Master, "What do you think of me?" Quick came the answer: "The Mother who is worshipped in the temple is the mother who has given birth to my body and is now living in the nahabat, and it is She again who is stroking my feet at this moment. Indeed, I always look on you as the personification of the Blissful Mother Kāli."

Sarada Devi, in the company of her husband, had rare spiritual experiences. She said: "I have no words to describe my wonderful exaltation of spirit as I watched him in his different moods. Under the influence of divine emotion he would sometimes talk on abstruse subjects, sometimes laugh, sometimes weep, and sometimes become perfectly motionless in samādhi. This would continue throughout the night. There was such an extraordinary divine presence in him that now and then I would shake with fear and wonder how the night would pass. Months went by in this way. Then one day he discovered that I had to keep awake the whole night lest, during my sleep, he should go into samādhi—for it might happen at any moment—, and so he asked me to sleep in the nahabat."

SUMMARY OF THE MASTER'S SPIRITUAL EXPERIENCES

We have now come to the end of Sri Ramakrishna's sādhanā, the period of his spiritual discipline. As a result of his supersensuous experiences he reached certain conclusions regarding himself and spirituality in general. His conclusions about himself may be summarized as follows:

First, he was an Incarnation of God, a specially commissioned person, whose spiritual experiences were for the benefit of humanity. Whereas it takes an ordinary man a whole life's struggle to realize one or two phases of God, he had in a few years realized God in all His phases.

Second, he knew that he had always been a free soul, that the various disciplines through which he had passed were really not necessary for his own liberation but were solely for the benefit of others. Thus the terms liberation and bondage were not applicable to him. As long as there are beings who consider themselves bound, God must come down to earth as an Incarnation to free them from bondage, just as a magistrate must visit any part of his district in which there is trouble.

Third, he came to foresee the time of his death. His words with respect to this matter were literally fulfilled.

About spirituality in general the following were his conclusions:

First, he was firmly convinced that all religions are true, that every doctrinal system represents a path to God. He had followed all the main paths and all had led him to the same goal. He was the first religious prophet recorded in history to preach the harmony of religions.

Second, the three great systems of thought known as Dualism, Qualified Non-dualism, and Absolute Non-dualism—Dvaita, Viśishtādvaita, and Advaita—he perceived to represent three stages in man's progress toward the Ultimate Reality. They were not contradictory but complementary and suited to different temperaments. For the ordinary man with strong attachment to the senses, a dualistic form of religion, prescribing a certain amount of material support, such as music and other symbols, is useful. A man of God-realization transcends the idea of worldly duties, but the ordinary mortal must perform his duties, striving to be unattached and to surrender the results to God. The mind can comprehend and describe the range of thought and experience up to the Viśishtādvaita, and no further. The Advaita, the last word in spiritual experience, is something to be felt in samādhi, for it transcends mind and speech. From the highest standpoint, the Absolute and Its manifestation are equally real—the Lord's Name, His Abode, and the Lord Himself are of the same spiritual Essence. Everything is Spirit, the difference being only in form.

Third, Sri Ramakrishna realized the wish of the Divine Mother that through him She should found a new Order, consisting of those who would uphold the universal doctrines illustrated in his life.

Fourth, his spiritual insight told him that those who were having their last birth on the mortal plane of existence and those who had sincerely called on the Lord even once in their lives must come to him.

During this period Sri Ramakrishna suffered several bereavements. The first was the death of a nephew named Akshay. After the young man's death Sri Ramakrishna said: "Akshay died before my very eyes. But it did not affect me in the least. I stood by and watched a man die. It was like a sword being drawn from its scabbard. I enjoyed the scene, and laughed and sang and danced over it. They removed the body and cremated it. But the next day as I stood there (*pointing to the southeast verandah of his room*), I felt a racking pain for the loss of Akshay, as if somebody were squeezing my heart like a wet towel. I wondered at it and thought that the Mother was teaching me a lesson. I was not much concerned even with my own body—much less with a relative. But if such was my pain at the loss of a nephew, how much more must be the grief of the householders at the loss of their near and dear ones!" In 1871 Mathur died, and some five years later Sambhu Mallick—who, after Mathur's passing away, had taken care of the Master's comfort. In 1873 died his elder brother Rameswar, and in 1876, his beloved mother. These bereavements left their imprint on the tender human heart of Sri Ramakrishna, albeit he had realized the immortality of the soul and the illusoriness of birth and death.

In March 1875, about a year before the death of his mother, the Master met Keshab Chandra Sen. The meeting was a momentous event for both Sri Ramakrishna and Keshab. Here the Master for the first time came into actual contact with a worthy representative of modern India.

BRĀHMO SAMĀJ

Keshab was the leader of the Brāhmo Samāj, one of the two great movements that, during the latter part of the nineteenth century, played an important part in shaping the course of the renascence of India. The founder of the Brāhmo movement had been the great Rājā Rammohan Roy (1774-1833). Though born in an orthodox brāhmin family, Rammohan Roy had shown great sympathy for Islām and Christianity. He had gone to Tibet in search of the Buddhist mysteries. He had extracted from Christianity its ethical system, but had rejected the divinity of Christ as he had denied the Hindu Incarnations. The religion of Islām influenced him, to a great extent, in the formulation of his monotheistic doctrines. But he always went back to the Vedas for his spiritual inspiration. The Brāhmo Samāj, which he founded in 1828, was dedicated to the "worship and adoration of the Eternal, the Unsearchable, the Immutable Being, who is the Author and Preserver of the Universe". The Samāj was open to all without distinction of colour, creed, caste, nation, or religion.

The real organizer of the Samāj was Devendranath Tagore (1817-1905), the father of the poet Rabindranath. His physical and spiritual beauty, aristocratic aloofness, penetrating intellect, and poetic sensibility made him the foremost leader of the educated Bengalis. These addressed him by the respectful epithet of Maharshi, the "Great Seer". The Maharshi was a Sanskrit scholar and, unlike Rājā Rammohan Roy, drew his inspiration entirely from the Upanishads. He was an implacable enemy of image worship and also fought to stop the infiltration of Christian ideas into the Samāj. He gave the movement its faith and ritual. Under his influence the

Brāhmo Samāj professed One Self-existent Supreme Being who had created the universe out of nothing, the God of Truth, Infinite Wisdom, Goodness, and Power, the Eternal and Omnipotent, the One without a Second. Man should love Him and do His will, believe in Him and worship Him, and thus merit salvation in the world to come.

By far the ablest leader of the Brāhmo movement was Keshab Chandra Sen (1838-1884). Unlike Rājā Rammohan Roy and Devendranath Tagore, Keshab was born of a middle-class Bengali family and had been brought up in an English school. He did not know Sanskrit and very soon broke away from the popular Hindu religion. Even at an early age he came under the spell of Christ and professed to have experienced the special favour of John the Baptist, Christ, and St. Paul. When he strove to introduce Christ to the Brāhmo Samāj, a rupture became inevitable with Devendranath. In 1868 Keshab broke with the older leader and founded the Brāhmo Samāj of India, Devendra retaining leadership of the first Brāhmo Samāj, now called the Ādi Samāj.

Keshab possessed a complex nature. When passing through a great moral crisis, he spent much of his time in solitude and felt that he heard the voice of God. When a devotional form of worship was introduced into the Brāhmo Samāj, he spent hours in singing kirtan with his followers. He visited England in 1870 and impressed the English people with his musical voice, his simple English, and his spiritual fervour. He was entertained by Queen Victoria. Returning to India, he founded centres of the Brāhmo Samāj in various parts of the country. Not unlike a professor of comparative religion in a European university, he began to discover, about the time of his first contact with Sri Ramakrishna, the harmony of religions. He became sympathetic toward the Hindu gods and goddesses, explaining them in a liberal fashion. Further, he believed that he was called by God to dictate to the world God's newly revealed law, the New Dispensation, the Navavidhān.

In 1878 a schism divided Keshab's Samāj. Some of his influential followers accused him of infringing the Brāhmo principles by marrying his daughter to a wealthy man before she had attained the marriageable age approved by the Samāj. This group seceded and established the Sādhāran Brāhmo Samāj, Keshab remaining the leader of the Navavidhān. Keshab now began to be drawn more and more toward the Christ ideal, though under the influence of Sri Ramakrishna his devotion to the Divine Mother also deepened. His mental oscillation between Christ and the Divine Mother of Hinduism found no position of rest. In Bengal and some other parts of India the Brāhmo movement took the form of unitarian Christianity, scoffed at Hindu rituals, and preached a crusade against image worship. Influenced by Western culture, it declared the supremacy of reason, advocated the ideals of the French Revolution, abolished the caste-system among its own members, stood for the emancipation of women, agitated for the abolition of early marriage, sanctioned the remarriage of widows, and encouraged various educational and social-reform movements. The immediate effect of the Brāhmo movement in Bengal was the checking of the proselytizing activities of the Christian missionaries. It also raised Indian culture in the estimation of its English masters. But it was an intellectual and eclectic religious ferment born of the necessity of the time. Unlike Hinduism, it was not founded on the deep inner experiences of sages and prophets. Its influence was confined to a comparatively few educated men and women of the country, and the vast masses of the Hindus remained outside it. It sounded monotonously only one of the notes in the rich gamut of the Eternal Religion of the Hindus.

ĀRYA SAMĀJ

The other movement playing an important part in the nineteenth-century religious revival of India was the Ārya Samāj. The Brāhmo Samāj, essentially a movement of compromise with European culture, tacitly admitted the superiority of the West. But the founder of the Ārya Samāj was a pugnacious Hindu sannyāsi who accepted the challenge of Islām and Christianity and was resolved to combat all foreign influence in India. Swami Dayananda (1824-1883) launched this movement in Bombay in 1875, and soon its influence was felt throughout western India. The Swami was a great scholar of the Vedas, which he explained as being strictly monotheistic. He preached against the worship of images and re-established the ancient Vedic sacrificial rites. According to him the Vedas were the ultimate authority on religion, and he accepted every word of them as literally true. The Ārya Samāj became a bulwark against the encroachments of Islām and Christianity, and its orthodox flavour appealed to many Hindu minds. It also assumed leadership in many movements of social reform. The caste-system became a target of its attack. Women it liberated from many of their social disabilities. The cause of education received from it a great impetus. It started agitation against early marriage and advocated the remarriage of Hindu widows. Its influence was strongest in the Punjab, the battle-ground of the Hindu and Islāmic cultures. A new fighting attitude was introduced into the slumbering Hindu society. Unlike the Brāhmo Samāj, the influence of the Ārya Samāj was not confined to the intellectuals. It was a force that spread to the masses. It was a dogmatic movement intolerant of those who disagreed with its views, and it emphasized only one way, the Ārya Samāj way, to the realization of Truth. Sri Ramakrishna met Swami Dayananda when the latter visited Bengal.

KESHAB CHANDRA SEN

Keshab Chandra Sen and Sri Ramakrishna met for the first time in the garden house of Jaygopal Sen at Belghariā, a few miles from Dakshineswar, where the great Brāhmo leader was staying with some of his disciples. In many respects the two were poles apart, though an irresistible inner attraction was to make them intimate friends. The Master had realized God as Pure Spirit and Consciousness, but he believed in the various forms of God as well. Keshab, on the other hand, regarded image worship as idolatry and gave allegorical explanations of the Hindu deities. Keshab was an orator and a writer of books and magazine articles; Sri Ramakrishna had a horror of lecturing and hardly knew how to write his own name. Keshab's fame spread far and wide, even reaching the distant shores of England; the Master still led a secluded life in the village of Dakshineswar. Keshab emphasized social reforms for India's regeneration; to Sri Ramakrishna God-realization was the only goal of life. Keshab considered himself a disciple of Christ and accepted in a diluted form the Christian sacraments and Trinity; Sri Rama-krishna was the simple child of Kāli, the Divine Mother, though he too, in a different way, acknowledged Christ's divinity. Keshab was a house-holder and took a real interest in the welfare of his children, whereas Sri Ramakrishna was a paramahamsa and completely indifferent to the life of the world. Yet, as their acquaintance ripened into friendship, Sri Rama-krishna and Keshab held each other in great love and respect. Years later, at the news of Keshab's death, the Master felt as if half his body had be-come paralyzed. Keshab's concepts of the harmony of religions and the Motherhood of God were deepened and enriched by his contact with Sri Ramakrishna.

Sri Ramakrishna, dressed in a red-bordered dhoti, one end of which was carelessly thrown over his left shoulder, came to Jaygopal's garden house accompanied by Hriday. No one took notice of the unostentatious visitor. Finally the Master said to Keshab, "People tell me you have seen God; so I have come to hear from you about God." A magnificent conversation fol-lowed. The Master sang a thrilling song about Kāli and forthwith went into samādhi. When Hriday uttered the sacred "Om" in his ears, he gradually came back to consciousness of the world, his face still radiating a divine brilliance. Keshab and his followers were amazed. The contrast between Sri Ramakrishna and the Brāhmo devotees was very interesting. There sat this small man, thin and extremely delicate. His eyes were illumined with an inner light. Good humour gleamed in his eyes and lurked in the corners of his mouth. His speech was Bengali of a homely kind with a slight, de-lightful stammer, and his words held men enthralled by their wealth of spiritual experience, their inexhaustible store of simile and metaphor, their power of observation, their bright and subtle humour, their wonderful catholicity, their ceaseless flow of wisdom. And around him now were the sophisticated men of Bengal, the best products of Western education, with Keshab, the idol of young Bengal, as their leader.

Keshab's sincerity was enough for Sri Ramakrishna. Henceforth the two saw each other frequently, either at Dakshineswar or at the temple of the Brāhmo Samāj. Whenever the Master was in the temple at the time of divine service, Keshab would request him to speak to the congregation. And Keshab would visit the saint, in his turn, with offerings of flowers and fruits.

OTHER BRĀHMO LEADERS

Gradually other Brāhmo leaders began to feel Sri Ramakrishna's influ-ence. But they were by no means uncritical admirers of the Master. They particularly disapproved of his ascetic renunciation and condemnation of "woman and gold".[7] They measured him according to their own ideals of

[7] See foot-note, p. 82.

the householder's life. Some could not understand his samādhi and described it as a nervous malady. Yet they could not resist his magnetic personality.

Among the Brāhmo leaders who knew the Master closely were Pratap Chandra Mazumdar, Vijaykrishna Goswami, Trailokyanath Sannyal, and Shivanath Shastri.

Shivanath, one day, was greatly impressed by the Master's utter simplicity and abhorrence of praise. He was seated with Sri Ramakrishna in the latter's room when several rich men of Calcutta arrived. The Master left the room for a few minutes. In the mean time Hriday, his nephew, began to describe his samādhi to the visitors. The last few words caught the Master's ear as he entered the room. He said to Hriday: "What a mean-spirited fellow you must be to extol me thus before these rich men! You have seen their costly apparel and their gold watches and chains, and your object is to get from them as much money as you can. What do I care about what they think of me? (Turning to the gentlemen) No, my friends, what he has told you about me is not true. It was not love of God that made me absorbed in God and indifferent to external life. I became positively insane for some time. The sādhus who frequented this temple told me to practise many things. I tried to follow them, and the consequence was that my austerities drove me to insanity." This is a quotation from one of Shivanath's books. He took the Master's words literally and failed to see their real import.

Shivanath vehemently criticized the Master for his other-worldly attitude toward his wife. He writes: "Ramakrishna was practically separated from his wife, who lived in her village home. One day when I was complaining to some friends about the virtual widowhood of his wife, he drew me to one side and whispered in my ear: 'Why do you complain? It is no longer possible; it is all dead and gone.' Another day as I was inveighing against this part of his teaching, and also declaring that our program of work in the Brāhmo Samāj includes women, that ours is a social and domestic religion, and that we want to give education and social liberty to women, the saint became very much excited, as was his way when anything against his settled conviction was asserted—a trait we so much liked in him—and exclaimed, 'Go, thou fool, go and perish in the pit that your women will dig for you.' Then he glared at me and said: 'What does a gardener do with a young plant? Does he not surround it with a fence, to protect it from goats and cattle? And when the young plant has grown up into a tree and it can no longer be injured by cattle, does he not remove the fence and let the tree grow freely?' I replied, 'Yes, that is the custom with gardeners.' Then he remarked, 'Do the same in your spiritual life; become strong, be full-grown; then you may seek them.' To which I replied, 'I don't agree with you in thinking that women's work is like that of cattle, destructive; they are our associates and helpers in our spiritual struggles and social progress'—a view with which he could not agree, and he marked his dissent by shaking his head. Then referring to the lateness of the hour he jocularly remarked, 'It is time for you to depart; take care, do not be late; otherwise your woman will not admit you into her room.' This evoked hearty laughter."

Pratap Chandra Mazumdar, the right-hand man of Keshab and an accom-

plished Brāhmo preacher in Europe and America, bitterly criticized Sri
Ramakrishna's use of uncultured language and also his austere attitude
toward his wife. But he could not escape the spell of the Master's personality. In the course of an article about Sri Ramakrishna, Pratap wrote in
the "Theistic Quarterly Review": "What is there in common between him
and me? I, a Europeanized, civilized, self-centred, semi-sceptical, so-called
educated reasoner, and he, a poor, illiterate, unpolished, half-idolatrous,
friendless Hindu devotee? Why should I sit long hours to attend to him, I,
who have listened to Disraeli and Fawcett, Stanley and Max Müller, and a
whole host of European scholars and divines? . . . And it is not I only, but
dozens like me, who do the same. . . . He worships Śiva, he worships Kāli,
he worships Rāma, he worships Krishna, and is a confirmed advocate of
Vedāntic doctrines. . . . He is an idolater, yet is a faithful and most devoted meditator on the perfections of the One Formless, Absolute, Infinite
Deity. . . . His religion is ecstasy, his worship means transcendental insight,
his whole nature burns day and night with a permanent fire and fever of a
strange faith and feeling. . . . So long as he is spared to us, gladly shall we
sit at his feet to learn from him the sublime precepts of purity, unworldli-
ness, spirituality, and inebriation in the love of God. . . . He, by his childlike bhakti, by his strong conceptions of an ever-ready Motherhood, helped
to unfold it [God as our Mother] in our minds wonderfully. . . . By
associating with him we learnt to realize better the divine attributes as scattered over the three hundred and thirty millions of deities of mythological
India, the gods of the Purānas."

The Brāhmo leaders received much inspiration from their contact with
Sri Ramakrishna. It broadened their religious views and kindled in their
hearts the yearning for God-realization; it made them understand and appreciate the rituals and symbols of Hindu religion, convinced them of the
manifestation of God in diverse forms, and deepened their thoughts about
the harmony of religions. The Master, too, was impressed by the sincerity
of many of the Brāhmo devotees. He told them about his own realizations
and explained to them the essence of his teachings, such as the necessity
of renunciation, sincerity in the pursuit of one's own course of discipline,
faith in God, the performance of one's duties without thought of results,
and discrimination between the Real and the unreal.

This contact with the educated and progressive Bengalis opened Sri
Ramakrishna's eyes to a new realm of thought. Born and brought up in a
simple village, without any formal education, and taught by the orthodox
holy men of India in religious life, he had had no opportunity to study
the influence of modernism on the thoughts and lives of the Hindus. He
could not properly estimate the result of the impact of Western education
on Indian culture. He was a Hindu of the Hindus, renunciation being to
him the only means to the realization of God in life. From the Brāhmos he
learnt that the new generation of India made a compromise between God
and the world. Educated young men were influenced more by the Western
philosophers than by their own prophets. But Sri Ramakrishna was not

dismayed, for he saw in this, too, the hand of God. And though he expounded
to the Brāhmos all his ideas about God and austere religious disciplines,
yet he bade them accept from his teachings only as much as suited their
tastes and temperaments.

THE MASTER'S YEARNING FOR HIS OWN DEVOTEES

Contact with the Brāhmos increased Sri Ramakrishna's longing to en-
counter aspirants who would be able to follow his teachings in their purest
form. "There was no limit", he once declared, "to the longing I felt at that
time. During the day-time I somehow managed to control it. The secular
talk of the worldly-minded was galling to me, and I would look wistfully
to the day when my own beloved companions would come. I hoped to find
solace in conversing with them and relating to them my own realizations.
Every little incident would remind me of them, and thoughts of them
wholly engrossed me. I was already arranging in my mind what I should say
to one and give to another, and so on. But when the day would come to a
close I would not be able to curb my feelings. The thought that another
day had gone by, and they had not come, oppressed me. When, during the
evening service, the temples rang with the sound of bells and conch-shells,
I would climb to the roof of the kuthi in the garden and, writhing in anguish
of heart, cry at the top of my voice: 'Come, my children! Oh, where are
you? I cannot bear to live without you.' A mother never longed so intensely
for the sight of her child, nor a friend for his companions, nor a lover for
his sweetheart, as I longed for them. Oh, it was indescribable! Shortly after
this period of yearning the devotees[8] began to come."

In the year 1879 occasional writings about Sri Ramakrishna by the Brāhmos, in the Brāhmo magazines, began to attract his future disciples from
the educated middle-class Bengalis, and they continued to come till 1884.
But others, too, came, feeling the subtle power of his attraction. They were
an ever shifting crowd of people of all castes and creeds: Hindus and
Brāhmos, Vaishnavas and Śāktas, the educated with university degrees and
the illiterate, old and young, mahārājās and beggars, journalists and artists,
pundits and devotees, philosophers and the worldly-minded, jnānis and yogis,
men of action and men of faith, virtuous women and prostitutes, office-
holders and vagabonds, philanthropists and self-seekers, dramatists and
drunkards, builders-up and pullers-down. He gave to them all, without stint,
from his illimitable store of realization. No one went away empty-handed.
He taught them the lofty knowledge of the Vedānta and the soul-melting
love of the Purāna. Twenty hours out of twenty-four he would speak without rest or respite. He gave to all his sympathy and enlightenment, and he
touched them with that strange power of the soul which could not but melt

[8] The word is generally used in the text to denote one devoted to God, a worshipper of the Personal God, or a follower of the path of love. A devotee of Sri
Ramakrishna is one who is devoted to Sri Ramakrishna and follows his teachings.
The word "disciple", when used in connexion with Sri Ramakrishna, refers to one
who had been initiated into spiritual life by Sri Ramakrishna and who regarded
him as his guru.

even the most hardened. And people understood him according to their powers of comprehension.

THE MASTER'S METHOD OF TEACHING

But he remained as ever the willing instrument in the hand of God, the child of the Divine Mother, totally untouched by the idea of being a teacher. He used to say that three ideas—that he was a guru, a father, and a master —pricked his flesh like thorns. Yet he was an extraordinary teacher. He stirred his disciples' hearts more by a subtle influence than by actions or words. He never claimed to be the founder of a religion or the organizer of a sect. Yet he was a religious dynamo. He was the verifier of all religions and creeds. He was like an expert gardener, who prepares the soil and removes the weeds, knowing that the plants will grow because of the inherent power of the seeds, producing each its appropriate flowers and fruits. He never thrust his ideas on anybody. He understood people's limitations and worked on the principle that what is good for one may be bad for another. He had the unusual power of knowing the devotees' minds, even their inmost souls, at the first sight. He accepted disciples with the full knowledge of their past tendencies and future possibilities. The life of evil did not frighten him, nor did religious squeamishness raise anybody in his estimation. He saw in everything the unerring finger of the Divine Mother. Even the light that leads astray was to him the light from God.

To those who became his intimate disciples the Master was a friend, companion, and playmate. Even the chores of religious discipline would be lightened in his presence. The devotees would be so inebriated with pure joy in his company that they would have no time to ask themselves whether he was an Incarnation, a perfect soul, or a yogi. His very presence was a great teaching; words were superfluous. In later years his disciples remarked that while they were with him they would regard him as a comrade, but afterwards would tremble to think of their frivolities in the presence of such a great person. They had convincing proof that the Master could, by his mere wish, kindle in their hearts the love of God and give them His vision.

Through all this fun and frolic, this merriment and frivolity, he always kept before them the shining ideal of God-Consciousness and the path of renunciation. He prescribed ascents steep or graded according to the powers of the climber. He permitted no compromise with the basic principles of purity. An aspirant had to keep his body, mind, senses, and soul unspotted; had to have a sincere love for God and an ever mounting spirit of yearning. The rest would be done by the Mother.

His disciples were of two kinds: the householders, and the young men, some of whom were later to become monks. There was also a small group of women devotees.

HOUSEHOLDER DEVOTEES

For the householders Sri Ramakrishna did not prescribe the hard path of total renunciation. He wanted them to discharge their obligations to their families. Their renunciation was to be mental. Spiritual life could not be acquired by flying away from responsibilities. A married couple should live like brother and sister after the birth of one or two children, devoting their time to spiritual talk and contemplation. He encouraged the householders, saying that their life was, in a way, easier than that of the monk, since it was more advantageous to fight the enemy from inside a fortress than in an open field. He insisted, however, on their repairing into solitude every now and then to strengthen their devotion and faith in God through prayer, japa, and meditation. He prescribed for them the companionship of sādhus. He asked them to perform their worldly duties with one hand, while holding to God with the other, and to pray to God to make their duties fewer and fewer so that in the end they might cling to Him with both hands. He would discourage in both the householders and the celibate youths any lukewarmness in their spiritual struggles. He would not ask them to follow indiscriminately the ideal of non-resistance, which ultimately makes a coward of the unwary.

FUTURE MONKS

But to the young men destined to be monks he pointed out the steep path of renunciation, both external and internal. They must take the vow of absolute continence and eschew all thought of greed and lust. By the practice of continence, aspirants develop a subtle nerve through which they understand the deeper mysteries of God. For them self-control is final, imperative, and absolute. The sannyāsis are teachers of men, and their lives should be totally free from blemish. They must not even look at a picture which may awaken their animal passions. The Master selected his future monks from young men untouched by "woman and gold" and plastic enough to be cast in his spiritual mould. When teaching them the path of renunciation and discrimination, he would not allow the householders to be anywhere near them.

RAM AND MANOMOHAN

The first two householder devotees to come to Dakshineswar were Ramchandra Dutta and Manomohan Mitra. A medical practitioner and chemist, Ram was sceptical about God and religion and never enjoyed peace of soul. He wanted tangible proof of God's existence. The Master said to him: "God really exists. You don't see the stars in the day-time, but that doesn't mean that the stars do not exist. There is butter in milk. But can anybody see it by merely looking at the milk? To get butter you must churn milk in a quiet and cool place. You cannot realize God by a mere wish; you must go through some mental disciplines." By degrees the Master awakened Ram's spirituality and the latter became one of his foremost lay disciples. It was Ram who introduced Narendranath to Sri Ramakrishna. Narendra was a relative of Ram.

Manomohan at first met with considerable opposition from his wife and other relatives, who resented his visits to Dakshineswar. But in the end the

unselfish love of the Master triumphed over worldly affection. It was Manomohan who brought Rakhal to the Master.

SURENDRA

Suresh Mitra, a beloved disciple whom the Master often addressed as
Surendra, had received an English education and held an important post in
an English firm. Like many other educated young men of the time, he
prided himself on his atheism and led a Bohemian life. He was addicted to
drinking. He cherished an exaggerated notion about man's free will. A victim of mental depression, he was brought to Sri Ramakrishna by Ramchandra Dutta. When he heard the Master asking a disciple to practise the
virtue of self-surrender to God, he was impressed. But though he tried thenceforth to do so, he was unable to give up his old associates and his drinking.
One day the Master said in his presence, "Well, when a man goes to an
undesirable place, why doesn't he take the Divine Mother with him?" And
to Surendra himself Sri Ramakrishna said: "Why should you drink wine as
wine? Offer it to Kāli, and then take it as Her prasād, as consecrated drink.
But see that you don't become intoxicated; you must not reel and your
thoughts must not wander. At first you will feel ordinary excitement, but
soon you will experience spiritual exaltation." Gradually Surendra's entire
life was changed. The Master designated him as one of those commissioned
by the Divine Mother to defray a great part of his expenses. Surendra's
purse was always open for the Master's comfort.

KEDAR

Kedarnath Chatterji was endowed with a spiritual temperament and had
tried various paths of religion, some not very commendable. When he met
the Master at Dakshineswar he understood the true meaning of religion.
It is said that the Master, weary of instructing devotees who were coming
to him in great numbers for guidance, once prayed to the Goddess Kāli:
"Mother, I am tired of speaking to people. Please give power to Kedar,
Girish, Ram, Vijay, and Mahendra to give them the preliminary instruction, so that just a little teaching from me will be enough." He was aware,
however, of Kedar's lingering attachment to worldly things and often
warned him about it.

HARISH

Harish, a young man in affluent circumstances, renounced his family and
took shelter with the Master, who loved him for his sincerity, singleness of
purpose, and quiet nature. He spent his leisure time in prayer and meditation, turning a deaf ear to the entreaties and threats of his relatives. Referring to his undisturbed peace of mind, the Master would say: "Real men
are dead to the world though living. Look at Harish. He is an example."
When one day the Master asked him to be a little kind to his wife, Harish
said: "You must excuse me on this point. This is not the place to show kindness. If I try to be sympathetic to her, there is a possibility of my forgetting
the ideal and becoming entangled in the world."

BHAVANATH

Bhavanath Chatterji visited the Master while he was still in his teens. His parents and relatives regarded Sri Ramakrishna as an insane person and tried their utmost to prevent him from becoming intimate with the Master. But the young boy was very stubborn and often spent nights at Dakshineswar. He was greatly attached to Narendra, and the Master encouraged their friendship. The very sight of him often awakened Sri Ramakrishna's spiritual emotion.

BALARAM BOSE

Balaram Bose came of a wealthy Vaishnava family. From his youth he had shown a deep religious temperament and had devoted his time to meditation, prayer, and the study of the Vaishnava scriptures. He was very much impressed by Sri Ramakrishna even at their first meeting. He asked Sri Ramakrishna whether God really existed and, if so, whether a man could realize Him. The Master said: "God reveals Himself to the devotee who thinks of Him as his nearest and dearest. Because you do not draw response by praying to Him once, you must not conclude that He does not exist. Pray to God, thinking of Him as dearer than your very self. He is much attached to His devotees. He comes to a man even before He is sought. There is none more intimate and affectionate than God." Balaram had never before heard God spoken of in such forceful words; every one of the words seemed true to him. Under the Master's influence he outgrew the conventions of the Vaishnava worship and became one of the most beloved of the disciples. It was at his home that the Master slept whenever he spent a night in Calcutta.

MAHENDRA OR M.

Mahendranath Gupta, better known as "M.", arrived at Dakshineswar in March 1882. He belonged to the Brāhmo Samāj and was headmaster of the Vidyāsāgar High School at Śyāmbāzār, Calcutta. At the very first sight the Master recognized him as one of his "marked" disciples. Mahendra recorded in his diary Sri Ramakrishna's conversations with his devotees. These are the first directly recorded words, in the spiritual history of the world, of a man recognized as belonging in the class of Buddha and Christ. The present volume is a translation of this diary. Mahendra was instrumental, through his personal contacts, in spreading the Master's message among many young and aspiring souls.

NAG MAHĀSHAY

Durgacharan Nag, also known as Nag Mahāshay, was the ideal householder among the lay disciples of Sri Ramakrishna. He was the embodiment of the Master's ideal of life in the world, unstained by worldliness. In spite of his intense desire to become a sannyāsi, Sri Ramakrishna asked him to live in the world in the spirit of a monk, and the disciple truly carried out this injunction. He was born of a poor family and even during his boyhood often sacrificed everything to lessen the sufferings of the needy. He had married at an early age and after his wife's death had married a second time to obey his father's command. But he once said to his wife: "Love on the physical level never lasts. He is indeed blessed who can give his love to God with his whole heart. Even a little attachment to the body endures for several births. So do not be attached to this cage of bone and flesh. Take shelter at the feet of the Mother and think of Her alone. Thus your life here and hereafter will be ennobled." The Master spoke of him as a "blazing light". He received every word of Sri Ramakrishna in dead earnest. One day he heard the Master saying that it was difficult for doctors, lawyers, and brokers to make much progress in spirituality. Of doctors he said, "If the mind clings to the tiny drops of medicine, how can it conceive of the Infinite?" That was the end of Durgacharan's medical practice and he threw his chest of medicines into the Ganges. Sri Ramakrishna assured him that he would not lack simple food and clothing. He bade him serve holy men. On being asked where he would find real holy men, the Master said that the sādhus themselves would seek his company. No sannyāsi could have lived a more austere life than Durgacharan.

GIRISH GHOSH

Girish Chandra Ghosh was a born rebel against God, a sceptic, a Bohemian, a drunkard. He was the greatest Bengali dramatist of his time, the father of the modern Bengali stage. Like other young men he had imbibed all the vices of the West. He had plunged into a life of dissipation and had become convinced that religion was only a fraud. Materialistic philosophy he justified as enabling one to get at least a little fun out of life. But a series of reverses shocked him and he became eager to solve the riddle of life. He had heard people say that in spiritual life the help of a guru was imperative and that the guru was to be regarded as God Himself. But Girish was too well acquainted with human nature to see perfection in a man. His first meeting with Sri Ramakrishna did not impress him at all. He returned home feeling as if he had seen a freak at a circus; for the Master, in a semi-conscious mood, had inquired whether it was evening, though the lamps were burning in the room. But their paths often crossed, and Girish could not avoid further encounters. The Master attended a performance in Girish's Star Theatre. On this occasion, too, Girish found nothing impressive about him. One day, however, Girish happened to see the Master dancing and singing with the devotees. He felt the contagion and wanted to join them, but restrained himself for fear of ridicule. Another day Sri Ramakrishna was about to give him spiritual instruction, when Girish said: "I don't want to listen to instructions. I have myself written many instructions. They are of no use to me. Please help me in a more tangible way if you can." This pleased the Master and he asked Girish to cultivate faith.

As time passed, Girish began to learn that the guru is the one who silently unfolds the disciple's inner life. He became a steadfast devotee of the Master.

He often loaded the Master with insults, drank in his presence, and took liberties which astounded the other devotees. But the Master knew that at heart Girish was tender, faithful, and sincere. He would not allow Girish to give up the theatre. And when a devotee asked him to tell Girish to give up drinking, he sternly replied: "That is none of your business. He who has taken charge of him will look after him. Girish is a devotee of heroic type. I tell you, drinking will not affect him." The Master knew that mere words could not induce a man to break deep-rooted habits, but that the silent influence of love worked miracles. Therefore he never asked him to give up alcohol, with the result that Girish himself eventually broke the habit. Sri Ramakrishna had strengthened Girish's resolution by allowing him to feel that he was absolutely free.

One day Girish felt depressed because he was unable to submit to any routine of spiritual discipline. In an exalted mood the Master said to him: "All right, give me your power of attorney. Henceforth I assume responsibility for you. You need not do anything." Girish heaved a sigh of relief. He felt happy to think that Sri Ramakrishna had assumed his spiritual responsibilities. But poor Girish could not then realize that he also, on his part, had to give up his freedom and make of himself a puppet in Sri Ramakrishna's hands. The Master began to discipline him according to this new attitude. One day Girish said about a trifling matter, "Yes, I shall do this." "No, no!" the Master corrected him. "You must not speak in that egotistic manner. You should say, 'God willing, I shall do it.'" Girish understood. Thenceforth he tried to give up all idea of personal responsibility and surrender himself to the Divine Will. His mind began to dwell constantly on Sri Ramakrishna. This unconscious meditation in time chastened his turbulent spirit.

The householder devotees generally visited Sri Ramakrishna on Sunday afternoons and other holidays. Thus a brotherhood was gradually formed, and the Master encouraged their fraternal feeling. Now and then he would accept an invitation to a devotee's home, where other devotees would also be invited. Kirtan would be arranged and they would spend hours in dance and devotional music. The Master would go into trances or open his heart in religious discourses and in the narration of his own spiritual experiences. Many people who could not go to Dakshineswar participated in these meetings and felt blessed. Such an occasion would be concluded with a sumptuous feast.

But it was in the company of his younger devotees, pure souls yet unstained by the touch of worldliness, that Sri Ramakrishna took greatest joy. Among the young men who later embraced the householder's life were Narayan, Paltu, the younger Naren, Tejchandra, and Purna. These visited the Master sometimes against strong opposition from home.

PURNA

Purna was a lad of thirteen, whom Sri Ramakrishna described as an Iśvarakoti, a soul born with special spiritual qualities...The Master said that

Purna was the last of the group of brilliant devotees who, as he once had seen in a trance, would come to him for spiritual illumination. Purna said to Sri Ramakrishna during their second meeting, "You are God Himself incarnated in flesh and blood." Such words coming from a mere youngster proved of what stuff the boy was made.

MAHIMACHARAN AND PRATAP HAZRA

Mahimacharan and Pratap Hazra were two devotees outstanding for their pretentiousness and idiosyncrasies. But the Master showed them his unfailing love and kindness, though he was aware of their shortcomings. Mahimacharan Chakravarty had met the Master long before the arrival of the other disciples. He had had the intention of leading a spiritual life, but a strong desire to acquire name and fame was his weakness. He claimed to have been initiated by Totapuri and used to say that he had been following the path of knowledge according to his guru's instructions. He possessed a large library of English and Sanskrit books. But though he pretended to have read them, most of the leaves were uncut. The Master knew all his limitations, yet enjoyed listening to him recite from the Vedas and other scriptures. He would always exhort Mahima to meditate on the meaning of the scriptural texts and to practise spiritual discipline.

Pratap Hazra, a middle-aged man, hailed from a village near Kāmārpukur. He was not altogether unresponsive to religious feelings. On a moment's impulse he had left his home, aged mother, wife, and children, and had found shelter in the temple garden at Dakshineswar, where he intended to lead a spiritual life. He loved to argue, and the Master often pointed him out as an example of barren argumentation. He was hypercritical of others and cherished an exaggerated notion of his own spiritual advancement. He was mischievous and often tried to upset the minds of the Master's young disciples, criticizing them for their happy and joyous life and asking them to devote their time to meditation. The Master teasingly compared Hazra to Jatilā and Kutilā, the two women who always created obstructions in Krishna's sport with the gopis, and said that Hazra lived at Dakshineswar to "thicken the plot" by adding complications.

SOME NOTED MEN

Sri Ramakrishna also became acquainted with a number of people whose scholarship or wealth entitled them everywhere to respect. He had met, a few years before, Devendranath Tagore, famous all over Bengal for his wealth, scholarship, saintly character, and social position. But the Master found him disappointing; for, whereas Sri Ramakrishna expected of a saint complete renunciation of the world, Devendranath combined with his saintliness a life of enjoyment. Sri Ramakrishna met the great poet Michael Madhusudan, who had embraced Christianity "for the sake of his stomach". To him the Master could not impart instruction, for the Divine Mother "pressed his tongue". In addition he met Mahārājā Jatindra Mohan Tagore, a titled aristocrat of Bengal; Kristodas Pal, the editor, social reformer, and patriot; Iswar Vidyāsāgar, the noted philanthropist and educator; Pundit

Shashadhar, a great champion of Hindu orthodoxy; Aswini Kumar Dutta, a headmaster, moralist, and leader of Indian Nationalism; and Bankim Chatterji, a deputy magistrate, novelist, and essayist, and one of the fashioners of modern Bengali prose. Sri Ramakrishna was not the man to be dazzled by outward show, glory, or eloquence. A pundit without discrimination he regarded as a mere straw. He would search people's hearts for the light of God, and if that was missing he would have nothing to do with them.

KRISTODAS PAL

The Europeanized Kristodas Pal did not approve of the Master's emphasis on renunciation and said: "Sir, this cant of renunciation has almost ruined the country. It is for this reason that the Indians are a subject nation today. Doing good to others, bringing education to the door of the ignorant, and above all, improving the material conditions of the country—these should be our duty now. The cry of religion and renunciation would, on the contrary, only weaken us. You should advise the young men of Bengal to resort only to such acts as will uplift the country." Sri Ramakrishna gave him a searching look and found no divine light within. "You man of poor understanding!" Sri Ramakrishna said sharply. "You dare to slight in these terms renunciation and piety, which our scriptures describe as the greatest of all virtues! After reading two pages of English you think you have come to know the world! You appear to think you are omniscient. Well, have you seen those tiny crabs that are born in the Ganges just when the rains set in? In this big universe you are even less significant than one of those small creatures. How dare you talk of *helping* the world? The Lord will look to that. You haven't the power in you to do it." After a pause the Master continued: "Can you explain to me how you can work for others? I know what you mean by helping them. To feed a number of persons, to treat them when they are sick, to construct a road or dig a well—isn't that all? These are good deeds, no doubt, but how trifling in comparison with the vastness of the universe! How far can a man advance in this line? How many people can you save from famine? Malaria has ruined a whole province; what could you do to stop its onslaught? God alone looks after the world. Let a man first realize Him. Let a man get the authority from God and be endowed with His power; then, and then alone, may he think of doing good to others. A man should first be purged of all egotism. Then alone will the Blissful Mother ask him to work for the world." Sri Ramakrishna mistrusted philanthropy that presumed to pose as charity. He warned people against it. He saw in most acts of philanthropy nothing but egotism, vanity, a desire for glory, a barren excitement to kill the boredom of life, or an attempt to soothe a guilty conscience. True charity, he taught, is the result of love of God—service to man in a spirit of worship.

MONASTIC DISCIPLES

The disciples whom the Master trained for monastic life were the following:

Narendranath Dutta (Swami Vivekananda)

Rakhal Chandra Ghosh (Swami Brahmananda)

Gopal Sur (Swami Advaitananda)

Baburam Ghosh (Swami Premananda)

Taraknath Ghoshal (Swami Shivananda)

Jogindranath Choudhury (Swami Jogananda)

Sashibhushan Chakravarty. (Swami Ramakrishnananda)

Saratchandra Chakravarty (Swami Saradananda)

Nitya Niranjan Sen (Swami Niranjanananda)

Kaliprasad Chandra (Swami Abhedananda)

Harinath Chattopadhyaya (Swami Turiyananda)

Sarada Prasanna (Swami Trigunatitananda)

Gangadhar Ghatak (Swami Akhandananda)

Subodh Ghosh (Swami Subodhananda)

Hariprasanna Chatterji (Swami Vijnanananda)

Latu (Swami Adbhutananda)

LATU

The first of these young men to come to the Master was Latu. Born of obscure parents, in Behar, he came to Calcutta in search of work and was engaged by Ramchandra Dutta as house-boy. Learning of the saintly Sri Ramakrishna, he visited the Master at Dakshineswar and was deeply touched by his cordiality. When he was about to leave, the Master asked him to take some money and return home in a boat or carriage. But Latu declared he had a few pennies and jingled the coins in his pocket. Sri Ramakrishna later requested Ram to allow Latu to stay with him permanently. Under Sri Ramakrishna's guidance Latu made great progress in meditation and was blessed with ecstatic visions, but all the efforts of the Master to give him a smattering of education failed. Latu was very fond of kirtan and other devotional songs but remained all his life illiterate.

RAKHAL

Even before Rakhal's coming to Dakshineswar, the Master had had visions of him as his spiritual son and as a playmate of Krishna at Vrindāvan. Rakhal was born of wealthy parents. During his childhood he developed wonderful spiritual traits and used to play at worshipping gods and goddesses. In his teens he was married to a sister of Manomohan Mitra, from whom he first heard of the Master. His father objected to his association with Sri Ramakrishna but afterwards was reassured to find that many celebrated people were visitors at Dakshineswar. The relationship between the Master and this beloved disciple was that of mother and child. Sri Ramakrishna allowed Rakhal many liberties denied to others. But he would not hesitate to chastise the boy for improper actions. At one time Rakhal felt a childlike jealousy because he found that other boys were receiving the Master's affection. He soon got over it and realized his guru as the Guru of the whole universe. The Master was worried to hear of his marriage, but was relieved to find that his wife was a spiritual soul who would not be a hindrance to his progress.

THE ELDER GOPAL

Gopal Sur of Sinthi came to Dakshineswar at a rather advanced age and was called the elder Gopal. He had lost his wife, and the Master assuaged his grief. Soon he renounced the world and devoted himself fully to meditation and prayer. Some years later Gopal gave the Master the ochre cloths with which the latter initiated several of his disciples into monastic life.

NARENDRA

To spread his message to the four corners of the earth Sri Ramakrishna needed a strong instrument. With his frail body and delicate limbs he could not make great journeys across wide spaces. And such an instrument was found in Narendranath Dutta, his beloved Naren, later known to the world as Swami Vivekananda. Even before meeting Narendranath, the Master had seen him in a vision as a sage, immersed in the meditation of the Absolute, who at Sri Ramakrishna's request had agreed to take human birth to assist him in his work.

Narendra was born in Calcutta on January 12, 1863, of an aristocratic kāyastha family. His mother was steeped in the great Hindu epics, and his father, a distinguished attorney of the Calcutta High Court, was an agnostic about religion, a friend of the poor, and a mocker at social conventions. Even in his boyhood and youth Narendra possessed great physical courage and presence of mind, a vivid imagination, deep power of thought, keen intelligence, an extraordinary memory, a love of truth, a passion for purity, a spirit of independence, and a tender heart. An expert musician, he also acquired proficiency in physics, astronomy, mathematics, philosophy, history, and literature. He grew up into an extremely handsome young man. Even as a child he practised meditation and showed great power of concentration. Though free and passionate in word and action, he took the vow of austere religious chastity and never allowed the fire of purity to be extinguished by the slightest defilement of body or soul.

As he read in college the rationalistic Western philosophers of the nineteenth century, his boyhood faith in God and religion was unsettled. He would not accept religion on mere faith; he wanted demonstration of God. But very soon his passionate nature discovered that mere Universal Reason was cold and bloodless. His emotional nature, dissatisfied with a mere abstraction, required a concrete support to help him in the hours of temptation. He wanted an external power, a guru, who by embodying perfection in the flesh would still the commotion of his soul. Attracted by the magnetic personality of Keshab, he joined the Brāhmo Samāj and became a singer in its choir. But in the Samāj he did not find the guru who could say that he had seen God.

In a state of mental conflict and torture of soul, Narendra came to Sri Ramakrishna at Dakshineswar. He was then eighteen years of age and had been in college two years. He entered the Master's room accompanied by some light-hearted friends. At Sri Ramakrishna's request he sang a few songs, pouring his whole soul into them, and the Master went into samādhi. A few minutes later Sri Ramakrishna suddenly left his seat, took Narendra by the hand, and led him to the screened verandah north of his room. They were alone. Addressing Narendra most tenderly, as if he were a friend of long acquaintance, the Master said: "Ah! You have come very late. Why have you been so unkind as to make me wait all these days? My ears are tired of hearing the futile words of worldly men. Oh, how I have longed to pour my spirit into the heart of someone fitted to receive my message!" He talked thus, sobbing all the time. Then, standing before Narendra with folded hands, he addressed him as Nārāyana, born on earth to remove the misery of humanity. Grasping Narendra's hand, he asked him to come again, alone, and very soon. Narendra was startled. "What is this I have come to see?" he said to himself. "He must be stark mad. Why, I am the son of Viswanath Dutta. How dare he speak this way to me?"

When they returned to the room and Narendra heard the Master speaking to others, he was surprised to find in his words an inner logic, a striking sincerity, and a convincing proof of his spiritual nature. In answer to Narendra's question, "Sir, have you seen God?" the Master said: "Yes, I have seen God. I have seen Him more tangibly than I see you. I have talked to Him more intimately than I am talking to you." Continuing, the Master said: "But, my child, who wants to see God? People shed jugs of tears for money, wife, and children. But if they would weep for God for only one day they would surely see Him." Narendra was amazed. These words he could not doubt. This was the first time he had ever heard a man saying that he had seen God. But he could not reconcile these words of the Master with the scene that had taken place on the verandah only a few minutes before. He concluded that Sri Ramakrishna was a monomaniac, and returned home rather puzzled in mind.

During his second visit, about a month later, suddenly, at the touch of the Master, Narendra felt overwhelmed and saw the walls of the room and everything around him whirling and vanishing. "What are you doing to me?" he cried in terror. "I have my father and mother at home." He saw his own ego and the whole universe almost swallowed in a nameless void. With a laugh the Master easily restored him. Narenda thought he might have been hypnotized, but he could not understand how a monomaniac could cast a spell over the mind of a strong person like himself. He returned home more confused than ever, resolved to be henceforth on his guard before this strange man.

But during his third visit Narendra fared no better. This time, at the Master's touch, he lost consciousness entirely. While he was still in that state, Sri Ramakrishna questioned him concerning his spiritual antecedents and whereabouts, his mission in this world, and the duration of his mortal life. The answers confirmed what the Master himself had known and inferred. Among other things, he came to know that Narendra was a sage who had already attained perfection, and that the day he learnt his real nature he would give up his body in yoga, by an act of will.

A few more meetings completely removed from Narendra's mind the last traces of the notion that Sri Ramakrishna might be a monomaniac or wily hypnotist. His integrity, purity, renunciation, and unselfishness were beyond question. But Narendra could not accept a man, an imperfect mortal, as his guru. As a member of the Brāhmo Samāj, he could not believe that a human intermediary was necessary between man and God. Moreover, he openly laughed at Sri Ramakrishna's visions as hallucinations. Yet in the secret chamber of his heart he bore a great love for the Master.

Sri Ramakrishna was grateful to the Divine Mother for sending him one who doubted his own realizations. Often he asked Narendra to test him as the money-changers test their coins. He laughed at Narendra's biting criticism of his spiritual experiences and samādhi. When at times Narendra's sharp words distressed him, the Divine Mother Herself would console him, saying: "Why do you listen to him? In a few days he will believe your every word." He could hardly bear Narendra's absences. Often he would weep bitterly for the sight of him. Sometimes Narendra would find the Master's love embarrassing; and one day he sharply scolded him, warning him that such infatuation would soon draw him down to the level of its object. The Master was distressed and prayed to the Divine Mother. Then he said to Narendra: "You rogue, I won't listen to you any more. Mother says that I love you because I see God in you, and the day I no longer see God in you I shall not be able to bear even the sight of you."

The Master wanted to train Narendra in the teachings of the non-dualistic Vedānta philosophy. But Narendra, because of his Brāhmo upbringing, considered it wholly blasphemous to look on man as one with his Creator. One day at the temple garden he laughingly said to a friend: "How silly! This jug is God! This cup is God! Whatever we see is God! And we too are God! Nothing could be more absurd." Sri Ramakrishna came out of his room and gently touched him. Spellbound, he immediately perceived that everything in the world was indeed God. A new universe opened around him. Returning home in a dazed state, he found there too that the food, the plate, the eater himself, the people around him, were all God. When he walked in the street, he saw that the cabs, the horses, the streams of people, the buildings, were all Brahman. He could hardly go about his day's business. His parents became anxious about him and thought him ill. And when the intensity of the experience abated a little, he saw the world as a dream. Walking in the public square, he would strike his head against the iron railings to know whether they were real. It took him a number of days to recover his normal self. He had a foretaste of the great experiences yet to come and realized that the words of the Vedānta were true.

At the beginning of 1884 Narendra's father suddenly died of heart-failure, leaving the family in a state of utmost poverty. There were six or seven mouths to feed at home. Creditors were knocking at the door. Relatives who had accepted his father's unstinted kindness now became enemies, some even bringing suit to deprive Narendra of his ancestral home. Actually starving and barefoot, Narendra searched for a job, but without success. He began to doubt whether anywhere in the world there was such a thing as unselfish sympathy. Two rich women made evil proposals to him and promised to put an end to his distress; but he refused them with contempt.

Narendra began to talk of his doubt of the very existence of God. His friends thought he had become an atheist and piously circulated gossip adducing unmentionable motives for his unbelief. His moral character was maligned. Even some of the Master's disciples partly believed the gossip, and Narendra told these to their faces that only a coward believed in God through fear of suffering or hell. But he was distressed to think that Sri Ramakrishna, too, might believe these false reports. His pride revolted. He said to himself: "What does it matter? If a man's good name rests on such slender foundations, I don't care." But later on he was amazed to learn that the Master had never lost faith in him. To a disciple who complained about Narendra's degradation, Sri Ramakrishna replied: "Hush, you fool! The Mother has told me it can never be so. I won't look at you if you speak that way again."

The moment came when Narendra's distress reached its climax. He had gone the whole day without food. As he was returning home in the evening he could hardly lift his tired limbs. He sat down in front of a house in sheer exhaustion, too weak even to think. His mind began to wander. Then, suddenly, a divine power lifted the veil over his soul. He found the solution of the problem of the coexistence of divine justice and misery, the presence of suffering in the creation of a blissful Providence. He felt bodily refreshed, his soul was bathed in peace, and he slept serenely.

Narendra now realized that he had a spiritual mission to fulfil. He resolved to renounce the world, as his grandfather had renounced it, and he came to Sri Ramakrishna for his blessing. But even before he had opened his mouth, the Master knew what was in his mind and wept bitterly at the thought of separation. "I know you cannot lead a worldly life," he said, "but for my sake live in the world as long as I live."

One day, soon after, Narendra requested Sri Ramakrishna to pray to the Divine Mother to remove his poverty. Sri Ramakrishna bade him pray to Her himself, for She would certainly listen to his prayer. Narendra entered the shrine of Kāli. As he stood before the image of the Mother, he beheld Her as a living Goddess, ready to give wisdom and liberation. Unable to ask Her for petty worldly things, he prayed only for knowledge and renunciation, love and liberation. The Master rebuked him for his failure to ask the Divine Mother to remove his poverty and sent him back to the temple. But Narendra, standing in Her presence, again forgot the purpose of his coming. Thrice he went to the temple at the bidding of the Master, and thrice he returned, having forgotten in Her presence why he had come. He was wondering about it when it suddenly flashed in his mind that this was all the work of Sri Ramakrishna; so now he asked the Master himself to remove his poverty, and was assured that his family would not lack simple food and clothing.

This was a very rich and significant experience for Narendra. It taught him that Śakti, the Divine Power, cannot be ignored in the world and that in the relative plane the need of worshipping a Personal God is imperative. Sri Ramakrishna was overjoyed with the conversion. The next day, sitting almost on Narendra's lap, he said to a devotee, pointing first to himself, then to Narendra: "I see I am this, and again that. Really I feel no difference. A stick floating in the Ganges seems to divide the water; but in reality the water is one. Do you see my point? Well, whatever is, is the Mother—isn't that so?" In later years Narendra would say: "Sri Rama-krishna was the only person who, from the time he met me, believed in me uniformly throughout. Even my mother and brothers did not. It was his unwavering trust and love for me that bound me to him for ever. He alone knew how to love. Worldly people only make a show of love for selfish ends."

TARAK

Others destined to be monastic disciples of Sri Ramakrishna came to Dakshineswar. Taraknath Ghoshal had felt from his boyhood the noble desire to realize God. Keshab and the Brāhmo Samāj had attracted him but proved inadequate. In 1882 he first met the Master at Ramchandra's house and was astonished to hear him talk about samādhi, a subject which always fascinated his mind. And that evening he actually saw a manifestation of that superconscious state in the Master. Tarak became a frequent visitor at Dakshineswar and received the Master's grace in abundance. The young boy often felt ecstatic fervour in meditation. He also wept profusely while meditating on God. Sri Ramakrishna said to him: "God favours those who can weep for Him. Tears shed for God wash away the sins of former births."

BABURAM

Baburam Ghosh came to Dakshineswar accompanied by Rakhal, his class-mate. The Master, as was often his custom, examined the boy's physiognomy and was satisfied about his latent spirituality. At the age of eight Baburam had thought of leading a life of renunciation, in the company of a monk, in a hut shut out from the public view by a thick wall of trees. The very sight of the Panchavati awakened in his heart that dream of boyhood. Baburam was tender in body and soul. The Master used to say that he was pure to his very bones. One day Hazra in his usual mischievous fashion advised Baburam and some of the other young boys to ask Sri Ramakrishna for some spiritual powers and not waste their life in mere gaiety and merri-ment. The Master, scenting mischief, called Baburam to his side and said: "What can you ask of me? Isn't everything that I have already yours? Yes, everything I have earned in the shape of realizations is for the sake of you all. So get rid of the idea of begging, which alienates by creating a distance. Rather realize your kinship with me and gain the key to all the treasures."

NIRANJAN

Nitya Niranjan Sen was a disciple of heroic type. He came to the Master when he was eighteen years old. He was a medium for a group of spiritual-ists. During his first visit the Master said to him: "My boy, if you think always of ghosts you will become a ghost, and if you think of God you will become God. Now, which do you prefer?" Niranjan severed all connexions with the spiritualists. During his second visit the Master embraced him and said warmly: "Niranjan, my boy, the days are flitting away. When will you realize God? This life will be in vain if you do not realize Him. When will you devote your mind wholly to God?" Niranjan was surprised to see the Master's great anxiety for his spiritual welfare. He was a young man endowed with unusual spiritual parts. He felt disdain for worldly pleasures and was totally guileless, like a child. But he had a violent temper. One day, as he was coming in a country boat to Dakshineswar, some of his fellow passengers began to speak ill of the Master. Finding his protest futile, Niranjan began to rock the boat, threatening to sink it in mid stream. That silenced the offenders. When he reported the incident to the Master, he was rebuked for his inability to curb his anger.

JOGINDRA

Jogindranath, on the other hand, was gentle to a fault. One day, under circumstances very like those that had evoked Niranjan's anger, he curbed his temper and held his peace instead of threatening Sri Ramakrishna's abusers. The Master, learning of his conduct, scolded him roundly. Thus to each the fault of the other was recommended as a virtue. The guru was striving to develop, in the first instance, composure, and in the second, mettle. The secret of his training was to build up, by a tactful recognition of the requirements of each given case, the character of the devotee.

Jogindranath came of an aristocratic brāhmin family of Dakshineswar. His father and relatives shared the popular mistrust of Sri Ramakrishna's sanity. At a very early age the boy developed religious tendencies, spending two or three hours daily in meditation, and his meeting with Sri Ramakrishna deepened his desire for the realization of God. He had a perfect horror of marriage. But at the earnest request of his mother he had had to yield, and he now believed that his spiritual future was doomed. So he kept himself away from the Master.

Sri Ramakrishna employed a ruse to bring Jogindra to him. As soon as the disciple entered the room, the Master rushed forward to meet the young man. Catching hold of the disciple's hand, he said: "What if you have married? Haven't I too married? What is there to be afraid of in that?" Touching his own chest he said: "If this [meaning himself] is propitious, then even a hundred thousand marriages cannot injure you. If you desire to lead a householder's life, then bring your wife here one day, and I shall see that she becomes a real companion in your spiritual progress. But if you want to lead a monastic life, then I shall eat up your attachment to the world." Jogin was dumbfounded at these words. He received new strength, and his spirit of renunciation was re-established.

SASHI AND SARAT

Sashi and Sarat were two cousins who came from a pious brāhmin family of Calcutta. At an early age they had joined the Brāhmo Samāj and had come under the influence of Keshab Sen. The Master said to them at their first meeting: "If bricks and tiles are burnt after the trade-mark has been stamped on them, they retain the mark for ever. Similarly, man should be stamped with God before entering the world. Then he will not become attached to worldliness." Fully aware of the future course of their life, he asked them not to marry. The Master asked Sashi whether he believed in God with form or in God without form. Sashi replied that he was not even sure about the existence of God; so he could not speak one way or the other. This frank answer very much pleased the Master.

Sarat's soul longed for the all-embracing realization of the Godhead. When the Master inquired whether there was any particular form of God he wished to see, the boy replied that he would like to see God in all the living beings of the world. "But", the Master demurred, "that is the last word in realization. One cannot have it at the very outset." Sarat stated calmly: "I won't be satisfied with anything short of that. I shall trudge on along the path till I attain that blessed state." Sri Ramakrishna was very much pleased.

HARINATH

Harinath had led the austere life of a brahmachāri even from his early boyhood—bathing in the Ganges every day, cooking his own meals, waking before sunrise, and reciting the Gītā from memory before leaving bed. He found in the Master the embodiment of the Vedānta scriptures. Aspiring to be a follower of the ascetic Śankara, he cherished a great hatred for women. One day he said to the Master that he could not allow even small girls to come near him. The Master scolded him and said: "You are talking like a fool. Why should you hate women? They are the manifestations of the Divine Mother. Regard them as your own mother and you will never feel their evil influence. The more you hate them, the more you will fall into their snares." Hari said later that these words completely changed his attitude toward women.

The Master knew Hari's passion for Vedānta. But he did not wish any of his disciples to become a dry ascetic or a mere bookworm. So he asked Hari to practise Vedānta in life by giving up the unreal and following the Real. "But it is not so easy", Sri Ramakrishna said, "to realize the illusoriness of the world. Study alone does not help one very much. The grace of God is required. Mere personal effort is futile. A man is a tiny creature after all, with very limited powers. But he can achieve the impossible if he prays to God for His grace." Whereupon the Master sang a song in praise of grace. Hari was profoundly moved and shed tears. Later in life Hari achieved a wonderful synthesis of the ideals of the Personal God and the Impersonal Truth.

GANGADHAR

Gangadhar, Harinath's friend, also led the life of a strict brahmachāri, eating vegetarian food cooked by his own hands and devoting himself to the study of the scriptures. He met the Master in 1884 and soon became a member of his inner circle. The Master praised his ascetic habit and attributed it to the spiritual disciplines of his past life. Gangadhar became a close companion of Narendra.

HARIPRASANNA

Hariprasanna, a college student, visited the Master in the company of his friends Sashi and Sarat. Sri Ramakrishna showed him great favour by initiating him into spiritual life. As long as he lived, Hariprasanna remembered and observed the following drastic advice of the Master: "Even if a woman is pure as gold and rolls on the ground for love of God, it is dangerous for a monk ever to look at her."

KALI

Kaliprasad visited the Master toward the end of 1883. Given to the practice of meditation and the study of the scriptures, Kali was particularly interested in yoga. Feeling the need of a guru in spiritual life, he came to the Master and was accepted as a disciple. The young boy possessed a rational mind and often felt sceptical about the Personal God. The Master said to him: "Your doubts will soon disappear. Others, too, have passed through such a state of mind. Look at Naren. He now weeps at the names of Rādhā and Krishna." Kali began to see visions of gods and goddesses. Very soon these disappeared and in meditation he experienced vastness, infinity, and the other attributes of the Impersonal Brahman.

SUBODH

Subodh visited the Master in 1885. At the very first meeting Sri Ramakrishna said to him: "You will succeed. Mother says so. Those whom She sends here will certainly attain spirituality." During the second meeting the Master wrote something on Subodh's tongue, stroked his body from the navel to the throat, and said, "Awake, Mother! Awake." He asked the boy to meditate. At once Subodh's latent spirituality was awakened. He felt a current rushing along the spinal column to the brain. Joy filled his soul.

SARADA

One more young man, Sarada Prasanna, completes the small band of the Master's disciples later to embrace the life of the wandering monk. With the exception of the elder Gopal, all of them were in their teens or slightly over. They came from middle-class Bengali families, and most of them were students in school or college. Their parents and relatives had envisaged for them bright worldly careers. They came to Sri Ramakrishna with pure bodies, vigorous minds, and uncontaminated souls. All were born with unusual spiritual attributes. Sri Ramakrishna accepted them, even at first sight, as his children, relatives, friends, and companions. His magic touch unfolded them. And later each according to his measure reflected the life of the Master, becoming a torch-bearer of his message across land and sea.

WOMAN DEVOTEES

With his woman devotees Sri Ramakrishna established a very sweet relationship. He himself embodied the tender traits of a woman: he had dwelt on the highest plane of Truth, where there is not even the slightest trace of sex; and his innate purity evoked only the noblest emotion in men and women alike. His woman devotees often said: "We seldom looked on Sri Ramakrishna as a member of the male sex. We regarded him as one of us. We never felt any constraint before him. He was our best confidant." They loved him as their child, their friend, and their teacher. In spiritual discipline he advised them to renounce lust and greed and especially warned them not to fall into the snares of men.

GOPĀL MĀ

Unsurpassed among the woman devotees of the Master in the richness of her devotion and spiritual experiences was Aghoremani Devi, an orthodox brāhmin woman. Widowed at an early age, she had dedicated herself completely to spiritual pursuits. Gopāla, the Baby Krishna, was her Ideal Deity, whom she worshipped following the vātsalya attitude of the Vaishnava religion, regarding Him as her own child. Through Him she satisfied her unassuaged maternal love, cooking for Him, feeding Him, bathing Him, and putting Him to bed. This sweet intimacy with Gopāla won her the sobriquet of Gopāl Mā, or Gopāla's Mother. For forty years she had lived on the bank of the Ganges in a small, bare room, her only companions being a threadbare copy of the *Rāmāyana* and a bag containing her rosary. At the age of sixty, in 1884, she visited Sri Ramakrishna at Dakshineswar. During the second visit, as soon as the Master saw her, he said: "Oh, you have come! Give me something to eat." With great hesitation she gave him some ordinary sweets that she had purchased for him on the way. The Master ate them with relish and asked her to bring him simple curries or sweets prepared by her own hands. Gopāl Mā thought him a queer kind of monk, for, instead of talking of God, he always asked for food. She did not want to visit him again, but an irresistible attraction brought her back to the temple garden. She carried with her some simple curries that she had cooked herself.

One early morning at three o'clock, about a year later, Gopāl Mā was about to finish her daily devotions, when she was startled to find Sri Ramakrishna sitting on her left, with his right hand clenched, like the hand of the image of Gopāla. She was amazed and caught hold of the hand, whereupon the figure vanished and in its place appeared the real Gopāla, her Ideal Deity. She cried aloud with joy. Gopāla begged her for butter. She pleaded her poverty and gave Him some dry coconut candies. Gopāla sat on her lap, snatched away her rosary, jumped on her shoulders, and moved all about the room. As soon as the day broke she hastened to Dakshineswar like an insane woman. Of course Gopāla accompanied her, resting His head on her shoulder. She clearly saw His tiny ruddy feet hanging over her breast. She entered Sri Ramakrishna's room. The Master had fallen into samādhi. Like a child, he sat on her lap, and she began to feed him with butter, cream, and other delicacies. After some time he regained consciousness and returned to his bed. But the mind of Gopāla's Mother was still roaming in another plane. She was steeped in bliss. She saw Gopāla frequently entering the Master's body and again coming out of it. When she returned to her hut, still in a dazed condition, Gopāla accompanied her.

She spent about two months in uninterrupted communion with God, the Baby Gopāla never leaving her for a moment. Then the intensity of her vision was lessened; had it not been, her body would have perished. The Master spoke highly of her exalted spiritual condition and said that such vision of God was a rare thing for ordinary mortals. The fun-loving Master one day confronted the critical Narendranath with this simple-minded woman. No two could have presented a more striking contrast. The Master knew of Narendra's lofty contempt for all visions, and he asked the old lady to narrate her experiences to Narendra. With great hesitation she told him her story. Now and then she interrupted her maternal chatter to ask Narendra: "My son, I am a poor ignorant woman. I don't understand anything. You are so learned. Now tell me if these visions of Gopāla are true." As Narendra listened to the story he was profoundly moved. He said, "Yes, mother, they are quite true." Behind his cynicism Narendra, too, possessed a heart full of love and tenderness.

THE MARCH OF EVENTS

In 1881 Hriday was dismissed from service in the Kāli temple, for an act of indiscretion, and was ordered by the authorities never again to enter the garden. In a way the hand of the Divine Mother may be seen even in this. Having taken care of Sri Ramakrishna during the stormy days of his spiritual discipline, Hriday had come naturally to consider himself the sole guardian of his uncle. None could approach the Master without his knowledge. And he would be extremely jealous if Sri Ramakrishna paid attention to anyone else. Hriday's removal made it possible for the real devotees of the Master to approach him freely and live with him in the temple garden.

During the week-ends the householders, enjoying a respite from their office duties, visited the Master. The meetings on Sunday afternoons were of the nature of little festivals. Refreshments were often served. Professional musicians now and then sang devotional songs. The Master and the devotees sang and danced, Sri Ramakrishna frequently going into ecstatic moods. The happy memory of such a Sunday would linger long in the minds of the devotees. Those whom the Master wanted for special instruction he would ask to visit him on Tuesdays and Saturdays. These days were particularly auspicious for the worship of Kāli.

The young disciples destined to be monks, Sri Ramakrishna invited on week-days, when the householders were not present. The training of the householders and of the future monks had to proceed along entirely different lines. Since M. generally visited the Master on week-ends, the *Gospel of Sri Ramakrishna* does not contain much mention of the future monastic disciples.

Finally, there was a handful of fortunate disciples, householders as well as youngsters, who were privileged to spend nights with the Master in his room. They would see him get up early in the morning and walk up and

7

down the room, singing in his sweet voice and tenderly communing with the Mother.

INJURY TO THE MASTER'S ARM

One day, in January 1884, the Master was going toward the pine-grove when he went into a trance. He was alone. There was no one to support him or guide his footsteps. He fell to the ground and dislocated a bone in his left arm. This accident had a significant influence on his mind, the natural inclination of which was to soar above the consciousness of the body. The acute pain in the arm forced his mind to dwell on the body and on the world outside. But he saw even in this a divine purpose; for, with his mind compelled to dwell on the physical plane, he realized more than ever that he was an instrument in the hand of the Divine Mother, who had a mission to fulfil through his human body and mind. He also distinctly found that in the phenomenal world God manifests Himself, in an inscrutable way, through diverse human beings, both good and evil. Thus he would speak of God in the guise of the wicked, God in the guise of the pious, God in the guise of the hypocrite, God in the guise of the lewd. He began to take a special delight in watching the divine play in the relative world. Sometimes the sweet human relationship with God would appear to him more appealing than the all-effacing Knowledge of Brahman. Many a time he would pray: "Mother, don't make me unconscious through the Knowledge of Brahman. Don't give me Brahmajnāna, Mother. Am I not Your child, and naturally timid? I must have my Mother. A million salutations to the Knowledge of Brahman! Give it to those who want it." Again he prayed: "O Mother, let me remain in contact with men! Don't make me a dried-up ascetic. I want to enjoy Your sport in the world." He was able to taste this very rich divine experience and enjoy the love of God and the company of His devotees because his mind, on account of the injury to his arm, was forced to come down to the consciousness of the body. Again, he would make fun of people who proclaimed him as a Divine Incarnation, by pointing to his broken arm. He would say, "Have you ever heard of God breaking His arm?" It took the arm about five months to heal.

BEGINNING OF HIS ILLNESS

In April 1885 the Master's throat became inflamed. Prolonged conversation or absorption in samādhi, making the blood flow into the throat, would aggravate the pain. Yet when the annual Vaishnava festival was celebrated at Pānihāti, Sri Ramakrishna attended it against the doctor's advice. With a group of disciples he spent himself in music, dance, and ecstasy. The illness took a turn for the worse and was diagnosed as "clergyman's sore throat". The patient was cautioned against conversation and ecstasies. Though he followed the physician's directions regarding medicine and diet, he could neither control his trances nor withhold from seekers the solace of his advice. Sometimes, like a sulky child, he would complain to the Mother about the crowds, who gave him no rest day or night. He was overheard to say to Her: "Why do You bring here all these worthless people, who are like milk diluted with five times its own quantity of water? My eyes are almost destroyed with blowing the fire to dry up the water. My health is gone. It is beyond my strength. Do it Yourself, if You want it done. This (*pointing to his own body*) is but a perforated drum, and if you go on beating it day in and day out, how long will it last?"

But his large heart never turned anyone away. He said, "Let me be condemned to be born over and over again, even in the form of a dog, if I can be of help to a single soul." And he bore the pain, singing cheerfully, "Let the body be preoccupied with illness, but, O mind, dwell for ever in God's Bliss!"

One night he had a hemorrhage of the throat. The doctor now diagnosed the illness as cancer. Narendra was the first to break this heart-rending news to the disciples. Within three days the Master was removed to Calcutta for better treatment. At Balaram's house he remained a week until a suitable place could be found at Śyāmpukur, in the northern section of Calcutta. During this week he dedicated himself practically without respite to the instruction of those beloved devotees who had been unable to visit him oftener at Dakshineswar. Discourses incessantly flowed from his tongue, and he often went into samādhi. Dr. Mahendra Sarkar, the celebrated homeopath of Calcutta, was invited to undertake his treatment.

ŚYĀMPUKUR

In the beginning of September 1885 Sri Ramakrishna was moved to Śyāmpukur. Here Narendra organized the young disciples to attend the Master day and night. At first they concealed the Master's illness from their guardians; but when it became more serious they remained with him almost constantly, sweeping aside the objections of their relatives and devoting themselves whole-heartedly to the nursing of their beloved guru. These young men, under the watchful eyes of the Master and the leadership of Narendra, became the antaranga bhaktas, the devotees of Sri Ramakrishna's inner circle. They were privileged to witness many manifestations of the Master's divine powers. Narendra received instructions regarding the propagation of his message after his death.

The Holy Mother—so Sarada Devi had come to be affectionately known by Sri Ramakrishna's devotees—was brought from Dakshineswar to look after the general cooking and to prepare the special diet of the patient. The dwelling space being extremely limited, she had to adapt herself to cramped conditions. At three o'clock in the morning she would finish her bath in the Ganges and then enter a small covered place on the roof, where she spent the whole day cooking and praying. After eleven at night, when the visitors went away, she would come down to her small bedroom on the first floor to enjoy a few hours' sleep. Thus she spent three months, working hard, sleeping little, and praying constantly for the Master's recovery.

At Śyāmpukur the devotees led an intense life. Their attendance on the Master was in itself a form of spiritual discipline. His mind was constantly soaring to an exalted plane of consciousness. Now and then they would catch the contagion of his spiritual fervour. They sought to divine the mean ing of this illness of the Master, whom most of them had accepted as an Incarnation of God. One group, headed by Girish with his robust optimism and great power of imagination, believed that the illness was a mere pretext to serve a deeper purpose. The Master had willed his illness in order to bring the devotees together and promote solidarity among them. As soon as this purpose was served, he would himself get rid of the disease. A second group thought that the Divine Mother, in whose hand the Master was an instrument, had brought about this illness to serve Her own mysterious ends. But the young rationalists, led by Narendra, refused to ascribe a super‚ natural cause to a natural phenomenon. They believed that the Master's body, a material thing, was subject, like all other material things, to physical laws. Growth, development, decay, and death were laws of nature to which the Master's body could not but respond. But though holding differing views, they all believed that it was to him alone that they must look for the attainment of their spiritual goal.

In spite of the physician's efforts and the prayers and nursing of the devotees, the illness rapidly progressed. The pain sometimes appeared to be unbearable. The Master lived only on liquid food, and his frail body was becoming a mere skeleton. Yet his face always radiated joy, and he continued to welcome the visitors pouring in to receive his blessing. When certain zealous devotees tried to keep the visitors away, they were told by Girish, "You cannot succeed in it; he has been born for this very purpose— to sacrifice himself for the redemption of others."

The more the body was devastated by illness, the more it became the habitation of the Divine Spirit. Through its transparency the gods and goddesses began to shine with ever increasing luminosity. On the day of the Kāli Pujā the devotees clearly saw in him the manifestation of the Divine Mother.

It was noticed at this time that some of the devotees were making an unbridled display of their emotions. A number of them, particularly among the householders, began to cultivate, though at first unconsciously, the art of shedding tears, shaking the body, contorting the face, and going into trances, attempting thereby to imitate the Master. They began openly to declare Sri Ramakrishna a Divine Incarnation and to regard themselves as his chosen people, who could neglect religious disciplines with impunity. Narendra's penetrating eye soon sized up the situation. He found out that some of these external manifestations were being carefully practised at home, while some were the outcome of malnutrition, mental weakness, or nervous debility. He mercilessly exposed the devotees who were pretending to have visions, and asked all to develop a healthy religious spirit. Narendra sang inspiring songs for the younger devotees, read with them the *Imitation of Christ* and the *Gītā*, and held before them the positive ideals of spirituality.

LAST DAYS AT COSSIPORE

When Sri Ramakrishna's illness showed signs of aggravation, the devotees, following the advice of Dr. Sarkar, rented a spacious garden house at Cossipore, in the northern suburbs of Calcutta. The Master was removed to this place on December 11, 1885.

It was at Cossipore that the curtain fell on the varied activities of the Master's life on the physical plane. His soul lingered in the body eight months more. It was the period of his great Passion, a constant crucifixion of the body and the triumphant revelation of the Soul. Here one sees the humanity and divinity of the Master passing and repassing across a thin border line. Every minute of those eight months was suffused with touching tenderness of heart and breath-taking elevation of spirit. Every word he uttered was full of pathos and sublimity.

It took the group only a few days to become adjusted to the new environment. The Holy Mother, assisted by Sri Ramakrishna's niece, Lakshmi Devi, and a few woman devotees, took charge of the cooking for the Master and his attendants. Surendra willingly bore the major portion of the expenses, other householders contributing according to their means. Twelve disciples were constant attendants of the Master: Narendra, Rakhal, Baburam, Niranjan, Jogin, Latu, Tarak, the elder Gopal, Kali, Sashi, Sarat, and the younger Gopal. Sarada, Harish, Hari, Gangadhar, and Tulasi visited the Master from time to time and practised sādhanā at home. Narendra, preparing for his law examination, brought his books to the garden house in order to continue his studies during the infrequent spare moments. He encouraged his brother disciples to intensify their meditation, scriptural studies, and other spiritual disciplines. They all forgot their relatives and their worldly duties.

Among the attendants Sashi was the embodiment of service. He did not practise meditation, japa, or any of the other disciplines followed by his brother devotees. He was convinced that service to the guru was the only religion for him. He forgot food and rest and was ever ready at the Master's bedside.

Pundit Shashadhar one day suggested to the Master that the latter could remove the illness by concentrating his mind on the throat, the scriptures having declared that yogis had power to cure themselves in that way. The Master rebuked the pundit. "For a scholar like you to make such a proposal!" he said. "How can I withdraw the mind from the Lotus Feet of God and turn it to this worthless cage of flesh and blood?" "For our sake at least", begged Narendra and the other disciples. "But", replied Sri Ramakrishna, "do you think I enjoy this suffering? I wish to recover, but that depends on the Mother."

NARENDRA: "Then please pray to Her. She must listen to you."

MASTER: "But I cannot pray for my body."

NARENDRA: "You must do it, for our sake at least."

MASTER: "Very well, I shall try."

A few hours later the Master said to Narendra: "I said to Her: 'Mother, I cannot swallow food because of my pain. Make it possible for me to eat a little.' She pointed you all out to me and said: 'What? You are eating enough through all these mouths. Isn't that so?' I was ashamed and could not utter another word." This dashed all the hopes of the devotees for the Master's recovery.

"I shall make the whole thing public before I go", the Master had said some time before. On January 1, 1886, he felt better and came down to the garden for a little stroll. It was about three o'clock in the afternoon. Some thirty lay disciples were in the hall or sitting about under the trees. Sri Ramakrishna said to Girish, "Well, Girish, what have you seen in me, that you proclaim me before everybody as an Incarnation of God?" Girish was not the man to be taken by surprise. He knelt before the Master and said with folded hands, "What can an insignificant person like myself say about the One whose glory even sages like Vyāsa and Vālmiki could not adequately measure?" The Master was profoundly moved. He said: "What more shall I say? I bless you all. Be illumined!" He fell into a spiritual mood. Hearing these words the devotees, one and all, became overwhelmed with emotion. They rushed to him and fell at his feet. He touched them all, and each received an appropriate benediction. Each of them, at the touch of the Master, experienced ineffable bliss. Some laughed, some wept, some sat down to meditate, some began to pray. Some saw light, some had visions of their Chosen Ideals, and some felt within their bodies the rush of spiritual power.

Narendra, consumed with a terrific fever for realization, complained to the Master that all the others had attained peace and that he alone was dissatisfied. The Master asked what he wanted. Narendra begged for samādhi, so that he might altogether forget the world for three or four days at a time. "You are a fool", the Master rebuked him. "There is a state even higher than that. Isn't it you who sing, 'All that exists art Thou'? First of all settle your family affairs and then come to me. You will experience a state even higher than samādhi."

The Master did not hide the fact that he wished to make Narendra his spiritual heir. Narendra was to continue the work after Sri Ramakrishna's passing. Sri Ramakrishna said to him: "I leave these young men in your charge. See that they develop their spirituality and do not return home." One day he asked the boys, in preparation for a monastic life, to beg their food from door to door without thought of caste. They hailed the Master's order and went out with begging-bowls. A few days later he gave the ochre cloth of the sannyāsi to each of them, including Girish, who was now second to none in his spirit of renunciation. Thus the Master himself laid the foundation of the future Ramakrishna Order of monks.

Sri Ramakrishna was sinking day by day. His diet was reduced to a minimum and he found it almost impossible to swallow. He whispered to M.: "I am bearing all this cheerfully, for otherwise you would be weeping. If you all say that it is better that the body should go rather than suffer this torture, I am willing." The next morning he said to his depressed disciples seated near the bed: "Do you know what I see? I see that God alone has become everything. Men and animals are only frameworks covered with skin, and it is He who is moving through their heads and limbs. I see that it is God Himself who has become the block, the executioner, and the victim for the sacrifice." He fainted with emotion. Regaining partial consciousness,

he said: "Now I have no pain. I am very well." Looking at Latu he said:
"There sits Latu resting his head on the palm of his hand. To me it is the
Lord who is seated in that posture."

The words were tender and touching. Like a mother he caressed Narendra
and Rakhal, gently stroking their faces. He said in a half whisper to M.,
"Had this body been allowed to last a little longer, many more souls would
have been illumined." He paused a moment and then said: "But Mother
has ordained otherwise. She will take me away lest, finding me guileless and
foolish, people should take advantage of me and persuade me to bestow on
them the rare gifts of spirituality." A few minutes later he touched his chest
and said: "Here are two beings. One is She and the other is Her devotee.
It is the latter who broke his arm, and it is he again who is now ill. Do you
understand me?" After a pause he added: "Alas! To whom shall I tell all
this? Who will understand me?" "Pain", he consoled them again, "is unavoidable as long as there is a body. The Lord takes on the body for the
sake of His devotees."

Yet one is not sure whether the Master's soul actually was tortured by this
agonizing disease. At least during his moments of spiritual exaltation—which
became almost constant during the closing days of his life on earth—he lost
all consciousness of the body, of illness and suffering. One of his attendants[9]
said later on: "While Sri Ramakrishna lay sick he never actually suffered
pain. He would often say: 'O mind! Forget the body, forget the sickness,
and remain merged in Bliss.' No, he did not really suffer. At times he would
be in a state when the thrill of joy was clearly manifested in his body. Even
when he could not speak he would let us know in some way that there was
no suffering, and this fact was clearly evident to all who watched him.
People who did not understand him thought that his suffering was very
great. What spiritual joy he transmitted to us at that time! Could such a
thing have been possible if he had been suffering physically? It was during
this period that he taught us again these truths: 'Brahman is always unattached. The three gunas are in It, but It is unaffected by them, just as the
wind carries odour yet remains odourless.' 'Brahman is Infinite Being, Infinite Wisdom, Infinite Bliss. In It there exist no delusion, no misery, no
disease, no death, no growth, no decay.' 'The Transcendental Being and
the being within are one and the same. There is one indivisible Absolute
Existence.' "

The Holy Mother secretly went to a Śiva temple across the Ganges to
intercede with the Deity for the Master's recovery. In a revelation she was
told to prepare herself for the inevitable end.

One day when Narendra was on the ground floor, meditating, the Master
was lying awake in his bed upstairs. In the depths of his meditation Narendra
felt as though a lamp were burning at the back of his head. Suddenly he
lost consciousness. It was the yearned-for, all-effacing experience of nirvikalpa
samādhi, when the embodied soul realizes its unity with the Absolute. After
a very long time he regained partial consciousness but was unable to find
his body. He could see only his head. "Where is my body?" he cried. The

[9] Latu, later known as Swami Adbhutananda.

elder Gopal entered the room and said, "Why, it is here, Naren!" But Narendra could not find it. Gopal, frightened, ran upstairs to the Master. Sri Ramakrishna only said: "Let him stay that way for a time. He has worried me long enough."

After another long period Narendra regained full consciousness. Bathed in peace, he went to the Master, who said: "Now the Mother has shown you everything. But this revelation will remain under lock and key, and I shall keep the key. When you have accomplished the Mother's work you will find the treasure again."

Some days later, Narendra being alone with the Master, Sri Ramakrishna looked at him and went into samādhi. Narendra felt the penetration of a subtle force and lost all outer consciousness. Regaining presently the normal mood, he found the Master weeping.

Sri Ramakrishna said to him: "Today I have given you my all and I am now only a poor fakir, possessing nothing. By this power you will do immense good in the world, and not until it is accomplished will you return." Henceforth the Master lived in the disciple.

Doubt, however, dies hard. After one or two days Narendra said to himself, "If in the midst of this racking physical pain he declares his Godhead, then only shall I accept him as an Incarnation of God." He was alone by the bedside of the Master. It was a passing thought, but the Master smiled. Gathering his remaining strength, he distinctly said, "He who was Rāma and Krishna is now, in this body, Ramakrishna—but not in your Vedāntic sense." Narendra was stricken with shame.

MAHĀSAMĀDHI

Sunday, August 15, 1886. The Master's pulse became irregular. The devotees stood by the bedside. Toward dusk Sri Ramakrishna had difficulty in breathing. A short time afterwards he complained of hunger. A little liquid food was put into his mouth; some of it he swallowed, and the rest ran over his chin. Two attendants began to fan him. All at once he went into samādhi of a rather unusual type. The body became stiff. Sashi burst into tears. But after midnight the Master revived. He was now very hungry and helped himself to a bowl of porridge. He said he was strong again. He sat up against five or six pillows, which were supported by the body of Sashi, who was fanning him. Narendra took his feet on his lap and began to rub them. Again and again the Master repeated to him, "Take care of these boys." Then he asked to lie down. Three times in ringing tones he cried the name of Kāli, his life's Beloved, and lay back. At two minutes past one there was a low sound in his throat and he fell a little to one side. A thrill passed over his body. His hair stood on end. His eyes became fixed on the tip of his nose. His face was lighted with a smile. The final ecstasy began. It was mahāsamādhi, total absorption, from which his mind never returned. Narendra, unable to bear it, ran downstairs.

Dr. Sarkar arrived the following noon and pronounced that life had departed not more than half an hour before. At five o'clock the Master's body was brought downstairs, laid on a cot, dressed in ochre clothes, and decorated with sandal-paste and flowers. A procession was formed. The passers-by wept as the body was taken to the cremation ground at the Barānagore Ghāt on the Ganges.

While the devotees were returning to the garden house, carrying the urn with the sacred ashes, a calm resignation came to their souls and they cried, "Victory unto the Guru!"

The Holy Mother was weeping in her room, not for her husband, but because she felt that Mother Kāli had left her. As she was about to put on the marks of a Hindu widow, in a moment of revelation she heard the words of faith, "I have only passed from one room to another."

The Gospel of
Sri Ramakrishna

Bhagavan Sri Ramakrishna

MAHENDRANATH GUPTA, OR M.
*(The recorder of The Gospel of
Sri Ramakrishna in Bengali)*

MASTER AND DISCIPLE

I T WAS ON A SUNDAY in spring, a few days after Sri Ramakrishna's birthday, that M. met him the first time. Sri Ramakrishna lived at the Kālibāri, the temple garden of Mother Kāli, on the bank of the Ganges at Dakshineswar.

M., being at leisure on Sundays, had gone with his friend Sidhu to visit several gardens at Barānagore. As they were walking in Prasanna Bannerji's garden, Sidhu said: "There is a charming place on the bank of the Ganges where a paramahamsa lives. Should you like to go there?" M. assented and they started immediately for the Dakshineswar temple garden. They arrived at the main gate at dusk and went straight to Sri Ramakrishna's room. And there they found him seated on a wooden couch, facing the east. With a smile on his face he was talking of God. The room was full of people, all seated on the floor, drinking in his words in deep silence.

M. stood there speechless and looked on. It was as if he were standing where all the holy places met and as if Śukadeva himself were speaking the word of God, or as if Sri Chaitanya were singing the name and glories of the Lord in Puri with Rāmānanda, Swarup, and the other devotees.

Sri Ramakrishna said: "When, hearing the name of Hari or Rāma once, you shed tears and your hair stands on end, then you may know for certain that you do not have to perform such devotions as the sandhyā any more. Then only will you have a right to renounce rituals; or rather, rituals will drop away of themselves. Then it will be enough if you repeat only the name of Rāma or Hari, or even simply Om." Continuing, he said, "The sandhyā merges in the Gāyatri, and the Gāyatri merges in Om."

M. looked around him with wonder and said to himself: "What a beautiful place! What a charming man! How beautiful his words are! I have no wish to move from this spot." After a few minutes he thought, "Let me see the place first; then I'll come back here and sit down."

As he left the room with Sidhu, he heard the sweet music of the evening service arising in the temple from gong, bell, drum, and cymbal. He could hear music from the nahabat, too, at the south end of the garden. The sounds travelled over the Ganges, floating away and losing themselves in the distance. A soft spring wind was blowing, laden with the fragrance of flowers; the moon had just appeared. It was as if nature and man together were preparing for the evening worship. M. and Sidhu visited the twelve Śiva temples, the Rādhākānta temple, and the temple of Bhavatārini. And as M. watched the services before the images his heart was filled with joy.

On the way back to Sri Ramakrishna's room the two friends talked. Sidhu told M. that the temple garden had been founded by Rāni Rasmani. He said that God was worshipped there daily as Kāli, Krishna, and Śiva, and that within the gates many sādhus and beggars were fed. When they reached Sri Ramakrishna's door again, they found it shut, and Brindē, the maid, standing outside. M., who had been trained in English manners and would not enter a room without permission, asked her, "Is the holy man in?" Brindē replied, "Yes, he's in the room."

M: "How long has he lived here?"

BRINDĒ: "Oh, he has been here a long time."

M: "Does he read many books?"

BRINDĒ: "Books? Oh, dear no! They're all on his tongue."

M. had just finished his studies in college. It amazed him to hear that Sri Ramakrishna read no books.

M: "Perhaps it is time for his evening worship. May we go into the room? Will you tell him we are anxious to see him?"

BRINDĒ: "Go right in, children. Go in and sit down."

Entering the room, they found Sri Ramakrishna alone, seated on the wooden couch. Incense had just been burnt and all the doors were shut. As he entered, M. with folded hands saluted the Master. Then, at the Master's bidding, he and Sidhu sat on the floor. Sri Ramakrishna asked them: "Where do you live? What is your occupation? Why have you come to Barānagore?" M. answered the questions, but he noticed that now and then the Master seemed to become absent-minded. Later he learnt that this mood is called bhāva, ecstasy. It is like the state of the angler who has been sitting with his rod: the fish comes and swallows the bait, and the float begins to tremble; the angler is on the alert; he grips the rod and watches the float steadily and eagerly; he will not speak to anyone. Such was the state of Sri Ramakrishna's mind. Later M. heard, and himself noticed, that Sri Ramakrishna would often go into this mood after dusk, sometimes becoming totally unconscious of the outer world.

M: "Perhaps you want to perform your evening worship. In that case may we take our leave?"

SRI RAMAKRISHNA (still in ecstasy): "No—evening worship? No, it is not exactly that."

After a little conversation M. saluted the Master and took his leave. "Come again", Sri Ramakrishna said.

On his way home M. began to wonder: "Who is this serene-looking man who is drawing me back to him? Is it possible for a man to be great without being a scholar? How wonderful it is! I should like to see him again. He himself said, 'Come again.' I shall go tomorrow or the day after."

M.'s second visit to Sri Ramakrishna took place on the southeast verandah at eight o'clock in the morning. The Master was about to be shaved, the barber having just arrived. As the cold season still lingered he had put on a moleskin shawl bordered with red. Seeing M., the Master said: "So you have come. That's good. Sit down here." He was smiling. He stammered a little when he spoke.

SRI RAMAKRISHNA (*to M.*): "Where do you live?"

M: "In Calcutta, sir."

SRI RAMAKRISHNA: "Where are you staying here?"

M: "I am at Barānagore at my older sister's—Ishan Kavirāj's house."

SRI RAMAKRISHNA: "Oh, at Ishan's? Well, how is Keshab now? He was very ill."

M: "Indeed, I have heard so too, but I believe he is well now."

SRI RAMAKRISHNA: "I made a vow to worship the Mother with green coconut and sugar on Keshab's recovery. Sometimes, in the early hours of the morning, I would wake up and cry before Her: 'Mother, please make Keshab well again. If Keshab doesn't live, whom shall I talk with when I go to Calcutta?' And so it was that I resolved to offer Her the green coconut and sugar.

"Tell me, do you know of a certain Mr. Cook who has come to Calcutta? Is it true that he is giving lectures? Once Keshab took me on a steamer, and this Mr. Cook, too, was in the party."

M: "Yes, sir, I have heard something like that; but I have never been to his lectures. I don't know much about him."

SRI RAMAKRISHNA: "Pratap's brother came here. He stayed a few days. He had nothing to do and said he wanted to live here. I came to know that he had left his wife and children with his father-in-law. He has a whole brood of them! So I took him to task. Just fancy! He is the father of so many children! Will people from the neighbourhood feed them and bring them up? He isn't even ashamed that someone else is feeding his wife and children, and that they have been left at his father-in-law's house. I scolded him very hard and asked him to look for a job. Then he was willing to leave here.

"Are you married?"

M: "Yes, sir."

SRI RAMAKRISHNA (*with a shudder*): "Oh, Ramlal![1] Alas, he is married!"

Like one guilty of a terrible offence, M. sat motionless; his eyes fixed on the ground. He thought, "Is it such a wicked thing to get married?"

The Master continued, "Have you any children?"

M. this time could hear the beating of his own heart. He whispered in a trembling voice, "Yes, sir, I have children."

Very sadly Sri Ramakrishna said, "Ah me! He even has children!"

Thus rebuked M. sat speechless. His pride had received a blow. After a few minutes Sri Ramakrishna looked at him kindly and said affectionately: "You see, you have certain good signs. I know them by looking at a person's forehead, his eyes, and so on. Tell me, now, what kind of person is your wife? Has she spiritual attributes, or is she under the power of avidyā?"

[1] A nephew of Sri Ramakrishna, and a priest in the Kāli temple.

M: "She is all right. But I am afraid she is ignorant."

MASTER (*with evident displeasure*): "And you are a man of knowledge!"

M. had yet to learn the distinction between knowledge and ignorance. Up to this time his conception had been that one got knowledge from books and schools. Later on he gave up this false conception. He was taught that to know God is knowledge, and not to know Him, ignorance. When Sri Rama-krishna exclaimed, "And you are a man of knowledge!", M.'s ego was again badly shocked.

MASTER: "Well, do you believe in God with form or without form?"

M., rather surprised, said to himself: "How can one believe in God with-out form when one believes in God with form? And if one believes in God without form, how can one believe that God has a form? Can these two contradictory ideas be true at the same time? Can a white liquid like milk be black?"

M: "Sir, I like to think of God as formless."

MASTER: "Very good. It is enough to have faith in either aspect. You believe in God without form; that is quite all right. But never for a moment think that this alone is true and all else false. Remember that God with form is just as true as God without form. But hold fast to your own con-viction."

The assertion that both are equally true amazed M.; he had never learnt this from his books. Thus his ego received a third blow; but since it was not yet completely crushed, he came forward to argue with the Master a little more.

M: "Sir, suppose one believes in God with form. Certainly He is not the clay image!"

MASTER (*interrupting*): "But why clay? It is an image of Spirit."

M. could not quite understand the significance of this "image of Spirit". "But, sir," he said to the Master, "one should explain to those who wor-ship the clay image that it is *not* God, and that, while worshipping it, they should have God in view and not the clay image. One should not worship clay."

MASTER (*sharply*): "That's the one hobby of you Calcutta people—giving lectures and bringing others to the light! Nobody ever stops to consider how to get the light himself. Who are you to teach others?

"He who is the Lord of the Universe will teach everyone. He alone teaches us, who has created this universe; who has made the sun and moon, men and beasts, and all other beings; who has provided means for their sustenance; who has given children parents and endowed them with love to bring them up. The Lord has done so many things—will He not show people the way to worship Him? If they need teaching, then He will be the Teacher. He is our Inner Guide.

"Suppose there is an error in worshipping the clay image; doesn't God know that through it He alone is being invoked? He will be pleased with that very worship. Why should you get a headache over it? You had better try for knowledge and devotion yourself."

This time M. felt that his ego was completely crushed. He now said to himself: "Yes, he has spoken the truth. What need is there for me to teach others? Have I known God? Do I really love Him? 'I haven't room enough for myself in my bed, and I am inviting my friend to share it with me!' I know nothing about God, yet I am trying to teach others. What a shame! How foolish I am! This is not mathematics or history or literature, that one can teach it to others. No, this is the deep mystery of God. What he says appeals to me."

This was M.'s first argument with the Master, and happily his last.

MASTER: "You were talking of worshipping the clay image. Even if the image *is* made of clay, there is need for that sort of worship. God Himself has provided different forms of worship. He who is the Lord of the Universe has arranged all these forms to suit different men in different stages of knowledge.

"The mother cooks different dishes to suit the stomachs of her different children. Suppose she has five children. If there is a fish to cook, she prepares various dishes from it—pilau, pickled fish, fried fish, and so on—to suit their different tastes and powers of digestion.

"Do you understand me?"

M. (*humbly*): "Yes, sir. How, sir, may we fix our minds on God?"

MASTER: "Repeat God's name and sing His glories, and keep holy company; and now and then visit God's devotees and holy men. The mind cannot dwell on God if it is immersed day and night in worldliness, in worldly duties and responsibilities; it is most necessary to go into solitude now and then and think of God. To fix the mind on God is very difficult, in the beginning, unless one practises meditation in solitude. When a tree is young it should be fenced all around; otherwise it may be destroyed by cattle.

"To meditate, you should withdraw within yourself or retire to a secluded corner or to the forest. And you should always discriminate between the Real and the unreal. God alone is real, the Eternal Substance; all else is unreal, that is, impermanent. By discriminating thus, one should shake off impermanent objects from the mind."

M. (*humbly*): "How ought we to live in the world?"

MASTER: "Do all your duties, but keep your mind on God. Live with all—with wife and children, father and mother—and serve them. Treat them as if they were very dear to you, but know in your heart of hearts that they do not belong to you.

"A maidservant in the house of a rich man performs all the household duties, but her thoughts are fixed on her own home in her native village. She brings up her master's children as if they were her own. She even speaks of them as 'my Rama' or 'my Hari'. But in her own mind she knows very well that they do not belong to her at all.

"The tortoise moves about in the water. But can you guess where her thoughts are? There on the bank, where her eggs are lying. Do all your duties in the world, but keep your mind on God.

"If you enter the world without first cultivating love for God, you will be entangled more and more. You will be overwhelmed with its danger, its grief, its sorrows. And the more you think of worldly things, the more you will be attached to them.

"First rub your hands with oil and then break open the jack-fruit; otherwise they will be smeared with its sticky milk. First secure the oil of divine love, and then set your hands to the duties of the world.

"But one must go into solitude to attain this divine love. To get butter from milk you must let it set into curd in a secluded spot: if it is too much disturbed, milk won't turn into curd. Next, you must put aside all other duties, sit in a quiet spot, and churn the curd. Only then do you get butter.

"Further, by meditating on God in solitude the mind acquires knowledge, dispassion, and devotion. But the very same mind goes downward if it dwells in the world. In the world there is only one thought: 'woman and gold'.[2]

"The world is water and the mind milk. If you pour milk into water they become one; you cannot find the pure milk any more. But turn the milk into curd and churn it into butter. Then, when that butter is placed in water, it will float. So, practise spiritual discipline in solitude and obtain the butter of knowledge and love. Even if you keep that butter in the water of the world the two will not mix. The butter will float.

"Together with this, you must practise discrimination. 'Woman and gold' is impermanent. God is the only Eternal Substance. What does a man get with money? Food, clothes, and a dwelling-place—nothing more. You cannot realize God with its help. Therefore money can never be the goal of life. That is the process of discrimination. Do you understand?"

M: "Yes, sir. I recently read a Sanskrit play called *Prabodha Chandrodaya*. It deals with discrimination."

MASTER: "Yes, discrimination about objects. Consider—what is there in money or in a beautiful body? Discriminate and you will find that even the body of a beautiful woman consists of bones, flesh, fat, and other disagreeable things. Why should a man give up God and direct his attention to such things? Why should a man forget God for their sake?"

M: "Is it possible to *see* God?"

---

[2] The term "woman and gold", which has been used throughout in a collective sense, occurs again and again in the teachings of Sri Ramakrishna to designate the chief impediments to spiritual progress. This favourite expression of the Master, "kāminikānchan", has often been misconstrued. By it he meant only "lust and greed", the baneful influence of which retards the aspirant's spiritual growth. He used the word "kāmini", or "woman", as a concrete term for the sex instinct when addressing his man devotees. He advised women, on the other hand, to shun "man". "Kānchan", or "gold", symbolizes greed, which is the other obstacle to spiritual life.

Sri Ramakrishna never taught his disciples to hate any woman, or womankind in general. This can be seen clearly by going through all his teachings under this head and judging them collectively. The Master looked on all women as so many images of the Divine Mother of the Universe. He paid the highest homage to womankind by accepting a woman as his guide while practising the very profound spiritual disciplines of Tantra. His wife, known and revered as the Holy Mother, was his constant companion and first disciple. At the end of his spiritual practice he literally worshipped his wife as the embodiment of the Goddess Kāli, the Divine Mother. After his passing away the Holy Mother became the spiritual guide not only of a large number of householders, but also of many monastic members of the Ramakrishna Order.

MASTER: "Yes, certainly. Living in solitude now and then, repeating God's name and singing His glories, and discriminating between the Real and the unreal—these are the means to employ to see Him."

M: "Under what conditions does one see God?"

MASTER: "Cry to the Lord with an intensely yearning heart and you will certainly see Him. People shed a whole jug of tears for wife and children. They swim in tears for money. But who weeps for God? Cry to Him with a real cry."

The Master sang:

> Cry to your Mother Śyāmā with a real cry, O mind!
> And how can She hold Herself from you?
> How can Śyāmā stay away?
> How can your Mother Kāli hold Herself away?
>
> O mind, if you are in earnest, bring Her an offering
> Of bel-leaves and hibiscus flowers;
> Lay at Her feet your offering
> And with it mingle the·fragrant sandal-paste of Love.

Continuing, he said: "Longing is like the rosy dawn. After the dawn out comes the sun. Longing is followed by the vision of God.

"God reveals Himself to a devotee who feels drawn to Him by the combined force of these three attractions: the attraction of worldly possessions for the worldly man, the child's attraction for its mother, and the husband's attraction for the chaste wife. If one feels drawn to Him by the combined force of these three attractions, then through it one can attain Him.

"The point is, to love God even as the mother loves her child, the chaste wife her husband, and the worldly man his wealth. Add together these three forces of love, these three powers of attraction, and give it all to God. Then you will certainly see Him.

"It is necessary to pray to Him with a longing heart. The kitten knows only how to call its mother, crying, 'Mew, mew!' It remains satisfied wherever its mother puts it. And the mother cat puts the kitten sometimes in the kitchen, sometimes on the floor, and sometimes on the bed. When it suffers it cries only, 'Mew, mew!' That's all it knows. But as soon as the mother hears this cry, wherever she may be, she comes to the kitten."

It was Sunday afternoon when M. came on his third visit to the Master. He had been profoundly impressed by his first two visits to this wonderful man. He had been thinking of the Master constantly, and of the utterly simple way he explained the deep truths of the spiritual life. Never before had he met such a man.

Sri Ramakrishna was sitting on the small couch. The room was filled with devotees,[3] who had taken advantage of the holiday to come to see the

---

[3] The word is generally used in the text to denote one devoted to God, a worshipper of the Personal God, or a follower of the path of love. A devotee of Sri Ramakrishna is one who is devoted to Sri Ramakrishna and follows his teachings.

Master. M. had not yet become acquainted with any of them; so he took his seat in a corner. The Master smiled as he talked with the devotees.

He addressed his words particularly to a young man of nineteen, named Narendranath,[4] who was a college student and frequented the Sādhāran Brāhmo Samāj. His eyes were bright, his words were full of spirit, and he had the look of a lover of God.

M. guessed that the conversation was about worldly men, who look down on those who aspire to spiritual things. The Master was talking about the great number of such people in the world, and about how to deal with them.

MASTER (to Narendra): "How do you feel about it? Worldly people say all kinds of things about the spiritually minded. But look here! When an elephant moves along the street, any number of curs and other small animals may bark and cry after it; but the elephant doesn't even look back at them. If people speak ill of you, what will you think of them?"

NARENDRA: "I shall think that dogs are barking at me."

MASTER (smiling): "Oh, no! You mustn't go that far, my child! (Laughter.) God dwells in all beings. But you may be intimate only with good people; you must keep away from the evil-minded. God is even in the tiger; but you cannot embrace the tiger on that account. (Laughter.) You may say, 'Why run away from a tiger, which is also a manifestation of God?' The answer to that is: 'Those who tell you to run away are also manifestations of God—and why shouldn't you listen to them?'

"Let me tell you a story. In a forest there lived a holy man who had many disciples. One day he taught them to see God in all beings and, knowing this, to bow low before them all. A disciple went to the forest to gather wood for the sacrificial fire. Suddenly he heard an outcry: 'Get out of the way! A mad elephant is coming!' All but the disciple of the holy man took to their heels. He reasoned that the elephant was also God in another form. Then why should he run away from it? He stood still, bowed before the animal, and began to sing its praises. The māhut of the elephant was shouting: 'Run away! Run away!' But the disciple didn't move. The animal seized him with its trunk, cast him to one side, and went on its way. Hurt and bruised, the disciple lay unconscious on the ground. Hearing what had happened, his teacher and his brother disciples came to him and carried him to the hermitage. With the help of some medicine he soon regained consciousness. Someone asked him, 'You knew the elephant was coming— why didn't you leave the place?' 'But', he said, 'our teacher has told us that God Himself has taken all these forms, of animals as well as men. Therefore, thinking it was only the elephant God that was coming, I didn't run away.' At this the teacher said: 'Yes, my child, it is true that the elephant God was coming; but the māhut God forbade you to stay there. Since all are mani-

---

The word "disciple", when used in connexion with Sri Ramakrishna, refers to one who had been initiated into spiritual life by Sri Ramakrishna and who regarded him as his guru.

[4] Subsequently world-famous as Swami Vivekananda.

festations of God, why didn't you trust the māhut's words? You should have heeded the words of the māhut God.' (*Laughter*.)

"It is said in the scriptures that water is a form of God. But some water is fit to be used for worship, some water for washing the face, and some only for washing plates or dirty linen. This last sort cannot be used for drinking or for a holy purpose. In like manner, God undoubtedly dwells in the hearts of all—holy and unholy, righteous and unrighteous; but a man should not have dealings with the unholy, the wicked, the impure. He must not be intimate with them. With some of them he may exchange words, but with others he shouldn't go even that far. He should keep aloof from such people."

A DEVOTEE: "Sir, if a wicked man is about to do harm, or actually does so, should we keep quiet then?"

MASTER: "A man living in society should make a show of tamas to protect himself from evil-minded people. But he should not harm anybody in anticipation of harm likely to be done him.

"Listen to a story. Some cowherd boys used to tend their cows in a meadow where a terrible poisonous snake lived. Everyone was on the alert for fear of it. One day a brahmachāri was going along the meadow. The boys ran to him and said: 'Revered sir, please don't go that way. A venomous snake lives over there.' 'What of it, my good children?' said the brahmachāri. 'I am not afraid of the snake. I know some mantras.' So saying, he continued on his way along the meadow. But the cowherd boys, being afraid, did not accompany him. In the mean time the snake moved swiftly toward him with upraised hood. As soon as it came near, he recited a mantra, and the snake lay at his feet like an earthworm. The brahmachāri said: 'Look here. Why do you go about doing harm? Come, I will give you a holy word. By repeating it you will learn to love God. Ultimately you will realize Him and so get rid of your violent nature.' Saying this, he taught the snake a holy word and initiated him into spiritual life. The snake bowed before the teacher and said, 'Revered sir, how shall I practise spiritual discipline?' 'Repeat that sacred word', said the teacher, 'and do no harm to anybody.' As he was about to depart, the brahmachāri said, 'I shall see you again.'

"Some days passed and the cowherd boys noticed that the snake would not bite. They threw stones at it. Still it showed no anger; it behaved as if it were an earthworm. One day one of the boys came close to it, caught it by the tail, and, whirling it round and round, dashed it again and again on the ground and threw it away. The snake vomited blood and became unconscious. It was stunned. It could not move. So, thinking it dead, the boys went their way.

"Late at night the snake regained consciousness. Slowly and with great difficulty it dragged itself into its hole; its bones were broken and it could scarcely move. Many days passed. The snake became a mere skeleton covered with a skin. Now and then, at night, it would come out in search of food. For fear of the boys it would not leave its hole during the day-time. Since receiving the sacred word from the teacher, it had given up doing harm to others. It maintained its life on dirt, leaves, or the fruit that dropped from the trees.

"About a year later the brahmachāri came that way again and asked after the snake. The cowherd boys told him that it was dead. But he couldn't believe them. He knew that the snake would not die before attaining the fruit of the holy word with which it had been initiated. He found his way to the place and, searching here and there, called it by the name he had given it. Hearing the teacher's voice, it came out of its hole and bowed before him with great reverence. 'How are you?' asked the brahmachāri. 'I am well, sir', replied the snake. 'But', the teacher asked, 'why are you so thin?' The snake replied: 'Revered sir, you ordered me not to harm anybody. So I have been living only on leaves and fruit. Perhaps that has made me thinner.'

"The snake had developed the quality of sattva; it could not be angry with anyone. It had totally forgotten that the cowherd boys had almost killed it.

"The brahmachāri said: 'It can't be mere want of food that has reduced you to this state. There must be some other reason. Think a little.' Then the snake remembered that the boys had dashed it against the ground. It said: 'Yes, revered sir, now I remember. The boys one day dashed me violently against the ground. They are ignorant, after all. They didn't realize what a great change had come over my mind. How could they know I wouldn't bite or harm anyone?' The brahmachāri exclaimed: 'What a shame! You are such a fool! You don't know how to protect yourself. I asked you not to bite, but I didn't forbid you to hiss. Why didn't you scare them by hissing?'

"So you must hiss at wicked people. You must frighten them lest they should do you harm. But never inject your venom into them. One must not injure others.

"In this creation of God there is a variety of things: men, animals, trees, plants. Among the animals some are good, some bad. There are ferocious animals like the tiger. Some trees bear fruit sweet as nectar, and others bear fruit that is poisonous. Likewise, among human beings, there are the good and the wicked, the holy and the unholy. There are some who are devoted to God, and others who are attached to the world.

"Men may be divided into four classes: those bound by the fetters of the world, the seekers after liberation, the liberated, and the ever-free.

"Among the ever-free we may count sages like Nārada. They live in the world for the good of others, to teach men spiritual truth.

"Those in bondage are sunk in worldliness and forgetful of God. Not even by mistake do they think of God.

"The seekers after liberation want to free themselves from attachment to the world. Some of them succeed and others do not.

"The liberated souls, such as the sādhus and mahātmās, are not entangled in the world, in 'woman and gold'. Their minds are free from worldliness. Besides, they always meditate on the Lotus Feet of God.

"Suppose a net has been cast into a lake to catch fish. Some fish are so clever that they are never caught in the net. They are like the ever-free. But most of the fish are entangled in the net. Some of them try to free themselves from it, and they are like those who seek liberation. But not all the fish that struggle succeed. A very few do jump out of the net, making a big splash in the water. Then the fishermen shout, 'Look! There goes a big one!' But most of the fish caught in the net cannot escape, nor do they make any effort to get out. On the contrary, they burrow into the mud with the net in their mouths and lie there quietly, thinking, 'We need not fear any more; we are quite safe here.' But the poor things do not know that the fishermen will drag them out with the net. These are like the men bound to the world.

"The bound souls are tied to the world by the fetters of 'woman and gold'. They are bound hand and foot. Thinking that 'woman and gold' will make them happy and give them security, they do not realize that it will lead them to annihilation. When a man thus bound to the world is about to die, his wife asks, 'You are about to go; but what have you done for me?' Again, such is his attachment to the things of the world that, when he sees the lamp burning brightly, he says: 'Dim the light. Too much oil is being used.' And he is on his death-bed!

"The bound souls never think of God. If they get any leisure they indulge in idle gossip and foolish talk, or they engage in fruitless work. If you ask one of them the reason, he answers, 'Oh, I cannot keep still; so I am making a hedge.' When time hangs heavy on their hands they perhaps start playing cards."

There was deep silence in the room.

A DEVOTEE: "Sir, is there no help, then, for such a worldly person?"

MASTER: "Certainly there is. From time to time he should live in the company of holy men, and from time to time go into solitude to meditate on God. Furthermore, he should practise discrimination and pray to God, 'Give me faith and devotion.' Once a person has faith he has achieved everything. There is nothing greater than faith.

(To Kedar) "You must have heard about the tremendous power of faith. It is said in the Purāna that Rāma, who was God Himself—the embodiment of Absolute Brahman—had to build a bridge to cross the sea to Ceylon. But Hanumān, trusting in Rāma's name, cleared the sea in one jump and reached the other side. He had no need of a bridge. (All laugh.)

"Once a man was about to cross the sea. Bibhishana wrote Rāma's name on a leaf, tied it in a corner of the man's wearing-cloth, and said to him: 'Don't be afraid. Have faith and walk on the water. But look here—the moment you lose faith you will be drowned.' The man was walking easily on the water. Suddenly he had an intense desire to see what was tied in his cloth. He opened it and found only a leaf with the name of Rāma written on it. 'What is this?' he thought. 'Just the name of Rāma!' As soon as doubt entered his mind he sank under the water.

"If a man has faith in God, then even if he has committed the most heinous sins—such as killing a cow, a brāhmin, or a woman—he will certainly be saved through his faith. Let him only say to God, 'O Lord, I will not repeat such an action', and he need not be afraid of anything."

When he had said this, the Master sang:

> If only I can pass away repeating Durgā's name,
> How canst Thou then, O Blessed One,
> Withhold from me deliverance,
> Wretched though I may be?
> I may have stolen a drink of wine, or killed a child unborn,
> Or slain a woman or a cow,
> Or even caused a brāhmin's death;
> But, though it all be true,
> Nothing of this can make me feel the least uneasiness;
> For through the power of Thy sweet name
> My wretched soul may still aspire
> Even to Brahmanhood.

Pointing to Narendra, the Master said: "You all see this boy. He behaves that way here. A naughty boy seems very gentle when with his father. But he is quite another person when he plays in the chāndni. Narendra and people of his type belong to the class of the ever-free. They are never entangled in the world. When they grow a little older they feel the awakening of inner consciousness and go directly toward God. They come to the world only to teach others. They never care for anything of the world. They are never attached to 'woman and gold'.

"The Vedas speak of the homā bird. It lives high up in the sky and there it lays its egg. As soon as the egg is laid it begins to fall; but it is so high up that it continues to fall for many days. As it falls it hatches, and the chick falls. As the chick falls its eyes open; it grows wings. As soon as its eyes open, it realizes that it is falling and will be dashed to pieces on touching the earth. Then it at once shoots up toward the mother bird high in the sky."

At this point Narendra left the room. Kedar, Prankrishna, M., and many others remained.

MASTER: "You see, Narendra excels in singing, playing on instruments, study, and everything. The other day he had a discussion with Kedar and tore his arguments to shreds. (All laugh.)

(To M.) "Is there any book in English on reasoning?"

M: "Yes, sir, there is. It is called Logic."

MASTER: "Tell me what it says."

M. was a little embarrassed. He said: "One part of the book deals with deduction from the general to the particular. For example: All men are mortal. Scholars are men. Therefore scholars are mortal. Another part deals with the method of reasoning from the particular to the general. For example: This crow is black. That crow is black. The crows we see everywhere are black. Therefore all crows are black. But there may be a fallacy in a conclusion arrived at in this way; for on inquiry one may find a white crow in some country. There is another illustration: If there is rain, there is or has been a cloud. Therefore rain comes from a cloud. Still another example: This man has thirty-two teeth. That man has thirty-two teeth. All the men we see have thirty-two teeth. Therefore men have thirty-two teeth. English logic deals with such inductions and deductions."

Sri Ramakrishna barely heard these words. While listening he became absent-minded. So the conversation did not proceed far.

When the meeting broke up, the devotees sauntered in the temple garden. M. went in the direction of the Panchavati. It was about five o'clock in the afternoon. After a while he returned to the Master's room. There, on the small north verandah, he witnessed an amazing sight.

Sri Ramakrishna was standing still, surrounded by a few devotees, and Narendra was singing. M. had never heard anyone except the Master sing so sweetly. When he looked at Sri Ramakrishna he was struck with wonder; for the Master stood motionless, with eyes transfixed. He seemed not even to breathe. A devotee told M. that the Master was in samādhi. M. had never before seen or heard of such a thing. Silent with wonder, he thought: "Is it possible for a man to be so oblivious of the outer world in the consciousness of God? How deep his faith and devotion must be to bring about such a state!"

Narendra was singing:

> Meditate, O my mind, on the Lord Hari,
> The Stainless One, Pure Spirit through and through.
> How peerless is the Light that in Him shines!
> How soul-bewitching is His wondrous form!
> How dear is He to all His devotees!
>
> Ever more beauteous in fresh-blossoming love
> That shames the splendour of a million moons,
> Like lightning gleams the glory of His form,
> Raising erect the hair for very joy.

The Master shuddered when this last line was sung. His hair stood on end, and tears of joy streamed down his cheeks. Now and then his lips parted in a smile. Was he seeing the peerless beauty of God, "that shames the splendour of a million moons"? Was this the vision of God, the Essence of Spirit? How much austerity and discipline, how much faith and devotion, must be necessary for such a vision!

The song went on:

> Worship His feet in the lotus of your heart;
> With mind serene and eyes made radiant
> With heavenly love, behold that matchless sight.

Again that bewitching smile. The body motionless as before, the eyes half shut, as if beholding a strange inner vision.

The song drew to a close. Narendra sang the last lines:

> Caught in the spell of His love's ecstasy,
> Immerse yourself for evermore, O mind,
> In Him who is Pure Knowledge and Pure Bliss.

The sight of the samādhi, and the divine bliss he had witnessed, left an indelible impression on M.'s mind. He returned home deeply moved. Now and then he could hear within himself the echo of those soul-intoxicating lines:

> Immerse yourself for evermore, O mind,
> In Him who is Pure Knowledge and Pure Bliss.

The next day, too, was a holiday for M. He arrived at Dakshineswar at three o'clock in the afternoon. Sri Ramakrishna was in his room; Narendra, Bhavanath, and a few other devotees were sitting on a mat spread on the floor. They were all young men of nineteen or twenty. Seated on the small couch, Sri Ramakrishna was talking with them and smiling.

No sooner had M. entered the room than the Master laughed aloud and said to the boys, "There! He has come again." They all joined in the laughter. M. bowed low before him and took a seat. Before this he had saluted the Master with folded hands, like one with an English education. But that day he learnt to fall down at his feet in orthodox Hindu fashion.

Presently the Master explained the cause of his laughter to the devotees. He said: "A man once fed a peacock with a pill of opium at four o'clock in the afternoon. The next day, exactly at that time, the peacock came back. It had felt the intoxication of the drug and returned just in time to have another dose." (*All laugh.*)

M. thought this a very apt illustration. Even at home he had been unable to banish the thought of Sri Ramakrishna for a moment. His mind was constantly at Dakshineswar and he had counted the minutes until he should go again.

In the mean time the Master was having great fun with the boys, treating them as if they were his most intimate friends. Peals of side-splitting laughter filled the room, as if it were a mart of joy. The whole thing was a revelation to M. He thought: "Didn't I see him only yesterday intoxicated with God? Wasn't he swimming then in the Ocean of Divine Love—a sight I had never seen before? And today the same person is behaving like an ordinary man! Wasn't it he who scolded me on the first day of my coming here? Didn't he admonish me, saying, 'And you are a man of knowledge!'? Wasn't it he who said to me that God with form is as true as God without form? Didn't he tell me that God alone is real and all else illusory? Wasn't it he who advised me to live in the world unattached, like a maidservant in a rich man's house?"

Sri Ramakrishna was having great fun with the young devotees; now and then he glanced at M. He noticed that M. sat in silence. The Master said to Ramlal: "You see, he is a little advanced in years, and therefore somewhat serious. He sits quiet while the youngsters are making merry." M. was then about twenty-eight years old.

The conversation drifted to Hanumān, whose picture hung on the wall in the Master's room.

Sri Ramakrishna said: "Just imagine Hanumān's state of mind. He didn't care for money, honour, creature comforts, or anything else. He longed only for God. When he was running away with the heavenly weapon that had been secreted in the crystal pillar, Mandodari began to tempt him with various fruits so that he might come down and drop the weapon.[5] But he couldn't be tricked so easily. In reply to her persuasions he sang this song:

> Am I in need of fruit?
> I have the Fruit that makes this life
> Fruitful indeed. Within my heart
> The Tree of Rāma grows,
> Bearing salvation for its fruit.

> Under the Wish-fulfilling Tree
> Of Rāma do I sit at ease,
> Plucking whatever fruit I will.
> But if you speak of fruit—
> No beggar, I, for common fruit.
> Behold, I go,
> Leaving a bitter fruit for you."

As Sri Ramakrishna was singing the song he went into samādhi. Again the half-closed eyes and motionless body that one sees in his photograph. Just a minute before, the devotees had been making merry in his company. Now all eyes were riveted on him. Thus for the second time M. saw the Master in samādhi.

After a long time the Master came back to ordinary consciousness. His face lighted up with a smile, and his body relaxed; his senses began to function in a normal way. He shed tears of joy as he repeated the holy name of Rāma. M. wondered whether this very saint was the person who a few minutes earlier had been behaving like a child of five.

The Master said to Narendra and M., "I should like to hear you speak and argue in English." They both laughed. But they continued to talk in their mother tongue. It was impossible for M. to argue any more before the Master. Though Sri Ramakrishna insisted, they did not talk in English.

At five o'clock in the afternoon all the devotees except Narendra and M. took leave of the Master. As M. was walking in the temple garden, he suddenly came upon the Master talking to Narendra on the bank of the goose-pond. Sri Ramakrishna said to Narendra: "Look here. Come a little more often. You are a new-comer. On first acquaintance people visit each other quite often, as is the case with a lover and his sweetheart. (*Narendra and M. laugh.*) So please come, won't you?"

Narendra, a member of the Brāhmo Samāj, was very particular about his promises. He said with a smile, "Yes, sir, I shall try."

As they were returning to the Master's room, Sri Ramakrishna said to M.: "When peasants go to market to buy bullocks for their ploughs, they can easily tell the good from the bad by touching their tails. On being touched there, some meekly lie down on the ground. The peasants recognize that these are without mettle and so reject them. They select only those bullocks

[5] The story referred to here is told in the *Rāmāyana*. Rāvana had received a boon as a result of which he could be killed only by a particular celestial weapon. This weapon was concealed in a crystal pillar in his palace. One day Hanumān, in the guise of an ordinary monkey, came to the palace and broke the pillar. As he was running away with the weapon, he was tempted with fruit by Mandodari, Rāvana's wife, so that he might give back the weapon. He soon assumed his own form and sang the song given in the text.

that frisk about and show spirit when their tails are touched. Narendra is like a bullock of this latter class. He is full of spirit within."

The Master smiled as he said this, and continued: "There are some people who have no grit whatever. They are like flattened rice soaked in milk—soft and mushy. No inner strength!"

It was dusk. The Master was meditating on God. He said to M.: "Go and talk to Narendra. Then tell me what you think of him."

Evening worship was over in the temples. M. met Narendra on the bank of the Ganges and they began to converse. Narendra told M. about his studying in college, his being a member of the Brāhmo Samāj, and so on.

It was now late in the evening and time for M.'s departure; but he felt reluctant to go and instead went in search of Sri Ramakrishna. He had been fascinated by the Master's singing and wanted to hear more. At last he found the Master pacing alone in the nātmandir in front of the Kāli temple. A lamp was burning in the temple on either side of the image of the Divine Mother. The single lamp in the spacious nātmandir blended light and darkness into a kind of mystic twilight, in which the figure of the Master could be dimly seen.

M. had been enchanted by the Master's sweet music. With some hesitation he asked him whether there would be any more singing that evening. "No, not tonight", said Sri Ramakrishna after a little reflection. Then, as if remembering something, he added: "But I'm going soon to Balaram Bose's house in Calcutta. Come there and you'll hear me sing." M. agreed to go.

MASTER: "Do you know Balaram Bose?"

M: "No, sir. I don't."

MASTER: "He lives in Bosepārā."

M: "Well, sir, I shall find him."

As Sri Ramakrishna walked up and down the hall with M., he said to him: "Let me ask you something. What do you think of me?"

M. remained silent. Again Sri Ramakrishna asked: "What do you think of me? How many ānnās of knowledge of God have I?"

M: "I don't understand what you mean by 'ānnās'. But of this I am sure: I have never before seen such knowledge, ecstatic love, faith in God, renunciation, and catholicity anywhere."

The Master laughed.

M. bowed low before him and took his leave. He had gone as far as the main gate of the temple garden when he suddenly remembered something and came back to Sri Ramakrishna, who was still in the nātmandir. In the dim light the Master, all alone, was pacing the hall, rejoicing in the Self— as the lion lives and roams alone in the forest.

In silent wonder M. surveyed that great soul.

MASTER (to M.): "What makes you come back?"

M: "Perhaps the house you asked me to go to belongs to a rich man. They may not let me in. I think I had better not go. I would rather meet you here."

MASTER: "Oh, no! Why should you think that? Just mention my name. Say that you want to see me; then someone will take you to me."

M. nodded his assent and, after saluting the Master, took his leave.

IN THE COMPANY OF DEVOTEES

A BOUT EIGHT O'CLOCK in the morning Sri Ramakrishna went as planned to Balaram Bose's house in Calcutta. It was the day of the Dola-yātrā. Ram, Manomohan, Rakhal,[1] Nityagopal, and other devotees were with him. M., too, came, as bidden by the Master.

The devotees and the Master sang and danced in a state of divine fervour. Several of them were in an ecstatic mood. Nityagopal's chest glowed with the upsurge of emotion, and Rakhal lay on the floor in ecstasy, completely unconscious of the world. The Master put his hand on Rakhal's chest and said: "Peace. Be quiet." This was Rakhal's first experience of ecstasy. He lived with his father in Calcutta and now and then visited the Master at Dakshineswar. About this time he had studied a short while in Vidyāsāgar's school at Śyāmpukur.

When the music was over, the devotees sat down for their meal. Balaram stood there humbly, like a servant. Nobody would have taken him for the master of the house. M. was still a stranger to the devotees, having met only Narendra at Dakshineswar.

A few days later M. visited the Master at Dakshineswar. It was between four and five o'clock in the afternoon. The Master and he were sitting on the steps of the Śiva temples. Looking at the temple of Rādhākānta, across the courtyard, the Master went into an ecstatic mood.

Since his nephew Hriday's dismissal from the temple, Sri Ramakrishna had been living without an attendant. On account of his frequent spiritual moods he could hardly take care of himself. The lack of an attendant caused him great inconvenience.

Sri Ramakrishna was talking to Kāli, the Divine Mother of the Universe. He said: "Mother, everyone says, 'My watch alone is right.' The Christians, the Brāhmos, the Hindus, the Mussalmāns, all say, 'My religion alone is true.' But, Mother, the fact is that nobody's watch is right. Who can truly understand Thee? But if a man prays to Thee with a yearning heart, he can reach Thee, through Thy grace, by any path. Mother, show me some time how the Christians pray to Thee in their churches. But Mother, what will people say if I go in? Suppose they make a fuss! Suppose they don't

---

[1] A beloved disciple of the Master, later known as Swami Brahmananda.

allow me to enter the Kāli temple again! Well then, show me the Christian worship from the door of the church."

Another day the Master was seated on the small couch in his room, with his usual beaming countenance. M. arrived with Kalikrishna, who did not know where his friend M. was taking him. He had only been told: "If you want to see a grog-shop, then come with me. You will see a huge jar of wine there." M. related this to Sri Ramakrishna, who laughed about it. The Master said: "The bliss of worship and communion with God is the true wine, the wine of ecstatic love. The goal of human life is to love God. Bhakti is the one essential thing. To know God through jnāna and reasoning is extremely difficult."

Then the Master sang:

Who is there that can understand what Mother Kāli is?
Even the six darśanas are powerless to reveal Her. . . .

The Master said, again: "The one goal of life is to cultivate love for God, the love that the milkmaids, the milkmen, and the cowherd boys of Vrindāvan felt for Krishna. When Krishna went away to Mathurā, the cowherds roamed about weeping bitterly because of their separation from Him."

Saying this the Master sang, with his eyes turned upward:

Just now I saw a youthful cowherd
With a young calf in his arms;
There he stood, by one hand holding
The branch of a young tree.
"Where are You, Brother Kānāi?" he cried;
But "Kānāi" scarcely could he utter;
"Kā" was as much as he could say.
He cried, "Where are You, Brother?"
And his eyes were filled with tears.

When M. heard this song of the Master's, laden with love, his eyes were moist with tears.

April 2, 1882

Sri Ramakrishna was sitting in the drawing-room of Keshab Chandra Sen's house in Calcutta; it was five o'clock in the afternoon. When Keshab was told of his arrival, he came to the drawing-room dressed to go out, for he was about to call on a sick friend. Now he cancelled his plan. The Master said to him: "You have so many things to attend to. Besides, you have to edit a newspaper. You have no time to come to Dakshineswar; so I have come to see you. When I heard of your illness I vowed green coconut and sugar to the Divine Mother for your recovery. I said to Her, 'Mother, if something happens to Keshab, with whom shall I talk in Calcutta?' "

Sri Ramakrishna spoke to Pratap and the other Brāhmo devotees. M. was seated near by. Pointing to him, the Master said to Keshab: "Will you

please ask him why he doesn't come to Dakshineswar any more? He repeatedly tells me he is not attached to his wife and children." M. had been
paying visits to the Master for about a month; his absence for a time from
Dakshineswar called forth this remark. Sri Ramakrishna had asked M. to
write to him, if his coming were delayed.

Pundit Samadhyayi was present. The Brāhmo devotees introduced him to
Sri Ramakrishna as a scholar well versed in the Vedas and the other
scriptures. The Master said, "Yes, I can see inside him through his eyes,
as one can see the objects in a room through the glass door."

Trailokya sang. Suddenly the Master stood up and went into samādhi,
repeating the Mother's name. Coming down a little to the plane of sense
consciousness, he danced and sang:

> I drink no ordinary wine, but Wine of Everlasting Bliss,
> As I repeat my Mother Kāli's name;
> It so intoxicates my mind that people take me to be drunk!
> First my guru gives molasses for the making of the Wine;
> My longing is the ferment to transform it.
> Knowledge, the maker of the Wine, prepares it for me then;
> And when it is done, my mind imbibes it from the bottle of the
> mantra,
> Taking the Mother's name to make it pure.
> Drink of this Wine, says Rāmprasād,[2] and the four fruits[3] of life
> are yours.

The Master looked at Keshab tenderly, as if Keshab were his very own.
He seemed to fear that Keshab might belong to someone else, that is to
say, that he might become a worldly person. Looking at him, the Master
sang again:

> We are afraid to speak, and yet we are afraid to keep still;
> Our minds, O Rādhā, half believe that we are about to lose you!
> We tell you the secret that we know—
> The secret whereby we ourselves, and others, with our help,
> Have passed through many a time of peril;
> Now it all depends on you.

Quoting the last part of the song, he said to Keshab: "That is to say,
renounce everything and call on God. He alone is real; all else is illusory.
Without the realization of God everything is futile. This is the great secret."

The Master sat down again and began to converse with the devotees.
For a while he listened to a piano recital, enjoying it like a child. Then he
was taken to the inner apartments, where he was served with refreshments
and the ladies saluted him.

As the Master was leaving Keshab's house, the Brāhmo devotees accompanied him respectfully to his carriage.

[2] The author of the song. It is customary for writers of devotional songs in India
to mention their names at the end of their songs.
[3] Dharma, artha, kāma, and moksha.

Sunday, April 9, 1882

Sri Ramakrishna was seated with his devotees in the drawing-room of
Prankrishna Mukherji's house in Calcutta; it was between one and two
o'clock in the afternoon. Since Colonel Viswanath[4] lived in that neighbourhood, the Master intended to visit him before going to see Keshab at the
Lily Cottage. A number of neighbours and other friends of Prankrishna
had been invited to meet Sri Ramakrishna. They were all eager to hear his
words.

MASTER: "God and His glory. This universe is His glory. People see His
glory and forget everything. They do not seek God, whose glory is this
world. All seek to enjoy 'woman and gold'. But there is too much misery
and worry in that. This world is like the whirlpool of the Viśālākshi.[5] Once
a boat gets into it there is no hope of its rescue. Again, the world is like a
thorny bush: you have hardly freed yourself from one set of thorns before
you find yourself entangled in another. Once you enter a labyrinth you find
it very difficult to get out. Living in the world, a man becomes seared, as it
were."

A DEVOTEE: "Then what is the way, sir?"

MASTER: "Prayer and the company of holy men. You cannot get rid of
an ailment without the help of a physician. But it is not enough to be in
the company of religious people only for a day. You should constantly seek
it, for the disease has become chronic. Again, you can't understand the pulse
rightly unless you live with a physician. Moving with him constantly, you
learn to distinguish between the pulse of phlegm and the pulse of bile."

DEVOTEE: "What is the good of holy company?"

MASTER: "It begets yearning for God. It begets love of God. Nothing
whatsoever is achieved in spiritual life without yearning. By constantly
living in the company of holy men, the soul becomes restless for God. This
yearning is like the state of mind of a man who has someone ill in the
family. His mind is in a state of perpetual restlessness, thinking how the
sick person may be cured. Or again, one should feel a yearning for God
like the yearning of a man who has lost his job and is wandering from one
office to another in search of work. If he is rejected at a certain place which
has no vacancy, he goes there again the next day and inquires, 'Is there any
vacancy today?'

"There is another way: earnestly praying to God. God is our very own.
We should say to Him: 'O God, what is Thy nature? Reveal Thyself to
me. Thou must show Thyself to me; for why else hast Thou created me?'
Some Sikh devotees once said to me, 'God is full of compassion.' I said:
'But why should we call Him compassionate? He is our Creator. What is
there to be wondered at if He is kind to us? Parents bring up their children.
Do you call that an act of kindness? They must act that way.' Therefore
we should force our demands on God. He is our Father and Mother, isn't

---

[4] The Resident of the Nepalese Government in Calcutta, and a devotee of the
Master.

[5] A stream near Sri Ramakrishna's birth-place.

He? If the son demands his patrimony and gives up food and drink in order to enforce his demand, then the parents hand his share over to him three years before the legal time. Or when the child demands some pice from his mother, and says over and over again: 'Mother, give me a couple of pice. I beg you on my knees!'—then the mother, seeing his earnestness, and unable to bear it any more, tosses the money to him.

"There is another benefit from holy company. It helps one cultivate discrimination between the Real and the unreal. God alone is the Real, that is to say, the Eternal Substance, and the world is unreal, that is to say, transitory. As soon as a man finds his mind wandering away to the unreal, he should apply discrimination. The moment an elephant stretches out its trunk to eat a plaintain-tree in a neighbour's garden, it gets a blow from the iron goad of the driver."

A NEIGHBOUR: "Why does a man have sinful tendencies?"

MASTER: "In God's creation there are all sorts of things. He has created bad men as well as good men. It is He who gives us good tendencies, and it is He again who gives us evil tendencies."

NEIGHBOUR: "In that case we aren't responsible for our sinful actions, are we?"

MASTER: "Sin begets its own result. This is God's law. Won't you burn your tongue if you chew a chilli? In his youth Mathur[a] led a rather fast life; so he suffered from various diseases before his death.

"One may not realize this in youth. I have looked into the hearth in the kitchen of the Kāli temple when logs are being burnt. At first the wet wood burns rather well. It doesn't seem then that it contains much moisture. But when the wood is sufficiently burnt, all the moisture runs back to one end. At last water squirts from the fuel and puts out the fire.

"So one should be careful about anger, passion, and greed. Take, for instance, the case of Hanumān. In a fit of anger he burnt Ceylon. At last he remembered that Sītā was living in the aśoka grove. Then he began to tremble lest the fire should injure her."

NEIGHBOUR: "Why has God created wicked people?"

MASTER: "That is His will, His play. In His māyā there exists avidyā as well as vidyā. Darkness is needed too. It reveals all the more the glory of light. There is no doubt that anger, lust, and greed are evils. Why, then, has God created them? In order to create saints. A man becomes a saint by conquering the senses. Is there anything impossible for a man who has subdued his passions? He can even realize God, through His grace. Again, see how His whole play of creation is perpetuated through lust.

"Wicked people are needed too. At one time the tenants of an estate became unruly. The landlord had to send Golak Choudhury, who was a ruffian. He was such a harsh administrator that the tenants trembled at the very mention of his name.

"There is need of everything. Once Sītā said to her Husband: 'Rāma, it would be grand if every house in Ayodhyā were a mansion! I find many

---

[a] The son-in-law of Rāni Rasmani, and a great devotee of Sri Ramakrishna, whom he provided with all the necessaries of life at the temple garden.

houses old and dilapidated.' 'But, my dear,' said Rāma, 'if all the houses were beautiful ones, what would the masons do?' (*Laughter*.) God has created all kinds of things. He has created good trees, and poisonous plants and weeds as well. Among the animals there are good, bad, and all kinds of creatures—tigers, lions, snakes, and so on."

NEIGHBOUR: "Sir, is it ever possible to realize God while leading the life of a householder?"

MASTER: "Certainly. But as I said just now, one must live in holy company and pray unceasingly. One should weep for God. When the impurities of the mind are thus washed away, one realizes God. The mind is like a needle covered with mud, and God is like a magnet. The needle cannot be united with the magnet unless it is free from mud. Tears wash away the mud, which is nothing but lust, anger, gréed, and other evil tendencies, and the inclination to worldly enjoyments as well. As soon as the mud is washed away, the magnet attracts the needle, tnat is to say, man realizes God. Only the pure in heart see God. A fever patient has an excess of the watery element in his system. What can quinine do for him unless that is removed?

"Why shouldn't one realize God while living in the world? But, as I said, one must live in holy company, pray to God, weeping for His grace, and now and then go into solitude. Unless the plants on a foot-path are protected at first by fences, they are destroyed by cattle."

NEIGHBOUR: "Then householders, too, will have the vision of God, won't they?"

MASTER: "Everybody will surely be liberated. But one should follow the instructions of the guru; if one follows a devious path, one will suffer in trying to retrace one's steps. It takes a long time to achieve liberation. A man may fail to obtain it in this life. Perhaps he will realize God only after many births. Sages like Janaka performed worldly duties. They performed them, bearing God in their minds, as a dancing-girl dances, keeping jars or trays on her head. Haven't you seen how the women in northwest India walk, talking and laughing while carrying water-pitchers on their heads?"

NEIGHBOUR: "You just referred to the instructions of the guru. How shall we find him?"

MASTER: "Anyone and everyone cannot be a guru. A huge timber floats on the water and can carry animals as well. But a piece of worthless wood sinks, if a man sits on it, and drowns him. Therefore in every age God incarnates Himself as the guru, to teach humanity. Satchidānanda alone is the guru.

"What is knowledge? And what is the nature of this ego? 'God alone is the Doer, and none else'—that is knowledge. I am not the doer; I am a mere instrument in His hand. Therefore I say: 'O Mother, Thou art the Operator and I am the machine. Thou art the Indweller and I am the house. Thou art the Driver and I am the carriage. I move as Thou movest me. I do as Thou makest me do. I speak as Thou makest me speak. Not I, not I, but Thou, but Thou.' "

From Prankrishna's house the Master went to Colonel Viswanath's and from there to the Lily Cottage.

VISIT TO VIDYĀSĀGAR

PUNDIT ISWAR CHANDRA VIDYĀSĀGAR was born in the village of Beersingh, not far from Kāmārpukur, Sri Ramakrishna's birth-place. He was known as a great scholar, educator, writer, and philanthropist. One of the creators of modern Bengali, he was also well versed in Sanskrit grammar and poetry. His generosity made his name a household word with his countrymen, most of his income being given in charity to widows, orphans, indigent students, and other needy people. Nor was his compassion limited to human beings: he stopped drinking milk for years so that the calves should not be deprived of it, and he would not drive in a carriage for fear of causing discomfort to the horses. He was a man of indomitable spirit, which he showed when he gave up the lucrative position of principal of the Sanskrit College of Calcutta because of a disagreement with the authorities. His affection for his mother was especially deep. One day, in the absence of a ferryboat, he swam a raging river at the risk of his life to fulfil her wish that he should be present at his brother's wedding. His whole life was one of utter simplicity. The title Vidyāsāgar, meaning "Ocean of Learning", was given him in recognition of his vast erudition.

Sri Ramakrishna had long wanted to visit Iswar Chandra Vidyāsāgar. Learning from M. that he was a teacher at Vidyāsāgar's school, the Master asked: "Can you take me to Vidyāsāgar? I should like very much to see him." M. told Iswar Chandra of Sri Ramakrishna's wish, and the pundit gladly agreed that M. should bring the Master, some Saturday afternoon at four o'clock. He only asked M. what kind of paramahamsa the Master was, saying, "Does he wear an ochre cloth?" M. answered: "No, sir. He is an unusual person. He wears a red-bordered cloth and polished slippers. He lives in a room in Rāni Rasmani's temple garden. In his room there is a couch with a mattress and mosquito net. He has no outer indication of holiness. But he doesn't know anything except God. Day and night he thinks of God alone."

On the afternoon of August 5 the Master left Dakshineswar in a hackney carriage, accompanied by Bhavanath, M., and Hazra. Vidyāsāgar lived in Bādurbāgan, in central Calcutta, about six miles from Dakshineswar. On the way Sri Ramakrishna talked with his companions; but as the carriage neared Vidyāsāgar's house his mood suddenly changed. He was overpowered with divine ecstasy. Not noticing this, M. pointed out the garden house where Rājā Rammohan Roy had lived. The Master was annoyed and said, "I don't care about such things now. He was going into an ecstatic state.

The carriage stopped in front of Vidyāsāgar's house. The Master alighted, supported by M., who then led the way. In the courtyard were many flowering plants. As the Master walked to the house he said to M., like a child, pointing to his shirt-button: "My shirt is unbuttoned. Will that offend Vidyāsāgar?" "Oh, no!" said M. "Don't be anxious about it. Nothing about you will be offensive. You don't have to button your shirt." He accepted the assurance simply, like a child.

Vidyāsāgar was about sixty-two years old, sixteen or seventeen years older than the Master. He lived in a two-storey house built in the English fashion, with lawns on all sides and surrounded by a high wall. After climbing the stairs to the second floor, Sri Ramakrishna and his devotees entered a room at the far end of which Vidyāsāgar was seated facing them, with a table in front of him. To the right of the table was a bench. Some friends of their host occupied chairs on the other two sides.

Vidyāsāgar rose to receive the Master. Sri Ramakrishna stood in front of the bench, with one hand resting on the table. He gazed at Vidyāsāgar, as if they had known each other before, and smiled in an ecstatic mood. In that mood he remained standing a few minutes. Now and then, to bring his mind back to normal consciousness, he said, "I shall have a drink of water."

In the mean time the young members of the household and a few friends and relatives of Vidyāsāgar had gathered around. Sri Ramakrishna, still in an ecstatic mood, sat on the bench. A young man, seventeen or eighteen years old, who had come to Vidyāsāgar to seek financial help for his education, was seated there. The Master sat down at a little distance from the boy, saying in an abstracted mood: "Mother, this boy is very much attached to the world. He belongs to Thy realm of ignorance."

Vidyāsāgar told someone to bring water and asked M. whether the Master would like some sweetmeats also. Since M. did not object, Vidyāsāgar himself went eagerly to the inner apartments and brought the sweets. They were placed before the Master. Bhavanath and Hazra also received their share. When they were offered to M., Vidyāsāgar said: "Oh, he is like one of the family. We needn't worry about him." Referring to a young devotee, the Master said to Vidyāsāgar: "He is a nice young man and is sound at the core. He is like the river Phalgu. The surface is covered with sand; but if you dig a little you will find water flowing underneath."

After taking some of the sweets, the Master, with a smile, began to speak to Vidyāsāgar. Meanwhile the room had become filled with people; some were standing and others were seated.

MASTER: "Ah! Today, at last, I have come to the ocean. Up till now I have seen only canals, marshes, or a river at the most. But today I am face to face with the sāgar, the ocean." (All laugh.)

VIDYĀSĀGAR (smiling): "Then please take home some salt water." (Laughter.)

MASTER: "Oh, no! Why salt water? You aren't the ocean of ignorance. You are the ocean of vidyā, knowledge. You are the ocean of condensed milk." (*All laugh.*)

VIDYĀSĀGAR: "Well, you may put it that way."

The pundit became silent. Sri Ramakrishna said: "Your activities are inspired by sattva. Though they are rājasic, they are influenced by sattva. Compassion springs from sattva. Though work for the good of others belongs to rajas, yet this rajas has sattva for its basis and is not harmful. Suka and other sages cherished compassion in their minds to give people religious instruction, to teach them about God. You are distributing food and learning. That is good too. If these activities are done in a selfless spirit they lead to God. But most people work for fame or to acquire merit. Their activities are not selfless. Besides, you are already a siddha."[1]

VIDYĀSĀGAR: "How is that, sir?"

MASTER (*laughing*): "When potatoes and other vegetables are well cooked, they become soft and tender. And you possess such a tender nature! You are so compassionate!" (*Laughter.*)

VIDYĀSĀGAR (*laughing*): "But when the paste of kalāi pulse is boiled it becomes all the harder."

MASTER: "But you don't belong to that class. Mere pundits are like diseased fruit that becomes hard and will not ripen at all. Such fruit has neither the freshness of green fruit nor the flavour of ripe. Vultures soar very high in the sky, but their eyes are fixed on rotten carrion on the ground. The book-learned are reputed to be wise, but they are attached to 'woman and gold'. Like the vultures, they are in search of carrion. They are attached to the world of ignorance. Compassion, love of God, and renunciation are the glories of true knowledge."

Vidyāsāgar listened to these words in silence. The others, too, gazed at the Master and were attentive to every word he said.

Vidyāsāgar was very reticent about giving religious instruction to others. He had studied Hindu philosophy. Once, when M. had asked him his opinion of it, Vidyāsāgar had said, "I think the philosophers have failed to explain what was in their minds." But in his daily life he followed all the rituals of Hindu religion and wore the sacred thread of a brāhmin. About God he had once declared: "It is indeed impossible to know Him. What, then, should be our duty? It seems to me that we should live in such a way that, if others followed our example, this very earth would be heaven. Everyone should try to do good to the world."

Sri Ramakrishna's conversation now turned to the Knowledge of Brahman.

MASTER: "Brahman is beyond vidyā and avidyā, knowledge and ignorance. It is beyond māyā, the illusion of duality.

"The world consists of the illusory duality of knowledge and ignorance. It contains knowledge and devotion, and also attachment to 'woman and gold'; righteousness and unrighteousness; good and evil. But Brahman is unattached to these. Good and evil apply to the jīva, the individual soul, as

[1] Literally, "perfect" or "boiled"; the word is applied both to the perfected soul and to boiled things.

do righteousness and unrighteousness; but Brahman is not at all affected by them.

"One man may read the *Bhāgavata* by the light of a lamp, and another may commit a forgery by that very light; but the lamp is unaffected. The sun sheds its light on the wicked as well as on the virtuous.

"You may ask, 'How, then, can one explain misery and sin and unhappiness?' The answer is that these apply only to the jīva. Brahman is unaffected by them. There is poison in a snake; but though others may die if bitten by it, the snake itself is not affected by the poison.

"What Brahman is cannot be described. All things in the world—the Vedas, the Purānas, the Tantras, the six systems of philosophy—have been defiled, like food that has been touched by the tongue, for they have been read or uttered by the tongue. Only one thing has not been defiled in this way, and that is Brahman. No one has ever been able to say what Brahman is."

VIDYĀSĀGAR (*to his friends*): "Oh! That is a remarkable statement. I have learnt something new today."

MASTER: "A man had two sons. The father sent them to a preceptor to learn the Knowledge of Brahman. After a few years they returned from their preceptor's house and bowed low before their father. Wanting to measure the depth of their knowledge of Brahman, he first questioned the older of the two boys. 'My child,' he said, 'you have studied all the scriptures. Now tell me, what is the nature of Brahman?' The boy began to explain Brahman by reciting various texts from the Vedas. The father did not say anything. Then he asked the younger son the same question. But the boy remained silent and stood with eyes cast down. No word escaped his lips. The father was pleased and said to him: 'My child, you have understood a little of Brahman. What It is cannot be expressed in words.'

"Men often think they have understood Brahman fully. Once an ant went to a hill of sugar. One grain filled its stomach. Taking another grain in its mouth it started homeward. On its way it thought, 'Next time I shall carry home the whole hill.' That is the way shallow minds think. They don't know that Brahman is beyond one's words and thought. However great a man may be, how much can he know of Brahman? Sukadeva and sages like him may have been big ants; but even they could carry at the utmost eight or ten grains of sugar!

"As for what has been said in the Vedas and the Purānas, do you know what it is like? Suppose a man has seen the ocean, and somebody asks him, 'Well, what is the ocean like?' The first man opens his mouth as wide as he can and says: 'What a sight! What tremendous waves and sounds!' The description of Brahman in the sacred books is like that. It is said in the Vedas that Brahman is of the nature of Bliss—It is Satchidānanda.

"Suka and other sages stood on the shore of this Ocean of Brahman and saw and touched the water. According to one school of thought they never plunged into it. Those who do, cannot come back to the world again.

"In samādhi one attains the Knowledge of Brahman—one realizes Brahman. In that state reasoning stops altogether, and man becomes mute. He has no power to describe the nature of Brahman.

"Once a salt doll went to measure the depth of the ocean. (*All laugh.*) It wanted to tell others how deep the water was. But this it could never do, for no sooner did it get into the water than it melted. Now who was there to report the ocean's depth?"

A DEVOTEE: "Suppose a man has obtained the Knowledge of Brahman in samādhi. Doesn't he speak any more?"

MASTER: "Śankarāchārya[2] retained the 'ego of Knowledge' in order to teach others. After the vision of Brahman a man becomes silent. He reasons about It as long as he has not realized It. If you heat butter in a pan on the stove, it makes a sizzling sound as long as the water it contains has not dried up. But when no trace of water is left the clarified butter makes no sound. If you put an uncooked cake of flour in that butter it sizzles again. But after the cake is cooked all sound stops. Just so, a man established in samādhi comes down to the relative plane of consciousness in order to teach others, and then he talks about God.

"The bee buzzes as long as it is not sitting on a flower. It becomes silent when it begins to sip the honey. But sometimes, intoxicated with the honey, it buzzes again.

"An empty pitcher makes a gurgling sound when it is dipped in water. When it fills up it becomes silent. (*All laugh.*) But if the water is poured from it into another pitcher, then you will hear the sound again. (*Laughter.*)

"The rishis of old attained the Knowledge of Brahman. One cannot have this so long as there is the slightest trace of worldliness. How hard the rishis laboured! Early in the morning they would go away from the hermitage, and would spend the whole day in solitude, meditating on Brahman. At night they would return to the hermitage and eat a little fruit or roots. They kept their minds aloof from the objects of sight, hearing, touch, and other things of a worldly nature. Only thus did they realize Brahman as their own inner consciousness.

"But in the Kaliyuga, man, being totally dependent on food for life, cannot altogether shake off the idea that he is the body. In this state of mind it is not proper for him to say, 'I am He.' When a man does all sorts of worldly things, he should not say, 'I am Brahman.' Those who cannot give up attachment to worldly things, and who find no means to shake off the feeling of 'I', should rather cherish the idea, 'I am God's servant; I am His devotee.' One can also realize God by following the path of devotion.

"The jnāni gives up his identification with worldly things, discriminating, 'Not this, not this'. Only then can he realize Brahman. It is like reaching the roof of a house by leaving the steps behind, one by one. But the vijnāni, who is more intimately acquainted with Brahman, realizes something more. He realizes that the steps are made of the same materials as the roof: bricks, lime, and brick-dust. That which is realized intuitively as Brahman, through the eliminating process of 'Not this, not this', is then found to have become

[2] One of the greatest philosophers of India.

the universe and all its living beings. The vijnāni sees that the Reality which is nirguna, without attributes, is also saguna, with attributes.

"A man cannot live on the roof a long time. He comes down again. Those who realize Brahman in samādhi come down also and find that it is Brahman that has become the universe and its living beings. In the musical scale there are the notes sā, re, gā, mā, pā, dhā, and ni; but one cannot keep one's voice on 'ni' a long time. The ego does not vanish altogether. The man coming down from samādhi perceives that it is Brahman that has become the ego, the universe, and all living beings. This is known as vijnāna.

"The path of knowledge leads to Truth, as does the path that combines knowledge and love. The path of love, too, leads to this goal. The way of love is as true as the way of knowledge. All paths ultimately lead to the same Truth. But as long as God keeps the feeling of ego in us, it is easier to follow the path of love.

"The vijnāni sees that Brahman is immovable and actionless, like Mount Sumeru. This universe consists of the three gunas—sattva, rajas, and tamas. They are in Brahman. But Brahman is unattached.

"The vijnāni further sees that what is Brahman is the Bhagavān, the Personal God. He who is beyond the three gunas is the Bhagavān, with His six supernatural powers. Living beings, the universe, mind, intelligence, love, renunciation, knowledge—all these are the manifestations of His power. (With a laugh) If an aristocrat has neither house nor property, or if he has been forced to sell them, one doesn't call him an aristocrat any more. (All laugh.) God is endowed with the six supernatural powers. If He were not, who would obey Him? (All laugh.)

"Just see how picturesque this universe is! How many things there are! The sun, moon, and stars; and how many varieties of living beings!—big and small, good and bad, strong and weak—some endowed with more power, some with less."

VIDYĀSĀGAR: "Has He endowed some with more power and others with less?"

MASTER: "As the All-pervading Spirit He exists in all beings, even in the ant. But the manifestations of His Power are different in different beings; otherwise, how can one person put ten to flight, while another can't face even one? And why do all people respect you? Have you grown a pair of horns? (Laughter.) You have more compassion and learning. Therefore people honour you and come to pay you their respects. Don't you agree with me?"

Vidyāsāgar smiled.

The Master continued: "There is nothing in mere scholarship. The object of study is to find means of knowing God and realizing Him. A holy man had a book. When asked what it contained, he opened it and showed that on all the pages were written the words 'Om Rāma', and nothing else.

"What is the significance of the Gītā? It is what you find by repeating the word ten times. It is then reversed into 'tāgi', which means a person who has renounced everything for God. And the lesson of the Gītā is: 'O man, renounce everything and seek God alone.' Whether a man is a monk or a householder, he has to shake off all attachment from his mind.

"Chaitanyadeva set out on a pilgrimage to southern India. One day he saw a man reading the *Gītā*. Another man, seated at a distance, was listening and weeping. His eyes were swimming in tears. Chaitanyadeva asked him, 'Do you understand all this?' The man said, 'No, revered sir, I don't understand a word of the text.' 'Then why are you crying?' asked Chaitanya. The devotee said: 'I see Arjuna's chariot before me. I see Lord Krishna and Arjuna seated in front of it, talking. I see this and I weep.'

"Why does a vijñāni keep an attitude of love toward God? The answer is that 'I-consciousness' persists. It disappears in the state of samādhi, no doubt, but it comes back. In the case of ordinary people the 'I' never disappears. You may cut down the aśwattha tree, but the next day sprouts shoot up. (*All laugh.*)

"Even after the attainment of Knowledge this 'I-consciousness' comes up, nobody knows from where. You dream of a tiger. Then you awake; but your heart keeps on palpitating! All our suffering is due to this 'I'. The cow cries, 'Hāmbā!', which means 'I'. That is why it suffers so much. It is yoked to the plough and made to work in rain and sun. Then it may be killed by the butcher. From its hide shoes are made, and also drums, which are mercilessly beaten. (*Laughter.*) Still it does not escape suffering. At last strings are made out of its entrails for the bows used in carding cotton. Then it no longer says, 'Hāmbā! Hāmbā!', 'I! I!', but 'Tuhu! Tuhu!', 'Thou! Thou!' Only then are its troubles over. O Lord, I am the servant; Thou art the Master. I am the child; Thou art the Mother.

"Once Rāma asked Hanumān, 'How do you look on Me?' And Hanumān replied: 'O Rāma, as long as I have the feeling of "I", I see that Thou art the whole and I am a part; Thou art the Master and I am Thy servant. But when, O Rāma, I have the knowledge of Truth, then I realize that Thou art I, and I am Thou.'

"The relationship of master and servant is the proper one. Since this 'I' must remain, let the rascal be God's servant.

" 'I' and 'mine'—these constitute ignorance. 'My house', 'my wealth', 'my learning', 'my possessions'—the attitude that prompts one to say such things comes of ignorance. On the contrary, the attitude born of Knowledge is: 'O God, Thou art the Master, and all these things belong to Thee. House, family, children, attendants, friends, are Thine.'

"One should constantly remember death. Nothing will survive death. We are born into this world to perform certain duties, like the people who come from the countryside to Calcutta on business. If a visitor goes to a rich man's garden, the superintendent says to him, 'This is our garden', 'This is our lake', and so forth. But if the superintendent is dismissed for some misdeed, he can't carry away even his mango-wood chest. He sends it secretly by the gate-keeper. (*Laughter.*)

"God laughs on two occasions. He laughs when the physician says to the patient's mother, 'Don't be afraid, mother; I shall certainly cure your boy.' God laughs, saying to Himself, 'I am going to take his life, and this man says he will save it!' The physician thinks he is the master, forgetting that God is the Master. God laughs again when two brothers divide their land with a string, saying to each other, 'This side is mine and that side is yours.' He laughs and says to Himself, 'The whole universe belongs to Me, but they say they own this portion or that portion.'

"Can one know God through reasoning? Be His servant, surrender yourself to Him, and then pray to Him.

(*To Vidyāsāgar, with a smile*) "Well, what is your attitude?"

VIDYĀSĀGAR (*smiling*): "Some day I shall confide it to you." (*All laugh.*)

MASTER (*laughing*): "God cannot be realized through mere scholarly reasoning."

Intoxicated with divine love, the Master sang:

> Who is there that can understand what Mother Kāli is?
> Even the six darśanas are powerless to reveal Her.
> It is She, the scriptures say, that is the Inner Self
> Of the yogi, who in Self discovers all his joy;
> She that, of Her own sweet will, inhabits every living thing.
>
> The macrocosm and microcosm rest in the Mother's womb;
> Now do you see how vast it is? In the Mulādhāra
> The yogi meditates on Her, and in the Sahasrāra:
> Who but Śiva has beheld Her as She really is?
> Within the lotus wilderness She sports beside Her Mate, the
>   Swan.[3]
>
> When man aspires to understand Her, Rāmprasād must smile;
> To think of knowing Her, he says, is quite as laughable
> As to imagine one can swim across the boundless sea.
> But while my mind has understood, alas! my heart has not;
> Though but a dwarf, it still would strive to make a captive of
>   the moon.

Continuing, the Master said: "Did you notice?

> The macrocosm and microcosm rest in the Mother's womb;
> Now do you see how vast it is?

"Again, the poet says:

> Even the six darśanas are powerless to reveal Her.

She cannot be realized by means of mere scholarship.

"One must have faith and love. Let me tell you how powerful faith is. A man was about to cross the sea from Ceylon to India. Bibhishana said to him: 'Tie this thing in a corner of your wearing-cloth, and you will cross the sea safely. You will be able to walk on the water. But be sure not to examine it, or you will sink.' The man was walking easily on the water of the sea—such is the strength of faith—when, having gone part of the way, he thought, 'What is this wonderful thing Bibhishana has given me, that I can walk even on the water?' He untied the knot and found only a leaf

[3] Śiva, the Absolute.

with the name of Rāma written on it. 'Oh, just this!' he thought, and instantly he sank.

"There is a popular saying that Hanumān jumped over the sea through his faith in Rāma's name, but Rāma Himself had to build a bridge

"If a man has faith in God, then he need not be afraid though he may have committed sin—nay, the vilest sin."

Then Sri Ramakrishna sang a song glorifying the power of faith:

> If only I can pass away repeating Durgā's name,
> How canst Thou then, O Blessed One,
> Withhold from me deliverance,
> Wretched though I may be? . . .

The Master continued: "Faith and devotion. One realizes God easily through devotion. He is grasped through ecstasy of love."

With these words the Master sang again:

> How are you trying, O my mind, to know the nature of God?
> You are groping like a madman locked in a dark room.
> He is grasped through ecstatic love; how can you fathom Him
>   without it?
> Only through affirmation, never negation, can you know Him;
> Neither through Veda nor through Tantra nor the six darśanas.
>
> It is in love's elixir only that He delights, O mind;
> He dwells in the body's inmost depths, in Everlasting Joy.
> And, for that love, the mighty yogis practise yoga from age to age;
> When love awakes, the Lord, like a magnet, draws to Him the soul.
>
> He it is, says Rāmprasād, that I approach as Mother;
> But must I give away the secret, here in the market-place?
> From the hints I have given, O mind, guess what that Being is!

While singing, the Master went into samādhi. He was seated on the bench, facing west, the palms of his hands joined together, his body erect and motionless. Everyone watched him expectantly. Vidyāsāgar, too, was speechless and could not take his eyes from the Master.

After a time Sri Ramakrishna showed signs of regaining the normal state. He drew a deep breath and said with a smile: "The means of realizing God are ecstasy of love and devotion—that is, one must love God. He who is Brahman is addressed as the Mother.

> He it is, says Rāmprasād, that I approach as Mother;
> But must I give away the secret, here in the market-place?
> From the hints I have given, O mind, guess what that Being is!

"Rāmprasād asks the mind only to guess the nature of God. He wishes it to understand that what is called Brahman in the Vedas is addressed by him as the Mother. He who is attributeless also has attributes. He who is Brahman is also Śakti. When thought of as inactive, He is called Brahman, and when thought of as the Creator, Preserver, and Destroyer, He is called the Primordial Energy, Kāli.

"Brahman and Śakti are identical, like fire and its power to burn. When we talk of fire we automatically mean also its power to burn. Again, the fire's power to burn implies the fire itself. If you accept the one you must accept the other.

"Brahman alone is addressed as the Mother. This is because a mother is an object of great love. One is able to realize God just through love. Ecstasy of feeling, devotion, love, and faith—these are the means. Listen to a song:

> As is a man's meditation, so is his feeling of love;
> As is a man's feeling of love, so is his gain;
> And faith is the root of all.
> If in the Nectar Lake of Mother Kāli's feet
> My mind remains immersed,
> Of little use are worship, oblations, or sacrifice.

"What is needed is absorption in God—loving Him intensely. The 'Nectar Lake' is the Lake of Immortality. A man sinking in It does not die, but becomes immortal. Some people believe that by thinking of God too much the mind becomes deranged; but that is not true. God is the Lake of Nectar, the Ocean of Immortality. He is called the 'Immortal' in the Vedas. Sinking in It, one does not die, but verily transcends death.

> Of little use are worship, oblations, or sacrifice.

If a man comes to love God, he need not trouble himself much about these activities. One needs a fan only as long as there is no breeze. The fan may be laid aside if the southern breeze blows. Then what need is there of a fan?

(To Vidyāsāgar) "The activities that you are engaged in are good. It is very good if you can perform them in a selfless spirit, renouncing egotism, giving up the idea that you are the doer. Through such action one develops love and devotion to God, and ultimately realizes Him.

"The more you come to love God, the less you will be inclined to perform action. When the daughter-in-law is with child, her mother-in-law gives her less work to do. As time goes by she is given less and less work. When the time of delivery nears, she is not allowed to do any work at all, lest it should hurt the child or cause difficulty at the time of birth.

"By these philanthropic activities you are really doing good to yourself. If you can do them disinterestedly, your mind will become pure and you will develop love of God. As soon as you have that love you will realize Him.

"Man cannot really help the world. God alone does that—He who has created the sun and the moon, who has put love for their children in parents' hearts, endowed noble souls with compassion, and holy men and devotees with divine love. The man who works for others, without any selfish motive, really does good to himself.

"There is gold buried in your heart, but you are not yet aware of it. It is covered with a thin layer of clay. Once you are aware of it, all these activities of yours will lessen. After the birth of her child, the daughter-in-law in the family busies herself with it alone. Everything she does is only for the child. Her mother-in-law doesn't let her do any household duties.

"Go forward. A wood-cutter once entered a forest to gather wood. A brahmachāri said to him, 'Go forward.' He obeyed the injunction and discovered some sandal-wood trees. After a few days he reflected, 'The holy man asked me to go forward. He didn't tell me to stop here.' So he went forward and found a silver-mine. After a few days he went still farther and discovered a gold-mine, and next, mines of diamonds and precious stones. With these he became immensely rich.

"Through selfless work, love of God grows in the heart. Then, through His grace, one realizes Him in course of time. God can be seen. One can talk to Him as I am talking to you."

In silent wonder they all sat listening to the Master's words. It seemed to them that the Goddess of Wisdom Herself, seated on Sri Ramakrishna's tongue, was addressing these words not merely to Vidyāsāgar, but to all humanity for its good.

It was nearly nine o'clock in the evening. The Master was about to leave.

MASTER (to Vidyāsāgar, with a smile): "The words I have spoken are really superfluous. You know all this; you simply aren't conscious of it. There are countless gems in the coffers of Varuna. But he himself isn't aware of them."

VIDYĀSĀGAR (with a smile): "You may say as you like."

MASTER (smiling): "Oh, yes. There are many wealthy people who don't know the names of all their servants, and are even unaware of many of the precious things in their houses." (All laugh.)

Everybody was delighted with the Master's conversation. Again addressing Vidyāsāgar, he said with a smile: "Please visit the temple garden some time—I mean the garden of Rasmani. It's a charming place."

VIDYĀSĀGAR: "Oh, of course I shall go. You have so kindly come here to see me, and shall I not return your visit?"

MASTER: "Visit me? Oh, never think of such a thing!"

VIDYĀSĀGAR: "Why, sir? Why do you say that? May I ask you to explain?"

MASTER (smiling): "You see, we are like small fishing-boats. (All smile.) We can ply in small canals and shallow waters and also in big rivers. But you are a ship. You may run aground on the way!" (All laugh.)

Vidyāsāgar remained silent. Sri Ramakrishna said with a laugh, "But even a ship can go there at this season."

VIDYĀSĀGAR (smiling): "Yes, this is the monsoon season." (All laugh.)

M. said to himself: "This is indeed the monsoon season of newly awakened love. At such times one doesn't care for prestige or formalities."

Sri Ramakrishna then took leave of Vidyāsāgar, who with his friends escorted the Master to the main gate, leading the way with a lighted candle in his hand. Before leaving the room, the Master prayed for the family's welfare, going into an ecstatic mood as he did so.

As soon as the Master and the devotees reached the gate, they saw an unexpected sight and stood still. In front of them was a bearded gentleman of fair complexion, aged about thirty-six. He wore his clothes like a Bengali, but on his head was a white turban tied after the fashion of the Śikhs. No sooner did he see the Master than he fell prostrate before him, turban and all.

When he stood up the Master said: "Who is this? Balaram? Why so late in the evening?"

BALARAM: "I have been waiting here a long time, sir."

MASTER: "Why didn't you come in?"

BALARAM: "All were listening to you. I didn't like to disturb you."

The Master got into the carriage with his companions.

VIDYĀSĀGAR (to M., softly): "Shall I pay the carriage hire?"

M: "Oh, don't bother, please. It is taken care of."

Vidyāsāgar and his friends bowed to Sri Ramakrishna, and the carriage started for Dakshineswar. But the little group, with the venerable Vidyāsāgar at their head holding the lighted candle, stood at the gate and gazed after the Master until he was out of sight.

4

ADVICE TO HOUSEHOLDERS

THE MASTER WAS CONVERSING with Kedar and some other devotees in his room in the temple garden. Kedar was a government official and had spent several years at Dacca, in East Bengal, where he had become a friend of Vijay Goswami. The two would spend a great part of their time together, talking about Sri Ramakrishna and his spiritual experiences. Kedar had once been a member of the Brāhmo Samāj. He followed the path of bhakti. Spiritual talk always brought tears to his eyes.

It was five o'clock in the afternoon. Kedar was very happy that day, having arranged a religious festival for Sri Ramakrishna. A singer had been hired by Ram, and the whole day passed in joy.

The Master explained to the devotees the secret of communion with God.

MASTER: "With the realization of Satchidānanda one goes into samādhi. Then duties drop away. Suppose I have been talking about the ostād and he arrives. What need is there of talking about him then? How long does the bee buzz around? So long as it isn't sitting on a flower. But it will not do for the sādhaka to renounce duties. He should perform his duties, such as worship, japa, meditation, prayer, and pilgrimage.

"If you see someone engaged in reasoning even after he has realized God, you may liken him to a bee, which also buzzes a little even while sipping honey from a flower."

The Master was highly pleased with the ostād's music. He said to the musician, "There is a special manifestation of God's power in a man who has any outstanding gift, such as proficiency in music."

MUSICIAN: "Sir, what is the way to realize God?"

MASTER: "Bhakti is the one essential thing. To be sure, God exists in all beings. Who, then, is a devotee? He whose mind dwells on God. But this is not possible as long as one has egotism and vanity. The water of God's grace cannot collect on the high mound of egotism. It runs down. I am a mere machine.

(*To Kedar and the other devotees*) "God can be realized through all paths. All religions are true. The important thing is to reach the roof. You can reach it by stone stairs or by wooden stairs or by bamboo steps or by a rope. You can also climb up by a bamboo pole.

"You may say that there are many errors and superstitions in another religion. I should reply: Suppose there are. Every religion has errors. Everyone thinks that his watch alone gives the correct time. It is enough to have yearning for God. It is enough to love Him and feel attracted to Him. Don't you know that God is the Inner Guide? He sees the longing of our heart and the yearning of our soul. Suppose a man has several sons. The older boys address him distinctly as 'Bābā' or 'Pāpā', but the babies can at best call him 'Bā' or 'Pā'. Now, will the father be angry with those who address him in this indistinct way? The father knows that they too are calling him, only they cannot pronounce his name well. All children are the same to the father. Likewise, the devotees call on God alone, though by different names. They call on one Person only. God is one, but His names are many."

Thursday, August 24, 1882

Sri Ramakrishna was talking to Hazra on the long northeast verandah of his room, when M. arrived. He saluted the Master reverently.

MASTER: "I should like to visit Iswar Chandra Vidyāsāgar a few times more. The painter first draws the general outlines and then puts in the details and colours at his leisure. The moulder first makes the image out of clay, then plasters it, then gives it a coat of whitewash, and last of all paints it with a brush. All these steps must be taken successively. Vidyāsāgar is fully ready, but his inner stuff is covered with a thin layer. He is now engaged in doing good works; but he doesn't know what is within himself. Gold is hidden within him. God dwells within us. If one knows that, one feels like giving up all activities and praying to God with a yearning soul."

So the Master talked with M.—now standing, now pacing up and down the long verandah.

MASTER: "A little spiritual discipline is necessary in order to know what lies within."

M: "Is it necessary to practise discipline all through life?"

MASTER: "No. But one must be up and doing in the beginning. After that one need not work hard. The helmsman stands up and clutches the rudder firmly as long as the boat is passing through waves, storms, high wind, or around the curves of a river; but he relaxes after steering through them. As soon as the boat passes the curves and the helmsman feels a favourable wind, he sits comfortably and just touches the rudder. Next he prepares to unfurl the sail and gets ready for a smoke. Likewise, the aspirant enjoys peace and calm after passing the waves and storms of 'woman and gold'.

"Some are born with the characteristics of the yogi; but they too should be careful. It is 'woman and gold' alone that is the obstacle; it makes them deviate from the path of yoga and drags them into worldliness. Perhaps they have some desire for enjoyment. After fulfilling their desire, they again direct their minds to God and thus recover their former state of mind, fit for the practise of yoga.

"Have you ever seen the spring trap for fish, called the 'satkā-kal'?"

M: "No, sir, I haven't seen it."

MASTER: "They use it in our part of the country. One end of a bamboo pole is fastened in the ground, and the other is bent over with a catch. From this end a line with a hook hangs over the water, with bait tied to the hook. When the fish swallows the bait, suddenly the bamboo jumps up and regains its upright position.

"Again, take a pair of scales, for example. If a weight is placed on one side, the lower needle moves away from the upper one. The lower needle is the mind, and the upper one, God. The meeting of the two is yoga.

"Unless the mind becomes steady there cannot be yoga. It is the wind of worldliness that always disturbs the mind, which may be likened to a candle-flame. If that flame doesn't move at all, then one is said to have attained yoga.

."'Woman and gold' alone is the obstacle to yoga. Always analyse what you see. What is there in the body of a woman? Only such things as blood, flesh, fat, entrails, and the like. Why should one love such a body?

"Sometimes I used to assume a rājasic mood in order to practise renunciation. Once I had the desire to put on a gold-embroidered robe, wear a ring on my finger, and smoke a hubble-bubble with a long pipe. Mathur Babu procured all these things for me. I wore the gold-embroidered robe and said to myself after a while, 'Mind! This is what is called a gold-embroidered robe.' Then I took it off and threw it away. I couldn't stand the robe any more. Again I said to myself, 'Mind! This is called a shawl, and this a ring, and this, smoking a hubble-bubble with a long pipe.' I threw those things away once for all, and the desire to enjoy them never arose in my mind again."

It was almost dusk. The Master and M. stood talking alone near the door on the southeast verandah.

MASTER (to M.): "The mind of the yogi is always fixed on God, always absorbed in the Self. You can recognize such a man by merely looking at him. His eyes are wide open, with an aimless look, like the eyes of the mother bird hatching her eggs. Her entire mind is fixed on the eggs, and there is a vacant look in her eyes. Can you show me such a picture?"

M: "I shall try to get one."

As evening came on, the temples were lighted up. Sri Ramakrishna was seated on his small couch, meditating on the Divine Mother. Then he chanted the names of God. Incense was burnt in the room, where an oil lamp had been lighted. Sounds of conch-shells and gongs came floating on the air as the evening worship began in the temple of Kāli. The light of the moon flooded all the quarters. The Master again spoke to M.

MASTER: "Perform your duties in an unselfish spirit. The work that Vidyāsāgar is engaged in is very good. Always try to perform your duties without desiring any result."

M: "Yes, sir. But may I know if one can realize God while performing one's duties? Can 'Rāma' and 'desire' coexist? The other day I read in a Hindi couplet: 'Where Rāma is, there desire cannot be; where desire is, there Rāma cannot be.'"

MASTER: "All, without exception, perform work. Even to chant the name and glories of God is work, as is the meditation of the non-dualist on 'I am He'. Breathing is also an activity. There is no way of renouncing work altogether. So do your work, but surrender the result to God."

M: "Sir, may I make an effort to earn more money?"

MASTER: "It is permissible to do so to maintain a religious family. You may try to increase your income, but in an honest way. The goal of life is not the earning of money, but the service of God. Money is not harmful if it is devoted to the service of God."

M: "How long should a man feel obliged to do his duty toward his wife and children?"

MASTER: "As long as they feel pinched for food and clothing. But one need not take the responsibility of a son when he is able to support himself. When the young fledgling learns to pick its own food, its mother pecks it if it comes to her for food."

M: "How long must one do one's duty?"

MASTER: "The blossom drops off when the fruit appears. One doesn't have to do one's duty after the attainment of God, nor does one feel like doing it then.

"If a drunkard takes too much liquor he cannot retain consciousness. If he takes only two or three glasses, he can go on with his work. As you advance nearer and nearer to God, He will reduce your activities little by little. Have no fear.

"Finish the few duties you have at hand, and then you will have peace. When the mistress of the house goes to bathe after finishing her cooking and other household duties, she won't come back, however you may shout after her."

M: "Sir, what is the meaning of the realization of God? What do you mean by God-vision? How does one attain it?"

MASTER: "According to the Vaishnavas the aspirants and the seers of God may be divided into different groups. These are the pravartaka, the sādhaka, the siddha, and the siddha of the siddha. He who has just set foot on the path may be called a pravartaka. He may be called a sādhaka who has for some time been practising spiritual disciplines, such as worship, japa, meditation, and the chanting of God's name and glories. He may be called a siddha who has known from his inner experience that God exists. An analogy is given in the Vedānta to explain this. The master of the house is asleep in a dark room. Someone is groping in the darkness to find him. He touches the couch and says, 'No, it is not he.' He touches the window and says, 'No, it is not he.' He touches the door and says, 'No, it is not he.' This is known in the Vedānta as the process of 'Neti, neti', 'Not this, not this'. At last his hand touches the master's body and he exclaims, 'Here he is!' In other words, he is now conscious of the 'existence' of the master. He has found him, but he doesn't yet know him intimately.

"There is another type, known as the siddha of the siddha, the 'supremely perfect'. It is quite a different thing when one talks to the master intimately, when one knows God very intimately through love and devotion. A siddha has undoubtedly attained God, but the 'supremely perfect' has known God very intimately.

"But in order to realize God, one must assume one of these attitudes: śānta, dāsya, sakhya, vātsalya, or madhur.

"Śānta, the serene attitude. The rishis of olden times had this attitude toward God. They did not desire any worldly enjoyment. It is like the single-minded devotion of a wife to her husband. She knows that her husband is the embodiment of beauty and love, a veritable Madan.

"Dāsya, the attitude of a servant toward his master. Hanumān had this attitude toward Rāma. He felt the strength of a lion when he worked for Rāma. A wife feels this mood also. She serves her husband with all her heart and soul. A mother also has a little of this attitude, as Yaśodā had toward Krishna.

"Sakhya, the attitude of friendship. Friends say to one another, 'Come here and sit near me.' Śridāma and other friends sometimes fed Krishna with fruit, part of which they had already eaten, and sometimes climbed on His shoulders.

"Vātsalya, the attitude of a mother toward her child. This was Yaśodā's attitude toward Krishna. The wife, too, has a little of this. She feeds her husband with her very life-blood, as it were. The mother feels happy only when the child has eaten to his heart's content. Yaśodā would roam about with butter in her hand, in order to feed Krishna.

"Madhur, the attitude of a woman toward her paramour. Rādhā had this attitude toward Krishna. The wife also feels it for her husband. This attitude includes all the other four."

M: "When one sees God does one see Him with these eyes?"

MASTER: "God cannot be seen with these physical eyes. In the course of spiritual discipline one gets a 'love body', endowed with 'love eyes', 'love ears', and so on. One sees God with those 'love eyes'. One hears the voice of God with those 'love ears'. One even gets a sexual organ made of love."

At these words M. burst out laughing. The Master continued, unannoyed, "With this 'love body' the soul communes with God."

M. again became serious.

MASTER: "But this is not possible without intense love of God. One sees nothing but God everywhere when one loves Him with great intensity. It is like a person with jaundice, who sees everything yellow. Then one feels, 'I am verily He.'

"A drunkard, deeply intoxicated, says, 'Verily I am Kāli!' The gopis, intoxicated with love, exclaimed, 'Verily I am Krishna!'

"One who thinks of God, day and night, beholds Him everywhere. It is like a man's seeing flames on all sides after he has gazed fixedly at one flame for some time."

"But that isn't the real flame", flashed through M.'s mind.

Sri Ramakrishna, who could read a man's inmost thought, said: "One doesn't lose consciousness by thinking of Him who is all Spirit, all Consciousness. Shivanath once remarked that too much thinking about God confounds the brain. Thereupon I said to him, 'How can one become un-conscious by thinking of Consciousness?'"

M: "Yes, sir, I realize that. It isn't like thinking of an unreal object. How can a man lose his intelligence if he always fixes his mind on Him whose very nature is eternal Intelligence?"

MASTER (*with pleasure*): "It is through God's grace that you understand that. The doubts of the mind will not disappear without His grace. Doubts do not disappear without Self-realization.

"But one need not fear anything if one has received the grace of God. It is rather easy for a child to stumble if he holds his father's hand; but there can be no such fear if the father holds the child's hand. A man does not have to suffer any more if God, in His grace, removes his doubts and reveals Himself to him. But this grace descends upon him only after he has prayed to God with intense yearning of heart and practised spiritual disci-pline. The mother feels compassion for her child when she sees him running about breathlessly. She has been hiding herself; now she appears before the child."

"But why should God make us run about?" thought M.

Immediately Sri Ramakrishna said: "It is His will that we should run about a little. Then it is great fun. God has created the world in play, as it were. This is called Mahāmāyā, the Great Illusion. Therefore one must take refuge in the Divine Mother, the Cosmic Power Itself. It is She who has bound us with the shackles of illusion. The realization of God is possible only when those shackles are severed."

The Master continued: "One must propitiate the Divine Mother, the Primal Energy, in order to obtain God's grace. God Himself is Mahāmāyā, who deludes the world with Her illusion and conjures up the magic of creation, preservation, and destruction. She has spread this veil of ignorance before our eyes. We can go into the inner chamber only when She lets us pass through the door. Living outside, we see only outer objects, but not that Eternal Being, Existence-Knowledge-Bliss Absolute. Therefore it is stated in the Purāna that deities like Brahmā praised Mahāmāyā for the destruction of the demons Madhu and Kaitabha.

"Sakti alone is the root of the universe. That Primal Energy has two aspects: vidyā and avidyā. Avidyā deludes. Avidyā conjures up 'woman and gold', which casts the spell. Vidyā begets devotion, kindness, wisdom, and love, which lead one to God. This avidyā must be propitiated, and that is the purpose of the rites of Sakti worship.[1]

"The devotee assumes various attitudes toward Sakti in order to pro-pitiate Her: the attitude of a handmaid, a 'hero', or a child. A hero's attitude is to please Her even as a man pleases a woman through intercourse.

"The worship of Sakti is extremely difficult. It is no joke. I passed two years as the handmaid and companion of the Divine Mother. But my natural attitude has always been that of a child toward its mother. I regard the breasts of any woman as those of my own mother.

"Women are, all of them, the veritable images of Sakti. In northwest

---

[1] In this worship a woman is regarded as the representation of the Divine Mother.

India the bride holds a knife in her hand at the time of marriage; in Bengal, a nut-cutter. The meaning is that the bridegroom, with the help of the bride, who is the embodiment of the Divine Power, will sever the bondage of illusion. This is the 'heroic' attitude. I never worshipped the Divine Mother that way. My attitude toward Her is that of a child toward its mother.

"The bride is the very embodiment of Śakti. Haven't you noticed, at the marriage ceremony, how the groom sits behind like an idiot? But the bride—she is so bold!

"After attaining God one forgets His external splendour, the glories of His creation. One doesn't think of God's glories after one has seen Him. The devotee, once immersed in God's Bliss, doesn't calculate any more about outer things. When I see Narendra, I don't need to ask him: 'What's your name? Where do you live?' Where is the time for such questions? Once a man asked Hanumān which day of the fortnight it was. 'Brother,' said Hanumān, 'I don't know anything of the day of the week, or the fortnight, or the position of the stars. I think of Rāma alone.'"

October 16, 1882

It was Monday, a few days before the Durgā Pujā, the festival of the Divine Mother. Sri Ramakrishna was in a very happy state of mind, for Narendra was with him. Narendra had brought two or three young members of the Brāhmo Samāj to the temple garden. Besides these, Rakhal, Ramlal, Hazra, and M. were with the Master.

Narendra had his midday meal with Sri Ramakrishna. Afterwards a temporary bed was made on the floor of the Master's room so that the disciples might rest awhile. A mat was spread, over which was placed a quilt covered with a white sheet. A few cushions and pillows completed the simple bed. Like a child, the Master sat near Narendranath on the bed. He talked with the devotees in great delight. With a radiant smile lighting his face, and his eyes fixed on Narendra, he was giving them various spiritual teachings, interspersing these with incidents from his own life.

MASTER: "After I had experienced samādhi, my mind craved intensely to hear only about God. I would always search for places where they were reciting or explaining the sacred books, such as the *Bhāgavata*, the *Mahābhārata*, and the *Adhyātma Rāmāyana*. I used to go to Krishnakishore to hear him read the *Adhyātma Rāmāyana*.

"What tremendous faith Krishnakishore had! Once, while at Vrindāvan, he felt thirsty and went to a well. Near it he saw a man standing. On being asked to draw a little water for him, the man said: 'I belong to a low caste, sir. You are a brāhmin. How can I draw water for you?' Krishnakishore said: 'Take the name of Śiva. By repeating His holy name you will make yourself pure.' The low-caste man did as he was told, and Krishnakishore, orthodox brāhmin that he was, drank that water. What tremendous faith!

"Once a holy man came to the bank of the Ganges and lived near the bathing-ghāt at Āriādaha, not far from Dakshineswar. We thought of paying him a visit. I said to Haladhari: 'Krishnakishore and I are going to see a holy man. Will you come with us?' Haladhari replied, 'What is the use of seeing a mere human body, which is no better than a cage of clay?' Haladhari was a student of the *Gītā* and Vedānta philosophy, and therefore referred to the holy man as a mere 'cage of clay'. I repeated this to Krishnakishore. With great anger he said: 'How impudent of Haladhari to make such a remark! How can he ridicule as a "cage of clay" the body of a man who constantly thinks of God, who meditates on Rāma, and has renounced all for the sake of the Lord? Doesn't he know that such a man is the embodiment of Spirit?' He was so upset by Haladhari's remarks that he would turn his face away from him whenever he met him in the temple garden, and stopped speaking to him.

"Once Krishnakishore asked me, 'Why have you cast off the sacred thread?' In those days of God-vision I felt as if I were passing through the great storm of Āswin,[2] and everything had blown away from me. No trace of my old self was left. I lost all consciousness of the world. I could hardly keep my cloth on my body, not to speak of the sacred thread! I said to Krishnakishore, 'Ah, you will understand if you ever happen to be as intoxicated with God as I was.'

"And it actually came to pass. He too passed through a God-intoxicated state, when he would repeat only the word 'Om' and shut himself up alone in his room. His relatives thought he was actually mad, and called in a physician. Ram Kavirāj of Nātāgore came to see him. Krishnakishore said to the physician, 'Cure me, sir, of my malady, if you please, but not of my Om.' (*All laugh.*)

"One day I went to see him and found him in a pensive mood. When I asked him about it, he said: 'The tax-collector was here. He threatened to dispose of my brass pots, my cups, and my few utensils, if I didn't pay the tax; so I am worried.' I said: 'But why should you worry about it? Let him take away your pots and pans. Let him arrest your body even. How will that affect you? For your nature is that of Kha!' (*Narendra and the others laugh.*) He used to say to me that he was the Spirit, all-pervading as the sky. He had got that idea from the *Adhyātma Rāmāyana*. I used to tease him now and then, addressing him as 'Kha'. Therefore I said to him that day, with a smile: 'You are Kha. Taxes cannot move you!'

"In that state of God-intoxication I used to speak out my mind to all. I was no respecter of persons. Even to men of position I was not afraid to speak the truth.

"One day Jatindra[3] came to the garden of Jadu Mallick. I was there too. I asked him: 'What is the duty of man? Isn't it our duty to think of God?' Jatindra replied: 'We are worldly people. How is it possible for us to achieve liberation? Even King Yudhisthira had to have a vision of hell.' This made me very angry. I said to him: 'What sort of man are you? Of all the incidents of Yudhisthira's life, you remember only his seeing hell. You don't remember his truthfulness, his forbearance, his patience, his discrimination, his

---

[2] The Master referred to the great cyclone of 1864.
[3] A titled aristocrat of Calcutta.

dispassion, his devotion to God.' I was about to say many more things, when Hriday stopped my mouth. After a little while Jatindra left the place, saying he had some other business to attend to.

"Many days later I went with Captain to see Rājā[4] Sourindra Tagore. As soon as I met him, I said, 'I can't address you as "Rājā", or by any such title, for I should be telling a lie.' He talked to me a few minutes, but even so our conversation was interrupted by the frequent visits of Europeans and others. A man of rājasic temperament, Sourindra was naturally busy with many things. Jatindra, his eldest brother, had been told of my coming, but he sent word that he had a pain in his throat and couldn't go out.

"One day, in that state of divine intoxication, I went to the bathing-ghāt on the Ganges at Barānagore. There I saw Jaya Mukherji repeating the name of God; but his mind was on something else. I went up and slapped him twice on the cheeks.

"At one time Rāni Rasmani was staying in the temple garden. She came to the shrine of the Divine Mother, as she frequently did when I worshipped Kāli, and asked me to sing a song or two. On this occasion, while I was singing, I noticed she was sorting the flowers for worship absent-mindedly. At once I slapped her on the cheeks. She became quite embarrassed and sat there with folded hands.

"Alarmed at this state of mind myself, I said to my cousin Haladhari: 'Just see my nature! How can I get rid of it?' After praying to the Divine Mother for some time with great yearning, I was able to shake off this habit.

"When one gets into such a state of mind, one doesn't enjoy any conversation but that about God. I used to weep when I heard people talk about worldly matters. When I accompanied Mathur Babu on a pilgrimage, we spent a few days in Benares at Raja Babu's house. One day I was seated in the drawing-room with Mathur Babu, Raja Babu, and others. Hearing them talk about various worldly things, such as their business losses and so forth, I wept bitterly and said to the Divine Mother: 'Mother, where have You brought me? I was much better off in the temple garden at Dakshineswar. Here I am in a place where I must hear about "woman and gold". But at Dakshineswar I could avoid it.' "

The Master asked the devotees, especially Narendra, to rest awhile, and he himself lay down on the smaller couch.

Late in the afternoon Narendra sang. Rakhal, Latu,[5] M., Hazra, and Priya, Narendra's Brāhmo friend, were present. The singing was accompanied by the drum:

> Meditate, O my mind, on the Lord Hari,
> The Stainless One, Pure Spirit through and through.
> How peerless is the light that in Him shines!
> How soul-bewitching is His wondrous form!
> How dear is He to all His devotees! . . .

[4] A title conferred on Sourindra by the Government of India. The word "rājā" really means "ruler of a kingdom".

[5] A young disciple of the Master, who later became a monk under the name of Swami Adbhutananda.

After this song Narendra sang:

> Oh, when will dawn for me that day of blessedness
> When He who is all Good, all Beauty, and all Truth,
> Will light the inmost shrine of my heart?
> When shall I sink at last, ever beholding Him,
> Into that Ocean of Delight?
> Lord, as Infinite Wisdom Thou shalt enter my soul,
> And my unquiet mind, made speechless by Thy sight,
> Will find a haven at Thy feet.
> In my heart's firmament, O Lord, Thou wilt arise
> As Blissful Immortality;
> And as, when the chakora beholds the rising moon,·
> It sports about for very joy,
> So, too, shall I be filled with heavenly happiness
> When Thou appearest unto me.
>
> Thou One without a Second, all Peace, the King of Kings!
> At Thy beloved feet I shall renounce my life
> And so at last shall gain life's goal;
> I shall enjoy the bliss of heaven while yet on earth!
> Where else is a boon so rare bestowed?
> Then shall I see Thy glory, pure and untouched by stain;
> As darkness flees from light, so will my darkest sins
> Desert me at Thy dawn's approach.
> Kindle in me, O Lord, the blazing fire of faith
> To be the pole-star of my life;
> O Succour of the weak, fulfil my one desire!
> Then shall I bathe both day and night
> In the boundless bliss of Thy Love, and utterly forget
> Myself, O Lord, attaining Thee.

Narendra sang again:

> With beaming face chant the sweet name of God
> Till in your heart the nectar overflows.
> Drink of it ceaselessly and share it with all!
> If ever your heart runs dry, parched by the flames
> Of worldly desire, chant the sweet name of God,
> And heavenly love will moisten your arid soul.
>
> Be sure, O mind, you never forget to chant
> His holy name: when danger stares in your face,
> Call on Him, your Father Compassionate;
> With His name's thunder, snap the fetters of sin!
> Come, let us fulfil our hearts' desires
> By drinking deep of Everlasting Joy,
> Made one with Him in Love's pure ecstasy.

Now Narendra and the devotees began to sing kirtan, accompanied by the drum and cymbals. They moved round and round the Master as they sang:

> Immerse yourself for evermore, O mind,
> In Him who is Pure Knowledge and Pure Bliss.

Next they sang:

> Oh, when will dawn for me that day of blessedness
> When He who is all Good, all Beauty, and all Truth
> Will light the inmost shrine of my heart? . . .

At last Narendra himself was playing on the drums, and he sang with the Master, full of joy:

> With beaming face chant the sweet name of God . . .

When the music was over, Sri Ramakrishna held Narendra in his arms a long time and said, "You have made us so happy today!" The flood-gate of the Master's heart was open so wide, that night, that he could hardly contain himself for joy. It was eight o'clock in the evening. Intoxicated with divine love, he paced the long verandah north of his room. Now and then he could be heard talking to the Divine Mother. Suddenly he said in an excited voice, "What can you do to me?" Was the Master hinting that māyā was helpless before him, since he had the Divine Mother for his support?

Narendra, M., and Priya were going to spend the night at the temple garden. This pleased the Master highly, especially since Narendra would be with him. The Holy Mother,[6] who was living in the nahabat, had prepared the supper. Surendra[7] bore the greater part of the Master's expenses. The meal was ready, and the plates were set out on the southeast verandah of the Master's room.

Near the east door of his room Narendra and the other devotees were gossiping.

NARENDRA: "How do you find the young men nowadays?"

M: "They are not bad; but they don't receive any religious instruction."

NARENDRA: "But from my experience I feel they are going to the dogs. They smoke cigarettes, indulge in frivolous talk, enjoy foppishness, play truant, and do everything of that sort. I have even seen them visiting questionable places."

M: "I didn't notice such things during our student days."

NARENDRA: "Perhaps you didn't mix with the students intimately. I have even seen them talking with people of immoral character. Perhaps they are on terms of intimacy with them."

M: "It is strange indeed."

NARENDRA: "I know that many of them form bad habits. It would be proper if the guardians of the boys, and the authorities, kept their eyes on these matters."

They were talking thus when Sri Ramakrishna came to them and asked with a smile, "Well, what are you talking about?"

NARENDRA: "I have been asking M. about the boys in the schools. The conduct of students nowadays isn't all that it should be."

The Master became grave and said to M. rather seriously: "This kind of

---

[6] By this name Sri Ramakrishna's wife was known among his devotees.

[7] The name by which Sri Ramakrishna addressed Suresh Mitra, a beloved householder disciple.

conversation is not good. It isn't desirable to indulge in any talk but talk
of God. You are their senior, and you are intelligent. You should not have
encouraged them to talk about such matters."

Narendra was then about nineteen years old, and M. about twenty-eight.
Thus admonished, M. felt embarrassed, and the others also fell silent.

While the devotees were enjoying their meal, Sri Ramakrishna stood by
and watched them with intense delight. That night the Master's joy was
very great.

After supper the devotees rested on the mat spread on the floor of the
Master's room. They began to talk with him. It was indeed a mart of joy.
The Master asked Narendra to sing the song beginning with the line: "In
Wisdom's firmament the moon of Love is rising full."

Narendra sang, and other devotees played the drums and cymbals:

> In Wisdom's firmament the moon of Love is rising full,
> And Love's flood-tide, in surging waves, is flowing everywhere.
> O Lord, how full of bliss Thou art! Victory unto Thee!
>
> On every side shine devotees, like stars around the moon;
> Their Friend, the Lord All-merciful, joyously plays with them;
> Behold! the gates of paradise today are open wide.
>
> The soft spring wind of the New Day raises fresh waves of joy;
> Gently it carries to the earth the fragrance of God's Love,
> Till all the yogis, drunk with bliss, are lost in ecstasy.
>
> Upon the sea of the world unfolds the lotus of the New Day,
> And there the Mother sits enshrined in blissful majesty.
> See how the bees are mad with joy, sipping the nectar there!
>
> Behold the Mother's radiant face, which so enchants the heart
> And captivates the universe! About Her Lotus Feet
> Bands of ecstatic holy men are dancing in delight.
>
> What matchless loveliness is Hers! What infinite content
> Pervades the heart when She appears! O brothers, says Premdās,
> I humbly beg you, one and all, to sing the Mother's praise!

Sri Ramakrishna sang and danced, and the devotees danced around him.
When the song was over, the Master walked up and down the northeast
verandah, where Hazra was seated with M. The Master sat down there.
He asked a devotee, "Do you ever have dreams?"

DEVOTEE: "Yes, sir. The other day I dreamt a strange dream. I saw the
whole world enveloped in water. There was water on all sides. A few boats
were visible, but suddenly huge waves appeared and sank them. I was about
to board a ship with a few others, when we saw a brāhmin walking over
that expanse of water. I asked him, 'How can you walk over the deep?' The
brāhmin said with a smile: 'Oh, there is no difficulty about that. There is a
bridge under the water.' I said to him, 'Where are you going?' 'To Bhawānipur, the city of the Divine Mother', he replied. 'Wait a little', I cried. 'I
shall accompany you.'"

MASTER: "Oh, I am thrilled to hear the story!"

DEVOTEE: "The brāhmin said: 'I am in a hurry. It will take you some time to get out of the boat. Good-bye. Remember this path and come after me.' "

MASTER: "Oh, my hair is standing on end! Please be initiated by a guru as soon as possible."

Shortly before midnight Narendra and the other devotees lay down on a bed made on the floor of the Master's room.

At dawn some of the devotees were up. They saw the Master, naked as a child, pacing up and down the room, repeating the names of the various gods and goddesses. His voice was sweet as nectar. Now he would look at the Ganges, now stop in front of the pictures hanging on the wall and bow down before them, chanting all the while the holy names in his sweet voice. He chanted: "Veda, Purāna, Tantra; Gītā, Gāyatri; Bhāgavata, Bhakta, Bhagavān." Referring to the *Gītā*, he repeated many times, "Tāgi, tāgi, tāgi."[8] Now and then he would say: "O Mother, Thou art verily Brahman, and Thou art verily Śakti. Thou art Purusha and Thou art Prakriti. Thou art Virāt. Thou art the Absolute, and Thou dost manifest Thyself as the Relative. Thou art verily the twenty-four cosmic principles."

In the mean time the morning service had begun in the temples of Kāli and Rādhākānta. Sounds of conch-shells and cymbals were carried on the air. The devotees came outside the room and saw the priests and servants gathering flowers in the garden for the divine service in the temples. From the nahabat floated the sweet melody of musical instruments, befitting the morning hours.

Narendra and the other devotees finished their morning duties and came to the Master. With a sweet smile on his lips Sri Ramakrishna was standing on the northeast verandah, close to his own room.

NARENDRA: "We noticed several sannyāsis belonging to the sect of Nānak in the Panchavati."

MASTER: "Yes, they arrived here yesterday. (*To Narendra*) I'd like to see you all sitting together on the mat."

As they sat there the Master looked at them with evident delight. He then began to talk with them. Narendra asked about spiritual discipline.

MASTER: "Bhakti, love of God, is the essence of all spiritual discipline. Through love one acquires renunciation and discrimination naturally."

NARENDRA: "Isn't it true that the Tantra prescribes spiritual discipline in the company of woman?"

MASTER: "That is not desirable. It is a very difficult path and often causes the aspirant's downfall. There are three such kinds of discipline. One may regard woman[9] as one's mistress or look on oneself as her handmaid or as her child. I look on woman as my mother. To look on oneself as her handmaid is also good; but it is extremely difficult to practise spiritual discipline looking on woman as one's mistress. To regard oneself as her child is a very pure attitude."

The sannyāsis belonging to the sect of Nānak entered the room and

---

[8] This word is formed by reversing the letters of "Gītā". "Tāgi" means "one who has renounced". Renunciation is the import of this sacred book.

[9] Woman is the symbol of the Divine Mother.

greeted the Master, saying, "Namo Nārāyanāya."[10] Sri Ramakrishna asked them to sit down.

MASTER: "Nothing is impossible for God. Nobody can describe His nature in words. Everything is possible for Him. There lived at a certain place two yogis who were practising spiritual discipline. The sage Nārada was passing that way one day. Realizing who he was, one of the yogis said: 'You have just come from God Himself. What is He doing now?' Nārada replied, 'Why, I saw Him making camels and elephants pass and repass through the eye of a needle.' At this the yogi said: 'Is that anything to wonder at? Everything is possible for God.' But the other yogi said: 'What? Making elephants pass through the eye of a needle—is that ever possible? You have never been to the Lord's dwelling-place.' "

At nine o'clock in the morning, while the Master was still sitting in his room, Manomohan arrived from Konnagar with some members of his family. In answer to Sri Ramakrishna's kind inquiries, Manomohan explained tnat he was taking them to Calcutta. The Master said: "Today is the first day of the Bengali month, an inauspicious day for undertaking a journey. I hope everything will be well with you." With a smile he began to talk of other matters.

When Narendra and his friends had finished bathing in the Ganges, the Master said to them earnestly: "Go to the Panchavati and meditate there under the banyan-tree. Shall I give you something to sit on?"

About half past ten Narendra and his Brāhmo friends were meditating in the Panchavati. After a while Sri Ramakrishna came to them. M., too, was present.

The Master said to the Brāhmo devotees: "In meditation one must be absorbed in God. By merely floating on the surface of the water, can you reach the gems lying at the bottom of the sea?"

Then he sang:

Taking the name of Kāli, dive deep down, O mind,
Into the heart's fathomless depths,
Where many a precious gem lies hid.
But never believe the bed of the ocean bare of gems
If in the first few dives you fail;
With firm resolve and self-control
Dive deep and make your way to Mother Kāli's realm.

Down in the ocean depths of heavenly Wisdom lie
The wondrous pearls of Peace, O mind;
And you yourself can gather them,
If you but have pure love and follow the scriptures' rule.
Within those ocean depths, as well,
Six alligators[11] lurk—lust, anger, and the rest—
Swimming about in search of prey.
Smear yourself with the turmeric of discrimination;
The very smell of it will shield you from their jaws.

[10] "Salutations to God." This is the way sādhus greet one another.
[11] The six passions: lust, anger, avarice, delusion, pride, and envy.

Upon the ocean bed lie strewn
Unnumbered pearls and precious gems;
Plunge in, says Rāmprasād, and gather up handfuls there!

Narendra and his friends came down from their seats on the raised plat-form of the Panchavati and stood near the Master. He returned to his room with them. The Master continued: "When you plunge in the water of the ocean, you may be attacked by alligators. But they won't touch you if your body is smeared with turmeric. There are no doubt six alligators—lust, anger, avarice, and so on—within you, in the 'heart's fathomless depths'. But pro-tect yourself with the turmeric of discrimination and renunciation, and they won't touch you.

"What can you achieve by mere lecturing and scholarship without dis-crimination and dispassion? God alone is real, and all else is unreal. God alone is substance, and all else is nonentity. That is discrimination.

"First of all set up God in the shrine of your heart, and then deliver lectures as much as you like. How will the mere repetition of 'Brahma' profit you if you are not imbued with discrimination and dispassion? It is the empty sound of a conch-shell.

"There lived in a village a young man named Padmalochan. People used to call him 'Podo', for short. In this village there was a temple in a very dilapidated condition. It contained no image of God. Aśwattha and other plants sprang up on the ruins of its walls. Bats lived inside, and the floor was covered with dust and the droppings of the bats. The people of the vil-lage had stopped visiting the temple. One day after dusk the villagers heard the sound of a conch-shell from the direction of the temple. They thought perhaps someone had installed an image in the shrine and was performing the evening worship. One of them softly opened the door and saw Pad-malochan standing in a corner, blowing the conch. No image had been set up. The temple hadn't been swept or washed. And filth and dirt lay every-where. Then he shouted to Podo:

You have set up no image here,
Within the shrine, O fool!
Blowing the conch, you simply make
Confusion worse confounded.
Day and night eleven bats
Scream there incessantly. . . .

"There is no use in merely making a noise if you want to establish the Deity in the shrine of your heart, if you want to realize God. First of all purify the mind. In the pure heart God takes His seat. One cannot bring the holy image into the temple if the droppings of bats are all around. The eleven bats are our eleven organs: five of action, five of perception, and the mind.

"First of all invoke the Deity, and then give lectures to your heart's content. First of all dive deep. Plunge to the bottom and gather up the gems. Then you may do other things. But nobody wants to plunge. People are without spiritual discipline and prayer, without renunciation and dispassion. They learn a few words and immediately start to deliver lectures. It is difficult to teach others. Only if a man gets a command from God, after realizing Him, is he entitled to teach."

Thus conversing, the Master came to the west end of the verandah. M. stood by his side. Sri Ramakrishna had repeated again and again that God cannot be realized without discrimination and renunciation. This made M. extremely worried. He had married and was then a young man of twenty-eight, educated in college in the Western way. Having a sense of duty, he asked himself, "Do discrimination and dispassion mean giving up 'woman and gold'?" He was really at a loss to know what to do.

M. (to the Master): "What should one do if one's wife says: 'You are neglecting me. I shall commit suicide.'?"

MASTER (in a serious tone): "Give up such a wife if she proves an obstacle in the way of spiritual life. Let her commit suicide or anything else she likes. The wife that hampers her husband's spiritual life is an ungodly wife."

Immersed in deep thought, M. stood leaning against the wall. Narendra and the other devotees remained silent a few minutes. The Master exchanged several words with them; then, suddenly going to M., he whispered in his ear: "But if a man has sincere love for God, then all come under his control —the king, wicked persons, and his wife. Sincere love of God on the husband's part may eventually help the wife to lead a spiritual life. If the husband is good, then through the grace of God the wife may also follow his example."

This had a most soothing effect on M.'s worried mind. All the while he had been thinking: "Let her commit suicide. What can I do?"

M. (to the Master): "This world is a terrible place indeed."

MASTER (to the devotees): "That is the reason Chaitanya said to his companion Nityānanda, 'Listen, brother, there is no hope of salvation for the worldly-minded.'"

On another occasion the Master had said to M. privately: "Yes, there is no hope for a worldly man if he is not sincerely devoted to God. But he has nothing to fear if he remains in the world after realizing God. Nor need a man have any fear whatever of the world if he attains sincere devotion by practising spiritual discipline now and then in solitude. Chaitanya had several householders among his devotees, but they were householders in name only, for they lived unattached to the world."

It was noon. The worship was over, and food offerings had been made in the temple. The doors of the temple were shut. Sri Ramakrishna sat down for his meal, and Narendra and the other devotees partook of the food offerings from the temple.

Sunday, October 22, 1882

It was the day of Vijayā, the last day of the celebration of the worship of Durgā, when the clay image is immersed in the water of a lake or river.

About nine o'clock in the morning M. was seated on the floor of the Master's room at Dakshineswar, near Sri Ramakrishna, who was reclining on the small couch. Rakhal was then living with the Master, and Narendra and Bhavanath visited him frequently. Baburam had seen him only once or twice.

MASTER: "Did you have any holiday during the Durgā Pujā?"

M: "Yes, sir. I went to Keshab's house every day for the first three days of the worship."

MASTER: "Is that so?"

M: "I heard there a very interesting interpretation of the Durgā Pujā."

MASTER: "Please tell me all about it."

M: "Keshab Sen held daily morning prayers in his house, lasting till ten or eleven. During these prayers he gave the inner meaning of the Durgā Pujā. He said that if anyone could realize the Divine Mother, that is to say, could install Mother Durgā in the shrine of his heart, then Lakshmi, Sarasvati, Kārtika, and Ganeśa[12] would come there of themselves. Lakshmi means wealth, Sarasvati knowledge, Kārtika strength, and Ganeśa success. By realizing the Divine Mother within one's heart, one gets all these without any effort whatever."

Sri Ramakrishna listened to the description, questioning M. now and then about the prayers conducted by Keshab. At last he said to M.: "Don't go hither and thither. Come here alone. Those who belong to the inner circle of my devotees will come only here. Boys like Narendra, Bhavanath, and Rakhal are my very intimate disciples. They are not to be thought lightly of. Feed[13] them one day. What do you think of Narendra?"

M: "I think very highly of him, sir."

MASTER: "Haven't you observed his many virtues? He is not only well versed in music, vocal and instrumental, but he is also very learned. Besides, he has controlled his passions and declares he will lead a celibate life. He has been devoted to God since his very boyhood.

"How are you getting along with your meditation nowadays? What aspect of God appeals to your mind—with form or without form?"

M: "Sir, now I can't fix my mind on God with form. On the other hand, I can't concentrate steadily on God without form."

MASTER: "Now you see that the mind cannot be fixed, all of a sudden, on the formless aspect of God. It is wise to think of God with form during the primary stages."

M: "Do you mean to suggest that one should meditate on clay images?"

MASTER: "Why clay? These images are the embodiments of Consciousness."

M: "Even so, one must think of hands, feet, and the other parts of the body. But again, I realize that the mind cannot be concentrated unless one meditates, in the beginning, on God with form. You have told me so. Well, God can easily assume different forms. May one meditate on the form of one's own mother?"

---

[12] According to Hindu mythology, Lakshmi and Sarasvati are the daughters, and Kārtika and Ganeśa the sons, of Durgā. Associated with the image of Durgā, they occupy positions on both sides of the Divine Mother.

[13] Feeding a holy man is considered a meritorious act.

MASTER: "Yes, the mother should be adored. She is indeed an embodiment of Brahman."

M. sat in silence. After a few minutes he asked the Master: "What does one feel while thinking of God without form? Isn't it possible to describe it?" After some reflection, the Master said, "Do you know what it is like?" He remained silent a moment and then said a few words to M. about one's experiences at the time of the vision of God with and without form.

MASTER: "You see, one must practise spiritual discipline to understand this correctly. Suppose there are treasures in a room. If you want to see them and lay hold of them, you must take the trouble to get the key and unlock the door. After that you must take the treasures out. But suppose the room is locked, and standing outside the door you say to yourself: 'Here I have opened the door. Now I have broken the lock of the chest. Now I have taken out the treasure.' Such brooding near the door will not enable you to achieve anything.

"You must practise discipline.

"The jnānis think of God without form. They don't accept the Divine Incarnation. Praising Sri Krishna, Arjuna said, 'Thou art Brahman Absolute.' Sri Krishna replied, 'Follow Me, and you will know whether or not I am Brahman Absolute.' So saying, Sri Krishna led Arjuna to a certain place and asked him what he saw there. 'I see a huge tree,' said Arjuna, 'and on it I notice fruits hanging like clusters of blackberries.' Then Krishna said to Arjuna, 'Come nearer and you will find that these are not clusters of blackberries, but clusters of innumerable Krishnas like Me, hanging from the tree.' In other words, Divine Incarnations without number appear and disappear on the tree of the Absolute Brahman.

"Kavirdās was strongly inclined to the formless God. At the mention of Krishna's name he would say: 'Why should I worship Him? The gopis would clap their hands while He performed a monkey dance.' (With a smile) But I accept God with form when I am in the company of people who believe in that ideal, and I also agree with those who believe in the formless God."

M. (smiling): "You are as infinite as He of whom we have been talking. Truly, no one can fathom your depth."

MASTER (smiling): "Ah! I see you have found it out. Let me tell you one thing. One should follow various paths. One should practise each creed for a time. In a game of satrancha a piece can't reach the centre square until it completes the circle; but once in the square it can't be overtaken by any other piece."

M: "That is true, sir.".

MASTER: "There are two classes of yogis: the vahudakas and the kutichakas. The vahudakas roam about visiting various holy places and have not yet found peace of mind. But the kutichakas, having visited all the sacred places, have quieted their minds. Feeling serene and peaceful, they settle down in one place and no longer move about. In that one place they are happy; they don't feel the need of going to any sacred place. If one of them ever visits a place of pilgrimage, it is only for the purpose of new inspiration.

"I had to practise each religion for a time—Hinduism, Islām, Christianity. Furthermore, I followed the paths of the Śāktas, Vaishnavas, and Vedāntists. I realized that there is only one God toward whom all are travelling; but the paths are different.

"While visiting the holy places, I would sometimes suffer great agony. Once I went with Mathur to Raja Babu's drawing-room in Benares. I found that they talked there only of worldly matters—money, real estate, and the like. At this I burst into tears. I said to the Divine Mother, weeping: 'Mother! Where hast Thou brought me? I was much better off at Dakshineswar.' In Allāhābād I noticed the same things that I saw elsewhere—the same ponds, the same grass, the same trees, the same tamarind-leaves.

"But one undoubtedly finds inspiration in a holy place. I accompanied Mathur Babu to Vrindāvan. Hriday and the ladies of Mathur's family were in our party. No sooner did I see the Kāliyadaman Ghāt than a divine emotion surged up within me. I was completely overwhelmed. Hriday used to bathe me there as if I were a small child.

"In the dusk I would walk on the bank of the Jamunā when the cattle returned along the sandy banks from their pastures. At the very sight of those cows the thought of Krishna would flash in my mind. I would run along like a madman, crying: 'Oh, where is Krishna? Where is my Krishna?'

"I went to Śyāmakunda and Rādhākunda[14] in a palanquin and got out to visit the holy Mount Govardhan. At the very sight of the mount I was over-powered with divine emotion and ran to the top. I lost all consciousness of the world around me. The residents of the place helped me to come down. On my way to the sacred pools of Śyāmakunda and Rādhākunda, when I saw the meadows, the trees, the shrubs, the birds, and the deer, I was over-come with ecstasy. My clothes became wet with tears. I said: 'O Krishna! Everything here is as it was in the olden days. You alone are absent.' Seated inside the palanquin I lost all power of speech. Hriday followed the palan-quin. He had warned the bearers to be careful about me.

"Gangāmāyi became very fond of me in Vrindāvan. She was an old woman who lived all alone in a hut near the Nidhuvan. Referring to my spiritual condition and ecstasy, she said, 'He is the very embodiment of Rādhā.' She addressed me as 'Dulāli'. When with her, I used to forget my food and drink, my bath, and all thought of going home. On some days Hriday used to bring food from home and feed me. Gangāmāyi also would serve me with food prepared by her own hands.

"Gangāmāyi used to experience trances. At such times a great crowd would come to see her. One day, in a state of ecstasy, she climbed on Hriday's shoulders.

"I didn't want to leave her and return to Calcutta. Everything was ar-ranged for me to stay with her. I was to eat double-boiled rice, and we were to have our beds on either side of the cottage. All the arrangements had been made, when Hriday said: 'You have such a weak stomach. Who will look after you?' 'Why,' said Gangāmāyi, 'I shall look after him. I'll nurse him.' As Hriday dragged me by one hand and she by the other, I remem-

[14] Places near Mathurā associated with the episode of Krishna and Rādhā.

bered my mother, who was then living alone here in the nahabat of the temple garden. I found it impossible to stay away from her, and said to Gangāmāyi, 'No, I must go.' I loved the atmosphere of Vrindāvan."

About eleven o'clock the Master took his meal, the offerings from the temple of Kāli. After taking his noonday rest he resumed his conversation with the devotees. Every now and then he uttered the holy word "Om" or repeated the sacred names of the deities.

After sunset the evening worship was performed in the temples. Since it was the day of Vijayā, the devotees first saluted the Divine Mother and then took the dust[15] of the Master's feet.

Tuesday, October 24, 1882

It was three or four o'clock in the afternoon. The Master was standing near the shelf where the food was kept, when Balaram and M arrived from Calcutta and saluted him. Sri Ramakrishna said to them with a smile: "I was going to take some sweets from the shelf, but no sooner did I put my hand on them than a lizard dropped on my body.[16] At once I removed my hand. (All laugh.)

"Oh, yes! One should observe all these things. You see, Rakhal is ill, and my limbs ache too. Do you know what's the matter? This morning as I was leaving my bed I saw[17] a certain person, whom I took for Rakhal. (All laugh.) Oh, yes! Physical features should be studied. The other day Narendra brought one of his friends, a man with only one good eye, though the other eye was not totally blind. I said to myself, 'What is this trouble that Narendra has brought with him?'

"A certain person comes here, but I can't eat any food that he brings. He works in an office at a salary of twenty rupees and earns another twenty by writing false bills. I can't utter a word in his presence, because he tells lies. Sometimes he stays here two or three days without going to his office. Can you guess his purpose? It is that I should recommend him to someone for a job somewhere else.

"Balaram comes from a family of devout Vaishnavas. His father, now an old man, is a pious devotee. He has a tuft of hair on his head, a rosary of tulsi beads round his neck, and a string of beads in his hand. He devotes his time to the repetition of God's name. He owns much property in Orissa and has built temples to Rādhā-Krishna in Kothār, Vrindāvan, and other places, establishing free guest-houses as well.

(To Balaram) "A certain person came here the other day. I understand he is the slave of that black hag of a wife. Why is it that people do not see God? It is because of the barrier of 'woman and gold'. How impudent he was to say to you the other day, 'A paramahamsa came to my father, who fed him with chicken curry!'[18]

[15] A form of reverent salutation in which one touches the feet of a superior with one's forehead.

[16] The dropping of a lizard on the body is considered an omen.

[17] Orthodox Hindus in Bengal believe that the first face seen in the morning indicates whether the day will bring good or evil.

[18] Orthodox Hindus are forbidden to eat chicken.

"In my present state of mind I can eat a little fish soup if it has been offered to the Divine Mother beforehand. I can't eat any meat, even if it is offered to the Divine Mother; but I taste it with the end of my finger lest She should be angry. (*Laughter.*)

"Well, can you explain this state of my mind? Once I was going from Burdwān to Kāmārpukur in a bullock-cart, when a great storm arose. Some people gathered near the cart. My companions said they were robbers. So I began to repeat the names of God, calling sometimes on Kāli, sometimes on Rāma, sometimes on Hanumān. What do you think of that?"

Was the Master hinting that God is one but is addressed differently by different sects?

MASTER (*to Balaram*): "Māyā is nothing but 'woman and gold'. A man living in its midst gradually loses his spiritual alertness. He thinks all is well with him. The scavenger carries a tub of night-soil on his head, and in course of time loses his repulsion to it. One gradually acquires love of God through the practice of chanting God's name and glories. (*To M.*) One should not be ashamed of chanting God's holy name. As the saying goes, 'One does not succeed so long as one has these three: shame, hatred, and fear.'

"At Kāmārpukur they sing kirtan very well. The devotional music is sung to the accompaniment of drums.

(*To Balaram*) "Have you installed any image at Vrindāvan?"

BALARAM: "Yes, sir. We have a grove where Krishna is worshipped."

MASTER: "I have been to Vrindāvan. The Nidhu Grove is very nice indeed."

THE MASTER AND KESHAB

IT WAS FRIDAY, the day of the Lakshmi Pujā. Keshab Chandra Sen had arranged a boat trip on the Ganges for Sri Ramakrishna.

About four o'clock in the afternoon the steamboat with Keshab and his Brāhmo followers cast anchor in the Ganges alongside the Kāli temple at Dakshineswar. The passengers saw in front of them the bathing-ghāt and the chāndni. To their left, in the temple compound, stood six temples of Śiva, and to their right another group of six Śiva temples. The white steeple of the Kāli temple, the tree-tops of the Panchavati, and the silhouette of pine-trees stood high against the blue autumn sky. The gardens between the two nahabats were filled with fragrant flowers, and along the bank of the Ganges were rows of flowering plants. The blue sky was reflected in the brown water of the river, the sacred Ganges, associated with the most ancient traditions of Āryan civilization. The outer world appeared soft and serene, and the hearts of the Brāhmo devotees were filled with peace.

Sri Ramakrishna was in his room talking with Vijay and Haralal. Some disciples of Keshab entered. Bowing before the Master, they said to him: "Sir, the steamer has arrived. Keshab Babu has asked us to take you there." A small boat was to carry the Master to the steamer. No sooner did he get into the boat than he lost outer consciousness in samādhi. Vijay was with him.

M. was among the passengers. As the boat came alongside the steamer, all rushed to the railing to have a view of Sri Ramakrishna. Keshab became anxious to get him safely on board. With great difficulty the Master was brought back to consciousness of the world and taken to a cabin in the steamer. Still in an abstracted mood, he walked mechanically, leaning on a devotee for support. Keshab and the others bowed before him, but he was not aware of them. Inside the cabin there were a few chairs and a table. He was made to sit on one of the chairs, Keshab and Vijay occupying two others. Some devotees were also seated, most of them on the floor, while many others had to stand outside. They peered eagerly through the door and windows. Sri Ramakrishna again went into deep samādhi and became totally unconscious of the outer world.

As the air in the room was stuffy because of the crowd of people, Keshab opened the windows. He was embarrassed to meet Vijay, since they had differed on certain principles of the Brāhmo Samāj and Vijay had separated himself from Keshab's organization, joining another society.

The Brāhmo devotees looked wistfully at the Master. Gradually he came back to sense consciousness; but the divine intoxication still lingered. He said to himself in a whisper: "Mother, why have You brought me here? They are hedged around and not free. Can I free them?" Did the Master find that the people assembled there were locked within the prison walls of the world? Did their helplessness make the Master address these words to the Divine Mother?

Sri Ramakrishna was gradually becoming conscious of the outside world. Nilmadhav of Ghāzipur and a Brāhmo devotee were talking about Pāvhāri Bābā. Another Brāhmo devotee said to the Master: "Sir, these gentlemen visited Pāvhāri Bābā. He lives in Ghāzipur. He is a holy man like yourself." The Master could hardly talk; he only smiled. The devotee continued, "Sir, Pāvhāri Bābā keeps your photograph in his room." Pointing to his body the Master said with a smile, "Just a pillow-case."

The Master continued: "But you should remember that the heart of the devotee is the abode of God. He dwells, no doubt, in all beings, but He especially manifests Himself in the heart of the devotee. A landlord may at one time or another visit all parts of his estate, but people say he is generally to be found in a particular drawing-room. The heart of the devotee is the drawing-room of God.

"He who is called Brahman by the jnānis is known as Ātman by the yogis and as Bhagavān by the bhaktas. The same brāhmin is called priest, when worshipping in the temple, and cook, when preparing a meal in the kitchen. The jnāni, sticking to the path of knowledge, always reasons about the Reality, saying, 'Not this, not this'. Brahman is neither 'this' nor 'that'; It is neither the universe nor its living beings. Reasoning in this way, the mind becomes steady. Then it disappears and the aspirant goes into samādhi. This is the Knowledge of Brahman. It is the unwavering conviction of the jnāni that Brahman alone is real and the world illusory. All these names and forms are illusory, like a dream. What Brahman is cannot be described. One cannot even say that Brahman is a Person. This is the opinion of the jnānis, the followers of Vedānta philosophy.

"But the bhaktas accept all the states of consciousness. They take the waking state to be real also. They don't think the world to be illusory, like a dream. They say that the universe is a manifestation of God's power and glory. God has created all these—sky, stars, moon, sun, mountains, ocean, men, animals. They constitute His glory. He is within us, in our hearts. Again, He is outside. The most advanced devotees say that He Himself has become all this—the twenty-four cosmic principles, the universe, and all living beings. The devotee of God wants to eat sugar, not to become sugar. (All laugh.)

"Do you know how a lover of God feels? His attitude is: 'O God, Thou art the Master, and I am Thy servant. Thou art the Mother, and I am Thy child.' Or again: 'Thou art my Father and Mother. Thou art the Whole, and I am a part.' He doesn't like to say, 'I am Brahman.'

"The yogi seeks to realize the Paramātman, the Supreme Soul. His ideal is the union of the embodied soul and the Supreme Soul. He withdraws his mind from sense-objects and tries to concentrate it on the Paramātman. Therefore, during the first stage of his spiritual discipline, he retires into solitude and with undivided attention practises meditation in a fixed posture.

"But the Reality is one and the same. The difference is only in name. He who is Brahman is verily Ātman, and again, He is the Bhagavān. He is Brahman to the followers of the path of knowledge, Paramātman to the yogis, and Bhagavān to the lovers of God."

The steamer had been going toward Calcutta; but the passengers, with their eyes fixed on the Master and their ears given to his nectar-like words, were oblivious of its motion. Dakshineswar, with its temples and gardens, was left behind. The paddles of the boat churned the waters of the Ganges with a murmuring sound. But the devotees were indifferent to all this. Spellbound, they looked on a great yogi, his face lighted with a divine smile, his countenance radiating love, his eyes sparkling with joy—a man who had renounced all for God and who knew nothing but God. Unceasing words of wisdom flowed from his lips.

MASTER: "The jnānis, who adhere to the non-dualistic philosophy of Vedānta, say that the acts of creation, preservation, and destruction, the universe itself and all its living beings, are the manifestations of Śakti, the Divine Power.[1] If you reason it out, you will realize that all these are as illusory as a dream. Brahman alone is the Reality, and all else is unreal. Even this very Śakti is unsubstantial, like a dream.

"But though you reason all your life, unless you are established in samādhi, you cannot go beyond the jurisdiction of Śakti. Even when you say, 'I am meditating', or 'I am contemplating', still you are moving in the realm of Śakti, within Its power.

"Thus Brahman and Śakti are identical. If you accept the one, you must accept the other. It is like fire and its power to burn. If you see the fire, you must recognize its power to burn also. You cannot think of fire without its power to burn, nor can you think of the power to burn without fire. You cannot conceive of the sun's rays without the sun, nor can you conceive of the sun without its rays.

"What is milk like? Oh, you say, it is something white. You cannot think of the milk without the whiteness, and again, you cannot think of the whiteness without the milk.

"Thus one cannot think of Brahman without Śakti, or of Śakti without Brahman. One cannot think of the Absolute without the Relative, or of the Relative without the Absolute.

"The Primordial Power is ever at play.[2] She is creating, preserving, and destroying in play, as it were. This Power is called Kāli. Kāli is verily Brahman, and Brahman is verily Kāli. It is one and the same Reality. When

---

[1] Known as māyā in the Vedānta philosophy.

[2] This idea introduces the elements of spontaneity and freedom in the creation.

we think of It as inactive, that is to say, not engaged in the acts of creation, preservation, and destruction, then we call It Brahman. But when It engages in these activities, then we call It Kāli or Śakti. The Reality is one and the same; the difference is in name and form.

"It is like water, called in different languages by different names, such as 'jal', 'pāni', and so forth. There are three or four ghāts on a lake. The Hindus, who drink water at one place, call it 'jal'. The Mussalmāns at another place call it 'pāni'. And the English at a third place call it 'water'. All three denote one and the same thing, the difference being in the name only. In the same way, some address the Reality as 'Allāh', some as 'God', some as 'Brahman', some as 'Kāli', and others by such names as 'Rāma', 'Jesus', 'Durgā', 'Hari'."

KESHAB (with a smile): "Describe to us, sir, in how many ways Kāli, the Divine Mother, sports in this world."

MASTER (with a smile): "Oh, She plays in different ways. It is She alone who is known as Mahā-Kāli, Nitya-Kāli, Śmaśāna-Kāli, Rakshā-Kāli, and Śyāmā-Kāli. Mahā-Kāli and Nitya-Kāli are mentioned in the Tantra philosophy. When there were neither the creation, nor the sun, the moon, the planets, and the earth, and when darkness was enveloped in darkness, then the Mother, the Formless One, Mahā-Kāli, the Great Power, was one with Mahā-Kāla, the Absolute.

"Śyāmā-Kāli has a somewhat tender aspect and is worshipped in the Hindu households. She is the Dispenser of boons and the Dispeller of fear. People worship Rakshā-Kāli, the Protectress, in times of epidemic, famine, earthquake, drought, and flood. Śmaśāna-Kāli is the embodiment of the power of destruction. She resides in the cremation ground, surrounded by corpses, jackals, and terrible female spirits. From Her mouth flows a stream of blood, from Her neck hangs a garland of human heads, and around Her waist is a girdle made of human hands.

"After the destruction of the universe, at the end of a great cycle, the Divine Mother garners the seeds for the next creation: She is like the elderly mistress of the house, who has a hotchpotch-pot in which she keeps different articles for household use. (All laugh.)

"Oh, yes! Housewives have pots like that, where they keep 'sea-foam',[3] blue pills, small bundles of seeds of cucumber, pumpkin, and gourd, and so on. They take them out when they want them. In the same way, after the destruction of the universe, my Divine Mother, the Embodiment of Brahman, gathers together the seeds for the next creation. After the creation the Primal Power dwells in the universe itself. She brings forth this phenomenal world and then pervades it. In the Vedas creation is likened to the spider and its web. The spider brings the web out of itself and then remains in it. God is the container of the universe and also what is contained in it.

"Is Kāli, my Divine Mother, of a black complexion? She appears black because She is viewed from a distance; but when intimately known She is no longer so. The sky appears blue at a distance; but look at it close by and you will find that it has no colour. The water of the ocean looks blue at a

[3] The Master perhaps referred to the cuttlefish bone found on the seashore. The popular belief is that it is hardened sea-foam.

distance, but when you go near and take it in your hand, you find that it is colourless."

The Master became intoxicated with divine love and sang:

> Is Kāli, my Mother, really black?
> The Naked One, of blackest hue,
> Lights the Lotus of the Heart. . . .

The Master continued: "Bondage and liberation are both of Her making. By Her māyā worldly people become entangled in 'woman and gold', and again, through Her grace they attain their liberation. She is called the Saviour, and the Remover of the bondage that binds one to the world."

Then the Master sang the following song[4] in his melodious voice:

> In the world's busy market-place, O Śyāmā, Thou art flying kites;
> High up they soar on the wind of hope, held fast by māyā's string.
> Their frames are human skeletons, their sails of the three gunas made;
> But all their curious workmanship is merely for ornament.
>
> Upon the kite-strings Thou hast rubbed the mānjā-paste[5] of world-liness,
> So as to make each straining strand all the more sharp and strong.
> Out of a hundred thousand kites, at best but one or two break free;
> And Thou dost laugh and clap Thy hands, O Mother, watching them!
>
> On favouring winds, says Rāmprasād, the kites set loose will speedily
> Be borne away to the Infinite, across the sea of the world.

The Master said: "The Divine Mother is always playful and sportive. This universe is Her play. She is self-willed and must always have Her own way. She is full of bliss. She gives freedom to one out of a hundred thousand."

A BRĀHMO DEVOTEE: "But, sir, if She likes, She can give freedom to all. Why, then, has She kept us bound to the world?"

MASTER: "That is Her will. She wants to continue playing with Her created beings. In a game of hide-and-seek[6] the running about soon stops if in the beginning all the players touch the 'granny'. If all touch her, then how can the game go on? That displeases her. Her pleasure is in continuing the game. Therefore the poet said:

> Out of a hundred thousand kites, at best but one or two break free;
> And Thou dost laugh and clap Thy hands, O Mother, watching them!

[4] The allusion of this song is to the well-known kite-flying competitions in India. Several people fly their kites and try to cut one another's kite-strings. Whoever has his string cut loses his kite and quits the game.

[5] A glue of barley and powdered glass.

[6] The allusion is to the Indian game of hide-and-seek, in which the leader, known as the "granny", bandages the eyes of the players and hides herself. The players are supposed to find her. If any player can touch her, the bandage is removed from his eyes and he is released from the game.

"It is as if the Divine Mother said to the human mind in confidence, with a sign from Her eye, 'Go and enjoy the world.' How can one blame the mind? The mind can disentangle itself from worldliness if, through Her grace, She makes it turn toward Herself. Only then does it become devoted to the Lotus Feet of the Divine Mother."

Whereupon Sri Ramakrishna, taking upon himself, as it were, the agonies of all householders, sang a song complaining to the Divine Mother:

> Mother, this is the grief that sorely grieves my heart,
> That even with Thee for Mother, and though I am wide awake,
> There should be robbery in my house.
> Many and many a time I vow to call on Thee,
> Yet when the time for prayer comes round, I have forgotten.
> Now I see it is all Thy trick.
>
> As Thou hast never given, so Thou receivest naught;
> Am I to blame for this, O Mother? Hadst Thou but given,
> Surely then Thou hadst received;
> Out of Thine own gifts I should have given to Thee.
> Glory and shame, bitter and sweet, are Thine alone;
> This world is nothing but Thy play.
> Then why, O Blissful One, dost Thou cause a rift in it?
>
> Says Rāmprasād: Thou hast bestowed on me this mind,
> And with a knowing wink of Thine eye
> Bidden it, at the same time, to go and enjoy the world.
> And so I wander here forlorn through Thy creation,
> Blasted, as it were, by someone's evil glance,
> Taking the bitter for the sweet,
> Taking the unreal for the Real.

The Master continued: "Men are deluded through Her māyā and have become attached to the world.

> Says Rāmprasād: Thou hast bestowed on me this mind,
> And with a knowing wink of Thine eye
> Bidden it, at the same time, to go and enjoy the world."

BRÂHMO DEVOTEE: "Sir, can't we realize God without complete renunciation?"

MASTER (*with a laugh*): "Of course you can! Why should you renounce everything? You are all right as you are, following the middle path—like molasses partly solid and partly liquid. Do you know the game of nax?[7] Having scored the maximum number of points, I am out of the game. I can't enjoy it. But you are very clever. Some of you have scored ten points, some six, and some five. You have scored just the right number; so you are not out of the game like me. The game can go on. Why, that's fine! (*All laugh.*)

"I tell you the truth: there is nothing wrong in your being in the world. But you must direct your mind toward God; otherwise you will not succeed.

---

[7] In the Indian card-game of nax the object is to stay in the game by scoring under seventeen points. Anyone scoring seventeen points or more has to retire.

Do your duty with one hand and with the other hold to God. After the duty is over, you will hold to God with both hands.

"It is all a question of the mind. Bondage and liberation are of the mind alone. The mind will take the colour you dye it with. It is like white clothes just returned from the laundry. If you dip them in red dye, they will be red. If you dip them in blue or green, they will be blue or green. They will take only the colour you dip them in, whatever it may be. Haven't you noticed that, if you read a little English, you at once begin to utter English words: *Foot fut it mit*?[8] Then you put on boots and whistle a tune, and so on. It all goes together. Or, if a scholar studies Sanskrit, he will at once rattle off Sanskrit verses. If you are in bad company, then you will talk and think like your companions. On the other hand, when you are in the company of devotees, you will think and talk only of God.

"The mind is everything. A man has his wife on one side and his daughter on the other. He shows his affection to them in different ways. But his mind is one and the same.

"Bondage is of the mind, and freedom is also of the mind. A man is free if he constantly thinks: 'I am a free soul. How can I be bound, whether I live in the world or in the forest? I am a child of God, the King of Kings. Who can bind me?' If bitten by a snake, a man may get rid of its venom by saying emphatically, 'There is no poison in me.' In the same way, by repeating with grit and determination, 'I am not bound, I am free', one really becomes so—one really becomes free.

"Once someone gave me a book of the Christians. I asked him to read it to me. It talked about nothing but sin. (*To Keshab*) Sin is the only thing one hears of at your Brāhmo Samāj, too. The wretch who constantly says, 'I am bound, I am bound' only succeeds in being bound. He who says day and night, 'I am a sinner, I am a sinner' verily becomes a sinner.

"One should have such burning faith in God that one can say: 'What? I have repeated the name of God, and can sin still cling to me? How can I be a sinner any more? How can I be in bondage any more?'

"If a man repeats the name of God, his body, mind, and everything become pure. Why should one talk only about sin and hell, and such things? Say but once, 'O Lord, I have undoubtedly done wicked things, but I won't repeat them.' And have faith in His name."

Sri Ramakrishna became intoxicated with divine love and sang:

> If only I can pass away repeating Durgā's name,
> How canst Thou then, O Blessed One,
> Withhold from me deliverance,
> Wretched though I may be? . . .

Then he said: "To my Divine Mother I prayed only for pure love. I offered flowers at Her Lotus Feet and prayed to Her: 'Mother, here is Thy virtue, here is Thy vice. Take them both and grant me only pure love for Thee. Here is Thy knowledge, here is Thy ignorance. Take them both and grant me only pure love for Thee. Here is Thy purity, here is Thy impurity.

---

[8] The Master was merely mimicking the sound of English.

Take them both, Mother, and grant me only pure love for Thee. Here is Thy dharma, here is Thy adharma. Take them both, Mother, and grant me only pure love for Thee.'

(*To the Brāhmo devotees*) "Now listen to a song by Rāmprasād:

> Come, let us go for a walk, O mind, to Kāli, the Wish-fulfilling Tree,
> And there beneath It gather the four fruits of life.
> Of your two wives, Dispassion and Worldliness,
> Bring along Dispassion only, on your way to the Tree,
> And ask her son Discrimination about the Truth.
>
> When will you learn-to lie, O mind, in the abode of Blessedness,
> With Cleanliness and Defilement on either side of you?
> Only when you have found the way
> To keep these wives contentedly under a single roof,
> Will you behold the matchless form of Mother Śyāmā.
>
> Ego and Ignorance, your parents, instantly banish from your sight;
> And should Delusion seek to drag you to its hole,
> Manfully cling to the pillar of Patience.
> Tie to the post of Unconcern the goats of Vice and Virtue,
> Killing them with the sword of Knowledge if they rebel.
>
> With the children of Worldliness, your first wife, plead from a goodly distance,
> And, if they will not listen, drown them in Wisdom's sea.
> Says Rāmprasād: If you do as I say,
> You can submit a good account, O mind, to the King of Death,
> And I shall be well pleased with you and call you my darling.

"Why shouldn't one be able to realize God in this world? King Janaka had such realization. Rāmprasād described the world as a mere 'framework of illusion'. But if one loves God's hallowed feet, then—

> This very world is a mansion of mirth;
> Here I can eat, here drink and make merry.
> Janaka's might was unsurpassed;
> What did he lack of the world or the Spirit?
> Holding to one as well as the other,
> He drank his milk from a brimming cup!

(*All laugh.*)

"But one cannot be a King Janaka all of a sudden. Janaka at first practised much austerity in solitude.

"Even if one lives in the world, one must go into solitude now and then. It will be of great help to a man if he goes away from his family, lives alone, and weeps for God even for three days. Even if he thinks of God for one day in solitude, when he has the leisure, that too will do him good. People shed a whole jug of tears for wife and children. But who cries for the Lord? Now and then one must go into solitude and practise spiritual discipline to realize God. Living in the world and entangled in many of its duties, the aspirant, during the first stage of spiritual life, finds many obstacles in the path of concentration. While the trees on the foot-path are young, they must be fenced around; otherwise they will be destroyed by cattle. The fence is necessary when the tree is young, but it can be taken away when the trunk is thick and strong. Then the tree won't be hurt even if an elephant is tied to it.

"The disease of worldliness is like typhoid. And there are a huge jug of water and a jar of savoury pickles in the typhoid patient's room. If you want to cure him of his illness, you must remove him from that room. The worldly man is like the typhoid patient. The various objects of enjoyment are the huge jug of water, and the craving for their enjoyment is his thirst. The very thought of pickles makes the mouth water; you don't have to bring them near. And he is surrounded with them. The companionship of woman is the pickles. Hence treatment in solitude is necessary.

"One may enter the world after attaining discrimination and dispassion. In the ocean of the world there are six alligators: lust, anger, and so forth. But you need not fear the alligators if you smear your body with turmeric before you go into the water. Discrimination and dispassion are the turmeric. Discrimination is the knowledge of what is real and what is unreal. It is the realization that God alone is the real and eternal Substance and that all else is unreal, transitory, impermanent. And you must cultivate intense zeal for God. You must feel love for Him and be attracted to Him. The gopis of Vrindāvan felt the attraction of Krishna. Let me sing you a song:

> Listen! The flute has sounded in yonder wood.
> There I must fly, for Krishna waits on the path.
> Tell me, friends, will you come along or no?
> To you my Krishna is merely an empty name;
> To me He is the anguish of my heart.
> You hear His flute-notes only with your ears,
> But, oh, I hear them in my deepest soul.
> I hear His flute calling: 'Rādhā, come out!
> Without you the grove is shorn of its loveliness.'"

The Master sang the song with tears in his eyes, and said to Keshab and the other Brāhmo devotees: "Whether you accept Rādhā and Krishna, or not, please do accept their attraction for each other. Try to create that same yearning in your heart for God. Yearning is all you need in order to realize Him."

Gradually the ebb-tide set in. The steamboat was speeding toward Calcutta. It passed under the Howrah Bridge and came within sight of the Botanical Garden. The captain was asked to go a little farther down the river. The passengers were enchanted with the Master's words, and most of them had no idea of time or of how far they had come.

Keshab began to serve some puffed rice and grated coconut. The guests held these in the folds of their wearing-cloths and presently started to eat. Everyone was joyful. The Master noticed, however, that Keshab and Vijay rather shrank from each other, and he was anxious to reconcile them.

MASTER (to Keshab): "Look here. There is Vijay. Your quarrel seems like the fight between Śiva and Rāma. Śiva was Rāma's guru. Though they fought with each other, yet they soon came to terms. But the grimaces of the ghosts, the followers of Śiva, and the gibberish of the monkeys, the followers of Rāma, would not come to an end! (*Loud laughter.*) Such quarrels take place even among one's own kith and kin. Didn't Rāma fight with His own sons, Lava and Kuśa? Again, you must have noticed how a mother and daughter, living together and having the same spiritual end in view, observe their religious fast separately on Tuesdays, each on her own account —as if the welfare of the mother were different from the welfare of the daughter. But what benefits the one benefits the other. In like manner, you have a religious society, and Vijay thinks he must have one too. (*Laughter.*) But I think all these are necessary. While Sri Krishna, Himself God Incarnate, played with the gopis at Vrindāvan, trouble-makers like Jatilā and Kutilā appeared on the scene. You may ask why. The answer is that the play does not develop without trouble-makers. (*All laugh.*) There is no fun without Jatilā and Kutilā. (*Loud laughter.*)

"Rāmānuja upheld the doctrine of Qualified Non-dualism. But his guru was a pure non-dualist. They disagreed with each other and refuted each other's arguments. That always happens. Still, to the teacher the disciple is his own."

All rejoiced in the Master's company and his words.

MASTER (*to Keshab*): "You don't look into people's natures before you make them your disciples, and so they break away from you.

"All men look alike, to be sure, but they have different natures. Some have an excess of sattva, others an excess of rajas, and still others an excess of tamas. You must have noticed that the cakes known as puli all look alike. But their contents are very different. Some contain condensed milk, some coconut kernel, and others mere boiled kalāi pulse. (*All laugh.*)

"Do you know my attitude? As for myself, I eat, drink, and live happily. The rest the Divine Mother knows. Indeed, there are three words that prick my flesh: 'guru', 'master', and 'father'.

"There is only one Guru, and that is Satchidānanda. He alone is the Teacher. My attitude toward God is that of a child toward its mother. One can get human gurus by the million. All want to be teachers. But who cares to be a disciple?

"It is extremely difficult to teach others. A man can teach only if God reveals Himself to him and gives the command. Nārada, Śukadeva, and sages like them had such a command from God, and Śankara had it too. Unless you have a command from God, who will listen to your words?

"Don't you know how easily the people of Calcutta get excited? The milk in the kettle puffs up and boils as long as the fire burns underneath. Take away the fuel and all becomes quiet. The people of Calcutta love sensations. You may see them digging a well at a certain place. They say they want water. But if they strike a stone they give up that place; they begin at another place. And there, perchance, they find sand; they give up the second place too. Next they begin at a third. And so it goes. But it won't do if a man only imagines that he has God's command.

"God does reveal Himself to man and speak. Only then may one receive

His command. How forceful are the words of such a teacher! They can move mountains. But mere lectures? People will listen to them for a few days and then forget them. They will never act upon mere words.

"At Kāmārpukur there is a small lake called the Hāldārpukur. Certain people used to befoul its banks every day. Others who came there in the morning to bathe would abuse the offenders loudly. But next morning they would find the same thing. The nuisance didn't stop. (All laugh.) The villagers finally informed the authorities about it. A constable was sent, who put up a notice on the bank which read: 'Commit no nuisance.' This stopped the miscreants at once. (All laugh.)

"To teach others, one must have a badge of authority; otherwise teaching becomes a mockery. A man who is himself ignorant starts out to teach others —like the blind leading the blind! Instead of doing good, such teaching does harm. After the realization of God one obtains an inner vision. Only then can one diagnose a person's spiritual malady and give instruction.

"Without the commission from God, a man becomes vain. He says to himself, 'I am teaching people.' This vanity comes from ignorance, for only an ignorant person feels that he is the doer. A man verily becomes liberated in life if he feels: 'God is the Doer. He alone is doing everything. I am doing nothing.' Man's sufferings and worries spring only from his persistent thought that he is the doer.

"You people speak of doing good to the world. Is the world such a small thing? And who are you, pray, to do good to the world? First realize God, see Him by means of spiritual discipline. If He imparts power, then you can do good to others; otherwise not."

A BRĀHMO DEVOTEE: "Then, sir, we must give up our activities until we realize God?"

MASTER: "No. Why should you? You must engage in such activities as contemplation, singing His praises, and other daily devotions."

BRĀHMO: "But what about our worldly duties—duties associated with our earning money, and so on?"

MASTER: "Yes, you can perform them too, but only as much as you need for your livelihood. At the same time, you must pray to God in solitude, with tears in your eyes, that you may be able to perform those duties in an unselfish manner. You should say to Him: 'O God, make my worldly duties fewer and fewer; otherwise, O Lord, I find that I forget Thee when I am involved in too many activities. I may think I am doing unselfish work, but it turns out to be selfish.' People who carry to excess the giving of alms, or the distributing of food among the poor, fall victims to the desire of acquiring name and fame.

"Sambhu Mallick once talked about establishing hospitals, dispensaries, and schools, making roads, digging public reservoirs, and so forth. I said to him: 'Don't go out of your way to look for such works. Undertake only those works that present themselves to you and are of pressing necessity—and those also in a spirit of detachment.' It is not good to become involved in many activities. That makes one forget God. Coming to the Kālighāt temple, some, perhaps, spend their whole time in giving alms to the poor. They have no time to see the Mother in the inner shrine! (*Laughter.*) First of all manage somehow to see the image of the Divine Mother, even by pushing through the crowd. Then you may or may not give alms, as you wish. You may give to the poor to your heart's content, if you feel that way. Work is only a means to the realization of God. Therefore I said to Sambhu, 'Suppose God appears before you; then will you ask Him to build hospitals and dispensaries for you?' (*Laughter.*) A lover of God never says that. He will rather say: 'O Lord, give me a place at Thy Lotus Feet. Keep me always in Thy company. Give me sincere and pure love for Thee.'

"Karmayoga is very hard indeed. In the Kaliyuga it is extremely difficult to perform the rites enjoined in the scriptures. Nowadays man's life is centred on food alone. He cannot perform many scriptural rites. Suppose a man is laid up with fever. If you attempt a slow cure with the old-fashioned indigenous remedies, before long his life may be snuffed out. He can't stand much delay. Nowadays the drastic 'D. Gupta'[9] mixture is appropriate. In the Kaliyuga the best way is bhaktiyoga, the path of devotion—singing the praises of the Lord, and prayer. The path of devotion alone is the religion for this age. (*To the Brāhmo devotees*) Yours also is the path of devotion. Blessed you are indeed that you chant the name of Hari and sing the Divine Mother's glories. I like your attitude. You don't call the world a dream, like the non-dualists. You are not Brahmajnānis like them; you are bhaktas, lovers of God. That you speak of Him as a Person is also good. You are devotees. You will certainly realize Him if you call on Him with sincerity and earnestness."

The boat cast anchor at Kayalāghāt and the passengers prepared to disembark. On coming outside they noticed that the full moon was up. The trees, the buildings, and the boats on the Ganges were bathed in its mellow light. A carriage was hailed for the Master, and M. and a few devotees got in with him. The Master asked for Keshab. Presently the latter arrived and inquired about the arrangements made for the Master's return to Dakshineswar. Then he bowed low and took leave of Sri Ramakrishna.

The carriage drove through the European quarter of the city. The Master enjoyed the sight of the beautiful mansions on both sides of the well lighted streets. Suddenly he said: "I am thirsty. What's to be done?" Nandalal, Keshab's nephew, stopped the carriage before the India Club and went upstairs to get some water. The Master inquired whether the glass had been well washed. On being assured that it had been, he drank the water.

As the carriage went along, the Master put his head out of the window and looked with childlike enjoyment at the people, the vehicles, the horses, and the streets, all flooded with moonlight. Now and then he heard European ladies singing at the piano. He was in a very happy mood.

The carriage arrived at the house of Suresh Mitra, who was a great devotee of the Master and whom he addressed affectionately as Surendra. He was not at home.

The members of the household opened a room on the ground floor for the Master and his party. The cab fare was to be paid. Surendra would

[9] A patent fever medicine containing a strong dose of quinine.

have taken care of it had he been there. The Master said to a devotee: "Why don't you ask the ladies to pay the fare? They certainly know that their master visits us at Dakshineswar. I am not a stranger to them." (*All laugh.*)

Narendra, who lived in that quarter of the city, was sent for. In the mean time Sri Ramakrishna and the devotees were invited to the drawing-room upstairs. The floor of the room was covered with a carpet and a white sheet. A few cushions were lying about. On the wall hung an oil painting especially painted for Surendra, in which Sri Ramakrishna was pointing out to Keshab the harmony of Christianity, Islām, Buddhism, Hinduism, and other religions. On seeing the picture Keshab had once said, "Blessed is the man who conceived the idea."

Sri Ramakrishna was talking joyously with the devotees, when Narendra arrived. This made the Master doubly happy. He said to his young disciple, "We had a boat trip with Keshab today. Vijay and many other Brāhmo devotees were there. (*Pointing to M.*) Ask him what I said to Keshab and Vijay about the mother and daughter observing their religious fast on Tuesdays, each on her own account, though the welfare of the one meant the welfare of the other. I also said to Keshab that trouble-makers like Jatilā and Kutilā were necessary to lend zest to the play. (*To M.*) Isn't that so?"

M: "Yes, sir. Quite so."

It was late. Surendra had not yet returned. The Master had to leave for the temple garden, and a cab was brought for him. M. and Narendra saluted him and took their leave. Sri Ramakrishna's carriage started for Dakshineswar through the moonlit streets.

THE MASTER WITH THE BRĀHMO
DEVOTEES (I)

I T WAS SATURDAY. The semi-annual Brāhmo festival, celebrated each autumn and spring, was being held in Benimadhav Pal's beautiful garden house at Sinthi, about three miles north of Calcutta. The house stood in a secluded place suited for contemplation. Trees laden with flowers, artificial lakes with grassy banks, and green arbours enhanced the beauty of the grounds. Just as the fleecy clouds were turning gold in the light of the setting sun, the Master arrived.

Many devotees had attended the morning devotions, and in the afternoon people from Calcutta and the neighbouring villages joined them. Shivanath, the great Brāhmo devotee whom the Master loved dearly, was one of the large gathering of members of the Brāhmo Samāj who had been eagerly awaiting Sri Ramakrishna's arrival.

When the carriage bringing the Master and a few devotees reached the garden house, the assembly stood up respectfully to receive him. There was a sudden silence, like that which comes when the curtain in a theatre is about to be rung up. People who had been conversing with one another now fixed their attention on the Master's serene face, eager not to lose one word that might fall from his lips.

At the sight of Shivanath the Master cried out joyously: "Ah! Here is Shivanath! You see, you are a devotee of God. The very sight of you gladdens my heart. One hemp-smoker feels very happy to meet another. Very often they embrace each other in an exuberance of joy."

The devotees burst out laughing.

MASTER: "Many people visit the temple garden at Dakshineswar. If I see some among the visitors indifferent to God, I say to them, 'You had better sit over there.' Or sometimes I say, 'Go and see the beautiful buildings.' (*Laughter.*)

"Sometimes I find that the devotees of God are accompanied by worthless people. Their companions are immersed in gross worldliness and don't enjoy spiritual talk at all. Since the devotees keep on, for a long time, talking with me about God, the others become restless. Finding it impossible to sit there

145

any longer, they whisper to their devotee friends: 'When shall we be going? How long will you stay here?' The devotees say: 'Wait a bit. We shall go after a little while.' Then the worldly people say in a disgusted tone: 'Well then, you can talk. We shall wait for you in the boat.' (*All laugh.*)

"Worldly people will never listen to you if you ask them to renounce everything and devote themselves whole-heartedly to God. Therefore Chaitanya and Nitāi, after some deliberation, made an arrangement to attract the worldly. They would say to such persons, 'Come, repeat the name of Hari, and you shall have a delicious soup of māgur fish and the embrace of a young woman.' Many people, attracted by the fish and the woman, would chant the name of God. After tasting a little of the nectar of God's hallowed name, they would soon realize that the 'fish soup' really meant the tears they shed for love of God, while the 'young woman' signified the earth. The embrace of the woman meant rolling on the ground in the rapture of divine love.

"Nitāi would employ any means to make people repeat Hari's name. Chaitanya said: 'The name of God has very great sanctity. It may not produce an immediate result, but one day it must bear fruit. It is like a seed that has been left on the cornice of a building. After many days the house crumbles, and the seed falls on the earth, germinates, and at last bears fruit.'

"As worldly people are endowed with sattva, rajas, and tamas, so also is bhakti characterized by the three gunas.

"Do you know what a worldly person endowed with sattva is like? Perhaps his house is in a dilapidated condition here and there. He doesn't care to repair it. The worship hall may be strewn with pigeon droppings and the courtyard covered with moss, but he pays no attention to these things. The furniture of the house may be old; he doesn't think of polishing it and making it look neat. He doesn't care for dress at all; anything is good enough for him. But the man himself is very gentle, quiet, kind, and humble; he doesn't injure anyone:

"Again, among the worldly there are people with the traits of rajas. Such a man has a watch and chain, and two or three rings on his fingers. The furniture of his house is all spick and span. On the walls hang portraits of the Queen, the Prince of Wales, and other prominent people; the building is whitewashed and spotlessly clean. His wardrobe is filled with a large assortment of clothes; even the servants have their livery, and all that.

"The traits of a worldly man endowed with tamas are sleep, lust, anger, egotism, and the like.

"Similarly, bhakti, devotion, has its sattva. A devotee who possesses it meditates on God in absolute secret, perhaps inside his mosquito net. Others think he is asleep. Since he is late in getting up, they think perhaps he has not slept well during the night. His love for the body goes only as far as appeasing his hunger, and that only by means of rice and simple greens. There is no elaborate arrangement about his meals, no luxury in clothes, and no display of furniture. Besides, such a devotee never flatters anybody for money.

"An aspirant possessed of rājasic bhakti puts a tilak[1] on his forehead and a necklace of holy rudrāksha beads, interspersed with gold ones, around his neck. (*All laugh.*) At worship he wears a silk cloth.

"A man endowed with tāmasic bhakti has burning faith. Such a devotee literally extorts boons from God, even as a robber falls upon a man and plunders his money. 'Bind! Beat! Kill!'—that is his way, the way of the dacoits."

Saying this, the Master began to sing in a voice sweet with rapturous love, his eyes turned upward:

> Why should I go to Gangā or Gayā, to Kāśi, Kānchi, or Prabhās,[2]
> So long as I can breathe my last with Kāli's name upon my lips?
> What need of rituals has a man, what need of devotions any more,
> If he repeats the Mother's name at the three holy hours?[3]
> Rituals may pursue him close, but never can they overtake him.
> Charity, vows, and giving of gifts do not appeal to Madan's[4] mind;
> The Blissful Mother's Lotus Feet are his whole prayer and sacrifice.
> Who could ever have conceived the power Her name possesses?
> Śiva Himself, the God of Gods, sings Her praise with His five
>   mouths!

The Master was beside himself with love for the Divine Mother. He sang with fiery enthusiasm:

> If only I can pass away repeating Durgā's name,
> How canst Thou then, O Blessed One,
> Withhold from me deliverance,
> Wretched though I may be? . . .

Then he said, "One must take the firm attitude: 'What? I have chanted the Mother's name. How can I be a sinner any more? I am Her child, heir to Her powers and glories.'

"If you can give a spiritual turn to your tamas, you can realize God with its help. Force your demands on God. He is by no means a stranger to you. He is indeed your very own.

"Again, you see, the quality of tamas can be used for the welfare of others. There are three classes of physicians: superior, mediocre, and inferior. The physician who feels the patient's pulse and just says to him, 'Take the medicine regularly' belongs to the inferior class. He doesn't care to inquire whether or not the patient has actually taken the medicine. The mediocre physician is he who in various ways persuades the patient to take the medicine, and says to him sweetly: 'My good man, how will you be cured unless you use the medicine? Take this medicine. I have made it for you myself.' But he who, finding the patient stubbornly refusing to take the medicine, forces it down his throat, going so far as to put his knee on the patient's

---

[1] A mark of sandal-paste or other material to denote one's religious affiliation.
[2] Five places of pilgrimage.
[3] Dawn, noon, and dusk.
[4] The author of the song.

chest, is the best physician. This is the manifestation of the tamas of the physician. It doesn't injure the patient; on the contrary, it does him good.

"Like the physicians, there are three types of religious teachers. The inferior teacher only gives instruction to the disciples but makes no inquiries about their progress. The mediocre teacher, for the good of the student, makes repeated efforts to bring the instruction home to him, begs him to assimilate it, and shows him love in many other ways. But there is a type of teacher who goes to the length of using force when he finds the student persistently unyielding; I call him the best teacher."

A BRĀHMO DEVOTEE: "Sir, has God forms or has He none?"

MASTER: "No one can say with finality that God is only 'this' and nothing else. He is formless, and again He has forms. For the bhakta He assumes forms. But He is formless for the jnāni, that is, for him who looks on the world as a mere dream. The bhakta feels that he is one entity and the world another. Therefore God reveals Himself to him as a Person. But the jnāni— the Vedāntist, for instance—always reasons, applying the process of 'Not this, not this'. Through this discrimination he realizes, by his inner perception, that the ego and the universe are both illusory, like a dream. Then the jnāni realizes Brahman in his own consciousness. He cannot describe what Brahman is.

"Do you know what I mean? Think of Brahman, Existence-Knowledge-Bliss Absolute, as a shoreless ocean. Through the cooling influence, as it were, of the bhakta's love, the water has frozen at places into blocks of ice. In other words, God now and then assumes various forms for His lovers and reveals Himself to them as a Person. But with the rising of the sun of Knowledge, the blocks of ice melt. Then one doesn't feel any more that God is a Person, nor does one see God's forms. What He is cannot be described. Who will describe Him? He who would do so disappears. He cannot find his 'I' any more.

"If one analyses oneself, one doesn't find any such thing as 'I'. Take an onion, for instance. First of all you peel off the red outer skin; then you find thick white skins. Peel these off one after the other, and you won't find anything inside.

"In that state a man no longer finds the existence of his ego. And who is there left to seek it? Who can describe how he feels in that state—in his own Pure Consciousness—about the real nature of Brahman? Once a salt doll went to measure the depth of the ocean. No sooner was it in the water than it melted. Now who was to tell the depth?

"There is a sign of Perfect Knowledge. Man becomes silent when It is attained. Then the 'I', which may be likened to the salt doll, melts in the Ocean of Existence-Knowledge-Bliss Absolute and becomes one with It. Not the slightest trace of distinction is left.

"As long as his self-analysis is not complete, man argues with much ado. But he becomes silent when he completes it. When the empty pitcher has been filled with water, when the water inside the pitcher becomes one with the water of the lake outside, no more sound is heard. Sound comes from the pitcher as long as the pitcher is not filled with water.

"People used to say in olden days that no boat returns after having once entered the black waters' of the ocean.

"All trouble and botheration come to an end when the 'I' dies. You may indulge in thousands of reasonings, but still the 'I' doesn't disappear. For people like you and me, it is good to have the feeling, 'I am a lover of God.'

"The Saguna Brahman is meant for the bhaktas. In other words, a bhakta believes that God has attributes and reveals Himself to men as a Person, assuming forms. It is He who listens to our prayers. The prayers that you utter are directed to Him alone. You are bhaktas, not jnānis or Vedāntists. It doesn't matter whether you accept God with form or not. It is enough to feel that God is a Person who listens to our prayers, who creates, preserves, and destroys the universe, and who is endowed with infinite power.

"It is easier to attain God by following the path of devotion."

BRĀHMO DEVOTEE: "Sir, is it possible for one to see God? If so, why can't we see Him?"

MASTER: "Yes, He can surely be seen. One can see His forms, and His formless aspect as well. How can I explain that to you?"

BRĀHMO DEVOTEE: "What are the means by which one can see God?"

MASTER: "Can you weep for Him with intense longing of heart? Men shed a jugful of tears for the sake of their children, for their wives, or for money. But who weeps for God? So long as the child remains engrossed with its toys, the mother looks after her cooking and other household duties. But when the child no longer relishes the toys, it throws them aside and yells for its mother. Then the mother takes the rice-pot down from the hearth, runs in haste, and takes the child in her arms."

BRĀHMO DEVOTEE: "Sir, why are there so many different opinions about the nature of God? Some say that God has form, while others say that He is formless. Again, those who speak of God with form tell us about His different forms. Why all this controversy?"

MASTER: "A devotee thinks of God as he sees Him. In reality there is no confusion about God. God explains all this to the devotee if the devotee only realizes Him somehow. You haven't set your foot in that direction. How can you expect to know all about God?

"Listen to a story. Once a man entered a wood and saw a small animal on a tree. He came back and told another man that he had seen a creature of a beautiful red colour on a certain tree. The second man replied: 'When I went into the wood, I also saw that animal. But why do you call it red? It is green.' Another man who was present contradicted them both and insisted that it was yellow. Presently others arrived and contended that it was grey, violet, blue, and so forth and so on. At last they started quarrelling among themselves. To settle the dispute they all went to the tree. They saw a man sitting under it. On being asked, he replied: 'Yes, I live under this tree and I know the animal very well. All your descriptions are true. Sometimes it appears red, sometimes yellow, and at other times blue, violet, grey, and so forth. It is a chameleon. And sometimes it has no colour at all. Now it has a colour, and now it has none.'

"In like manner, one who constantly thinks of God can know His real nature; he alone knows that God reveals Himself to seekers in various forms and aspects. God has attributes; then again He has none. Only the man who lives under the tree knows that the chameleon can appear in various colours, and he knows, further, that the animal at times has no colour at all. It is the others who suffer from the agony of futile argument.

"Kabir used to say, 'The formless Absolute is my Father, and God with form is my Mother.'

"God reveals Himself in the form which His devotee loves most. His love for the devotee knows no bounds. It is written in the Purāna that God assumed the form of Rāma for His heroic devotee, Hanumān.

"The forms and aspects of God disappear when one discriminates in accordance with the Vedānta philosophy. The ultimate conclusion of such discrimination is that Brahman alone is real and this world of names and forms illusory. It is possible for a man to see the forms of God, or to think of Him as a Person, only so long as he is conscious that he is a devotee. From the standpoint of discrimination this 'ego of a devotee' keeps him a little away from God.

"Do you know why images of Krishna or Kāli are three and a half cubits high? Because of distance. Again, on account of distance the sun appears to be small. But if you go near it you will find the sun so big that you won't be able to comprehend it. Why have images of Krishna and Kāli a dark-blue colour? That too is on account of distance, like the water of a lake, which appears green, blue, or black from a distance. Go near, take the water in the palm of your hand, and you will find that it has no colour. The sky also appears blue from a distance. Go near and you will see that it has no colour at all.

"Therefore I say that in the light of Vedāntic reasoning Brahman has no attributes. The real nature of Brahman cannot be described. But so long as your individuality is real, the world also is real, and equally real are the different forms of God and the feeling that God is a Person.

"Yours is the path of bhakti. That is very good; it is an easy path. Who can fully know the infinite God? and what need is there of knowing the Infinite? Having attained this rare human birth, my supreme need is to develop love for the Lotus Feet of God.

"If a jug of water is enough to remove my thirst, why should I measure the quantity of water in a lake? I become drunk on even half a bottle of wine—what is the use of my calculating the quantity of liquor in the tavern? What need is there of knowing the Infinite?

"The various states of mind of the Brahmajnāni are described in the Vedas. The path of knowledge is extremely difficult. One cannot obtain jnāna if one has the least trace of worldliness and the slightest attachment to 'woman and gold'. This is not the path for the Kaliyuga.

"The Vedas speak of seven planes where the mind dwells. When the mind is immersed in worldliness it dwells in the three lower planes—at the navel, the organ of generation, and the organ of evacuation. In that state the mind loses all its higher visions—it broods only on 'woman and gold'. The fourth plane of the mind is at the heart. When the mind dwells there, one has the first glimpse of spiritual consciousness. One sees light all around. Such a man, perceiving the divine light, becomes speechless with wonder and says: 'Ah! What is this? What is this?' His mind does not go downward to the objects of the world.

"The fifth plane of the mind is at the throat. When the mind reaches this, the aspirant becomes free from all ignorance and illusion. He does not enjoy talking or hearing about anything but God. If people talk about worldly things, he leaves the place at once.

"The sixth plane is at the forehead. When the mind reaches it, the aspirant sees the form of God day and night. But even then a little trace of ego remains. At the sight of that incomparable beauty of God's form, one becomes intoxicated and rushes forth to touch and embrace it. But one doesn't succeed. It is like the light inside a lantern. One feels as if one could touch the light, but one cannot on account of the pane of glass.

"In the top of the head is the seventh plane. When the mind rises there, one goes into samādhi. Then the Brahmajnāni directly perceives Brahman. But in that state his body does not last many days. He remains unconscious of the outer world. If milk is poured into his mouth, it runs out. Dwelling on this plane of consciousness, he gives up his body in twenty-one days. That is the condition of the Brahmajnāni. But yours is the path of devotion. That is a very good and easy path.

"Once a man said to me, 'Sir, can you teach me quickly the thing you call samādhi?' (All laugh.)

"After a man has attained samādhi all his actions drop away. All devotional activities, such as worship, japa, and the like, as well as all worldly duties, cease to exist for such a person. At the beginning there is much ado about work. As a man makes progress toward God, the outer display of his work becomes less and less—so much so that he cannot even sing the name and glories of God. (To Shivanath) As long as you were not here at the meeting, people talked a great deal about you and discussed your virtues. But no sooner did you arrive here than all that stopped. Now the very sight of you makes everyone happy. People now simply say, 'Ah! Here is Shivanath Babu.' All other talk about you has stopped.

"After attaining samādhi, I once went to the Ganges to perform tarpan. But as I took water in the palm of my hand, it trickled down through my fingers. Weeping, I said to Haladhari, 'Cousin, what is this?' Haladhari replied, 'It is called galitahasta[5] in the holy books.' After the vision of God, such duties as the performance of tarpan drop away.

"In the kirtan the devotee first sings, 'Nitāi āmār mātā hāti.'[6] As the devotional mood deepens, he simply sings, 'Hāti! Hāti!' Next, all he can sing is 'Hāti'. And last of all he simply sings, 'Hā!' and goes into samādhi. The man who has been singing all the while then becomes speechless.

"Again, at a feast given to the brāhmins one at first hears much noise of talking. When the guests sit on the floor with leaf-plates in front of them, much of the noise ceases. Then one hears only the cry, 'Bring some luchi!'

---

[5] Literally, "inert and benumbed hand".
[6] "My Nitāi dances like a mad elephant."

As they partake of the luchi and other dishes, three quarters of the noise subsides. When the curd, the last course, appears, one hears only the sound 'soop, soop' as the guests eat the curd with their fingers. Then there is practically no noise. Afterwards all retire to sleep, and absolute silence reigns.

"Therefore I say, at the beginning of religious life a man makes much ado about work, but as his mind dives deeper into God, he becomes less active. Last of all comes the renunciation of work, followed by samādhi.

"Generally the body does not remain alive after the attainment of samādhi. The only exceptions are such sages as Nārada, who keep their bodies alive in order to bring spiritual light to others. It is also true of Divine Incarnations, like Chaitanya. After the well is dug, one generally throws away the spade and the basket. But some keep them in order to help their neighbours. The great souls who retain their bodies after samādhi feel compassion for the suffering of others. They are not so selfish as to be satisfied with their own illumination. You are well aware of the nature of selfish people. If you ask them to spit at a particular place, they won't, lest it should do you good. If you ask them to bring a sweetmeat worth a cent from the store, they will perhaps lick it on the way back. (All laugh.)

"But the manifestations of Divine Power are different in different beings. Ordinary souls are afraid to teach others. A piece of worthless timber may itself somehow float across the water, but it sinks even under the weight of a bird. Sages like Nārada are like a heavy log of wood, which not only floats on the water but also can carry men, cows, and even elephants.

(To Shivanath and the other Brāhmo devotees) "Can you tell me why you dwell so much on the powers and glories of God? I asked the same thing of Keshab Sen. One day Keshab and his party came to the temple garden at Dakshineswar. I told them I wanted to hear how they lectured. A meeting was arranged in the paved courtyard above the bathing-ghāt on the Ganges, where Keshab gave a talk. He spoke very well. I went into a trance. After the lecture I said to Keshab, 'Why do you so often say such things as: "O God, what beautiful flowers Thou hast made! O God, Thou hast created the heavens, the stars, and the ocean!" and so on?' Those who love splendour themselves are fond of dwelling on God's splendour.

"Once a thief stole the jewels from the images in the temple of Rādhākānta. Mathur Babu entered the temple and said to the Deity: 'What a shame, O God! You couldn't save Your own ornaments.' 'The idea!' I said to Mathur. 'Does He who has Lakshmi for His handmaid and attendant ever lack any splendour? Those jewels may be precious to you, but to God they are no better than lumps of clay. Shame on you! You shouldn't have spoken so meanly. What riches can you give to God to magnify His glory?'

"Therefore I say, a man seeks the person in whom he finds joy. What need has he to ask where that person lives, the number of his houses, gardens, relatives, and servants, or the amount of his wealth? I forget everything when I see Narendra. Never, even unwittingly, have I asked him where he lived, what his father's profession was, or the number of his brothers.

"Dive deep in the sweetness of God's Bliss. What need have we of His infinite creation and unlimited glory?"

The Master sang:

> Dive deep, O mind, dive deep in the Ocean of God's Beauty;
> If you descend to the uttermost depths,
> There you will find the gem of Love.
>
> Go seek, O mind, go seek Vrindāvan in your heart,
> Where with His loving devotees
> Sri Krishna sports eternally.
>
> Light up, O mind, light up true wisdom's shining lamp,
> And let it burn with steady flame
> Unceasingly within your heart.
>
> Who is it that steers your boat across the solid earth?
> It is your guru, says Kubir;
> Meditate on his holy feet.

Sri Ramakrishna continued: "It is also true that after the vision of God the devotee desires to witness His līlā. After the destruction of Rāvana at Rāma's hands, Nikashā, Rāvana's mother, began to run away for fear of her life. Lakshmana said to Rāma: 'Revered Brother, please explain this strange thing to me. This Nikashā is an old woman who has suffered a great deal from the loss of her many sons, and yet she is so afraid of losing her own life that she is taking to her heels!' Rāma bade her come near, gave her assurance of safety, and asked her why she was running away. Nikashā answered: 'O Rāma, I am able to witness all this līlā of Yours because I am still alive. I want to live longer so that I may see the many more things You will do on this earth.' (All laugh.)

(To Shivanath) "I like to see you. How can I live unless I see pure-souled devotees? I feel as if they had been my friends in a former incarnation."

A BRĀHMO DEVOTEE: "Sir, do you believe in the reincarnation of the soul?"

MASTER: "Yes, they say there is something like that. How can we understand the ways of God through our small intellects? Many people have spoken about reincarnation; therefore I cannot disbelieve it. As Bhishma lay dying on his bed of arrows, the Pāndava brothers and Krishna stood around him. They saw tears flowing from the eyes of the great hero. Arjuna said to Krishna: 'Friend, how surprising it is! Even such a man as our grandsire Bhishma—truthful, self-restrained, supremely wise, and one of the eight Vasus—weeps, through māyā, at the hour of death.' Sri Krishna asked Bhishma about it. Bhishma replied: 'O Krishna, You know very well that this is not the cause of my grief. I am thinking that there is no end to the Pāndavas' sufferings, though God Himself is their charioteer.[7] A thought like this makes me feel that I have understood nothing of the ways of God, and so I weep.'"

It was about half past eight when the evening worship began in the prayer hall. Soon the moon rose in the autumn sky and flooded the trees and creepers of the garden with its light. After prayer the devotees began to sing. Sri Ramakrishna was dancing, intoxicated with love of God. The Brāhmo devotees danced around him to the accompaniment of drums and cymbals.

Krishna, an Incarnation of God, was Arjuna's charioteer.

All appeared to be in a very joyous mood. The place echoed and re-echoed with God's holy name.

When the music had stopped, Sri Ramakrishna prostrated himself on the ground and, making salutations to the Divine Mother again and again, said: "Bhāgavata—Bhakta—Bhagavān! My salutations at the feet of the jnānis! My salutations at the feet of the bhaktas! I salute the bhaktas who believe in God with form, and I salute the bhaktas who believe in God without form. I salute the knowers of Brahman of olden times. And my salutations at the feet of the modern knowers of Brahman of the Brāhmo Samāj!"

Then the Master and the devotees enjoyed a supper of delicious dishes, which Benimadhav, their host, had provided.

Wednesday, November 15, 1882

Sri Ramakrishna, accompanied by Rakhal and several other devotees, came to Calcutta in a carriage and called for M. at the school where he was teaching. Then they all set out for the Maidān. Sri Ramakrishna wanted to see the Wilson Circus. As the carriage rolled along the crowded Chitpore Road, his joy was very great. Like a little child he leaned first out of one side of the carriage and then out of the other, talking to himself as if addressing the passers-by. To M. he said: "I find the attention of the people fixed on earthly things. They are all rushing about for the sake of their stomachs. No one is thinking of God."

They arrived at the circus. Tickets for the cheapest seats were purchased. The devotees took the Master to a high gallery, and they all sat on a bench. He said joyfully: "Ha! This is a good place. I can see the show well from here." There were exhibitions of various feats. A horse raced around a circular track over which large iron rings were hung at intervals. The circus rider, an Englishwoman, stood on one foot on the horse's back, and as the horse passed under the rings, she jumped through them, always alighting on one foot on the horse's back. The horse raced around the entire circle, and the woman never missed the horse or lost her balance.

When the circus was over, the Master and the devotees stood outside in the field, near the carriage. Since it was a cold night he covered his body with his green shawl.

Sri Ramakrishna said to M.: "Did you see how that Englishwoman stood on one foot on her horse, while it ran like lightning? How difficult a feat that must be! She must have practised a long time. The slightest carelessness and she would break her arms or legs; she might even be killed. One faces the same difficulty leading the life of a householder. A few succeed in it through the grace of God and as a result of their spiritual practice. But most people fail. Entering the world, they become more and more involved in it; they drown in worldliness and suffer the agonies of death. A few only, like Janaka, have succeeded, through the power of their austerity, in leading the spiritual life as householders. Therefore spiritual practice is extremely necessary; otherwise one cannot rightly live in the world."

The Master got into the carriage with the devotees and went to Balaram Bose's house. He was taken with his companions to the second floor. It was evening and the lamps were lighted. The Master described the feats he had seen at the circus. Gradually other devotees gathered, and soon he was engaged in spiritual talk with them.

The conversation turned to the caste-system. Sri Ramakrishna said: "The caste-system can be removed by one means only, and that is the love of God. Lovers of God do not belong to any caste. The mind, body, and soul of a man become purified through divine love. Chaitanya and Nityānanda scattered the name of Hari to everyone, including the pariah, and embraced them all. A brāhmin without this love is no longer a brāhmin. And a pariah with the love of God is no longer a pariah. Through bhakti an untouchable becomes pure and elevated."

Speaking of householders entangled in worldliness, the Master said: "They are like the silk-worm. They can come out of the cocoon of their worldly life if they wish. But they can't bear to; for they themselves have built the cocoon with great love and care. So they die there. Or they are like the fish in a trap. They can come out of it by the way they entered, but they sport inside the trap with other fish and hear the sweet sound of the murmuring water and forget everything else. They don't even make an effort to free themselves from the trap. The lisping of children is the murmur of the water, and the other fish are relatives and friends. Only one or two make good their escape by running away. They are the liberated souls."

The Master then sang:

> When such delusion veils the world, through Mahāmāyā's spell,
> That Brahmā is bereft of sense,
> And Vishnu loses consciousness,
> What hope is left for men?

> The narrow channel first is made, and there the trap is set;
> But open though the passage lies,
> The fish, once safely through the gate,
> Do not come out again.

> The silk-worm patiently prepares its closely spun cocoon;
> Yet even though a way leads forth,
> Encased within its own cocoon,
> The worm remains to die.

The Master continued: "Man may be likened to grain. He has fallen between the millstones and is about to be crushed. Only the few grains that stay near the peg escape. Therefore men should take refuge at the peg, that is to say, in God. Call on Him. Sing His name. Then you will be free. Otherwise you will be crushed by the King of Death."

The Master sang again:

> Mother! Mother! My boat is sinking, here in the ocean of this
>   world;
> Fiercely the hurricane of delusion rages on every side!
> Clumsy is my helmsman, the mind; stubborn my six oarsmen, the
>   passions;
> Into a pitiless wind
> I sailed my boat, and now it is sinking!

Split is the rudder of devotion; tattered is the sail of faith;
Into my boat the waters are pouring! Tell me, what shall I do?
For with my failing eyes, alas! nothing but darkness do I see.
Here in the waves I will swim,
O Mother, and cling to the raft of Thy name!

Mr. Viswas had been sitting in the room a long time; he now left. He had once been wealthy but had squandered everything in an immoral life. Finally he had become indifferent to his wife and children. Referring to Mr. Viswas, the Master said: "He is an unfortunate wretch. A householder has his duties to discharge, his debts to pay: his debt to the gods, his debt to his ancestors, his debt to the rishis, and his debt to wife and children. If a wife is chaste, then her husband should support her; he should also bring up their children until they are of age. Only a monk must not save; the bird and the monk do not provide for the morrow. But even a bird provides when it has young. It brings food in its bill for its chicks."

BALARAM: "Mr. Viswas now wants to cultivate the company of holy people."

MASTER (with a smile): "A monk's kamandalu goes to the four principal holy places[8] with him, but it still tastes bitter. Likewise, it is said that the Malaya breeze turns all trees into sandal-wood. But there are a few exceptions,· such as the cotton-tree, the aśwattha, and the hog plum.

"Some frequent the company of holy men in order to smoke hemp. Many monks smoke it, and these householders stay with them, prepare the hemp, and partake of the prasād."

Thursday, November 16, 1882

The Master had come to Calcutta. In the evening he went to the house of Rajmohan, a member of the Brāhmo Samāj, where Narendra and some of his young friends used to meet and worship according to the Brāhmo ceremonies. Sri Ramakrishna wanted to see their worship. He was accompanied by M. and a few other devotees.

The Master was very happy to see Narendra and expressed a desire to watch the young men at their worship. Narendra sang and then the worship began. One of the young men conducted it. He prayed, "O Lord, may we give up everything and be absorbed in Thee!" Possibly the youth was inspired by the Master's presence and so talked of utter renunciation. Sri Ramakrishna remarked in a whisper, "Much likelihood there is of that!"

Rajmohan served the Master with refreshments.

Sunday, November 19, 1882

It was the auspicious occasion of the Jagaddhātri Pujā, the festival of the Divine Mother. Sri Ramakrishna was invited to Surendra's house in Calcutta; but first he went to the house of Manomohan in the neighbourhood. The Master was seated in Manomohan's parlour. He said: "God very

---

[8] At the four cardinal points of India, namely, Kedārnāth in the Himālayas, Dwārakā in the west, Rāmeśwar in the south, and Puri in the east.

much relishes the bhakti of the poor and the lowly, just as the cow relishes fodder mixed with oil-cake. King Duryodhana showed Krishna the splendour of his wealth and riches, but Krishna accepted the hospitality of the poor Vidura. God is fond of His devotees. He runs after the devotee as the cow after the calf."

The Master sang:

> And, for that love, the mighty yogis practise yoga from age to age;
> When love awakes, the Lord, like a magnet, draws to Him the soul.

Then he said: "Chaitanya used to shed tears of joy at the very mention of Krishna's name. God alone is the real Substance; all else is illusory. Man can realize God if he wants to, but he madly craves the enjoyment of 'woman and gold'. The snake has a precious stone[9] in its head, but it is perfectly satisfied to eat a mere frog.

"Bhakti is the one essential thing. Who can ever know God through reasoning? I want love of God. What do I care about knowing His infinite glories? One bottle of wine makes me drunk. What do I care about knowing how many gallons there are in the grog-shop? One jar of water is enough to quench my thirst. I don't need to know the amount of water there is on earth."

Sri Ramakrishna arrived at Surendra's house. Many devotees had assembled there, including Surendra's elder brother, who was a judge.

MASTER (to Surendra's brother): "You are a judge. That is very good. But remember, everything happens through God's power. It is He who has given you your high position; that is how you became a judge. People think it is they who are great. The water from the roof flows through a spout that is shaped like a lion's head. It looks as if the lion were bringing the water out through its mouth. But look at the source of the water! A cloud gathers in the sky and rain falls on the roof; then the water flows through the pipe and at last comes out through the spout."

SURENDRA'S BROTHER: "The Brāhmo Samāj preaches the freedom of women and the abolition of the caste-system. What do you think about these matters?"

MASTER: "Men feel that way when they are just beginning to develop spiritual yearning. A storm raises clouds of dust, and one cannot distinguish between the different trees—the mango, the hog plum, and the tamarind. But after the storm blows over, one sees clearly. After the first storm of divine passion is quelled, one gradually understands that God alone is the Highest Good, the Eternal Substance, and that all else is transitory. One cannot grasp this without tapasyā and the company of holy men. What is the use of merely reciting the written parts for the drum? It is very difficult to put them into practice on the instrument. What can be accomplished by a mere lecture? It is austerity that is necessary. By that alone can one comprehend.

"You asked about caste distinctions. There is only one way to remove them, and that is by love of God. Lovers of God have no caste. Through this

[9] A folk belief in Bengal.

divine love the untouchable becomes pure, the pariah no longer remains a pariah. Chaitanya embraced all, including the pariahs.

"The members of the Brāhmo Samāj sing the name of Hari. That is very good. Through earnest prayer one receives the grace of God and realizes Him. God can be realized by means of all paths. The same God is invoked by different names."

SURENDRA'S BROTHER: "Sir, what do you think of Theosophy?"

MASTER: "I have heard that man can acquire superhuman powers through it and perform miracles. I saw a man who had brought a ghost under control. The ghost used to procure various things for his master. What shall I do with superhuman powers? Can one realize God through them? If God is not realized then everything becomes false."

November 1882

It was about four o'clock in the afternoon when Sri Ramakrishna arrived in Calcutta to attend the annual festival of the Brāhmo Samāj, which was to be celebrated at Manilal Mallick's house. Besides M. and other devotees of the Master, Vijay Goswami and a number of Brāhmos were present. Elaborate arrangements had been made to make the occasion a success. Vijay was to conduct the worship.

The kathak recited the life of Prahlāda from the Purāna. Its substance was as follows: Hiranyakaśipu, Prahlāda's father, was king of the demons. He bore great malice toward God and put his own son through endless tortures for leading a religious life. Afflicted by his father, Prahlāda prayed to God, "O God, please give my father holy inclinations."

At these words the Master wept. He went into an ecstatic mood. Afterwards he began to talk to the devotees.

MASTER: "Bhakti is the only essential thing. One obtains love of God by constantly chanting His name and singing His glories. Ah! What a devotee Shivanath is! He is soaked in the love of God, like a cheese-cake in syrup.

"One should not think, 'My religion alone is the right path and other religions are false.' God can be realized by means of all paths. It is enough to have sincere yearning for God. Infinite are the paths and infinite the opinions.

"Let me tell you one thing. God can be seen. The Vedas say that God is beyond mind and speech. The meaning of this is that God is unknown to the mind attached to worldly objects. Vaishnavcharan[10] used to say, 'God is known by the mind and intellect that are pure.' Therefore it is necessary to seek the company of holy men, practise prayer, and listen to the instruction of the guru. These purify the mind. Then one sees God. Dirt can be removed from water by a purifying agent. Then one sees one's reflection in it. One cannot see one's face in a mirror if the mirror is covered with dirt.

"After the purification of the heart one obtains divine love. Then one sees God, through His grace. One can teach others if one receives that command from God after seeing Him. Before that one should not 'lecture'. There is a song that says:

[10] A noted devotee of the Vaishnava sect and an admirer of Sri Ramakrishna.

You have set up no image here,
Within the shrine, O fool!
Blowing the conch, you simply make
Confusion worse confounded.

"You should first cleanse the shrine of your heart. Then you should install the Deity and arrange worship. As yet nothing has been done. What can you achieve by blowing the conch-shell[11] and simply making a loud noise?"

Vijay sat on a raised stool and conducted the worship according to the rules of the Brāhmo Samāj. Afterwards he sat by the Master.

MASTER (to Vijay): "Will you tell me one thing? Why did you harp so much on sin? By repeating a hundred times, 'I am a sinner', one verily becomes a sinner. One should have such faith as to be able to say, 'What? I have taken the name of God; how can I be a sinner?' God is our Father and Mother. Tell Him, 'O Lord, I have committed sins, but I won't repeat them.' Chant His name and purify your body and mind. Purify your tongue by singing God's holy name."

December 1882

In the afternoon Sri Ramakrishna was seated on the west porch of his room in the temple garden at Dakshineswar. Among others, Baburam, Ramdayal, and M. were present. These three were going to spend the night with the Master. M. intended to stay the following day also, for he was having his Christmas holidays. Baburam had only recently begun to visit the Master.

MASTER (to the devotees): "A man becomes liberated even in this life when he knows that God is the Doer of all things. Once Keshab came here with Sambhu Mallick. I said to him, 'Not even a leaf moves except by the will of God.' Where is man's free will? All are under the will of God. Nangtā was a man of great knowledge, yet even he was about to drown himself in the Ganges. He stayed here eleven months. At one time he suffered from stomach trouble. The excruciating pain made him lose control over himself, and he wanted to drown himself in the river. There was a long shoal near the bathing-ghāt. However far he went into the river, he couldn't find water above his knees. Then he understood everything[12] and came back. At one time I was very ill and was about to cut my throat with a knife. Therefore I say: 'O Mother, I am the machine and Thou art the Operator; I am the chariot and Thou art the Driver. I move as Thou movest me; I do as Thou makest me do.' "

The devotees sang kirtan in the Master's room:

Dwell, O Lord, O Lover of bhakti,
In the Vrindāvan of my heart,
And my devotion unto Thee
Will be Thy Rādhā, dearly loved;

[11] The conch-shell is blown during the temple service.
[12] He realized that man is not free even to kill himself, that everything depends on the will of the Divine Mother. See Introduction, p. 31.

My body will be Nanda's home,
My tenderness will be Yaśodā,
My longing for deliverance
Will be Thy gentle gopi maids.

Lift the Govardhan of my sin
And slay my six unyielding passions,
Fierce as the demons sent by Kamśa!
Sweetly play the flute[13] of Thy grace,
Charming the milch cow of my mind;
Abide in the pasture of my soul.

Dwell by the Jamunā of my yearning,
Under the banyan of my hope,
For ever gracious to Thy servant;
And, if naught but the cowherds' love
Can hold Thee in Vrindāvan's vale,
Then, Lord, let Dāśarathi, too,
Become Thy cowherd and Thy slave.

Again they sang:

Sing, O bird that nestles deep within my heart!
Sing, O bird that sits on the Kalpa-Tree of Brahman!
Sing God's everlasting praise.
Taste, O bird, of the four fruits of the Kalpa-Tree,
Dharma, artha, kāma, moksha.
Sing, O bird, "He alone is the Comfort of my soul!"
Sing, O bird, "He alone is my life's enduring Joy!"
O thou wondrous bird of my life,
Sing aloud in my heart! Unceasingly sing, O bird!
Sing for evermore, even as the thirsty chātak
Sings for the raindrop from the cloud.

A devotee from Nandanbāgān entered the room with his friends. The Master looked at him and said, "Everything inside him can be seen through his eyes, as one sees the objects in a room through a glass door." This devotee and his brothers always celebrated the anniversary of the Brāhmo Samāj at their house in Nandanbāgān. Sri Ramakrishna had taken part in these festivals.

The evening worship began in the temples. The Master was seated on the small couch in his room, absorbed in meditation. He went into an ecstatic mood and said a little later: "Mother, please draw him to Thee. He is so modest and humble! He has been visiting Thee." Was the Master referring to Baburam, who later became one of his foremost disciples?

The Master explained the different kinds of samādhi to the devotees. The conversation then turned to the joy and suffering of life. Why did God create so much suffering?

M: "Once Vidyāsāgar said in a mood of pique: 'What is the use of calling on God? Just think of this incident: At one time Chenghiz Khan plundered

[13] A reference to Sri Krishna's pastoral life.

a country and imprisoned many people. The number of prisoners rose to about a hundred thousand. The commander of his army said to him: "Your Majesty, who will feed them? It is risky to keep them with us. It will be equally dangerous to release them. What shall I do?" Chenghiz Khan said: "That's true. What can be done? Well, have them killed." The order was accordingly given to cut them to pieces. Now, God saw this slaughter, didn't He? But He didn't stop it in any way. Therefore I don't need God, whether He exists or not. I don't derive any good from Him.' "

MASTER: "Is it possible to understand God's action and His motive? He creates, He preserves, and He destroys. Can we ever understand why He destroys? I say to the Divine Mother: 'O Mother, I do not need to understand. Please give me love for Thy Lotus Feet.' The aim of human life is to attain bhakti. As for other things, the Mother knows best. I have come to the garden to eat mangoes. What is the use of my calculating the number of trees, branches, and leaves? I only eat the mangoes; I don't need to know the number of trees and leaves."

Baburam, M., and Ramdayal slept that night on the floor of the Master's room.

It was an early hour of the morning, about two or three o'clock. The room was dark. Sri Ramakrishna was seated on his bed and now and then conversed with the devotees.

MASTER: "Remember that dayā, compassion, and māyā, attachment, are two different things. Attachment means the feeling of 'my-ness' toward one's relatives. It is the love one feels for one's parents, one's brother, one's sister, one's wife and children. Compassion is the love one feels for all beings of the world. It is an attitude of equality. If you see anywhere an instance of compassion, as in Vidyāsāgar, know that it is due to the grace of God. Through compassion one serves all beings. Māyā also comes from God. Through māyā God makes one serve one's relatives. But one thing should be remembered: māyā keeps us in ignorance and entangles us in the world, whereas dayā makes our hearts pure and gradually unties our bonds.

"God cannot be realized without purity of heart. One receives the grace of God by subduing the passions—lust, anger, and greed. Then one sees God. I tried many things in order to conquer lust.

"When I was ten or eleven years old and lived at Kāmārpukur, I first experienced samādhi. As I was passing through a paddy-field, I saw something and was overwhelmed. There are certain characteristics of God-vision. One sees light, feels joy, and experiences the upsurge of a great current in one's chest, like the bursting of a rocket."

The next day Baburam and Ramdayal returned to Calcutta. M. spent the day and the night with the Master.

December 1882

It was afternoon. The Master was sitting in his room at Dakshineswar with M. and one or two other devotees. Several Mārwāri devotees arrived and saluted the Master. They requested Sri Ramakrishna to give them spiritual instruction. He smiled.

MASTER (*to the Mārwāri devotees*): "You see, the feeling of 'I' and 'mine' is the result of ignorance. But to say, 'O God, Thou art the Doer; all these belong to Thee' is the sign of Knowledge. How can you say such a thing as 'mine'? The superintendent of the garden says, 'This is my garden.' But if he is dismissed because of some misconduct, then he does not have the courage to take away even such a worthless thing as his mango-wood box. Anger and lust cannot be destroyed. Turn them toward God. If you must feel desire and temptation, then desire to realize God, feel tempted by Him. Discriminate and turn the passions away from worldly objects. When the elephant is about to devour a plaintain-tree in someone's garden, the māhut strikes it with his iron-tipped goad.

"You are merchants. You know how to improve your business gradually. Some of you start with a castor-oil factory. After making some money at that, you open a cloth shop. In the same way, one makes progress toward God. It may be that you go into solitude, now and then, and devote more time to prayer.

"But you must remember that nothing can be achieved except in its proper time. Some persons must pass through many experiences and perform many worldly duties before they can turn their attention to God; so they have to wait a long time. If an abscess is lanced before it is soft, the result is not good; the surgeon makes the opening when it is soft and has come to a head. Once a child said to its mother: 'Mother, I am going to sleep now. Please wake me up when I feel the call of nature.' 'My child,' said the mother, 'when it is time for that, you will wake up yourself. I shan't have to wake you.'"

The Mārwāri devotees generally brought offerings of fruit, candy, and other sweets for the Master. But Sri Ramakrishna could hardly eat them. He would say: "They earn their money by falsehood. I can't eat their offerings." He said to the Mārwāris: "You see, one can't strictly adhere to truth in business. There are ups and downs in business. Nānak once said, 'I was about to eat the food of unholy people, when I found it stained with blood.' A man should offer only pure things to holy men. He shouldn't give them food earned by dishonest means. God is realized by following the path of truth. One should always chant His name. Even while one is performing one's duties, the mind should be left with God. Suppose I have a carbuncle on my back. I perform my duties, but the mind is drawn to the carbuncle. It is good to repeat the name of Rāma. 'The same Rāma who was the son of King Daśaratha has created this world. Again, as Spirit, He pervades all beings. He is very near us; He is both within and without.'"

THE MASTER AND VIJAY GOSWAMI

IT WAS AFTERNOON. Sri Ramakrishna was sitting on his bed after a short noonday rest. Vijay, Balaram, M., and a few other devotees were sitting on the floor with their faces toward the Master. They could see the sacred river Ganges through the door. Since it was winter all were wrapped up in warm clothes. Vijay had been suffering from colic and had brought some medicine with him.

Vijay was a paid preacher in the Sādhāran Brāhmo Samāj, but there were many things about which he could not agree with the Samāj authorities. He came from a very noble family of Bengal noted for its piety and other spiritual qualities. Advaita Goswāmi, one of his remote ancestors, had been an intimate companion of Sri Chaitanya. Thus the blood of a great lover of God flowed in Vijay's veins. As an adherent of the Brāhmo Samāj, Vijay no doubt meditated on the formless Brahman; but his innate love of God, inherited from his distinguished ancestors, had merely been waiting for the proper time to manifest itself in all its sweetness. Thus Vijay was irresistibly attracted by the God-intoxicated state of Sri Ramakrishna and often sought his company. He would listen to the Master's words with great respect, and they would dance together in an ecstasy of divine love.

It was a week-day. Generally devotees came to the Master in large numbers on Sundays; hence those who wanted to have intimate talks with him visited him on week-days.

A boy named Vishnu, living in Āriādaha, had recently committed suicide by cutting his throat with a razor. The talk turned to him.

MASTER: "I felt very badly when I heard of the boy's passing away. He was a pupil in a school and he used to come here. He would often say to me that he couldn't enjoy worldly life. He had lived with some relatives in the western provinces and at that time used to meditate in solitude, in the meadows, hills, and forests. He told me he had visions of many divine forms.

"Perhaps this was his last birth. He must have finished most of his duties in his previous birth. The little that had been left undone was perhaps finished in this one.

"One must admit the existence of tendencies inherited from previous births. There is a story about a man who practised the śava-sādhanā.[1] He worshipped the Divine Mother in a deep forest. First he saw many terrible visions. Finally a tiger attacked and killed him. Another man, happening to pass and seeing the approach of the tiger, had climbed a tree. Afterwards he got down and found all the arrangements for worship at hand. He performed some purifying ceremonies and seated himself on the corpse. No sooner had he done a little japa than the Divine Mother appeared before him and said: 'My child, I am very much pleased with you. Accept a boon from Me.' He bowed low at the Lotus Feet of the Goddess and said: 'May I ask You one question, Mother? I am speechless with amazement at Your action. The other man worked so hard to get the ingredients for Your worship and tried to propitiate You for such a long time, but You didn't condescend to show him Your favour. And I, who don't know anything of worship, who have done nothing, who have neither devotion nor knowledge nor love, and who haven't practised any austerities, am receiving so much of Your grace.' The Divine Mother said with a laugh: 'My child, you don't remember your previous births. For many births you tried to propitiate Me through austerities. As a result of those austerities all these things have come to hand, and you have been blessed with My vision. Now ask Me your boon.'"

A DEVOTEE: "I am frightened to hear of the suicide."

MASTER: "Suicide is a heinous sin, undoubtedly. A man who kills himself must return again and again to this world and suffer its agony.

"But I don't call it suicide if a person leaves his body after having the vision of God. There is no harm in giving up one's body that way. After attaining Knowledge some people give up their bodies. After the gold image has been cast in the clay mould, you may either preserve the mould or break it.

"Many years ago a young man of about twenty used to come to the temple garden from Barānagore; his name was Gopal Sen. In my presence he used to experience such intense ecstasy that Hriday had to support him for fear he might fall to the ground and break his limbs. That young man touched my feet one day and said: 'Sir, I shall not be able to see you any more. Let me bid you good-bye.' A few days later I learnt that he had given up his body.

"It is said that there are four classes of human beings: the bound, those aspiring after liberation, the liberated, and the ever-perfect.

"This world is like a fishing-net. Men are the fish, and God, whose māyā has created this world, is the fisherman. When the fish are entangled in the net, some of them try to tear through its meshes in order to get their liberation. They are like the men striving after liberation. But by no means all of them escape. Only a few jump out of the net with a loud splash, and then people say, 'Ah! There goes a big one!' In like manner, three or four men attain liberation. Again, some fish are so careful by nature that they are never caught in the net; some beings of the ever-perfect class, like Nārada,

---

[1] A religious practice prescribed by the Tantra, in which the aspirant uses a śava, or corpse, as his seat for meditation.

are never entangled in the meshes of worldliness. Most of the fish are trapped; but they are not conscious of the net and of their imminent death. No sooner are they entangled than they run headlong, net and all, trying to hide themselves in the mud. They don't make the least effort to get free. On the contrary, they go deeper and deeper into the mud. These fish are like the bound men. They are still inside the net, but they think they are quite safe there. A bound creature is immersed in worldliness, in 'woman and gold', having gone deep into the mire of degradation. But still he believes he is quite happy and secure. The liberated, and the seekers after liberation, look on the world as a deep well. They do not enjoy it. Therefore, after the attainment of Knowledge, the realization of God, some give up their bodies. But such a thing is rare indeed.

"The bound creatures, entangled in worldliness, will not come to their senses at all. They suffer so much misery and agony, they face so many dangers, and yet they will not wake up.

"The camel loves to eat thorny bushes. The more it eats the thorns, the more the blood gushes from its mouth. Still it must eat thorny plants and will never give them up. The man of worldly nature suffers so much sorrow and affliction, but he forgets it all in a few days and begins his old life over again. Suppose a man has lost his wife or she has turned unfaithful. Lo! He marries again.

"Or take the instance of a mother: her son dies and she suffers bitter grief; but after a few days she forgets all about it. The mother, so overwhelmed with sorrow a few days before, now attends to her toilet and puts on her jewelry. A father becomes bankrupt through the marriage of his daughters, yet he goes on having children year after year. People are ruined by litigation, yet they go to court all the same. There are men who cannot feed the children they have, who cannot clothe them or provide decent shelter for them; yet they have more children every year.

"Again, the worldly man is like a snake trying to swallow a mole. The snake can neither swallow the mole nor give it up. The bound soul may have realized that there is no substance to the world—that the world is like a hog plum, only stone and skin—but still he cannot give it up and turn his mind to God.

"I once met a relative of Keshab Sen, fifty years old. He was playing cards. As if the time had not yet come for him to think of God!

"There is another characteristic of the bound soul. If you remove him from his worldly surroundings to a spiritual environment, he will pine away. The worm that grows in filth feels very happy there. It thrives in filth. It will die if you put it in a pot of rice."

All remained silent.

VIJAY: "What must the bound soul's condition of mind be in order to achieve liberation?"

MASTER: "He can free himself from attachment to 'woman and gold' if, by the grace of God, he cultivates a spirit of strong renunciation. What is this strong renunciation? One who has only a mild spirit of renunciation says, 'Well, all will happen in the course of time; let me now simply repeat the name of God.' But a man possessed of a strong spirit of renunciation feels restless for God, as the mother feels for her own child. A man of strong renunciation seeks nothing but God. He regards the world as a deep well and feels as if he were going to be drowned in it. He looks on his relatives as venomous snakes; he wants to fly away from them. And he does go away. He never thinks, 'Let me first make some arrangement for my family and then I shall think of God.' He has great inward resolution.

"Let me tell you a story about strong renunciation. At one time there was a drought in a certain part of the country. The farmers began to cut long channels to bring water to their fields. One farmer was stubbornly determined. He took a vow that he would not stop digging until the channel connected his field with the river. He set to work. The time came for his bath, and his wife sent their daughter to him with oil. 'Father,' said the girl, 'it is already late. Rub your body with oil and take your bath.' 'Go away!' thundered the farmer. 'I have too much to do now.' It was past midday, and the farmer was still at work in his field. He didn't even think of his bath. Then his wife came and said: 'Why haven't you taken your bath? The food is getting cold. You overdo everything. You can finish the rest tomorrow or even today after dinner.' The farmer scolded her furiously and ran at her, spade in hand, crying: 'What? Have you no sense? There's no rain. The crops are dying. What will the children eat? You'll all starve to death. I have taken a vow not to think of bath and food today before I bring water to my field.' The wife saw his state of mind and ran away in fear. Through a whole day's back-breaking labour the farmer managed by evening to connect his field with the river. Then he sat down and watched the water flowing into his field with a murmuring sound. His mind was filled with peace and joy. He went home, called his wife, and said to her, 'Now give me some oil and prepare me a smoke.' With serene mind he finished his bath and meal, and retired to bed, where he snored to his heart's content. The determination he showed is an example of strong renunciation.

"Now, there was another farmer who was also digging a channel to bring water to his field. His wife, too, came to the field and said to him: 'It's very late. Come home. It isn't necessary to overdo things.' The farmer didn't protest much, but put aside his spade and said to his wife, 'Well, I'll go home since you ask me to.' (*All laugh.*) That man never succeeded in irrigating his field. This is a case of mild renunciation.

"As without strong determination the farmer cannot bring water to his field, so also without intense yearning a man cannot realize God. (*To Vijay*) Why don't you come here now as frequently as before?"

VIJAY: "Sir, I wish to very much, but I am not free. I have accepted work in the Brāhmo Samāj."

MASTER: "It is 'woman and gold' that binds man and robs him of his freedom. It is woman that creates the need for gold. For woman one man becomes the slave of another, and so loses his freedom. Then he cannot act as he likes.

"The priests in the temple of Govindaji at Jaipur were celibates at first, and at that time they had fiery natures. Once the King of Jaipur sent for them, but they didn't obey him. They said to the messenger, 'Ask the king to come to see us.' After consultation, the king and his ministers arranged marriages for them. From then on the king didn't have to send for them. They would come to him of themselves and say: 'Your Majesty, we have come with our blessings. Here are the sacred flowers of the temple. Deign to accept them.' They came to the palace, for now they always wanted money for one thing or another: the building of a house, the rice-taking ceremony of their babies, or the rituals connected with the beginning of their children's education.

"There is the story of the twelve hundred nedās[2] and thirteen hundred nedis.[3] Virabhadra, the son of Nityānanda Goswāmi, had thirteen hundred 'shaven-headed' disciples. They attained great spiritual powers. That alarmed their teacher. 'My disciples have acquired great spiritual powers', thought Virabhadra. 'Whatever they say to people will come to pass. Wherever they go they may create alarming situations; for people offending them unwittingly will come to grief.' Thinking thus, Virabhadra one day called them to him and said, 'See me after performing your daily devotions on the bank of the Ganges.' These disciples had such a high spiritual nature that, while meditating, they would go into samādhi and be unaware of the river water flowing over their heads during the flood-tide. Then the ebb-tide would come and still they would remain absorbed in meditation.

"Now, one hundred of these disciples had anticipated what their teacher would ask of them. Lest they should have to disobey his injunctions, they had quickly disappeared from the place before he summoned them. So they did not go to Virabhadra with the others. The remaining twelve hundred disciples went to the teacher after finishing their meditation. Virabhadra said to them: 'These thirteen hundred nuns will serve you. I ask you to marry them.' 'As you please, revered sir', they said. 'But one hundred of us have gone away.' Thenceforth each of these twelve hundred disciples had a wife. Consequently they all lost their spiritual power. Their austerities did not have their original fire. The company of woman robbed them of their spirituality because it destroyed their freedom.

(To Vijay) "You yourself perceive how far you have gone down by being a servant of others. Again, one finds that people with many university degrees, scholars with their vast English education, accept service under their English masters and are daily trampled under their boots. The one cause of all this is woman. They have married and set up a 'gay fair' with their wives and children. Now they cannot go back, much as they would like to. Hence all these insults and humiliations, all this suffering from slavery.

"Once a man realizes God through intense dispassion, he is no longer attached to woman. Even if he must lead the life of a householder, he is free from fear of and attachment to woman. Suppose there are two magnets, one big and the other small. Which one will attract the iron? The big one,

---

[2] Literally, "shaven-headed". Among the Vaishnava devotees, those who renounce the world shave their heads.
[3] Vaishnava nuns.

of course. God is the big magnet. Compared to Him, woman is a small one. What can 'woman' do?"

A DEVOTEE: "Sir, shall we hate women then?"

MASTER: "He who has realized God does not look upon a woman with the eye of lust; so he is not afraid of her. He perceives clearly that women are but so many aspects of the Divine Mother. He worships them all as the Mother Herself.

(*To Vijay*) "Come here now and then. I like to see you very much."

VIJAY: "I have to do my various duties in the Brāhmo Samāj; that is why I can't always come here. But I shall visit you whenever I find it possible."

MASTER (*to Vijay*): "The task of a religious teacher is indeed difficult. One cannot teach men without a direct command from God. People won't listen to you if you teach without such authority. Such teaching has no force behind it. One must first of all attain God through spiritual discipline or some other means. Thus armed with authority from God, one can deliver lectures.

"After receiving the command from God, one can be a teacher and give lectures anywhere. He who receives authority from God also receives power from Him. Only then can he perform the difficult task of a teacher.

"An insignificant tenant was once engaged in a lawsuit with a big landlord. People realized that there was a powerful man behind the tenant. Perhaps another big landlord was directing the case from behind. Man is an insignificant creature. He cannot fulfil the difficult task of a teacher without receiving power direct from God."

VIJAY: "Don't the teachings of the Brāhmo Samāj bring men salvation?"

MASTER: "How is it ever possible for one man to liberate another from the bondage of the world? God alone, the Creator of this world-bewitching māyā, can save men from māyā. There is no other refuge but that great Teacher, Satchidānanda. How is it ever possible for men who have not realized God or received His command, and who are not strengthened with divine strength, to save others from the prison-house of the world?

"One day as I was passing the Panchavati on my way to the pine-grove, I heard a bullfrog croaking. I thought it must have been seized by a snake. After some time, as I was coming back, I could still hear its terrified croaking. I looked to see what was the matter, and found that a water-snake had seized it. The snake could neither swallow it nor give it up. So there was no end to the frog's suffering. I thought that had it been seized by a cobra it would have been silenced after three croaks at the most. As it was only a water-snake, both of them had to go through this agony. A man's ego is destroyed after three croaks, as it were, if he gets into the clutches of a real teacher. But if the teacher is an 'unripe' one, then both the teacher and the disciple undergo endless suffering. The disciple cannot get rid either of his ego or of the shackles of the world. If a disciple falls into the clutches of an incompetent teacher, he doesn't attain liberation."

VIJAY: "Sir, why are we bound like this? Why don't we see God?"

MASTER: "Māyā is nothing but the egotism of the embodied soul. This egotism has covered everything like a veil. 'All troubles come to an end when the ego dies.' If by the grace of God a man but once realizes that he is not the doer, then he at once becomes a jīvanmukta. Though living in the body, he is liberated. He has nothing else to fear.

"This māyā, that is to say, the ego, is like a cloud. The sun cannot be seen on account of a thin patch of cloud; when that disappears one sees the sun. If by the grace of the guru one's ego vanishes, then one sees God.

"Rāma, who is God Himself, was only two and a half cubits ahead of Lakshmana. But Lakshmana couldn't see Him because Sītā stood between them. Lakshmana may be compared to the jīva, and Sītā to māyā. Man cannot see God on account of the barrier of māyā. Just look: I am creating a barrier in front of my face with this towel. Now you can't see me, even though I am so near. Likewise, God is the nearest of all, but we cannot see Him on account of this covering of māyā.

"The jīva is nothing but the embodiment of Satchidānanda. But since māyā, or ego, has created various upādhis, he has forgotten his real Self.

"Each upādhi changes man's nature. If he wears a fine black-bordered cloth, you will at once find him humming Nidhu Babu's love-songs. Then playing-cards and a walking-stick follow. If even a sickly man puts on high boots, he begins to whistle and climbs the stairs like an Englishman, jumping from one step to another. If a man but holds a pen in his hand, he scribbles on any paper he can get hold of—such is the power of the pen!

"Money is also a great upādhi. The possession of money makes such a difference in a man! He is no longer the same person. A brāhmin used to frequent the temple garden. Outwardly he was very modest. One day I went to Konnagar with Hriday. No sooner did we get off the boat than we noticed the brāhmin seated on the bank of the Ganges. We thought he had been enjoying the fresh air. Looking at us, he said: 'Hello there, priest! How do you do?' I marked his tone and said to Hriday: 'The man must have got some money. That's why he talks that way.' Hriday laughed.

"A frog had a rupee, which he kept in his hole. One day an elephant was going over the hole, and the frog, coming out in a fit of anger, raised his foot, as if to kick the elephant, and said, 'How dare you walk over my head?' Such is the pride that money begets!

"One can get rid of the ego after the attainment of Knowledge. On attaining Knowledge one goes into samādhi, and the ego disappears. But it is very difficult to obtain such Knowledge.

"It is said in the Vedas that a man experiences samādhi when his mind ascends to the seventh plane. The ego can disappear only when one goes into samādhi. Where does the mind of a man ordinarily dwell? In the first three planes. These are at the organs of evacuation and generation, and at the navel. Then the mind is immersed only in worldliness, attached to 'woman and gold'. A man sees the light of God when his mind dwells in the plane of the heart. He sees the light and exclaims: 'Ah! What is this? What is this?' The next plane is at the throat. When the mind dwells there he likes to hear and talk only of God. When the mind ascends to the next plane, in the forehead, between the eyebrows, he sees the form of Satchidānanda and desires to touch and embrace It. But he is unable to do so It is like the light in a lantern, which you can see but cannot touch. You feel as if you were touching the light, but in reality you are not. When the mind reaches the seventh plane, then the ego vanishes completely and the man goes into samādhi."

VIJAY: "What does a man see when he attains the Knowledge of Brahman after reaching the seventh plane?"

MASTER: "What happens when the mind reaches the seventh plane cannot be described.

"Once a boat enters the 'black waters' of the ocean, it does not return. Nobody knows what happens to the boat after that. Therefore the boat cannot give us any information about the ocean.

"Once a salt doll went to measure the depth of the ocean. No sooner did it enter the water than it melted. Now who could tell how deep the ocean was? That which could have told about its depth had melted. Reaching the seventh plane, the mind is annihilated; man goes into samādhi. What he feels then cannot be described in words.

"The 'I' that makes one a worldly person and attaches one to 'woman and gold' is the 'wicked I'. The intervention of this ego creates the difference between jīva and Ātman. Water appears to be divided into two parts if one puts a stick across it. But in reality there is only one water. It appears as two on account of the stick. This 'I' is the stick. Remove the stick and there remains only one water as before.

"Now, what is this 'wicked I'? It is the ego that says: 'What? Don't they know me? I have so much money! Who is wealthier than I?' If a thief robs such a man of only ten rupees, first of all he wrings the money out of the thief, then he gives him a good beating. But the matter doesn't end there: the thief is handed over to the police and is eventually sent to jail. The 'wicked I' says: 'What? Doesn't the rogue know whom he has robbed? To steal my ten rupees! How dare he?' "

VIJAY: "If without destroying the 'I' a man cannot get rid of attachment to the world and consequently cannot experience samādhi, then it would be wise for him to follow the path of Brahmajnāna to attain samādhi. If the 'I' persists in the path of devotion, then one should rather choose the path of knowledge."

MASTER: "It is true that one or two can get rid of the 'I' through samādhi; but these cases are very rare. You may indulge in thousands of reasonings, but still the 'I' comes back. You may cut the peepal-tree to the very root today, but you will notice a sprout springing up tomorrow. Therefore if the 'I' must remain, let the rascal remain as the 'servant I'. As long as you live, you should say, 'O God, Thou art the Master and I am Thy servant.' The 'I' that feels, 'I am the servant of God, I am His devotee' does not injure one. Sweet things cause acidity of the stomach, no doubt, but sugar candy is an exception.

"The path of knowledge is very difficult. One cannot obtain Knowledge unless one gets rid of the feeling that one is the body. In the Kaliyuga the life of man is centred on food. He cannot get rid of the feeling that he is the body, and the ego. Therefore the path of devotion is prescribed for this cycle.

This is an easy path. You will attain God if you sing His name and glories and pray to Him with a longing heart. There is not the least doubt about it.

"Suppose you draw a line on the surface of water with a bamboo stick. The water appears to be divided into two parts; but the line doesn't remain for any length of time. The 'servant I' or the 'devotee I' or the 'child I' is only a line drawn with the ego and is not real."

VIJAY (to the Master): "Sir, you ask us to renounce the 'wicked I'. Is there any harm in the 'servant I'?"

MASTER: "The 'servant I'—that is, the feeling, 'I am the servant of God, I am the devotee of God'—does not injure one. On the contrary, it helps one to realize God."

VIJAY: "Well, sir, what becomes of the lust, anger, and other passions of one who keeps the 'servant I'?"

MASTER: "If a man truly feels like that, then he has only the semblance of lust, anger, and the like. If, after attaining God, he looks on himself as the servant or the devotee of God, then he cannot injure anyone. By touching the philosopher's stone a sword is turned into gold. It keeps the appearance of a sword but cannot injure.

"When the dry branch of a coconut palm drops to the ground, it leaves only a mark on the trunk indicating that once there was a branch at that place. In like manner, he who has attained God keeps only an appearance of ego; there remains in him only a semblance of anger and lust. He becomes like a child. A child has no attachment to the three gunas—sattva, rajas, and tamas. He becomes as quickly detached from a thing as he becomes attached to it. You can cajole him out of a cloth worth five rupees with a doll worth an ānnā, though at first he may say with great determination: 'No, I won't give it to you. My daddy bought it for me.' Again, all persons are the same to a child. He has no feeling of high and low in regard to persons. So he doesn't discriminate about caste. If his mother tells him that a particular man should be regarded as an elder brother, the child will eat from the same plate with him, though the man may belong to the low caste of a blacksmith. The child doesn't know hate, or what is holy or unholy.

"Even after attaining samādhi, some retain the 'servant ego' or the 'devotee ego'. The bhakta keeps this 'I-consciousness'. He says, 'O God, Thou art the Master and I am Thy servant; Thou art the Lord and I am Thy devotee.' He feels that way even after the realization of God. His 'I' is not completely effaced. Again, by constantly practising this kind of 'I-consciousness', one ultimately attains God. This is called bhaktiyoga.

"One can attain the Knowledge of Brahman, too, by following the path of bhakti. God is all-powerful. He may give His devotee Brahmajnāna also, if He so wills. But the devotee generally doesn't seek the Knowledge of the Absolute. He would rather have the consciousness that God is the Master and he the servant, or that God is the Divine Mother and he the child."

VIJAY: "But those who discriminate according to the Vedānta philosophy also realize Him in the end, don't they?"

MASTER: "Yes, one may reach Him by following the path of discrimination too: that is called jnānayoga. But it is an extremely difficult path. I have told you already of the seven planes of consciousness. On reaching the seventh plane the mind goes into samādhi. If a man acquires the firm knowledge that Brahman alone is real and the world illusory, then his mind merges in samādhi. But in the Kaliyuga the life of a man depends entirely on food. How can he have the consciousness that Brahman alone is real and the world illusory? In the Kaliyuga it is difficult to have the feeling, 'I am not the body, I am not the mind, I am not the twenty-four cosmic principles; I am beyond pleasure and pain, I am above disease and grief, old age and death.' However you may reason and argue, the feeling that the body is identical with the soul will somehow crop up from an unexpected quarter. You may cut a peepal-tree to the ground and think it is dead to its very root, but the next morning you will find a new sprout shooting up from the dead stump. One cannot get rid of this identification with the body; therefore the path of bhakti is best for the people of the Kaliyuga. It is an easy path.

"And, 'I don't want to become sugar; I want to eat it.' I never feel like saying, 'I am Brahman.' I say, 'Thou art my Lord and I am Thy servant.' It is better to make the mind go up and down between the fifth and sixth planes, like a boat racing between two points. I don't want to go beyond the sixth plane and keep my mind a long time in the seventh. My desire is to sing the name and glories of God. It is very good to look on God as the Master and oneself as His servant. Further, you see, people speak of the waves as belonging to the Ganges; but no one says that the Ganges belongs to the waves. The feeling, 'I am He', is not wholesome. A man who entertains such an idea, while looking on his body as the Self, causes himself great harm. He cannot go forward in spiritual life; he drags himself down. He deceives himself as well as others. He cannot understand his own state of mind.

"But it isn't any and every kind of bhakti that enables one to realize God. One cannot realize God without premā-bhakti. Another name for premā-bhakti is rāga-bhakti.[4] God cannot be realized without love and longing. Unless one has learnt to love God, one cannot realize Him.

"There is another kind of bhakti, known as vaidhi-bhakti, according to which one must repeat the name of God a fixed number of times, fast, make pilgrimages, worship God with prescribed offerings, make so many sacrifices, and so forth and so on. By continuing such practices a long time one gradually acquires rāga-bhakti. God cannot be realized until one has rāga-bhakti. One must love God. In order to realize God one must be completely free from worldliness and direct all of one's mind to Him.

"But some acquire rāga-bhakti directly. It is innate in them. They have it from their very childhood. Even at an early age they weep for God. An instance of such bhakti is to be found in Prahlāda. Vaidhi-bhakti is like moving a fan to make a breeze. One needs the fan to make the breeze. Similarly, one practises japa, austerity, and fasting, in order to acquire love of God. But the fan is set aside when the southern breeze blows of itself.

---

[4] Supreme love, which makes one attached only to God.

Such actions as japa and austerity drop away when one spontaneously feels love and attachment for God. Who, indeed, will perform the ceremonies enjoined in the scriptures, when mad with love of God?

"Devotion to God may be said to be 'green' so long as it doesn't grow into love of God; but it becomes 'ripe' when it has grown into such love.

"A man with 'green' bhakti cannot assimilate spiritual talk and instruction; but one with 'ripe' bhakti can. The image that falls on a photographic plate covered with black film[5] is retained. On the other hand, thousands of images may be reflected on a bare piece of glass, but not one of them is retained. As the object moves away, the glass becomes the same as it was before. One cannot assimilate spiritual instruction unless one has already developed love of God."

VIJAY: "Is bhakti alone sufficient for the attainment of God, for His vision?"

MASTER: "Yes, one can see God through bhakti alone. But it must be 'ripe' bhakti, premā-bhakti and rāga-bhakti. When one has that bhakti, one loves God even as the mother loves the child, the child the mother, or the wife the husband.

"When one has such love and attachment for God, one doesn't feel the attraction of māyā to wife, children, relatives, and friends. One retains only compassion for them. To such a man the world appears a strange land, a place where he has merely to perform his duties. It is like a man's having his real home in the country, but coming to Calcutta for work; he has to rent a house in Calcutta for the sake of his duties. When one develops love of God, one completely gets rid of one's attachment to the world and worldly wisdom.

"One cannot see God if one has even the slightest trace of worldliness. Match-sticks, if damp, won't strike fire though you rub a thousand of them against the match-box. You only waste a heap of sticks. The mind soaked in worldliness is such a damp match-stick. Once Sri Rādhā said to her friends that she saw Krishna everywhere—both within and without. The friends answered: 'Why, we don't see Him at all. Are you delirious?' Rādhā said, 'Friends, paint your eyes with the collyrium of divine love, and then you will see Him.'

(To Vijay) "It is said in a song of your Brāhmo Samāj:

> O Lord, is it ever possible to know Thee without love,
> However much one may perform worship and sacrifice?

"If the devotee but once feels this attachment and ecstatic love for God, this mature devotion and longing, then he sees God in both His aspects, with form and without form."

VIJAY: "How can one see God?"

MASTER: "One cannot see God without purity of heart. Through attachment to 'woman and gold' the mind has become stained—covered with dirt, as it were. A magnet cannot attract a needle if the needle is covered with mud. Wash away the mud and the magnet will draw it. Likewise, the dirt

[5] Silver nitrate.

of the mind can be washed away with the tears of our eyes. This stain is removed if one sheds tears of repentance and says, 'O God, I shall never again do such a thing.' Thereupon God, who is like the magnet, draws to Himself the mind, which is like the needle. Then the devotee goes into samādhi and obtains the vision of God.

"You may try thousands of times, but nothing can be achieved without God's grace. One cannot see God without His grace. Is it an easy thing to receive the grace of God? One must altogether renounce egotism; one cannot see God as long as one feels, 'I am the doer.' Suppose, in a family, a man has taken charge of the store-room; then if someone asks the master, 'Sir, will you yourself kindly give me something from the store-room?', the master says to him: 'There is already someone in the store-room. What can I do there?'

"God doesn't easily appear in the heart of a man who feels himself to be his own master. But God can be seen the moment His grace descends. He is the Sun of Knowledge. One single ray of His has illumined the world with the light of knowledge. That is how we are able to see one another and acquire varied knowledge. One can see God only if He turns His light toward His own face.

"The police sergeant goes his rounds in the dark of night with a lantern[6] in his hand. No one sees his face; but with the help of that light the sergeant sees everybody's face, and others, too, can see one another. If you want to see the sergeant, however, you must pray to him: 'Sir, please turn the light on your own face. Let me see you.' In the same way one must pray to God: 'O Lord, be gracious and turn the light of knowledge on Thyself, that I may see Thy face.'

"A house without light indicates poverty. So one must light the lamp of Knowledge in one's heart. As it is said in a song:

> Lighting the lamp of Knowledge in the chamber of your heart,
> Behold the face of the Mother, Brahman's Embodiment."

As Vijay had brought medicine with him, the Master asked a devotee to give him some water. He was indeed a fountain of infinite compassion. He had arranged for Vijay's boat fare, since the latter was too poor to pay it. Vijay, Balaram, M., and the other devotees left for Calcutta in a country boat.

Monday, January 1, 1883

At eight o'clock in the morning Sri Ramakrishna was seated on a mat spread on the floor of his room at Dakshineswar. Since it was a cold day, he had wrapped his body in his moleskin shawl. Prankrishna and M. were seated in front of him. Rakhal, too, was in the room. Prankrishna was a high government official and lived in Calcutta. Since he had had no offspring by his first wife, with her permission he had married a second time. By the second wife he had a son. Because he was rather stout, the Master addressed

[6] A reference to the lantern carried by the night-watch, which has dark glass on three sides.

him now and then as "the fat brāhmin". He had great respect for Sri Ramakrishna. Though a householder, Prankrishna studied the Vedānta and had
been heard to say: "Brahman alone is real and the world illusory. I am He."
The Master used to say to him: "In the Kaliyuga the life of a man depends
on food. The path of devotion prescribed by Nārada is best for this age."

A devotee had brought a basket of jilipi for the Master, which the latter
kept by his side. Eating a bit of the sweets, he said to Prankrishna with a
smile: "You see, I chant the name of the Divine Mother; so I get all these
good things to eat. (Laughter.) But She doesn't give such fruits as gourd or
pumpkin. She bestows the fruit of Amrita, Immortality—knowledge, love,
discrimination, renunciation, and so forth."

A boy six or seven years old entered the room. The Master himself became
like a child. He covered the contents of the basket with the palm of his
hand, as a child does to conceal sweets from another child lest the latter
should snatch them. Then he put the basket aside.

Suddenly the Master went into samādhi and sat thus a long time. His
body was transfixed, his eyes wide open and unwinking, his breathing hardly
perceptible. After a long time he drew a deep breath, indicating his return
to the world of sense.

MASTER (to Prankrishna): "My Divine Mother is not only formless,
She has forms as well. One can see Her forms. One can behold Her incomparable beauty through feeling and love. The Mother reveals Herself to Her
devotees in different forms.

"I saw Her yesterday. She was clad in a seamless ochre-coloured garment,
and She talked with me.

"She came to me another day as a Mussalmān girl six or seven years old.
She had a tilak on her forehead and was naked. She walked with me, joking
and frisking like a child.

"At Hriday's house I had a vision of Gaurānga. He wore a black-bordered
cloth.

"Haladhari used to say that God is beyond both Being and Non-being. I
told the Mother about it and asked Her, 'Then is the divine form an illusion?' The Divine Mother appeared to me in the form of Rati's mother and
said, 'Do thou remain in bhāva.'[7] I repeated this to Haladhari. Now and
then I forget Her command and suffer. Once I broke my teeth because I
didn't remain in bhāva. So I shall remain in bhāva unless I receive a revelation from heaven or have a direct experience to the contrary. I shall follow
the path of love. What do you say?"

PRANKRISHNA: "Yes, sir."

MASTER: "But why should I ask you about it? There is Someone within
me who does all these things through me. At times I used to remain in a
mood of Godhood and would enjoy no peace of mind unless I were being
worshipped.

[7] A rare state of divine exaltation, when the devotee, after realizing the Absolute,
remains in the borderland between the Absolute and the Relative; in this state he sees
that both the Absolute and the Relative, as the two aspects of the Godhead, are real.

"I am the machine and God is the Operator. I act as He makes me act. I speak as He makes me speak.

> Keep your raft, says Rāmprasād, afloat on the sea of life,
> Drifting up with the flood-tide, drifting down with the ebb.

"It is like the cast-off leaf before a gale; sometimes it is blown to a good place and sometimes into the gutter, according to the direction of the wind.

"As the weaver said in the story: 'The robbery was committed by the will of Rāma, I was arrested by the police by the will of Rāma, and again, by the will of Rāma, I was set free.'

"Hanumān once said to Rāma: 'O Rāma, I have taken refuge in Thee. Bless me that I may have pure devotion to Thy Lotus Feet and that I may not be caught in the spell of Thy world-bewitching māyā.'

"Once a dying bullfrog said to Rāma: 'O Rāma, when caught by a snake I cry for Your protection. But now I am about to die, struck by Your arrow. Hence I am silent.'

"I used to see God directly with these very eyes, just as I see you. Now I see divine visions in trance.

"After realizing God a man becomes like a child. One acquires the nature of the object one meditates upon. The nature of God is like that of a child. As a child builds up his toy house and then breaks it down, so God acts while creating, preserving, and destroying the universe. Further, as the child is not under the control of any guna, so God is beyond the three gunas—sattva, rajas, and tamas. That is why paramahamsas keep five or ten children with them, that they may assume their nature."

Sitting on the floor in the room was a young man from Āgarpārā about twenty-two years old. Whenever he came to the temple garden, he would take the Master aside, by a sign, and whisper his thoughts to him. He was a new-comer. That day he was sitting on the floor near the Master.

MASTER (to the young man): "A man can change his nature by imitating another's character. He can get rid of a passion like lust by assuming the feminine mood. He gradually comes to act exactly like a woman. I have noticed that men who take female parts in the theatre speak like women or brush their teeth like women while bathing. Come again on a Tuesday or Saturday.

(To Prankrishna) "Brahman and Sakti are inseparable. Unless you accept Sakti, you will find the whole universe unreal—'I', 'you', house, buildings, and family. The world stands solid because the Primordial·Energy stands behind it. If there is no supporting pole, no framework can be made, and without the framework there can be no beautiful image of Durgā.

"Without giving up worldliness a man cannot awaken his spiritual consciousness, nor can he realize God. He cannot but be a hypocrite as long as he has even a trace of worldly desire. God cannot be realized without guilelessness.

> Cherish love within your heart; abandon cunning and deceit:
> Through service, worship, selflessness, does Rāma's blessed vision
>   come.

Even those engaged in worldly activities, such as office work or business, should hold to the truth. Truthfulness alone is the spiritual discipline in the Kaliyuga."

PRANKRISHNA: "Yes, sir. It is said in the *Mahānirvāna Tantra*: 'O Goddess, this religion enjoins it upon one to be truthful, self-controlled, devoted to the welfare of others, unagitated, and compassionate.'"

MASTER: "Yes. But these ideas must be assimilated."

Sri Ramakrishna was sitting on the small couch. He was in an ecstatic mood and looked at Rakhal. Suddenly he was filled with the tender feeling of parental love toward his young disciple and spiritual child. Presently he went into samādhi. The devotees sat speechless, looking at the Master with wondering eyes.

Regaining partial consciousness, the Master said: "Why is my spiritual feeling kindled at the sight of Rakhal? The more you advance toward God, the less you will see of His glories and grandeur. The aspirant at first has a vision of the Goddess with ten arms;[8] there is a great display of power in that image. The next vision is that of the Deity with two arms; there are no longer ten arms holding various weapons and missiles. Then the aspirant has a vision of Gopāla, in which there is no trace of power. It is the form of a tender child. Beyond that there are other visions also. The aspirant then sees only Light.

"Reasoning and discrimination vanish after the attainment of God and communion with Him in samādhi. How long does a man reason and discriminate? As long as he is conscious of the manifold, as long as he is aware of the universe, of embodied beings, of 'I' and 'you'. He becomes silent when he is truly aware of Unity. This was the case with Trailanga Swami.[9]

"Have you watched a feast given to the brāhmins? At first there is a great uproar. But the noise lessens as their stomachs become more and more filled with food. When the last course of curd and sweets is served, one hears only the sound 'soop, soop' as they scoop up the curd in their hands. There is no other sound. Next is the stage of sleep—samādhi. There is no more uproar.

(*To M. and Prankrishna*) "Many people talk of Brahmajnāna, but their minds are always preoccupied with lower things: house, buildings, money, name, and sense pleasures. As long as you stand at the foot of the Monument,[10] so long do you see horses, carriages, Englishmen, and English-women. But when you climb to its top, you behold the sky and the ocean stretching to infinity. Then you do not enjoy buildings, carriages, horses, or men. They look like ants.

"All such things as attachment to the world and enthusiasm for 'woman and gold' disappear after the attainment of the Knowledge of Brahman. Then comes the cessation of all passions. When the log burns, it makes a crackling noise and one sees the flame. But when the burning is over and

---

[8] The allusion is to the image of Durga.

[9] A noted monk of Benares whom the Master once met. The Swami observed a vow of silence.

[10] A reference to the Ochterloney Monument in Calcutta.

only ash remains, then no more noise is heard. Thirst disappears with the destruction of attachment. Finally comes peace.

"The nearer you come to God, the more you feel peace. Peace, peace, peace—supreme peace! The nearer you come to the Ganges, the more you feel its coolness. You will feel completely soothed when you plunge into the river.

"But the universe and its created beings, and the twenty-four cosmic principles, all exist because God exists. Nothing remains if God is eliminated. The number increases if you put many zeros after the figure one; but the zeros don't have any value if the one is not there."

The Master continued: "There are some who come down, as it were, after attaining the Knowledge of Brahman—after samādhi—and retain the 'ego of Knowledge' or the 'ego of Devotion', just as there are people who, of their own sweet will, stay in the market-place after the market breaks up. This was the case with sages like Nārada. They kept the 'ego of Devotion' for the purpose of teaching men. Śankarāchārya kept the 'ego of Knowledge' for the same purpose.

"God cannot be realized if there is the slightest attachment to the things of the world. A thread cannot pass through the eye of a needle if the tiniest fibre sticks out.

"The anger and lust of a man who has realized God are only appearances. They are like a burnt string. It looks like a string, but a mere puff blows it away.

"God is realized as soon as the mind becomes free from attachment. Whatever appears in the Pure Mind is the voice of God. That which is Pure Mind is also Pure Buddhi; that, again, is Pure Ātman, because there is nothing pure but God. But in order to realize God one must go beyond dharma and adharma."

The Master sang in his melodious voice:

Come, let us go for a walk, O mind, to Kāli, the Wish-fulfilling
    Tree,
And there beneath It gather the four fruits of life. . . .

Sri Ramakrishna went out on the southeast verandah of his room and sat down. Prankrishna and the other devotees accompanied him. Hazra, too, was sitting there. The Master said to Prankrishna with a smile: "Hazra is not a man to be trifled with. If one finds the big dargāh here,[11] then Hazra is the smaller dargāh." All laughed at the Master's words. A certain gentleman, Navakumar by name, came to the door and stood there. At sight of the devotees he immediately left. "Oh! Egotism incarnate!" Sri Ramakrishna remarked.

About half past nine in the morning Prankrishna took leave of the Master. Soon afterwards a minstrel sang some devotional songs to the accompaniment of a stringed instrument. The Master was listening to the songs when Kedar Chatterji, a householder devotee, entered the room clad in his office clothes. He was a man of devotional temperament and cherished the

[11] Referring to himself.

attitude of the gopis of Vrindāvan. Words about God would make him weep.

The sight of Kedar awakened in the Master's mind the episode of Vrindāvan in Sri Krishna's life. Intoxicated with divine love, the Master stood up and sang, addressing Kedar:

> Tell me, friend, how far is the grove
> Where Krishna, my Beloved, dwells?
> His fragrance reaches me even here;
> But I am tired and can walk no farther. . . .

Sri Ramakrishna assumed the attitude of Sri Rādhā to Krishna and went into deep samādhi while singing the song. He stood there, still as a picture on canvas, with tears of divine joy running down his cheeks.

Kedar knelt before the Master. Touching his feet, he chanted a hymn:

> We worship the Brahman-Consciousness in the Lotus of the Heart,
> The Undifferentiated, who is adored by Hari, Hara, and Brahmā;
> Who is attained by yogis in the depths of their meditation;
> The Scatterer of the fear of birth and death,
> The Essence of Knowledge and Truth, the Primal Seed of the world.

After a time the Master regained consciousness of the relative world. Soon Kedar took his leave and returned to his office in Calcutta.

At midday Ramlal brought the Master a plate of food that had been offered in the Kāli temple. Like a child he ate a little of everything.

Later in the afternoon several Mārwāri devotees entered the Master's room, where Rakhal and M. also were seated.

A Mārwāri devotee: "Sir, what is the way?"

Master: "There are two ways. One is the path of discrimination, the other is that of love. Discrimination means to know the distinction between the Real and the unreal. God alone is the real and permanent Substance; all else is illusory and impermanent. The magician alone is real; his magic is illusory. This is discrimination.

"Discrimination and renunciation. Discrimination means to know the distinction between the Real and the unreal. Renunciation means to have dispassion for the things of the world. One cannot acquire them all of a sudden. They must be practised every day. One should renounce 'woman and gold' mentally at first. Then, by the will of God, one can renounce it both mentally and outwardly. It is impossible to ask the people of Calcutta to renounce all for the sake of God. One has to tell them to renounce mentally.

"Through the discipline of constant practice one is able to give up attachment to 'woman and gold'. That is what the Gītā says. By practice one acquires uncommon power of mind. Then one doesn't find it difficult to subdue the sense-organs and to bring anger, lust, and the like under control. Such a man behaves like a tortoise, which, once it has tucked in its limbs, never puts them out. You cannot make the tortoise put its limbs out again, though you chop it to pieces with an axe."

MĀRWĀRI DEVOTEE: "Revered sir, you just mentioned two paths. What is the other path?"

MASTER: "The path of bhakti, or zealous love of God. Weep for God in solitude, with a restless soul, and ask Him to reveal Himself to you.

> Cry to your Mother Śyāmā with a real cry, O mind!
> And how can She hold Herself from you?"

MĀRWĀRI DEVOTEE: "Sir, what is the meaning of the worship of the Personal God? And what is the meaning of God without form or attribute?"

MASTER: "As you recall your father by his photograph, so likewise the worship of the image reveals in a flash the nature of Reality.

"Do you know what God with form is like? Like bubbles rising on an expanse of water, various divine forms are seen to rise out of the Great Ākāśa of Consciousness. The Incarnation of God is one of these forms. The Primal Energy sports, as it were, through the activities of a Divine Incarnation.

"What is there in mere scholarship? God can be attained by crying to Him with a longing heart. There is no need to know many things.

"He who is an āchārya has to know different things. One needs a sword and shield to kill others; but to kill oneself, a needle or a nail-knife suffices.

"One ultimately discovers God by trying to know who this 'I' is. Is this 'I' the flesh, the bones, the blood, or the marrow? Is it the mind or the buddhi? Analysing thus, you realize at last that you are none of these. This is called the process of 'Neti, neti', 'Not this, not this'. One can neither comprehend nor touch the Ātman. It is without qualities or attributes.

"But, according to the path of devotion, God has attributes. To a devotee Krishna is Spirit, His Abode is Spirit, and everything about Him is Spirit."

The Mārwāri devotees saluted the Master and took their leave.

At the approach of evening Sri Ramakrishna went out to look at the sacred river. The lamp was lighted in his room. The Master chanted the hallowed name of the Divine Mother and meditated on Her. Then the evening worship began in the various temples. The sound of gongs, floating on the air, mingled with the murmuring voice of the river. Peace and blessedness reigned everywhere.

THE MASTER'S BIRTHDAY
CELEBRATION AT
DAKSHINESWAR

Sunday, February 18, 1883

SRI RAMAKRISHNA arrived at Govinda Mukherji's house at Belgharia, near
Calcutta. Besides Narendra, Ram, and other devotees, some of Govinda's
neighbours were present. The Master first sang and danced with the
devotees. After the kirtan they sat down. Many saluted the Master. Now
and then he would say, "Bow before God."

"It is God alone", he said, "who has become all this. But in certain places—
for instance, in a holy man—there is a greater manifestation than in others.
You may say, there are wicked men also. That is true, even as there are
tigers and lions; but one need not hug the 'tiger God'. One should keep
away from him and salute him from a distance. Take water, for instance.
Some water may be drunk, some may be used for worship, some for bathing,
and some only for washing dishes."

A NEIGHBOUR: "Revered sir, what are the doctrines of Vedānta?"

MASTER: "The Vedāntist says, 'I am He.' Brahman is real and the world
illusory. Even the 'I' is illusory. Only the Supreme Brahman exists.

"But the 'I' cannot be got rid of. Therefore it is good to have the feeling,
'I am the servant of God, His son, His devotee.'

"For the Kaliyuga the path of bhakti is especially good. One can realize
God through bhakti too. As long as one is conscious of the body, one is also
conscious of objects. Form, taste, smell, sound, and touch—these are the
objects. It is extremely difficult to get rid of the consciousness of objects. And
one cannot realize 'I am He' as long as one is aware of objects.

"The sannyāsi is very little conscious of worldly objects. But the householder is always engrossed in them. Therefore it is good for him to feel,
'I am the servant of God.'"

NEIGHBOUR: "Sir, we are sinners. What will happen to us?"

MASTER: "All the sins of the body fly away if one chants the name of
God and sings His glories. The birds of sin dwell in the tree of the body.
Singing the name of God is like clapping your hands. As, at a clap of the

hands, the birds in the tree fly away, so do our sins disappear at the chanting of God's name and glories.

"Again, you find that the water of a reservoir dug in a meadow is evaporated by the heat of the sun. Likewise, the water of the reservoir of sin is dried up by the singing of the name and glories of God.

"You must practise it every day. The other day, at the circus, I saw a horse running at top speed, with an Englishwoman standing on one foot on its back. How much she must have practised to acquire that skill!

"Weep at least once to see God.

"These, then, are the two means: practice and passionate attachment to God, that is to say, restlessness of the soul to see Him."

Sri Ramakrishna began his midday meal with the devotees. It was about one o'clock. A devotee sang in the courtyard below:

> Awake, Mother! Awake! How long Thou hast been asleep
> In the lotus of the Mulādhāra!
> Fulfil Thy secret function, Mother:
> Rise to the thousand-petalled lotus within the head,
> Where mighty Śiva has His dwelling;
> Swiftly pierce the six lotuses
> And take away my grief, O Essence of Consciousness!

Hearing the song, Sri Ramakrishna went into samādhi; his whole body became still, and his hand remained touching the plate of food. He could eat no more. After a long time his mind came down partially to the plane of the sense world, and he said, "I want to go downstairs." A devotee led him down very carefully. Still in an abstracted mood, he sat near the singer. The song had ended. The Master said to him very humbly, "Sir, I want to hear the chanting of the Mother's name again."

The musician sang:

> Awake, Mother! Awake! How long Thou hast been asleep
> In the lotus of the Mulādhāra! . . .

The Master again went into ecstasy.

February 25, 1883

After his noon meal the Master conversed with the devotees. Ram, Kedar, Nityagopal, M., and others had arrived from Calcutta. Rakhal, Harish, Latu, and Hazra were living with the Master. Mr. Choudhury, who had three or four university degrees and was a government officer, was also present. He had recently lost his wife and had visited the Master several times for peace of mind.

MASTER (to Ram and the other devotees): "Devotees like Rakhal, Narendra, and Bhavanath may be called nityasiddha. Their spiritual consciousness has been awake since their very birth. They assume human bodies only to impart spiritual illumination to others.

"There is another class of devotees, known as kripāsiddha, that is to say, those on whom the grace of God descends all of a sudden and who at once

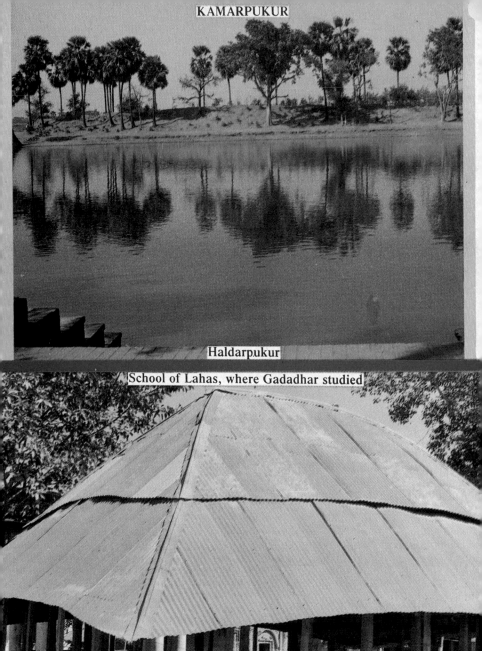

KAMARPUKUR

Haldarpukur

School of Lahas, where Gadadhar studied

attain His vision and Knowledge. Such people may be likened to a room that has been dark a thousand years, which, when a lamp is brought into it, becomes light immediately, not little by little.

"Those who lead a householder's life should practise spiritual discipline; they should pray eagerly to God in solitude. (*To Mr. Choudhury*) God cannot be realized through scholarship. Who, indeed, can understand the things of the Spirit through reason? No, all should strive for devotion to the Lotus Feet of God.

"Infinite are the glories of God! How little can you fathom them! Can you ever find out the meaning of God's ways?

"Bhishma was none other than one of the eight Vasus, but even he shed tears on his bed of arrows. He said: 'How astonishing! God Himself is the companion of the Pāndava brothers, and still there is no end to their troubles and sorrows!' Who can ever understand the ways of God?

"A man thinks, 'I have practised a little prayer and austerity; so I have gained a victory over others.' But victory and defeat lie with God. I have seen a prostitute dying in the Ganges and retaining consciousness[1] to the end."

MR. CHOUDHURY: "How can one see God?"

MASTER: "Not with these eyes. God gives one divine eyes; and only then can one behold Him. God gave Arjuna divine eyes so that he might see His Universal Form.[2]

"Your philosophy is mere speculation. It only reasons. God cannot be realized that way.

"God cannot remain unmoved if you have rāga-bhakti, that is, love of God with passionate attachment to Him. Do you know how fond God is of His devotees' love? It is like the cow's fondness for fodder mixed with oil-cake. The cow gobbles it down greedily.

"Rāga-bhakti is pure love of God, a love that seeks God alone and not any worldly end. Prahlāda had it. Suppose you go to a wealthy man every day, but you seek no favour of him; you simply love to see him. If he wants to show you favour, you say: 'No, sir. I don't need anything. I came just to see you.' Such is love of God for its own sake. You simply love God and don't want anything from Him in return."

Saying this, the Master sang:

> Though I[3] am never loath to grant salvation,
> I hesitate indeed to grant pure love.
> Whoever wins pure love surpasses all;
> He is adored by men;
> He triumphs over the three worlds. . . .

He continued, "The gist of the whole thing is that one must develop passionate yearning for God and practise discrimination and renunciation."

MR. CHOUDHURY: "Sir, is it not possible to have the vision of God without the help of a guru?"

[1] Dying in the Ganges while retaining full consciousness is considered by the Hindus an act of great spiritual merit and the result of pious living.
[2] An allusion to the eleventh chapter of the *Bhagavad Gītā*.
[3] The song represents Sri Krishna's words.

MASTER: "Satchidānanda Himself is the Guru. At the end of the śava-sādhanā, just when the vision of the Ishta is about to take place, the guru appears before the aspirant and says to him, 'Behold! There is your Ishta.' Saying this, the guru merges in the Ishta. He who is the guru is also the Ishta. The guru is the thread that leads to God. Women perform a ritualistic worship known as the 'Ananta-vrata', the object of worship being the Infinite. But actually the Deity worshipped is Vishnu. In Him are the 'infinite' forms of God.

(To Ram and the other devotees) "If you asked me which form of God you should meditate upon, I should say: Fix your attention on that form which appeals to you most; but know for certain that all forms are the forms of one God alone.

"Never harbour malice toward anyone. Śiva, Kāli, and Hari are but different forms of that One. He is blessed indeed who has known all as one.

> Outwardly he appears as Śiva's devotee,
> But in his heart he worships Kāli, the Blissful Mother,
> And with his tongue he chants aloud Lord Hari's name.

"The body does not endure without a trace of lust, anger, and the like. You should try to reduce them to a minimum."

Looking at Kedar, the Master said: "He is very nice. He accepts both the Absolute and the Relative. He believes in Brahman, but he also accepts the gods and Divine Incarnations in human form."

In Kedar's opinion Sri Ramakrishna was such an Incarnation.

Looking at Nityagopal, the Master said to the devotees, "He is in a lofty mood.

(To Nityagopal) "Don't go there too often. You may go once in a while. She may be a devotee, but she is a woman too. Therefore I warn you.

"The sannyāsi must observe very strict discipline. He must not look even at the picture of a woman. But this rule doesn't apply to householders. An aspirant should not associate with a woman, even though she is very much devoted to God. A sannyāsi, even though he may have subdued his passions, should follow this discipline to set an example to householders.

"Worldly people learn renunciation by seeing the complete renunciation of a monk; otherwise they sink more and more. A sannyāsi is a world teacher."

Friday, March 9, 1883

About nine o'clock in the morning the Master was seated in his room with Rakhal, M., and a few other devotees. It was the day of the new moon. As usual with him on such days, Sri Ramakrishna entered again and again into communion with the Divine Mother. He said to the devotees: "God alone exists, and all else is unreal. The Divine Mother has kept all deluded by Her māyā. Look at men. Most of them are entangled in worldliness. They suffer so much, but still they have the same attachment to 'woman and gold'. The camel eats thorny shrubs, and blood gushes from its mouth; still it will eat thorns. While suffering pain at the time of delivery, a woman says, 'Ah! I shall never go to my husband again.' But afterwards she forgets.

"The truth is that no one seeks God. There are people who eat the prickly leaves of the pineapple and not the fruit."

DEVOTEE: "Sir, why has God put us in the world?"

MASTER: "The world is the field of action. Through action one acquires knowledge. The guru instructs the disciple to perform certain works and refrain from others. Again, he advises the pupil to perform action without desiring the result. The impurity of the mind is destroyed through the performance of duty. It is like getting rid of a disease by means of medicine, under the instruction of a competent physician.

"Why doesn't God free us from the world? Ah, He will free us when the disease is cured. He will liberate us from the world when we are through with the enjoyment of 'woman and gold'. Once a man registers his name in the hospital, he cannot run away. The doctor will not let him go away unless his illness is completely cured."

During these days Sri Ramakrishna's heart overflowed with motherly love like the love Yaśodā felt for Krishna. So he kept Rakhal with him. Rakhal felt toward the Master as a child feels toward its mother. He would sit leaning on the Master's lap as a young child leans on its mother while sucking her breast.

Rakhal was thus seated by the Master when a man entered the room and said that a high tide was coming in the Ganges. The Master and the devotees ran to the Panchavati to see it. At the sight of a boat being tossed by the tide, Sri Ramakrishna exclaimed: "Look! Look! I hope nothing happens to it."

They all sat in the Panchavati. The Master asked M. to explain the cause of the tide. M. drew on the ground the figures of the sun, moon, and earth and tried to explain gravitation, ebb-tide, flood-tide, new moon, full moon, eclipse, and so forth.

MASTER (to M.): "Stop it! I can't follow you. It makes me dizzy. My head is aching. Well, how can they know of things so far off?

"You see, during my childhood I could paint well; but arithmetic would make my head spin. I couldn't learn simple arithmetic."

Sri Ramakrishna returned to his room with the devotees. Looking at a picture of Yaśodā, on the wall, he said: "It is not well done. She looks like a garland-seller."

The Master enjoyed a nap after his noon meal. Adhar and other devotees gradually gathered. This was Adhar's first visit. He was a deputy magistrate and about thirty years old.

ADHAR (to the Master): "Sir, I have a question to ask. Is it good to sacrifice animals before the Deity? It certainly involves killing."

MASTER: "The śāstra prescribes sacrifice on special occasions. Such sacrifice is not harmful. Take, for instance, the sacrifice of a goat on the eighth day of the full or new moon.

"I am now in such a state of mind that I cannot watch a sacrifice. Also I cannot eat meat offered to the Divine Mother. Therefore I first touch my finger to it, then to my head, lest She should be angry with me.

"Again, in a certain state of mind I see God in all beings, even in an ant. At that time, if I see a living being die, I find consolation in the thought that it is the death of the body, the soul being beyond life and death.

"One should not reason too much; it is enough if one loves the Lotus Feet of the Mother. Too much reasoning throws the mind into confusion. You get clear water if you drink from the surface of a pool. Put your hand deeper and stir the water, and it becomes muddy. Therefore pray to God for devotion.

"Behind Dhruva's devotion there was desire. He practised austerities to gain his father's kingdom. But Prahlāda's love for God was motiveless—a love that sought no return."

A DEVOTEE: "How can one realize God?"

MASTER: "Through that kind of love. But one must force one's demand on God. One should be able to say: 'O God, wilt Thou not reveal Thyself to me? I will cut my throat with a knife.' This is the tamas of bhakti."

DEVOTEE: "Can one see God?"

MASTER: "Yes, surely. One can see both aspects of God—God with form and without form. One can see God with form, the Embodiment of Spirit. Again, God can be directly perceived in a man with a tangible form. Seeing an Incarnation of God is the same as seeing God Himself. God is born on earth as man in every age."

March 11, 1883

It was Sri Ramakrishna's birthday. Many of his disciples and devotees wanted to celebrate the happy occasion at the Dakshineswar temple garden.

From early morning the devotees streamed in, alone or in parties. After the morning worship in the temples sweet music was played in the nahabat. It was springtime. The trees, creepers, and plants were covered with new leaves and blossoms. The very air seemed laden with joy. And the hearts of the devotees were glad on this auspicious day.

M. arrived early in the morning and found the Master talking smilingly to Bhavanath, Rakhal, and Kalikrishna. M. prostrated himself before him.

MASTER (to M.): "I am glad you have come."

(To the devotees) "One cannot be spiritual as long as one has shame, hatred, or fear. Great will be the joy today. But those fools who will not sing or dance, mad with God's name, will never attain God. How can one feel any shame or fear when the names of God are sung? Now sing, all of you."

Bhavanath and his friend Kalikrishna sang:

> Thrice blessed is this day of joy!
> May all of us unite, O Lord,
> To preach Thy true religion here
> In India's holy land!
> Thou dwellest in each human heart;
> Thy name, resounding everywhere,

Fills the four corners of the sky.
Today Thy devotees proclaim
Thy boundless majesty.

We seek not wealth or friends or fame,
O Lord! No other hope is ours.
For Thee alone Thy devotees
Long with unflagging love.
Safe at Thy feet, what fear have we
Of death or danger? We have found
The Fount of Immortality.
To Thee the victory, O Lord!
To Thee the victory!

As Sri Ramakrishna listened to the song with folded hands, his mind soared to a far-off realm. He remained absorbed in meditation a long time. After a while Kalikrishna whispered something to Bhavanath. Then he bowed before the Master and rose. Sri Ramakrishna was surprised. He asked, "Where are you going?"

BHAVANATH: "He is going away on a little business."

MASTER: "What is it about?"

BHAVANATH: "He is going to the Barānagore Workingmen's Institute."

MASTER: "It's his bad luck. A stream of bliss will flow here today. He could have enjoyed it. But how unlucky!"

Sri Ramakrishna did not feel well; so he decided not to bathe in the Ganges. About nine o'clock a few jars of water were taken from the river, and with the help of the devotees he finished his bath on the verandah east of his room.

After bathing, the Master put on a new wearing-cloth, all the while chanting the name of God. Accompanied by one or two disciples he walked across the courtyard to the temple of Kāli, still chanting Her hallowed name. His eyes had an indrawn look, like that of a bird hatching her eggs.

On entering the temple, he prostrated himself before the image and worshipped the Divine Mother. But he did not observe any ritual of worship. Now he would offer flowers and sandal-paste at the feet of the image, and now he would put them on his own head. After finishing the worship in his own way, he asked Bhavanath to carry the green coconut that had been offered to the Mother. He also visited the images of Rādhā and Krishna in the Vishnu temple.

When the Master returned to his room, he found that other devotees had arrived, among them Ram, Nityagopal, and Kedar. They all saluted the Master, who greeted them cordially.

He asked Nityagopal, "Will you eat something now?" "Yes", the devotee answered. Nityagopal, who was twenty-three or twenty-four years old and unmarried, was like a child. His mind was always soaring in the spiritual realm. He visited the Master sometimes alone and sometimes in Ram's company. The Master had observed the spiritual state of his mind and had become very fond of him. He remarked now and then that Nityagopal was in the state of a paramahamsa.

After Nityagopal had finished eating, the Master took him aside and gave him various instructions.

A certain woman, about thirty-one years old and a great devotee, often visited Sri Ramakrishna and held him in high respect. She had been much impressed by Nityagopal's spiritual state and, looking upon him as her own son, often invited him to her house.

MASTER (to Nityagopal): "Do you go there?"

NITYAGOPAL (like a child): "Yes, I do. She takes me."

MASTER: "Beware, holy man! Go there once in a great while, but not frequently; otherwise you will slip from the ideal. Māyā is nothing but 'woman and gold'. A holy man must live away from woman. All sink there. 'Even Brahmā and Vishnu struggle for life in that whirlpool.' "

Nityagopal listened to these words attentively.

M. (to himself): "How strange! This young man has developed the state of a paramahamsa. That is what the Master says now and then. Is there still a possibility of his falling into danger in spite of his high spiritual state? What an austere rule is laid down for a sādhu! He may slip from his ideal by associating intimately with women. How can an ordinary man expect to attain liberation unless such a high ideal is set by holy men? The woman in question is very devout; but still there is danger. Now I understand why Chaitanya punished his disciple, the younger Haridās, so severely. In spite of his teacher's prohibition, Haridās conversed with a widow devotee. But he was a sannyāsi. Therefore Chaitanya banished him. What a severe punishment! How hard is the rule for one who has accepted the life of renunciation! Again, what love the Master cherishes for this devotee! He is warning him even now, lest he should run into danger in the future."

"Beware, holy man!" These words of the Master echoed in the hearts of the devotees, like the distant rumbling of thunder.

The Master went with the devotees to the northeast verandah of his room. Among them was a householder from the village of Dakshineswar, who studied Vedānta philosophy at home. He had been discussing Om with Kedar before the Master. He said, "This Eternal Word, the Anāhata Sabda, is ever present both within and without."

MASTER: "But the Word is not enough. There must be something indicated by the Word. Can your name alone make me happy? Complete happiness is not possible for me unless I see you."

DEVOTEE: "That Eternal Word itself is Brahman."

MASTER (to Kedar): "Oh, don't you understand? He upholds the doctrine of the rishis of olden times. They once said to Rāma: 'O Rāma, we know You only as the son of Daśaratha. Let sages like Bharadvāja worship You as God Incarnate. We want to realize Brahman, the Indivisible Existence-Knowledge-Bliss Absolute.' At these words Rāma smiled and went away."

KEDAR: "Those rishis could not recognize Rāma as an Incarnation of God. They must have been fools."

MASTER (seriously): "Please don't say such a thing. People worship God

according to their tastes and temperaments. The mother cooks the same fish
differently for her children, that each one may have what suits his stomach.
For some she cooks the rich dish of pilau. But not all the children can digest
it. For those with weak stomachs she prepares soup. Some, again, like fried
fish or pickled fish. It depends on one's taste.

"The rishis followed the path of jnāna. Therefore they sought to realize
Brahman, the Indivisible Existence-Knowledge-Bliss Absolute. But those who
follow the path of devotion seek an Incarnation of God, to enjoy the sweetness of bhakti. The darkness of the mind disappears when God is realized.
In the Purāna it is said that it was as if a hundred suns were shining when
Rāma entered the court. Why, then, weren't the courtiers burnt up? It was
because the brilliance of Rāma was not like that of a material object. As
the lotus blooms when the sun rises, so the lotus of the heart of the people
assembled in the court burst into blossom."

As the Master uttered these words, standing before the devotees, he suddenly fell into an ecstatic mood. His mind was withdrawn from external
objects. No sooner did he say, "the lotus of the heart burst into blossom",
than he went into deep samādhi. He stood motionless, his countenance
beaming and his lips parted in a smile.

After a long time he returned to the normal consciousness of the world.
He drew a long breath and repeatedly chanted the name of Rāma, every
word showering nectar into the hearts of the devotees. The Master sat down,
the others seating themselves around him.

MASTER (to the devotees): "Ordinary people do not recognize the advent
of an Incarnation of God. He comes in secret. Only a few of His intimate
disciples can recognize Him. That Rāma was both Brahman Absolute and a
perfect Incarnation of God in human form was known only to twelve rishis.
The other sages said to Him, 'Rāma, we know You only as Daśaratha's son.'

"Can everyone comprehend Brahman, the Indivisible Existence-Knowledge-
Bliss Absolute? He alone has attained perfect love of God who, having
reached the Absolute, keeps himself in the realm of the Relative in order
to enjoy the divine līlā. A man can describe the ways and activities of the
Queen[4] if he has previously visited her in England. Only then will his
description of the Queen be correct. Sages like Bharadvāja adored Rāma and
said: 'O Rāma, You are nothing but the Indivisible Satchidānanda. You
have appeared before us as a human being, but You look like a man because
You have shrouded Yourself with Your own māyā.' These rishis were great
devotees of Rāma and had supreme love for God."

Presently some devotees from Konnagar arrived, singing kirtan to the
accompaniment of drums and cymbals. As they reached the northeast
verandah of Sri Ramakrishna's room, the Master joined in the music, dancing with them intoxicated with divine joy. Now and then he went into
samādhi, standing still as a statue. While he was in one of these states of
divine unconsciousness, the devotees put thick garlands of jasmine around
his neck. The enchanting form of the Master reminded the devotees of
Chaitanya, another Incarnation of God. The Master passed alternately

[4] Queen Victoria.

through three moods of divine consciousness: the inmost, when he completely lost all knowledge of the outer world; the semi-conscious, when he danced with the devotees in an ecstasy of love; and the conscious, when he joined them in loud singing. It was indeed a sight for the gods, to see the Master standing motionless in samādhi, with fragrant garlands hanging from his neck, his countenance beaming with love, and the devotees singing and dancing around him.

When it was time for his noon meal, Sri Ramakrishna put on a new yellow cloth and sat on the small couch. His golden complexion, blending with his yellow cloth, enchanted the eyes of the devotees.

After his meal Sri Ramakrishna rested a little on the small couch. Inside and outside his room crowded the devotees, among them Kedar, Suresh, Ram, Manomohan, Girindra, Rakhal, Bhavanath, and M. Rakhal's father was also present.

A Vaishnava goswāmi was seated in the room. The Master said to him: "Well, what do you say? What is the way?"

GOSWĀMI: "Sir, the chanting of God's name is enough. The scriptures emphasize the sanctity of God's name for the Kaliyuga."

MASTER: "Yes, there is no doubt about the sanctity of God's name. But can a mere name achieve anything, without the yearning love of the devotee behind it? One should feel great restlessness of soul for the vision of God. Suppose a man repeats the name of God mechanically, while his mind is absorbed in 'woman and gold'. Can he achieve anything? Mere muttering of magic words doesn't cure one of the pain of a spider or scorpion sting. One must also apply the smoke of burning cow-dung."[5]

GOSWĀMI: "But what about Ajāmila then? He was a great sinner; there was no sin he had not indulged in. But he uttered the name of Nārāyana on his death-bed, calling his son, who also had that name. And thus he was liberated."

MASTER: "Perhaps Ajāmila had done many spiritual things in his past births. It is also said that he once practised austerity; besides, those were the last moments of his life. What is the use of giving an elephant a bath? It will cover itself with dirt and dust again and become its former self. But if someone removes the dust from its body and gives it a bath just before it enters the stable, then the elephant remains clean.

"Suppose a man becomes pure by chanting the holy name of God, but immediately afterwards commits many sins. He has no strength of mind. He doesn't take a vow not to repeat his sins. A bath in the Ganges undoubtedly absolves one of all sins; but what does that avail? They say that the sins perch on the trees along the bank of the Ganges. No sooner does the man come back from the holy waters than the old sins jump on his shoulders from the trees. (All laugh.) The same old sins take possession of him again. He is hardly out of the water before they fall upon him.

"Therefore I say, chant the name of God, and with it pray to Him that you may have love for Him. Pray to God that your attachment to such

[5] A primitive medicine used by the villagers for scorpion bites.

transitory things as wealth, name, and creature comforts may become less and less every day.

(*To the goswāmi*) "With sincerity and earnestness one can realize God through all religions. The Vaishnavas will realize God, and so will the Śāktas, the Vedāntists, and the Brāhmos. The Mussalmāns and Christians will realize Him too. All will certainly realize God if they are earnest and sincere.

"Some people indulge in quarrels, saying, 'One cannot attain anything unless one worships our Krishna', or, 'Nothing can be gained without the worship of Kāli, our Divine Mother', or, 'One cannot be saved without accepting the Christian religion.' This is pure dogmatism. The dogmatist says, 'My religion alone is true, and the religions of others are false.' This is a bad attitude. God can be reached by different paths.

"Further, some say that God has form and is not formless. Thus they start quarrelling. A Vaishnava quarrels with a Vedāntist.

"One can rightly speak of God only after one has seen Him. He who has seen God knows really and truly that God has form and that He is formless as well. He has many other aspects that cannot be described.

"Once some blind men chanced to come near an animal that someone told them was an elephant. They were asked what the elephant was like. The blind men began to feel its body. One of them said the elephant was like a pillar; he had touched only its leg. Another said it was like a winnowing-fan; he had touched only its ear. In this way the others, having touched its tail or belly, gave their different versions of the elephant. Just so, a man who has seen only one aspect of God limits God to that alone. It is his conviction that God cannot be anything else.

(*To the goswāmi*) "How can you say that the only truth about God is that He has form? It is undoubtedly true that God comes down to earth in a human form, as in the case of Krishna. And it is true as well that God reveals Himself to His devotees in various forms. But it is also true that God is formless; He is the Indivisible Existence-Knowledge-Bliss Absolute. He has been described in the Vedas both as formless and as endowed with form. He is also described there both as attributeless and as endowed with attributes.

"Do you know what I mean? Satchidānanda is like an infinite ocean. Intense cold freezes the water into ice, which floats on the ocean in blocks of various forms. Likewise, through the cooling influence of bhakti, one sees forms of God in the Ocean of the Absolute. These forms are meant for the bhaktas, the lovers of God. But when the Sun of Knowledge rises, the ice melts; it becomes the same water it was before. Water above and water below, everywhere nothing but water. Therefore a prayer in the *Bhāgavata* says: 'O Lord, Thou hast form, and Thou art also formless. Thou walkest before us, O Lord, in the shape of a man; again, Thou hast been described in the Vedas as beyond words and thought.'

"But you may say that for certain devotees God assumes eternal forms. There are places in the ocean where the ice doesn't melt at all. It assumes the form of quartz."

KEDAR: "It is said in the *Bhāgavata* that Vyāsa asked God's forgiveness for his three transgressions. He said: 'O Lord, Thou art formless, but I have thought of Thee in my meditation as endowed with form; Thou art beyond speech, but I have sung Thee hymns; Thou art the All-pervading Spirit, but I have made pilgrimages to sacred places. Be gracious, O Lord, and forgive these three transgressions of mine.'"

MASTER: "Yes, God has form and He is formless too. Further, He is beyond both form and formlessness. No one can limit Him."

Rakhal's father was sitting in the room. At that time Rakhal was staying with the Master. After his mother's death his father had married a second time. Now and then he came to Dakshineswar because of Rakhal's being there. He did not raise much objection to his son's living with the Master. Being a wealthy man of the world, he was always involved in litigation. There were lawyers and deputy magistrates among Sri Ramakrishna's visitors. Rakhal's father found it profitable to cultivate their acquaintance, since he expected to be benefited by their counsels in worldly matters.

Now and then the Master cast a glance at Rakhal's father. It was his cherished desire that Rakhal should live with him permanently at Dakshineswar.

MASTER (*to Rakhal's father and the devotees*): "Ah, what a nice character Rakhal has developed! Look at his face and every now and then you will notice his lips moving. Inwardly he repeats the name of God, and so his lips move.

"Youngsters like him belong to the class of the ever-perfect. They are born with God-Consciousness. No sooner do they grow a little older than they realize the danger of coming in contact with the world. There is the parable of the homā bird in the Vedas. The bird lives high up in the sky and never descends to earth. It lays its egg in the sky, and the egg begins to fall. But the bird lives in such a high region that the egg hatches while falling. The fledgling comes out and continues to fall. But it is still so high that while falling it grows wings and its eyes open. Then the young bird perceives that it is dashing down toward the earth and will be instantly killed. The moment it sees the ground, it turns and shoots up toward its mother in the sky. Then its one goal is to reach its mother.

"Youngsters like Rakhal are like that bird. From their very childhood they are afraid of the world, and their one thought is how to reach the Mother, how to realize God.

"You may ask, 'How is it possible for these boys, born of worldly parents and living among the worldly-minded, to develop such knowledge and devotion?' It can be explained. If a pea falls into a heap of dung, it germinates into a pea-plant none the less. The peas that grow on that plant serve many useful purposes. Because it was sown in dung, will it produce another kind of plant?

"Ah, what a sweet nature Rakhal has nowadays! And why shouldn't it be so? If the yam is a good one, its shoots also become good. (*All laugh.*) Like father like son."

M. (aside to Girindra): "How well he has explained God with and without form! Do the Vaishnavas believe only in God with form?"

GIRINDRA: "Perhaps so. They are one-sided."

M: "Did you understand what he meant by the 'eternal form' of God? That 'quartz'? I couldn't grasp it well."

MASTER (to M.): "Well, what are you talking about?"

M. and Girindra smiled and remained silent.

Later in the afternoon the devotees were singing in the Panchavati, where the Master joined them. They sang together in praise of the Divine Mother:

> High in the heaven of the Mother's feet, my mind was soaring
>   like a kite,
> When came a blast of sin's rough wind that drove it swiftly toward
>   the earth.
> Māyā disturbed its even flight by bearing down upon one side,
> And I could make it rise no more.
> Entangled in the twisting string of love for children and for wife,
> Alas! my kite was rent in twain.
>
> It lost its crest of wisdom soon and downward plunged as I let it go;
> How could it hope to fly again, when all its top was torn away?
> Though fastened with devotion's cord, it came to grief in playing
>   here;
> Its six opponents[6] worsted it.
> Now Nareschandra rues this game of smiles and tears, and thinks
>   it better
> Never to have played at all.

The singing continued. Sri Ramakrishna danced with the devotees. They sang:

> The black bee of my mind is drawn in sheer delight
> To the blue lotus flower of Mother Śyāmā's feet,
> The blue flower of the feet of Kāli, Śiva's Consort;
> Tasteless, to the bee, are the blossoms of desire.
> My Mother's feet are black, and black, too, is the bee;
> Black is made one with black! This much of the mystery
> My mortal eyes behold, then hastily retreat.
> But Kamalākānta's hopes are answered in the end;
> He swims in the Sea of Bliss, unmoved by joy or pain.

The kirtan went on:

> O Mother, what a machine[7] is this that Thou hast made!
> What pranks Thou playest with this toy
> Three and a half cubits high!
> Hiding Thyself within, Thou holdest the guiding string;
> But the machine, not knowing it,
> Still believes it moves by itself.
> Whoever finds the Mother remains a machine no more;

[6] The six passions.
[7] The human body.

15

Yet some machines have even bound
The Mother Herself with the string of Love.

It was a very happy day for all.

The Master, accompanied by M., was coming back to his room, when he met Trailokya, a Brāhmo devotee, on the way. Trailokya bowed before the Master.

MASTER: "They are singing in the Panchavati. Won't you go there?"

TRAILOKYA: "What shall I do there?"

MASTER: "Why, you will enjoy the music."

TRAILOKYA: "I have been there already."

MASTER: "Well, well! That's good."

It was about six o'clock in the evening. The Master was sitting with the devotees on the southeast verandah of his room.

MASTER: "A holy man who has renounced the world will of course chant the name of God. That is only natural. He has no other duties to perform. If he meditates on God it shouldn't surprise anybody. On the other hand, if he fails to think of God or chant His holy name, then people will think ill of him.

"But it is a great deal to his credit if a householder utters the name of the Lord. Think of King Janaka. What courage he had, indeed! He fenced with two swords, the one of Knowledge and the other of work. He possessed the perfect Knowledge of Brahman and also was devoted to the duties of the world. An unchaste woman attends to the minutest duties of the world, but her mind always dwells on her paramour.

"The constant company of holy men is necessary. The holy man introduces one to God."

KEDAR: "Yes, sir. The great soul is born in the world for the redemption of humanity. He leads others to God, just as a locomotive engine takes along with it a long train of carriages. Or again, he is like a river or lake that quenches the thirst of many people."

The devotees were ready to return home. One by one they saluted the Master. At the sight of Bhavanath Sri Ramakrishna said: "Don't go away today. The very sight of you inspires me." Bhavanath had not yet entered into worldly life. A youth of twenty, he had a fair complexion and handsome features. He shed tears of joy on hearing the name of God. The Master looked on him as the embodiment of Nārāyana.

Thursday, March 29, 1883

The Master had taken a little rest after his noon meal, when a few devotees arrived from Calcutta, among them Amrita and the well-known singer of the Brāhmo Samāj, Trailokya.

Rakhal was not feeling well. The Master was greatly worried about him and said to the devotees: "You see, Rakhal is not well. Will soda-water help him? What am I to do now? Rakhal, please take the prasād from the Jagannāth temple."

Even as he spoke these words the Master underwent a strange transformation. He looked at Rakhal with the infinite tenderness of a mother and affectionately uttered the name of Govinda.[8] Did he see in Rakhal the manifestation of God Himself? The disciple was a young boy of pure heart who had renounced all attraction to lust and greed. And Sri Ramakrishna was intoxicated day and night with love of God. At the sight of Rakhal his eyes expressed the tender feelings of a mother, a love like that which had filled the heart of Mother Yaśodā at the sight of the Baby Krishna. The devotees gazed at the Master in wonder as he went into deep samādhi. As his soul soared into the realm of Divine Consciousness, his body became motionless, his eyes were fixed on the tip of his nose, and his breathing almost ceased.

An unknown Bengali, dressed in the ochre cloth of a monk, entered the room and sat on the floor. The Master's mind was coming down to the ordinary plane of consciousness. Presently he began to talk, though the spell of samādhi still lingered.

MASTER (*at the sight of the ochre cloth*): "Why this gerruā? Should one put on such a thing for a mere fancy? A man once said, 'I have exchanged the *Chandi* for a drum.' At first he used to sing the holy songs of the *Chandi*; now he beats the drum. (*All laugh.*)

"There are three or four varieties of renunciation. Afflicted with miseries at home, one may put on the ochre cloth of a monk; but that renunciation doesn't last long. Again, a man out of work puts on an ochre wearing-cloth and goes off to Benares. After three months he writes home: 'I have a job here. I shall come home in a few days. Don't worry about me.' Again, a man may have everything he wants. He lacks nothing, yet he does not enjoy his possessions. He weeps for God alone. That is real renunciation.

"No lie of any sort is good. A false garb, even though a holy one, is not good. If the outer garb does not correspond to the inner thought, it gradually brings ruin. Uttering false words or doing false deeds, one gradually loses all fear. Far better is the white cloth of a householder. Attachment to worldliness, occasional lapses from the ideal, and an outer garb of gerruā—how dreadful!

"It is not proper for a righteous person to tell a lie or do something false even in a dramatic performance. Once I went to Keshab's house to see the performance of a play called *Nava-Vrindāvan*. They brought something on the stage which they called the 'Cross'. Another actor sprinkled water, which they said was the 'Water of Peace'. I saw a third actor staggering and reeling in the role of a drunkard."

A BRĀHMO DEVOTEE: "It was K—."

MASTER: "It is not good for a devotee to play such parts. It is bad for the mind to dwell on such subjects for a long while. The mind is like white linen fresh from the laundry; it takes the colour in which you dip it. If it is associated with falsehood for a long time, it will be stained with falsehood.

"Another day I went to Keshab's house to see the play called *Nimāi-sannyās*.[9] Some flattering disciples of Keshab spoiled the whole performance.

[8] A name of Krishna. According to the Master, Rakhal, in one of his previous incarnations, had been a cowherd of Vrindāvan and an intimate companion of Sri Krishna.

[9] A play describing Sri Chaitanya's embracing of the monastic life.

One of them said to Keshab, 'You are the Chaitanya of the Kaliyuga.' Keshab pointed to me and asked with a smile, 'Then who is he?' I replied: 'Why, I am the servant of your servant. I am a speck of the dust of your feet.' Keshab had a desire for name and fame.

(*To Amrita and Trailokya*) "Youngsters like Narendra and Rakhal are ever-perfect. Every time they are born they are devoted to God. An ordinary man acquires a little devotion after austerities and a hard struggle. But these boys have love of God from the very moment of their birth. They are like the natural image of Śiva, which springs forth from the earth and is not set up by human hands.

"The ever-perfect form a class by themselves. Not all birds have crooked beaks. The ever-perfect are never attached to the world. There is the instance of Prahlāda.

"Ordinary people practise spiritual discipline and cultivate devotion to God; but they also become attached to the world and are caught in the glamour of 'woman and gold'. They are like flies, which sit on a flower or a sweetmeat and light on filth as well.

"But the ever-perfect are like bees, which light only on flowers and sip the honey. The ever-perfect drink only the Nectar of Divine Bliss. They are never inclined to worldly pleasures.

"The devotion of the ever-perfect is not like the ordinary devotion that one acquires as a result of strenuous spiritual discipline. Ritualistic devotion consists in repeating the name of God and performing worship in a prescribed manner. It is like crossing a rice-field in a roundabout way along the balk. Again, it is like reaching a near-by village by boat in a roundabout way along a winding river.

"One does not follow the injunctions of ceremonial worship when one develops rāga-bhakti, when one loves God as one's own. Then it is like crossing a rice-field after the harvest. You don't have to walk along the balk. You can go straight across the field in any direction.

"When the country is flooded deep with water, one doesn't have to follow the winding river. Then the fields are deep under water. You can row your boat straight to the village.

"Without this intense attachment, this passionate love, one cannot realize God."

AMRITA: "Sir, how do you feel in samādhi?"

MASTER: "You may have heard that the cockroach, by intently meditating on the brahmara, is transformed into a brahmara. Do you know how I feel then? I feel like a fish released from a pot into the water of the Ganges."

AMRITA: "Don't you feel at that time even a trace of ego?"

MASTER: "Yes, generally a little of it remains. However hard you may rub a grain of gold against a grindstone, still a bit of it always remains. Or again, take the case of a big fire; the ego is like one of its sparks. In samādhi I lose outer consciousness completely; but God generally keeps a little trace of ego in me for the enjoyment of divine communion. Enjoyment is possible only when 'I' and 'you' remain.

"Again, sometimes God effaces even that trace of 'I'. Then one experiences jaḍa samādhi or nirvikalpa samādhi. That experience cannot be described. A salt doll went to measure the depth of the ocean, but before it had gone far into the water it melted away. It became entirely one with the water of the ocean. Then who was to come back and tell the ocean's depth?"

ADVICE TO THE BRĀHMOS

SRI RAMAKRISHNA was visiting Balaram in Calcutta, with Narendra, Bhavanath, Rakhal, M., and others. Balaram, at the Master's bidding, had invited some of the young devotees to lunch. Sri Ramakrishna often said to him, "Feed them now and then; that will confer on you the merit of feeding holy men." The Master looked on his young disciples, yet untouched by "woman and gold", as veritable embodiments of God.

A few days earlier Sri Ramakrishna had been to Keshab's house with Narendra and Rakhal to see a performance of the play entitled *Nava-Vrindāvan*. Narendra had taken part in the performance, in which Keshab had played the role of Pāvhāri Bābā.

MASTER: "Keshab came on the stage in the role of a holy man and sprinkled the 'Water of Peace'. But I didn't like it. The idea of sprinkling such water on a theatrical stage after a performance!

"Another gentleman played the part of Sin. That is not good either. One should not commit sin; one should not even feign it."

The Master wanted to hear Narendra sing. The young disciple was not feeling well, but at the Master's earnest request he sang to the accompaniment of the tānpurā:

> Sing, O bird that nestles deep within my heart!
> Sing, O bird that sits on the Kalpa-Tree of Brahman!
> Sing God's everlasting praise. . . .

Then he sang:

> Brahman, Joy of the whole universe, Supreme Effulgence;
> God beginningless, Lord of the world, the very Life of life! . . .

And again:

> O King of Kings, reveal Thyself to me!
> I crave Thy mercy. Cast on me Thy glance!
> At Thy dear feet I dedicate my life,
> Seared in the fiery furnace of this world.
>
> My heart, alas, is deeply stained with sin;
> Ensnared in māyā, I am all but dead.

Compassionate Lord! Revive my fainting soul
With the life-giving nectar of Thy grace.

Narendra continued:

Upon the tray of the sky blaze bright
The lamps of sun and moon;
Like diamonds shine the glittering stars
To deck Thy wondrous form.
The sweet Malaya breeze blows soft,
For fragrant incense smoke;
The moving air sways to and fro
The fan before Thy holy face;
Like gleaming votive lights
The fresh and flowery groves appear.

How wonderful Thy worship is,
O Slayer of birth and death!
The sacred Om, from space arisen,
Is the resounding drum.
My mind craves nectar day and night
At Hari's Lotus Feet;
Oh, shower the waters of Thy grace
On thirsty Nānak, blessed Lord;
And may Thy hallowed name
Become his everlasting home!

He sang again:

In Wisdom's firmament the moon of Love is rising full,
And Love's flood-tide, in surging waves, is flowing everywhere.
O Lord, how full of bliss Thou art! Victory unto Thee! . . .

Then at the Master's bidding Bhavanath sang:

Where is a friend like Thee, O Essence of Mercy?
Where is another friend like Thee
To stand by me through pain and pleasure?
Who, among all my friends, forgives my failings,
Bringing me comfort for my grief,
Soothing my spirit in its terror?

Thou art the Helmsman who dost steer life's craft
Across the world's perilous sea;
Thy grace it is alone, O Lord,
That silences my raging passions' storm.
Thou pourest out the waters of peace
Upon my burning, penitent soul;
And Thine is the bosom that will shelter me
When every other friend I own
Deserts me in my dying hour.

Narendra said to the Master with a smile, referring to Bhavanath, "He has given up fish and betel-leaf."[1]

[1] Hindu religious aspirants often renounce these, since they are considered luxuries detrimental to spiritual progress.

MASTER: "Why so? What is the matter with fish and betel-leaf? They aren't harmful. The renunciation of 'woman and gold' is the true renunciation.

"Where is Rakhal?"

A DEVOTEE: "He is asleep, sir."

MASTER (*with a smile*): "Once a man went to a certain place to see a theatrical performance, carrying a mat under his arm. Hearing that it would be some time before the performance began, he spread the mat on the floor and fell asleep. When he woke up it was all over. (*All laugh.*) Then he returned home with the mat under his arm."

Ramdayal was very ill and lay in bed in another room. The Master went there to inquire about him.

About four o'clock in the afternoon some members of the Brāhmo Samāj arrived. The Master began to converse with them.

A BRĀHMO: "Sir, have you read the *Panchadaśi?*"

MASTER: "At first one should hear books like that and indulge in reasoning. But later on—

> Cherish my precious Mother Śyāmā
> Tenderly within, O mind;
> May you and I alone behold Her,
> Letting no one else intrude.

"One should hear the scriptures during the early stages of spiritual discipline. After attaining God there is no lack of knowledge. Then the Divine Mother supplies it without fail.

"A child spells out every word as he writes, but later on he writes fluently.

"The goldsmith is up and doing while melting gold. As long as the gold hasn't melted, he works the bellows with one hand, moves the fan with the other, and blows through a pipe with his mouth. But the moment the gold melts and is poured into the mould, he is relieved of all anxiety.

"Mere reading of the scriptures is not enough. A person cannot understand the true significance of the scriptures if he is attached to the world.

> Though with intense delight I learnt many poems and dramas,
> I have forgotten them all, entrapped in Krishna's love.

"Keshab enjoys the world and practises yoga as well. Living in the world, he directs his mind to God."

A devotee described the Convocation of Calcutta University, saying that the meeting looked like a forest of human heads.

MASTER: "The feeling of the Divine is awakened in me when I see a great crowd of people. Had I seen that meeting, I should have been overwhelmed with spiritual fervour."

Sunday, April 8, 1883

It was Sunday morning. The Master, looking like a boy, was seated in his room, and near him was another boy, his beloved disciple Rakhal. M.

entered and saluted the Master. Ramlal also was in the room, and Kishori, Manilal Mallick, and several other devotees gathered by and by.

Manilal Mallick, a business man, had recently been to Benares, where he owned a bungalow.

MASTER: "So you have been to Benares. Did you see any holy men there?"

MANILAL: "Yes, sir. I paid my respects to Trailanga Swami, Bhaskarananda, and others."

MASTER: "Tell us something about them."

MANILAL: "Trailanga Swami is living in the same temple where he lived before—on the Manikarnikā Ghāt, near the Benimādhav Minaret. People say he was formerly in a more exalted spiritual state. He could perform many miracles. Now he has lost much of that power."

MASTER: "That is the criticism of worldly people."

MANILAL: "Trailanga Swami keeps a strict vow of silence. Unlike him, Bhaskarananda is friendly with all."

MASTER: "Did you have any conversation with Bhaskarananda?"

MANILAL: "Yes, sir. We had a long talk. Among other things we discussed the problem of good and evil. He said to me: 'Don't follow the path of evil. Give up sinful thoughts. That is how God wants us to act. Perform only those duties that are virtuous.'"

MASTER: "Yes, that is also a path, meant for worldly-minded people. But those whose spiritual consciousness has been awakened, who have realized that God alone is real and all else illusory, cherish a different ideal. They are aware that God alone is the Doer and others are His instruments.

"Those whose spiritual consciousness has been awakened never make a false step. They do not have to reason in order to shun evil. They are so full of love of God that whatever action they undertake is a good action. They are fully conscious that they are not the doers of their actions, but mere servants of God. They always feel: 'I am the machine and He is the Operator. I do as He does through me. I speak as He speaks through me. I move as He moves me.'

"Fully awakened souls are beyond virtue and vice. They realize that it is God who does everything.

"There was a monastery in a certain place. The monks residing there went out daily to beg their food. One day a monk, while out for his alms, saw a landlord beating a man mercilessly. The compassionate monk stepped in and asked the landlord to stop. But the landlord was filled with anger and turned his wrath against the innocent monk. He beat the monk till he fell unconscious on the ground. Someone reported the matter to the monastery. The monks ran to the spot and found their brother lying there. Four or five of them carried him back and laid him on a bed. He was still unconscious. The other monks sat around him sad at heart; some were fanning him. Finally someone suggested that he should be given a little milk to drink. When it was poured into his mouth he regained consciousness. He opened his eyes and looked around. One of the monks said, 'Let us see whether he is fully conscious and can recognize us.' Shouting into his ear, he said,

'Revered sir, who is giving you milk?' 'Brother,' replied the holy man in a low voice, 'He who beat me is now giving me milk.'

"But one does not attain such a state of mind without the realization of God."

MANILAL: "Sir, what you have just said applies to a man of a very lofty spiritual state. I talked on such topics in a general way with Bhaskarananda."

MASTER: "Does he live in a house?"

MANILAL: "Yes, sir. He lives with a devotee."

MASTER: "How old is he now?"

MANILAL: "About fifty-five."

MASTER: "Did you talk about anything else?"

MANILAL: "I asked him how to cultivate bhakti. He said: 'Chant the name of God. Repeat the name of Rāma.'"

MASTER: "That is very good."

The worship was over in the temples and the bells rang for the food offerings in the shrines. As it was a summer noon the sun was very hot. The flood-tide began in the Ganges and a breeze came up from the south. Sri Ramakrishna was resting in his room after his meal.

The people of Basirhāt, Rakhal's birth-place, had been suffering from a severe drought during the summer months.

MASTER (to Manilal): "Rakhal says that the people in his native village have been suffering seriously from a scarcity of water. Why don't you build a reservoir there? That will do the people good. (Smiling) You have so much money; what will you do with all your wealth? But they say that telis[2] are very calculating." (All laugh.)

Manilal was truly a calculating man, though he suffered no lack of money. In later years he set up an endowment of twenty-five thousand rupees for the maintenance of poor students.

Manilal made no answer to these words of the Master about his caste characteristics. Later on, in the course of the conversation, he remarked casually: "Sir, you referred to a reservoir. You might as well have confined yourself to that suggestion. Why allude to the 'oil-man caste' and all that?"

Some of the devotees smiled to themselves. The Master laughed.

Presently a few elderly members of the Brāhmo Samāj arrived. The room was full of devotees. Sri Ramakrishna was sitting on his bed, facing the north. He kept smiling, and talked to the Brāhmo devotees in a joyous mood.

MASTER: "You talk glibly about prema. But is it such a commonplace thing? There are two characteristics of prema. First, it makes one forget the world. So intense is one's love of God that one becomes unconscious of outer things. Chaitanya had this ecstatic love; he 'took a wood for the sacred grove of Vrindāvan and the ocean for the dark waters of the Jamunā'. Second, one has no feeling of 'my-ness' toward the body, which is so dear to man. One wholly gets rid of the feeling that the body is the soul.

"There are certain signs of God-realization. The man in whom longing

[2] The oil-man caste to which Manilal belonged. It is a comparatively low caste in Hindu society in Bengal.

for God manifests its glories is not far from attaining Him. What are the glories of that longing? They are discrimination, dispassion, compassion for living beings, serving holy men, loving their company, chanting the name and glories of God, telling the truth, and the like. When you see those signs of longing in an aspirant, you can rightly say that for him the vision of God is not far to seek.

"The state of a servant's house will tell you unmistakably whether his master has decided to visit it. First, the rubbish and jungle around the house are cleared up. Second, the soot and dirt are removed from the rooms. Third, the courtyard, floors, and other places are swept clean. Finally the master himself sends various things to the house, such as a carpet, a hubble-bubble for smoking, and the like. When you see these things arriving, you conclude that the master will very soon come."

A DEVOTEE: "Sir, should one first practise discrimination to attain self-control?"

MASTER: "That is also a path. It is called the path of vichāra, reasoning. But the inner organs[3] are brought under control naturally through the path of devotion as well. It is rather easily accomplished that way. Sense pleasures appear more and more tasteless as love for God grows. Can carnal pleasure attract a grief-stricken man and woman the day their child has died?"

DEVOTEE: "How can I develop love for God?"

MASTER: "Repeat His name, and sins will disappear. Thus you will destroy lust, anger, the desire for creature comforts, and so on."

DEVOTEE: "How can I take delight in God's name?"

MASTER: "Pray to God with a yearning heart that you may take delight in His name. He will certainly fulfil your heart's desire."

So saying, the Master sang a song in his sweet voice, pleading with the Divine Mother to show Her grace to suffering men:

> O Mother, I have no one else to blame:
> Alas! I sink in the well these very hands have dug.
> With the six passions for my spade,
> I dug a pit in the sacred land of earth;
> And now the dark water of death gushes forth!
> How can I save myself, O my Redeemer?
>
> Surely I have been my own enemy;
> How can I now ward off this dark water of death?
> Behold, the waters rise to my chest!
> How can I save myself? O Mother, save me!
> Thou art my only Refuge; with Thy protecting glance
> Take me across to the other shore of the world.

The Master sang again:

> What a delirious fever is this that I suffer from!
> O Mother, Thy grace is my only cure.
> False pride is the fever that racks my wasted form;
> "I" and "mine" are my cry. Oh, what a wicked delusion!

[3] Mind (manas), intelligence (buddhi), mind-stuff (chitta), and ego (ahamkāra).

My quenchless thirst for wealth and friends is never-ceasing;
How, then, shall I sustain my life?
Talk about things unreal, this is my wretched delirium,
And I indulge in it always, O Giver of all good fortune!

My eyes in seeming sleep are closed, my stomach is filled
With the vile worms of cruelty.
Alas! I wander about absorbed in unmeaning deeds;
Even for Thy holy name I have no taste, O Mother!
I doubt that I shall ever be cured of this malady.

Then the Master said: " 'Even for Thy holy name I have no taste.' A typhoid patient has very little chance of recovery if he loses all taste for food; but his life need not be despaired of if he enjoys food even a little. That is why one should cultivate a taste for God's name. Any name will do—Durgā, Krishna, or Śiva. Then if, through the chanting of the name, one's attachment to God grows day by day, and joy fills the soul, one has nothing to fear. The delirium will certainly disappear; the grace of God will certainly descend.

" 'As is a man's feeling of love, so is his gain.' Once two friends were going along the street, when they saw some people listening to a reading of the Bhāgavata. 'Come, friend', said the one to the other. 'Let us hear the sacred book.' So saying he went in and sat down. The second man peeped in and went away. He entered a house of ill fame. But very soon he felt disgusted with the place. 'Shame on me!' he said to himself. 'My friend has been listening to the sacred word of Hari; and see where I am!' But the friend who had been listening to the Bhāgavata also became disgusted. 'What a fool I am!' he said. 'I have been listening to this fellow's blah-blah, and my friend is having a grand time.' In course of time they both died. The messenger of Death came for the soul of the one who had listened to the Bhāgavata and dragged it off to hell. The messenger of God came for the soul of the one who had been to the house of prostitution and led it up to heaven.

"Verily, the Lord looks into a man's heart and does not judge him by what he does or where he lives. 'Krishna accepts a devotee's inner feeling of love.'

"In the Kartābhajā sect, the teacher, while giving initiation, says to the disciple, 'Now everything depends on your mind.' According to this sect, 'He who has the right mind finds the right way and also achieves the right end.' It was through the power of his mind that Hanumān leapt over the sea. 'I am the servant of Rāma; I have repeated the holy name of Rāma. Is there anything impossible for me?'—that was Hanumān's faith.

"Ignorance lasts as long as one has ego. There can be no liberation so long as the ego remains. 'O God, Thou art the Doer and not I'—that is knowledge.

"By being lowly one can rise high. The chātak bird makes its nest on low ground, but it soars very high in the sky. Cultivation is not possible on high land; in low land water accumulates and makes cultivation possible.

"One must take the trouble to seek the company of holy persons. In his own home a man hears only worldly talk; the disease of worldliness has become chronic with him. The caged parrot sitting on its perch repeats, 'Rāma! Rāma!' But let it fly to the forest and it will squawk in its usual way.

"Mere possession of money doesn't make a nobleman. One sign of the mansion of a nobleman is that all the rooms are lighted. The poor cannot afford much oil, and consequently cannot have so many lights. This shrine of the body should not be left dark; one should illumine it with the lamp of Wisdom.

> Lighting the lamp of Knowledge in the chamber of your heart,
> Behold the face of the Mother, Brahman's Embodiment.

"Everyone can attain Knowledge. There are two entities: jīvātmā, the individual soul, and Paramātmā, the Supreme Soul. Through prayer all individual souls can be united to the Supreme Soul. Every house has a connection for gas, and gas can be obtained from the main storage-tank of the Gas Company. Apply to the Company, and it will arrange for your supply of gas. Then your house will be lighted.

"In some people spiritual consciousness has already been awakened; but they have special marks. They do not enjoy hearing or talking about anything but God. They are like the chātak, which prays for rain-water though the seven oceans, the Ganges, the Jamunā, and the rivers near it are all filled with water. It won't drink anything but rain-water, even though its throat is burning with thirst."

The Master wanted to hear a few songs. Ramlal and a brāhmin official of the temple garden sang:

> Dwell, O Lord, O Lover of bhakti,
> In the Vrindāvan of my heart,
> And my devotion unto Thee
> Will be Thy Rādhā, dearly loved. . . .

And again:

> The dark cloud of the summer storm fades into nothingness,
> When, flute in hand and a smile on His lips,
> Lighting the world with His loveliness,
> Krishna, the Dark One, appears.

> His dazzling yellow robe outgleams even the lightning's glare;
> A wreath of wild-flowers interwoven
> Gently swings from His youthful breast
> And softly kisses His feet.

> See, there He stands, the Lord of life, the Moon of Nanda's line,
> Outshining all the moons in heaven
> And with the splendour of His rays
> Flooding the Jamunā's bank!

> He stands there, stealing the maidens' hearts; He lures them from
>   hearth and home.
> Krishna enters my own heart's shrine,
> And with His flute-note steals away
> My wisdom, life, and soul.

To whom shall Gangā Nārāyana pour out his tale of woe?
Ah, friend, you might have understood
Had you but gone to the Jamunā's bank
To fill your water-jar!

Again they sang:

High in the heaven of the Mother's feet, my mind was soaring
    like a kite,
When came a blast of sin's rough wind that drove it swiftly toward
    the earth. . . .

MASTER (*to the devotees*): "As the tiger devours other animals, so does
the 'tiger of zeal for the Lord' eat up lust, anger, and the other passions.
Once this zeal grows in the heart, lust and the other passions disappear.
The gopis of Vrindāvan had that state of mind because of their zeal for
Krishna.

"Again, this zeal for God is compared to collyrium. Rādhā said to her
friends, 'I see Krishna everywhere.' They replied, 'Friend, you have painted
your eyes with the collyrium of love; that is why you see Krishna everywhere.'

"They say that when your eyes are painted with collyrium made from
the ashes of a frog's head you see snakes everywhere.

"They are indeed bound souls who constantly dwell with 'woman and
gold' and do not think of God even for a moment. How can you expect
noble deeds of them? They are like mangoes pecked by a crow, which may
not be offered to the Deity in the temple, and which even men hesitate
to eat.

"Bound souls, worldly people, are like silk-worms. The worms can cut
through their cocoons if they want, but having woven the cocoons themselves, they are too much attached to them to leave them. And so they
die there.

"Free souls are not under the control of 'woman and gold'. There are
some silk-worms that cut through the cocoon they have made with such great
care. But they are few and far between.

"It is māyā that deludes. Only a few become spiritually awakened and
are not deluded by the spell of māyā. They do not come under the control
of 'woman and gold'.

"There are two classes of perfect souls: those who attain perfection
through spiritual practice, and those who attain it through the grace of God.
Some farmers irrigate their fields with great labour. Only then can they
grow crops. But there are some who do not have to irrigate at all; their fields
are flooded by rain. They don't have to go to the trouble of drawing water.
One must practise spiritual discipline laboriously, in order to avoid the
clutches of māyā. Those who attain liberation through the grace of God do
not have to labour. But they are few indeed.

"Then there is the class of the ever-perfect. They are born in each life
with their spiritual consciousness already awakened. Think of a spring
whose outlet is obstructed. While looking after various things in the garden,

the plumber accidentally clears it and the water gushes out. Yet people are amazed to see the first manifestations of an ever-perfect soul's zeal for God. They say, 'Where was all this devotion and renunciation and love?'"

The conversation turned to the spiritual zeal of devotees, as illustrated in the earnestness of the gopis of Vrindāvan. Ramlal sang:

> Thou art my All in All, O Lord!—the Life of my life, the Essence
>> of essence;
> In the three worlds I have none else but Thee to call my own.
> Thou art my peace, my joy, my hope; Thou my support, my
>> ·wealth, my glory;
> Thou my wisdom and my strength.
>
> Thou art my home, my place of rest; my dearest friend, my next of
>> kin;
> My present and my future, Thou; my heaven and my salvation.
> Thou art my scriptures, my commandments; Thou art my ever
>> gracious Guru;
> Thou the Spring of my boundless bliss.
>
> Thou art the Way, and Thou the Goal; Thou the Adorable One,
>> O Lord!
> Thou art the Mother tender-hearted; Thou the chastising Father;
> Thou the Creator and Protector; Thou the Helmsman who dost
>> steer
> My craft across the sea of life.

MASTER (to the devotees): "Ah! What a beautiful song!—'Thou art my All in All.'"

Ramlal sang again, this time describing the pangs of the gopis on being separated from their beloved Krishna:[4]

> Hold not, hold not the chariot's wheels!
> Is it the wheels that make it move?
> The Mover of its wheels is Krishna,
> By whose will the worlds are moved. . . .

The Master went into deep samādhi. His body was motionless; he sat with folded hands as in his photograph. Tears of joy flowed from the corners of his eyes. After a long time his mind came down to the ordinary plane of consciousness. He mumbled something, of which only a word now and then could be heard by the devotees in the room. He was saying: "Thou art I, and I am Thou—Thou eatest—Thou—I eat! . . . What is this confusion Thou hast created?"

Continuing, the Master said: "I see everything like a man with jaundiced eyes! I see Thee alone everywhere. O Krishna, Friend of the lowly! O Eternal Consort of my soul! O Govinda!"

As he uttered the words "Eternal Consort of my soul" and "Govinda", the Master again went into samādhi. There was complete silence in the

---

[4] When Krishna mounted His chariot to go away to Mathurā, the gopis clung to the wheels and would not let the chariot move.

room. The eager and unsatiated eyes of the devotees were fixed on the Master, a God-man of infinite moods.

Adhar Sen arrived with several of his friends. He was a deputy magistrate, about thirty years old. This was his second visit to the Master. He was accompanied by his friend Saradacharan, who was extremely unhappy because of the death of his eldest son. A retired deputy inspector of schools, Saradacharan devoted himself to meditation and prayer. Adhar had brought his friend to the Master for consolation in his afflicted state of mind.

Coming down from samādhi, the Master found the eyes of the devotees fixed on him. He muttered to himself, still in an abstracted mood.

Then, addressing the devotees, Sri Ramakrishna said: "The spiritual wisdom of worldly people is seen only on rare occasions. It is like the flame of a candle. No, it is rather like a single ray of the sun passing through a chink in a wall. Worldly people chant the name of God, but there is no zeal behind it. It is like children's swearing by God, having learnt the word from the quarrels of their aunts.

"Worldly people have no grit. If they succeed in an undertaking, it is all right, but if they don't succeed, it scarcely bothers them at all. When they need water they begin to dig a well. But as soon as they strike a stone they give up digging there and begin at another place. Perhaps they come to a bed of sand. Finding nothing but sand, they give that place up too. How can they succeed in getting water unless they continue to dig persistently where they started?

"Man reaps the harvest of his own past actions. Hence you read in the song:

> O Mother, I have no one else to blame:
> Alas! I sink in the well these very hands have dug.

" 'I' and 'mine'—that is ignorance. By discriminating you will realize that what you call 'I' is really nothing but Ātman. Reason it out. Are you the body or the flesh or something else? At the end you will know that you are none of these. You are free from attributes. Then you will realize that you have never been the doer of any action, that you have been free from virtue and faults alike, that you are beyond righteousness and unrighteousness.

"From ignorance a man says, 'This is gold and this is brass.' But a man of Knowledge says, 'It is all gold.'

"Reasoning stops when one sees God. But there are instances of people who have realized God and who still continue to reason. Again, there are people who, even after having seen God, chant His name with devotion and sing His glories.

"How long does a child cry? So long as it is not sucking at its mother's breast. As soon as it is nursed it stops crying. Then the child feels only joy. Joyously it drinks the milk from its mother's breast. But it is also true that, while drinking, the child sometimes plays and laughs.

"It is God alone who has become everything. But in man He manifests Himself the most. God is directly present in the man who has the pure heart of a child and who laughs and cries and dances and sings in divine ecstasy."

By this time Sri Ramakrishna had become better acquainted with Adhar, who related the cause of his friend's grief. The Master sang, as if to himself:

To arms! To arms, O man! Death storms your house in battle array!
Bearing the quiver of knowledge, mount the chariot of devotior,
Bend the bow of your tongue with the bow-string of love;
And aim at him the shaft of Mother Kāli's holy name.
Here is a ruse for the fray: You need no chariot or charioteer;
Fight your foe from the Ganges' bank, and he is easily slain.

Then he said: "What can you do? Be ready for Death. Death has entered the house. You must fight him with the weapon of God's holy name. God alone is the Doer. I say: 'O Lord, I do as Thou doest through me. I speak as Thou speakest through me. I am the machine and Thou art the Operator. I am the house and Thou art the Indweller. I am the engine and Thou art the Engineer.' Give your power of attorney to God. One doesn't come to grief through letting a good man assume one's responsibilities. Let His will be done.

"But isn't your grief for your son only natural? The son is one's own self reborn. Lakshmana ran to Rāvana when the latter fell dead on the battle-field. Looking at Rāvana's body, he found that every one of his bones was full of holes. Thereupon he said to Rāma: 'O Rāma, glory be to Your arrows! There is no spot in Rāvana's body that they have not pierced.' 'Brother,' replied Rāma, 'the holes you see in his bones are not from My arrows. Grief for his sons has pierced them through and through. These holes are the marks of his grief. It has penetrated his very bones.'

"But house, wife, and children are all transitory; they have only a momentary existence. The palm-tree alone is real. One or two fruits have dropped off. Why lament?

"God is engaged in three kinds of activity: creation, preservation, and destruction. Death is inevitable. All will be destroyed at the time of dissolution. Nothing will remain. At that time the Divine Mother will gather up the seeds for the future creation, even as the elderly mistress of the house keeps in her hotchpotch-pot little bags of cucumber seeds, 'sea-foam', blue pills, and other miscellaneous things. The Divine Mother will take Her seeds out again at the time of the new creation."

Sri Ramakrishna began to talk with Adhar on the verandah north of his room.

MASTER (to Adhar): "You are a deputy magistrate. Remember that you have obtained your position through the grace of God. Do not forget Him, but remember that all men must one day walk down the same path.[5] We stay in the world only a couple of days.

"This world is our field of activity. We are born here to perform certain duties. People have their homes in the country but come to Calcutta to work.

"It is necessary to do a certain amount of work. This is a kind of discipline. But one must finish it speedily. While melting gold, the goldsmith uses

[5] Adhar Sen passed away eighteen months after this conversation. At the news of his death the Master wept before the Mother a long time. Adhar was a great devotee of Sri Ramakrishna, who referred to him as his own relative.

everything—the bellows, the fan, and the pipe—so that he may have the hot fire he needs to melt the metal. After the melting is over, he relaxes and asks his attendant to prepare a smoke for him. All this time his face has been hot and perspiring; but now he can smoke.

"One must have stern determination; then alone is spiritual practice possible. One must make a firm resolve.

"There is great power in the seed of God's name. It destroys ignorance. A seed is tender, and the sprout soft; still it pierces the hard ground. The ground breaks and makes way for the sprout.

"The mind becomes very much distracted if one lives long in the midst of 'woman and gold'. Therefore one must be very careful. But monks do not have much to fear. The real sannyāsi lives away from 'woman and gold'. Therefore through the practice of spiritual discipline he can always fix his mind on God.

"True sannyāsis, those who are able to devote their minds constantly to God, are like bees, which light only on flowers and sip their honey. Those who live in the world, in the midst of 'woman and gold', may direct their attention to God; but sometimes their minds dwell also on 'woman and gold'. They are like common flies, which light on a piece of candy, then on a sore or filth.

"Always keep your mind fixed on God. In the beginning you must struggle a little; later on you will enjoy your pension."

Sunday, April 15, 1883

Surendra, a beloved lay disciple of the Master, had invited him to his house on the auspicious occasion of the Annapurnā Pujā. It was about six o'clock when Sri Ramakrishna arrived there with some of his devotees. The image of the Divine Mother had been installed in the worship hall. At Her feet lay hibiscus flowers and vilwa-leaves; from Her neck hung a garland of flowers. Sri Ramakrishna entered the hall and bowed down before the image. Then he went to the open courtyard, where he sat on a carpet, surrounded by his devotees and disciples. A few bolsters lay on the carpet, which was covered with a white linen sheet. He was asked to lean against one of these, but he pushed it aside.

MASTER (to the devotees): "To lean against a bolster![6] You see, it is very difficult to give up vanity. You may discriminate, saying that the ego is nothing at all; but still it comes, nobody knows from where. A goat's legs jerk for a few moments even after its head has been cut off. Or perhaps you are frightened in a dream; you shake off sleep and are wide awake, but still you feel your heart palpitating. Egotism is exactly like that. You may drive it away, but still it appears from somewhere. Then you look sullen and say: 'What! I have not been shown proper respect!' "

KEDAR: " 'One should be lowlier than a straw and patient as a tree.' "

MASTER: "As for me, I consider myself as a speck of the dust of the devotee's feet."

Vaidyanath arrived. He was a well-educated man, a lawyer of the High

6 Rich and aristocratic persons seeking comfort generally sit in this fashion.

Court of Calcutta. With folded hands he saluted the Master and took his seat at one side.

SURENDRA (to the Master): "He is one of my relatives."

MASTER: "Yes, I see he has a nice nature."

SURENDRA: "He has come here because he wants to ask you a question or two."

MASTER (to Vaidyanath): "All that you see is the manifestation of God's Power. No one can do anything without this Power. But you must remember that there is not an equal manifestation of God's Power in all things. Vidyāsāgar once asked me whether God endowed some with greater power than others. I said to him: 'If there are no greater and lesser manifestations of His Power, then why have we taken the trouble to visit you? Have you grown two horns?' So it stands to reason that God exists in all beings as the All-pervasive Power; but the manifestations of His Power are different in different beings."

VAIDYANATH: "Sir, I have a doubt. People speak of free will. They say that a man can do either good or evil according to his will. Is it true? Are we really free to do whatever we like?"

MASTER: "Everything depends on the will of God. The world is His play. He has created all these different things—great and small, strong and weak, good and bad, virtuous and vicious. This is all His māyā, His sport. You must have observed that all the trees in a garden are not of the same kind.

"As long as a man has not realized God, he thinks he is free. It is God Himself who keeps this error in man. Otherwise sin would have multiplied. Man would not have been afraid of sin, and there would have been no punishment for it.

"But do you know the attitude of one who has realized God? He feels: 'I am the machine, and Thou, O Lord, art the Operator. I am the house and Thou art the Indweller. I am the chariot and Thou art the Driver. I move as Thou movest me; I speak as Thou makest me speak.'

(To Vaidyanath): "It is not good to argue. Isn't that so?"

VAIDYANATH: "Yes, sir. The desire to argue disappears when a man attains wisdom."

The Master, out of his stock of a dozen English words, said, "Thank you!" in the most charming way, and all laughed.

MASTER (to Vaidyanath): "You will make spiritual progress. People don't trust a man when he speaks about God. Even if a great soul affirms that he has seen God, still the average person will not accept his words. He says to himself, 'If this man has really seen God, then let him show Him to me.' But can a man learn to feel a person's pulse in one day? He must go about with a physician for many days; only then can he distinguish the different pulses. He must be in the company of those with whom the examination of the pulse has become a regular profession.

"Can anyone and everyone pick out a yarn of a particular count? If you are in that trade, you can distinguish in a moment a forty-count thread from a forty-one."

The kirtan was about to begin. Some Vaishnavas were seated on one side with their mridangas and cymbals. A drummer began to play on his instrument preparatory to the singing. The sweet and melodious sound of the mridanga filled the courtyard, calling to mind the ecstatic kirtan of Sri Gaurānga. The Master passed into a deep spiritual state. Now and then he looked at the drummer and said, "Ah! Ah! My hair is all standing on end."

The singers asked what kind of song they should sing. The Master said humbly, "Something about Gaurānga, if you please."

The kirtan began. They sang about the celestial beauty of Sri Gaurānga:

> The beauty of Gaurānga's face
> Glows brighter than the brightest gold;
> His smile illumines all the world.
> Who cares for even a million moons
> Shining in the blue autumn sky?

The chief musician added improvised lines as they sang: "O friend, his face shines like the full moon!" "But it does not wane nor has it any stain." "It illumines the devotee's heart." Again he improvised: "His face is bathed with the essence of a million moons."

At these words the Master went into deep samādhi. After a short while he regained consciousness of the sense world. Then he suddenly stood up, overpowered by his spiritual mood, and sang improvised lines with the professionals, thinking himself to be a milkmaid of Vrindāvan gone mad with the beauty of Sri Krishna's form: "Whose fault is it—my mind's or His beauty's?" "In the three worlds I see nothing but my beloved Krishna."

The Master danced and sang. All remained spellbound as they watched. The chief musician sang the words of a gopi: "O flute, pray stop. Can you not go to sleep?" One of the musicians added a new line: "How can it sleep? It rests on Krishna's lips."

The Master sat down. The music went on. They sang, assuming the mood of Rādhā: "My eyes are blinded. My ears are deaf. I have lost the power of smell. All my senses are paralysed. But, alas, why am I left alone?"

Finally the musicians sang of the union of Rādhā and Krishna:

> Rādhā and Krishna are joined at last in the Nidhu Grove of
>   Vrindāvan;
> Incomparable their beauty, and limitless their love!
> The one half shines like yellow gold, the other like bluest sapphire;
> Round the neck, on one side, a wild-flower garland hangs,
> And, on the other, there swings a necklace of precious gems.
> A ring of gold adorns one ear, a ring of shell the other;
> Half of the brow is bright as the blazing midday sun,
> The other softly gleams with the glow of the rising moon.
> Upon one half of the head a graceful peacock feather stands,
> And, from the other half, there hangs a braid of hair.

As the music came to a close the Master said, "Bhāgavata—Bhakta—Bhagavān", and bowed low to the devotees seated on all sides. He touched with his forehead the ground made holy by the singing of the sacred music. It was now about half past nine in the evening. Surendra entertained the

Master and the devotees with a sumptuous feast. When it was time to take leave of their host, the Master, the devotees, and Surendra entered the worship hall and stood before the image.

SURENDRA (to the Master): "No one has sung anything about the Divine Mother today."

MASTER (pointing to the image): "Ah! Look at the beauty of the hall. The light of the Divine Mother seems to have lighted the whole place. Such a sight fills the heart with joy. Grief and desire for pleasure disappear.

"But can one not see God as formless Reality? Of course one can. But not if one has 'the slightest trace of worldliness. The rishis of olden times renounced everything and then contemplated Satchidānanda, the Indivisible Brahman.

"The Brahmajnānis of modern times[7] sing of God as 'immutable, homogeneous'. It sounds very dry to me. It seems as if the singers themselves don't enjoy the sweetness of God's Bliss. One doesn't want a refreshing drink made with sugar candy if one is satisfied with mere coarse treacle.

"Just see how happy you are, looking at this image of the Deity. But those who always cry after the formless Reality do not get anything. They realize nothing either inside or outside."

The Master sang a song to the Divine Mother:

> O Mother, ever blissful as Thou art,
> Do not deprive Thy worthless child of bliss!
> My mind knows nothing but Thy Lotus Feet.
> The King of Death scowls at me terribly;
> Tell me, Mother, what shall I say to him?
>
> It was my heart's desire to sail my boat
> Across the ocean of this mortal life,
> O Durgā, with Thy name upon my lips.
> I never dreamt that Thou wouldst drown me here
> In the dark waters of this shoreless sea.
>
> Both day and night I swim among its waves,
> Chanting Thy saving name; yet even so
> There is no end, O Mother, to my grief.
> If I am drowned this time, in such a plight,
> No one will ever chant Thy name again.

Again he sang:

> Repeat, O mind, my Mother Durgā's hallowed name!
> Whoever treads the path, repeating "Durgā! Durgā!",
> Śiva Himself protects with His almighty trident.
> Thou art the day, O Mother! Thou art the dusk and the night.
> Sometimes Thou art man, and sometimes woman art Thou.
> Thou mayest even say to me: "Step aside! Go away!"
> Yet I shall cling to Thee, O Durgā! Unto Thy feet
> As Thine anklets I shall cling, making their tinkling sound.

A reference to the members of the Brāhmo Samāj.

Mother, when as the Kite[8] Thou soarest in the sky,
There, in the water beneath, as a minnow I shall be swimming;
Upon me Thou wilt pounce, and pierce me through with Thy claws.
Thus, when the breath of life forsakes me in Thy grip,
Do not deny me the shelter of Thy Lotus Feet!

The Master saluted the divine image. As he came down the steps, he called softly to Rakhal: "Where are my shoes? Are they missing?"

As the Master got into the carriage, Surendra and the other devotees bowed down before him. Then the carriage started for Dakshineswar. The moon still lighted the streets.

[8] According to Hindu mythology the Divine Mother at one time took the form of a bird similar to the kite.

THE MASTER WITH THE BRĀHMO
DEVOTEES (II)

SRI RAMAKRISHNA paid a visit to Benimadhav Pal's garden house at Sinthi, near Calcutta, on the occasion of the semi-annual festival of the Brāhmo Samāj. Many devotees of the Samāj were present and sat around the Master. Now and then some of them asked him questions.

A BRĀHMO DEVOTEE: "Sir, what is the way?"

MASTER: "Attachment to God, or, in other words, love for Him. And secondly, prayer."

BRĀHMO DEVOTEE: "Which one is the way—love or prayer?"

MASTER: "First love, and then prayer."

The Master sang:

> Cry to your Mother Śyāmā with a real cry, O mind!
> And how can She hold Herself from you?
> How can Śyāmā stay away? . . .

Continuing, the Master said: "And one must always chant the name and glories of God and pray to Him. An old metal pot must be scrubbed every day. What is the use of cleaning it only once? Further, one must practise discrimination and renunciation; one must be conscious of the unreality of the world."

BRĀHMO: "Is it good to renounce the world?"

MASTER: "Not for all. Those who have not yet come to the end of their enjoyments should not renounce the world. Can one get drunk on two ānnās' worth of wine?"

BRĀHMO: "Then should they lead a worldly life?"

MASTER: "Yes, they should try to perform their duties in a detached way. Before you break the jack-fruit open, rub your hands with oil, so that the sticky milk will not smear them. The maidservant in a rich man's house performs all her duties, but her mind dwells on her home in the country. This is an example of doing duty in a detached way. You should renounce the world only in mind. But a sannyāsi should renounce the world both inwardly and outwardly."

BRĀHMO: "What is the meaning of the 'end of enjoyments'?"

MASTER: "I mean the enjoyment of 'woman and gold'. It is risky to put a typhoid patient in a room where pitchers of water and jugs of pickled tamarind are kept. Most people don't feel any longing for God unless they have once passed through the experience of wealth, name, fame, creature comforts, and the like, that is to say, unless they have seen through these enjoyments."

BRĀHMO: "Who is really bad, man or woman?"

MASTER: "As there are women endowed with vidyāśakti, so also there are women with avidyāśakti. A woman endowed with spiritual attributes leads a man to God, but a woman who is the embodiment of delusion makes him forget God and drowns him in the ocean of worldliness.

"This universe is created by the Mahāmāyā[1] of God. Mahāmāyā contains both vidyāmāyā, the illusion of knowledge, and avidyāmāyā, the illusion of ignorance. Through the help of vidyāmāyā one cultivates such virtues as the taste for holy company, knowledge, devotion, love, and renunciation. Avidyāmāyā consists of the five elements and the objects of the five senses— form, flavour, smell, touch, and sound. These make one forget God."

BRĀHMO: "If the power of avidyā is the cause of ignorance, then why has God created it?"

MASTER: "That is His play. The glory of light cannot be appreciated without darkness. Happiness cannot be understood without misery. Knowledge of good is possible because of knowledge of evil.

"Further, the mango grows and ripens on account of the covering skin. You throw away the skin when the mango is fully ripe and ready to be eaten. It is possible for a man to attain gradually to the Knowledge of Brahman because of the covering skin of māyā. Māyā in its aspects of vidyā and avidyā may be likened to the skin of the mango. Both are necessary."

BRĀHMO: "Sir, is it good to worship God with form, an image of the Deity made of clay?"

MASTER: "You do not accept God with form. That is all right. The image is not meant for you. For you it is good to deepen your feeling toward your own Ideal. From the worshippers of the Personal God you should learn their yearning—for instance, Sri Krishna's attraction for Rādhā. You should learn from the worshippers of the Personal God their love for their Chosen Ideal. When the believers in the Personal God worship the images of Kāli and Durgā, with what feeling they cry from the depths of their souls, 'Mother! O Mother!' How much they love the Deity! You should accept that feeling. You don't have to accept the image."

BRĀHMO: "How does one cultivate the spirit of dispassion? Why don't all attain it?"

MASTER: "Dispassion is not possible unless there is satiety through enjoyment. You can easily cajole a small child with candies or toys. But after eating the candies and finishing its play, it cries, 'I want to go to my mother.' Unless you take the child to its mother, it will throw away the toy and scream at the top of its voice."

The members of the Brāhmo Samāj are opposed to the traditional guru

[1] The inscrutable Power of Illusion.

system of orthodox Hinduism. Therefore the Brāhmo devotee asked the Master about it.

BRĀHMO: "Is spiritual knowledge impossible without a guru?"

MASTER: "Satchidānanda alone is the Guru. If a man in the form of a guru awakens spiritual consciousness in you, then know for certain that it is God the Absolute who has assumed that human form for your sake. The guru is like a companion who leads you by the hand. After the realization of God, one loses the distinction between the guru and the disciple. That creates a very difficult situation; there the guru and the disciple do not see each other.'[2] It was for this reason that Janaka said to Śukadeva, 'Give me first my teacher's fee if you want me to initiate you into the Knowledge of Brahman.' For the distinction between the teacher and the disciple ceases to exist after the disciple attains to Brahman. The relationship between them remains as long as the disciple does not see God."

It was dusk. Some of the Brāhmo devotees said to the Master, "Perhaps it is time for your evening devotions."

MASTER: "No, it isn't exactly that. One should pass through these disciplines in the beginning. Later one doesn't need the rituals of formal worship or to follow the injunctions."

After dusk the preacher of the Brāhmo Samāj conducted the service from the pulpit. The service was interspersed with recitations from the Upanishads and the singing of Brāhmo songs.

After the service the Master and the preacher conversed.

MASTER: "Well, it seems to me that both the formless Deity and God with form are real. What do you say?"

PREACHER: "Sir, I compare the formless God to the electric current, which is not seen with the eyes but can be felt."

MASTER: "Yes, both are true. God with form is as real as God without form. Do you know what describing God as being formless only is like? It is like a man's playing only a monotone on his flute, though it has seven holes. But on the same instrument another man plays different melodies. Likewise, in how many ways the believers in a Personal God enjoy Him! They enjoy Him through many different attitudes: the serene attitude, the attitude of a servant, a friend, a mother, a husband, or a lover.

"You see, the thing is somehow or other to get into the Lake of the Nectar of Immortality. Suppose one person gets into It by propitiating the Deity with hymns and worship, and you are pushed into It. The result will be the same. Both of you will certainly become immortal.

"I give the Brāhmos the illustration of water and ice. Satchidānanda is like an endless expanse of water. The water of the great ocean in cold regions freezes into blocks of ice. Similarly, through the cooling influence of divine love, Satchidānanda assumes forms for the sake of the bhaktas. The rishis had the vision of the supersensuous Spirit-form and talked with It. But devotees acquire a 'love body', and with its help they see the Spirit-form of the Absolute.

[2] Because the aspirant realizes, at that time, the oneness of existence and hence does not perceive the separate existence of the teacher.

"It is also said in the Vedas that Brahman is beyond mind and words. The heat of the sun of Knowledge melts the ice-like form of the Personal God. On attaining the Knowledge of Brahman and communing with It in nirvikalpa samādhi, one realizes Brahman, the Infinite, without form or shape and beyond mind and words.

"The nature of Brahman cannot be described. About It one remains silent. Who can explain the Infinite in words? However high a bird may soar, there are regions higher still. What do you say?"

PREACHER: "Yes, sir, it is so stated in the Vedānta philosophy."

MASTER: "Once a salt doll went to the ocean to measure its depth. But it could not come back to give a report. According to one school of thought, sages like Śukadeva saw and touched the Ocean of Brahman, but did not plunge into It.

"Once I said to Vidyāsāgar, 'Everything else but Brahman has been polluted, as it were, like food touched by the tongue.' In other words, no one has been able to describe what Brahman is. A thing once uttered by the tongue becomes polluted. Vidyāsāgar, great pundit though he was, was highly pleased with my remarks.

"It is said that there are places near Kedār[3] that are covered with eternal snow; he who climbs too high cannot come back. Those who have tried to find out what there is in the higher regions, or what one feels there, have not come back to tell us about it.

"After having the vision of God man is overpowered with bliss. He becomes silent. Who will speak? Who will explain?

"The king lives beyond seven gates. At each gate sits a man endowed with great power and glory. At each gate the visitor asks, 'Is this the king?' The gate-keeper answers, 'No. Not this, not this.' The visitor passes through the seventh gate and becomes overpowered with joy. He is speechless. This time he doesn't have to ask, 'Is this the king?' The mere sight of him removes all doubts."

PREACHER: "Yes, sir, it is so described in Vedānta."

MASTER: "When the Godhead is thought of as creating, preserving, and destroying, It is known as the Personal God, Saguna Brahman, or the Primal Energy, Ādyāśakti. Again, when It is thought of as beyond the three gunas, then It is called the Attributeless Reality, Nirguna Brahman, beyond speech and thought; this is the Supreme Brahman, Parabrahman.

"Under the spell of God's māyā man forgets his true nature. He forgets that he is heir to the infinite glories of his Father. This divine māyā is made up of three gunas. And all three are robbers; for they rob man of all his treasures and make him forget his true nature. The three gunas are sattva, rajas, and tamas. Of these, sattva alone points the way to God. But even sattva cannot take a man to God.

"Let me tell you a story. Once a rich man was passing through a forest, when three robbers surrounded him and robbed him of all his wealth. After snatching all his possessions from him, one of the robbers said: 'What's the good of keeping the man alive? Kill him.' Saying this, he was about to

---

[3] A high peak in the Himālayas, which is a place of pilgrimage for the Hindus.

strike their victim with his sword, when the second robber interrupted and said: 'There's no use in killing him. Let us bind him fast and leave him here. Then he won't be able to tell the police.' Accordingly the robbers tied him with a rope, left him, and went away.

"After a while the third robber returned to the rich man and said: 'Ah! You're badly hurt, aren't you? Come, I'm going to release you.' The third robber set the man free and led him out of the forest. When they came near the highway, the robber said, 'Follow this road and you will reach home easily.' 'But you must come with me too', said the man. 'You have done so much for me. We shall all be happy to see you at our home.' 'No,' said the robber, 'it is not possible for me to go there. The police will arrest me.' So saying, he left the rich man after pointing out his way.

"Now, the first robber, who said: 'What's the good of keeping the man alive? Kill him', is tamas. It destroys. The second robber is rajas, which binds a man to the world and entangles him in a variety of activities. Rajas makes him forget God. Sattva alone shows the way to God. It produces virtues like compassion, righteousness, and devotion. Again, sattva is like the last step of the stairs. Next to it is the roof. The Supreme Brahman is man's own abode. One cannot attain the Knowledge of Brahman unless one transcends the three gunas."

PREACHER: "You have given us a fine talk, sir."

MASTER (with a smile): "Do you know the nature of devotees? When one devotee meets another, he says, 'Let me speak and you listen; and when you speak I shall listen.' You are a preacher and teach so many people! You are a steamship, and I am a mere fishing-boat." (All laugh.)

Wednesday, May 2, 1883

About five o'clock in the afternoon Sri Ramakrishna arrived at the temple of the Brāhmo Samāj in Nandanbāgan, accompanied by M., Rakhal, and a few other devotees. At first the Master sat in the drawing-room on the ground floor, where the Brāhmo devotees gradually assembled. Rabindranath Tagore and a few other members of the Tagore family were present on this occasion.

Sri Ramakrishna was asked to go to the worship hall on the second floor. A dais had been built on the eastern side of the room. There were a few chairs and a piano in the hall. The Brāhmo worship was to begin at dusk.

As soon as the Master entered the worship hall he bowed low before the dais. Having taken his seat, he said to M. and the other devotees, "Narendra once asked me, 'What good is there in bowing before the Brāhmo Samāj temple?' The sight of the temple recalls to my mind God alone; then God-Consciousness is kindled in my mind. God is present where people talk about Him. One feels there the presence of all the holy places. Places of worship recall God alone to my mind.

"Once a devotee was overwhelmed with ecstasy at the sight of a bāblā-tree. The idea flashed in his mind that the handle of the axe used in the garden of the temple of Rādhākānta was made from the wood of the bāblā. Another devotee had such devotion for his guru that he would be overwhelmed with divine feeling at the sight of his guru's neighbours. Krishna-consciousness would be kindled in Rādhā's mind at the sight of a cloud, a blue dress,[4] or a painting of Krishna. She would become restless and cry like a mad person, 'Krishna, where art Thou?'"

GHOSAL: "But madness is not desirable."

MASTER: "What do you mean? Was Rādhā's madness the madness that comes from brooding over worldly objects and makes one unconscious? One attains that madness by meditating on God. Haven't you heard of love-madness and knowledge madness?"

A BRĀHMO DEVOTEE: "How can one realize God?"

MASTER: "By directing your love to Him and constantly reasoning that God alone is real and the world illusory. The aśwattha tree alone is permanent; its fruit is transitory."

BRĀHMO: "We have passions like anger and lust. What shall we do with these?"

MASTER: "Direct the six passions to God. The impulse of *lust* should be turned into the desire to have intercourse with Ātman. Feel *angry* at those who stand in your way to God. Feel *greedy* for Him. If you must have the feeling of *I and mine*, then associate it with God. Say, for instance, 'My Rāma, my Krishna.' If you must have *pride*, then feel like Bibhishana, who said, 'I have touched the feet of Rāma with my head; I will not bow this head before anyone else.'"

BRĀHMO: "If it is God that makes me do everything, then I am not responsible for my sins."

MASTER (*with a smile*): "Yes, Duryodhana also said that. 'O Krishna, I do what Thou, seated in my heart, makest me do.' If a man has the firm conviction that God alone is the Doer and he is His instrument, then he cannot do anything sinful. He who has learnt to dance correctly never makes a false step. One cannot even believe in the existence of God until one's heart becomes pure."

Sri Ramakrishna looked at the devotees assembled in the worship hall and said: "It is very good to gather in this way, now and then, and think of God and sing His name and glories. But the worldly man's yearning for God is momentary. It lasts as long as a drop of water on a red-hot frying-pan."

The worship was about to begin, and the big hall was filled with Brāhmo devotees. Some of the Brāhmo ladies sat on chairs, with music books in their hands. The songs of the Brāhmo Samāj were sung to the accompaniment of harmonium and piano. Sri Ramakrishna's joy was unbounded. The invocation was followed by a prayer, and then the worship began. The āchāryas, seated on the platform, recited from the Vedas:

> Om. Thou art our Father. Give us right knowledge; do not destroy us! We bow to Thee.

The Brāhmo devotees chanted in chorus with the āchāryas:

> Om. Brahman is Truth, Knowledge, Infinity. It shines as Bliss and

[4] Krishna had a dark-blue complexion.

Immortality. Brahman is Peace, Blessedness, and the One without a Second; It is pure and unstained by sin.

The āchāryas chanted in praise of God:

Om. O Reality, Cause of the Universe, we bow to Thee!

Then the āchāryas chanted their prayer together:

From the unreal lead us to the Real; from darkness lead us to Light; from death lead us to Immortality. Reach us through and through, O Rudra, and protect us evermore with Thy Compassionate Face.

As Sri Ramakrishna heard these hymns, he went into a spiritual mood. After this an āchārya read a paper.

The worship was over. Most of the devotees went downstairs or to the courtyard for fresh air while the refreshments were being made ready. It was about nine o'clock in the evening. The hosts were so engrossed with the other invited guests that they forgot to pay any attention to Sri Ramakrishna.

MASTER (to Rakhal and the other devotees): "What's the matter? Nobody is paying any attention to us!"

RAKHAL (angrily): "Sir, let us leave here and go to Dakshineswar."

MASTER (with a smile): "Keep quiet! The carriage hire is three rupees and two ānnās. Who will pay that? Stubbornness won't get us anywhere. You haven't a penny, and you are making these empty threats! Besides, where shall we find food at this late hour of the night?"

After a long time dinner was announced. The devotees were asked to take their seats. The Master, with Rakhal and the others, followed the crowd to the second floor. No room could be found for him inside the hall. Finally, with great difficulty, a place was found for him in a dusty corner. A brāhmin woman served some curry, but Sri Ramakrishna could not eat it. He ate luchi with salt and took some sweets.

There was no limit to the Master's kindness. The hosts were mere young-sters; how could he be displeased with them, even though they did not show him proper respect? Further, it would have been inauspicious for the house-hold if a holy man had left the place without taking food. Finally, the feast had been prepared in the name of God.

Sri Ramakrishna got into a carriage: but who was to pay the hire? The hosts could not be found. Referring to this incident afterwards, the Master said to the devotees, jokingly: "The boys went to our hosts for the carriage hire. First they were put out, but at last they managed to get together three rupees. Our hosts refused to pay the extra two ānnās and said, 'No, that will do.'"

Sunday, May 13, 1883

The Master paid a visit to the Hari-Bhakti-Pradāyini Sabhā of Kānshāri-pāra, in Calcutta, on the anniversary day of that religious society.

Kirtan and other forms of devotional music had been arranged for the occasion. The songs centred round the Vrindāvan episode of Sri Krishna's

life. The theme was Rādhā's pique because of Sri Krishna's having visited
Chandrāvali, another of the gopis of Vrindāvan. Rādhā's friends tried to
console her and said to her: "Why are you piqued? It seems you are not
thinking of Krishna's happiness, but only of your own." Rādhā said to them:
"I am not angry at His going to Chandrāvali's grove. But why should He go
there? She doesn't know how to take care of Him."

May 20, 1883

The following Sunday a kirtan was arranged at the house of Ram, one
of the Master's householder devotees. Sri Ramakrishna graced the occasion
with his presence. The musicians sang about Rādhā's pangs at her separation
from Krishna:

> Rādhā said to her friends: "I have loved to see Krishna from my
> childhood. My finger-nails are worn off from counting the days on them
> till I shall see Him. Once He gave me a garland. Look, it has withered,
> but I have not yet thrown it away. Alas! Where has the Moon of
> Krishna risen now? Has that Moon gone away from my firmament,
> afraid of the Rāhu[5] of my pique? Alas! Shall I ever see Krishna again?
> O my beloved Krishna, I have never been able to look at You to my
> heart's complete satisfaction. I have only one pair of eyes; they blink and
> so hinder my vision. And further, on account of streams of tears I could
> not see enough of my Beloved. The peacock feather on the crown of
> His head shines like arrested lightning. The peacocks, seeing Krishna's
> dark-cloud complexion, would dance in joy, spreading their tails. O
> friends, I shall not be able to keep my life-breath. After my death, place
> my body on a branch of the dark tamāla tree and inscribe on my body
> Krishna's sweet name."

The Master said: "God and His name are identical; that is the reason Rādhā
said that. There is no difference between Rāma and His holy name."

May 27, 1883

Sri Ramakrishna was in his room at Dakshineswar, conversing with the
devotees. It was about nine o'clock in the morning.

MASTER (*to M. and the other devotees*): "It is not good to harbour malice.
The Śāktas, the Vaishnavas, and the Vedāntists quarrel among themselves.
That is not wise. Padmalochan was court pundit of the Mahārājā of Burdwān.
Once at a meeting the pundits were discussing whether Śiva was superior
to Brahmā, or Brahmā to Śiva. Padmalochan gave an appropriate reply. 'I
don't know anything about it', said he. 'I haven't talked either to Śiva or to
Brahmā.'

"If people feel sincere longing, they will find that all paths lead to God.
But one should have nishthā, single-minded devotion. It is also described as
chaste and unswerving devotion to God. It is like a tree with only one trunk
shooting straight up. Promiscuous devotion is like a tree with five branches.

[5] A monster in Hindu mythology, said to cause the eclipse by devouring the sun
and the moon.

Such was the single-minded devotion of the gopis to Krishna that they didn't care to look at anyone but the Krishna they had seen at Vrindāvan—the Shepherd Krishna, bedecked with a garland of yellow wild-flowers and wearing a peacock feather on His crest. At the sight of Krishna at Mathurā with a turban on His head and dressed in royal robes, the gopis pulled down their veils. They would not look at His face. 'Who is this man?' they said. 'Should we violate our chaste love for Krishna by talking to him?'

"The devotion of the wife to her husband is also an instance of unswerving love. She feeds her brothers-in-law as well, and looks after their comforts, but she has a special relationship with her husband. Likewise, one may have that single-minded devotion to one's own religion; but one should not on that account hate other faiths. On the contrary, one should have a friendly attitude toward them."

The Master bathed in the Ganges and then went to the Kāli temple with M. He sat before the image and offered flowers at the feet of the Divine Mother. Now and then he put flowers on his own head and meditated.

After a long time he stood up. He was in a spiritual mood and danced before the image, chanting the name of Kāli. Now and again he said: "O Mother! O Destroyer of suffering! O Remover of grief and agony!" Was he teaching people thus to pray to the Mother of the Universe with a yearning heart, in order to get rid of the suffering inevitable in physical life?

Sri Ramakrishna returned to his room and sat on the west porch. Rakhal, M., Nakur Vaishnav, and other devotees were with him. Nakur had been known to the Master for about twenty-five years. He was a devotee of Gaurānga and had a small shop which Sri Ramakrishna had often visited when he first came to Calcutta from Kāmārpukur.

Still overpowered with divine ecstasy, the Master sang:

O Kāli, my Mother full of Bliss! Enchantress of the almighty Śiva!
In Thy delirious joy Thou dancest, clapping Thy hands together!
Eternal One! Thou great First Cause, clothed in the form of the
    Void!
Thou wearest the moon upon Thy brow.
Where didst Thou find Thy garland of heads before the universe
    was made?
Thou art the Mover of all that move, and we are but Thy helpless
    toys;
We move alone as Thou movest us and speak as through us Thou
    speakest.
But worthless Kamalākānta says, fondly berating Thee:
Confoundress! With Thy flashing sword
Thoughtlessly Thou hast put to death my virtue and my sin alike!

He sang again:

Mother, Thou art our sole Redeemer,
Thou the Support of the three gunas,
Higher than the most high.
Thou art compassionate, I know,
Who takest away our bitter grief.

Sandhyā art Thou, and Gāyatri;
Thou dost sustain this universe.
Mother, the Help art Thou
Of those that have no help but Thee,
O Eternal Beloved of Śiva!

Thou art in earth, in water Thou;
Thou liest at the root of all.
In me, in every creature,
Thou hast Thy home; though clothed with form,
Yet art Thou formless Reality.

The Master sang a few more songs in praise of the Divine Mother. Then he said to the devotees: "It is not always best to tell householders about the sorrows of life. They want bliss. Those who suffer from chronic poverty can go without food for a day or two. But it is not wise to talk about the sorrows and miseries of life to those who suffer if their food is delayed a few minutes. Vaishnavcharan used to say: 'Why should one constantly dwell on sin? Be merry!' "

While the Master was resting after his midday meal, Manohor Goswami, a singer of kirtan, arrived. He sang about the ecstatic love of Gaurānga and the divine episode of Vrindāvan. The Master was absorbed in a deep spiritual mood. He tore off his shirt and said, to the melody of the kirtan, assuming the attitude of Rādhā: "O Krishna, my Beloved! O friends, bring Krishna to me. Then you will be real friends. Or take me to Him, and I will be your slave for ever."

The musician sat spellbound at Sri Ramakrishna's ecstasy; then he said with folded hands, "Won't you please rid me of my worldliness?"

MASTER: "You are like the holy man who went about the city after first finding a lodging. You are a sweet person and express many sweet ideas."

MUSICIAN: "Sir, I am like the bullock that only carries the bag of sugar but cannot taste it. Alas, I myself do not enjoy the sweetness of divine bliss."

The melodious music went on, and all were filled with joy.

Saturday, June 2, 1883

Sri Ramakrishna had been invited to visit the homes of his devotees Balaram, Adhar, and Ram in Calcutta. Devotional music had been arranged by Adhar and Ram. The Master was accompanied in the carriage by Rakhal, M., and others.

As they drove along, Sri Ramakrishna said to the devotees: "You see, sin flies away when love of God grows in a man's heart, even as the water of the reservoir dug in a meadow dries up under the heat of the sun. But one cannot love God if one feels attracted to worldly things, to 'woman and gold'. Merely taking the vow of monastic life will not help a man if he is attached to the world. It is like swallowing your own spittle after spitting it out on the ground."

After a few minutes the Master continued: "The members of the Brāhmo

Samāj do not accept God with form. Narendra says that God with form is a mere idol. He says further: 'What? He[6] still goes to the Kāli temple!' "

Sri Ramakrishna and his party arrived at Balaram's house. Yajnanath of Nandanbāgān came to invite the Master to his house at four o'clock in the afternoon. Sri Ramakrishna agreed to go if he felt well. After Yajnanath's departure the Master went into an ecstatic mood. He said to the Divine Mother: "Mother, what is all this? Stop! What are these things Thou art showing to me? What is it that Thou dost reveal to me through Rakhal and others? The form is disappearing. But, Mother, what people call 'man' is only a pillow-case, nothing but a pillow-case. Consciousness is Thine alone.

"The modern Brahmajnānis have not tasted Thy sweet bliss. Their eyes look dry and so do their faces. They won't achieve anything without ecstatic love of God.

"Mother, once I asked Thee to give me a companion just like myself. Is that why Thou hast given me Rakhal?"

The Master went to Adhar's house, where arrangements were being made for the kirtan. Many devotees and neighbours had gathered in Adhar's drawing-room, anxious to listen to the Master's words.

MASTER (*to the devotees*): "Both worldliness and liberation depend on God's will. It is God alone who has kept man in the world in a state of ignorance; and man will be free when God, of His own sweet will, calls him to Himself. It is like the mother calling the child at meal-time, when he is out playing. When the time comes for setting a man free, God makes him seek the company of holy men. Further, it is God who makes him restless for spiritual life."

A NEIGHBOUR: "What kind of restlessness, sir?"

MASTER: "Like the restlessness of a clerk who has lost his job. He makes the round of the offices daily and asks whether there is any vacancy. When that restlessness comes, man longs for God. A fop, seated comfortably with one leg over the other, chewing betel-leaf and twirling his moustaches—a carefree dandy—, cannot attain God."

NEIGHBOUR: "Can one get this longing for God through frequenting the company of holy men?"

MASTER: "Yes, it is possible. But not for a confirmed scoundrel. A sannyāsi's kamandalu, made of bitter gourd, travels with him to the four great places of pilgrimage but still does not lose its bitterness."

The kirtan began. The musician sang of Sri Krishna's life in Vrindāvan:

> RĀDHĀ: "Friend, I am about to die. Give me back my Krishna."
> FRIEND: "But, Rādhā, the cloud of Krishna was ready to burst into rain. It was yourself who blew it away with the strong wind of your pique. You are certainly not happy to see Krishna happy; or why were you piqued?"
> RĀDHĀ: "But this pride was not mine. My pride has gone away with Him who made me proud."

After the music Sri Ramakrishna conversed with the devotees.

[6] Referring to the Master.

MASTER: "The gopis worshipped Kātyāyani in order to be united with Sri Krishna. Everyone is under the authority of the Divine Mother, Mahāmāyā, the Primal Energy. Even the Incarnations of God accept the help of māyā to fulfil their mission on earth. Therefore they worship the Primal Energy. Don't you see how bitterly Rāma wept for Sītā? 'Brahman weeps, ensnared in the meshes of māyā.'

"Vishnu incarnated Himself as a sow in order to kill the demon Hiranyāksha. After killing the demon, the sow remained quite happy with her young ones. Forgetting her real nature, she was suckling them very contentedly. The gods in heaven could not persuade Vishnu to relinquish His sow's body and return to the celestial regions. He was absorbed in the happiness of His beast form. After consulting among themselves, the gods sent Śiva to the sow. Śiva asked the sow, 'Why have you forgotten yourself?' Vishnu replied through the sow's body, 'Why, I am quite happy here.' Thereupon with a stroke of his trident Śiva destroyed the sow's body, and Vishnu went back to heaven."

From Adhar's house Sri Ramakrishna went to Ram's house. Ramchandra Dutta, one of the chief householder disciples of the Master, lived in Calcutta. He had been one of the first to announce the Master as an Incarnation of God. The Master had visited his house a number of times and unstintingly praised the devotion and generosity of this beloved disciple. A few of the Master's disciples made Ram's house virtually their own dwelling-place.

Ram had arranged a special festival to celebrate the Master's visit. The small courtyard was nicely decorated. A kathak, seated on a raised platform, was reciting from the *Bhāgavata* when the Master arrived. Ram greeted him respectfully and seated him near the reader. The disciple was extremely happy. The kathak was in the midst of the story of King Harischandra.

The great King Harischandra of the Purāna was the embodiment of generosity. No one ever went away from him empty-handed. Now, the sage Viśwāmitra, wanting to test the extent of the king's charity, extracted from him a promise to grant any boon that he might ask. Then the sage asked for the gift of the sea-girt world, of which Harischandra was king. Without the slightest hesitation the king gave away his kingdom. Then Viśwāmitra demanded the auxiliary fee, which alone makes charity valid and meritorious.

The kathak continued his recitation:

Viśwāmitra said to the king: "O King, you have given away the entire world, which was your kingdom. It now belongs to me; you cannot claim any place here. But you may live in Benares, which belongs to Śiva. I shall lead you there with your wife Śaibyā, and Rohitāśva, your son. There you can procure the auxiliary fee that you owe me." The royal family, accompanied by the sage, reached Benares and visited the temple of Śiva.

At the very mention of Śiva, the Master went into spiritual mood and repeated the holy name several times indistinctly.

The kathak continued:

The king could not procure the fee and was compelled to sell Śaibyā, his royal consort, to a brāhmin. With her went Prince Rohitāśva. But since even that was not enough to redeem his pledge to the sage, Harischandra sold himself to an untouchable who kept a cremation ground. He was ordered to supervise the cremations.

One day, while plucking flowers for his brāhmin master, Prince Rohitāśva was bitten by a venomous snake and that very night died. The cruel brāhmin would not leave his bed to help the poor mother cremate the body. The night was dark and stormy. Lightning rent the black clouds. Śaibyā started for the cremation ground alone, carrying the body of her son in her arms. Smitten with fear and overpowered with grief, the queen filled heaven and earth with her wailing. Arriving at the cremation ground, she did not recognize her husband, who demanded the usual fee for the cremation. Śaibyā was penniless and wept bitterly at her unending misfortunes. The impenetrable darkness was illumined only by the terrible flames of the cremation pyres. Above her the thunder roared, and before her the uncouth guardian of the cremation ground demanded his fee. She who had once been queen of the world sat there with her only child dead and cold on her lap.

The devotees burst into tears and loudly lamented this tragic episode of a royal life. And what was the Master doing? He was listening to the recital with rapt attention. Tear-drops appeared in his eyes and he wiped them away.

The kathak continued:

When the queen, wailing bitterly, uttered the name of her husband, Harischandra at once recognized his wife and son. Then the two wept for the dead prince. Yet in all these misfortunes the king never once uttered a word of regret for his charity.

Finally the sage Viśwāmitra appeared and told them that he had only wanted to put the king's charitable impulses to a crucial test. Then, through his spiritual power, the sage brought the prince back to life and returned to the king his lost kingdom.

Sri Ramakrishna asked the kathak to recite the episode of Uddhava, the friend and devotee of Krishna.

At the request of Krishna, Uddhava had gone to Vrindāvan to console the cowherds and the gopis, who were sore at heart because of their separation from their beloved Krishna.

The kathak said:

When Uddhava arrived at Vrindāvan, the gopis and cowherd boys ran to him eagerly and asked him: "How is our Krishna? Has He forgotten us altogether? Doesn't He even speak our names?" So saying, some of them wept. Others accompanied him to various places in Vrindāvan still filled with Krishna's sweet memory. They said: "Here it was that Krishna lifted up Mount Govardhan, and here He killed the demons sent by the evil-minded Kaṃsa. In this meadow He tended His cows; here on the bank of the Jamunā He sported with the gopis. Here

He played with the cowherd boys, and here in these groves He met the gopis secretly." Uddhava said to them: "Why are you so grief-stricken at Krishna's absence? He resides in all beings as their indwelling Spirit. He is God Himself, and nothing can exist without God." "But", said the gopis, "we do not understand all that. We can neither read nor write. We know only our Krishna of Vrindāvan, who played with us here in so many ways." Uddhava said: "Krishna is God Himself. By meditating on Him, man escapes from birth and death in the world and attains liberation." The gopis said: "We do not understand big words like 'liberation'. We want to see the Krishna of our hearts."

The Master listened to the story from the *Bhāgavata* with great attention and said at last, "Yes, the gopis were right."

Then he sang:

> Though I[7] am never loath to grant salvation,
> I hesitate indeed to grant pure love.
> Whoever wins pure love surpasses all;
> He is adored by men;
> He triumphs over the three worlds.

> Listen, Chandrāvali![8] I shall tell you of love:
> Mukti a man may gain, but rare is bhakti.
> Solely for pure love's sake did I become
> King Vali's door-keeper
> Down in his realm in the nether world.[9]

> Alone in Vrindāvan can pure love be found;
> Its secret none but the gopas and gopis know.
> For pure love's sake I dwelt in Nanda's house;
> Taking him as My father,
> I carried his burdens on My head.

The Master said to the kathak: "The gopis had ecstatic love, unswerving and single-minded devotion to one ideal. Do you know the meaning of devotion that is not loyal to one ideal? It is devotion tinged with intellectual knowledge. It makes one feel: 'Krishna has become all these. He alone is the Supreme Brahman. He is Rāma, Śiva, and Śakti.' But this element of knowledge is not present in ecstatic love of God. Once Hanumān came to Dwārakā and wanted to see Sītā and Rāma. Krishna said to Rukmini, His queen, 'You had better assume the form of Sītā; otherwise there will be no escape from the hands of Hanumān.'[10]

"Once the Pāndava brothers performed the Rājasuya sacrifice. All the kings placed Yudhisthira on the royal throne and bowed low before him in homage. But Bibhishana, the King of Ceylon, said, 'I bow down to Nārāyana and to none else.' At these words the Lord Krishna bowed down to

[7] The song represents Sri Krishna's words.
[8] One of the gopis of Vrindāvan.
[9] An allusion to the story of Vali, narrated in the Purāna. He was punished by the Lord for his excessive charity and was condemned to rule over the nether world. But he succeeded in extracting from the Lord the boon that He would be his door-keeper.
[10] Because Rāma and Sītā were Hanumān's Chosen Ideals.

Yudhisthira. Only then did Bibhishana prostrate himself, crown and all, before him.

"Do you know what devotion to one ideal is like? It is like the attitude of a daughter-in-law in the family. She serves all the members of the family—her brothers-in-law, father-in-law, husband, and so forth—, bringing them water to wash their feet, fetching their towels, arranging their seats, and the like; but with her husband she has a special relationship.

"There are two elements in this ecstatic love: 'I-ness' and 'my-ness'. Yaśodā used to think: 'Who would look after Gopāla if I did not? He will fall ill if I do not serve Him.' She did not look on Krishna as God. The other element is 'my-ness'. It means to look on God as one's own—'my Gopāla'. Uddhava said to Yaśodā: 'Mother, your Krishna is God Himself. He is the Lord of the Universe and not a common human being.' 'Oh!' exclaimed Yaśodā. 'I am not asking you about your Lord of the Universe. I want to know how my Gopāla fares. Not the Lord of the Universe, but my Gopāla.'

"How faithful to Krishna the gopis were! After many entreaties to the door-keeper, the gopis entered the royal court in Mathurā, where Krishna was seated as king. The door-keeper took them to Him; but at the sight of King Krishna wearing the royal turban, the gopis bent down their heads and said among themselves: 'Who is this man with a turban on his head? Should we violate our chaste love for Krishna by talking to him? Where is our beloved Krishna with the yellow robe and the bewitching crest with the peacock feather?'

"Did you observe the single-minded love of the gopis for Krishna? The ideal of Vrindāvan is unique. I am told that the people of Dwārakā worship Krishna, the companion of Arjuna, but reject Rādhā."

A DEVOTEE: "Which is the better, ecstatic love or love mixed with knowledge?"

MASTER: "It is not possible to develop ecstatic love of God unless you love Him very deeply and regard Him as your very own.

"Listen to a story. Once three friends were going through a forest, when a tiger suddenly appeared before them. 'Brothers,' one of them exclaimed, 'we are lost!' 'Why should you say that?' said the second friend. 'Why should we be lost? Come, let us pray to God.' The third friend said: 'No. Why should we trouble God about it? Come, let us climb this tree.'

"The friend who said, 'We are lost!' did not know that there is a God who is our Protector. The friend who asked the others to pray to God was a jnāni. He was aware that God is the Creator, Preserver, and Destroyer of the world. The third friend, who didn't want to trouble God with prayers and suggested climbing the tree, had ecstatic love of God. It is the very nature of such love that it makes a man think himself stronger than his Beloved. He is always alert lest his Beloved should suffer. The one desire of his life is to keep his Beloved from even being pricked in the foot by a thorn."

Ram served the Master and the devotees with delicious sweets.

WITH THE DEVOTEES AT DAK-SHINESWAR (I)

Monday, June 4, 1883

ABOUT NINE O'CLOCK in the morning the devotees began to arrive at the temple garden. Sri Ramakrishna was sitting on the porch of his room facing the Ganges. M., who had spent the previous night with the Master, sat near him. Balaram and several other devotees were present. Rakhal lay on the floor, resting his head on the Master's lap. For the past few days the Master had been regarding Rakhal as the Baby Krishna.

Seeing Trailokya[1] passing on his way to the Kāli temple, Sri Ramakrishna asked Rakhal to get up. Trailokya bowed to the Master.

MASTER *(to Trailokya)*: "Was there no yātrā performance last night?"[2]

TRAILOKYA: "No, sir. We couldn't conveniently arrange it."

MASTER: "What is done is done. But please see that this doesn't happen again. The traditions of the temple should be properly observed."

Trailokya gave a suitable reply and went on his way. After a while Ram Chatterji, the priest of the Vishnu temple, came up to Sri Ramakrishna.

MASTER: "Well, Ram, I told Trailokya that the yātrā performance should not be omitted again. Was I right in saying that?"

RAM: "What of it, sir? Of course you were right. The traditions should be observed."

The Master asked Balaram to stay for his midday meal. Before the meal Sri Ramakrishna described to the devotees the days of his God-intoxication. Rakhal, M., Ramlal, and a few others were present.

MASTER: "Now and then Hazra comes forward to teach me. He says to me, 'Why do you think so much about the youngsters?' One day, as I was going to Balaram's house in a carriage, I felt greatly troubled about it. I said to the Divine Mother: 'Mother, Hazra admonishes me for worrying about Narendra and the other young boys. He asks me why I forget God and think about these youngsters.' No sooner did this thought arise in my mind

---

[1] The son of Mathur and grandson of Rāni Rasmani. He had become proprietor of the temple in 1871.

[2] A special worship of the Divine Mother had taken place that night in the Kāli temple. On similar occasions in previous years the proprietors of the temple had arranged the performance of the yātrā.

than the Divine Mother revealed to me in a flash that it is She Herself who
has become man. But She manifests Herself most clearly through a pure
soul. At this vision I went into samādhi. Afterwards I felt angry with Hazra.
I said to myself, 'That rascal made me miserable.' Then I thought: 'But why
should I blame the poor man? How is he to know?'

"I know these youngsters to be Nārāyana Himself. At my first meeting
with Narendra I found him completely indifferent to his body. When I
touched his chest with my hand, he lost consciousness of the outer world.
Regaining consciousness, Narendra said: 'Oh, what have you done to me?
I have my father and mother at home!' The same thing happened at Jadu
Mallick's house. As the days passed I longed more and more to see him. My
heart yearned for him. One day at that time I said to Bholanath:[3] 'Can you
tell me why I should feel this way? There is a boy called Narendra, of the
kāyastha caste. Why should I feel so restless for him?' Bholanath said: 'You
will find the explanation in the Mahābhārata. On coming down to the plane
of ordinary consciousness, a man established in samādhi enjoys himself in
the company of sāttvic people. He feels peace of mind at the sight of such
men.' When I heard this my mind was set at ease. Now and then I would
sit alone and weep for the sight of Narendra.

"Oh, what a state of mind I passed through! When I first had that experience, I could not perceive the coming and going of day or night. People said
I was insane. What else could they say? They made me marry. I was then in
a state of God-intoxication. At first I felt worried about my wife. Then I
thought she too would eat and drink and live like me.

"I visited my father-in-law's house. They arranged a kirtan. It was a great
religious festival, and there was much singing of God's holy name. Now and
then I would wonder about my future. I would say to the Divine Mother,
'Mother, I shall take my spiritual experiences to be real if the landlords of
the country show me respect.' They too came of their own accord and talked
with me.

"Oh, what an ecstatic state it was! Even the slightest suggestion would
awaken my spiritual consciousness. I worshipped the 'Beautiful' in a girl
fourteen years old. I saw that she was the personification of the Divine
Mother. At the end of the worship I bowed before her and offered a rupee at
her feet. One day I witnessed a Rāmlīlā performance. I saw the performers
to be the actual Sītā, Rāma, Lakshmana, Hanumān, and Bibhishana. Then I
worshipped the actors and actresses who played those parts.

"At that time I used to invite maidens here and worship them. I found
them to be embodiments of the Divine Mother Herself.

"One day I saw a woman in blue standing near the bakul-tree. She was a
prostitute. But she instantly kindled in me the vision of Sītā. I forgot the
woman. I saw that it was Sītā herself on her way to meet Rāma after her
rescue from Rāvana in Ceylon. For a long time I remained in samādhi, unconscious of the outer world.

"Another day I had gone to the Maidān in Calcutta for fresh air. A great
crowd had assembled there to watch a balloon ascension. Suddenly I saw an

[3] A clerk at the Dakshineswar temple garden.

English boy leaning against a tree. As he stood there his body was bent in three places. The vision of Krishna came before me in a flash. I went into samādhi.

"Once, at Sihore, I fed the cowherd boys. I put sweetmeats into their hands. I saw that these boys were actually the cowherd boys of Vrindāvan, and I partook of the sweetmeats from their hands.

"At that time I was almost unconscious of the outer world. Mathur Babu kept me at his Jānbāzār mansion a few days. While living there I regarded myself as the handmaid of the Divine Mother. The ladies of the house didn't feel at all bashful with me. They felt as free before me as women feel before a small boy or girl. I used to escort Mathur's daughter to her husband's chamber with the maidservant.

"Even now the slightest thing awakens God-Consciousness in me. Rakhal used to repeat the name of God half aloud. At such times I couldn't control myself. It would rouse my spiritual consciousness and overwhelm me."

Sri Ramakrishna went on describing the different experiences he had had while worshipping the Divine Mother as Her handmaid. He said: "Once I imitated a professional woman singer for a man singer. He said my acting was quite correct and asked me where I had learnt it." The Master repeated his imitation for the devotees, and they burst into laughter.

After his noon meal the Master took a short rest. Manilal Mallick, an old member of the Brāhmo Samāj, entered the room and sat down after saluting the Master, who was still lying on his bed. Manilal asked him questions now and then, and the Master, still half asleep, answered with a word or two. Manilal said that Shivanath admired Nityagopal's spiritual state. The Master asked in a sleepy tone what they thought of Hazra.

Then Sri Ramakrishna sat up on his bed and told Manilal about Bhavanath's devotion to God.

MASTER: "Ah, what an exalted state he is in! He has hardly begun to sing about God before his eyes fill with tears. The very sight of Harish made him ecstatic. He said that Harish was very lucky. He made the remark because Harish was spending a few days here, now and then, away from his home."

Sri Ramakrishna asked M., "Well, what is the cause of bhakti? Why should the spiritual feeling of young boys like Bhavanath be awakened?" M. remained silent.

MASTER: "The fact is, all men may look alike from the outside, but some of them have fillings of 'condensed milk'. Cakes may have fillings of condensed milk or powdered black grams, but they all look alike from the outside. The desire to know God, ecstatic love of Him, and such other spiritual qualities are the 'condensed milk'."

Sri Ramakrishna spoke reassuringly to the devotees.

MASTER (to M.): "Some think: 'Oh, I am a bound soul. I shall never acquire knowledge and devotion.' But if one receives the guru's grace, one has nothing to fear. Once a tigress attacked a flock of goats. As she sprang on her prey, she gave birth to a cub and died. The cub grew up in the company of the goats. The goats ate grass and the cub followed their example.

They bleated; the cub bleated too. Gradually it grew to be a big tiger. One day another tiger attacked the same flock. It was amazed to see the grass-eating tiger. Running after it, the wild tiger at last seized it, whereupon the grass-eating tiger began to bleat. The wild tiger dragged it to the water and said: 'Look at your face in the water. It is just like mine. Here is a little meat. Eat it.' Saying this, it thrust some meat into its mouth. But the grass-eating tiger would not swallow it and began to bleat again. Gradually, however, it got the taste for blood and came to relish the meat. Then the wild tiger said: 'Now you see there is no difference between you and me. Come along and follow me into the forest.'

"So there can be no fear if the guru's grace descends on one. He will let you know who you are and what your real nature is.

"If the devotee practises spiritual discipline a little, the guru explains everything to him. Then the disciple understands for himself what is real and what is unreal. God alone is real, and the world is illusory.

"One night a fisherman went into a garden and cast his net into the lake in order to steal some fish. The owner heard him and surrounded him with his servants. They brought lighted torches and began to search for him. In the mean time the fisherman smeared his body with ashes and sat under a tree, pretending to be a holy man. The owner and his men searched a great deal but could not find the thief. All they saw was a holy man covered with ashes, meditating under a tree. The next day the news spread in the neighbourhood that a great sage was staying in the garden. People gathered there and saluted him with offerings of fruit, flowers, and sweets. Many also offered silver and copper coins. 'How strange!' thought the fisherman. 'I am not a genuine holy man, and still people show such devotion to me. I shall certainly realize God if I become a true sādhu. There is no doubt about it.'

"If a mere pretence of religious life can bring such spiritual awakening, you can imagine the effect of real sādhanā. In that state you will surely realize what is real and what is unreal. God alone is real, and the world is illusory."

One of the devotees said to himself: "Is the world unreal, then? The fisherman, to be sure, renounced worldly life. What, then, will happen to those who live in the world? Must they too renounce it?" Sri Ramakrishna, who could see into a man's innermost thought, said very tenderly: "Suppose an office clerk has been sent to jail. He undoubtedly leads a prisoner's life there. But when he is released from jail, does he cut capers in the street? Not at all. He gets a job as a clerk again and goes on working as before. Even after attaining Knowledge through the guru's grace, one can very well live in the world as a jīvanmukta." Thus did Sri Ramakrishna reassure those who were living as householders.

MANILAL: "Sir, where shall I meditate on God when I perform my daily worship?"

MASTER: "Why, the heart is a splendid place. Meditate on God there."

Manilal, a member of the Brāhmo Samāj, believed in a formless God. Addressing him, the Master said: "Kabir used to say: 'God with form is my Mother, the formless God my Father. Whom should I blame? Whom should

I adore? The two sides of the scales are even.' During the day-time Haladhari used to meditate on God with form, and at night on the formless God. Whichever attitude you adopt, you will certainly realize God if you have firm faith. You may believe in God with form or in God without form, but your faith must be sincere and whole-hearted. Sambhu Mallick used to come on foot from Bāghbāzār to his garden house at Dakshineswar. One day a friend said to him: 'It is risky to walk such a long distance. Why don't you come in a carriage?' At that Sambhu's face turned red and he exclaimed: 'I set out repeating the name of God! What danger can befall me?' Through faith alone one attains everything. I used to say, 'I shall take all this[4] to be true if I meet a certain person or if a certain officer of the temple garden talks to me.' What I would think of would invariably come to pass."

M. had studied English logic. In the chapters on fallacies he had read that only superstitious people believed in the coincidence of morning dreams with actual events. Therefore he asked the Master, "Was there never any exception?"

MASTER: "No. At that time everything happened that way. I would repeat the name of God and believe that a certain thing would happen, and it would invariably come to pass. (To Manilal) But you must remember, unless one is guileless and broad-minded, one cannot have such faith. Bony people, the hollow-eyed, the cross-eyed—people with physical traits like those cannot easily acquire faith. What can a man do if there are evil omens on all sides?"

It was dusk. The maidservant entered the room and burnt incense. Manilal and some other devotees left for Calcutta. M. and Rakhal were in the room. The Master was seated on his small couch absorbed in meditation on the Divine Mother. There was complete silence.

After a time Bhagavati, an old maidservant of the temple proprietor, entered the room and saluted the Master from a distance. Sri Ramakrishna bade her sit down. The Master had known her for many years. In her younger days she had lived a rather immoral life; but the Master's compassion was great. Soon he began to converse with her.

MASTER: "Now you are pretty old. Have you been feeding the Vaishnavas and holy men, and thus spending your money in a noble way?"

BHAGAVATI (smiling): "How can I say that?"[5]

MASTER: "Have you been to Vrindāvan, Benares, and the other holy places?"

BHAGAVATI (shrinkingly): "How can I say that?—I have built a bathing-place, and my name is inscribed there on a slab."

MASTER: "Indeed!"

BHAGAVATI: "Yes, sir. My name, 'Srimati Bhagavati Dasi', is written there."

MASTER (with a smile): "How nice!"

Emboldened by the Master's words, Bhagavati approached and saluted him, touching his feet. Like a man stung by a scorpion, Sri Ramakrishna stood up and cried out, "Govinda! Govinda!" A big jar of Ganges water stood

---

[4] His spiritual experiences.
[5] She meant "yes". In India it is customary not to mention one's meritorious deeds.

in a corner of the room. He hurried there, panting, and washed with the holy water the spot the maidservant had touched. The devotees in the room were amazed to see this incident. Bhagavati sat as if struck dead.

Sri Ramakrishna consoled her and said in a very kindly tone, "You should salute me from a distance." In order to relieve her mind of all embarrassment, the Master said tenderly, "Listen to a few songs."

The Master then sang about the Divine Mother:

> The black bee of my mind is drawn in sheer delight
> To the blue lotus flower of Mother Śyāmā's feet. . . .

Then he sang:

> High in the heaven of the Mother's feet, my mind was soaring like
>   a kite,
> When came a gust of sin's rough wind that drove it swiftly toward
>   the earth. . . .

Again:

> Dwell, O mind, within yourself;
> Enter no other's home.
> If you but seek there, you will find
> All you are searching for.
>
> God, the true Philosopher's Stone,
> Who answers every prayer,
> Lies hidden deep within your heart,
> The richest gem of all.
>
> How many pearls and precious stones
> Are scattered all about
> The outer court that lies before
> The chamber of your heart!

Tuesday, June 5, 1883

Rakhal and Hazra were staying with the Master in the temple garden at Dakshineswar. M., too, had been there since the previous Sunday. As it was a week-day there were only a few devotees in the room. Generally people gathered there in large numbers on Sundays or holidays.

It was afternoon. Sri Ramakrishna was telling the devotees about his experiences during his God-intoxicated state.

MASTER (*to M.*): "Oh, what a state I passed through! At that time I didn't eat my meals here. I would enter the house of a brāhmin in the village or at Barānagore or at Āriādaha. Generally it would be past meal-time. I would just sit down there without saying a word. If the members of the household asked me why I had come, I would simply say, 'I want something to eat.' Now and then I would go, uninvited of course, to Ram Chatterji's house at Ālambāzār or to the Choudhurys at Dakshineswar. But I didn't relish the food at the Choudhurys' house.

"One day I begged Mathur to take me to Devendra Tagore's house. I said: 'Devendra chants the name of God. I want to see him. Will you take me there?' Mathur Babu was a very proud man. How could one expect him to go to another man's house uninvited? At first he hesitated. But then he said: 'All right. Devendra and I were fellow students. I will take you to him.'

"Another day I learnt of a good man named Dina Mukherji, living at Bāghbāzār near the bridge. He was a devotee. I asked Mathur to take me there. Finding me insistent, he took me to Dina's house in a carriage. It was a small place. The arrival of a rich man in a big carriage embarrassed the inmates. We too were embarrassed. That day Dina's son was being invested with the sacred thread. The house was crowded, and there was hardly any place for Dina to receive us. We were about to enter a side room, when someone cried out: 'Please don't go into that room. There are ladies there.' It was really a distressing situation. Returning, Mathur Babu said, 'Father, I shall never listen to you again.' I laughed.

"Oh, what a state I passed through! Once Kumar Singh gave a feast to the sādhus and invited me too. I found a great many holy men assembled there. When I sat down for the meal, several sādhus asked me about myself. At once I felt like leaving them and sitting alone. I wondered why they should bother about all that. The sādhus took their seats. I began to eat before they had started. I heard several of them remark, 'Oh! What sort of man is this?'"

It was about five o'clock in the afternoon. Sri Ramakrishna was sitting on the steps of his verandah. Hazra, Rakhal, and M. were near him. Hazra had the attitude of a Vedāntist: "I am He."

MASTER (to Hazra): "Yes, all one's confusion comes to an end if one only realizes that it is God who manifests Himself as the atheist and the believer, the good and the bad, the real and the unreal; that it is He who is present in waking and in sleep; and that He is beyond all these.

"There was a farmer to whom an only son was born when he was rather advanced in age. As the child grew up, his parents became very fond of him. One day the farmer was out working in the fields, when a neighbour told him that his son was dangerously ill—indeed, at the point of death. Returning home he found the boy dead. His wife wept bitterly, but his own eyes remained dry. Sadly the wife said to her neighbours, 'Such a son has passed away, and he hasn't even one tear to shed!' After a long while the farmer said to his wife: 'Do you know why I am not crying? Last night I dreamt I had become a king, and the father of seven princes. These princes were beautiful as well as virtuous. They grew in stature and acquired wisdom and knowledge in the various arts. Suddenly I woke up. Now I have been wondering whether I should weep for those seven children or this one boy.' To the jnānis the waking state is no more real than the dream state.

"God alone is the Doer. Everything happens by His will."

HAZRA: "But it is very difficult to understand that. Take the case of the sādhu of Bhukailās. How people tortured him and, in a way, killed him! They had found him in samādhi. First they buried him, then they put him under water, and then they branded him with a hot iron. Thus they brought him back to consciousness of the world. But in the end the sādhu died as a result of these tortures. He undoubtedly suffered at the hands of men, though, as you say, he died by the will of God."

MASTER: "Man must reap the fruit of his own karma. But as far as the death of that holy man is concerned, it was brought about by the will of God. The kavirājs prepare makaradhvaja[6] in a bottle. The bottle is covered with clay and heated in the fire. The gold inside the bottle melts and combines with the other ingredients, and the medicine is made. Then the physicians break the bottle carefully and take out the medicine. When the medicine is made, what difference does it make whether the bottle is preserved or broken? So people think that the holy man was killed. But perhaps his inner stuff had been made. After the realization of God, what difference does it make whether the body lives or dies?

"The sādhu of Bhukailās was in samādhi. There are many kinds of samādhi. My own spiritual experiences tally with the words I heard from a sādhu of Hrishikesh. Sometimes I feel the rising of the spiritual current inside me, as though it were the creeping of an ant. Sometimes it feels like the movement of a monkey jumping from one branch to another. Again, sometimes it feels like a fish swimming in water. Only he who experiences it knows what it is like. In samādhi one forgets the world. When the mind comes down a little, I say to the Divine Mother: 'Mother, please cure me of this. I want to talk to people.'

"None but the Iśvarakotis can return to the plane of relative consciousness after attaining samādhi. Some ordinary men attain samādhi through spiritual discipline; but they do not come back. But when God Himself is born as a man, as an Incarnation, holding in His hand the key to others' liberation, then for the welfare of humanity the Incarnation returns from samādhi to consciousness of the world."

M. (to himself): "Does the Master hold in his hand the key to man's liberation?"

HAZRA: "The one thing needful is to please God. What does it matter whether an Incarnation of God exists or not?"

It was the day of the new moon. Gradually night descended and dense darkness enveloped the trees and the temples. A few lights shone here and there in the temple garden. The black sky was reflected in the waters of the Ganges.

The Master went to the verandah south of his room. A spiritual mood was the natural state of his mind. The dark night of the new moon, associated with the black complexion of Kāli, the Divine Mother, intensified his spiritual exaltation. Now and then he repeated "Om" and the name of Kāli. He lay down on a mat and whispered to M.

MASTER: "Yes, God can be seen. X— has had a vision of God. But don't tell anyone about it. Tell me, which do you like better, God with form, or the formless Reality?"

M: "Sir, nowadays I like to think of God without form. But I am also

---

[6] An Indian medicine made of mercury and sulphur, in the preparation of which gold acts as a catalytic agent.

beginning to understand that it is God alone who manifests Himself through different forms."

MASTER: "Will you take me in a carriage some day to Mati Seal's garden house at Belgharia? When you throw puffed rice into the lake there, the fish come to the surface and eat it. Ah! I feel so happy to see them sport in the water. That will awaken your spiritual consciousness too. You will feel as if the fish of the human soul were playing in the Ocean of Satchidananda. In the same manner, I go into an ecstatic mood when I stand in a big meadow. I feel like a fish released from a bowl into a lake.

"Spiritual discipline is necessary in order to see God. I had to pass through very severe discipline. How many austerities I practised under the bel-tree! I would lie down under it, crying to the Divine Mother, 'O Mother, reveal Thyself to me.' The tears would flow in torrents and soak my body."

M: "You practised so many austerities, but people expect to realize God in a moment! Can a man build a wall simply by moving his finger around his home?"

MASTER (with a smile): "Amrita says that one man lights a fire and ten bask in its heat. I want to tell you something else. It is good to remain on the plane of the Lila after reaching the Nitya."

M: "You once said that one comes down to the plane of the Lila in order to enjoy the divine play."

MASTER: "No, not exactly that. The Lila is real too.

"Let me tell you something. Whenever you come here, bring a trifle with you.[7] Perhaps I shouldn't say it; it may look like egotism. I also told Adhar Sen that he should bring a pennyworth of something with him. I asked Bhavanath to bring a pennyworth of betel-leaf. Have you noticed Bhavanath's devotion? Narendra and he seem like man and woman. He is devoted to Narendra. Bring Narendra here with you in a carriage, and also bring some sweets with you. It will do you good.

"Knowledge and love—both are paths leading to God. Those who follow the path of love have to observe a little more outer purity. But the violation of this by a man following the path of knowledge cannot injure him. It is destroyed in the fire of knowledge. Even a banana tree is burnt up when it is thrown into a roaring fire.

"The jnanis follow the path of discrimination. Sometimes it happens that, discriminating between the Real and the unreal, a man loses his faith in the existence of God. But a devotee who sincerely yearns for God does not give up his meditation even though he is invaded by atheistic ideas. A man whose father and grandfather have been farmers continues his farming even though he doesn't get any crop in a year of drought."

Lying on the mat and resting his head on a pillow, Sri Ramakrishna continued the conversation. He said to M: "My legs are aching. Please stroke them gently." Thus, out of his infinite compassion, the Master allowed his disciple to render him personal service.

[7] The Hindu scriptures command the householder to visit a holy man with suitable presents.

June 8, 1883

It was a summer day. The evening service in the Kāli temple was over. Sri Ramakrishna stood before the image of the Divine Mother and waved the fan a few minutes.

Ram, Kedar Chatterji, and Tarak arrived from Calcutta with flowers and sweets. Kedar was about fifty years old. At first he had frequented the Brāhmo Samāj and joined other religious sects in his search for God, but later on he had accepted the Master as his spiritual guide. He was an accountant in a government office and lived in a suburb of Calcutta.

Tarak was a young man of twenty-four. His wife had died shortly after their marriage. He hailed from the village of Bārāsat not far from Calcutta. His father, a highly spiritual soul, had visited Sri Ramakrishna many times. Tarak often went to Ram's house and used to go to Dakshineswar in the company of Ram and Nityagopal. He worked in a business firm, but his attitude toward the world was one of utter indifference.

As Sri Ramakrishna came out of the temple, he saw Ram, Kedar, M., Tarak, and other devotees standing outside. He showed his affection for Tarak by touching his chin. He was very happy to see him.

Returning to his room, the Master sat on the floor in an ecstatic mood, with his legs stretched before him. Ram and Kedar decorated his feet with flowers and garlands. The Master was in samādhi.

Kedar believed in certain queer practices of a religious sect to which he had once belonged. He held the Master's big toe in his hand, believing that in this way the Master's spiritual power would be transmitted to him. As Sri Ramakrishna regained partial consciousness, he said, "Mother, what can he do to me by holding my toe?" Kedar sat humbly with folded hands. Still in an ecstatic mood, the Master said to Kedar: "Your mind is still attracted by 'woman and gold'. What is the use of saying you don't care for it? Go forward. Beyond the forest of sandal-wood there are many more things: mines of silver, gold, diamonds, and other precious stones. Having a glimpse of spirituality, don't think you have attained everything." The Master was again in an ecstatic mood. He said to the Divine Mother, "Mother, take him away." At these words Kedar's throat dried up. In a frightened tone he said to Ram, "What is the Master saying?"

At the sight of Rakhal, Sri Ramakrishna was again overpowered with a spiritual mood. He said to his beloved disciple: "I have been here many days. When did you come?"

Was the Master hinting that he was an Incarnation of God, and Rakhal his divine companion, a member of the inner circle of devotees?

Sunday, June 10, 1883

The Master was sitting in his room with Rakhal, M., Latu, Kishori, Ramlal, Hazra, and other devotees. It was about ten o'clock in the morning.

Describing his early life, Sri Ramakrishna said to them: "During my younger days the men and women of Kāmārpukur were equally fond of me. They loved to hear me sing. I could imitate other people's gestures and conversation, and I used to entertain them that way. The women would put aside things for me to eat. No one distrusted me. Everybody took me in as one of the family.

"But I was like a happy pigeon. I used to frequent only happy families. I would run away from a place where I saw misery and suffering.

"One or two young boys of the village were my close friends. I was very intimate with some of them; but now they are totally immersed in worldliness. A few of them visit me here now and then and say, 'Goodness! He seems to be just the same as he was in the village school!' While I was at school, arithmetic would throw me into confusion, but I could paint very well and could also model small images of the deities.

"I loved to visit the free eating-places maintained for holy men and the poor, and would watch them for hours.

"I loved to hear the reading of sacred books such as the *Rāmāyaṇa* and *Bhāgavata*. If the readers had any affectations, I could easily imitate them and would entertain others with my mimicry.

"I understood the behaviour of women very well and imitated their words and intonations. I could easily recognize immoral women. Immoral widows part their hair in the middle and perform their toilet with great care. They have very little modesty. The way they sit is so different! But let's not talk of worldly things any more."

The Master asked Ramlal to sing. Ramlal sang:

> Who is this terrible Woman, dark as the sky at midnight?
> Who is this Woman dancing over the field of battle,
> Like a blue lotus that floats on a crimson sea of blood?
> Who is She, clad alone in the Infinite for a garment,
> Rolling Her three great eyes in frenzy and savage fury?
> Under the weight of Her tread the earth itself is trembling!
> Śiva, Her mighty Husband, who wields the fearful trident,
> Lies like a lifeless corpse beneath Her conquering feet.

The next song described the grief of Mandodari at the death of her husband Rāvana. As he listened to it the Master shed tears of sorrow and said: "Once, when I entered the pine-grove over there, I heard the boatmen on the Ganges singing that song and wept bitterly for a long time. I had to be brought back to my room."

Ramlal sang about the love of the gopis for Sri Krishna. Akrura was about to drive Sri Krishna in a chariot from Vrindāvan to Mathurā. The gopis would not let Him go. Some held the wheels of the chariot; some lay down in front of it. They blamed Akrura, not knowing that Sri Krishna was leaving them of His own will. Akrura was explaining this to the gopis. Ramlal sang:

> Hold not, hold not the chariot's wheels!
> Is it the wheels that make it move?
> The Mover of its wheels is Krishna,
> By whose will the worlds are moved. . . .

About the gopis, the Master said: "What deep love, what ecstatic devotion they had for Krishna! Rādhā painted the picture of Sri Krishna with her own hand, but did not paint His legs lest He should run away to Mathurā! I used to sing these songs very often during my boyhood. I could reproduce the whole drama from memory."

After his meal Sri Ramakrishna sat on the couch. He had not yet found time to rest. The devotees began to assemble. One party arrived from Manirāmpur and another from Belgharia. Some of the devotees said, "We have disturbed your rest."

MASTER: "Oh, no! What you say applies only to a rājasic man. About him people say, 'Ah, now he will enjoy his sleep.'"

The devotees from Manirāmpur asked the Master how to realize God.

MASTER: "You must practise spiritual discipline a little. It will not do simply to say that milk contains butter. You must let the milk set into curd and then churn it. Only then can you get butter from it. Spiritual aspirants must go into solitude now and then. After acquiring love of God in solitude, they may live in the world. If one is wearing a pair of shoes, one can easily walk over thorns.

"The most important thing is faith.

> As is a man's meditation, so is his feeling of love;
> As is a man's feeling of love, so is his gain;
> And faith is the root of all.

If one has faith one has nothing to fear."

A DEVOTEE: "Sir, is it necessary to have a guru?"

MASTER: "Yes, many need a guru. But a man must have faith in the guru's words. He succeeds in spiritual life by looking on his guru as God Himself. Therefore the Vaishnavas speak of Guru, Krishna, and Vaishnava.[8]

"One should constantly repeat the name of God. The name of God is highly effective in the Kaliyuga. The practice of yoga is not possible in this age, for the life of a man depends on food. Clap your hands while repeating God's name, and the birds of your sin will fly away.

"One should always seek the company of holy men. The nearer you approach the Ganges, the cooler the breeze will feel. Again, the nearer you go to a fire, the hotter the air will feel.

"But one cannot achieve anything through laziness and procrastination. People who desire worldly enjoyment say about spiritual progress: 'Well, it will all happen in time. We shall realize God some time or other.'

"I said to Keshab Sen: 'When a father sees that his son has become restless for his inheritance, he gives him his share of the property even three years before the legal time. A mother keeps on cooking while the baby is in bed sucking its toy. But when it throws the toy away and cries for her, she puts down the rice-pot and takes the baby in her arms and nurses it.' I said all this to Keshab.

"It is said that, in the Kaliyuga, if a man can weep for God one day and one night, he sees Him.

[8] The Master meant that the guru, Krishna, and the Vaishnava were to be equally revered. One should honour the Vaishnava because God dwells in his heart.

"Feel piqued at God and say to Him: 'You have created me. Now You must reveal Yourself to me.' Whether you live in the world or elsewhere, always fix your mind on God. The mind soaked in worldliness may be compared to a wet match-stick. You won't get a spark, however much you may rub it. Ekalavya placed the clay image of Drona, his teacher, in front of him and thus learnt archery.[9]

"Go forward. The wood-cutter, following the instructions of the holy man, went forward and found in the forest sandal-wood and mines of silver and gold; and going still farther, he found diamonds and other precious stones.

"The ignorant are like people living in a house with clay walls. There is very little light inside, and they cannot see outside at all. But those who enter the world after attaining the Knowledge of God are like people living in a house made of glass. For them both inside and outside are light. They can see things outside as well as inside.

"Nothing exists except the One. That One is the Supreme Brahman. So long as He keeps the 'I' in us, He reveals to us that it is He who, as the Primal Energy, creates, preserves, and destroys the universe.

"That which is Brahman is also the Primal Energy. Once a king asked a yogi to impart Knowledge to him in one word. The yogi said, 'All right; you will get Knowledge in one word.' After a while a magician came to the king. The king saw the magician moving two of his fingers rapidly and heard him exclaim, 'Behold, O King! Behold.' The king looked at him amazed when, after a few minutes, he saw the two fingers becoming one. The magician moved that one finger rapidly and said, 'Behold, O King! Behold.' The implication of the story is that Brahman and the Primal Energy at first appear to be two. But after attaining the Knowledge of Brahman one does not see the two. Then there is no differentiation; it is One, without a second —Advaita—non-duality."

The Master was very happy to see a musician who had come with the devotees from Belgharia. Some time before, Sri Ramakrishna had gone into an ecstatic mood on hearing his devotional music. At the Master's request the musician sang a few songs, one of which described the awakening of the Kundalini and the six centres:

Awake, Mother! Awake! How long Thou hast been asleep
In the lotus of the Mulādhāra!
Fulfil Thy secret function, Mother:
Rise to the thousand-petalled lotus within the head,
Where mighty Śiva has His dwelling;
Swiftly pierce the six lotuses
And take away my grief, O Essence of Consciousness!

[9] The story is in the *Mahābhārata*. Drona refused to teach Ekalavya archery because the latter belonged to a low caste. Thereupon Ekalavya went to the forest and practised archery before the clay image of Drona, whom he regarded as his teacher. In course of time he became an expert archer. When Drona discovered that he excelled even Arjuna, Drona's most beloved disciple, in this art, he asked Ekalavya to give him his thumb as the teacher's fee. By carrying out this order, Ekalavya demonstrated his spirit of self-sacrifice and also his love for his teacher.

MASTER: "The song speaks of the Kundalini's passing through the six centres. God is both within and without. From within He creates the various states of mind. After passing through the six centres, the jīva goes beyond the realm of māyā and becomes united with the Supreme Soul. This is the vision of God.

"One cannot see God unless māyā steps aside from the door. Rāma, Lakshmana, and Sītā were walking together. Rāma was in front, Sītā walked in the middle, and Lakshmana followed them. But Lakshmana could not see Rāma because Sītā was between them. In like manner,' man cannot see God because māyā is between them. (*To Mani Mallick*) But māyā steps aside from the door when God shows His grace to the devotee. When the visitor stands before the door, the door-keeper says to the master, 'Sir, command us, and we shall let him pass.'

"There are two schools of thought: the Vedānta and the Purāna. According to the Vedānta this world is a 'framework of illusion', that is to say, it is all illusory, like a dream. But according to the Purāna, the books of devotion, God Himself has become the twenty-four cosmic principles. Worship God both within and without.

"As long as God keeps the awareness of 'I' in us, so long do sense-objects exist; and we cannot very well speak of the world as a dream. There is fire in the hearth; therefore the rice and pulse and potatoes and the other vegetables jump about in the pot. They jump about as if to say: 'We are here! We are jumping!' This body is the pot. The mind and intelligence are the water. The objects of the senses are the rice, potatoes, and other vegetables. The 'I-consciousness' identified with the senses says, 'I am jumping about.' And Satchidānanda is the fire.

"Hence the Bhakti scriptures describe this very world as a 'mansion of mirth'. Rāmprasād sang in one of his songs, 'This world is a framework of illusion.' Another devotee gave the reply, 'This very world is a mansion of mirth.' As the saying goes, 'The devotee of Kāli, free while living, is full of Eternal Bliss.' The bhakta sees that He who is God has also become māyā. Again, He Himself has become the universe and all its living beings. The bhakta sees God, māyā, the universe, and the living beings as one. Some devotees see everything as Rāma: it is Rāma alone who has become everything. Some see everything as Rādhā and Krishna. To them it is Krishna alone who has become the twenty-four cosmic principles. It is like seeing everything green through green glasses.

"But the Bhakti scriptures admit that the manifestations of Power are different in different beings. It is Rāma who has become everything, no doubt; but He manifests Himself more in some than in others. There is one kind of manifestation of Rāma in the Incarnation of God, and another in men. Even the Incarnations are conscious of the body. Embodiment is due to māyā. Rāma wept for Sītā. But the Incarnation of God puts a bandage over His eyes by His own will, like children playing blindman's buff. The children stop playing when their mother calls them. It is quite different, however, with the ordinary man. The cloth his eyes are bandaged with is fastened to his back with screws, as it were. There are eight fetters. Shame, hatred, fear, caste, lineage, good conduct, grief, and secretiveness—these are the eight fetters. And they cannot be unfastened without the help of a guru."

A DEVOTEE: "Sir, please bless us."

MASTER: "God is in all beings. But you must apply to the Gas Company. It will connect the storage-tank with the pipe in your house.

"One must pray earnestly. It is said that one can realize God by directing to Him the combined intensity of three attractions, namely, the child's attraction for the mother, the husband's attraction for the chaste wife, and the attraction of worldly possessions for the worldly man.

"There are certain signs by which you can know a true devotee of God. His mind becomes quiet as he listens to his teacher's instruction, just as the poisonous snake is quieted by the music of the charmer. I don't mean the cobra. There is another sign. A real devotee develops the power of assimilating instruction. An image cannot be impressed on bare glass, but only on glass stained with a black solution, as in photography. The black solution is devotion to God. There is a third sign of a true devotee. The true devotee has controlled his senses. He has subdued his lust. The gopis were free from lust.

"You are talking about your leading a householder's life. Suppose you are a householder. It rather helps in the practice of spiritual discipline. It is like fighting from inside a fort. The Tāntriks sometimes use a corpse in their religious rites. Now and then the dead body frightens them by opening its mouth. That is why they keep fried rice and grams near them, and from time to time they throw some of the grains into the corpse's mouth. Thus pacifying the corpse, they repeat the name of the Deity without any worry. Likewise, the householder should pacify his wife and the other members of his family. He should provide them with food and other necessities. Thus he removes the obstacles to his practice of spiritual discipline.

"Those who still have a few worldly experiences to enjoy should lead a householder's life and pray to God. That is why Nityānanda allowed the worldly to enjoy catfish soup and the warm embrace of a young woman while repeating God's name.

"But it is quite different with genuine sannyāsis. A bee lights on flowers and on nothing else. To the chātak all water except rain is tasteless. It will drink no other water, but looks up agape for the rain that falls when the star Svāti is in the ascendant. It drinks only that water. A real sannyāsi will not enjoy any kind of bliss except the Bliss of God. The bee lights only on flowers. The real monk is like a bee, whereas the householder devotee is like a common fly, which lights on a festering sore as well as on a sweetmeat.

"You have taken so much trouble to come here. You must be seeking God. But almost everyone is satisfied simply by seeing the garden. Only one or two look for its owner. People enjoy the beauty of the world; they do not seek its Owner.

(Pointing to the singer) "A little while ago he sang a song describing the six centres. These are dealt with in Yoga. There are two kinds of yoga: hathayoga and rājayoga. The hathayogi practises physical exercises. His goal is to acquire supernatural powers: longevity and the eight psychic powers. These are his aims. But the aim of rājayoga is the attainment of devotion, ecstatic love, knowledge, and renunciation. Of these two, rājayoga is the better.

"There is much similarity between the seven 'planes' described in the Vedānta and the six 'centres' of Yoga. The first three planes of the Vedas may be compared to the first three Yogic centres, namely, Mulādhāra, Svādhisthāna, and Manipura. With ordinary people the mind dwells in these three planes, at the organs of evacuation and generation and at the navel. When the mind ascends to the fourth plane, the centre designated in Yoga as Anāhata, it sees the individual soul as a flame. Besides, it sees light. At this the aspirant cries: 'Ah! What is this? Ah! What is this?'

"When the mind rises to the fifth plane, the aspirant wants to hear only about God. This is the Viśuddha centre of Yoga. The sixth plane and the centre known by the yogi as Ājnā are one and the same. When the mind rises there, the aspirant sees God. But still there is a barrier between God and the devotee. It is like the barrier of glass in a lantern, which keeps one from touching the light. King Janaka used to give instruction about Brahma-jnāna from the fifth plane. Sometimes he dwelt on the fifth plane, and sometimes on the sixth.

"After passing the six centres the aspirant arrives at the seventh plane. Reaching it, the mind merges in Brahman. The individual soul and the Supreme Soul become one. The aspirant goes into samādhi. His consciousness of the body disappears. He loses the knowledge of the outer world. He does not see the manifold any more. His reasoning comes to a stop.

"Trailanga Swami once said that because a man reasons he is conscious of multiplicity, of variety. Attaining samādhi, one gives up the body in twenty-one days. Spiritual consciousness is not possible without the awakening of the Kundalini.

"A man who has realized God shows certain characteristics. He becomes like a child or a madman or an inert thing or a ghoul. Further, he is firmly convinced that he is the machine and God is its Operator, that God alone is the Doer and all others are His instruments. As some Sikh devotees once said to me, even the leaf moves because of God's will. One should be aware that everything happens by the will of Rāma. The weaver said: 'The price of the cloth, by the will of Rāma, is one rupee six ānnās. By the will of Rāma the robbery was committed. By the will of Rāma the robbers were arrested. By the will of Rāma I too was arrested by the police. And at last, by the will of Rāma, I was released.'"

It was dusk. Sri Ramakrishna had had no rest since his midday meal. He had talked unceasingly to the devotees about God. At last the visitors took their leave and went home.

Friday, June 15, 1883

It was a holiday on account of the Hindu religious festival Dasaharā. Among the devotees who visited Sri Ramakrishna at Dakshineswar that day were Adhar, M., and Rakhal's father. Rakhal's father's father-in-law was also present. All were seated on the floor of the Master's room.

Rakhal's father's father-in-law was a devotee of God. He asked the Master, "Sir, can one realize God while leading the life of a householder?"

MASTER (*with a smile*): "Why not? Live in the world like a mudfish. The mudfish lives in the mud but itself remains unstained. Or live in the world like a loose woman. She attends to her household duties, but her mind is always on her sweetheart. Do your duties in the world, fixing your mind on God. But this is extremely difficult. I said to the members of the Brāhmo Samāj: 'Suppose a typhoid patient is kept in a room where there are jars of pickles and pitchers of water. How can you expect the patient to recover? The very thought of spiced pickles brings water to one's mouth.' To a man, woman is like that pickle. The craving for worldly things, which is chronic in man, is like the patient's craving for water. There is no end to this craving. The typhoid patient says, 'I shall drink a whole pitcher of water.' The situation is very difficult. There is so much confusion in the world. If you go this way, you are threatened with a shovel; if you go that way, you are threatened with a broomstick; again, in another direction, you are threatened with a shoe-beating. Besides, one cannot think of God unless one lives in solitude. The goldsmith melts gold to make ornaments. But how can he do his work well if he is disturbed again and again? Suppose you are separating rice from bits of husk. You must do it all by yourself. Every now and then you have to take the rice in your hand to see how clean it is. But how can you do your work well if you are called away again and again?"

A DEVOTEE: "What then is the way, sir?"

MASTER: "There *is* a way. One succeeds if one develops a strong spirit of renunciation. Give up at once, with determination, what you know to be unreal. Once, when I was seriously ill, I was taken to the physician Gangaprasad Sen. He said to me: 'I shall give you a medicine, but you mustn't drink any water. You may take pomegranate juice.' Everyone wondered how I could live without water; but I was determined not to drink it. I said to myself: 'I am a paramahamsa and not a goose. I shall drink only milk.'[10]

"You have to spend a few days in solitude. If you but touch the 'granny'[11] you are safe. Turn yourself into gold and then live wherever you please. After realizing God and divine love in solitude, one may live in the world as well. (*To Rakhal's father*) That is why I ask the youngsters to stay with me; for they will develop love of God by staying here a few days. After that they can very well lead the life of a householder."

DEVOTEE: "If God is responsible for everything, then why should people speak of good and evil, virtue and vice? One commits sin also by the will of God, isn't that so?"

ANOTHER DEVOTEE: "How can we understand the will of God?"

MASTER: "There is no doubt that virtue and vice exist in the world; but

---

[10] A paramahamsa is one belonging to the highest order of monks; the word also means "swan". There is a popular tradition in India that a swan can separate the milk from a mixture of milk and water. It is said that a secretion of acid turns the milk into curd, which the swan eats, leaving the water.

[11] An allusion to the game of hide-and-seek. See foot-note 6, p. 136.

God Himself is unattached to them. There may be good and bad smells in the air, but the air is not attached to them. The very nature of God's creation is that good and evil, righteousness and unrighteousness, will always exist in the world. Among the trees in the garden one finds mango and jack-fruit, and hog plum too. Haven't you noticed that even wicked men are needed? Suppose there are rough tenants on an estate; then the landlord must send a ruffian to control them."

The conversation again turned to the life of the householder.

MASTER (*to the devotees*): "You see, by leading a householder's life a man needlessly dissipates his mental powers. The loss he thus incurs can be made up if he takes to monastic life. The first birth is a gift of the father; then comes the second birth, when one is invested with the sacred thread. There is still another birth at the time of being initiated into monastic life. The two obstacles to spiritual life are 'woman' and 'gold'. Attachment to 'woman' diverts one from the way leading to God. Man doesn't know what it is that causes his downfall. Once, while going to the Fort,[12] I couldn't see at all that I was driving down a sloping road; but when the carriage went inside the Fort, I realized how far down I had come. Alas! Women keep men deluded. Captain says, 'My wife is full of wisdom.' The man possessed by a ghost does not realize it. He says, 'Why, I am all right!' "

The devotees listened to these words in deep silence.

MASTER: "It is not lust alone that one should be afraid of in the life of the world. There is also anger. Anger arises when obstacles are placed in the way of desire."

M: "At meal-time, sometimes a cat stretches out its paw to take the fish from my plate. But I cannot show any resentment."

MASTER: "Why? You may even beat it once in a while. What's the harm? A worldly man should hiss, but he shouldn't pour out his venom. He mustn't actually injure others. But he should make a show of anger to protect himself from enemies. Otherwise they will injure him. But a sannyāsi need not even hiss."

A DEVOTEE: "I find it is extremely difficult for a householder to realize God. How few people can lead the life you prescribe for them! I haven't found any."

MASTER: "Why should that be so? I have heard of a deputy magistrate named Pratap Singh. He is a great man. He has many virtues: compassion and devotion to God. He meditates on God. Once he sent for me. Certainly there are people like him.

"The practice of discipline is absolutely necessary. Why shouldn't a man succeed if he practises sādhanā? But he doesn't have to work hard if he has real faith—faith in his guru's words. Once Vyāsa was about to cross the Jamunā, when the gopis also arrived there, wishing to go to the other side. But no ferry-boat was in sight. They said to Vyāsa, 'Revered sir, what shall we do now?' 'Don't worry', said Vyāsa. 'I will take you across. But I am very hungry. Have you anything for me to eat?' The gopis had plenty of milk, cream, and butter with them. Vyāsa ate it all. Then the gopis asked, 'Well,

[12] A reference to the fort in Calcutta.

sir, what about crossing the river?' Vyāsa stood on the bank of the Jamunā and said, 'O Jamunā, if I have not eaten anything today, then may your waters part so that we may all walk to the other side.' No sooner did the sage utter these words than the waters of the Jamunā parted. The gopis were speechless with wonder. 'He ate so much just now,' they said to themselves, 'and he says, "If I have not eaten anything . . ."!' Vyāsa had the firm conviction that it was not himself, but the Nārāyana who dwelt in his heart, that had partaken of the food.

"Sankarāchārya was a Brahmajnāni, to be sure. But at the beginning he too had the feeling of differentiation. He didn't have absolute faith that everything in the world is Brahman. One day as he was coming out of the Ganges after his bath, he saw an untouchable, a butcher, carrying a load of meat. Inadvertently the butcher touched his body. Sankara shouted angrily, 'Hey there! How dare you touch me?' 'Revered sir,' said the butcher, 'I have not touched you, nor have you touched me. The Pure Self cannot be the body nor the five elements nor the twenty-four cosmic principles.' Then Sankara came to his senses. Once Jadabharata was carrying King Rahugana's palanquin and at the same time giving a discourse on Self-Knowledge. The king got down from the palanquin and said to Jadabharata, 'Who are you, pray?' The latter answered, 'I am Not this, not this—I am the Pure Self.' He had perfect faith that he was the Pure Self.

" 'I am He', 'I am the Pure Self'—that is the conclusion of the jnānis. But the bhaktas say, 'The whole universe is the glory of God.' Who would recognize a wealthy man without his power and riches? But it is quite different when God Himself, gratified by the aspirant's devotion, says to him, 'You are the same as Myself.' Suppose a king is seated in his court, and his cook enters the hall, sits on the throne, and says, 'O King, you and I are the same!' People will certainly call him a madman. But suppose one day the king, pleased with the cook's service, says to him: 'Come, sit beside me. There is nothing wrong in that. There is no difference between you and me.' Then, if the cook sits on the throne with the king, there is no harm in it. It is not good for ordinary people to say, 'I am He'. The waves belong to the water. Does the water belong to the waves?

"The upshot of the whole thing is that, no matter what path you follow, yoga is impossible unless the mind becomes quiet. The mind of a yogi is under his control; he is not under the control of his mind. When the mind is quiet the prāna stops functioning. Then one gets kumbhaka. One may have the same kumbhaka through bhaktiyoga as well: the prāna stops functioning through love of God too. In the kirtan the musician sings, 'Nitāi āmār mātā hāti!'[13] Repeating this, he goes into a spiritual mood and cannot sing the whole sentence. He simply sings, 'Hāti! Hāti!' When the mood deepens he sings only, 'Hā! Hā!' Thus his prāna stops through ecstasy, and kumbhaka follows.

"Suppose a man is sweeping a courtyard with his broom, and another man comes and says to him: 'Hello! So-and-so is no more. He is dead.' Now,

---

[13] "My Nitāi dances like a mad elephant!"

if the dead person was not related to the sweeper, the latter goes on with his work, remarking casually: 'Ah! That's too bad. He is dead. He was a good fellow.' The sweeping goes on all the same. But if the dead man was his relative, then the broom drops from his hand. 'Ah!' he exclaims, and he too drops to the ground. His prāna has stopped functioning. He can neither work nor think. Haven't you noticed, among women, that if one of them looks at something or listens to something in speechless amazement, the other women say to her, 'What? Are you in ecstasy?' In this instance, too, the prāna has stopped functioning, and so she remains speechless, with mouth agape.

"It will not do merely to repeat, 'I am He, I am He.' There are certain signs of a jnāni. Narendra has big protruding eyes. (*Pointing to a devotee*) He also has good eyes and forehead.

"All men are by no means on the same level. It is said that there are four classes of men: the bound, the struggling, the liberated, and the ever-free. It is also not a fact that all men have to practise spiritual discipline. There are the ever-free and those who achieve perfection through spiritual discipline. Some realize God after much spiritual austerity, and some are perfect from their very birth. Prahlāda is an example of the ever-free.

"Eternally perfect sages like Prahlāda also practise meditation and prayer. But they have realized the *fruit*, God-vision, even before their spiritual practice. They are like gourds and pumpkins, which grow fruit first and then flowers.

(*Looking at Rakhal's father*) "Even though an eternally perfect soul is born in a low family, still he retains his innate perfection. He cannot do anything else. A pea germinating in a heap of cow-dung still grows into a pea-plant.

"God has given to some greater power than to others. In one man you see it as the light of a lamp, in another, as the light of a torch. One word of Vidyāsāgar's revealed to me the utmost limit of his intelligence. When I told him of the different manifestations of God's Power in different beings, he said to me, 'Sir, has God then given greater power to some than to others?' At once I said: 'Yes, certainly He has. If there are not different degrees of manifestation of His Power, then why should your name be known far and wide? You see, we have come to you after hearing of your knowledge and compassion. You haven't grown two horns, have you?' With all his fame and erudition, Vidyāsāgar said such a childish thing as 'Has God given greater power to some than to others?' The truth is that when the fisherman draws his net, he first catches big fish like trout and carp; then he stirs up the mud with his feet, and small fish come out—minnows, mud-fish, and so on. So also, unless a man knows God, 'minnows' and the like gradually come out from within him. What can one achieve through mere scholarship?"

Sunday, June 17, 1883

Sri Ramakrishna was resting in his room in the temple garden at Dakshineswar. It was afternoon. Adhar and M. arrived and saluted the

Master. A Tāntrik devotee also came in. Rakhal, Hazra, and Ramlal were staying with Sri Ramakrishna.

MASTER (*to the devotees*): "Why shouldn't one be able to attain spirituality, living the life of a householder? But it is extremely difficult. Sages like Janaka entered the world after attaining Knowledge. But still the world is a place of terror. Even a detached householder has to be careful. Once Janaka bent down his head at the sight of a bhairavi. He shrank from seeing a woman. The bhairavi said to him: 'Janaka, I see you have not yet attained Knowledge. You still differentiate between man and woman.'

"If you move about in a room filled with soot, you will soil your body, however slightly, no matter how clever you may be. I have seen householder devotees filled with spiritual emotion while performing their daily worship wearing their silk clothes. They maintain that attitude even until they take their refreshments after the worship. But afterwards they become their old selves again. They display their rājasic and tāmasic natures.

"Sattva begets bhakti. Even bhakti has three aspects: sattva, rajas, and tamas. The sattva of bhakti is pure sattva. When a devotee acquires it he doesn't direct his mind to anything but God. He pays only as much attention to his body as is absolutely necessary for its protection.

"But a paramahamsa is beyond the three gunas. Though they exist in him, yet they are practically non-existent. Like a child, he is not under the control of any of the gunas. That is why paramahamsas allow small children to come near them—in order to assume their nature.

"Paramahamsas may not lay things up; but this rule does not apply to householders. They must provide for their families."

TĀNTRIK DEVOTEE: "Is a paramahamsa aware of virtue and vice?"

MASTER: "Keshab Sen also asked that question. I said to him, 'If I explain that to you, then you won't be able to keep your society together.' 'In that case we had better stop here', said Keshab.

"Do you know the significance of virtue and vice? A paramahamsa sees that it is God who gives us evil tendencies as well as good tendencies. Haven't you noticed that there are both sweet and bitter fruits? Some trees give sweet fruit, and some bitter or sour. God has made the mango-tree, which yields sweet fruit, and also the hog plum, which yields sour fruit."

TĀNTRIK: "Yes, sir. That is true. On the hill-top one sees extensive rose gardens, reaching as far as the eye can see."

MASTER: "The paramahamsa realizes that all these—good and bad, virtue and vice, real and unreal—are only the glories of God's māyā. But these are very deep thoughts. One realizing this cannot keep an organization together or anything like that."

TĀNTRIK: "But the law of karma exists, doesn't it?"

MASTER: "That also is true. Good produces good, and bad produces bad. Don't you get the hot taste if you eat chillies? But these are all God's līlā, His play."

TĀNTRIK: "Then what is the way for us? We shall have to reap the result of our past karma, shall we not?"

MASTER: "That may be so. But it is different with the devotees of God. Listen to a song:

> O mind, you do not know how to farm!
> Fallow lies the field of your life.
> If you had only worked it well,
> How rich a harvest you might reap!
> Hedge it about with Kāli's name
> If you would keep your harvest safe;
> This is the stoutest hedge of all,
> For Death himself cannot come near it.
>
> Sooner or later will dawn the day
> When you must forfeit your precious field;
> Gather, O mind, what fruit you may.
> Sow for your seed the holy name
> Of God that your guru has given to you,
> Faithfully watering it with love;
> And if you should find the task too hard,
> Call upon Rāmprasād for help.

He sang again:

> I have securely blocked the way by which the King of Death will
>   come;
> Henceforward all my doubts and fears are set at naught for ever.
> Śiva Himself is standing guard at the nine doorways of my house,[14]
> Which has one Pillar[15] for support, and three ropes[16] to secure it.
> The Lord has made His dwelling-place the thousand-petalled
>   lotus flower
> Within the head, and comforts me with never-ceasing care.

The Master continued: "Anyone who dies in Benares, whether a brāhmin or a prostitute, will become Śiva. When a man sheds tears at the name of Hari, Kāli, or Rāma, then he has no further need of the sandhyā and other rites. All actions drop away of themselves. The fruit of action does not touch him."

Again the Master sang:

> As is a man's meditation, so is his feeling of love;
> As is a man's feeling of love, so is his gain;
> And faith is the root of all.
> If in the Nectar Lake of Mother Kāli's feet
> My mind remains immersed,
> Of little use are worship, oblations, or sacrifice.

He sang another song:

> Why should I go to Gangā or Gayā, to Kāśi, Kānchi, or Prabhās,
> So long as I can breathe my last with Kāli's name upon my
>   lips? . . .

[14] The body with its nine apertures, such as eyes, ears, nose, mouth, etc.
[15] Brahman.
[16] The three gunas.

Then he said, "When a man merges himself in God, he can no longer retain wicked or sinful tendencies."

TĀNTRIK: "You have said rightly that he keeps only the 'Knowledge ego'."

MASTER: "Yes, he keeps only the 'Knowledge ego', the 'devotee ego', the 'servant ego', and the 'good ego'. His 'wicked ego' disappears."

TĀNTRIK: "Today you have destroyed many of our doubts."

MASTER: "All doubts disappear when one realizes the Self.

"Assume the tāmasic aspect of bhakti. Say with force: 'What? I have uttered the names of Rāma and Kāli. How can I be in bondage any more? How can I be affected by the law of karma?'"

The Master sang:

> If only I can pass away repeating Durgā's name,
> How canst Thou then, O Blessed One,
> Withhold from me deliverance,
> Wretched though I may be?
> I may have stolen a drink of wine, or killed a child unborn,
> Or slain a woman or a cow,
> Or even caused a brāhmin's death;
> But, though it all be true,
> Nothing of this can make me feel the least uneasiness;
> For through the power of Thy sweet name
> My wretched soul may still aspire
> Even to Brahmanhood.

The Master continued: "Faith! Faith! Faith! Once a guru said to his pupil, 'Rāma alone has become everything.' When a dog began to eat the pupil's bread, he said to it: 'O Rāma, wait a little. I shall butter Your bread.' Such was his faith in the words of his guru.

"Worthless people do not have any faith. They always doubt. But doubts do not disappear completely till one realizes the Self.

"In genuine love of God there is no desire. Only through such love does one speedily realize God. Attainment of supernatural powers and so on— these are desires. Krishna once said to Arjuna: 'Friend, you cannot realize God if you acquire even one of the eight supernatural powers. They will only add a little to your power.'"

TĀNTRIK: "Sir, why don't the rituals of Tantra bear fruit nowadays?"

MASTER: "It is because people cannot practise them with absolute correctness and devotion."

In conclusion the Master said: "Love of God is the one essential thing. A true lover of God has nothing to fear, nothing to worry about. He is aware that the Divine Mother knows everything. The cat handles the mouse one way, but its own kitten a very different way."

THE FESTIVAL AT PĀNIHĀTI

Monday, June 18, 1883

SRI RAMAKRISHNA had been invited to the great religious festival at Pānihāti, near Calcutta. This "Festival of the Flattened Rice" was inaugurated by Raghunāth Dās, a disciple of Sri Chaitanya. It is said that Raghunāth used to run away from home, secretly practise his devotions, and enjoy the bliss of spiritual ecstasy. One day Nityānanda said to him: "Thief! You run away from home and enjoy the love of God all alone. You hide it from us. I shall punish you today. You must arrange a religious festival and entertain the devotees with flattened rice." Since then the festival has been annually celebrated at Pānihāti by the Vaishnavas. Thousands of the followers of Sri Chaitanya participate in it. Its chief feature is the singing of the names and glories of God, and the dancing of the devotees in religious fervour. The centre of the festivity is the temple of Rādhā-Krishna, built on the bank of the Ganges.

The Master had been invited to the festival by Mani Sen, who was the custodian of the temple. Ram, M., Rakhal, Bhavanath, and a few other disciples went with the Master in a carriage. On his way to Pānihāti Sri Ramakrishna was in a light mood and joked with the youngsters. But as soon as the carriage reached the place of the festival, the Master, to the utter amazement of the devotees, shot into the crowd. He joined the kirtan party of Navadvip Goswami, Mani Sen's guru, and danced, totally forgetting the world. Every now and then he stood still in samādhi, carefully supported by Navadvip Goswami for fear he might fall to the ground. Thousands of devotees were gathered together for the festival. Wherever one looked there was a forest of human heads. The crowd seemed to become infected by the Master's divine fervour and swayed to and fro, chanting the name of God, until the very air seemed to reverberate with it. Drums, cymbals, and other instruments produced melodious sounds. The atmosphere became intense with spiritual fervour. The devotees felt that Gaurānga himself was being manifested in the person of Sri Ramakrishna. Flowers were showered from all sides on his feet and head. The shouting of the name of Hari was heard even at a distance, like the rumbling of the ocean.

Sri Ramakrishna entered by turn into all the moods of ecstasy. In deep samādhi he stood still, his face radiating a divine glow. In the state of partial consciousness he danced, sometimes gently and sometimes with the vigour of a lion. Again, regaining consciousness of the world, he sang, himself leading the chorus:

> Behold, the two brothers[1] have come, who weep while chanting
>   Hari's name,
> The brothers who dance in ecstasy and make the world dance in
>   His name!
> Behold them, weeping themselves, and making the whole world
>   weep as well,
> The brothers who, in return for blows, offer to sinners Hari's love.
> Behold them, drunk with Hari's love, who make the world drunk
>   as well!
> Behold, the two brothers have come, who once were Kānāi and
>   Balāi of Braja,
> They who would steal the butter out of the pots of the gopi maids.
> Behold, the two have come, who shatter all the rules of caste,
> Embracing everyone as brother, even the outcaste shunned by men;
> Who lose themselves in Hari's name, making the whole world mad;
> Who are none other than Hari Himself, and chant His hallowed
>   name!
> Behold them, who saved from their sinful ways the ruffians Jagāi
>   and Mādhāi,[2]
> They who cannot distinguish between a friend and an enemy!
> Behold the two brothers, Gaur and Nitāi, who come again to save
>   mankind.

Again the Master sang:

> See how all Nadiā is shaking
> Under the waves of Gaurānga's love! . . .

The crowd, with the Master in the centre, surged toward the temple of Rādhā-Krishna. Only a small number could enter. The rest stood outside the portal and jostled with one another to have a look at Sri Ramakrishna. In a mood of intoxication he began to dance in the courtyard of the shrine. Every now and then his body stood transfixed in deep samādhi. Hundreds of people around him shouted the name of God, and thousands outside caught the strain and raised the cry with full-throated voices. The echo travelled over the Ganges, striking a note in the hearts of people in the boats on the holy river, and they too chanted the name of God.

When the kirtan was over, Mani Sen took Sri Ramakrishna and Navadvip Goswami into a room and served them with refreshments. Afterwards Ram, M., and the other devotees were also served with the prasād.

In the afternoon, the Master was sitting in Mani Sen's drawing-room with the devotees. Navadvip was also near him. Mani offered the carriage hire to Sri Ramakrishna. Pointing to Ram and the others, the Master said: "Why

---

[1] Gaurānga and Nityānanda.

[2] At one time Nityānanda was beaten by the ruffians Jagāi and Mādhāi, who later were converted to spiritual life by his love.

should they accept it from you? They earn money." He became engaged in conversation with Navadvip.

MASTER: "Bhakti matured becomes bhāva. Next is mahābhāva, then prema, and last of all is the attainment of God. Gaurānga experienced the states of mahābhāva and prema. When prema is awakened, a devotee completely forgets the world; he also forgets his body, which is so dear to a man. Gaurānga experienced prema. He jumped into the ocean, thinking it to be the Jamunā. The ordinary jīva does not experience mahābhāva or prema. He goes only as far as bhāva. But Gaurānga experienced all three states. Isn't that so?"

NAVADVIP: "Yes, sir, that is true. The inmost state, the semi-conscious state, and the conscious state."

MASTER: "In the inmost state he would remain in samādhi, unconscious of the outer world. In the semi-conscious state he could only dance. In the conscious state he chanted the name of God."

Navadvip introduced his son to the Master. The young man was a student of the scriptures. He saluted Sri Ramakrishna.

NAVADVIP: "He studies the scriptures at home. Previously one hardly saw a copy of the Vedas in this country. Max Müller has translated them; so people can now read these books."

MASTER: "Too much study of the scriptures does more harm than good. The important thing is to know the essence of the scriptures. After that, what is the need of books? One should learn the essence and then dive deep in order to realize God.

"The Divine Mother has revealed to me the essence of the Vedānta. It is that Brahman alone is real and the world illusory. The essence of the Gītā is what you get by repeating the word ten times. The word becomes reversed. It is then 'tāgi', which refers to renunciation. The essence of the Gītā is: 'O man, renounce everything and practise spiritual discipline for the realization of God.' "

NAVADVIP: "But how can we persuade our minds to renounce?"

MASTER: "You are a goswāmi. It is your duty to officiate as priest in the temple. You cannot renounce the world; otherwise, who would look after the temple and its services? You have to renounce mentally.

"It is God Himself who has kept you in the world to set an example to men. You may resolve in your mind a thousand times to renounce the world, but you will not succeed. God has given you such a nature that you must perform your worldly duties.

"Krishna said to Arjuna: 'What do you mean, you will not fight? By your mere will you cannot desist from fighting. Your very nature will make you fight.' "

At the mere mention of Krishna and Arjuna the Master went into samādhi. In the twinkling of an eye his body became motionless and his eyeballs transfixed, while his breathing could scarcely be noticed. At this sudden transformation Navadvip and his son and the other devotees looked at the Master in mute wonder.

Regaining partial consciousness, he said to Navadvip: "Yoga and bhoga.

You goswāmis have both. Now your only duty is to call on God and pray to Him sincerely: 'O God, I don't want the glories of Thy world-bewitching māyā. I want Thee alone!' God dwells in all beings, undoubtedly. That being the case, who may be called His devotee? He who dwells in God, he who has merged his mind and life and innermost soul in God."

The Master returned to the sense plane. Referring to his samādhi, he said to Navadvip: "Some say that this state of mine is a disease. I say to them, 'How can one become unconscious by thinking of Him whose Consciousness has made the whole world conscious?' "

Mani Sen said good-bye to the invited brāhmins and Vaishnavas with suitable gifts of money. He offered five rupees to Sri Ramakrishna. The latter said that he could not possibly accept any money. But Mani insisted. The Master then asked him in the name of his guru not to press him. Mani requested him again to accept the offering. Sri Ramakrishna asked M., in a distressed voice, whether he should take the money. The disciple made a vehement protest and said, "No, sir. By no means."

Friends of Mani Sen gave the money to Rakhal, requesting him to buy some mangoes and sweets for the Master. Sri Ramakrishna said to M.: "I have definitely said to Mani that I would not accept the money. I feel free now. But Rakhal has accepted it. His is now the responsibility."

Sri Ramakrishna, accompanied by the devotees, took a carriage to return to Dakshineswar. They were going to pass the temple garden of Mati Seal on the way. For a long time the Master had been asking M. to take him to the reservoir in the garden in order that he might teach him how to meditate on the formless God. There were tame fish in the reservoir. Nobody harmed them. Visitors threw puffed rice and other bits of food into the water, and the big fish came in swarms to eat the food. Fearlessly the fish swam in the water and sported there joyously.

Coming to the reservoir, the Master said to M.: "Look at the fish. Meditating on the formless God is like swimming joyfully like these fish, in the Ocean of Bliss and Consciousness."

Monday, June 25, 1883

Sri Ramakrishna was at Balaram Bose's house in Calcutta. Rakhal and M were seated near him. The Master was in ecstasy. He conversed with the devotees in an abstracted mood.

MASTER: "Let me assure you that a man can realize his Inner Self through sincere prayer. But to the extent that he has the desire to enjoy worldly objects, his vision of the Self becomes obstructed."

M: "Yes, sir. You always ask us to plunge into God."

MASTER (*joyously*): "Yes! That's it. Let me tell you that the realization of Self is possible for all, without any exception."

M: "That is true, sir. But God is the Doer. He works through different beings in different ways, according to their capacity to manifest the Divine. God gives to some full spiritual consciousness, and others He keeps in ignorance."

MASTER: "No, that is not so. One should pray to God with a longing heart. God certainly listens to prayer if it is sincere. There is no doubt about it."

A DEVOTEE: "Yes, sir. There is this 'I-consciousness' in us; therefore we must pray."

MASTER (to M.): "A man should reach the Nitya, the Absolute, by following the trail of the Līlā, the Relative. It is like reaching the roof by the stairs. After realizing the Absolute, he should climb down to the Relative and live on that plane in the company of devotees, charging his mind with the love of God. This is my final and most mature opinion.

"God has different forms, and He sports in different ways. He sports as Iśvara, deva, man, and the universe. In every age He descends to earth in human form, as an Incarnation, to teach people love and devotion. There is the instance of Chaitanya. One can taste devotion and love of God only through His Incarnations. Infinite are the ways of God's play, but what I need is love and devotion. I want only the milk. The milk comes through the udder of the cow. The Incarnation is the udder."

Was Sri Ramakrishna hinting that he was an Incarnation of God? Did he suggest that those who saw him saw God? Did he thus speak about himself when speaking of Chaitanya?

It was a hot day in June 1883. Sri Ramakrishna was sitting on the steps of the Śiva temples in the temple garden. M. arrived with ice and other offerings and sat down on the steps after saluting the Master.

MASTER (to M.): "The husband of Mani Mallick's granddaughter was here. He read in a book[3] that God could not be said to be quite wise and omniscient; otherwise, why should there be so much misery in the world? As regards death, it would be much better to kill a man all at once, instead of putting him through slow torture. Further, the author writes that if he himself were the Creator, he would have created a better world."

M. listened to these words in surprise and made no comment.

MASTER (to M.): "Can a man ever understand God's ways? I too think of God sometimes as good and sometimes as bad. He has kept us deluded by His great illusion. Sometimes He wakes us up and sometimes He keeps us unconscious. One moment the ignorance disappears, and the next moment it covers our mind. If you throw a brick-bat into a pond covered with moss, you get a glimpse of the water. But a few moments later the moss comes dancing back and covers the water.

"One is aware of pleasure and pain, birth and death, disease and grief, as long as one is identified with the body. All these belong to the body alone, and not to the Soul. After the death of the body, perhaps God carries one to a better place. It is like the birth of the child after the pain of delivery. Attaining Self-Knowledge, one looks on pleasure and pain, birth and death, as a dream.

"How little we know! Can a one-seer pot hold ten seers of milk? If ever a salt doll ventures into the ocean to measure its depth, it cannot come back and give us the information. It melts into the water and disappears."

[3] The autobiography of John Stuart Mill.

At dusk the evening service began in the different temples. The Master was sitting on the small couch in his room, absorbed in contemplation of the Divine Mother. Several devotees also were there. M. was going to spend the night with the Master.

A little later Sri Ramakrishna began to talk to a devotee privately, on the verandah north of his room. He said: "It is good to meditate in the small hours of the morning and at dawn. One should also meditate daily after dusk." He instructed the devotee about meditation on the Personal God and on the Impersonal Reality.

After a time he sat on the semicircular porch west of his room. It was about nine o'clock.

MASTER: "Those who come here will certainly have all their doubts removed. What do you say?"

M: "That is true, sir."

A boat was moving in the Ganges, far away from the bank. The boatman began to sing. The sound of his voice floating over the river reached the Master's ears, and he went into a spiritual mood. The hair on his body stood on end. He said to M., "Just feel my body." M. was greatly amazed. He thought: "The Upanishads describe Brahman as permeating the universe and the ether. Has that Brahman, as sound, touched the Master's body?"

After a time Sri Ramakrishna began to converse again.

MASTER: "Those who come here must have been born with good tendencies. Isn't that true?"

M: "It is true, sir."

MASTER: "Adhar must have good tendencies."

M: "That goes without saying."

MASTER: "A guileless man easily realizes God. There are two paths: the path of righteousness and the path of wickedness. One should follow the path of righteousness."

M: "That is true, sir. If a thread has a single fibre sticking out, it cannot pass through the eye of a needle."

MASTER: "If a man finds a hair in the food he is chewing, he spits out the entire morsel."

M: "But you say that the man who has realized God cannot be injured by evil company. A blazing fire burns up even a plantain-tree."

Saturday, July 14, 1883

Sri Ramakrishna arrived at Adhar's house in Calcutta. Rakhal, M., and other devotees were with the Master. Adhar had arranged to have Rajnarayan, the famous singer, and his party, recite the *Chandi*.

Rajnarayan began the recital in the worship hall. He sang:

> I have surrendered my soul at the fearless feet of the Mother;
> Am I afraid of Death any more? . . .

As the Master listened, he became filled with divine fervour and joined the musicians. Now and then he improvised an appropriate line. Suddenly he went into *samādhi* and stood still.

The singer sang again:

Who is the Woman yonder who lights the field of battle?
Darker Her body gleams even than the darkest storm-cloud,
And from Her teeth there flash the lightning's blinding flames!
Dishevelled Her hair is flying behind as She rushes about,
Undaunted in this war between the gods and the demons.
Laughing Her terrible laugh, She slays the fleeing asuras,
And with Her dazzling flashes She bares the horror of war.

How beautiful on Her brow the drops of moisture appear!
About Her dense black hair the bees are buzzing in swarms;
The moon has veiled its face, beholding this Sea of Beauty.
Tell me, who can She be, this Sorceress? Wonder of wonders!
Śiva Himself, like a corpse, lies vanquished at Her feet.
Kamalākānta has guessed who She is, with the elephant's gait;
She is none other than Kāli, Mother of all the worlds.

Sri Ramakrishna was in deep samādhi.

Saturday, July 21, 1883

It was about four o'clock in the afternoon when Sri Ramakrishna, with Ramlal and one or two other devotees, started from Dakshineswar for Calcutta in a carriage. As the carriage passed the gate of the Kāli temple, they met M. coming on foot with four mangoes in his hand. The carriage stopped and M. saluted the Master. Sri Ramakrishna was going to visit some of his devotees in Calcutta.

MASTER (*to M., with a smile*): "Come with us. We are going to Adhar's house."

M. got joyfully into the carriage. Having received an English education, he did not believe in the tendencies inherited from previous births. But he had admitted a few days before that it was on account of Adhar's good tendencies from past births that he showed such great devotion to the Master. Later on he had thought about this subject and had discovered that he was not yet completely convinced about inherited tendencies. He had come to Dakshineswar that day to discuss the matter with Sri Ramakrishna.

MASTER: "Well, what do you think of Adhar?"

M: "He has great yearning for God."

MASTER: "Adhar, too, speaks very highly of you."

M. remained silent awhile and then began to speak of past tendencies.

M: "I haven't much faith in rebirth and inherited tendencies. Will that in any way injure my devotion to God?"

MASTER: "It is enough to believe that all is possible in God's creation. Never allow the thought to cross your mind that your ideas are the only true ones, and that those of others are false. Then God will explain everything.

"What can a man understand of God's activities? The facets of God's creation are infinite. I do not try to understand God's actions at all. I have heard that everything is possible in God's creation, and I always bear that in mind. Therefore I do not give a thought to the world, but meditate on

God alone Once Hanumān was asked, 'What day of the lunar month is it?' Hanumān said: 'I don't know anything about the day of the month, the position of the moon and stars, or any such things. I think of Rāma alone.'

"Can one ever understand the work of God? He is so near; still it is not possible for us to know Him. Balarāma did not realize that Krishna was God."

M: "That is true, sir."

MASTER: "God has covered all with His māyā. He doesn't let us know anything. Māyā is 'woman and gold'. He who puts māyā aside to see God, can see Him. Once, when I was explaining God's actions to someone, God suddenly showed me the lake at Kāmārpukur. I saw a man removing the green scum and drinking the water. The water was clear as crystal. God revealed to me that Satchidānanda is covered by the scum of māyā. He who puts the green scum aside can drink the water.

"Let me tell you a very secret experience. Once I had entered the wood near the pine-grove, and was sitting there, when I had a vision of something like the hidden door of a chamber. I couldn't see the inside of the chamber. I tried to bore a hole in the door with a nail-knife, but did not succeed. As I bored, the earth fell back into the hole and filled it. Then suddenly I made a very big opening."

Uttering these words, the Master remained silent. After a time he said: "These are very profound words. I feel as if someone were pressing my mouth. . . . I have seen with my own eyes that God dwells even in the sexual organ. I saw Him once in the sexual intercourse of a dog and a bitch.

"The universe is conscious on account of the Consciousness of God. Sometimes I find that this Consciousness wriggles about, as it were, even in small fish."

The carriage came to the crossing at Shovābāzār in Calcutta. The Master continued, saying, "Sometimes I find that the universe is saturated with the Consciousness of God, as the earth is soaked with water in the rainy season.

"Well, I see so many visions, but I never feel vain about them."

M. (with a smile): "That you should speak of vanity, sir!"

MASTER: "Upon my word, I don't feel vanity even in the slightest degree."

M: "There once lived a man in Greece, Socrates by name. A voice from heaven said that he was wise among men. Socrates was amazed at this revelation. He meditated on it a long time in solitude and then realized its significance. He said to his friends, 'I alone of all people have understood that I do not know anything.' But every man believes he is wise. In reality all are ignorant."

MASTER: "Now and then I think, 'What is it I know that makes so many people come to me?' Vaishnavcharan was a great pundit. He used to say to me: 'I can find in the scriptures all the things you talk about. But do you know why I come to you? I come to hear them from your mouth.'"

M: "All your words tally with the scriptures. Navadvip Goswami also said that the other day at the festival at Pānihāti. You told us that day that by repeating the word 'Gītā' a number of times one reverses it and it becomes 'tāgi', which refers to renunciation. Renunciation is the essence of the

Gitā. Navadvip Goswami supported your statement from the grammatical standpoint."

MASTER: "Have you found anyone else resembling me—any pundit or holy man?"

M: "God has created you with His own hands, whereas He has made others by machine. All others He has created according to law."

MASTER (*laughing, to Ramlal and the other devotees*): "Listen to what he is saying!"

Sri Ramakrishna laughed for some time, and said at last, "Really and truly I have no pride—no, not even the slightest bit."

M: "Knowledge does us good in one respect at least; it makes us feel that we do not know anything, that we are nothing."

MASTER: "Right you are! I am nothing. I am nobody.

"Do you believe in English astronomy?"

M: "It is possible to make new discoveries by applying the laws of Western astronomy. Observing the irregular movement of Uranus, the astronomers looked through their telescopes and discovered Neptune shining in the sky. They can also foretell eclipses."

MASTER: "Yes, that is so."

The carriage drove on. They were approaching Adhar's house. Sri Ramakrishna said to M., "Dwell in the truth and you will certainly realize God."

M: "You said the other day to Navadvip Goswami: 'O God, I want Thee. Please do not delude me with Thy world-bewitching māyā. I want to realize Thee.'"

MASTER: "Yes, one should be able to say that from one's innermost soul."

Sri Ramakrishna arrived at Adhar's house and took a seat in the parlour. Ramlal, Adhar, M., and the other devotees sat near him. Rakhal was staying with his father in Calcutta.

MASTER (*to Adhar*): "Didn't you let Rakhal know that I was coming?"

ADHAR: "Yes, sir. I have sent him word."

Finding that the Master was eager to see Rakhal, Adhar at once sent his carriage to fetch him. Adhar had been yearning to see the Master that day, but he had not definitely known that Sri Ramakrishna was coming.

ADHAR: "You haven't been here for a long time. I prayed to God today that you might come. I even shed tears."

The Master was pleased and said with a smile, "You don't mean that!"

It was dusk and the lamps were lighted. Sri Ramakrishna saluted the Divine Mother with folded hands and sat quietly absorbed in meditation. Then he began to chant the names of God in his sweet voice: "Govinda! Govinda! Satchidānanda! Hari! Hari!" Every word he uttered showered nectar on the ears of the devotees.

Ramlal sang in praise of Kāli, the Divine Mother:

Thy name, I have heard, O Consort of Śiva, is the destroyer of
    our fear,
And so on Thee I cast my burden: Save me! Save me, O kindly
    Mother!

Out of Thy womb the world is born, and Thou it is that dost
pervade it.
Art Thou Kālī? Art Thou Rādhā? Who can ever rightly say?

Mother, in every living creature Thou dost have Thy dwelling-
place;
As Kundalini Thou dost live in the lotus of the Mulādhāra.
Above it lies the Svādhisthāna, where the four-petalled lotus
blooms;
There also Thou dost make Thy home, O mystic power of
Kundalini,
In the four petals of that flower, and in Vajrāsana's six petals.
At the navel is Manipura, the blue ten-petalled lotus flower;
Through the pathway of Sushumnā, Thou dost ascend and enter
there.
O Lady of the lotuses, in lotus blossoms Thou dost dwell!

Beyond them lies the Lake of Nectar, in the region of the heart,
Where the twelve-petalled lotus flower enchants the eye with
scarlet flame.
When Thou dost open it, O Mother, touching it with Thy Lotus
Feet,
The age-long darkness of the heart instantly scatters at Thy sight.
Above, in the throat, is the sixteen-petalled lotus flower, of smoky
hue;
Within the petals of this flower there lies concealed a subtle space,
Transcending which, one sees at length the universe in Space
dissolve.
And higher yet, between the eyebrows, blossoms the lotus of two
petals,
Where the mind of man remains a prisoner and past controlling;
From this flower the mind desires to watch the sportive play of life.

Highest of all, within the head, the soul-enthralling centre is,
Where shines the thousand-petalled lotus, Mahādeva's dwelling-
place.
Having ascended to His throne, O Spouse of Śiva, sit beside Him!
Thou art the Primal Power, O Mother! She whose senses are
controlled;
The yogis meditate on Thee as Umā, great Himālaya's daughter.

Thou who art the Power of Śiva! Put to death my ceaseless
cravings;
Grant that I never fall again into the ocean of this world.
Mother, Thou art the Primal Power, Thou the five cosmic prin-
ciples;
Who can ever hope to know Thee, who art beyond all principles?
Only for Thy bhaktas' sake dost Thou assume Thy various forms;
But when Thy devotee's five senses merge in the five elements,
Mother, it is Thyself alone that he beholds as formless Truth.

As Ramlal sang the lines:

Above, in the throat, is the sixteen-petalled lotus flower, of smoky
hue;

Within the petals of this flower there lies concealed a subtle space,
Transcending which, one sees at length the universe in Space
dissolve,

the Master said to M.: "Listen. This is known as the vision of Satchidānanda,
the Formless Brahman. The Kundalini, rising above the Viśuddha chakra,
enables one to see everything as ākāśa."

M: "Yes, sir."

MASTER: "One attains the Absolute by going beyond the universe and its
created beings conjured up by māyā. By passing beyond the Nāda one goes
into samādhi. By repeating 'Om' one goes beyond the Nāda and attains
samādhi."

Adhar served Sri Ramakrishna with fruits and sweets. The Master left for
Jadu Mallick's house.

Sri Ramakrishna entered the room in Jadu's house where the Divine
Mother was worshipped. He stood before the image, which had been decorated with flowers, garlands, and sandal-paste, and which radiated a heavenly
beauty and splendour. Lights were burning before the pedestal. A priest was
seated before the image. The Master asked one of his companions to offer a
rupee in the shrine, according to the Hindu custom.

Sri Ramakrishna stood a long time with folded hands before the blissful
image, the devotees standing behind him. Gradually he went into samādhi,
his body becoming motionless and his eyes fixed.

With a long sigh he came back to the world of the senses and said, still
intoxicated with divine fervour, "Mother, good-bye." But he could not leave
the place. He remained standing there. Addressing Ramlal, he said: "Please
sing that song. Then I shall be all right."

Ramlal sang:

O Mother, Consort of Śiva, Thou hast deluded this world. . . .

The Master went to the drawing-room with the devotees. Every now and
then he said, "O Mother, please dwell in my heart!" Jadu was sitting in the
drawing-room with his friends. The Master sat down, still in an ecstatic
mood, and sang:

O Mother, ever blissful as Thou art,
Do not deprive Thy worthless child of bliss! . . .

Finishing the song, he said to Jadu, still in a state of divine fervour: "Well,
sir, what shall I sing? Shall I sing 'Mother, am I Thine eight-months child'?"
He sang:

Mother, am I Thine eight-months child?[4] Thy red eyes cannot
frighten me!
My riches are Thy Lotus Feet, which Śiva holds upon His breast;
Yet, when I seek my heritage, I meet with excuses and delays.
A deed of gift I hold in my heart, attested by Thy Husband Śiva;
I shall sue Thee, if I must, and with a single point shall win.

[4] A premature child is generally weak and fearful.

If Thou dost oppose me, Thou wilt learn what sort of mother's
    son I am.
This bitterly contested suit between the Mother and Her son—
What sport it is! says Rāmprasād. I shall not cease tormenting Thee
Till Thou Thyself shalt yield the fight and take me in Thine arms
    at last.

Coming down nearly to a normal state, the Master said, "I shall take some of the Divine Mother's prasād." Then he ate a little of it.

Jadu Mallick was sitting near him with several friends, among whom were a few of his flatterers.

MASTER (with a smile): "Well, why do you keep these buffoons with you?"

JADU (with a smile): "Suppose they are. Won't you redeem them?"

MASTER (smiling): "The water of the Ganges cannot purify a wine-jar."

Jadu had promised the Master that he would arrange a recital of the Chandi in his house. Some time had elapsed, but he had not yet kept his promise.

MASTER: "Well, what about the recital of the Chandi?"

JADU: "I have been busy with many things; I haven't been able to arrange it."

MASTER: "How is that? A man gives his word and doesn't take it back! 'The words of a man are like the tusks of the elephant: they come out but do not go back.' A man must be true to his word. What do you say?"

JADU (with a smile): "You are right."

MASTER: "You are a shrewd man. You do a thing after much calculation. You are like the brāhmin who selects a cow that eats very little, supplies plenty of dung, and gives much milk." (All laugh.)

After a time he said to Jadu: "I now understand your nature. It is half warm and half cold. You are devoted to God and also to the world."

The Master and his devotees were served by Jadu with sweets and fruit, and then the party left for the home of Khelat Ghosh.

Khelat Ghosh's house was a big mansion, but it looked deserted. As the Master entered the house he fell into an ecstatic mood. M., Ramlal, and a few other devotees were with him. Their host was Khelat Ghosh's brother-in-law. He was an old man, a Vaishnava. His body was stamped with the name of God, according to the Vaishnava custom, and he carried in his hand a small bag containing his rosary. He had visited the Master, now and then, at Dakshineswar. But most of the Vaishnavas held narrow religious views; they criticized the Vedāntists and the followers of the Śiva cult. Sri Ramakrishna soon began to speak.

MASTER: "It is not good to feel that one's own religion alone is true and all others are false. God is one only, and not two. Different people call on Him by different names: some as Āllāh, some as God, and others as Krishna, Śiva, and Brahman. It is like the water in a lake. Some drink it at one place and call it 'jal', others at another place and call it 'pāni', and still others at a third place and call it 'water'. The Hindus call it 'jal', the Christians 'water', and the Mussalmāns 'pāni'. But it is one and the same thing. Opinions are but paths. Each religion is only a path leading to God, as rivers come from different directions and ultimately become one in the one ocean.

"The Truth established in the Vedas, the Purāṇas, and the Tantras is but one Satchidānanda. In the Vedas It is called Brahman, in the Purāṇas It is called Krishna, Rāma, and so on, and in the Tantras It is called Śiva. The one Satchidānanda is called Brahman, Krishna, and Śiva."

The devotees were silent.

A VAISHNAVA DEVOTEE: "Sir, why should one think of God at all?"

MASTER: "If a man really has that knowledge,[5] then he is indeed liberated though living in a body.

"Not all, by any means, believe in God. They simply talk. The worldly-minded have heard from someone that God exists and that everything happens by His will; but it is not their inner belief.

"Do you know what a worldly man's idea of God is like? It is like the children's swearing by God when they quarrel. They have heard the word while listening to their elderly aunts quarrelling.

"Is it possible for all to comprehend God? God has created the good and the bad, the devoted and the impious, the faithful and the sceptical. The wonders that we see all exist in His creation. In one place there is more manifestation of His Power, in another less. The sun's light is better reflected by water than by earth, and still better by a mirror. Again, there are different levels among the devotees of God: superior, mediocre, and inferior. All this has been described in the Gītā."

VAISHNAVA: "True, sir."

MASTER: "The inferior devotee says, 'God exists, but He is very far off, up there in heaven.' The mediocre devotee says, 'God exists in all beings as life and consciousness.' The superior devotee says: 'It is God Himself who has become everything; whatever I see is only a form of God. It is He alone who has become māyā, the universe, and all living beings. Nothing exists but God.'"

VAISHNAVA: "Does anyone ever attain that state of mind?"

MASTER: "One cannot attain it unless one has seen God. But there are signs that a man has had the vision of God. A man who has seen God sometimes behaves like a madman: he laughs, weeps, dances, and sings. Sometimes he behaves like a child, a child five years old—guileless, generous, without vanity, unattached to anything, not under the control of any of the gunas, always blissful. Sometimes he behaves like a ghoul: he doesn't differentiate between things pure and things impure; he sees no difference between things clean and things unclean. And sometimes he is like an inert thing, staring vacantly: he cannot do any work; he cannot strive for anything."

Was the Master making a veiled reference to his own states of mind?

MASTER (to the Vaishnava devotee): "The feeling of 'Thee and Thine' is the outcome of Knowledge; 'I and mine' comes from ignorance. Knowledge makes one feel: 'O God, Thou art the Doer and I am Thy instrument.

[5] The knowledge that God exists within and without and everywhere. In that case, thinking of God is superfluous.

O God, to Thee belongs all—body, mind, house, family, living beings, and the universe. All these are Thine. Nothing belongs to me.'

"An ignorant person says, 'Oh, God is there—very far off.' The man of Knowledge knows that God is right here, very near, in the heart; that He has assumed all forms and dwells in all hearts as their Inner Controller."

Sunday, July 22, 1883

Taking advantage of the holiday, many householder devotees visited Sri Ramakrishna in his room at the Dakshineswar temple garden. The young devotees, mostly students, generally came on week-days. Sometimes the Master asked his intimate disciples to come on a Tuesday or a Saturday, days that he considered very auspicious for special religious instruction. Adhar, Rakhal, and M. had come from Calcutta in a hired carriage.

Sri Ramakrishna had enjoyed a little rest after his midday meal. The room had an atmosphere of purity and holiness. On the walls hung pictures of gods and goddesses, among them one of Christ rescuing the drowning Peter. Outside the room were plants laden with fragrant flowers, and the Ganges could be seen flowing toward the south. The Master was seated on the small couch, facing the north, and the devotees sat on mats and carpets spread on the floor. All eyes were directed toward him. Mani Mallick, an old Brāhmo devotee about sixty-five years of age, came to pay his respects to the Master. He had returned a few months earlier from a pilgrimage to Benares and was recounting his experiences to Sri Ramakrishna.

MANI MALLICK: "A monk whom I met in Benares said that no religious experience is possible without the control of the sense-organs. Nothing could be achieved by merely crying, 'God! God!' "

MASTER: "Do you understand the views of teachers like him? According to them, one must first practise spiritual discipline: self-restraint, self-control, forbearance, and the like. Their aim is to attain Nirvāna. They are followers of Vedānta. They constantly discriminate, saying, 'Brahman alone is real, and the world illusory.' But this is an extremely difficult path. If the world is illusory, then you too are illusory. The teacher who gives the instruction is equally illusory. His words, too, are as illusory as a dream.

"But this experience is beyond the reach of the ordinary man. Do you know what it is like? If you burn camphor nothing remains. When wood is burnt at least a little ash is left. Finally, after the last analysis, the devotee goes into samādhi. Then he knows nothing whatsoever of 'I', 'you', or the universe.

"Padmalochan was a man of deep wisdom. He had great respect for me, though at that time I constantly repeated the name of the Divine Mother. He was the court pundit of the Mahārājā of Burdwan. Once he came to Calcutta and went to live in a garden house near Kāmārhāti. I felt a desire to see him and sent Hriday there to learn if the pundit had any vanity. I was told that he had none. Then I met him. Though a man of great knowledge and scholarship, he began to weep on hearing me sing Rāmprasād's devotional songs. We talked together a long while; conversation with nobody else gave me such satisfaction. He said to me, 'Give up the

desire for the company of devotees; otherwise people of all sorts will come
to you and make you deviate from your spiritual ideal.' Once he entered into
a controversy, by correspondence, with Utshavānanda, Vaishnavcharan's
guru. He told me an interesting incident. Once a meeting was called to
decide which of the two deities, Śiva or Brahmā, was the greater. Unable to
come to any decision, the pundits at last referred the matter to Padmalochan.
With characteristic guilelessness he said: 'How do I know? Neither I nor
any of my ancestors back to the fourteenth generation have seen Śiva or
Brahmā.' About the renunciation of 'woman and gold', he said to me one
day: 'Why have you given up those things? Such distinctions as "This is
money and that is clay" are the outcome of ignorance.' What could I say
to that? I replied: 'I don't know all these things, my dear sir. But for my
part, I cannot relish such things as money and the like.'

"There was a pundit who was tremendously vain. He did not believe
in the forms of God. But who can understand the inscrutable ways of the
Divine? God revealed Himself to him as the Primal Power. This vision
made the pundit unconscious for a long time. After regaining partial consciousness he uttered only the sound 'Kā! Kā! Kā!' He could not fully pronounce 'Kāli'."

A DEVOTEE: "Sir, you met Pundit Vidyāsāgar. What did you think of
him?"

MASTER: "Vidyāsāgar has both scholarship and charity, but he lacks inner
vision. Gold lies hidden within him. Had he but found it out, his activities
would have been reduced; finally they would have stopped altogether. Had
he but known that God resides in his heart, his mind would have been
directed to God in thought and meditation. Some persons must perform
selfless work a long time before they can practise dispassion and direct
their minds to the spiritual ideal and at last be absorbed in God.

"The activities that Vidyāsāgar is engaged in are good. Charity is very
noble. There is a great deal of difference between dayā, compassion, and
māyā, attachment. Dayā is good, but not māyā. Māyā is love for one's relatives—one's wife, children, brother, sister, nephew, father, and mother. But
dayā is the same love for all created beings without any distinction."

M: "Is dayā also a bondage?"

MASTER: "Yes, it is. But that concept is something far beyond the ordinary man. Dayā springs from sattva. Sattva preserves, rajas creates, and
tamas destroys. But Brahman is beyond the three gunas. It is beyond
Prakriti.

"None of the three gunas can reach Truth; they are like robbers, who
cannot come to a public place for fear of being arrested. Sattva, rajas, and
tamas are like so many robbers.

"Listen to a story. Once a man was going through a forest, when three
robbers fell upon him and robbed him of all his possessions. One of the
robbers said, 'What's the use of keeping this man alive?' So saying, he was
about to kill him with his sword, when the second robber interrupted him,
saying: 'Oh, no! What is the use of killing him? Tie him hand and foot
and leave him here.' The robbers bound his hands and feet and went away.

After a while the third robber returned and said to the man: 'Ah, I am sorry. Are you hurt? I will release you from your bonds.' After setting the man free, the thief said: Come with me. I will take you to the public highway.' After a long time they reached the road. Then the robber said: 'Follow this road. Over there is your house.' At this the man said: 'Sir, you have been very good to me. Come with me to my house.' 'Oh, no!' the robber replied. 'I can't go there. The police will know it.'

"This world itself is the forest. The three robbers prowling here are sattva, rajas, and tamas. It is they that rob a man of the Knowledge of Truth. Tamas wants to destroy him. Rajas binds him to the world. But sattva rescues him from the clutches of rajas and tamas. Under the protection of sattva, man is rescued from anger, passion, and the other evil effects of tamas. Further, sattva loosens the bonds of the world. But sattva also is a robber. It cannot give him the ultimate Knowledge of Truth, though it shows him the road leading to the Supreme Abode of God. Setting him on the path, sattva tells him: 'Look yonder. There is your home.' Even sattva is far away from the Knowledge of Brahman.

"What Brahman is cannot be described. Even he who knows It cannot talk about It. There is a saying that a boat, once reaching the 'black waters' of the ocean, cannot come back.

"Once four friends, in the course of a walk, saw a place enclosed by a wall. The wall was very high. They all became eager to know what was inside. One of them climbed to the top of the wall. What he saw on looking inside made him speechless with wonder. He only cried, 'Ah! Ah!' and dropped in. He could not give any information about what he saw. The others, too, climbed the wall, uttered the same cry, 'Ah! Ah!', and jumped in. Now who could tell what was inside?

"Sages like Jadabharata and Dattātreya, after realizing Brahman, could not describe It. A man's 'I' completely disappears when he goes into samādhi after attaining the Knowledge of Brahman. That is why Rāmprasād sang, addressing his mind:

> If you should find the task too hard,
> Call upon Rāmprasād for help.

The mind must completely merge itself in Knowledge. But that is not enough. 'Rāmprasād', that is, the principle of 'I', must vanish too. Then alone does one get the Knowledge of Brahman."

A DEVOTEE: "Sir, is it possible then that Śukadeva did not have the ultimate Knowledge?"

MASTER: "According to some people, Śukadeva only saw and touched the Ocean of Brahman; he did not dive into It. That is why he could return to the world and impart religious instruction. According to others, he returned to the world of name and form, after attaining the Knowledge of Brahman, for the purpose of teaching others. He had to recite the Bhāgavata to King Parikshit and had to teach people in various ways; therefore God did not destroy his 'I' altogether. God kept in him the 'ego of Knowledge'."

DEVOTEE: "Can one keep up an organization after attaining the Knowledge of Brahman?"

MASTER: "Once I talked to Keshab Sen about the Knowledge of Brahman. He asked me to explain it further. I said, 'If I proceed further, then you won't be able to preserve your organization and following.' 'Then please stop here!' replied Keshab. (*All laugh.*) But still I said to Keshab: ' "I" and "mine" indicate ignorance. Without ignorance one cannot have such a feeling as "I am the doer; these are my wife, children, possessions, name and fame".' Thereupon Keshab said, 'Sir, if one gave up the "I", nothing whatsoever would remain.' I reassured him and said: 'I am not asking you to give up all of the "I". You should give up only the "unripe, I". The "unripe I" makes one feel: "I am the doer. These are my wife and children. I am a teacher." Renounce this "unripe I" and keep the "ripe I", which will make you feel that you are the servant of God, His devotee, and that God is the Doer and you are His instrument.' "

DEVOTEE: "Can the 'ripe I' form an organization?"

MASTER: "I said to Keshab Sen that the 'I' that says, 'I am a leader, I have formed this party, I am teaching people', is the 'unripe I'. It is very difficult to preach religion. It is not possible to do so without receiving the commandment of God. The permission of God is necessary. Sukadeva had a command from God to recite the *Bhāgavata*. If, after realizing God, a man gets His command and becomes a preacher or teacher, then that preaching or teaching does no harm. His 'I' is not 'unripe'; it is 'ripe'.

"I asked Keshab to give up this 'unripe I'. The ego that feels, 'I am the servant of God and lover of God' does not injure one. I said to him: 'You have been constantly talking of your organization and your followers. But people also go away from your organization.' Keshab answered: 'It is true, sir. After staying in it several years, people go to another organization. What is worse, on deserting me they abuse me right and left.' 'Why don't you study their nature?' I said. 'Is there any good in making anybody and everybody a disciple?'

"I said to Keshab further: 'You should accept the Divine Mother, the Primal Energy. Brahman is not different from Its Śakti. What is Brahman is also Śakti. As long as a man remains conscious of the body, he is conscious of duality. It is only when a man tries to describe what he sees that he finds duality.' Keshab later on recognized Kāli.

"One day when Keshab was here with his disciples, I said to him that I would like to hear him preach. He delivered a lecture in the chāndni. Then we all sat by the bathing-ghāt and had a long conversation. I said to him: 'It is Bhagavān alone who in one form appears as bhakta, and in another as the *Bhāgavata*. Please repeat "Bhāgavata—Bhakta—Bhagavān".' Keshab and his disciples repeated the words. Then I asked him to repeat 'Guru—Krishna —Vaishnava'. Thereupon Keshab said: 'Sir, I should not go so far now. People will say that I have become an orthodox Hindu.'

"It is extremely difficult to go beyond the three gunas. One cannot reach that state without having realized God. Man dwells in the realm of māyā. Māyā does not permit him to see God. It has made him a victim of ignorance.

"Once Hriday brought a bull-calf here. I saw, one day, that he had tied it with a rope in the garden, so that it might graze there. I asked him, 'Hriday, why do you tie the calf there every day?' 'Uncle,' he said, 'I am going to send this calf to our village. When it grows strong I shall yoke it to the plough.' As soon as I heard these words I was stunned to think: 'How inscrutable is the play of the divine māyā! Kāmārpukur and Sihore[6] are so far away from Calcutta! This poor calf must go all that way. Then it will grow, and at length it will be yoked to the plough. This is indeed the world! This is indeed māyā!' I fell down unconscious. Only after a long time did I regain consciousness."

It was three or four o'clock in the afternoon. M. found Sri Ramakrishna seated on the couch in an abstracted mood. After some time he heard him talking to the Divine Mother. The Master said, "O Mother, why hast Thou given him only a particle?" Remaining silent a few moments, he added: "I understand it, Mother. That little bit will be enough for him and will serve Thy purpose. That little bit will enable him to teach people."

Did the Master thus transmit spiritual powers to his disciples? Did he thus come to know that his disciples, after him, would go out into the world as teachers of men?

Rakhal was in the room. Sri Ramakrishna was still in a state of partial consciousness when he said to Rakhal: "You were angry with me, weren't you? Do you know why I made you angry? There was a reason. Only then would the medicine work. The surgeon first brings an abscess to a head. Only then does he apply a herb so that it may burst and dry up."

After a pause he went on: "Yes, I have found Hazra to be like a piece of dry wood. Then why does he live here? This has a meaning too. The play is enlivened by the presence of trouble-makers like Jatilā and Kutilā.

(To M.) "One must accept the forms of God. Do you know the meaning of the image of Jagaddhātri? She is the Bearer of the Universe. Without Her support and protection the universe would fall from its place and be destroyed. The Divine Mother, Jagaddhātri, reveals Herself in the heart of óne who can control the mind, which may be compared to an elephant."

RAKHAL: "The mind is a mad elephant."

MASTER: "Therefore the lion, the carrier of the Divine Mother, keeps it under control."[7]

It was dusk. The evening service began in the temples. Sri Ramakrishna was chanting the names of the gods and goddesses. He was seated on the small couch, with folded hands, and became absorbed in contemplation of the Divine Mother. The world outside was flooded with moonlight, and the devotees inside the Master's room sat in silence and looked at his serene face.

In the mean time Govinda of Belghariā and some of his friends had entered the room. Sri Ramakrishna was still in a semi-conscious state. After a few

---

[6] Hriday's birth-place.

[7] In the image of Jagaddhātri, the lion, Her carrier, is seen keeping an elephant under control.

minutes he said to the devotees: "Tell me your doubts. I shall explain everything."

Govinda and the other devotees looked thoughtful.

GOVINDA: "Revered sir, why does the Divine Mother have a black complexion?"[8]

MASTER: "You see Her as black because you are far away from Her. Go near and you will find Her devoid of all colour. The water of a lake appears black from a distance. Go near and take the water in your hand, and you will see that it has no colour at all. Similarly, the sky looks blue from a distance. But look at the atmosphere near you; it has no colour. The nearer you come to God, the more you will realize that He has neither name nor form. If you move away from the Divine Mother, you will find Her blue, like the grass-flower. Is Śyāmā male or female? A man once saw the image of the Divine Mother wearing a sacred thread.[9] He said to the worshipper: 'What? You have put the sacred thread on the Mother's neck!' The worshipper said: 'Brother, I see that you have truly known the Mother. But I have not yet been able to find out whether She is male or female; that is why I have put the sacred thread on Her image.'

"That which is Śyāmā is also Brahman. That which has form, again, is without form. That which has attributes, again, has no attributes. Brahman is Śakti; Śakti is Brahman. They are not two. These are only two aspects, male and female, of the same Reality, Existence-Knowledge-Bliss Absolute."

GOVINDA: "What is the meaning of 'yogamāyā'?"

MASTER: "It signifies the yoga, or union, of Purusha[10] and Prakriti.[11] Whatever you perceive in the universe is the outcome of this union. Take the image of Śiva and Kālī. Kālī stands on the bosom of Śiva; Śiva lies under Her feet like a corpse; Kālī looks at Śiva. All this denotes the union of Purusha and Prakriti. Purusha is inactive; therefore Śiva lies on the ground like a corpse. Prakriti performs all Her activities in conjunction with Purusha. Thus She creates, preserves, and destroys. That is also the meaning of the conjoined images of Rādhā and Krishna. On account of that union, again, the images are slightly inclined toward each other.

"To denote this union, Sri Krishna wears a pearl in His nose, Rādhā a blue stone in hers. Rādhā has a fair complexion, bright as the pearl. Sri Krishna's is blue. For this reason Rādhā wears the blue stone. Further, Krishna's apparel is yellow, and Rādhā's blue.

"Who is the best devotee of God? It is he who sees, after the realization of Brahman, that God alone has become all living beings, the universe, and the twenty-four cosmic principles. One must discriminate at first, saying 'Not this, not this', and reach the roof. After that one realizes that the steps are made of the same materials as the roof, namely, brick, lime, and brick-dust. The devotee realizes that it is Brahman alone that has become all these—the living beings, the universe, and so on.

[8] A reference to the image of Kālī.
[9] The images of male deities only are invested with the sacred thread.
[10] The male aspect of Reality; the Soul, or Absolute.
[11] The female aspect of Reality; Primordial Nature, or Power.

"Mere dry reasoning—I spit on it! I have no use for it! (*The Master spits on the ground.*)

"Why should I make myself dry through mere reasoning? May I have unalloyed love for the Lotus Feet of God as long as the consciousness of 'I' and 'you' remains with me!

(*To Govinda*) "Sometimes I say, 'Thou art verily I, and I am verily Thou.' Again I feel, 'Thou art Thou.' Then I do not find any trace of 'I'. It is Śakti alone that becomes flesh as God Incarnate. According to one school of thought, Rāma and Krishna are but two waves in the Ocean of Absolute Bliss and Consciousness.

"Chaitanya, Consciousness, is awakened after Advaita-jnāna, the Knowledge of the non-dual Brahman. Then one perceives that God alone exists in all beings as Consciousness. After this realization comes Ānanda, Bliss. Advaita, Chaitanya, and Nityānanda.[12]

(*To M.*) "Let me ask you not to disbelieve in the forms of God. Have faith in God's forms. Meditate on that form of God which appeals to your mind.

(*To Govinda*) "The fact is that one does not feel the longing to know or see God as long as one wants to enjoy worldly objects. The child forgets everything when he plays with his toys. Try to cajole him away from play with a sweetmeat; you will not succeed. He will eat only a bit of it. When he relishes neither the sweetmeat nor his play, then he says, 'I want to go to my mother.' He doesn't care for the sweetmeat any more. If a man whom he doesn't know and has never seen says to the child, 'Come along; I shall take you to your mother', the child follows him. The child will go with anyone who will carry him to his mother.

"The soul becomes restless for God when one is through with the enjoyment of worldly things. Then a person has only one thought—how to realize God. He listens to whatever anyone says to him about God."

M. (*to himself*): "Alas! The soul becomes restless for God only when one is through with the enjoyment of worldly things."

August 18, 1883

Sri Ramakrishna was at Balaram Bose's house in Calcutta. He was explaining the mystery of Divine Incarnation to the devotees.

MASTER: "In order to bring people spiritual knowledge, an Incarnation of God lives in the world in the company of devotees, cherishing an attitude of love for God. It is like going up and coming down the stairs after having once reached the roof. In order to reach the roof, other people should follow the path of devotion, as long as they have not attained Knowledge and become free of desire. The roof can be reached only when all desires are done away with. The shopkeeper does not go to bed before finishing his accounts. He goes to sleep only when his accounts are finished.

(*To M.*) "A man will certainly succeed if he will take the plunge. Success is sure for such a man.

---

[12] Non-duality, Consciousness, and Eternal Bliss.

"Well, what do you think of the worship conducted by Keshab, Shivanath, and the other Brāhmo leaders?"

M: "They are satisfied, as you say, with describing the garden, but they seldom speak of seeing the Master of the garden. Describing the garden is the beginning and end of their worship."

MASTER: "You are right. Our only duty is to seek the Master of the garden and speak to Him. The only purpose of life is to realize God."

Sri Ramakrishna then went to Adhar's house. After dusk he sang and danced in Adhar's drawing-room. M., Rakhal, and other devotees were present. After the music he sat down, still in an ecstatic mood. He said to Rakhal: "This religious fervour[13] is not like rain in the rainy season, which comes in torrents and goes in torrents. It is like an image of Śiva that has not been set up by human hands but is a natural one that has sprung up, as it were, from the bowels of the earth. The other day you left Dakshineswar in a temper. I prayed to the Divine Mother to forgive you."

The Master was still in an abstracted mood and said to Adhar, "My son, meditate on the Deity whose name you chanted." With these words he touched Adhar's tongue with his finger and wrote something on it. Did the Master thereby impart spirituality to Adhar?

[13] Referring to himself.

THE MASTER AND M.

IT WAS SUNDAY, the first day after the full moon. Sri Ramakrishna was resting after his noon meal. The midday offering had been made in the temples, and the temple doors were closed.

In the early afternoon the Master sat up on the small couch in his room. M. prostrated himself before him and sat on the floor. The Master was talking to him on the philosophy of Vedānta.

MASTER (to M.): "Self-Knowledge is discussed in the *Ashtāvakra Samhitā*. The non-dualists say, 'Soham', that is, 'I am the Supreme Self.' This is the view of the sannyāsis of the Vedāntic school. But this is not the right attitude for householders, who are conscious of doing everything themselves. That being so, how can they declare, 'I am That, the actionless Supreme Self'? According to the non-dualists the Self is unattached. Good and bad, virtue and vice, and the other pairs of opposites, cannot in any way injure the Self, though they undoubtedly afflict those who have identified themselves with their bodies. Smoke soils the wall, certainly, but it cannot in any way affect ākāśa, space. Following the Vedāntists of this class, Krishnakishore used to say, 'I am Kha', meaning ākāśa. Being a great devotee, he could say that with some justification; but it is not becoming for others to do so.

"But to feel that one is a free soul is very good. By constantly repeating, 'I am free, I am free', a man verily becomes free. On the other hand, by constantly repeating, 'I am bound, I am bound', he certainly becomes bound to worldliness. The fool who says only, 'I am a sinner, I am a sinner', verily drowns himself in worldliness. One should rather say: 'I have chanted the name of God. How can I be a sinner? How can I be bound?'

(To M.) "You see, I am very much depressed today. Hriday has written me that he is very ill. Why should I feel dejected about it? Is it because of māyā or dayā?"

M. could not find suitable words for a reply, and remained silent.

MASTER: "Do you know what māyā is? It is attachment to relatives—parents, brother and sister, wife and children, nephew and niece. Dayā means love for all created beings. Now what is this, my feeling about Hriday? Is it māyā or dayā? But Hriday did so much for me: he served me

274

whole-heartedly and nursed me when I was ill. But later he tormented me
also. The torment became so unbearable that once I was about to commit
suicide by jumping into the Ganges from the top of the embankment. But
he did much to serve me. Now my mind will be at rest if he gets some
money. But whom shall I ask for it? Who likes to speak about such things
to our rich visitors?"

At two or three o'clock in the afternoon Adhar Sen and Balaram
arrived. After saluting Sri Ramakrishna, they sat on the floor and asked
him if he was well. The Master said, "Yes, I am well physically, but a little
troubled in mind." He did not refer to Hriday and his troubles.

The conversation turned to the Goddess Simhavāhini.

MASTER: "Yes, I visited the Goddess. She is worshipped by one of the
branches of the Mallick family of Calcutta. This branch of the family is now
in straitened circumstances, and the house they live in is dilapidated. The
walls and floor are spotted with moss and pigeon-droppings, and the cement
and plaster are crumbling. But other branches of the Mallick family are well
off. This branch has no signs of prosperity. (*To M.*) Well, what does that
signify?"

M. remained silent.

MASTER: "The thing is that everyone must reap the result of his past
karma. One must admit the influence of tendencies inherited from past
births and the result of the prārabdha karma. Nevertheless, in that dilapidated
house I saw the face of the Goddess radiating a divine light. One must believe
in the Divine Presence in the image.

"Once I went to Vishnupur. The rājā of that place has several fine
temples. In one of them there is an image of the Divine Mother, called
Mrinmayi.[1] There are several lakes near the temple, known as the Lālbāndh,
Krishnabāndh, and so on. In the water of one of the lakes I could smell the
ointments that women use for their hair. How do you explain that? I didn't
know at that time that the woman devotees offer ointments to the Goddess
Mrinmayi while visiting Her temple. Near the lake I went into samādhi,
though I had not yet seen the image in the temple. In that state I saw the
divine form from the waist up, rising from the water."

In the mean time other devotees had arrived. Someone referred to the
political revolution and civil war in Kābul. A devotee said that Yakub Khān,
the Āmir of Afghanistan, had been deposed. He told the Master that the
. mir was a great devotee of God.

MASTER: "But you must remember that pleasure and pain are the characteristics of the embodied state. In Kavi Kankan's *Chandi* it is written that
Kāluvir was sent to prison and a heavy stone placed on his chest. Yet Kālu
was born as a result of a boon from the Divine Mother of the Universe.
Thus pleasure and pain are inevitable when the soul accepts a body. Again,
take the case of Srimanta, who was a great devotee. Though his mother,
Khullanā, was very much devoted to the Divine Mother, there was no end
to his troubles. He was almost beheaded. There is also the instance of the
wood-cutter who was a great lover of the Divine Mother. She appeared

[1] For the legend connected with this temple, see p. 797.

before him and showed him much grace and love; but he had to continue his profession of wood-cutting and earn his livelihood by that arduous work. Again, while Devaki, Krishna's mother, was in prison, she had a vision of God Himself endowed with four hands, holding mace, discus, conch-shell, and lotus. But with all that she couldn't get out of prison."

M: "Why speak only of getting out of prison? This body is the source of all our troubles. Devaki should have been freed from the body."

MASTER: "The truth is that one must reap the result of the prārabdha karma. The body remains as long as the results of past actions do not completely wear away. Once a blind man bathed in the Ganges and as a result was freed from his sins. But his blindness remained all the same. (All laugh.) It was because of his evil deeds in his past birth that he had to undergo that affliction."

M: "Yes, sir. The arrow that has already left the bow is beyond our control."

MASTER: "However much a bhakta may experience physical joy and sorrow, he always has knowledge and the treasure of divine love. This treasure never leaves him. Take the Pāndava brothers for instance. Though they suffered so many calamities, they did not lose their God-Consciousness even once. Where can you find men like them, endowed with so much knowledge and devotion?"

Just then Narendra and Colonel Viswanath Upadhyaya entered the room. Narendra was then twenty-two years old and studying in college. They saluted the Master and sat down. The Master requested Narendra to sing. The tānpurā hung on the west wall of the room. The devotees fixed their eyes on Narendra as he began to tune the drums.

MASTER (to Narendra): "The drums don't sound as well as before."

CAPTAIN: "They are now full. Therefore they are quiet, like a vessel filled with water. Or they are like a holy man, who remains silent when his heart is full of God-Consciousness."

MASTER: "But what about sages like Nārada?"

CAPTAIN: "They talked because they were moved by the sufferings of others."

MASTER: "You are right. After attaining samādhi, Nārada, Śukadeva, and others came down a few steps, as it were, to the plane of normal consciousness and broke their silence out of compassion for the sufferings of others and to help them."

Narendra began to sing:

Oh, when will dawn for me that day of blessedness
When He who is all Good, all Beauty, and all Truth,
Will light the inmost shrine of my heart?
When shall I sink at last, ever beholding Him,
Into that Ocean of Delight? . . .

No sooner had the Master heard a few words of the song than he went into deep samādhi. He sat with folded hands, facing the east. His body was erect and his mind completely bereft of worldly consciousness. His breath had almost stopped. With unwinking eyes he sat motionless as a picture on a canvas. His mind had dived deep into the Ocean of God's Beauty.

Narendra left the room and went to the east verandah, where Hazra was seated on a blanket, with a rosary in his hand. They fell to talking. Other devotees arrived. The Master came down from samādhi and looked around. He could not find Narendra. The tānpurā was lying on the floor. He noticed that the earnest eyes of the devotees were riveted on him.

MASTER (referring to Narendra): "He has lighted the fire. Now it doesn't matter whether he stays in the room or goes out.

(To Captain and the other devotees) "Attribute to yourselves the bliss of God-Consciousness; then you too will experience ineffable joy. The bliss of God-Consciousness always exists in you. It is only hidden by the veiling and projecting power of māyā.[2] The less you are attached to the world, the more you love God."

CAPTAIN: "The farther you proceed toward your home in Calcutta, the farther you leave Benares behind. Again, the farther you proceed toward Benares, the farther behind you leave your home."

MASTER: "As Rādhā advanced toward Krishna, she could smell more and more of the sweet fragrance of His body. The nearer you approach to God, the more you feel His love. As the river approaches the ocean it increasingly feels the flow of the tides.

"The jnāni experiences God-Consciousness within himself; it is like the upper Ganges, flowing in only one direction. To him the whole universe is illusory, like a dream; he is always established in the Reality of Self. But with the lover of God the case is different. His feeling does not flow in only one direction. He feels both the ebb-tide and the flood-tide of divine emotion. He laughs and weeps and dances and sings in the ecstasy of God. The lover of God likes to sport with Him. In the Ocean of God-Consciousness he sometimes swims, sometimes goes down, and sometimes rises to the surface—like pieces of ice in the water. (Laughter.)

"The jnāni seeks to realize Brahman. But the ideal of the bhakta is the Personal God—a God endowed with omnipotence and with the six treasures. Yet Brahman and Sakti are, in fact, not different. That which is the Blissful Mother is, again, Existence-Knowledge-Bliss Absolute. They are like the gem and its lustre. When one speaks of the lustre of the gem, one thinks of the gem; and again, when one speaks of the gem, one refers to its lustre. One cannot conceive of the lustre of the gem without thinking of the gem, and one cannot conceive of the gem without thinking of its lustre.

"Existence-Knowledge-Bliss Absolute is one, and one only. But It is associated with different limiting adjuncts on account of the different degrees of Its manifestation. That is why one finds various forms of God. The devotee sings, 'O my Divine Mother, Thou art all these!' Wherever you see actions, like creation, preservation, and dissolution, there is the manifestation of Sakti. Water is water whether it is calm or full of waves and bubbles. The Absolute alone is the Primordial Energy, which creates, preserves, and

---

[2] The veiling power of māyā hides the Reality; the projecting power of māyā creates the names and forms of the manifold universe.

destroys. Thus it is the same 'Captain', whether he remains inactive or performs his worship or pays a visit to the Governor General. Only we designate him by different names at different times."

CAPTAIN: "Yes, sir, that is so."

MASTER: "I said those words to Keshab Sen."

CAPTAIN: "Keshab is not an orthodox Hindu. He adopts manners and customs according to his own whim. He is a well-to-do gentleman and not a holy man."

MASTER (to the other devotees): "Captain forbids me to go to see Keshab."

CAPTAIN: "But, sir, you act as you will. What can I do?"

MASTER (sharply): "Why shouldn't I go to see Keshab? You feel at ease when you go to the Governor General's house,[3] and for money at that. Keshab thinks of God and chants His name. Isn't it you who are always saying that God Himself has become the universe and all its living beings? Doesn't God dwell in Keshab also?"

With these words the Master left the room abruptly and went to the northeast verandah. Captain and the other devotees remained, waiting for his return. M. accompanied the Master to the verandah, where Narendra was talking with Hazra. Sri Ramakrishna knew that Hazra always indulged in dry philosophical discussions. Hazra would say: "The world is unreal, like a dream. Worship, food offerings to the Deity, and so forth, are only hallucinations of the mind. The aim of spiritual life is to meditate on one's own real Self." Then he would repeat, "I am He." But, with all that, he had a soft corner in his heart for money, material things, and people's attention.

Sri Ramakrishna smiled and said to Hazra and Narendra, "Hello! What are you talking about?"

NARENDRA (smiling): "Oh, we are discussing a great many things. They are rather too deep for others."

MASTER (with a smile): "But Pure Knowledge and Pure Love are one and the same thing. Both lead the aspirants to the same goal. The path of love is much the easier."

Narendra quoted a song:

> O Mother, make me mad with Thy love!
> What need have I of knowledge or reason?

Narendra said to M. that he had been reading a book by Hamilton, who wrote: "A learned ignorance is the end of philosophy and the beginning of religion."

MASTER (to M.): "What does that mean?"

Narendra explained the sentence in Bengali. The Master beamed with joy and said in English, "Thank you! Thank you!" Everyone laughed at the charming way he said these words. They knew that his English vocabulary consisted of only half a dozen words.

It was almost dusk when most of the devotees, including Narendra, took leave of the Master. Sri Ramakrishna went out and looked at the Ganges

---

[3] According to orthodox Hindu custom, an Englishman is a mlechchha, one outside the pale of Hindu society. The touch of a mlechchha pollutes a Hindu.

for a few minutes from the west porch. Two priests were bathing in preparation for the evening worship. Young men of the village were strolling in the garden or standing on the concrete embankment, gazing at the murmuring river. Others, perhaps more thoughtful, were walking about in the solitude of the Panchavati.

It became dark. The maidservant lighted the lamp in Sri Ramakrishna's room and burnt incense. The evening worship began in the twelve temples of Śiva and in the shrines of Krishna and Kāli.

As it was the first day after the full moon, the moonlight soon flooded the tops of the trees and temples, and touched with silver the numberless waves of the sacred river.

The Master returned to his room. After bowing to the Divine Mother, he clapped his hands and chanted the sweet names of God. A number of holy pictures hung on the walls of the room. Among others, there were pictures of Dhruva, Prahlāda, Kāli, Rādhā-Krishna, and the coronation of Rāma. The Master bowed low before the pictures and repeated the holy names. Then he repeated the holy words, "Brahma—Ātmā—Bhagavān; Bhāgavata—Bhakta—Bhagavān; Brahma—Śakti, Śakti—Brahma; Veda, Purāna, Tantra, Gītā, Gāyatri." Then he said: "I have taken refuge at Thy feet, O Divine Mother; not I, but Thou. I am the machine and Thou art the Operator", and so on.

While the Master was meditating in this fashion on the Divine Mother, a few devotees, coming in from the garden, gathered in his room. Sri Ramakrishna sat down on the small couch. He said to the devotees: "Narendra, Bhavanath, Rakhal, and devotees like them belong to the group of the nityasiddhas; they are eternally free. Religious practice on their part is superfluous. Look at Narendra. He doesn't care about anyone. One day he was going with me in Captain's carriage. Captain wanted him to take a good seat, but Narendra didn't even look at him. He is independent even of me. He doesn't tell me all he knows, lest I should praise his scholarship before others. He is free from ignorance and delusion. He has no bonds. He is a great soul. He has many good qualities. He is expert in music, both as a singer and player, and is also a versatile scholar. Again, he keeps his passions under control and says that he will never marry. There is a close friendship between Narendra and Bhavanath; they are just like man and woman. Narendra doesn't come here very often. That is good, for I am overwhelmed by his presence."

Monday, August 20, 1883

Sri Ramakrishna was sitting on his bed, inside the mosquito net, meditating. It was about eight o'clock in the evening. M. was sitting on the floor with his friend Hari Babu. Hari, a young man of twenty-eight, had lost his wife about eleven years before and had not married a second time. He was much devoted to his parents, brothers, and sisters.

Hazra was living at Dakshineswar. Rakhal lived with the Master, though now and then he stayed at Adhar's house. Narendra, Bhavanath, Adhar, M., Ram, Manomohan, and other devotees visited the Master almost every week.

Hriday, Sri Ramakrishna's nephew, was ill in his home in the country. The Master was worried about him. One of the devotees had sent him a little money, but the Master did not know it.

When Sri Ramakrishna came out of the mosquito net and sat on the small couch, the devotees saluted him.

MASTER (to M.): "I was meditating inside the net. It occurred to me that meditation, after all, was nothing but the imagining of a form, and so I did not enjoy it. One gets satisfaction if God reveals Himself in a flash. Again, I said to myself, 'Who is it that meditates, and on whom does he meditate?'"

M: "Yes, sir. You said that God Himself has become everything—the universe and all living beings. Even he who meditates is God."

MASTER: "What is more, one cannot meditate unless God wills it. One can meditate when God makes it possible for one to do so. What do you say?"

M: "True, sir. You feel like that because there is no 'I' in you. When there is no ego, one feels like that."

MASTER: "But it is good to have a trace of ego, which makes it possible for a man to feel that he is the servant of God. As long as a man thinks that it is he who is doing his duties, it is very good for him to feel that God is the Master and he God's servant. When one is conscious of doing work, one should establish with God the relationship of servant and Master."

M. was always reflecting on the nature of the Supreme Brahman.

MASTER (to M.): "Like the ākāśa, Brahman is without any modification. It has become manifold because of Śakti. Again, Brahman is like fire, which itself has no colour. The fire appears white if you throw a white substance into it, red if you throw a red, black if you throw a black. The three gunas —sattva, rajas, and tamas—belong to Śakti alone. Brahman Itself is beyond the three gunas. What Brahman is cannot be described. It is beyond words. That which remains after everything is eliminated by the Vedāntic process of 'Not this, not this', and which is of the nature of Bliss, is Brahman.

"Suppose the husband of a young girl has come to his father-in-law's house and is seated in the drawing-room with other young men of his age. The girl and her friends are looking at them through the window. Her friends do not know her husband and ask her, pointing to one young man, 'Is that your husband?' 'No', she answers, smiling. They point to another young man and ask if he is her husband. Again she answers no. They repeat the question, referring to a third, and she gives the same answer. At last they point to her husband and ask, 'Is he the one?' She says neither yes nor no, but only smiles and keeps quiet. Her friends realize that he is her husband.

"One becomes silent on realizing the true nature of Brahman.

(To M.) "Well, why do I talk so much?"

M: "You talk in order to awaken the spiritual consciousness of the devotees. You once said that when an uncooked luchi is dropped into boiling ghee it makes a sizzling noise."

The Master began to talk to M. about Hazra.

MASTER: "Do you know the nature of a good man? He never troubles others. He doesn't harass people. The nature of some people is such that when they go to a feast they want special seats. A man who has true devotion to God never makes a false step, never gives others trouble for nothing.

"It is not good to live in the company of bad people. A man should stay away from them and thus protect himself. (*To M.*) Isn't that so?"

M: "Yes, sir. The mind sinks far down in the company of the wicked. But it is quite different with a hero, as you say."

MASTER: "How is that?"

M: "When a fire is feeble it goes out when even a small stick is thrown into it; but a blazing fire is not affected even if a plantain-tree is thrown into it. The tree itself is burnt to ashes."

The Master asked M. about his friend Hari Babu.

M: "He has come here to pay you his respects. He lost his wife long ago."

MASTER (*to Hari*): "What kind of work do you do?"

M: "Nothing in particular. But at home he takes good care of his parents and his brothers and sisters."

MASTER (*with a smile*): "How is that? You are like 'Elder, the pumpkin-cutter'. You are neither a man of the world nor a devotee of God. That is not good. You must have seen the sort of elderly man who lives in a family and is always ready, day or night, to entertain the children. He sits in the parlour and smokes the hubble-bubble. With nothing in particular to do, he leads a lazy life. Now and again he goes to the inner court and cuts a pumpkin; for, since women do not cut pumpkins, they send the children to ask him to come and do it. That is the extent of his usefulness—hence his nickname, 'Elder, the pumpkin-cutter'.

"You must do 'this' as well as 'that'. Do your duties in the world, and also fix your mind on the Lotus Feet of the Lord. Read books of devotion like the *Bhāgavata* or the life of Chaitanya when you are alone and have nothing else to do."

It was about ten o'clock. Sri Ramakrishna finished a light supper of farina pudding and one or two luchis. After saluting him, M. and his friend took their leave.

Friday, September 7, 1883

Sri Ramakrishna and M. were talking in the Master's room at half past seven in the evening. No one else was present.

MASTER: "The other day I went to Calcutta. As I drove along the streets in the carriage, I observed that everyone's attention was fixed on low things. Everyone was brooding over his stomach and running after nothing but food. Everyone's mind was turned to 'woman and gold'. I saw only one or two with their attention fixed on higher things, with their minds turned to God."

M: "The present age has aggravated this stomach-worry. Trying to imitate the English, people have turned their attention to more luxuries; therefore their wants have also increased."

MASTER: "What do the English think about God?"

M: "They believe in a formless God."

MASTER: "That is also one of our beliefs."

For a time Master and disciple remained silent. Then Sri Ramakrishna began to describe his experiences of Brahman.

MASTER: "One day I had the vision of Consciousness, non-dual and indivisible. At first it had been revealed to me that there were innumerable men, animals, and other creatures. Among them there were aristocrats, the English, the Mussalmāns, myself, scavengers, dogs, and also a bearded Mussalmān with an earthenware tray of rice in his hand. He put a few grains of rice into everybody's mouth. I too tasted a little.

"Another day I saw rice, vegetables, and other food-stuff, and filth and dirt as well, lying around. Suddenly the soul came out of my body and, like a flame, touched everything. It was like a protruding tongue of fire and tasted everything once, even the excreta. It was revealed to me that all these are one Substance, the non-dual and indivisible Consciousness.

"Another day[4] it was revealed to me that I had devotees—my intimate companions, my very own. Thereafter I would climb to the roof of the kuthi as soon as the bells and the conch-shells of the evening service sounded in the temples, and cry out with a longing heart: 'Oh, where are you all? Come here! I am dying to see you!'

(To M.) "Well, what do you think of these visions?"

M: "God sports through you. This I have realized, that you are the instrument and God is the Master. God has created other beings as if with a machine, but yourself with His own hands."

MASTER: "Well, Hazra says that after the vision of God one acquires the six divine powers."

M: "Those who seek pure love don't want powers."

MASTER: "Perhaps Hazra was a poor man in his previous life, and that is why he wants so much to see the manifestation of power. He wants to know what I talk about with the cook. He says to me: 'You don't have to talk to the cook. I shall talk to the manager of the temple myself and see that you get everything you want.' (M. laughs aloud.) He talks to me that way and I say nothing."

M: "Many a time you have said that a devotee who loves God for the sake of love does not care to see God's powers. A true devotee wants to see God as Gopāla.[5] In the beginning God becomes the magnet, and the devotee the needle. But in the end the devotee himself becomes the magnet, and God the needle; that is to say, God becomes small to His devotee."

MASTER: "Yes, it is just like the sun at dawn. You can easily look at that sun. It doesn't dazzle the eyes; rather it satisfies them. God becomes tender for the sake of His devotees. He appears before them, setting aside His powers."

Both remained silent for some time.

M: "Why should your visions not be real? If they are unreal, then the

---

[4] This happened before any of the Master's intimate disciples came to him.

[5] The Baby Krishna, bereft of all divine powers.

world is still more unreal; for there is only one mind that is the instrument of perception. Your pure mind sees those visions, and our ordinary minds see worldly objects."

MASTER: "I see that you have grasped the idea of unreality. Well, tell me what you think of Hazra."

M: "Oh, I don't know." (*The Master laughs.*)

MASTER: "Well, do you find me to be like anybody else?"

M: "No, sir."

MASTER: "Like any other paramahamsa?"

M: "No, sir. You can't be compared to anybody else."

MASTER (*smiling*): "Have you heard of a tree called the 'achina'?"[6]

M: "No, sir."

MASTER: "There is a tree called by that name. But nobody knows what it is."

M: "Likewise, it is not possible to recognize you. The more a man understands you, the more uplifted he will be."

M. was silent. He said to himself: "The Master referred to 'the sun at dawn' and 'the tree unrecognizable by man'. Did he mean an Incarnation of God? Is this the play of God through man? Is the Master himself an Incarnation? Was this why he cried to the devotees from the roof of the kuthi: 'Where are you? Come to me!'?"

Sri Ramakrishna was sitting on the steps of the southeast verandah of the Kāli temple. Rakhal, M., and Hazra were with him. He talked light-heartedly about his boyhood days.

When it was dusk he returned to his room and sat down on the small couch. Soon he went into samādhi and in that state began to talk to the Divine Mother. He said: "Mother, what is all this row about? Shall I go there? I shall go if You take me." The Master was to go to a devotee's house. Was it for this that he was asking the Divine Mother's permission?

Again he spoke to Her, perhaps praying about an intimate disciple: "Mother, please make him stainless. Well, Mother, why have You given him only a particle?" Remaining silent a moment, he said: "Oh, I see. That will be enough for Your work."

In the same state he said, addressing the devotees: "That which is Brahman is verily Śakti. I address That, again, as the Mother. I call It Brahman when It is inactive, and Śakti when It creates, preserves, and destroys. It is like water, sometimes still and sometimes covered with waves. The Incarnation of God is a part of the līlā of Śakti. The purpose of the Divine Incarnation is to teach man ecstatic love for God. The Incarnation is like the udder of the cow, the only place milk is to be got. God incarnates Himself as man. There is a great accumulation of divinity in an Incarnation, like the accumulation of fish in a deep hollow in a lake."

Some of the devotees wondered, "Is Sri Ramakrishna an Incarnation of God, like Krishna, Chaitanya, and Christ?"

[6] Literally, "unrecognizable".

Sunday, September 9, 1883

Sri Ramakrishna had finished his midday meal and was sitting on the small couch. Rakhal, M., and Ratan were sitting on the floor. Ratan was the steward of Jadu Mallick's garden house and was devoted to the Master. Now and then Ram Chatterji and Hazra passed in or out of the room. It was about two o'clock.

Ratan told the Master that a yātrā performance by Nilkantha had been arranged in Jadu Mallick's house in Calcutta.

RATAN (*to the Master*): "You must go. The date has been set."

MASTER: "That's good. I want to go. Nilkantha sings with great devotion."

A DEVOTEE: "That is true, sir."

MASTER: "Tears flow from his eyes as he sings. (*To Ratan*) I am thinking of spending the night in Calcutta when I go to see the yātrā."

RATAN: "That will be fine."

Ram Chatterji and the other devotees asked Ratan about a theft in Jadu Mallick's house.

RATAN: "Yes, the golden sandals of the Deity were stolen from the shrine room in Jadu Babu's house. It has created an uproar. They are going to try to discover the thief by means of a 'charmed plate'. Everybody will sit in one room, and the plate will move in the direction of the man who stole the sandals."

MASTER (*with a smile*): "How does the plate move? By itself?"

RATAN: "No. A man presses it to the ground."

A DEVOTEE: "It is a kind of sleight of hand. It is a clever trick."

MASTER: "The real cleverness is the cleverness by which one realizes God. That trick is the best of all tricks."

As the conversation went on, several Bengali gentlemen entered the room and, after saluting the Master, sat down. One of them was already known to Sri Ramakrishna. These gentlemen followed the cult of Tantra. The Master knew that one of them indulged in immoral acts in the name of religion. The Tantra rituals, under certain conditions, allow the mixing of men and women devotees. But Sri Ramakrishna regarded all women, even prostitutes, as manifestations of the Divine Mother. He addressed them all as "Mother".

MASTER (*with a smile*): "Where is Achalananda? My ideal is different from that of Achalananda and his disciples. As for myself, I look on all women as my mother."

The visiting gentlemen sat silent.

MASTER: "Every woman is a mother to me. Achalananda used to stay here now and then. He would drink a great deal of consecrated wine. Hearing about my attitude toward women, he stubbornly justified his own views. He insisted again and again: 'Why should you not recognize the attitude of a "hero" toward women? Won't you admit the injunctions of Śiva? Śiva Himself is the author of the Tantra, which prescribes various disciplines, including the "heroic".' I said to him: 'But, my dear sir, I don't know. I don't like these ideas. To me every woman is a mother.'

"Achalananda did not support his own children. He said to me, 'God will support them.' I said nothing. But this is the way I felt about it: 'Who will support your children? I hope your renunciation of wife and children is not a way of earning money. People will think you are a holy man because you have renounced everything; so they will give you money. In that way you will earn plenty of money.'

"Spiritual practice with a view to winning a lawsuit and earning money, or to helping others win in court and acquire property, shows a very mean understanding.

"Money enables a man to get food and drink, build a house, worship the Deity, serve devotees and holy men, and help the poor when he happens to meet them. These are the good uses of money. Money is not meant for luxuries or creature comforts or for buying a position in society.

"People practise various Tāntrik disciplines to acquire supernatural powers. How mean such people are! Krishna said to Arjuna, 'Friend, by acquiring one of the eight siddhis you may add a little to your power, but you will not be able to realize Me.' One cannot get rid of māyā as long as one exercises supernatural powers. And māyā begets egotism.

"Body and wealth are impermanent. Why go to so much trouble for their sakes? Just think of the plight of the hathayogis. Their attention is fixed on one ideal only—longevity. They do not aim at the realization of God at all. They practise such exercises as washing out the intestines, drinking milk through a tube, and the like, with that one aim in view.

"There was once a goldsmith whose tongue suddenly turned up and stuck to his palate. He looked like a man in samādhi. He became completely inert and remained so a long time. People came to worship him. After several years, his tongue suddenly returned to its natural position, and he became conscious of things as before. So he went back to his work as a goldsmith. (All laugh.)

"These are physical things and have nothing to do with God. There was a man who knew eighty-two postures and talked big about yoga-samādhi. But inwardly he was drawn to 'woman and gold'. Once he found a bank-note worth several thousand rupees. He could not resist the temptation, and swallowed it, thinking he would get it out somehow later on. The note was got out of him all right, but he was sent to jail for three years. In my guilelessness I used to think that the man had made great spiritual progress. Really, I say it upon my word!

"Mahendra Pal of Sinthi once gave Ramlal five rupees. Ramlal told me about it after he had gone. I asked him what the gift was for, and Ramlal said 'that it was meant for me. I thought it might enable me to pay off some of my debt for milk. That night I went to bed and, if you will believe me, I suddenly woke up with a pain. I felt as if a cat were scratching inside my chest. I at once went to Ramlal and asked him: 'For whom did Mahendra give this money? Was it for your aunt?[7] 'No,' said Ramlal, 'it is meant for you.' I said to him, 'Go and return the money at once, or I shall have no peace of mind.' Ramlal returned the money early in the morning and I felt relieved.

[7] Referring to the Holy Mother, Sri Ramakrishna's wife.

"Once a rich man came here and said to me: 'Sir, you must do something so that I may win my lawsuit. I have heard of your reputation and so I have come here.' 'My dear sir,' I said to him, 'you have made a mistake. I am not the person you are looking for; Achalananda is your man.'

"A true devotee of God does not care for such things as wealth or health. He thinks: 'Why should I practise spiritual austerities for creature comforts, money, or name and fame? These are all impermanent. They last only a day or two.' "

The visiting gentlemen took leave of the Master after saluting him. When they had departed, Sri Ramakrishna smiled and said to M., "You can never make a thief listen to religion. (All laugh.)

"Well, what do you think of Narendra?"

M: "He is splendid."

MASTER: "Yes. His intelligence is as great as his learning. Besides, he is gifted in music, both as a singer and player. Then too, he has control over his passions. He says he will never marry."

M: "You once said that one who constantly talks of his sin really becomes a sinner; he cannot extricate himself from sin. But if a man has firm faith that he is the son of God, then he makes rapid strides in spiritual life."

MASTER: "Yes, faith. What tremendous faith Krishnakishore had! He used to say: 'I have spoken the name of God once. That is enough. How can I remain a sinner? I have become pure and stainless.' One day Haladhari said: 'Even Ajāmila had to perform austerities to gratify God. Can one receive the grace of God without austerities? What will one gain by speaking the name of Nārāyana only once?' At these remarks Krishnakishore's anger knew no bounds. The next time he came to this garden to pick flowers he wouldn't even look at Haladhari.

"Haladhari's father was a great devotee. At bathing-time he would stand waist-deep in the water and meditate on God, uttering the sacred mantra; then the tears would flow from his eyes.

"One day a holy man came to the bathing-place on the Ganges at Āriādaha. We talked about seeing him. Haladhari said, 'What shall we gain by seeing the body of a man, a mere cage made of the five elements?' Krishnakishore 'heard about it and said: 'What? Did Haladhari ask what would be gained by visiting a holy man? By repeating the name of Krishna or Rāma a man transforms his physical body into a spiritual body. To such a man everything is the embodiment of Spirit. To him Krishna is the embodiment of Spirit, and His sacred Abode is the embodiment of Spirit.' He also said, 'A man who utters the name of Krishna or Rāma even once reaps the result of a hundred sandhyās.'

"One of his sons chanted the name of Rāma on his death-bed. Krishnakishore said, 'He has nothing to worry about; he has chanted the name of Rāma.' But now and then he wept. After all, it was the death of his own son.

"Nothing whatsoever is achieved by the performance of worship, japa, and devotions, without faith. Isn't that so?"

M: "Yes, sir. That is true."

MASTER: "I see people coming to the Ganges to bathe. They talk their heads off about everything under the sun. The widowed aunt says: 'Without me they cannot perform the Durgā Pujā. I have to look after even the smallest detail. Again, I have to supervise everything when there is a marriage festival in the family, even the bed of the bride and groom.' "

M: "Why should we blame them? How else will they pass the time?"

MASTER (*with a smile*): "Some people have their shrine rooms in their attics. The women arrange the offerings and flowers and make the sandal-paste. But, while doing so, they never say a word about God. The burden of the conversation is: 'What shall we cook today? I couldn't get good vegetables in the market. That curry was delicious yesterday. That boy is my cousin. Hello there! Have you that job still? Don't ask me how I am. My Hari is no more.' Just fancy! They talk of such things in the shrine room at the time of worship!"

M: "Yes, sir, it is so in the majority of cases. As you say, can one who has passionate yearning for God continue formal worship and devotions for long?"

Sri Ramakrishna and M. were now conversing alone.

M: "Sir, if it is God Himself who has become everything, then why do people have so many different feelings?"

MASTER: "Undoubtedly God exists in all beings as the All-pervading Spirit, but the manifestations of His Power are different in different beings. In some places there is a manifestation of the power of Knowledge; in others, of the power of ignorance. In some places there is a greater manifestation of power than in others. Don't you see that among human beings there are cheats and gamblers, to say nothing of men who are like tigers. I think of them as the 'cheat God', the 'tiger God'."

M. (*with a smile*): "We should salute them from a distance. If we go near the 'tiger God' and embrace him, he may devour us."

MASTER: "He and His Power, Brahman and Its Power—nothing else exists but this. In a hymn to Rāma, Nārada said: 'O Rāma, You are Śiva, and Sītā is Bhagavati; You are Brahmā, and Sītā is Brahmāni; You are Indra, and Sītā is Indrāni; You are Nārāyana, and Sītā is Lakshmi. O Rāma, You are the symbol of all that is masculine, and Sītā of all that is feminine.' "

M: "Sir, what is the Spirit-form of God like?"

Sri Ramakrishna reflected a moment and said softly: "Shall I tell you what it is like? It is like water. . . . One understands all this through spiritual discipline.

"Believe in the form of God. It is only after attaining Brahmajnāna that one sees non-duality, the oneness of Brahman and Its Śakti. Brahman and Śakti are identical, like fire and its power to burn. When a man thinks of fire, he must also think of its power to burn. Again, when he thinks of the power to burn, he must also think of fire. Further, Brahman and Śakti are like milk and its whiteness, water and its wetness.

"But there is a stage beyond even Brahmajnāna. After jnāna comes vijnāna. He who is aware of knowledge is also aware of ignorance. The sage Vaśishtha was stricken with grief at the death of his hundred sons. Asked by Lakshmana why a man of knowledge should grieve for such a reason, Rāma said, 'Brother, go beyond both knowledge and ignorance.' He who has knowledge has ignorance also. If a thorn has entered your foot, get another thorn and with its help take out the first; then throw away the second also."

M: "Should one throw away both knowledge and ignorance?"

MASTER: "Yes. That is why one should acquire vijnāna. You see, he who is aware of light is also aware of darkness. He who is aware of happiness is also aware of suffering. He who is aware of virtue is also aware of vice. He who is aware of good is also aware of evil. He who is aware of holiness is also aware of unholiness. He who is aware of 'I' is also aware of 'you'.

"What is vijnāna? It is knowing God in a special way. The awareness and conviction that fire exists in wood is jnāna, knowledge. But to cook rice on that fire, eat the rice, and get nourishment from it is vijnāna. To know by one's inner experience that God exists is jnāna. But to talk to Him, to enjoy Him as Child, as Friend, as Master, as Beloved, is vijnāna. The realization that God alone has become the universe and all living beings is vijnāna.

"According to one school of thought, God cannot be seen. Who sees whom? Is God outside you, that you can see Him? One sees only oneself. Having once entered the 'black waters' of the ocean, the ship does not come back and so cannot describe what it experiences."

M: "It is true, sir. As you say, having climbed to the top of the monument, one becomes unaware of what is below: horses and carriages, men and women, houses, shops and offices, and so on."

MASTER: "I don't go to the Kāli temple nowadays. Is that an offence? At one time Narendra used to say, 'What? He still goes to the Kāli temple!' "

M: "Every day you are in a new state of mind. How can you ever offend God?"

MASTER: "Someone said to Sen, about Hriday: 'He is very ill. Please bring two pieces of cloth and a couple of shirts for him. We will send them to his village.' Sen offered only two rupees. How do you explain that? He has so much money, and yet he is so miserly! What do you say to that?"

M: "Those who seek God cannot behave that way—I mean those whose goal is the attainment of Knowledge."

MASTER: "God alone is the Reality and all else is unreal."

Saturday, September 22, 1883

Sri Ramakrishna was seated in the drawing-room of Adhar's house in Calcutta, with Rakhal, Adhar, M., Ishan, and other devotees. Many gentlemen of the neighbourhood were also present. It was afternoon.

The Master was very fond of Ishan. He had been a superintendent in the Accountant General's office, and later on his children also occupied high government positions. One of them was a class-mate of Narendra. Ishan's purse was always open for the poor and needy. When he retired from service, he devoted his time to spiritual practices and charity. He often visited Sri Ramakrishna at Dakshineswar.

MASTER (*to Ishan*): "Please tell us the story of the boy who posted the letter."

ISHAN (*with a smile*): "A boy once heard that God is our Creator. So he wrote a letter to God, setting forth his prayers, and posted it. The address he put on the envelope was 'Heaven'."

MASTER (*with a smile*): "Did you hear that story? One succeeds in spiritual life when one develops a faith like that boy's. (*To Ishan*) Tell us about the renunciation of activities."

ISHAN: "After the attainment of God, religious duties such as the sandyhā drop away. One day some people were sitting on the bank of the Ganges performing the sandyhā. But one of them abstained from it. On being asked the reason, he said: 'I am observing aśoucha. I cannot perform the sandyhā ceremony.[8] In my case the defilement is due to both a birth and a death. My mother, Ignorance, is dead, and my son, Self-Knowledge, has been born.'"

MASTER: "Tell us, also, how caste distinctions drop away when one attains Self-Knowledge."

ISHAN: "Sankarāchārya was once climbing the steps after finishing his bath in the Ganges, when he saw just in front of him an untouchable who had a pack of dogs with him. 'You have touched me!' said Śankara. 'Revered sir,' said the pariah, 'I have not touched you, nor have you touched me. The Self is the Inner Ruler of all beings and cannot be contaminated. Is there any difference between the sun's reflection in wine and its reflection in the Ganges?'"

MASTER (*with a smile*): "And about harmony: how one can realize God through all paths."

ISHAN (*smiling*): "Both Hari and Hara are derived from the same root.[9] The difference is only in the pratyaya.[10] In reality, He who is Hari is also Hara. If a man has faith in God, then it doesn't matter whom he worships."

MASTER: "And please tell us also how the heart of the sādhu is the greatest of all."

ISHAN: "This earth is the largest thing we see anywhere around us. But larger than the earth is the ocean, and larger than the ocean is the sky. But Vishnu, the Godhead, has covered earth, sky, and the nether world with one of His feet. And that foot of Vishnu is enshrined in the sādhu's heart. Therefore the heart of a holy man is the greatest of all."

The devotees were delighted with Ishan's words.

Ishan intended to retire to a solitary place and practise a special discipline of the Gāyatri, through which Brahman is invoked. But the Master said that the Knowledge of Brahman was not possible without the complete destruction of worldliness. Further, he said that it was impossible for a man

---

[8] Aśoucha is a temporary defilement caused by the birth or death of a blood relative. A man observing aśoucha cannot perform the sandyhā, or daily worship.

[9] The root "hri", from which both words are derived. Further, Hari and Hara are two manifestations of the same Godhead. Hari is a name of Vishnu, the Ideal Deity of the Vaishnavas, and Hara a name of Śiva, the Ideal Deity of the Śaivas.

[10] There is a pun on this word, which means both "faith" and "inflection".

totally to withdraw his mind from the objects of the senses in the Kaliyuga, when his life was dependent on food. That is why the Master discouraged people from attempting the Vedic worship of Brahman and asked them to worship Śakti, the Divine Mother, who is identical with Brahman.

MASTER (to Ishan): "Why do you waste your time simply repeating 'Neti, neti'? Nothing whatsoever can be specified about Brahman, except that It exists.

"Whatever we see or think about is the manifestation of the glory of the Primordial Energy, the Primal Consciousness. Creation, preservation, and destruction, living beings and the universe, and further, meditation and the meditator, bhakti and prema—all these are manifestations of the glory of that Power.

"But Brahman is identical with Its Power. On returning from Ceylon, Hanumān praised Rāma, saying: 'O Rāma, You are the Supreme Brahman, and Sītā is Your Śakti. You and She are identical.' Brahman and Śakti are like the snake and its wriggling motion. Thinking of the snake, one must think of its wriggling motion, and thinking of its wriggling motion, one must think of the snake. Or they are like milk and its whiteness. Thinking of milk, one has to think of its colour, that is, whiteness, and thinking of the whiteness of milk, one has to think of milk itself. Or they are like water and its wetness. Thinking of water, one has to think of its wetness, and thinking of the wetness of water, one has to think of water.

"This Primal Power, Mahāmāyā, has covered Brahman. As soon as the covering is withdrawn, one realizes: 'I am what I was before', 'I am Thou; Thou art I'.

"As long as that covering remains, the Vedāntic formula 'I am He', that is, man is the Supreme Brahman, does not rightly apply. The wave is part of the water, but the water is not part of the wave. As long as that covering remains, one should call on God as Mother. Addressing God, the devotee should say, 'Thou art the Mother and I am Thy child; Thou art the Master and I am Thy servant.' It is good to have the attitude of the servant toward the master. From this relationship of master and servant spring up other attitudes: the attitude of serene love for God, the attitude of friend toward friend, and so forth. When the master loves his servant, he may say to him, 'Come, sit by my side; there is no difference between you and me.' But if the servant comes forward of his own will to sit by the master, will not the master be angry?

"God's play on earth as an Incarnation is the manifestation of the glory of the Chitśakti, the Divine Power. That which is Brahman is also Rāma, Krishna, and Śiva."

ISHAN: "Yes, sir. Both Hari and Hara are derived from the same root. The difference lies only in the pratyaya."

MASTER: "Yes, there is only One without a second. The Vedas speak of It as 'Om Satchidānanda Brahma', the Purānas as 'Om Satchidānanda Krishna', and the Tantra as 'Om Satchidānanda Śiva'.

"The Chitśakti, as Mahāmāyā, has deluded all with ignorance. It is said in the *Adhyātma Rāmāyana* that when the rishis saw Rāma, they prayed to Him in these words only: 'O Rāma, please do not delude us with Your world-bewitching māyā.'"

ISHAN: "What is this māyā?"

MASTER: "Whatever you see, think, or hear is māyā. In a word, 'woman and gold' is the covering of māyā.

"There is no harm in chewing betel-leaf, eating fish, smoking, or rubbing the body with oil. What will one achieve by renouncing only these things? The one thing needful is the renunciation of 'woman and gold'. That renunciation is the real and supreme renunciation. Householders should go into solitude now and then, to practise spiritual discipline in order to culti-vate devotion to God; they should renounce mentally. But the sannyāsi should renounce both mentally and physically.

"I once said to Keshab, 'How can a typhoid patient be cured if he remains in a room where a pitcher of water and a jar of pickles are kept?' Now and then one should live in solitude."

A DEVOTEE: "Sir, what do you think of the Navavidhān? It seems to me like a hotchpotch of everything."

MASTER: "Some say it is a modern thing. That sets me wondering: 'Then is the God of the Brāhmo Samāj a new God?' The Brāhmos speak of their cult as the Navavidhān, as a New Dispensation. Well, it may be so. Who knows? There are six systems of philosophy; so perhaps it is like one of these.

"But do you know where those who speak of the formless God make their mistake? It is where they say that God is formless only, and that those who differ with them are wrong.

"But I know that God is both with and without form. And He may have many more aspects. It is possible for Him to be everything.

(*To Ishan*) "The Chitśakti, Mahāmāyā, has become the twenty-four cosmic principles. One day as I was meditating, my mind wandered away to Rashke's house. He is a scavenger. I said to my mind, 'Stay there, you rogue!' The Divine Mother revealed to me that the men and women in this house were mere masks; inside them was the same Divine Power, Kundalini, that rises up through the six spiritual centres of the body.

"Is the Primal Energy man or woman? Once at Kāmārpukur I saw the worship of Kāli in the house of the Lahas. They put a sacred thread[11] on the image of the Divine Mother. One man asked, 'Why have they put the sacred thread on the Mother's person?' The master of the house said: 'Brother, I see that you have rightly understood the Mother. But I do not yet know whether the Divine Mother is male or female.'

"It is said that Mahāmāyā swallowed Śiva. When the six centres in Her were awakened, Śiva came out through Her thigh. Then Śiva created the Tantra philosophy.

"Take refuge in the Chitśakti, the Mahāmāyā."

ISHAN: "Please bestow your grace on me."

MASTER: "Say to God with a guileless heart, 'O God, reveal Thyself to

[11] See foot-note 9, p. 271.

me.' And weep. Pray to God, 'O God, keep my mind away from "woman and gold".' And dive deep. Can a man get pearls by floating or swimming on the surface? He must dive deep.

"One must get instruction from a guru. Once a man was looking for a stone image of Śiva. Someone said to him: 'Go to a certain river. There you will find a tree. Near it is a whirlpool. Dive into the water there, and you will find the image of Śiva.' So I say that one must get instruction from a teacher."

ISHAN: "That is true, sir."

MASTER: "It is Satchidānanda that comes to us in the form of the guru. If a man is initiated by a human guru, he will not achieve anything if he regards his guru as a mere man. The guru should be regarded as the direct manifestation of God. Only then can the disciple have faith in the mantra given by the guru. Once a man has faith he achieves all. The śudra Ekalavya learnt archery in the forest before a clay image of Drona. He worshipped the image as the living Drona; that by itself enabled him to attain mastery in archery.

"Don't mix intimately with brāhmin pundits. Their only concern is to earn money. I have seen brāhmin priests reciting the *Chandi* while performing the swastyayana. It is hard to tell whether they are reading the sacred book or something else. They turn half the pages without reading them. (*All laugh.*)

"A nail-knife suffices to kill oneself. One needs sword and shield to kill others. That is the purpose of the śastras.

"One doesn't really need to study the different scriptures. If one has no discrimination, one doesn't achieve anything through mere scholarship, even though one studies all the six systems of philosophy. Call on God, crying to Him secretly in solitude. He will give all that you need."

Sri Ramakrishna had heard that Ishan was building a house on the bank of the Ganges for the practice of spiritual discipline. He asked Ishan eagerly: "Has the house been built? Let me tell you that the less people know of your spiritual life, the better it will be for you. Devotees endowed with śattva meditate in a secluded corner or in a forest, or withdraw into the mind. Sometimes they meditate inside the mosquito net."

Now and then Ishan invited Hazra to his house. Hazra had a craze for outward purity. Sri Ramakrishna often discouraged him in this.

MASTER (*to Ishan*): "Let me tell you another thing. Don't be over-fastidious about outward purity. Once a sādhu felt very thirsty. A water-carrier was carrying water in his skin water-bag, and offered the water to the holy man. The sādhu asked if the skin was clean. The carrier said: 'Revered sir, my skin bag is perfectly clean. But inside *your skin* are all sorts of filthy things. That is why I can ask you to drink water from my skin. It won't injure you.' By 'your skin', the carrier meant the body, the belly, and so forth.

"Have faith in the name of God. Then you won't need even to go to holy places."

Sri Ramakrishna sang, intoxicated with divine fervour:

> Why should I go to Gangā or Gayā, to Kāśi, Kānchi, or Prabhās,
> So long as I can breathe my last with Kāli's name upon my
>   lips? . . .

Ishan remained silent.

MASTER (*to Ishan*): "Tell me if you have any more doubts."

ISHAN: "You said everything when you spoke of faith."

MASTER: "God can be realized by true faith alone. And the realization is hastened if you believe everything about God. The cow that picks and chooses its food gives milk only in dribblets, but if she eats all kinds of plants, then her milk flows in torrents.

"Once I heard a story. A man heard the command of God that he should see his Ideal Deity in a ram. He at once believed it. It is God who exists in all beings.

"A guru said to his disciple, 'It is Rāma alone who resides in all bodies.' The disciple was a man of great faith. One day a dog snatched a piece of bread from him and started to run away. He ran after the dog, with a jar of butter in his hand, and cried again and again: 'O Rāma, stand still a minute. That bread hasn't been buttered.'

"What tremendous faith Krishnakishore had! He used to say, 'By chanting "Om Krishna, Om Rāma", one gets the result of a million sandhyās.' Once he said to me secretly, 'I don't like the sandhyā and other devotions any more; but don't tell anyone.'

"Sometimes I too feel that way. The Mother reveals to me that She Herself has become everything. One day I was coming from the pine-grove toward the Panchavati. A dog followed me. I stood still for a while near the Panchavati. The thought came to my mind that the Mother might say something to me through that dog.

"You were absolutely right when you said that through faith alone one achieves all."

ISHAN: "But we are householders."

MASTER: "What if you are? Through His grace even the impossible becomes possible. Rāmprasād sang, 'This world is a mere framework of illusion.' Another man composed a song by way of reply:

> This very world is a mansion of mirth;
> Here I can eat, here drink and make merry.
> Janaka's might was unsurpassed;
> What did he lack of the world or the Spirit?
> Holding to one as well as the other,
> He drank his milk from a brimming cup!

"One should first realize God through spiritual discipline in solitude, and then live in the world. Only then can one be a King Janaka. What can you achieve otherwise?

"Further, take the case of Śiva. He has everything—Kārtika, Ganeśa, Lakshmi, and Sarasvati. Still, sometimes He dances in a state of divine fervour, chanting the name of Rāma, and sometimes He is absorbed in samādhi."

14

INSTRUCTION TO VAISHNAVAS
AND BRĀHMOS

Sunday, September 23, 1883

SRI RAMAKRISHNA was sitting in his room at Dakshineswar with Rakhal, M., and other devotees. Hazra sat on the porch outside. The Master was conversing with the devotees.

MASTER (*to a devotee*): "Narendra doesn't like even you, nowadays. (*To M.*) Why didn't he come to see me at Adhar's house?

"How versatile Narendra is! He is gifted in singing, in playing on instruments, and in studies. He is independent and doesn't care about anybody. The other day he was returning to Calcutta with Captain in his carriage. Captain begged Narendra to sit beside him, but he took a seat opposite. He didn't even look at Captain.

"What can a man achieve through mere scholarship? What is needed is prayer and spiritual discipline. Gauri of Indesh was both a scholar and a devotee. He was a worshipper of the Divine Mother. Now and then he would be overpowered with spiritual fervour. When he chanted a hymn to the Mother, the pundits would seem like earth-worms beside him. I too would be overcome with ecstasy.

"At first he was a bigoted worshipper of Śakti. He used to pick up tulsi-leaves[1] with a couple of sticks, so as not to touch them with his fingers. (*All laugh.*) Then he went home. When he came back he didn't behave that way any more. He gave remarkable interpretations of Hindu mythology. He would say that the ten heads of Rāvana represented the ten organs. Kumbhakarna was the symbol of tamas, Rāvana of rajas, and Bibhishana of sattva. That was why Bibhishana obtained favour with Rāma."

After the Master's midday meal, while he was resting, Ram, Tarak,[2] and some other devotees arrived from Calcutta.

Nityagopal, Tarak, and several others were staying with Ram, a householder disciple of the Master. Nityagopal was always in an exalted spiritual mood. Tarak's mind, too, was always indrawn; he seldom exchanged words

---

[1] These leaves are sacred to Vishnu. The bigoted worshipper of Śakti hates everything associated with Vishnu, and *vice versa*.

[2] A monastic disciple of the Master, known later as Swami Shivananda.

with others. Ram looked after their physical needs. Rakhal now and then spent a few days at Adhar's house.

RAM (to the Master): "We have been taking lessons on the drum."

MASTER (to Ram): "Nityagopal too?"

RAM: "No, sir. He plays a little."

MASTER: "And Tarak?"

RAM: "He knows a good deal."

MASTER: "Then he won't keep his eyes on the ground so much. If the mind is much directed to something else, it doesn't dwell deeply on God."

RAM: "I have been studying the drum only to accompany the kirtan."

MASTER (to M.): "I hear that you too are taking singing lessons. Is that so?"

M: "No, sir. I just open my mouth now and then."

MASTER: "Have you practised that song: 'O Mother, make me mad with Thy love'? If you have, please sing it. The song expresses my ideal perfectly."

The conversation turned to Hazra's hatred for certain people, which Sri Ramakrishna did not like.

MASTER (to the devotees): "I used frequently to visit a certain house at Kāmārpukur. The boys of the family were of my age. The other day they came here and spent two or three days with me. Their mother, like Hazra, used to hate people. Then something happened to her foot, and gangrene set in. On account of the foul smell, no one could enter her room. I told the incident to Hazra and asked him not to hate anyone."

Toward evening, as Sri Ramakrishna was standing in the northwest corner of the courtyard, he went into samādhi. In those days the Master remained almost always in an ecstatic state. He would lose consciousness of the world at the slightest suggestion from outside. But for scant conversation with visiting devotees, he remained in an indrawn mood and was unable to perform his daily worship and devotions.

Coming down to the relative world, he began to talk to the Divine Mother, still standing where he was. "O Mother," he said, "worship has left me, and japa also. Please see, Mother, that I do not become an inert thing. Let my attitude toward God be that of the servant toward the master. O Mother, let me talk about Thee and chant Thy holy name. I want to sing Thy glories. Give me a little strength of body that I may move about, that I may go to places where Thy devotees live, and sing Thy name."

In the morning Sri Ramakrishna had been to the Kāli temple to offer flowers at the Mother's feet.

Continuing, the Master said: "O Mother, I offered flowers at Thy feet this morning. I thought: 'That is good. My mind is again going back to formal worship.' Then why do I feel like this now? Why art Thou turning me into a sort of inert thing?"

The moon had not yet risen. It was a dark night. The Master, still in an abstracted mood, sat on the small couch in his room and continued his talk with the Divine Mother. He said: "Why this special discipline of the Gāyatri? Why this jumping from this roof to that? . . . Who told him to do it? Perhaps he is doing it of his own accord. . . . Well, he will practise a little of that discipline."

The previous day Sri Ramakrishna had discouraged Ishan· about Vedic worship, saying that it was not suitable for the Kaliyuga. He had asked Ishan to worship God as the Divine Mother.

The Master said to M., "Are these all my fancies, or are they real?" M. remained silent with wonder at the Master's intimate relationship with the Divine Mother. He thought She must be within us as well as without. Indeed She must be very near us; or why should the Master speak to Her in a whisper?

Wednesday, September 26, 1883

There were very few devotees with the Master, for most of them came on Sundays. Rakhal and Latu were living with him the greater part of the time. M. arrived in the afternoon and found the Master seated on the small couch. The conversation turned to Narendra.

MASTER (*to M.*): "Have you seen Narendra lately? (*With a smile*) He said of me: 'He still goes to the Kāli temple. But he will not when he truly understands.' His people are very much dissatisfied with him because he comes here now and then. The other day he came here in a hired carriage, and Surendra paid for it. Narendra's aunt almost had a row with Surendra about it."

The Master left the couch and went to the northeast verandah, where Hazra, Kishori, Rakhal, and a few other devotees were sitting.

MASTER (*to M.*): "How is it that you are here today? Have you no school?"

M: "Our school closed today at half past one."

MASTER: "Why so early?"

M: "Vidyāsāgar visited the school. He owns the school. So the boys get a half holiday whenever he comes."

MASTER: "Why doesn't Vidyāsāgar keep his word? 'If one who holds to truth and looks on woman as his mother does not realize God, then Tulsi is a liar.'[3] If a man holds to truth he will certainly realize God. The other day Vidyāsāgar said he would come here and visit me. But he hasn't kept his word.

"There is a big difference between a scholar and a holy man. The mind of a mere scholar is fixed on 'woman and gold', but the sādhu's mind is on the Lotus Feet of Hari. A scholar says one thing and does another. But it is quite a different matter with a sādhu. The words and actions of a man who has given his mind·to the Lotus Feet of God are altogether different. In Benares I saw a young sannyāsi who belonged to the sect of Nānak. He was the same age as you. He used to refer to me as the 'loving monk'. His sect has a monastery in Benares. I was invited there one day. I found that the mohant was like a housewife. I asked him, 'What is the way?' 'For the Kaliyuga,' he said, 'the path of devotion as enjoined by Nārada.' He was reading a book. When the reading was over, he recited: 'Vishnu is in water,

[3] A quotation from the sayings of Tulsidās, a great sage and poet.

Vishnu is on land, Vishnu is on the mountain top; the whole world is pervaded by Vishnu.' At the end he said, 'Peace! Peace! Abiding Peace!'

"One day he was reading the *Gītā*. He was so strict about his monastic rules that he would not read a holy book looking at a worldly man. So he turned his face toward me and his back on Mathur, who was also present. It was this holy man who told me of Nārada's path of devotion as suited to the people of the Kaliyuga."

M: "Are not sādhus of his class followers of the Vedānta?"

MASTER: "Yes, they are. But they also accept the path of devotion. The fact is that in the Kaliyuga one cannot wholly follow the path laid down in the Vedas. Once a man said to me that he would perform the puraścharana of the Gāyatri. I said: 'Why don't you do that according to the Tantra? In the Kaliyuga the discipline of Tantra is very efficacious.'

"It is extremely difficult to perform the rites enjoined in the Vedas. Further, at the present time people lead the life of slaves.[4] It is said that those who serve others for twelve years or so become slaves. They acquire the traits of those they serve. While serving their masters they acquire the rajas, the tamas, the spirit of violence, the love of luxury, and the other traits of their masters. Not only do they serve their masters, but they also enjoy a pension after their term of service is over.

"Once a Vedāntic monk came here. He used to dance at the sight of a cloud. He would go into an ecstasy of joy over a rain-storm. He would get very angry if anyone went near him when he meditated. One day I came to him while he was meditating, and that made him very cross. He discriminated constantly, 'Brahman alone is real and the world is illusory.' Since the appearance of diversity is due to māyā, he walked about with a prism from a chandelier in his hand. One sees different colours through the prism; in reality there is no such thing as colour. Likewise, nothing exists, in reality, except Brahman. But there is an appearance of the manifold because of māyā, egoism. He would not look at an object more than once, lest he should be deluded by māyā and attachment. He would discriminate, while taking his bath, at the sight of birds flying in the sky. He knew grammar. He stayed here for three days. One day he heard the sound of a flute near the embankment and said that a man who had realized Brahman would go into samādhi at such a sound."

While talking about the monk, the Master showed his devotees the manners and movements of a paramahamsa: the gait of a child, face beaming with laughter, eyes swimming in joy, and body completely naked. Then he again took his seat on the small couch and poured out his soul-enthralling words.

MASTER (*to M.*): "I learnt Vedānta from Nangtā: 'Brahman alone is real; the world is illusory.' The magician performs his magic. He produces a mango-tree which even bears mangoes. But this is all sleight of hand. The magician alone is real."

M: "It seems that the whole of life is a long sleep. This much I understand, that we are not seeing things rightly. We perceive the world with a

[4] Perhaps the Master was referring to the foreign rule in India.

mind by which we cannot comprehend even the nature of the sky. So how can our perceptions be correct?"

MASTER: "There is another way of looking at it. We do not see the sky rightly. It looks as if the sky were touching the ground at the horizon. How can a man see correctly? His mind is delirious, like the mind of a typhoid patient."

The Master sang in his sweet voice:

> What a delirious fever is this that I suffer from!
> O Mother, Thy grace is my only cure. . . .

Continuing, the Master said: "Truly it is a state of delirium. Just see how worldly men quarrel among themselves. No one knows what they quarrel about. Oh, how they quarrel! 'May such and such a thing befall you!' How much shouting! How much abuse!"

M: "I said to Kishori: 'The box is empty; there is nothing inside. But two men pull at it from either side, thinking the box contains money.' Well, the body alone is the cause of all this mischief, isn't it? The jnānis see all this and say to themselves, 'What a relief one feels when this pillow-case of the body drops off.'"

The Master and M. went toward the Kāli temple.

MASTER: "Why should you say such things? This world may be a 'framework of illusion', but it is also said that it is a 'mansion of mirth'. Let the body remain. One can also turn this world into a mansion of mirth."

M: "But where is unbroken bliss in this world?"

MASTER: "Yes, where is it?"

Sri Ramakrishna stood in front of the shrine of Kāli and prostrated himself before the Divine Mother. M. followed him. Then the Master sat on the lower floor in front of the shrine room, facing the blissful image, and leaned against a pillar of the nātmandir. He wore a red-bordered cloth, part of which was on his shoulder and back. M. sat by his side.

M: "Since there is no unbroken happiness in the world, why should one assume a body at all? I know that the body is meant only to reap the results of past action. But who knows what sort of action it is performing now? The unfortunate part is that we are being crushed."

MASTER: "If a pea falls into filth, it grows into a pea-plant none the less."

M: "But still there are the eight bonds."

MASTER: "They are not eight bonds, but eight fetters. But what if they are? These fetters fall off in a moment, by the grace of God. Do you know what it is like? Suppose a room has been kept dark a thousand years. The moment a man brings a light into it, the darkness vanishes. Not little by little. Haven't you seen the magician's feat? He takes a string with many knots, and ties one end to something, keeping the other in his hand. Then he shakes the string once or twice, and immediately all the knots come undone. But another man cannot untie the knots however he may try. All the knots of ignorance come undone in the twinkling of an eye, through the guru's grace.

"Well, can you tell me why Keshab Sen has changed so much lately? He used to come here very often. He learnt here how to bow low before a holy man. One day I told him that one should not salute a holy man as he had been doing. Harish says rightly: 'All the cheques must be approved here. Only then will they be cashed in the bank.'" (*Laughter.*)

M. listened to these words breathlessly. He began to realize that Satchidānanda, in the form of the guru, passes the "cheque".

MASTER: "Do not reason. Who can ever know God? I have heard it from Nangtā, once for all, that this whole universe is only a fragment of Brahman.

"Hazra is given to too much calculation. He says, 'This much of God has become the universe and this much is the balance.' My head aches at his calculations. I know that I know nothing. Sometimes I think of God as good, and sometimes as bad. What can I know of Him?"

M: "It is true, sir. Can anyone ever know God? Each thinks, with his little bit of intelligence, that he has understood all of God. As you say, an ant went to a sugar hill and, finding that one grain of sugar filled its stomach, thought that the next time it would take the entire hill into its hole."

MASTER: "Who can ever know God? I don't even try. I only call on Him as Mother. Let Mother do whatever She likes. I shall know Her if it is Her will; but I shall be happy to remain ignorant if She wills otherwise. My nature is that of a kitten. It only cries, 'Mew, mew!' The rest it leaves to its mother. The mother cat puts the kitten sometimes in the kitchen and sometimes on the master's bed. The young child wants only his mother. He doesn't know how wealthy his mother is, and he doesn't even want to know. He knows only, 'I have a mother; why should I worry?' Even the child of the maidservant knows that he has a mother. If he quarrels with the son of the master, he says: 'I shall tell my mother. I have a mother.' My attitude, too, is that of a child."

Suddenly Sri Ramakrishna caught M.'s attention and said, touching his own chest: "Well, there must be something here. Isn't that so?"

M. looked wonderingly at the Master. He said to himself: "Does the Mother Herself dwell in the Master's heart? Is it the Divine Mother who has assumed this human body for the welfare of humanity?"

Sri Ramakrishna was praying to the Divine Mother: "O Mother! O Embodiment of Om! Mother, how many things people say about Thee! But I don't understand any of them. I don't know anything, Mother. I have taken refuge at Thy feet. I have sought protection in Thee. O Mother, I pray only that I may have pure love for Thy Lotus Feet, love that seeks no return. And Mother, do not delude me with Thy world-bewitching māyā. I seek Thy protection. I have taken refuge in Thee."

The evening worship in the temples was over. Sri Ramakrishna was again seated in his room with M.

M. had been visiting the Master for the past two years and had received his grace and blessings. He had been told that God was both with form and without form, that He assumed forms for the sake of His devotees. To the worshipper of the formless God, the Master said: "Hold to your conviction, but remember that all is possible with God. He has form, and again, He is formless. He can be many things more."

MASTER (to M.): "You have accepted an ideal, that of God without form—isn't that so?"

M: "Yes, sir. But I also believe what you say—that all is possible with God. It is quite possible for God to have forms."

MASTER: "Good. Remember further that, as Consciousness, He pervades the entire universe of the living and non-living."

M: "I think of Him as the consciousness in conscious beings."

MASTER: "Stick to that ideal now. There is no need of tearing down and changing one's attitude. You will gradually come to realize that the consciousness in conscious beings is the Consciousness of God. He alone is Consciousness.

"Let me ask you one thing. Do you feel attracted to money and treasures?"

M: "No, sir. But I think of earning money in order to be free from anxiety, to be able to think of God without worry."

MASTER: "Oh, that's perfectly natural."

M: "Is it greed? I don't think so."

MASTER: "You are right. Otherwise, who will look after your children? What will become of them if you feel that you are not the doer?"

M: "I have heard that one cannot attain Knowledge as long as one has the consciousness of duty. Duty is like the scorching sun."

MASTER: "Keep your present attitude. It will be different when the consciousness of duty drops away of itself."

They remained silent a few minutes.

M: "To enter the world after attaining partial knowledge! Why, it is like dying in full consciousness, as in cholera!"

MASTER: "Oh, Rām! Rām!"

The idea in M.'s mind was that just as a cholera patient feels excruciating pain at the time of death, because of retaining consciousness, so also a jnāni with partial knowledge must feel extremely miserable leading the life of the world, which he knows to be illusory.

M: "People who are completely ignorant are like typhoid patients, who remain unconscious at the time of death and so do not feel the pain."

MASTER: "Tell me, what does one attain through money? Jaygopal Sen is such a wealthy man; but he complains that his children don't obey him."

M: "Is poverty the only painful thing in the world? There are the six passions besides. Then disease and grief."

MASTER: "And also name and fame, the desire to win people's recognition. Well, what do you think my attitude is?"

M: "It is like that of a man just awakened from sleep. He becomes aware of himself. You are always united with God."

MASTER: "Do you ever dream of me?"

M: "Yes, sir. Many times."

MASTER: "How? Did you dream of me as giving you instruction?"

M. remained silent.

MASTER: "If you ever see me instructing you, then know that it is Satchidānanda Himself that does so."

M. related his dream experiences to Sri Ramakrishna, who listened to them attentively.

MASTER (*to M.*): "That is very good. Don't reason any more. You are a follower of Śakti."

Wednesday, October 10, 1883

Adhar had invited the Master to come to his house on the occasion of the Durgā Pujā festival. It was the third day of the worship of the Divine Mother. When Sri Ramakrishna arrived at Adhar's house, he found Adhar's friend Sarada, Balaram's father, and Adhar's neighbours and relatives waiting for him.

The Master went into the worship hall to see the evening worship. When it was over, he remained standing there in an abstracted mood and sang in praise of the Divine Mother:

> Out of my deep affliction rescue me, O Redeemer!
> Terrified by the threats of the King of Death am I!
> Left to myself, I shall perish soon;
> Save me, oh, save me now, I pray!
>
> Mother of all the worlds! Thou, the Support of mankind!
> Thou, the Bewitcher of all, the Mother of all that has life!
> Vrindāvan's charming Rādhā art Thou,
> Dearest playmate of Braja's Beloved.
>
> Blissful comrade of Krishna, well-spring of Krishna's līlā,
> Child of Himālaya, best of the gopis, beloved of Govinda!
> Sacred Gangā, Giver of moksha!
> Śakti! The universe sings Thy praise.
>
> Thou art the Spouse of Śiva, the Ever-blessed, the All;
> Sometimes Thou takest form and sometimes art absolute.
> Eternal Beloved of Mahādeva,
> Who can fathom Thine infinite glories?

The Master went to Adhar's drawing-room on the second floor and took a seat, surrounded by the guests. Still in a mood of divine fervour, he said: "Gentlemen, I have eaten. Now go and enjoy the feast." Was the Master hinting that the Divine Mother had partaken of Adhar's offering? Did he identify himself with the Divine Mother and therefore say, "I have eaten"?

Then, addressing the Divine Mother, he continued: "Shall I eat, O Mother? Or will You eat? O Mother, the very Embodiment of the Wine of Divine Bliss!" Did the Master look on himself as one with the Divine Mother? Had the Mother incarnated Herself as the Son to instruct mankind in the ways of God? Was this why the Master said, "I have eaten"?

In that state of divine ecstasy Sri Ramakrishna saw the six centres in his body, and the Divine Mother dwelling in them. He sang a song to that effect.

Again he sang:

> My mind is overwhelmed with wonder,
> Pondering the Mother's mystery;
> Her very name removes
> The fear of Kāla, Death himself;
> Beneath Her feet lies Mahā-Kāla.

> Why should Her hue be kāla, black?
> Many the forms of black, but She
> Appears astoundingly black;
> When contemplated in the heart,
> She lights the lotus that blossoms there.

> Her form is black, and She is named
> Kāli, the Black One. Blacker than black
> Is She! Beholding Her,
> Man is bewitched for evermore;
> No other form can he enjoy.

> In wonderment asks Rāmprasād:
> Where dwells this Woman so amazing?
> At Her mere name, his mind
> Becomes at once absorbed in Her,
> Though he has never yet beheld Her.

The fear of the devotees flies away if they but seek shelter at the feet of the Divine Mother. Was that why the Master sang the following song?

> I have surrendered my soul at the fearless feet of the Mother;
> Am I afraid of Death any more?
> Unto the tuft of hair on my head
> Is tied the almighty mantra, Mother Kāli's name.
> My body I have sold in the market-place of the world
> And with it have bought Sri Durgā's name.

> Deep within my heart I have planted the name of Kāli,
> The Wish-fulfilling Tree of heaven;
> When Yama, King of Death, appears,
> To him I shall open my heart and show it growing there.
> I have cast out from me my six unflagging foes;[5]
> Ready am I to sail life's sea,
> Crying, "To Durgā, victory!"

Sarada was stricken with grief on account of his son's death. So Adhar had taken him to Dakshineswar to visit the Master. Sarada was a devotee of Sri Chaitanya. Sri Ramakrishna looked at him and was inspired with the ideal of Gaurānga.

He sang:[6]

> Why has My body turned so golden? It is not time for this to be:
> Many the ages that must pass, before as Gaurānga I appear.
> Here in the age of Dwāpara My sport is not yet at an end;
> How strange this transformation is!

[5] The six passions.
[6] The song represents the words of Gaurānga in the mood of Krishna. Gaurānga, who had a golden complexion, is regarded as an Incarnation of Krishna.

The peacock glistens, all of gold; and golden, too, the cuckoo
  gleams!
Everything around Me here has turned to gold! Naught else
  appears
But gold, whichever way I look.
What can it mean, this miracle, that everything I see is gold?

Ah, I can guess its meaning now:
Rādhā has come to Mathurā,[7] and that is why My skin is gold.
For she is like the brahmara,[8] and so has given Me her hue.
Dark blue My body was but now; yet in the twinkling of an eye
It turned to gold. Have I become Rādhā by contemplating her?

I cannot imagine where I am—in Mathurā or Navadvip.
But how could this have come to pass?
Not yet is Balarāma born as Nitāi, nor has Nārada
Become Śrivas, nor Yaśodā as Mother Sachi yet returned.
Then why should I, among them all, alone assume a golden face?
Not yet is Father Nanda born as Jagannāth;[9] then why should I
Be thus transmuted into gold?
Perhaps because in Mathurā sweet Rādhā has appeared, My skin
Has borrowed Gaurānga's golden hue.

Sri Ramakrishna sang again, still overpowered with the ideal of Gaurānga:

Surely Gaurānga is lost in a state of blissful ecstasy;
In an exuberance of joy, he laughs and weeps and dances and
  sings.
He takes a wood for Vrindāvan, the Ganges for the blue Jamunā;
Loudly he sobs and weeps. Yet, though he is all gold without,
He is all black within—black with the blackness of Krishna!

The Master continued to sing, assuming the attitude of a woman devotee
infatuated with love for Gaurānga:

> Why do my neighbours raise such a scandal?
> Why do they cast aspersions upon me
> Simply because of Gaurānga?
> How can they understand my feelings?
> How can I ever explain?
> Can I ever explain at all?
> Alas, to whom shall I explain it?
> Ah, but they make me die of shame!
>
> Once on a time, at the house of Śrivas,
> Gorā was loudly singing the kirtan,
> When, on the ground of the courtyard,
> Falling, he rolled in an ecstasy.
> I, who was standing near him,
> Seeing him where he lay entranced,

[7] The capital of Krishna's kingdom, where He lived after leaving Vrindāvan.

[8] According to a Hindu legend, the cockroach, by intently meditating upon the
brahmara, becomes transformed into the latter.

[9] Sachi and Jagannāth were Gaurānga's parents; Yaśodā and Nanda were Krishna's
parents.

Was suddenly lost to outward sense,
Until the wife of Śrivās revived me.

Another day, in the bhaktas' procession,
Gorā was sweetly singing the kirtan;
Clasping the outcastes to him,
He softened the unbelievers' hearts.
Through Nadiā's market-place
He chanted Lord Hari's holy name.
I followed the throng, and from close by
Caught a glimpse of his golden feet.

Once by the Ganges' bank he stood,
His body bright as the sun and moon,
Charming all with his beauty.
I too had come, to fetch some water,
And, as I looked from one side,
My water-jar slipped and fell to the ground.
My sister-in-law, the gossip, saw me,
And now she is spreading it everywhere.

Balaram's father was a Vaishnava; hence the Master also sang of the divine love of the gopis for their beloved Krishna:

I have not found my Krishna, O friend! How cheerless my home
    without Him!
Ah, if Krishna could only be the hair upon my head,
Carefully I should braid it then, and deck it with bakul-flowers;
Carefully I should fashion the braids out of my Krishna-hair.
Krishna is black, and black is my hair; black would be one with
    black!

Ah, if Krishna could only be the ring I wear in my nose,
Always from my nose He would hang, and my two lips could touch
    Him.
But it can never be, alas! Why should I idly dream?
Why should Krishna care at all to be the ring in my nose?

Ah, if Krishna could only be the bracelets on my arms,
Always He would cling to my wrists, and proudly I should walk,
Shaking my bracelets to make them sound, shaking my arms to
    show them;
Down the king's highway I should walk, wearing my Krishn
    bracelets.

Balaram's father was a wealthy man with estates in different parts of Orissa. An orthodox member of the Vaishnava sect, he had built temples and arranged for distribution of food to the pilgrims at various holy places. He had been spending the last years of his life in Vrindāvan. The Vaishnavas, for the most part, are bigoted in their religious views. Some of them harbour malicious feelings toward the followers of the Tantra and Vedānta. But Sri Ramakrishna never encouraged such a narrow outlook. According to his teachings, through earnestness and yearning all lovers of God will ultimately reach the same goal. The Master began the conversation in order to broaden the religious views of Balaram's father.

MASTER (to M.): "Once I thought, 'Why should I be one-sided?' Therefore I was initiated into Vaishnavism in Vrindāvan and took the garb of a Vaishnava monk. I spent three days practising the Vaishnava discipline. Again, at Dakshineswar I was initiated into the mystery of Rāma worship. I painted my forehead with a long mark and put on a string with a diamond round my neck. But after a few days I gave them up.

"A certain man had a tub. People would come to him to have their clothes dyed. The tub contained a solution of dye. Whatever colour a man wanted for his cloth, he would get by dipping the cloth in the tub. One man was amazed to see this and said to the dyer, 'Please give me the dye you have in your tub.'"

Was the Master hinting that people professing different religions would come to him and have their spiritual consciousness awakened according to their own ideals?

MASTER (to Balaram's father): "Don't read books any more. But you may read books on devotion, such as the life of Chaitanya.`

"The whole thing is to love God and taste His sweetness. He is sweetness and the devotee is its enjoyer. The devotee drinks the sweet Bliss of God. Further, God is the lotus and the devotee the bee. The devotee sips the honey of the lotus.

"As a devotee cannot live without God, so also God cannot live without His devotee. Then the devotee becomes the sweetness, and God its enjoyer. The devotee becomes the lotus, and God the bee. It is the Godhead that has become these two in order to enjoy Its own Bliss. That is the significance of the episode of Rādhā and Krishna.[10]

"At the beginning of spiritual life the devotee should observe such rites as pilgrimage, putting a string of beads around his neck, and so forth. But outward ceremonies gradually drop off as he attains the goal, the vision of God. Then his only activity is the repetition of God's name, and contemplation and meditation on Him.

"The pennies equivalent to sixteen rupees make a great heap. But sixteen silver coins do not look like such a big amount. Again, the quantity becomes much smaller when you change the sixteen rupees into one gold mohur. And if you change the gold into a tiny piece of diamond, people hardly notice it."

Orthodox Vaishnavas insist on the outer insignia of religion. They criticize any devotee who does not wear these marks. Was that why the Master said that, after the vision of God, a devotee becomes indifferent to outer marks, giving up formal worship when the goal of spiritual life is attained?

MASTER (to Balaram's father): "The Kartābhajās group the devotees into four classes: the pravartaka, the sadhaka, the siddha, and the siddha of the siddha. The pravartaka, the beginner, puts the mark of his religion on his

[10] According to one school of the Vaishnava religion, the Supreme God Himself became Rādhā and Krishna in order to enjoy the bliss of their mutual communion.

forehead, wears a string of beads around his neck, and observes other outer conventions. The sādhaka, the struggling devotee, does not care so much for elaborate rites. An example of this class is the Bāul. The siddha, the perfect, firmly believes that God exists. The siddha of the siddha, the supremely perfect, like Chaitanya, not only has realized God but also has become intimate with Him and talks with Him all the time. This is the last limit of realization.

"There are many kinds of spiritual aspirants. Those endowed with sattva perform their spiritual practices secretly. They look like ordinary people, but they meditate inside the mosquito net.

"Aspirants endowed with rajas exhibit outward pomp—a string of beads around the neck, a mark on the forehead, an ochre robe, a silk cloth, a rosary with a gold bead, and so on. They are like stall-keepers advertising their wares with signboards.

"All religions and all paths call upon their followers to pray to one and the same God. Therefore one should not show disrespect to any religion or religious opinion. It is God alone who is called Satchidānanda Brahman in the Vedas, Satchidānanda Krishna in the Purānas, and Satchidānanda Śiva in the Tantras. It is one and the same Satchidānanda.

"There are different sects of Vaishnavas. That which is called Brahman in the Vedas is called Ālekh-Niranjan by one Vaishnava sect. 'Ālekh' means That which cannot be pointed out or perceived by the sense-organs. According to this sect, Rādhā and Krishna are only two bubbles of the Ālekh.

"According to the Vedānta,[11] there is no Incarnation of God. The Vedāntists say that Rāma and Krishna are but two waves in the Ocean of Satchidānanda.

"In reality there are not two. There is only One. A man may call on God by any name; if he is sincere in his prayer he will certainly reach Him. He will succeed if he has longing."

As Sri Ramakrishna spoke these words to the devotees, he was overwhelmed with divine fervour. Coming down to partial consciousness of the world, he said to Balaram's father, "Are you the father of Balaram?"

All sat in silence. Balaram's aged father was silently telling his beads.

MASTER (to M. and the others): "Well, these people practise so much japa and go to so many sacred places, but why are they like this? Why do they make no progress? In their case it seems as if the year consists of eighteen months.

"Once I said to Harish: 'What is the use of going to Benares if one does not feel restless for God? And if one feels that longing, then this very place is Benares.'

"They make so many pilgrimages and repeat the name of God so much, but why do they not realize anything? It is because they have no longing for God. God reveals Himself to the devotee if only he calls upon Him with a longing heart.

"At the beginning of a yātrā performance much light-hearted restlessness

11 A reference to the Advaita Vedānta.

is to be observed on the stage. At that time one does not see Krishna. Next the sage Nārada enters with his flute and sings longingly, 'O Govinda! O my Life! O my Soul!' Then Krishna can no longer remain away and appears with the cowherd boys."

Tuesday, October 16, 1883

Sri Ramakrishna was in his room with Rakhal, Balaram's father, Beni Pal, M., Mani Mallick, Ishan, Kishori, and other devotees.

MASTER: "Liberal-minded devotees accept all the forms of God: Krishna, Kāli, Śiva, Rāma, and so on."

BALARAM'S FATHER: "Yes, sir. It is like a woman's recognizing her husband, whatever clothes he wears."

MASTER: "But again, there is a thing called nishthā, single-minded devotion. When the gopis went to Mathurā they saw Krishna with a turban on His head. At this they pulled down their veils and said, 'Who is this man? Where is *our* Krishna with the peacock feather on His crest and the yellow cloth on His body?' Hanumān also had that unswerving devotion. He came to Dwārakā in the cycle of Dwāpara. Krishna said to Rukmini, His queen, 'Hanumān will not be satisfied unless he sees the form of Rāma.' So, to please Hanumān, Krishna assumed the form of Rāma.

"But, my dear sir, I am in a peculiar state of mind. My mind constantly descends from the Absolute to the Relative, and again ascends from the Relative to the Absolute.

"The attainment of the Absolute is called the Knowledge of Brahman. But it is extremely difficult to acquire. A man cannot acquire the Knowledge of Brahman unless he completely rids himself of his attachment to the world. When the Divine Mother was born as the daughter of King Himālaya, She showed Her various forms to Her father. The king said, 'I want to see Brahman.' Thereupon the Divine Mother said: 'Father, if that is your desire, then you must seek the company of holy men. You must go into solitude, away from the world, and now and then live in holy company.'

"The manifold has come from the One alone, the Relative from the Absolute. There is a state of consciousness where the many disappears, and the One, as well; for the many must exist as long as the One exists. Brahman is without comparison. It is impossible to explain Brahman by analogy. It is between light and darkness. It is Light, but not the light that we perceive, not material light.

"Again, when God changes the state of my mind, when He brings my mind down to the plane of the Relative, I perceive that it is He who has become all these—the Creator, māyā, the living beings, and the universe.

"Again, sometimes He shows me that He has created the universe and all living beings. He is the Master, and the universe His garden.

"'He is the Master, and the universe and all its living beings belong to Him'—that is Knowledge. And, 'I am the doer', 'I am the guru', 'I am the father'—that is ignorance. 'This is my house; this is my family; this is my wealth; these are my relatives'—this also is ignorance."

BALARAM'S FATHER: "That is true, sir."

MASTER: "As long as you do not feel that God is the Master, you must come back to the world, you must be born again and again. There will be no rebirth when you can truly say, 'O God, Thou art the Master.' As long as you cannot say, 'O Lord, Thou alone art real', you will not be released from the life of the world. This going and coming, this rebirth, is inevitable. There will be no liberation. Further, what can you achieve by saying, 'It is mine'? The manager of an estate may say, 'This is our garden; these are our couches and furniture.' But when he is dismissed by the master, he hasn't the right to take away even a chest of worthless mango-wood given to him for his use.

"The feeling of 'I and mine' has covered the Reality. Because of this we do not see Truth. Attainment of Chaitanya, Divine Consciousness, is not possible without the knowledge of Advaita, Non-duality. After realizing Chaitanya one enjoys Nityānanda, Eternal Bliss. One enjoys this Bliss after attaining the state of a paramahamsa.

"Vedānta does not recognize the Incarnation of God. According to it, Chaitanyadeva is only a bubble of the non-dual Brahman

"Do you know what the vision of Divine Consciousness is like? It is like the sudden illumination of a dark room when a match is struck.

"The Incarnation of God is accepted by those who follow the path of bhakti. A woman belonging to the Kartābhajā sect observed my condition and remarked: 'You have inner realization. Don't dance and sing too much. Ripe grapes must be preserved carefully in cotton. The mother-in-law lessens her daughter-in-law's activities when the daughter-in-law is with child. One characteristic of God-realization is that the activities of a man with such realization gradually drop away. Inside this man [meaning Sri Ramakrishna] is the real Jewel.'

"Watching me eat, she remarked, 'Sir, are you yourself eating, or are you feeding someone else?'

"The feeling of ego has covered the Truth. Narendra once said, 'As the "I" of man recedes, the "I" of God approaches.' Kedar says, 'The more clay there is in the jar, the less water it holds.'

"Krishna said to Arjuna: 'Brother, you will not realize Me if you possess even one of the eight siddhis.' These give only a little power. With healing and the like one may do only a little good to others. Isn't that true?

"Therefore I prayed to the Divine Mother for pure love only, a love that does not seek any return. I never asked for occult powers."

While talking thus, Sri Ramakrishna went into samādhi. He sat there motionless, completely forgetful of the outer world. Then, coming down to the sense world, he sang:

> Ah, friend! I have not found Him yet, whose love has driven me
> mad. . . .

At the Master's request, Ramlal sang a song describing how Chaitanya embraced the monastic life:

Oh, what a vision I have beheld in Keshab Bhārati's[12] hut!
Gorā, in all his matchless grace,
Shedding tears in a thousand streams!
Like a mad elephant
He dances in ecstasy and sings,
Drunk with an overwhelming love.

Rolling flat upon the ground and swimming in his tears,
He weeps and shouts Lord Hari's name,
Piercing the very heavens with his cries,
Loud as a lion's roar;
Then most humbly he begs men's love,
To feel himself the servant of God.

Shorn of his locks, he has put on the yogi's ochre robe;
Even the hardest heart must melt
To see his pure and heavenly love.
Smitten by man's deep woe,
He has abandoned everything
And pours out love unstintingly.

Oh, would that Premdās were his slave and, passing from
          door to door,
Might sing Gaurānga's endless praise!

The Master asked Mani Mallick to quote the words of Tulsidās to the effect that one who had developed love of God could not observe caste distinctions.

MANI: "'The throat of the chātak bird is pierced with thirst. All around are the waters of the Ganges, the Jamunā, the Saraju, and of innumerable other rivers and lakes; but the bird will not touch any of these. It only looks up expectantly for the rain that falls when the star Svāti is in the ascendant.'"

MASTER: "That means that love for the Lotus Feet of God is alone real, and all else illusory."

MANI: "Tulsi also said: 'At the touch of the philosopher's stone, the eight metals become gold. Likewise all castes, even the butcher and the untouchable, become pure by repeating Hari's name. Without Hari's name the people of the four castes are but butchers.'"

MASTER: "The hide that the scriptures forbid one to touch can be taken inside the temple after it has been tanned.

"Man becomes pure by repeating the name of God. Therefore one should practise the chanting of God's name. I said to Jadu Mallick's mother: 'In the hour of death you will think only of worldly things—of family, children, executing the will, and so forth. The thought of God will not come to your mind. The way to remember God in the hour of death is to practise, now, the repetition of His name and the chanting of His glories. If one keeps up this practice, then in the hour of death one will repeat the name of God. When the cat pounces upon the bird, the bird only squawks and does not say, 'Rāma, Rāma, Harē-Krishna'.

"It is good to prepare for death. One should constantly think of God and

[12] The monastic teacher of Sri Chaitanya.

chant His name in solitude during the last years of one's life. If the elephant is put into the stable after its bath it is not soiled again by dirt and dust."

Balaram's father, Mani Mallick, and Beni Pal were all elderly men. Did the Master give this instruction especially for their benefit?

MASTER: "Why do I ask you to think of God and chant His name in solitude? Living in the world day and night, one suffers from worries. Haven't you noticed brother killing brother for a foot of land? The Śikhs said to me, 'The cause of all worry and confusion is these three: land, woman, and money.'

"You are leading a householder's life. Why should you be afraid of the world? When Rāma said to Daśaratha that He was going to renounce the world, it worried His father, and the king sought counsel of Vaśishtha. Vaśishtha said to Rāma: 'Rāma, why should You give up the world? Reason with me. Is this world outside God? What is there to renounce and what is there to accept? Nothing whatever exists but God. It is Brahman alone that appears as Iśvara, māyā, living beings, and the universe.' "

BALARAM'S FATHER: "It is very difficult, sir."

MASTER: "The aspirant, while practising spiritual discipline, looks upon the world as a 'framework of illusion'. Again, after the attainment of Knowledge, the vision of God, this very world becomes to him a 'mansion of mirth'.

"It is written in the books of the Vaishnavas: 'God can be attained through faith alone; reasoning pushes Him far away.' Faith alone!

"What faith Krishnakishore had! At Vrindāvan a low-caste man drew water for him from a well. Krishnakishore said to him, 'Repeat the name of Śiva.' After the man had repeated the name of Śiva, Krishnakishore unhesitatingly drank the water. He used to say, 'If a man chants the name of God, does he need to spend money any more for the atonement of his sins? How foolish!' He was amazed to see people worshipping God with the sacred tulsi-leaf in order to get rid of their illnesses. At the bathing-ghāt here he said to us, 'Please bless me, that I may pass my days repeating Rāma's holy name.' Whenever I went to his house he would dance with joy at the sight of me. Rāma said to Lakshmana, 'Brother, whenever you find people singing and dancing in the ecstasy of divine love, know for certain that I am there.' Chaitanya is an example of such ecstatic love. He laughed and wept and danced and sang in divine ecstasy. He was an Incarnation. God incarnated Himself through Chaitanya."

Sri Ramakrishna sang a song describing the divine love of Chaitanya. Then Balaram's father, Mani Mallick, Beni Pal, and several other devotees took leave of the Master.

In the evening, devotees from Kānsāritolā, Calcutta, arrived. The Master danced and sang with them in a state of divine fervour. After dancing, he went into a spiritual mood and said, "I shall go part of the way myself." Kishori came forward to massage his feet, but the Master did not allow anyone to touch him.

Ishan arrived. The Master was seated, still in a spiritual mood. After a

while he became engaged in talk with Ishan. It was Ishan's desire to practise
the purascharana of the Gāyatri.

MASTER (to Ishan): "Follow your own intuition. I hope there is no more
doubt in your mind. Is there any? The path of the Vedas is not meant for
the Kaliyuga. The path of Tantra is efficacious."

ISHAN: "I have almost resolved to perform an atonement ceremony."

MASTER: "Do you mean to say that one cannot follow the path of Tantra?
That which is Brahman is also Śakti, Kāli.

> Knowing the secret that Kāli is one with the highest Brahman,
> I have discarded, once for all, both righteousness and sin."

ISHAN: "It is mentioned in a hymn in the *Chandi* that Brahman alone is
the Primal Energy. Brahman is identical with Śakti."

MASTER: "It will not do simply to express that idea in words. Only when
you assimilate it will all be well with you.

"When the heart becomes pure through the practice of spiritual discipline,
then one rightly feels that God alone is the Doer. He alone has become mind,
life, and intelligence. We are only His instruments.

> Thou it is that holdest the elephant in the mire;
> Thou, that helpest the lame man scale the loftiest hill.

"When your heart becomes pure, then you will realize that it is God who
makes us perform such rites as the purascharana.

> Thou workest Thine own work; men only call it theirs.

"All doubts disappear after the realization of God. Then the devotee meets
the favourable wind. He becomes free from worry. He is like the boatman
who, when the favourable wind blows, unfurls the sail, holds the rudder
lightly, and enjoys a smoke."

Ishan took his leave and Sri Ramakrishna talked with M. No one else was
present. He asked M. what he thought of Narendra, Rakhal, Adhar, and
Hazra, and whether they were guileless. "And", asked the Master, "what do
you think of me?"

M. said: "You are simple and at the same time deep. It is extremely difficult to understand you."

Sri Ramakrishna laughed.

November 26, 1883

It was the day of the annual festival of the Sinduriāpatti Brāhmo Samāj.
The ceremony was to be performed in Manilal Mallick's house. The worship
hall was beautifully decorated with flowers, wreaths, and evergreens, and
many devotees were assembled, eagerly awaiting the worship. Their enthusiasm had been greatly heightened by the news that Sri Ramakrishna was
going to grace the occasion with his presence. Keshab, Vijay, Shivanath, and
other leaders of the Brāhmo Samāj held him in high respect. His God-
intoxicated state of mind, his intense love of spiritual life, his burning faith,
his intimate communion with God, and his respect for women, whom he

regarded as veritable manifestations of the Divine Mother, together with the unsullied purity of his character, his complete renunciation of worldly talk, his love and respect for all religious faiths, and his eagerness to meet devotees of all creeds, attracted the members of the Brāhmo Samāj to him. Devotees came that day from far-off places to join the festival, for it would give them a chance to get a glimpse of the Master and listen to his inspiring talk.

Sri Ramakrishna arrived at the house before the worship began, and became engaged in conversation with Vijaykrishna Goswami and the other devotees. The lamps were lighted and the divine service was about to begin.

The Master asked if Shivanath would come to the festival. A Brāhmo devotee said that he had other important things to do and was not coming.

MASTER: "I feel very happy when I see Shivanath. He always seems to be absorbed in the bliss of bhakti. Further, a man who is respected by so many surely possesses some divine power. But he has one great defect: he doesn't keep his word. Once he said to me that he would come to Dakshineswar, but he neither came nor sent me word. That is not good. It is said that truthfulness alone constitutes the spiritual discipline of the Kaliyuga. If a man clings tenaciously to truth he ultimately realizes God. Without this regard for truth, one gradually loses everything. If by chance I say that I will go to the pine-grove, I must go there even if there is no further need of it, lest I lose my attachment to truth. After my vision of the Divine Mother, I prayed to Her, taking a flower in my hands: 'Mother, here is Thy knowledge and here is Thy ignorance. Take them both, and give me only pure love. Here is Thy holiness and here is Thy unholiness. Take them both, Mother, and give me pure love. Here is Thy good and here is Thy evil. Take them both, Mother, and give me pure love. Here is Thy righteousness and here is Thy unrighteousness. Take them both, Mother, and give me pure love.' I mentioned all these, but I could not say: 'Mother, here is Thy truth and here is Thy falsehood. Take them both.' I gave up everything at Her feet but could not bring myself to give up truth."

Soon the service began according to the rules of the Brāhmo Samāj. The preacher was seated on the dais. After the opening prayer he recited holy texts of the Vedas and was joined by the congregation in the invocation to the Supreme Brahman. They chanted in chorus: "Brahman is Truth, Knowledge, and Infinity. It shines as Bliss and Immortality. Brahman is Peace, Blessedness, the One without a Second; It is pure and unstained by sin." The minds of the devotees were stilled, and they closed their eyes in meditation.

The Master went into deep samādhi. He sat there transfixed and speechless. After some time he opened his eyes, looked around, and suddenly stood up with the words "Brahma! Brahma!" on his lips. Soon the devotional music began, accompanied by drums and cymbals. In a state of divine fervour the Master began to dance with the devotees. Vijay and the other Brāhmos danced around him. The guests and the devotees were enchanted. Many of them drank the sweet bliss of God's name and forgot the world. The happiness of the material world appeared bitter to them, at least for the time being.

After the kirtan all sat around the Master, eager to hear his words.

MASTER: "It is difficult to lead the life of a householder in a spirit of detachment. Once Pratap[13] said to me: 'Sir, we follow the example of King Janaka. He led the life of a householder in a detached spirit. We shall follow him.' I said to him: 'Can one be like King Janaka by merely wishing it? How many austerities he practised in order to acquire divine knowledge! He practised the most intense form of asceticism for many years and only then returned to the life of the world.'

"Is there, then, no hope for householders? Certainly there is. They must practise spiritual discipline in solitude for some days. Thus they will acquire knowledge and devotion. Then it will not hurt them to lead the life of the world. But when you practise discipline in solitude, keep yourself entirely away from your family. You must not allow your wife, son, daughter, mother, father, sister, brother, friends, or relatives near you. While thus practising discipline in solitude, you should think: 'I have no one else in the world. God is my all.' You must also pray to Him, with tears in your eyes, for knowledge and devotion.

"If you ask me how long you should live in solitude away from your family, I should say that it would be good for you if you could spend even one day in such a manner. Three days at a time are still better. One may live in solitude for twelve days, a month, three months, or a year, according to one's convenience and ability. One hasn't much to fear if one leads the life of a householder after attaining knowledge and devotion.

"If you break a jack-fruit after rubbing your hands with oil, then its sticky milk will not smear your hands. While playing the game of hide-and-seek, you are safe if you but once touch the 'granny'. Be turned into gold by touching the philosopher's stone. After that you may remain buried underground a thousand years; when you are taken out you will still be gold.

"The mind is like milk. If you keep the mind in the world, which is like water, then the milk and water will get mixed. That is why people keep milk in a quiet place and let it set into curd, and then churn butter from it. Likewise, through spiritual discipline practised in solitude, churn the butter of knowledge and devotion from the milk of the mind. Then that butter can easily be kept in the water of the world. It will not get mixed with the world. The mind will float detached on the water of the world."

Vijay had just returned from Gayā, where he had spent a long time in solitude and holy company. He had put on the ochre robe of a monk and was in an exalted state of mind, always indrawn. He was sitting before the Master with his head bent down, as if absorbed in some deep thought.

Casting his benign glance on Vijay, the Master said: "Vijay, have you found your room?

"Let me tell you a parable: Once two holy men, in the course of their wanderings, entered a city. One of them, with wondering eyes and mouth agape, was looking at the market-place, the stalls, and the buildings, when he met his companion. The latter said: 'You seem to be filled with wonder at the city. Where is your baggage?' He replied: 'First of all I found a room.

[13] Pratap Chandra Mazumdar, a celebrated leader of the Brāhmo Samāj.

I put my things in it, locked the door, and felt totally relieved. Now I am going about the city enjoying all the fun.'

"So I am asking you, Vijay, if you have found your room. (*To M. and the others*) You see, the spring in Vijay's heart has been covered all these days. Now it is open.

(*To Vijay*) "Well, Shivanath is always in trouble and turmoil. He has to write for magazines and perform many other duties. Worldly duties bring much worry and anxiety along with them.

"It is narrated in the *Bhāgavata* that the Avadhuta had twenty-four gurus, one of whom was a kite. In a certain place the fishermen were catching fish. A kite swooped down and snatched a fish. At the sight of the fish, about a thousand crows chased the kite and made a great noise with their cawing. Whichever way the kite flew with the fish, the crows followed it. The kite flew to the south and the crows followed it there. The kite flew to the north and still the crows followed after it. The kite went east and west, but with the same result. As the kite began to fly about in confusion, lo, the fish dropped from its mouth. The crows at once let the kite alone and flew after the fish. Thus relieved of its worries, the kite sat on the branch of a tree and thought: 'That wretched fish was at the root of all my troubles. I have now got rid of it and therefore I am at peace.'

"The Avadhuta learnt this lesson from the kite, that as long as a man has the fish, that is, worldly desires, he must perform actions and consequently suffer from worry, anxiety, and restlessness. No sooner does he renounce these desires than his activities fall away and he enjoys peace of soul.

"But work without any selfish motive is good. It does not create any worry. But it is very difficult to be totally unselfish. We may think that our work is selfless, but selfishness comes, unknown to us, from no one knows where. But if a man has already undergone great spiritual discipline, then as a result of it he may be able to do work without any selfish motive. After the vision of God a man can easily do unselfish work. In most cases action drops away after the attainment of God. Only a few, like Nārada, work to bring light to mankind.

"The Avadhuta accepted a bee as another teacher. Bees accumulate their honey by days of hard labour. But they cannot enjoy their honey, for a man soon breaks the comb and takes it away. The Avadhuta learnt this lesson from the bees, that one should not lay things up. Sādhus should depend one hundred per cent on God. They must not gather for the morrow. But this does not apply to the householder. He must bring up his family; therefore it is necessary for him to provide. Birds and monks do not hoard. Yet birds also hoard after their chicks are hatched: they collect food in their beaks for their young ones.

"Let me tell you one thing, Vijay. Don't trust a sādhu if he keeps bag and baggage with him and a bundle of clothes with many knots. I have seen such sādhus under the banyan tree in the Panchavati. Two or three of them were seated there. One was picking over lentils, some were sewing their clothes, and all were gossiping about a feast they had enjoyed in a rich man's house. They said among themselves, 'That rich man spent a hundred thousand rupees on the feast and fed the sādhus sumptuously with cake, sweets, and many such delicious things.' " (All laugh.)

VIJAY: "It is true, sir. I have seen such sādhus at Gayā. They are called the lotāwalla sādhus[14] of Gayā."

MASTER (to Vijay): "When love of God is awakened, work drops away of itself. If God makes some men work, let them work. It is now time for you to give up everything. Renounce all and say, 'O mind, may you and I alone behold the Mother, letting no one else intrude.' "

Saying this, Sri Ramakrishna began to sing in his soul-enthralling voice:

> Cherish my precious Mother Śyāmā
> Tenderly within, O mind;
> May you and I alone behold Her,
> Letting no one else intrude.
>
> O mind, in solitude enjoy Her,
> Keeping the passions all outside;
> Take but the tongue, that now and again
> It may cry out, "O Mother! Mother!"
>
> Suffer no breath of base desire
> To enter and approach us there,
> But bid true knowledge stand on guard,
> Alert and watchful evermore.

The Master said to Vijay: "Surrender yourself completely to God, and set aside all such things as fear and shame. Give up such feelings as, 'What will people think of me if I dance in the ecstasy of God's holy name?' The saying, 'One cannot have the vision of God as long as one has these three— shame, hatred, and fear', is very true. Shame, hatred, fear, caste, pride, secretiveness, and the like are so many bonds. Man is free when he is liberated from all these.

"When bound by ties one is jīva, and when free from ties one is Śiva. Prema, ecstatic love of God, is a rare thing.

"First of all one acquires bhakti. Bhakti is single-minded devotion to God, like the devotion a wife feels for her husband. It is very difficult to have unalloyed devotion to God. Through such devotion one's mind and soul merge in Him.

"Then comes bhāva, intense love. Through bhāva a man becomes speechless. His nerve currents are stilled. Kumbhaka comes by itself. It is like the case of a man whose breath and speech stop when he fires a gun.

"But prema, ecstatic love, is an extremely rare thing. Chaitanya had that love. When one has prema one forgets all outer things. One forgets the world. One even forgets one's own body, which is so dear to a man."

The Master began to sing:

> Oh, when will dawn the blessed day
> When tears of joy will flow from my eyes
> As I repeat Lord Hari's name?
> Oh, when will dawn the blessed day

[14] Sādhus carrying water-pots.

When all my craving for the world
Will vanish straightway from my heart,
And with the thrill of His holy name
All of my hair will stand on end?
Oh, when will dawn that blessed day?

So the talk of divine things was proceeding, when some invited Brāhmo devotees entered the room. There were among them a few pundits and high government officials.

Sri Ramakrishna had said that bhāva stills the nerve currents of the devotee. He continued: "When Arjuna was about to shoot at the target, the eye of a fish, his eyes were fixed on the eye of the fish, and on nothing else. He didn't even notice any part of the fish except the eye. In such a state the breathing stops and one experiences kumbhaka.

"Another characteristic of God-vision is that a great spiritual current rushes up along the spine and goes toward the brain. If then the devotee goes into samādhi, he sees God."

Looking at the Brāhmo devotees who had just arrived, the Master said: "Mere pundits, devoid of divine love, talk incoherently. Pundit Samadhyayi once said, in the course of his sermon: 'God is dry. Make Him sweet by your love and devotion.' Imagine! To describe Him as dry, whom the Vedas declare as the Essence of Bliss! It makes one feel that the pundit didn't know what God really is. That was why his words were so incoherent.

"A man once said, 'There are many horses in my uncle's cow-shed.' From that one could know that the man had no horses at all. No one keeps a horse in a cow-shed.

"Some people pride themselves on their riches and power—their wealth, honour, and social position. But these are only transitory. Nothing will remain with you in death.

"There is a song that runs:

Remember this, O mind! Nobody is your own:
Vain is your wandering in this world.
Trapped in the subtle snare of māyā as you are,
Do not forget the Mother's name.

Only a day or two men honour you on earth
As lord and master; all too soon
That form, so honoured now, must needs be cast away,
When Death, the Master, seizes you.

Even your beloved wife, for whom, while yet you live,
You fret yourself almost to death,
Will not go with you then; she too will say farewell,
And shun your corpse as an evil thing.

"One must not be proud of one's money. If you say that you are rich, then one can remind you that there are richer men than you, and others richer still, and so on. At dusk the glow-worm comes out and thinks that it lights the world. But its pride is crushed when the stars appear in the sky. The stars feel that they give light to the earth. But when the moon rises the stars fade in shame. The moon feels that the world smiles at its light and that it lights the earth. Then the eastern horizon becomes red, and the sun rises. The moon fades and after a while is no longer seen.

"If wealthy people would think that way, they would get rid of their pride in their wealth."

Manilal had provided a sumptuous feast in celebration of the festival. He entertained the Master and the other guests with great love and attention. It was late at night when they returned to their homes.

15

LAST VISIT TO KESHAB

Wednesday, November 28, 1883

A T TWO O'CLOCK in the afternoon, M. was pacing the foot-path of the Circular Road in front of the Lily Cottage, where Keshab Chandra Sen lived. He was eagerly awaiting the arrival of Sri Rama-krishna. Keshab's illness had taken a serious turn, and there was very little chance of his recovery. Since the Master loved Keshab dearly, he was coming from Dakshineswar to pay him a visit.

On the east side of the Circular Road was Victoria College, where the ladies of Keshab's Brāhmo Samāj and their daughters received their education. To the north of the college was a spacious garden house inhabited by an English family. M. noticed that there was a commotion in the house and wondered what was going on. Presently a hearse arrived with the drivers dressed in black, and the members of the household appeared, looking very sad. There had been a death in the family.

"Whither does the soul go, leaving behind this mortal body?" Pondering the age-old question, M. waited, watching the carriages that came from the north.

About five o'clock a carriage stopped in front of the Lily Cottage and Sri Ramakrishna got out with Latu and several other devotees, including Rakhal. He was received by Keshab's relatives, who led him and the devotees upstairs to the verandah south of the drawing-room. The Master seated himself on a couch.

After a long wait he became impatient to see Keshab. Keshab's disciples said that he was resting and would be there presently. Sri Ramakrishna became more and more impatient and said to Keshab's disciples: "Look here, what need is there of his coming to me? Why can't I go in and see him?"

PRASANNA (*humbly*): "Sir, he will come in a few minutes."

MASTER: "Go away! It is you who are making all this fuss. Let me go in."

Prasanna began to talk about Keshab in order to divert the Master's attention. He said: "Keshab is now an altogether different person. Like you, sir, he talks to the Divine Mother. He hears what the Mother says, and laughs and cries."

When he was told that Keshab talked to the Divine Mother and laughed and cried, the Master became ecstatic. Presently he went into samādhi.

It was winter and the Master was wearing a green flannel coat with a shawl thrown over it. He sat straight, with his eyes fixed, deep in ecstasy. A long time passed in this way. There was no indication of his returning to the normal plane of consciousness.

Gradually it became dark. Lamps were lighted in the drawing-room, where the Master was now to go. While he was slowly coming down to the plane of ordinary consciousness, he was taken there, though with great difficulty. The room was well furnished. At the sight of the furniture, the Master muttered to himself, "These things were necessary before, but of what use are they now?" Seeing Rakhal, he said, "Oh, hello! Are you here?" Then, seating himself on a couch, he again lost consciousness of the outer world, and, looking around as if seeing someone, he said: "Hello, Mother! I see that You too have come. How You are showing off in Your Benares sāri! Don't bother me now, please. Sit down and be quiet."

The Master was in a state of intense divine intoxication. In the well-lighted room the Brāhmo devotees sat around the Master; Latu, Rakhal, and M. remained near him. He was saying to himself, still filled with divine fervour: "The body and the soul! The body was born and it will die. But for the soul there is no death. It is like the betel-nut. When the nut is ripe it does not stick to the shell. But when it is green it is difficult to separate it from the shell. After realizing God, one does not identify oneself any more with the body. Then one knows that body and soul are two different things."

At this moment Keshab entered the room. He came through the east door. Those who remembered the man who had preached in the Town Hall or the Brāhmo Samāj temple were shocked to see this skeleton covered with skin. He could hardly stand. He walked holding to the wall for support. With great difficulty he sat down in front of the couch. In the mean time Sri Ramakrishna had got down from the couch and was sitting on the floor. Keshab bowed low before the Master and remained in that position a long time, touching the Master's feet with his forehead. Then he sat up. Sri Ramakrishna was still in a state of ecstasy. He muttered to himself. He talked to the Divine Mother.

Raising his voice, Keshab said: "I am here, sir. I am here." He took Sri Ramakrishna's left hand and stroked it gently. But the Master was in deep samādhi, completely intoxicated with divine love. A stream of words came from his lips as he talked to himself, and the devotees listened to him spellbound.

MASTER: "As long as a man associates himself with upādhis, so long he sees the manifold, such as Keshab, Prasanna, Amrita, and so on; but on attaining Perfect Knowledge he sees only one Consciousness everywhere. The same Perfect Knowledge, again, makes him realize that the one Consciousness has become the universe and its living beings and the twenty-four cosmic principles. But the manifestations of Divine Power are different in different beings. It is He, undoubtedly, who has become everything; but in some cases there is a greater manifestation than in others.

"Vidyāsāgar once asked me, 'Can it be true that God has endowed some with greater power and some with less?' I replied: 'If that were not so, how is it that one man may be stronger than fifty? If that were not the case, again, how is it that we have all come here to see you?'

"The soul through which God sports is endowed with His special power. The landlord may reside in any part of his estate, but he is generally to be found in a particular drawing-room. The devotee is God's drawing-room. God loves to sport in the heart of His devotee. It is there that His special · power is manifest.

"What is the sign of such a devotee? When you see a man doing great works, you may know that God's special power is manifested through him.

"The Primordial Power and the Supreme Brahman are identical. You can never think of the one without the other. They are like the gem and its brilliance. One cannot think of the brilliance without the gem, or of the gem without its brilliance. Again, it is like the snake and its wriggling motion. One cannot think of the wriggling motion without the snake, or of the snake without its wriggling motion.

"It is the Primordial Power that has become the universe and its living beings and the twenty-four cosmic principles. It is a case of involution and evolution.[1]

"Why do I feel so restless for Rakhal, Narendra, and the other youngsters? Hazra once asked me, 'When will you think of God if you are always anxious about these boys?' (*Keshab and the others smile.*) That worried me greatly. I prayed to the Divine Mother: 'Mother, see what a fix I am in! Hazra scolds me because I worry about these young men.' Afterwards I asked Bholanath about it. He said to me that such a state of mind is described in the *Mahābhārata*. How else will a man established in samādhi occupy his mind in the phenomenal world, after coming down from samādhi? That is why he seeks the company of devotees endowed with sattva. I gave a sigh of relief when Bholanath told me of the *Mahābhārata*.

"Hazra is not to blame. During the period of struggle one should follow the method of discrimination—'Not this, not this'—and direct the whole mind to God. But the state of perfection is quite different. After reaching God one reaffirms what formerly one denied. To extract butter you must separate it from the buttermilk. Then you discover that butter and buttermilk are intrinsically related to one another. They belong to the same stuff. The butter is not essentially different from the buttermilk, nor the buttermilk essentially different from the butter. After realizing God one knows definitely that it is He who has become everything. In some objects He is manifested more clearly, and in others less clearly.

"When a flood comes from the ocean, all the land is deep under water. Before the flood, the boat could have reached the ocean only by following the winding course of the river. But after the flood, one can row straight to the ocean. One need not take a roundabout course. After the harvest has been reaped, one need not take the roundabout course along the balk of the field. One can cross the field at any point.

[1] That is to say, before the creation, the universe and its living beings and the twenty-four cosmic principles lie involved in the Primordial Power, and after the creation these gradually evolve from It.

"After the realization of God, He is seen in all beings. But His greater manifestation is in man. Again, among men, God manifests Himself more clearly in those devotees who are sāttvic, in those who have no desire whatever to enjoy 'woman and gold'. Where can a man of samādhi rest his mind, after coming down from the plane of samādhi? That is why he feels the need of seeking the company of pure-hearted devotees, endowed with sattva and free from attachment to 'woman and gold'. How else could such a person occupy himself in the relative plane of consciousness?

"He who is Brahman is the Ādyāśakti, the Primal Energy. When inactive He is called Brahman, the Purusha; He is called Śakti, or Prakriti, when engaged in creation, preservation, and destruction. These are the two aspects of Reality: Purusha and Prakriti. He who is the Purusha is also Prakriti. Both are the embodiment of Bliss.

"If you are aware of the Male Principle, you cannot ignore the Female Principle. He who is aware of the father must also think of the mother. (Keshab laughs.) He who knows darkness also knows light. He who knows night also knows day. He who knows happiness also knows misery. You understand this, don't you?"

KESHAB: "Yes, sir. I do."

MASTER: "My Mother! Who is my Mother? Ah, She is the Mother of the Universe. It is She who creates and preserves the world, who always protects Her children, and who grants whatever they desire: dharma, artha, kāma, moksha. A true son cannot live away from his mother. The mother knows everything. The child only eats, drinks, and makes merry; he doesn't worry himself about the things of the world."

KESHAB: "Yes, sir. It is quite true."

While talking, Sri Ramakrishna regained the normal consciousness of the world. With a smile on his face he conversed with Keshab. The roomful of men watched them eagerly, and listened to their words. Everybody was amazed to find that neither Keshab nor the Master inquired about each other's health. They talked only of God.

MASTER (to Keshab): "Why do the members of the Brāhmo Samāj dwell so much on God's glories? Is there any great need of repeating such things as 'O God, Thou hast created the moon, the sun, and the stars'? Most people are filled with admiration for the garden only. How few care to see its owner! Who is greater, the garden or its owner?

"After a few drinks at a tavern, do I care to know how many gallons of wine are stored there? One bottle is enough for me.

"When I met Narendra, I never asked him: 'Who is your father? How many houses does he own?'

"Shall I tell you the truth? Man loves his own riches, and so he thinks that God loves His, too. He thinks that God will be pleased if we glorify His riches. Once Sambhu said to me, 'Please bless me, that I may die leaving my riches at the Lotus Feet of God.' I answered: 'These are riches only to you. What riches can you offer God? To Him these are mere dust and straw.'

"Once a thief broke into the temple of Vishnu and robbed the image of its jewels. Mathur Babu and I went to the temple to see what was the matter. Addressing the image, Mathur said bitterly: 'What a shame, Lord! You are so worthless! The thief took all the ornaments from Your body, and You couldn't do a thing about it.' Thereupon I said to Mathur: 'Shame on you! How improper your words are! To God, the jewels you talk so much about are only lumps of clay. Lakshmi, the Goddess of Fortune, is . His Consort. Do you mean to say that He should spend sleepless nights because a thief has taken your few rupees? You mustn't say such things.'

"Can one ever bring God under control through wealth? He can be tamed only through love. What does He want? Certainly not wealth! He wants from His devotees love, devotion, feeling, discrimination, and renunciation.

"One looks on God exactly according to one's own inner feeling. Take, for instance, a devotee with an excess of tamas. He thinks that the Divine Mother eats goat. So he slaughters one for Her. Again, the devotee endowed with rajas cooks rice and various other dishes for the Mother. But the sāttvic devotee doesn't make any outer show of his worship. People don't even know he is worshipping. If he has no flowers, he worships God with mere Ganges water and the leaves of the bel-tree. His food offering to the Deity consists of sweetened puffed rice or a few candies. Occasionally he cooks a little rice pudding for the Deity.

"There is also another class of devotees, those who are beyond the three gunas. They have the nature of a child. Their worship consists in chanting God's name—just His name.

(To Keshab, with a smile) "Why is it that you are ill? There is a reason for it. Many spiritual feelings have passed through your body; therefore it has fallen ill. At the time an emotion is aroused, one understands very little about it. The blow that it delivers to the body is felt only after a long while. I have seen big steamers going by on the Ganges, at the time hardly noticing their passing. But oh, my! What a terrific noise is heard after a while, when the waves splash against the banks! Perhaps a piece of the bank breaks loose and falls into the water.

"An elephant entering a hut creates havoc within and ultimately shakes it down. The elephant of divine emotion enters the hut of this body and shatters it to pieces.

"Do you know what actually happens? When a house is on fire, at first a few things inside burn. Then comes the great commotion. Just so, the fire of Knowledge at first destroys such enemies of spiritual life as passion, anger, and so forth. Then comes the turn of ego. And lastly a violent commotion is seen in the physical frame.

"You may think that everything is going to be over. But God will not release you as long as the slightest trace of your illness is left. You simply cannot leave the hospital if your name is registered there. As long as the illness is not perfectly cured, the doctor won't give you a permit to go. Why did you register your name in the hospital at all?" (All laugh.)

Keshab laughed again and again at the Master's allusion to the hospital. Then Sri Ramakrishna spoke of his own illness. (To Keshab) ."Hriday used to say, 'Never before have I seen such ecstasy for God, and never before have I seen such illness.' I was then seriously ill with stubborn diarrhoea. It was as if millions of ants were gnawing at my brain. But all the same, spiritual talk went on day and night. Dr. Rama of Natagore was called in to see me. He found me discussing spiritual truth. 'What a mad-man!' he said. 'Nothing is left of him but a few bones, and still he is reasoning like that!' "

MASTER (to Keshab): "All depends on God's will.

> O Mother, all is done after Thine own sweet will;
> Thou art in truth self-willed, Redeemer of mankind!
> Thou workest Thine own work; men only call it theirs.

"In order to take full advantage of the dew, the gardener removes the soil from the Basra rose down to the very root. The plant thrives better on account of the moisture. Perhaps that is why you too are being shaken to the very root. (Keshab and the Master laugh.) It may be that you will do tremendous things when you come back.

"Whenever I hear that you are ill I become extremely restless. After hearing of your last illness I used to weep to the Divine Mother in the small hours of the morning. I prayed to Her, 'O Mother, if anything happens to Keshab, with whom, then, shall I talk in Calcutta?' Coming to Calcutta, I offered fruits and sweets to the Divine Mother with a prayer for your well-being."

The devotees were deeply touched to hear of Sri Ramakrishna's love for Keshab and his longing for the Brāhmo leader.

MASTER: "But this time, to tell the truth, I didn't feel anxious to that extent. Only for two or three days did I feel a little worried."

Keshab's venerable mother came to the east door of the room, the same door through which Keshab had entered. Umanath said aloud to the Master, "Sir, here is mother saluting you."

Sri Ramakrishna smiled. Umanath said again, "Mother asks you to bless Keshab that he may be cured of his illness."

MASTER (to Keshab's mother): "Please pray to the Divine Mother, who is the Bestower of all bliss. She will take away your troubles.

(To Keshab) "Don't spend long hours in the inner apartments. You will sink down and down in the company of women. You will feel better if you hear only talk of God."

The Master uttered these words in a serious voice and then began to laugh like a boy. He said to Keshab, "Let me see your hand." He weighed it playfully, like a child. At last he said: "No, your hand is light. Hypocrites have heavy hands." (All laugh.)

Umanath again said to the Master from the door, "Mother asks you to bless Keshab."

MASTER (gravely): "What can I do? God alone blesses all. 'Thou workest Thine own work; men only call it theirs.'

"God laughs on two occasions. He laughs when two brothers divide land between them. They put a string across the land and say to each other, 'This side is mine, and that side is yours.' God laughs and says to Himself, 'Why, this whole universe is Mine; and about a little clod they say, "This side is mine, and that side is yours"!'

"God laughs again when the physician says to the mother weeping bitterly because of her child's desperate illness: 'Don't be afraid, mother. I shall cure your child.' The physician does not know that no one can save the child if God wills that he should die." (*All are silent.*)

Just then Keshab was seized with a fit of coughing, which lasted for a long time. The sight of his suffering made everyone sad. He became exhausted and could stay no longer. He bowed low before the Master and left the room, holding to the wall as before.

Some refreshments had been arranged for the Master. Keshab's eldest son was seated near him. Amrita introduced the boy and requested Sri Ramakrishna to bless him. The Master said, "It is not given to me to bless anyone." With a sweet smile he stroked the boy's body gently.

AMRITA (*with a smile*): "All right, then do as you please."

MASTER (*to the devotees*): "I cannot say such a thing as 'May you be healed.' I never ask the Divine Mother to give me the power of healing. I pray to Her only for pure love.

"Is Keshab a small person? He is respected by all, seekers after wealth as well as holy men. Once I visited Dayananda, who was then staying at a garden house. I saw he was extremely anxious about Keshab's coming; he went out every few minutes to see whether he had arrived. I learnt later on that Keshab had made an appointment with him that day. Keshab, I understood, had no faith in the sacrifices and the deities mentioned in the Vedas. Referring to this, Dayananda said: 'Why, the Lord has created so many things. Could He not make deities as well?'"

Continuing, the Master said: "Keshab is free from the pride of a small-minded religious teacher. To many people he has said, 'If you have any doubts, go there[2] to have them solved.' It is my way, too, to say: 'What shall I do with people's respect? Let Keshab's virtues increase a millionfold.' Keshab is certainly a great man. Everyone respects him, seekers after wealth as well as holy men." Thus did Sri Ramakrishna praise Keshab before the latter's disciples.

After partaking of the refreshments the Master was ready to leave. The Brāhmo devotees accompanied him to the cab, which was standing in the street. While coming down the stairs the Master noticed that there was no light on the ground floor. He said to Amrita and Keshab's other disciples: "These places should be well lighted. A house without light becomes stricken with poverty. Please see that it doesn't happen again."

Then Sri Ramakrishna left for Dakshineswar with one or two devotees.

On his way to Dakshineswar from Keshab's cottage Sri Ramakrishna stopped at Jaygopal Sen's house. It was about seven o'clock in the evening.

[2] To Sri Ramakrishna.

In the drawing-room Jaygopal's relatives and neighbours had gathered. Vaikuntha, Jaygopal's brother, said to the Master: "Sir, we are worldly people. Please give us some advice."

MASTER: "Do your duty to the world after knowing God. With one hand hold to the Lotus Feet of the Lord and with the other do your work."

VAIKUNTHA: "Is the world unreal?"

MASTER: "Yes, it is unreal as long as one has not realized God. Through ignorance man forgets God and speaks always of 'I' and 'mine'. He sinks down and down, entangled in māyā, deluded by 'woman and gold'. Māyā robs him of his knowledge to such an extent that he cannot find the way of escape, though such a way exists.

"Listen to a song:

> When such delusion veils the world, through Mahāmāyā's spell,
> That Brahmā is bereft of sense
> And Vishnu loses consciousness,
> What hope is left for men? . . .

"You all know from your experience how impermanent the world is. Look at it this way. How many people have come into the world and again passed away! People are born and they die. This moment the world is and the next it is not. It is impermanent. Those you think to be your very own will not exist for you when you close your eyes in death. Again, you see people who have no immediate relatives, and yet for the sake of a grandson they will not go to Benares to lead a holy life. 'Oh, what will become of my Haru then?' they argue.

> The narrow channel first is made, and there the trap is set;
> But open though the passage lies,
> The fish, once safely through the gate,
> Do not come out again.

> Yet even though a way leads forth,
> Encased within its own cocoon,
> The worm remains to die.

This kind of world is illusory and impermanent."

A NEIGHBOUR: "Why, sir, should one hold to God with one hand and to the world with the other? Why should one even stretch out one hand to hold to the world, if it is impermanent?"

MASTER: "The world is not impermanent if one lives there after knowing God. Listen to another song:

> O mind, you do not know how to farm!
> Fallow lies the field of your life.
> If you had only worked it well,
> How rich a harvest you might reap!
> Hedge it about with Kāli's name
> If you would keep your harvest safe;
> This is the stoutest hedge of all,
> For Death himself cannot come near it. . . .

"Did you listen to the song?

> Hedge it about with Kāli's name
> If you would keep your harvest safe.

Surrender yourself to God and you will achieve everything.

> This is the stoutest hedge of all,
> For Death himself cannot come near it.

"Yes, it is a strong hedge indeed. If you but realize God, you won't see the world as unsubstantial. He who has realized God knows that God Himself has become the world and all living beings. When you feed your child, you should feel that you are feeding God. You should look on your father and mother as veritable manifestations of God and the Divine Mother, and serve them as such. If a man enters the world after realizing God, he does not generally keep up physical relations with his wife. Both of them are devotees; they love to talk only of God and pass their time in spiritual conversation. They serve other devotees of God, for they know that God alone has become all living beings; and, knowing this, they devote their lives to the service of others."

NEIGHBOUR: "But, sir, such a husband and wife are not to be found anywhere."

MASTER: "Yes, they can be found, though they may be very rare. Worldly people cannot recognize them. In order to lead such a life both husband and wife must be spiritual. It is possible to lead such a life if both of them have tasted the Bliss of God. God's special grace is necessary to create such a couple; otherwise there will always be misunderstanding between them. In that case the one has to leave the other. Life becomes very miserable if husband and wife do not agree. The wife will say to her husband day and night: 'Why did my father marry me to such a person? I can't get enough to eat or to feed my children. I haven't clothes enough to cover my body or to give to my children. I haven't received a single piece of jewelry from you. How happy you have made me! Ah! You keep your eyes closed and mutter the name of God! Now do give up all these crazy ideas.'"

DEVOTEE: "There are such obstacles, certainly. Besides, the children may be disobedient. There is no end of difficulties. Now, sir, what is the way?"

MASTER: "It is extremely difficult to practise spiritual discipline and at the same time lead a householder's life. There are many handicaps: disease, grief, poverty, misunderstanding with one's wife, and disobedient, stupid, and stubborn children. I don't have to give you a list of them.

"But still there is a way out. One should pray to God, going now and then into solitude, and make efforts to realize Him."

NEIGHBOUR: "Must one leave home then?"

MASTER: "No, not altogether. Whenever you have leisure, go into solitude for a day or two. At that time don't have any relations with the outside world and don't hold any conversation with worldly people on worldly affairs. You must live either in solitude or in the company of holy men."

NEIGHBOUR: "How can one recognize a holy man?"

MASTER: "He who has surrendered his body, mind, and innermost self to God is surely a holy man. He who has renounced 'woman and gold' is surely a holy man. He is a holy man who does not regard woman with the eyes of a worldly person. He never forgets to look upon a woman as his mother, and to offer her his worship if he happens to be near her. The holy man constantly thinks of God and does not indulge in any talk except about spiritual things. Furthermore, he serves all beings, knowing that God resides in everybody's heart. These, in general, are the signs of a holy man."

NEIGHBOUR: "Must one always live in solitude?"

MASTER: "Haven't you seen the trees on the foot-path along a street? They are fenced around as long as they are very young; otherwise cattle destroy them. But there is no longer any need of fences when their trunks grow thick and strong. Then they won't break even if an elephant is tied to them. Just so, there will be no need for you to worry and fear if you make your mind as strong as a thick tree-trunk. First of all try to acquire discrimination. Break the jack-fruit open only after you have rubbed your hands with oil; then its sticky milk won't smear them."

NEIGHBOUR: "What is discrimination?"

MASTER: "Discrimination is the reasoning by which one knows that God alone is real and all else is unreal. Real means eternal, and unreal means impermanent. He who has acquired discrimination knows that God is the only Substance and all else is non-existent. With the awakening of this spirit of discrimination a man wants to know God. On the contrary, if a man loves the unreal—such things as creature comforts, name, fame, and wealth—, then he doesn't want to know God, who is of the very nature of Reality. Through discrimination between the Real and the unreal one seeks to know God.

"Listen to a song:

> Come, let us go for a walk, O mind, to Kāli, the Wish-fulfilling
>   Tree,
> And there beneath It gather the four fruits of life.
> Of your two wives, Dispassion and Worldliness,
> Bring along Dispassion only, on your way to the Tree,
> And ask her son Discrimination about the Truth. . . .

"By turning the mind within oneself one acquires discrimination, and through discrimination one thinks of Truth. Then the mind feels the desire to 'go for a walk to Kāli, the Wish-fulfilling Tree.' Reaching that Tree, that is to say, going near to God, you can without any effort gather four fruits, namely, dharma, artha, kāma, and moksha. Yes, after realizing God, one can also get, if one so desires, dharma, artha, and kāma, which are necessary for leading the worldly life."

NEIGHBOUR: "Then why should one call the world māyā?"

MASTER: "As long as one has not realized God, one should renounce the world, following the process of 'Neti, neti'. But he who has attained God knows that it is God who has become all this. Then he sees that

God, māyā, living beings, and the universe form one whole. God includes the universe and its living beings. Suppose you have separated the shell, flesh, and seeds of a bel-fruit and someone asks you the weight of the fruit. Will you leave aside the shell and the seeds, and weigh only the flesh? Not at all. To know the real weight of the fruit, you must weigh the whole of it—the shell, the flesh, and the seeds. Only then can you tell its real weight. The shell may be likened to the universe, and the seeds to living beings. While one is engaged in discrimination one says to oneself that the universe and the living beings are non-Self and unsubstantial. At that time one thinks of the flesh alone as the substance, and the shell and seeds as unsubstantial. But after discrimination is over, one feels that all three parts of the fruit together form a unity. Then one further realizes that the stuff that has produced the flesh of the fruit has also produced the shell and seeds. To know the real nature of the bel-fruit one must know all three.

"It is the process of evolution and involution. The world, after its dissolution, remains involved in God; and God, at the time of creation, evolves as the world. Butter goes with buttermilk, and buttermilk goes with butter. If there is a thing called buttermilk, then butter also exists; and if there is a thing called butter, then buttermilk also exists. If the Self exists, then the non-Self must also exist.

"The phenomenal world belongs to that very Reality to which the Absolute belongs; again, the Absolute belongs to that very Reality to which the phenomenal world belongs. He who is realized as God has also become the universe and its living beings. One who knows the Truth knows that it is He alone who has become father and mother, child and neighbour, man and animal, good and bad, holy and unholy, and so forth."

NEIGHBOUR: "Then is there no virtue and no sin?"

MASTER: "They both exist and do not exist. If God keeps the ego in a man, then He keeps in him the sense of differentiation and also the sense of virtue and sin. But in a rare few He completely effaces the ego, and these go beyond virtue and sin, good and bad. As long as a man has not realized God, he retains the sense of differentiation and the knowledge of good and bad. You may say: 'Virtue and sin are the same to me. I am doing only as God bids me.' But you know in your heart of hearts that those are mere words. No sooner do you commit an evil deed than you feel a palpitation in your heart. Even after God has been realized, He keeps in the mind of the devotee, if He so desires, the feeling of the 'servant ego'. In that state the devotee says, 'O God, Thou art the Master and I am Thy servant.' Such a devotee enjoys only spiritual talk and spiritual deeds. He does not enjoy the company of ungodly people. He does not care for any work that is not of a holy nature. So you see that God keeps the sense of differentiation even in such a devotee."

NEIGHBOUR: "You ask us, sir, to live in the world after knowing God. Can God really be known?"

MASTER: "God cannot be known by the sense-organs or by this mind;

but He can be known by the pure mind, the mind that is free from worldly desires."

NEIGHBOUR: "Who can know God?"

MASTER: "Right. Who can really know Him? But as for us, it is enough to know as much of Him as we need. What need have I of a whole well of water? One jar is more than enough for me. An ant went to a sugar hill. Did it need the entire hill? A grain or two of sugar was more than enough."

NEIGHBOUR: "Sir, we are like typhoid patients. How can we be satisfied with one jar of water? We feel like knowing the whole of God."

MASTER: "That's true. But there is also medicine for typhoid."

NEIGHBOUR: "What is that medicine, sir?"

MASTER: "The company of holy men, repeating the name of God and singing His glories, and unceasing prayer. I prayed to the Divine Mother: 'Mother, I don't seek knowledge. Here, take Thy knowledge, take Thy ignorance. Give me only pure love for Thy Lotus Feet.' I didn't ask for anything else.

"As is the disease, so must the remedy be. The Lord says in the *Gītā*: 'O Arjuna, take refuge in Me. I shall deliver you from all sins.' Take shelter at His feet. He will give you right understanding. He will take entire responsibility for you. Then you will get rid of the typhoid. Can one ever know God with such a mind as this? Can one pour four seers of milk into a one-seer pot? Can we ever know God unless He lets us know Him? Therefore I say, take shelter in God. Let Him do whatever He likes. He is self-willed. What power is there in a man?"

WITH THE DEVOTEES AT
DAKSHINESWAR (II)

SRI RAMAKRISHNA was seated on the small couch in his room with Adhar, Manomohan, Rakhal, M., Harish, and other devotees. It was about two o'clock in the afternoon. The Master was describing to them the exalted state of Sri Chaitanya.

MASTER: "Chaitanya experienced three states of mind. First, the conscious state, when his mind dwelt on the gross and the subtle. Second, the semi-conscious state, when his mind entered the causal body and was absorbed in the bliss of divine intoxication. Third, the inmost state, when his mind was merged in the Great Cause.

"This agrees very well with the five koshas, or 'sheaths', described in the Vedanta. The gross body corresponds to the annamayakosha and the pranamayakosha, the subtle body to the manomayakosha and the vijnanamayakosha, and the causal body to the anandamayakosha. The Mahakarana, the Great Cause, is beyond the five sheaths. When Chaitanya's mind merged in That, he would go into samadhi. This is called the nirvikalpa or jada samadhi.

"While conscious of the outer world, Chaitanya sang the name of God; while in the state of partial consciousness, he danced with the devotees; and while in the inmost state of consciousness, he remained absorbed in samadhi."

M. (to himself): "Is the Master hinting at the different states of his own mind? There is much similarity between Chaitanya and the Master."

MASTER: "Chaitanya was Divine Love incarnate. He came down to earth to teach people how to love God. One achieves everything when one loves God. There is no need of hathayoga."

A DEVOTEE: "Sir, what is hathayoga like?"

MASTER: "A man practising hathayoga dwells a great deal on his body. He washes his intestines by means of a bamboo tube through his anus. He draws ghee and milk through his sexual organ. He learns how to manipulate his tongue by performing exercises. He sits in a fixed posture and now and then levitates. All these are actions of prana. A magician was performing his feats when his tongue turned up and clove to the roof of his mouth.

Immediately his body became motionless. People thought he was dead. He was buried and remained many years in the grave. After a long time the grave somehow broke open. Suddenly the man regained consciousness of the world and cried out, 'Come delusion! Come confusion!'[1] (*All laugh.*) All these are actions of prāna.

"The Vedāntists do not accept hathayoga. There is also rājayoga. Rājayoga describes how to achieve union with God through the mind—by means of discrimination and bhakti. This yoga is good. Hathayoga is not good. The life of a man in the Kaliyuga is dependent on food."

Sri Ramakrishna was standing in the road by the side of the nahabat. He was on his way to his room, having come from the pine-grove. He saw M. seated on the verandah of the nahabat, behind the fence, absorbed in meditation.

MASTER: "Hello! You are here? You will get results very soon. If you practise a little, then someone will come forward to help you."

M. looked up at the Master, startled; he remained sitting on the floor.

MASTER: "The time is ripe for you. The mother bird does not break the shell of the egg until the right time arrives. What I told you is indeed your Ideal."

Sri Ramakrishna again mentioned to M. his spiritual Ideal.

MASTER: "It is not necessary for all to practise great austerity. But I went through great suffering. I used to lie on the ground with my head resting on a mound for a pillow. I hardly noticed the passing of the days. I only called on God and wept, 'O Mother! O Mother!'"

M. had been visiting Sri Ramakrishna for the past two years. Since he had been educated along English lines, he had acquired a fondness for Western philosophy and science, and had liked to hear Keshab and other scholars lecture. Sri Ramakrishna would address him now and then as the "Englishman". Since coming to Sri Ramakrishna, M. had lost all relish for lectures and for books written by English scholars. The only thing that appealed to him now was to see the Master day and night, and hear the words that fell from his blessed lips. M. constantly dwelt on certain of Sri Ramakrishna's sayings. The Master had said, "One can certainly see God through the practice of spiritual discipline", and again, "The vision of God is the only goal of human life."

MASTER (*to M.*): "If you practise only a little, someone will come forward to tell you the right path. Observe the ekādaśi.

"You are my very own, my relative; otherwise, why should you come here so frequently? While listening to the kirtan, I had a vision of Rakhal in the midst of Sri Krishna's companions in Vrindāvan. Narendra belongs to a very high level. Hirananda[2] too; how childlike his nature is! What a sweet disposition he has! I want to see him too.

[1] Magicians, while performing their feats, cry in this way in order to cast a spell on the spectators.

[2] A devotee of the Master from Sindh.

"Once I saw the companions of Chaitanya, not in a trance but with these very eyes. Formerly I was in such an exalted state of mind that I could see all these things with my naked eyes; but now I see them in samādhi. I saw the companions of Chaitanya with these naked eyes. I think I saw you there, and Balaram too. You must have noticed that when I see certain people I jump up with a start. Do you know why? A man feels that way when he sees his own people after a long time.

"I used to pray to the Mother, crying: 'Mothei, if I do not find the devotees I'll surely die. Please bring them to me immediately.' In those days whatever desire arose in my mind would come to pass. I planted a tulsi-grove in the Panchavati in order to practise japa and meditation. I wanted very much to fence it around with bamboo sticks. Soon afterwards a bundle of bamboo sticks and some string were carried by the flood-tide of the Ganges right in front of the Panchavati. A temple servant noticed them and joyfully told me.

"In that state of divine exaltation I could no longer perform the formal worship. 'Mother,' I said, 'who will look after me? I haven't the power to take care of myself. I want to listen only to talk about Thee. I want to feed Thy devotees. I want to give a little help to those whom I chance to meet. How will all that be possible, Mother? Give me a rich man to stand by me.' That is why Mathur Babu did so much to serve me.

"I said further, 'Certainly I shall not have any children, Mother. But it is my desire that a boy with sincere love for God should always remain with me. Give me such a boy.' That is the reason Rakhal came here. Those whom I think of as my own are part and parcel of me."

The Master started again for the Panchavati accompanied by M. No one else was with them. Sri Ramakrishna with a smile narrated to him various incidents of the past years of his life.

MASTER: "You see, one day I saw a strange figure covering the whole space from the Kāli temple to the Panchavati. Do you believe this?"

M. remained silent with wonder. He plucked one or two leaves from a branch in the Panchavati and put them in his pocket.

MASTER: "See there—that branch has been broken. I used to sit under it."

M: "I took a young twig from that tree—I have it at home."

MASTER (with a smile): "Why?"

M: "I feel happy when I look at it. After all this is over, this place will be considered very holy."

MASTER (smiling): "What kind of holy place? Like Pānihāti?"

Almost every year, for some time past, the Master had been attending the religious festival at Pānihāti.

It was evening. Sri Ramakrishna was sitting on the small couch in his room, absorbed in meditation on the Divine Mother. The evening worship in the temples began, with the music of gong and conch-shell. M. was going to spend the night with the Master.

After a time Sri Ramakrishna asked M. to read from the *Bhaktamāla*, a book about the Vaishnava saints.

M. read:

There was a king named Jayamal who loved Krishna with all his heart. He followed with unfailing devotion all the rites and ceremonies associated with the adoration of Krishna, whom he worshipped under the name of Śyāmalasundara. Completely satisfied with his own Ideal Deity, he never directed his attention to any other god or goddess. One of the inflexible rules of his devotions was to worship the Deity daily till almost midday. He would never deviate from this practice, even at the risk of his wealth or his kingdom. Learning this secret, an enemy king invaded the kingdom during the morning hours. Jayamal's soldiers could not fight without his command; so they watched the invasion silently. Slowly the enemy surrounded the moat of the capital; yet Jayamal did not come out of his shrine room. His mother came to him and wept bitterly, trying to persuade the king to fight. He said to her calmly: "Why are you worried? Śyāmalasundara gave me this kingdom. What can I do if He has decided to take it away? On the other hand, none will be able to do me harm if He protects me. Our own efforts are vain!"

And actually, in the mean time, Śyāmalasundara, the Deity Himself, had taken the king's horse from the stable and had ridden fully armed to the field. Alone He faced the hostile king and alone destroyed his army. Having crushed the enemy forces, the Deity returned to the temple and fastened the horse near by.

Jayamal, on completing his worship, came out and discovered the horse there, panting and covered with sweat. "Who has been riding my horse?" he demanded. "Who brought it to the temple?" The officers declared they knew nothing about it. In a pensive mood the king proceeded to the battle-field with his army and there found the enemy, with the exception of its leader, lying dead. He was staring uncomprehendingly at the scene, when the enemy king approached, worshipped him, and said: "Please permit me to tell you something. How could I fight? You have a warrior who could conquer the entire world. I do not want your wealth or your kingdom; indeed, I will gladly give you my own, if you will tell me about that Blue Warrior, your friend. No sooner did I turn my eyes on him than he cast a spell on my heart and soul."

Jayamal then realized it had been none other than Śyāmalasundara that had appeared on the battle-field. The enemy king understood too. He worshipped Jayamal and through his blessings received Krishna's grace.

MASTER: "Do you believe all that? Do you believe Krishna rode on that horse and killed Jayamal's enemies?"

M: "I believe that Jayamal, Krishna's devotee, prayed to Him with a yearning heart. But I don't know whether the enemy really saw Him coming to the battle-field on a horse. Krishna might have come there riding the horse, but I do not know whether they really saw Him."

MASTER (*with a smile*): "The book contains nice stories about devotees. But it is one-sided. Also, it abuses those who differ with its views."

The following morning the Master and M. were talking in the garden.
M: "Then I shall stay here."

MASTER: "Well, you all come here so often. What does it mean? People visit a holy man once at the most. But you all come here so often. What is the significance of that?"

M. remained silent. The Master himself gave the reply.

MASTER: "Could you come here unless you belonged to my inner circle? That means you all are my own relatives, my own people—like father and son, brother and sister.

"I do not tell you everything. If I did, would you come here any more?

"Once Śukadeva went to Janaka to be instructed in the Knowledge of Brahman. Janaka said, 'First give me my fee.' 'But', said Śukadeva, 'why should I give you the fee before receiving the instruction?' Janaka laughed and said: 'Will you be conscious of guru and disciple after attaining Brahma-jñāna? That is why I asked you to give me the fee first.' "

It was night. The moon rose, flooding all the quarters with its silvery light. M. was walking alone in the garden of the temple. On one side of the path stood the Panchavati, the bakul-grove, the nahabat, and the Master's room, and on the other side flowed the Ganges, reflecting millions of broken moons on its rippling surface.

M. said to himself: "Can one really see God? The Master says it is possible. He says that, if one makes a little effort, then someone comes forward and shows the way. Well, I am married. I have children. Can one realize God in spite of all that?"

M. reflected awhile and continued his soliloquy: "Surely one can. Otherwise, why should the Master say so? Why shouldn't it be possible through the grace of God?

"Here is the world around me—the sun, moon, stars, living beings, and the twenty-four cosmic principles. How did they come into existence? Who is their Creator? What am I to Him? Life is indeed vain without this knowledge.

"Sri Ramakrishna is certainly the best of men. In all my life I have not seen another great soul like him. He must have seen God. Otherwise, how could he talk with God day and night, addressing Him so intimately as 'Mother'? Otherwise, how could he love God so intimately? Such is his love for God that he forgets the outer world. He goes into samādhi and remains like a lifeless thing. Again, in the ecstasy of that love, he laughs and cries and dances and sings."

Friday, December 14, 1883

At nine o'clock in the morning Sri Ramakrishna was standing on the southeast verandah near the door of his room, with Ramlal by his side. Rakhal and Latu were moving about. M. arrived and prostrated himself before the Master. Sri Ramakrishna said to him affectionately: "You have come. That's very good. Today is an auspicious day."

It was the last day of the Bengali month and the day of the full moon. M. was going to spend a few days with the Master practising spiritual discipline. The Master had said to him, "If an aspirant practises a little spiritual discipline, then someone comes forward to help him."

The Master had said to M: "You should not eat every day at the guest-house of the Kāli temple. The guest-house is intended to supply free food to monks and the destitute. Bring your own cook with you." M. had accordingly done so. The Master arranged a place for the man to cook and he asked Ramlal to speak to the milkman about milk.

A little later Ramlal began to read from the *Adhyātma Rāmāyana*. The Master and M. listened while he read:

> Rāma had married Sītā after breaking the great bow of Śiva. On the way to Ayodhyā with His bride, Rāma was confronted by the warrior sage Paraśurāma, who was about to make trouble for Him. Paraśurāma threw a bow at Rāma and challenged Him to string it. Daśaratha, Rāma's father, was seized with fear. With a smile, Rāma took the bow in His left hand and strung it. Then, twanging the bow-string, He fixed an arrow and asked Paraśurāma where to shoot it. That curbed the pride of the warrior sage. Prostrating himself before Rāma, Paraśurāma worshipped Him as the Supreme Brahman.

As Sri Ramakrishna listened to Paraśurāma's hymn, he went into a spiritual mood and now and then chanted the name of Rāma in his melodious voice.

Then the Master asked Ramlal to read about Guhaka. Ramlal read:

> Guhaka, the pariah, was chief of the untouchables and an intimate friend of Rāma. When Rāma, Sītā, and Lakshmana were starting into the forest to redeem Daśaratha's pledge, Guhaka ferried them across the river. Rāma embraced Guhaka tenderly and told him He was going to spend fourteen years in exile, wearing the bark of trees and eating the herbs, fruits, and roots that grew in the woods. He promised to visit Guhaka again on His way back to Ayodhyā after the period of exile was over. The pariah king waited patiently. But when the fourteenth year had run out and Rāma had not returned, Guhaka lighted a funeral pyre. He was on the point of entering it when Hanumān arrived as Rāma's messenger. In a celestial chariot Rāma and Sītā soon appeared, and Guhaka's joy was unbounded.

After the midday meal Sri Ramakrishna lay down on his bed to rest. M. was seated on the floor. Presently Dr. Shyama and a few devotees arrived. The Master sat up on the bed and began to converse with them.

MASTER: "It is by no means necessary for a man always to be engaged in his duties. Actions drop away when one realizes God, as the flower drops of itself when the fruit appears.

"He who has realized God no longer performs religious duties such as the sandhyā. In his case the sandhyā merges in the Gāyatri. When that happens, it is enough for a person to repeat just the Gāyatri mantra. Then the Gāyatri merges in Om. After that one no longer chants even the Gāyatri; it is enough then to chant simply Om. How long should a man practise such devotions as the sandhyā? As long as he does not feel a thrill in his body and shed tears of joy while repeating the name of Rāma or of Hari. People worship God to win money or a lawsuit. That is not good."

A DEVOTEE: "We find that everyone strives after money. Even Keshab Sen married his daughter to a prince."

MASTER: "Keshab's case is quite different. God provides everything for a genuine devotee, even without his making any effort. The son of a real king gets his monthly allowance. I am not talking of lawyers and men of that sort, who go through suffering in order to earn money, and who become slaves of others to that end. I am speaking of a real prince. A true devotee has no desire. He does not care for money. Money comes to him of itself. The Gītā describes such a devotee as 'content with what comes to him without effort'. A good brāhmin, without any personal motive, can accept food even from the house of an untouchable. He does not desire it; it comes of its own accord."

A DEVOTEE: "Sir, how should one live in the world?"

MASTER: "Live in the world as the mudfish lives in the mud. One develops love of God by going away from the world into solitude, now and then, and meditating on God. After that one can live in the world unattached. The mud is there, and the fish has to live in it, but its body is not stained by the mud. Such a man can lead the life of a householder in a spirit of detachment."

The Master noticed that M. was listening to his words with great attention.

MASTER (looking at M.): "One can realize God if one feels intense dispassion for worldly things. A man with such dispassion feels that the world is like a forest on fire. He regards his wife and children as a deep well. If he really feels that kind of dispassion, he renounces home and family. It is not enough for him to live in the world in a spirit of detachment.

"'Woman and gold' alone is māyā. If māyā is once recognized, it feels ashamed of itself and takes to flight. A man put on a tiger skin and tried to frighten another man. But the latter said: 'Ah! I have recognized you! You are our Hare.' At that the man dressed in the skin went away smiling to frighten someone else.

"All women are the embodiments of Śakti. It is the Primal Power that has become women and appears to us in the form of women. It is said in the Adhyātma Rāmāyana that Nārada and others praised Rāma, saying: 'O Rāma, Thou alone art all that we see as male, and Sītā, all that we see as female. Thou art Indra, and Sītā is Indrāni; Thou art Śiva, and Sītā is Śivāni: Thou art man, and Sītā is woman. What more need I say? Thou alone dost exist wherever there is a male, and Sītā wherever there is a female.'

(To the devotees) "One cannot renounce by the mere wish. There are prārabdha karma—inherited tendencies—and the like. Once a yogi said to a king, 'Live with me in the forest and think of God.' The king replied: 'That I cannot very well do. I could live with you, but I still have the desire for enjoyment. If I live in this forest, perhaps I shall create a kingdom even here. I still have desires.'

"Natabar Panja used to look after his cows in this garden during his boyhood. He had many desires. Hence he has established a castor-oil factory and earned a great deal of money. He has a prosperous castor-oil business at Ālambāzār.

"There is one sect that prescribes spiritual discipline in company with women. I was once taken to the women belonging to the Kartābhajā sect. They all sat around me. I addressed them as 'mother'. At that they whispered among themselves: 'He is still a pravartaka. He doesn't know the way.' According to that sect the pravartaka is the beginner. Then comes the sādhaka, the struggling aspirant, and last of all the siddha of the siddha, the supremely perfect. A woman walked over to Vaishnavcharan and sat near him. Asked about it, he answered, 'She feels just like a young girl.' One quickly strays from the religious path by looking on woman as wife. But to regard her as mother is a pure attitude."

Some of the devotees took leave of the Master, saying that they were going to visit the temple of Kāli and several of the other temples.

M. went walking alone in the Panchavati and other places in the temple garden. He thought about the Master's assurance that God can be easily realized, and about his exhortation to lead a life of intense renunciation, and his saying that māyā, when recognized, takes to flight.

At half past three in the afternoon M. again entered the Master's room and sat on the floor. A teacher from the Broughton Institution had come with several students to pay a visit to Sri Ramakrishna. They were conversing together. Now and then the teacher asked questions. The conversation was about the worship of images.

MASTER (to the teacher): "What is wrong with image worship? The Vedānta says that Brahman manifests Itself where there is 'Existence, Light, and Love'. Therefore nothing exists but Brahman.

"How long do small girls play with their dolls? As long as they are not married and do not live with their husbands. After marriage they put the dolls away in a box. What further need is there of worshipping the image after the vision of God?"

The Master glanced at M. and said: "One attains God when one feels yearning for Him. An intense restlessness is needed. Through it the whole mind goes to God.

"A man had a daughter who became a widow when she was very young. She had never known her husband. She noticed the husbands of other girls and said one day to her father, 'Where is my husband?' The father replied: 'Govinda[3] is your husband. He will come to you if you call Him.' At these words the girl went to her room, closed the door, and cried to Govinda, saying: 'O Govinda, come to me! Show Yourself to me! Why don't You come?' God could not resist the girl's piteous cry and appeared before her.

"One must have childlike faith—and the intense yearning that a child

[3] A name of Krishna.

feels to see its mother. That yearning is like the red sky in the east at dawn. After such a sky the sun must rise. Immediately after that yearning one sees God.

"Let me tell you the story of a boy named Jatila. He used to walk to school through the woods, and the journey frightened him. One day he told his mother of his fear. She replied: 'Why should you be afraid? Call Madhusudana.'[4] 'Mother,' asked the boy, 'who is Madhusudana?' The mother said, 'He is your Elder Brother.' One day after this, when the boy again felt afraid in the woods, he cried out, 'O Brother Madhusudana!' But there was no response. He began to weep aloud: 'Where are You, Brother Madhusudana? Come to me. I am afraid.' Then God could no longer stay away. He appeared before the boy and said: 'Here I am. Why are you frightened?' And so saying He took the boy out of the woods and showed him the way to school. When He took leave of the boy, God said: 'I will come whenever you call Me. Do not be afraid.' One must have this faith of a child, this yearning.

"A brāhmin used to worship his Family Deity daily with food offerings. One day he had to go away on business. As he was about to leave the house, he said to his young son: 'Give the offering to the Deity today. See that God is fed.' The boy offered food in the shrine, but the image remained silent on the altar. It would neither talk nor eat. The boy waited a long time, but still the image did not move. But the boy firmly believed that God would come down from His throne, sit on the floor, and partake of the food. Again and again he prayed to the Deity, saying: 'O Lord, come down and eat the food. It is already very late. I cannot sit here any longer.' But the image did not utter a word. The boy burst into tears and cried: 'O Lord, my father asked me to feed You. Why won't You come down? Why won't You eat from my hands?' The boy wept for some time with a longing soul. At last the Deity, smiling, came down from the altar and sat before the meal and ate it. After feeding the Deity, the boy came out of the shrine room. His relatives said: 'The worship is over. Now bring away the offering.' 'Yes,' said the boy, 'the worship is over. But God has eaten everything.' 'How is that?' asked the relatives. The boy replied innocently, 'Why, God has eaten the food.' They entered the shrine and were speechless with wonder to see that the Deity had really eaten every bit of the offering."

Late in the afternoon Sri Ramakrishna was talking to M. They were standing on the south side of the nahabat. Since it was winter the Master was wrapped in his woolen shawl.

MASTER: "Where will you sleep? In the hut in the Panchavati?"

M: "Won't they let me have the room on the upper floor of the nahabat?"

M. selected the nahabat because he had a poetic temperament. From there he could see the sky, the Ganges, the moonlight, and the flowers in the garden.

MASTER: "Oh, they'll let you have it. But I suggested the Panchavati

---

[4] A name of Krishna.

because so much contemplation and meditation have been practised[5] there
and the name of God has been chanted there so often."

It was evening. Incense was burning in the Master's room. He was sitting
on the small couch, absorbed in meditation. M. was sitting on the floor with
Rakhal, Latu, and Ramlal.

The Master said to M., "The sum and substance of the whole thing is to
cultivate devotion for God and love Him." At Sri Ramakrishna's request
Ramlal sang a few songs, the Master himself singing the first line of each.

Ramlal sang:

> Oh, what a vision I have beheld in Keshab Bhārati's hut!
> Gorā, in all his matchless grace,
> Shedding tears in a thousand streams!
> Like a mad elephant
> He dances in ecstasy and sings,
> Drunk with an overwhelming love. . . .

Then he sang:

> Though I[6] am never loath to grant salvation,
> I hesitate indeed to grant pure love.
> Whoever wins pure love surpasses all;
> He is adored by men;
> He triumphs over the three worlds. . . .

Sri Ramakrishna said to Ramlal, "Sing that one—'Gaur and Nitāi, ye
blessed brothers'." Ramlal began the song and the Master joined him:

> Gaur and Nitāi, ye blessed brothers!
> I have heard how kind you are,
> And therefore I have come to you.
> When I visited Benares,
> Śiva, Lord of Kāśi, told me
> Of the Parabrahman's birth,
> As man, in Mother Sachi's home.
> O Brahman, Thee I recognize!
> Many a sādhu have I seen,
> But never one so kind as you.

> Once at Braja you were born
> As Kānāi and Balāi, His brother;
> Now, once more, in Nadiā,
> As Gaur and Nitāi do you appear,
> Hiding the shapes that then you wore.
> In Braja's pastures running freely,
> Once you frolicked; now, for play,
> You roll on the ground in Nadiā,
> Chanting aloud Lord Hari's name.

[5] During the period of his sādhanā Sri Ramakrishna practised spiritual discipline
in the hut in the Panchavati.
[6] The song represents Sri Krishna's words.

Laughing, shouting, once you played
At Braja with your cowherd friends;
And now you chant Lord Hari's name.

O Gaur, how cleverly you hide
The dark-blue form[7] you wore at Braja!
But your slanting eyes betray you.
Through the blessing of your name
The sinner is set free, they say;
And so my soul is filled with hope.
Now with eager heart I hasten
To your feet: Lord! I implore you,
Keep me safe within their shadow.

You redeemed Jagāi and Mādhāi,
Wretched sinners though they were;
I pray you, do the same for me.
I have heard that you embrace
All men as brothers, even the outcaste,
Whispering in the ears of all
Lord Hari's life-renewing name.

Late at night M. sat alone in the nahabat. The sky, the river, the garden, the steeples of the temples, the trees, and the Panchavati were flooded with moonlight. Deep silence reigned everywhere, broken only by the melodious murmuring of the Ganges. M. was meditating on Sri Ramakrishna.

At three o'clock in the morning M. left his seat. He proceeded toward the Panchavati as Sri Ramakrishna had suggested. He did not care for the nahabat any more and resolved to stay in the hut in the Panchavati.

Suddenly he heard a distant sound, as if someone were wailing piteously, "Oh, where art Thou, Brother Madhusudana?" The light of the full moon streamed through the thick foliage of the Panchavati, and as he proceeded he saw at a distance one of the Master's disciples sitting alone in the grove, crying helplessly, "Oh, where art Thou, Brother Madhusudana?"

Silently M. watched him.

Saturday, December 15, 1883

M. had been staying at Dakshineswar with Sri Ramakrishna. The Master was sitting in his room, listening to the life of Prahlāda, which Ramlal was reading from the *Bhaktamāla*. M. was sitting on the floor. Rakhal, Latu, and Harish were also in the room, and Hazra was on the verandah. While listening to the story of Prahlāda's love for God, Sri Ramakrishna went into an ecstatic mood.

Hiranyakaśipu, the king of the demons and father of Prahlāda, had put his son to endless torture to divert the boy's mind from the love of God. But through divine grace all the king's attempts to kill Prahlāda were ineffective. At last God appeared, assuming the form of Nrisimha, the Man-lion, and killed Hiranyakaśipu. The gods were frightened at the rage and roaring of the Man-lion and thought that the destruction of the world was imminent.

[7] An allusion to Krishna's dark-blue complexion; Gaurānga's complexion was golden.

They sent Prahlāda to pacify the Deity. The boy sang a hymn to Him in words of love, and the Man-lion, moved by affection, licked Prahlāda's body.

Still in an ecstatic mood, the Master said, "Ah! Ah! What love for the devotee!" The Master went into deep samādhi. He sat there motionless. A tear-drop could be seen at the corner of each of his eyes.

The Master came down to the plane of the sense world and spoke to M., expressing his abhorrence for those who, while practising spiritual discipline, enjoyed sex-life.

MASTER: "Aren't you ashamed of yourself? You have children, and still you enjoy intercourse with your wife. Don't you hate yourself for thus leading an animal life? Don't you hate yourself for dallying with a body which contains only blood, phlegm, filth, and excreta? He who contemplates the Lotus Feet of God looks on even the most beautiful woman as mere ash from the cremation ground. To enjoy a body which will not last and which consists of such impure ingredients as intestines, bile, flesh, and bone! Aren't you ashamed of yourself?"

M. sat there silently, hanging his head in shame.

MASTER: "A man who has tasted even a drop of God's ecstatic love looks on 'woman and gold' as most insignificant. He who has tasted syrup made from sugar candy regards a drink made from treacle as a mere trifle. One gradually obtains that love for God if one but prays to Him with a yearning heart and always chants His name and glories."

The Master was in an ecstasy of love. He began to dance about the room and sing:

> Who is singing Hari's name upon the sacred Ganges' bank?
> Is it Nitāi that has come, the giver of heavenly love? . . .

It was ten o'clock in the morning. Ramlal had finished the daily worship in the Kāli temple. The Master went to the temple accompanied by M. Entering the shrine, the Master sat before the image. He offered a flower or two at the feet of the Divine Mother. Then he put a flower on his own head and began to meditate. He sang a song to the Divine Mother:

> Thy name, I have heard, O Consort of Śiva, is the destroyer of
> our fear,
> And so on Thee I cast my burden: Save me! Save me, O kindly
> Mother! . . .

Sri Ramakrishna returned from the Kāli temple and sat on the southeast verandah of his room. He ate some refreshments which had been offered at the temple, and the devotees also received a share.

Rakhal sat by the Master and read about Lord Erskine from *Self-Help* by Smiles.

MASTER (*to M.*): "What does the book say?"

M: "It says that Lord Erskine performed his duty without desiring any result for himself. Disinterested duty."

MASTER: "That is very good. But the characteristic of a man of Perfect Knowledge is that he doesn't keep a single book with him. He carries all his

Knowledge on the tip of his tongue. There's the instance of Śukadeva. Books—I mean the scriptures—contain a mixture of sand and sugar. The sādhu takes the sugar, leaving aside the sand. He takes only the essence."

Vaishnavcharan, the musician, arrived and sang a few devotional songs. M. spent the night in the nahabat.

Sunday, December 16, 1883

Sri Ramakrishna was seated with M. on the semicircular porch of his room at about ten o'clock in the morning. The fragrance of gardenias, jasmines, oleanders, roses, and other flowers filled the air. The Master was singing, looking at M:

> Thou must save me, sweetest Mother! Unto Thee I come for
> refuge,
> Helpless as a bird imprisoned in a cage.
> I have done unnumbered wrongs, and aimlessly I roam about,
> Misled by māyā's spell, bereft of wisdom's light,
> Comfortless as a mother cow whose calf has wandered far away.

MASTER: "But why? Why should I live like a 'bird imprisoned in a cage'? Fie! For shame!"

. As the Master said these words he went into an ecstatic mood. His body became motionless and his mind stopped functioning; tears streamed down his cheeks. After a while he said, "O Mother, make me like Sītā, completely forgetful of everything—body and limbs—,totally unconscious of hands, feet, and sense-organs—only the one thought in her mind, 'Where is Rāma?' "

Was the Master inspired by the ideal of Sītā to teach M. the yearning that a devotee should feel for God? Sītā's very life was centred in Rāma. Completely absorbed in the thought of Rāma, Sītā forgot even the body, which is so dear to all.

At four o'clock in the afternoon Mr. Mukherji, a relative of Prankrishna, arrived in the company of a brāhmin well versed in the scriptures.

MUKHERJI: "I am very happy to meet you, sir."

MASTER: "God dwells in all beings. He is the gold in all. In some places it is more clearly manifest than in others. God dwells in the worldly-minded, no doubt, but He is hidden there, like gold under deep layers of clay."

MUKHERJI: "Sir, what is the difference between worldly and other-worldly things?"

MASTER: "While striving for the realization of God, the aspirant has to practise renunciation, applying the logic of 'Neti, neti'—'Not this, not this'. But after attaining the vision of God, he realizes that God alone has become all things.

"At one time Rāma was overpowered by the spirit of renunciation. Daśaratha, worried at this, went to the sage Vaśishtha and begged him to persuade Rāma not to give up the world. The sage came to Rāma and found him in a gloomy mood. The fire of intense renunciation had been raging in the Prince's mind. Vaśishtha said: 'Rāma, why should You renounce the world? Is the world outside God? Reason with me.' Rāma realized that the world had evolved from the Supreme Brahman. So He said nothing.

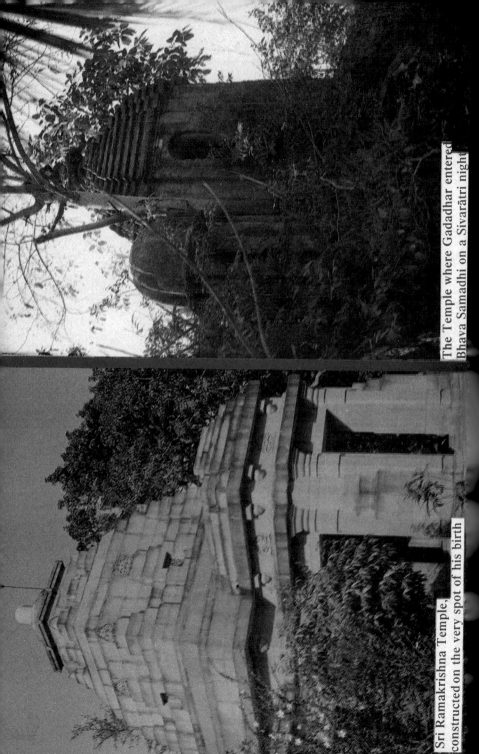

The Temple where Gadadhar entered Bhava Samadhi on a Sivarátri night

Sri Ramakrishna Temple, constructed on the very spot of his birth

The mango tree planted by Sri Ramakrishna

Family Deities: Sītalā, Raghuvīr and Rameswar Śiva

"Buttermilk is made from the same substance as butter. One who realizes this knows that butter goes with buttermilk and buttermilk with butter. After separating the butter with great effort—that is to say, after attaining Brahmajnāna—you will realize that as long as butter exists, buttermilk also must exist. Wherever there is butter there must be buttermilk as well. As long as one feels that Brahman exists, one must also be aware that the universe, living beings, and the twenty-four cosmic principles exist as well.

"What Brahman is cannot be described in words. Everything has been polluted, like food that has touched the tongue—that is, everything has been described in words. But no one has been able to describe Brahman. It is therefore unpolluted. I said this to Vidyāsāgar and he was delighted.

"But the Knowledge of Brahman cannot be realized if the aspirant is worldly-minded even in the slightest degree. He succeeds in acquiring this Knowledge only when his mind is totally free from 'woman and gold'. Pārvati once said to Her father, 'Father, seek the company of holy men if you want the Knowledge of Brahman.'"

Addressing Mr. Mukherji, Sri Ramakrishna said: "You are rich, and still you call on God. That is very good indeed. It is said in the *Gītā* that those who fall from the path of yoga are born in their next birth as devotees of God in rich families."

Mr. Mukherji quoted the line from the *Gītā*.

MASTER: "God, if He so desires, can keep a jnāni in the world too. The world and all living beings have been created by His will. But He is self-willed."

MUKHERJI (*with a smile*): "How can God have any will? Does He lack anything?"

MASTER (*with a smile*): "What's wrong in that? Water is water whether it is still or in waves. The snake is a snake whether it is coiled up motionless or wriggles along. A man is the same man whether sitting still or engaged in action.

"How can you eliminate from the Reality the universe and its living beings? If you do that, It will lack Its full weight. You cannot find out the total weight of the bel-fruit if you eliminate the seeds and shell.

"Brahman is unattached. One finds good and bad smells in the air, but the air itself is untainted. Brahman and Śakti are identical. It is the Primordial Power that has become the world and all living beings."

MUKHERJI: "Why does one deviate from the path of yoga?"

MASTER: "As the saying goes: 'In my mother's womb I was in a state of yoga; coming into the world, I have eaten its clay. The midwife has cut one shackle, the navel cord; but how shall I cut the shackle of māyā?'

"Māyā is nothing but 'woman' and 'gold'. A man attains yoga when he has freed his mind from these two. The Self—the Supreme Self—is the magnet; the individual self is the needle. The individual self experiences the state of yoga when it is attracted by the Supreme Self to Itself. But the magnet cannot attract the needle if the needle is covered with clay; it can draw the needle only when the clay is removed. The clay of 'woman' and 'gold' must be removed."

MUKHERJI: "How can one remove it?"

MASTER: "Weep for God with a longing heart. Tears shed for Him will wash away the clay. When you have thus freed yourself from impurity, you will be attracted by the magnet. Only then will you attain yoga."

MUKHERJI: "Priceless words!"

MASTER: "If a man is able to weep for God, he will see Him. He will go into samādhi. Perfection in yoga is samādhi. A man achieves kumbhaka without any yogic exercise if he but weeps for God. The next stage is samādhi.

"There is another method—that of meditation. In the Sahasrāra, Śiva manifests Himself in a special manner. The aspirant should meditate on Him. The body is like a tray; the mind and buddhi are like water. The Sun of Satchidānanda is reflected in this water. Meditating on the reflected sun, one sees the Real Sun through the grace of God.

"But the worldly man must constantly live in the company of holy men. It is necessary for all, even for sannyāsis. But it is especially necessary for the householder. His disease has become chronic because he has to live constantly in the midst of 'woman and gold'."

MUKHERJI: "Yes, sir. The disease has indeed become chronic."

MASTER: "Give God the power of attorney. Let Him do whatever He wants. Be like a kitten and cry to Him with a fervent heart. The mother cat puts the kitten wherever she wants to. The kitten doesn't know anything. It is left sometimes on the bed and sometimes near the hearth."

MUKHERJI: "It is good to read sacred books like the *Gītā*."

MASTER: "But what will you gain by mere reading? Some have heard of milk, some have seen it, and there are some, besides, who have drunk it. God can indeed be seen; what is more, one can talk to Him.

"The first stage is that of the beginner. He studies and hears. Second is the stage of the struggling aspirant. He prays to God, meditates on Him, and sings His name and glories. The third stage is that of the perfect soul. He has seen God, realized Him directly and immediately in his inner Consciousness. Last is the stage of the supremely perfect, like Chaitanya. Such a devotee establishes a definite relationship with God, looking on Him as his Son or Beloved."

M., Rakhal, Jogin, Latu, and the other devotees were entranced by these words of divine realization.

Mr. Mukherji and his friend were taking leave of the Master. After saluting him, they stood up. The Master also stood up to show them courtesy.

MUKHERJI (*smiling*): "That you should stand up or sit down!"

MASTER (*smiling*): "But what's the harm? Water is water whether it is placid or in waves. I am like a cast-off leaf in the wind. The wind blows that leaf wherever it lists. I am the machine and God is its Operator."

Mr. Mukherji and his friend left the room. M. thought: "According to the Vedānta all is like a dream. Are all these—the ego, the universe, and the living beings—unreal then?"

M. had studied a little of the Vedānta. He also had read the German philosophers, such as Kant and Hegel, whose writings are only a faint echo of the Vedānta. But Sri Ramakrishna did not arrive at his conclusions by reasoning, as do ordinary scholars. It was the Divine Mother of the Universe who revealed the Truth to him. These were the thoughts that passed through M.'s mind.

A little later Sri Ramakrishna and M. were conversing on the porch west of the Master's room. No one else was there. It was a late winter afternoon, and the sun had not yet gone below the horizon.

M: "Is the world unreal?"

MASTER: "Why should it be unreal? What you are asking is a matter for philosophical discussion.

"In the beginning, when a man reasons following the Vedāntic method of 'Not this, not this', he realizes that Brahman is not the living beings, not the universe, not the twenty-four cosmic principles. All these things become like dreams to him. Then comes the affirmation of what has been denied, and he feels that God Himself has become the universe and all living beings.

"Suppose you are climbing to the roof by the stairs. As long as you are aware of the roof, you are also aware of the stairs. He who is aware of the high is also aware of the low. But after reaching the roof you realize that the stairs are made of the same materials—brick, lime, and brick-dust—as the roof.

"Further, I have given the illustration of the bel-fruit. Both changeability and unchangeability belong to one and the same Reality.

"The ego cannot be done away with. As long as 'I-consciousness' exists, living beings and the universe must also exist. After realizing God, one sees that it is He Himself who has become the universe and the living beings. But one cannot realize this by mere reasoning.

"Śiva has two states of mind. First, the state of samādhi, when He is transfixed in the Great Yoga. He is then Ātmārāma, satisfied in the Self. Second, the state when He descends from samādhi and keeps a trace of ego. Then He dances about, chanting, 'Rāma, Rāma!'"

Did the Master describe Śiva to hint at his own state of mind?

It was evening. Sri Ramakrishna was meditating on the Divine Mother and chanting Her holy name. The devotees also went off to solitary places and meditated on their Chosen Ideals. Evening worship began at the temple garden in the shrines of Kāli, Rādhā-Krishna, and Śiva.

It was the second day of the dark fortnight of the moon. Soon the moon rose in the sky, bathing temples, trees, flowers, and the rippling surface of the Ganges in its light. The Master was sitting on the couch and M. on the floor. The conversation turned to the Vedānta.

MASTER (to M.): "Why should the universe be unreal? That is a speculation of the philosophers. After realizing God, one sees that it is God Himself who has become the universe and all living beings.

"The Divine Mother revealed to me in the Kāli temple that it was She who had become everything. She showed me that everything was full of Consciousness. The Image was Consciousness, the altar was Consciousness, the water-vessels were Consciousness, the door-sill was Consciousness, the marble floor was Consciousness—all was Consciousness.

"I found everything inside the room soaked, as it were, in Bliss—the Bliss of Satchidānanda. I saw a wicked man in front of the Kāli temple; but in him also I saw the Power of the Divine Mother vibrating.

"That was why I fed a cat with the food that was to be offered to the Divine Mother. I clearly perceived that the Divine Mother Herself had become everything—even the cat. The manager of the temple garden wrote to Mathur Babu saying that I was feeding the cat with the offering intended for the Divine Mother. But Mathur Babu had insight into the state of my mind. He wrote back to the manager: 'Let him do whatever he likes. You must not say anything to him.'

"After realizing God, one sees all this aright—that it is He who has become the universe, living beings, and the twenty-four cosmic principles. But what remains when God completely effaces the ego cannot be described in words. As Rāmprasād said in one of his songs, 'Then alone will you know whether you are good or I am good!' I get into even that state now and then.

"A man sees a thing in one way through reasoning and in an altogether different way when God Himself shows it to him."

Monday, December 17, 1883

It was about eight o'clock in the morning. Sri Ramakrishna was in his room with M., when Dr. Madhu arrived and sat down beside the Master on the small couch. He was an elderly man and full of wit. He used to visit the Master when the latter felt indisposed.

MASTER: "The whole thing in a nutshell is that one must develop ecstatic love for Satchidānanda. What kind of love? How should one love God? Gauri used to say that one must become like Sītā to understand Rāma; like Bhagavati, the Divine Mother, to understand Bhagavān, Śiva. One must practise austerity, as Bhagavati did, in order to attain Śiva. One must cultivate the attitude of Prakriti in order to realize Purusha—the attitude of a friend, a handmaid, or a mother.

"I saw Sītā in a vision. I found that her entire mind was concentrated on Rāma. She was totally indifferent to everything—her hands, her feet, her clothes, her jewels. It seemed that Rāma had filled every bit of her life and she could not remain alive without Rāma."

M: "Yes, sir. She was mad with love for Rāma."

MASTER: "Mad! That's the word. One must become mad with love in order to realize God. But that love is not possible if the mind dwells on 'woman and gold'. Sex-life with a woman! What happiness is there in that? The realization of God gives ten million times more happiness. Gauri used to say that when a man attains ecstatic love of God all the pores of the skin, even the roots of the hair, become like so many sexual organs, and in every pore the aspirant enjoys the happiness of communion with the Ātman.

"One must call on God with a longing heart. One must learn from the guru how God can be realized. Only if the guru himself has attained Perfect Knowledge can he show the way.

"A man gets rid of all desires when he has Perfect Knowledge. He becomes like a child five years old. Sages like Dattātreya and Jaḍabharata had the nature of a child."

M: "One hears about them. But there were many others like them that the world doesn't hear about."

MASTER: "Yes. The jnāni gets rid of all desire. If any is left, it does not hurt him. At the touch of the philosopher's stone the sword is transformed into gold. Then that sword cannot do any killing. Just so, the jnāni keeps only a semblance of anger and passion. They are anger and passion only in name and cannot injure him."

M: "Yes, sir. The jnāni goes beyond the three gunas, as you say. He is not under the control of any of the gunas—sattva, rajas, or tamas. All these three are so many robbers, as it were."

MASTER: "Yes, one must assimilate that."

M: "In this world there are perhaps not more than three or four men of Perfect Knowledge."

MASTER: "Why do you say that? One sees many holy men and sannyāsis in the monasteries of upper India."

M: "Well, I too can become a sannyāsi like one of those."

The Master fixed his gaze on M. and said, "By renouncing everything?"

M: "What can a man achieve unless he gets rid of māyā? What will a man gain by merely being a sannyāsi, if he cannot subdue māyā?"

Both remained silent a few minutes.

M: "Sir, what is the nature of the divine love transcending the three gunas?"

MASTER: "Attaining that love, the devotee sees everything full of Spirit and Consciousness. To him 'Krishna is Consciousness, and His sacred Abode is also Consciousness'. The devotee, too, is Consciousness. Everything is Consciousness. Very few people attain such love."

DR. MADHU: "The love transcending the three gunas means, in other words, that the devotee is not under the control of any of the gunas."

MASTER (smiling): "Yes, that's it. He becomes like a child five years old, not under the control of any of the gunas."

The Master was resting after his noon meal. Mani Mallick arrived and saluted him. Sri Ramakrishna remained lying on the couch and said a word or two to Mani.

MANI: "I hear you visited Keshab Sen."

MASTER: "Yes. How is he now?"

MANI: "He hasn't recovered to any extent from his illness."

MASTER: "I found him to be very rājasic. I had to wait a long time before I could see him."

The Master sat up on the couch and continued his conversation with the devotees.

MASTER (to M.): "I became mad for Rāma. I used to walk about carrying an image of Rāmlālā[8] given to me by a monk. I bathed it, fed it, and laid it down to sleep. I carried it wherever I went. I became mad for Rāmlālā."

[8] A brass image of the Boy Rāma.

M. AT DAKSHINESWAR (I)

Tuesday, December 18, 1883

SRI RAMAKRISHNA was seated in his room with his devotees. He spoke highly of Devendranath Tagore's love of God and renunciation, and then said, pointing to Rakhal and the other young devotees, "Devendra is a good man; but blessed indeed are those young aspirants who, like Sukadeva, practise renunciation from their very boyhood and think of God day and night without being involved in worldly life.

"The worldly man always has some desire or other, though at times he shows much devotion to God. Once Mathur Babu was entangled in a lawsuit. He said tó me in the shrine of Kāli, 'Sir, please offer this flower to the Divine Mother.' I offered it unsuspectingly, but he firmly believed that he would attain his objective if I offered the flower.

"What devotion Rati's mother had! How often she used to come here and how much she served me! She was a Vaishnava. One day she noticed that I ate the food offered at the Kāli temple, and that stopped her coming. Her devotion to God was one-sided. It isn't possible to understand a person right away."

It was a winter morning, and the Master was sitting near the east door of his room, wrapped in his moleskin shawl. He looked at the sun and suddenly went into samādhi. His eyes stopped blinking and he lost all consciousness of the outer world. After a long time he came down to the plane of the sense world. Rakhal, Hazra, M., and other devotees were seated near him.

MASTER (to Hazra): "The state of samādhi is certainly inspired by love. Once, at Syāmbāzār, they arranged a kirtan at Natavar Goswami's house. There I had a vision of Krishna and the gopis of Vrindāvan. I felt that my subtle body was walking at Krishna's heels.

"I went into samādhi when similar devotional songs were sung at the Hari Sabhā in Jorāshānko in Calcutta. That day they feared I might give up the body."

After the Master had finished his bath, he again spoke of the ecstatic love of the gopis. He said to M. and the other devotees: "One should accept the fervent attachment of the gopis to their beloved Krishna. Sing songs like this:

> Tell me, friend, how far is the grove
> Where Krishna, my Beloved, dwells?
> His fragrance reaches me even here;
> But I am tired and can walk no farther."

Again he sang:

> I am not going home, O friend,
> For there it is hard for me to chant my Krishna's name. . . .

Sri Ramakrishna had vowed to offer green coconut and sugar to Siddheśvari, the Divine Mother, for Rakhal's welfare. He asked M. whether he would pay for the offerings.

That afternoon the Master, accompanied by M., Rakhal, and some other devotees, set out in a carriage for the temple of Siddheśvari in Calcutta. On the way the offerings were purchased. On reaching the temple, the Master asked the devotees to offer the fruit and sugar to the Divine Mother. They saw the priests and their friends playing cards in the temple. Sri Ramakrishna said: "To play cards in a temple! One should think of God here."

From the temple the Master went to Jadu Mallick's house. Jadu was surrounded by his admirers, well-dressed dandies. He welcomed the Master.

MASTER (with a smile): "Why do you keep so many clowns and flatterers with you?"

JADU (smiling): "That you may liberate them." (Laughter.)

MASTER: "Flatterers think that the rich man will loosen his purse-strings for them. But it is very difficult to get anything from him. Once a jackal saw a bullock and would not give up his company. The bullock roamed about and the jackal followed him. The jackal thought: 'There hang the bullock's testicles. Some time or other they will drop to the ground and I shall eat them.' When the bullock slept on the ground, the jackal lay down too, and when the bullock moved about, the jackal followed him. Many days passed in this way, but the bullock's testicles still clung to his body. The jackal went away disappointed. (All laugh.) That also happens to flatterers."

Jadu and his mother served refreshments to Sri Ramakrishna and the devotees.

Wednesday, December 19, 1883

It was nine o'clock in the morning. Sri Ramakrishna was talking to M. near the bel-tree at Dakshineswar. This tree, under which the Master had practised the most austere sādhanā, stood in the northern end of the temple garden. Farther north ran a high wall, and just outside was the government magazine. West of the bel-tree was a row of tall pines that rustled in the wind. Below the trees flowed the Ganges, and to the south could be seen the sacred grove of the Panchavati. The dense trees and underbrush hid the temples. No noise of the outside world reached the bel-tree.

MASTER (to M.): "But one cannot realize God without renouncing 'woman and gold'."

M: "Why? Did not Vaśishtha say to Rāma, 'O Rāma, You may renounce the world if the world is outside God'?"

MASTER (smiling): "He said that to Rāma so that Rāma might destroy Rāvana. Rāma accepted the life of a householder and married to fulfil that mission."

M. stood there like a log, stunned and speechless.

Sri Ramakrishna went to the Panchavati on his way back to his room. M. accompanied him. It was then about ten o'clock.

M: "Sir, is there no spiritual discipline leading to realization of the Impersonal God?"

MASTER: "Yes, there is. But the path is extremely difficult. After intense austerities the rishis of olden times realized God as their innermost consciousness and experienced the real nature of Brahman. But how hard they had to work! They went out of their dwellings in the early morning and all day practised austerities and meditation. Returning home at nightfall, they took a light supper of fruit and roots.

"But an aspirant cannot succeed in this form of spiritual discipline if his mind is stained with worldliness even in the slightest degree. The mind must withdraw totally from all objects of form, taste, smell, touch, and sound. Only thus does it become pure. The Pure Mind is the same as the Pure Ātman. But such a mind must be altogether free from 'woman and gold'. When it becomes pure, one has another experience. One realizes: 'God alone is the Doer, and I am His instrument.' One does not feel oneself to be absolutely necessary to others either in their misery or in their happiness.

"Once a wicked man beat into unconsciousness a monk who lived in a monastery. On regaining consciousness he was asked by his friends, 'Who is feeding you milk?' The monk said, 'He who beat me is now feeding me.'"

M: "Yes, sir. I know that story."

MASTER: "It is not enough to know it. One must assimilate its meaning. It is the thought of worldly objects that prevents the mind from going into samādhi. One becomes established in samādhi when one is completely rid of worldliness. It is possible for me to give up the body in samādhi; but I have a slight desire to enjoy the love of God and the company of His devotees. Therefore I pay a little attention to my body.

"There is another kind of samādhi, called unmanā samādhi. One attains it by suddenly gathering the dispersed mind. You understand what that is, don't you?"

M: "Yes, sir."

MASTER: "Yes. It is the sudden withdrawal of the dispersed mind to the Ideal. But that samādhi does not last long. Worldly thoughts intrude and destroy it. The yogi slips down from his yoga.

"At Kāmārpukur I have seen the mongoose living in its hole up in the wall. It feels snug there. Sometimes people tie a brick to its tail; then the pull of the brick makes it come out of its hole. Every time the mongoose tries to be comfortable inside the hole, it has to come out because of the pull of the brick. Such is the effect of brooding on worldly objects that it makes the yogi stray from the path of yoga.

"Worldly people may now and then experience samādhi. The lotus blooms, no doubt, when the sun is up; but its petals close again when the sun is covered by a cloud. Worldly thought is the cloud."

M: "Isn't it possible to develop both jnāna and bhakti by the practice of spiritual discipline?"

MASTER: "Through the path of bhakti a man may attain them both. If it is necessary, God gives him the Knowledge of Brahman. But a highly qualified aspirant may develop both jnāna and bhakti at the same time. Such is the case with the Iśvarakotis—Chaitanya for example. But the case of ordinary devotees is different.

"There are five kinds of light: the light of a lamp, the light of various kinds of fire, the light of the moon, the light of the sun, and lastly the combined light of the sun and the moon. Bhakti is the light of the moon, and jnāna the light of the sun.

"Sometimes it is seen that the sun has hardly set when the moon rises in the sky. In an Incarnation of God one sees, at the same time, the sun of Knowledge and the moon of Love.

"Can everyone, by the mere wish, develop Knowledge and Love at the same time? It depends on the person. One bamboo is more hollow than another. Is it possible for all to comprehend the nature of God? Can a one-seer pot hold five seers of milk?"

M: "But what about the grace of God? Through His grace a camel can pass through the eye of a needle."

MASTER: "But is it possible to obtain God's grace just like that? A beggar may get a penny, if he asks for it. But suppose he asks you right off for his train fare. How about that?"

M. stood silent. The Master, too, remained silent. Suddenly he said: "Yes, it is true. Through the grace of God some may get both jnāna and bhakti."

M. saluted the Master and went back to the bel-tree.

At midday, finding that M. had not yet returned, Sri Ramakrishna started toward the bel-tree; but on reaching the Panchavati he met M. carrying his prayer carpet and water-jug. M. saluted the Master.

Sri Ramakrishna said to M: "I was coming to look for you. Because of your delay I thought you might have scaled the wall and run away. I watched your eyes this morning and felt apprehensive lest you should go away like Narayan Shastri. Then I said to myself: 'No, he won't run away. He thinks a great deal before doing anything.'"

The same night the Master talked to M., Rakhal, Latu, Harish, and a few other devotees.

MASTER (to M.): "Some people give a metaphysical interpretation of the Vrindāvan episode of Sri Krishna's life. What do you say about it?"

M: "There are various opinions. What if there are? You have told us the story of Bhishmadeva's weeping, on his bed of arrows, because he could not understand anything of God's ways.

"Again, you have told us that Hanumān used to say: 'I don't know any thing about the day of the week, the position of the stars, and so forth. I only meditate on Rāma.'

"Further, you have said to us that in the last analysis there are two things only: Brahman and Its Power. You have also said that, after the attainment of Brahmajnāna, a man realizes these two to be One, the One that has no two."

MASTER: "Yes, that is true. Your ideal is to reach the goal. You may reach it by going either through a thorny forest or along a good road.

"Diverse opinions certainly exist. Nangtā used to say that the monks could not be feasted because of the diversity of their views. Once a feast was arranged for the sannyāsis. Monks belonging to many sects were invited. Everyone claimed that his sect should be fed first, but no conclusion could be arrived at. At last they all went away and the food had to be given to the prostitutes."

M: "Totapuri was indeed a great soul."

MASTER: "But Hazra says he was an ordinary man. There's no use in discussing these things. Everyone says that his watch alone gives the correct time.

"You see, Narayan Shastri developed a spirit of intense renunciation. He was a great scholar. He gave up his wife and went away. A man attains yoga when he completely effaces 'woman and gold' from his mind. With some, the characteristics of the yogi are well marked.

"I shall have to tell you something of the six centres. The mind of the yogi passes through these, and he realizes God through His grace. Have you heard of the six centres?"

M: "These are the 'seven planes' of the Vedānta."

MASTER: "Not the Vedānta, but the Vedas. Do you know what the six centres are like? They are the 'lotuses' in the subtle body. The yogis see them. They are like the fruits and leaves of a wax tree."

M: "Yes, sir. The yogis can perceive them. I have read that there is a kind of glass through which a tiny object looks very big. Likewise, through yoga one can see those subtle lotuses."

Following Sri Ramakrishna's direction, M. spent the night in the hut at the Panchavati. In the early hours of the morning he was singing alone:

> I am without the least benefit of prayer and austerity, O Lord!
> I am the lowliest of the lowly; make me pure with Thy hallowed
>   touch.
> One by one I pass my days in hope of reaching Thy Lotus Feet,
> But Thee, alas, I have not found. . . .

Suddenly M. glanced toward the window and saw the Master standing there. Sri Ramakrishna's eyes became heavy with tears as M. sang the line:

> I am the lowliest of the lowly; make me pure with Thy hallowed
>   touch.

M. sang again:

> I shall put on the ochre robe and ear-rings made of conch-shell;
> Thus, in the garb of a yogini, from place to place I shall wander,
> Till I have found my cruel Hari. . . .

M. saw that the Master was walking with Rakhal.

Friday, December 21, 1883

In the morning the Master and M. were conversing alone under the bel-tree. The Master told him many secrets of spiritual discipline, exhorting him to renounce "woman and gold". He further said that the mind at times becomes one's guru.

After his midday meal the Master went to the Panchavati wearing a beautiful yellow robe. Two or three Vaishnava monks were there, clad in the dress of their sect.

In the afternoon a monk belonging to the sect of Nānak arrived. He was a worshipper of the formless God. Sri Ramakrishna asked him to meditate as well on God with form. The Master said to him: "Dive deep; one does not get the precious gems by merely floating on the surface. God is without form, no doubt; but He also has form. By meditating on God with form one speedily acquires devotion; then one can meditate on the formless God. It is like throwing a letter away, after learning its contents, and then setting out to follow its instructions."

Saturday, December 22, 1883

Rakhal, Harish, M., and Latu had been staying with Sri Ramakrishna at Dakshineswar. About nine o'clock in the morning the Master was sitting with them on the southeast verandah of his room, when Balaram's father and Devendra Ghosh of Śyāmpukur arrived.

A DEVOTEE: "Sir, how does one obtain love for God?"

MASTER: "Go forward. The king dwells beyond the seven gates. You can see him only after passing through all the gates.

"At the time of the installation of Annapurnā at Chānak, I said to Dwarika Babu: 'Large fish live in the deep water of a big lake. Throw some spiced bait into the water; then the fish will come, attracted by its smell; now and then they will make the water splash. Devotion and ecstatic love are like the spiced bait.

"God sports in the world as man. He incarnates Himself as man—as in the case of Krishna, Rāma, and Chaitanya. Once I said to Keshab: 'The greatest manifestation of God is in man. There are small holes in the balk of a field, where crabs and fish accumulate in the rainy season. If you want to find them you must seek them in the holes. If you seek God, you must seek Him in the Incarnations.'

"The Divine Mother of the Universe manifests Herself through this three-and-a-half cubit man. There is a song that says:

> O Mother, what a machine is this that Thou hast made!
> What pranks Thou playest with this toy
> Three and a half cubits high! . . .

"One needs spiritual practice in order to know God and recognize Divine Incarnations. Big fish live in the large lake, but to see them one must throw spiced bait in the water. There is butter in milk, but one must churn the milk to get it. There is oil in mustard-seed, but one must press the seed to extract the oil."

DEVOTEE: "Has God form, or is He formless?"

MASTER: "Wait, wait! First of all you must go to Calcutta; then only will you know where the Maidān, the Asiatic Society, and the Bengal Bank are located. If you want to go to the brāhmin quarter of Khardaha, you must first of all go to Khardaha.

"Why should it not be possible to practise the discipline of the formless God? But it is very difficult to follow that path. One cannot follow it without renouncing 'woman and gold'. There must be complete renunciation, both inner and outer. You cannot succeed in this path if you have the slightest trace of worldliness.

"It is easy to worship God with form. But it is not as easy as all that.

"One should not discuss the discipline of the Impersonal God or the path of knowledge with a bhakta. Through great effort perhaps he is just cultivating a little devotion. You will injure it if you explain away everything as a mere dream.

"Kabir was a worshipper of the Impersonal God. He did not believe in Śiva, Kāli, or Krishna. He used to make fun of them and say that Kāli lived on the offerings of rice and banana, and that Krishna danced like a monkey when the gopis clapped their hands. (All laugh.)

"One who worships God without form perhaps sees at first the deity with ten arms, then the deity with four arms, then the Baby Krishna with two arms. At last he sees the Indivisible Light and merges in It.

"It is said that sages like Dattātreya and Jadabharata did not return to the relative plane after having the vision of Brahman. According to some people, Śukadeva tasted only a drop of that Ocean of Brahman-Consciousness. He saw and heard the rumbling of the waves of that Ocean, but he did not dive into It.

"A brahmachāri once said to me, 'One who goes beyond Kedār cannot keep his body alive.' Likewise, a man cannot preserve his body after attaining Brahmajnāna.[1] The body drops off in twenty-one days.

"There was an infinite field beyond a high wall. Four friends tried to find out what was beyond the wall. Three of them, one after the other, climbed the wall, saw the field, burst into loud laughter, and dropped to the other side. These three could not give any information about the field. Only the fourth man came back and told people about it. He is like those who retain their bodies, even after attaining Brahmajnāna, in order to teach others. Divine Incarnations belong to this class.

"Pārvati was born as the daughter of King Himālaya. After Her birth She revealed to the king Her various divine forms. The father said: 'Well,

[1] In the case of an ordinary aspirant the body drops off after he attains the Knowledge of Brahman, but this is not so in the case of a Divine Incarnation, because He is born with a special mission to teach mankind.

Daughter, You have shown me all these forms. That is nice. But You have another aspect, which is Brahman. Please show me that.' 'Father,' replied Pārvati, 'if you seek the Knowledge of Brahman, then renounce the world and live in the company of holy men.' But King Himālaya insisted. Thereupon Pārvati revealed Her Brahman-form, and immediately the king fell down unconscious.

"All that I have just said belongs to the realm of reasoning. Brahman alone is real and the world illusory—that is reasoning. And everything but Brahman is like a dream. But this is an extremely difficult path. To one who follows it even the divine play in the world becomes like a dream and appears unreal; his 'I' also vanishes. The followers of this path do not accept the Divine Incarnation. It is a very difficult path. The lovers of God should not hear much of such reasoning.

"That is why God incarnates Himself as man and teaches people the path of devotion. He exhorts people to cultivate self-surrender to God. Following the path of devotion, one realizes everything through His grace—both Knowledge and Supreme Wisdom.

"God sports in this world. He is under the control of His devotee. 'Syāmā, the Divine Mother, is Herself tied by the cord of the love of Her devotee.'

"Sometimes God becomes the magnet and the devotee the needle, and sometimes the devotee becomes the magnet and God the needle. The devotee attracts God to him. God is the Beloved of His devotee and is under his control.

"According to one school, the gopis of Vrindāvan, like Yaśodā, had believed in the formless God in their previous births; but they did not derive any satisfaction from this belief. That is why later on they enjoyed so much bliss in the company of Sri Krishna in the Vrindāvan episode of His life. One day Krishna said to the gopis: 'Come along. I shall show you the Abode of the Eternal. Let us go to the Jamunā for a bath.' As they dived into the water of the river, they at once saw Goloka. Next they saw the Indivisible Light. Thereupon Yaśodā exclaimed: 'O Krishna, we don't care for these things any more. We would like to see You in Your human form. I want to take You in my arms and feed You.'

"So the greatest manifestation of God is through His Incarnations. The devotee should worship and serve an Incarnation of God as long as He lives in a human body. 'At the break of day He disappears into the secret chamber of His House.'

"Not all, by any means, can recognize an Incarnation of God. Assuming a human body, the Incarnation falls a victim to disease, grief, hunger, thirst, and all such things, like ordinary mortals. Rāma wept for Sītā. 'Brahman weeps, entrapped in the snare of the five elements.'

"It is said in the Purāna that God, in His Incarnation as the Sow, lived happily with His young ones even after the destruction of Hiranyāksha.[2] As the Sow, He nursed them and forgot all about His abode in heaven. At

[2] According to Hindu mythology, God incarnated Himself as a sow in order to save the world from the iniquities of the demon Hiranyāksha.

last Siva killed the sow body with his trident, and God, laughing aloud, went to His own abode."

In the afternoon Bhavanath arrived. Rakhal, M., Harish, and other devotees were in the room.

MASTER (to Bhavanath): "To love an Incarnation of God—that is enough. Ah, what ecstatic love the gopis had for Krishna!"

Sri Ramakrishna began to sing, assuming the attitude of the gopis:

O Krishna! You are the Soul of my soul. . . .

Then he sang:

I am not going home, O friend,
For there it is hard for me to chant my Krishna's name. . .

And again:

O Friend, that day I stood at my door as You were going to the woods. . . .

Continuing, the Master said: "When Krishna suddenly disappeared in the act of dancing and playing with the gopis, they were beside themselves with grief. Looking at a tree, they said: 'O tree, you must be a great hermit. You must have seen Krishna. Otherwise, why do you stand there motionless, as if absorbed in samādhi?' Looking at the earth covered with green grass, they said: 'O earth, you must have seen Krishna. Otherwise, why does your hair stand on end? You must have enjoyed the thrill of His touch.' Looking at the mādhavi creeper, they said, 'O mādhavi, give us back our Mādhava!' The gopis were intoxicated with ecstatic love for Krishna. Akrura came to Vrindāvan to take Krishna and Balarāma to Mathurā. When they mounted the chariot, the gopis clung to the wheels. They would not let the chariot move."

Saying this, Sri Ramakrishna sang, assuming the attitude of Akrura:

Hold not, hold not the chariot's wheels!
Is it the wheels that make it move?
The Mover of its wheels is Krishna,
By whose will the worlds are moved. . . .

MASTER: " 'Is it the wheels that make it move?' 'By whose will the worlds are moved.' 'The driver moves the chariot at his Master's bidding.' I feel deeply touched by these lines."

Sunday, December 23, 1883

At nine o'clock in the morning Sri Ramakrishna was seated on the southwest porch of his room, with Rakhal, Latu, M., Harish, and some other devotees. M. had now been nine days with the Master at Dakshineswar. Earlier in the morning Manomohan had arrived from Konnagar on his way to Calcutta. Hazra, too, was present.

A Vaishnava was singing. Referring to one of the songs, Sri Ramakrishna said: "I didn't enjoy that song very much. The songs of the earlier writers seem to me to have more of the right spirit. Once I sang for Nangtā at the Panchavati: 'To arms! To arms, O man! Death storms your house in battle array.' I sang another: 'O Mother, I have no one else to blame: Alas! I sink in the well these very hands have dug.'

"Nangtā, the Vedāntist, was a man of profound knowledge. The song moved him to tears though he didn't understand its meaning. Padmalochan also wept when I sang the songs of Rāmprasād about the Divine Mother. And he was truly a great pundit."

After the midday meal Sri Ramakrishna rested a few minutes in his room. M. was sitting on the floor. The Master was delighted to hear the music that was being played in the nahabat. He then explained to M. that Brahman alone has become the universe and all living beings.

MASTER: "Referring to a certain place, someone once said to me: 'Nobody sings the name of God there. It has no holy atmosphere.' No sooner did he say this than I perceived that it was God alone who had become all living beings. They appeared as countless bubbles or reflections in the Ocean of Satchidānanda.

"Again, I find sometimes that living beings are like so many pills made of Indivisible Consciousness. Once I was on my way to Burdwan from Kāmārpukur. At one place I ran to the meadow to see how living beings are sustained. I saw ants crawling there. It appeared to me that every place was filled with Consciousness."

Hazra entered the room and sat on the floor.

MASTER: "Again, I perceive that living beings are like different flowers with various layers of petals. They are also revealed to me as bubbles, some big, some small."

While describing in this way the vision of different divine forms, the Master went into an ecstatic state and said, "I have become! I am here!" Uttering these words he went into samādhi. His body was motionless. He remained in that state a long time and then gradually regained partial consciousness of the world. He began to laugh like a boy and pace the room. His eyes radiated bliss as if he had seen a wondrous vision. His gaze was not fixed on any particular object, and his face beamed with joy. Still pacing the room, the Master said: "I saw the paramahamsa who stayed under the banyan tree walking thus with just such a smile. Am I too in that state of mind?"

He sat on the small couch and engaged in conversation with the Divine Mother.

MASTER: "I don't even care to know. Mother, may I have pure love for Thy Lotus Feet!

(*To M.*) "One attains this state immediately after freeing oneself of all grief and desire.

(*To the Divine Mother*) "Mother, Thou hast done away with my worship. Please see, Mother, that I don't give up all desire. Mother, the paramahamsa is but a child. Doesn't a child need a mother? Therefore Thou art the Mother and I am the child. How can the child live without the Mother?"

Sri Ramakrishna was talking to the Divine Mother in a voice that would have melted even a stone. Again he addressed Her, saying: "Mere knowledge of Advaita! I spit on it! Thou dost exist as long as Thou dost keep the ego in me. The paramahamsa is but a child. Doesn't a child need a mother?"

M. sat there speechless and looked at the divine manifestation in the Master. He said to himself: "The Master is an ocean of mercy that knows no motive. He has kept himself in the state of a paramahamsa that he might, as teacher, awaken the spiritual consciousness of myself and other earnest souls."

M. further thought: "The Master says, 'Advaita—Chaitanya—Nityānanda'; that is to say, through the knowledge of the Non-dual Brahman one attains Consciousness and enjoys Eternal Bliss. The Master has not only attained the knowledge of non-duality but is in a state of Eternal Bliss. He is always drunk with ecstatic love for the Mother of the Universe."

With folded hands Hazra looked at the Master and said every now and then: "How blessed you are! How blessed you are!"

MASTER (to Hazra): "But you have hardly any faith; you simply live here to add to the play, like Jatilā and Kutilā."

In the afternoon M. paced the temple garden alone. He was deeply absorbed in the thought of the Master and was pondering the Master's words concerning the attainment of the exalted state of the paramahamsa, after the elimination of grief and desire. M. said to himself: "Who is this Sri Ramakrishna, acting as my teacher? Has God embodied Himself for our welfare? The Master himself says that no one but an Incarnation can come down to the phenomenal plane from the state of nirvikalpa samādhi."

Monday, December 24, 1883

At eight o'clock in the morning Sri Ramakrishna and M. were talking together in the pine-grove at the northern end of the temple garden. This was the eleventh day of M.'s stay with the Master.

It was winter. The sun had just risen. The river was flowing north with the tide. Not far off could be seen the bel tree where the Master had practised great spiritual austerities. Sri Ramakrishna faced the east as he talked to his disciple and told him about the Knowledge of Brahman.

MASTER: "The formless God is real, and equally real is God with form. Nangtā used to instruct me about the nature of Satchidānanda Brahman. He would say that It is like an infinite ocean—water everywhere, to the right, left, above, and below. Water enveloped in water. It is the Water of the Great Cause, motionless. Waves spring up when It becomes active. Its activities are creation, preservation, and destruction.

"Again, he used to say that Brahman is where reason comes to a stop. There is the instance of camphor. Nothing remains after it is burnt—not even a trace of ash.

"Brahman is beyond mind and speech. A salt doll entered the ocean to measure its depth; but it did not return to tell others how deep the ocean was. It melted in the ocean itself.

"The rishis once said to Rāma: 'O Rāma, sages like Bharadvāja may very well call you an Incarnation of God, but we cannot do that. We adore the

Word-Brahman.[3] We do not want the human form of God.' Rāma smiled and went away, pleased with their adoration.

"But the Nitya and the Līlā are the two aspects of the same Reality. As I have said before, it is like the roof and the steps leading to it. The Absolute plays in many ways: as Iśvara, as the gods, as man, and as the universe. The Incarnation is the play of the Absolute as man. Do you know how the Absolute plays as man? It is like the rushing down of water from a big roof through a pipe; the power of Satchidānanda—nay, Satchidānanda Itself—descends through the conduit of a human form as water descends through the pipe. Only twelve sages, Bharadvāja and the others, recognized Rāma as an Incarnation of God. Not everyone can recognize an Incarnation.

"It is God alone who incarnates Himself as man to teach people the ways of love and knowledge. Well, what do you think of me?

"Once my father went to Gayā. There Raghuvir said to him in a dream, 'I shall be born as your son.' Thereupon my father said to Him: 'O Lord, I am a poor brāhmin. How shall I be able to serve You?' 'Don't worry about it', Raghuvir replied. 'It will be taken care of.'

"My sister, Hriday's mother, used to worship my feet with flowers and sandal-paste. One day I placed my foot on her head and said to her, 'You will die in Benares.'

"Once Mathur Babu said to me: 'Father, there is nothing inside you but God. Your body is like an empty shell. It may look from outside like a pumpkin, but inside there is nothing—neither flesh nor seed. Once I saw you as someone moving with a veil on.'

(*To M.*) "I am shown everything beforehand. Once I saw Gaurānga and his devotees singing kirtan in the Panchavati. I think I saw Balaram there and you too.

"I wanted to know the experiences of Gaurānga and was shown them at Śyāmbāzār in our native district. A crowd gathered; they even climbed the trees and the walls; they stayed with me day and night. For seven days I had no privacy whatever. Thereupon I said to the Divine Mother, 'Mother, I have had enough of it.'

"I am at peace now. I shall have to be born once more. Therefore I am not giving all knowledge to my companions. (*With a smile*) Suppose I give you all knowledge; will you then come to me again so willingly?

"I recognized you on hearing you read the *Chaitanya Bhāgavat*.[4] You are my own. The same substance, like father and son. All of you are coming here again. When you pull one part of the kalmi creeper, all the branches come toward you. You are all relatives—like brothers. Suppose Rakhal, Harish, and the others had gone to Puri, and you were there too. Would you live separately?

"Before you came here, you didn't know who you were. Now you will know. It is God who, as the guru, makes one know.

"Nangtā told the story of the tigress and the herd of goats. Once a tigress attacked a herd of goats. A hunter saw her from a distance and killed her.

[3] Om, the symbol of Brahman.
[4] A life of Chaitanya.

The tigress was pregnant and gave birth to a cub as she expired. The cub began to grow in the company of the goats. At first it was nursed by the she-goats, and later on, as it grew bigger, it began to eat grass and bleat like the goats. Gradually the cub became a big tiger; but still it ate grass and bleated. When attacked by other animals, it would run away, like the goats. One day a fierce-looking tiger attacked the herd. It was amazed to see a tiger in the herd eating grass and running away with the goats at its approach. It left the goats and caught hold of the grass-eating tiger, which began to bleat and tried to run away. But the fierce tiger dragged it to the water and said: 'Now look at your face in the water. You see, you have the pot-face of a tiger; it is exactly like mine.' Next it pressed a piece of meat into its mouth. At first the grass-eating tiger refused to eat the meat. Then it got the taste of the meat and relished it. At last the fierce tiger said to the grass-eater: 'What a disgrace! You lived with the goats and ate grass like them!' And the other was really ashamed of itself.

"Eating grass is like enjoying 'woman and gold'. To bleat and run away like a goat is to behave like an ordinary man. Going away with the new tiger is like taking shelter with the guru, who awakens one's spiritual consciousness, and recognizing him alone as one's relative. To see one's face rightly is to know one's real Self."

Sri Ramakrishna stood up. There was silence all around, disturbed only by the gentle rustling of the pine-needles and the murmuring of the Ganges. The Master went to the Panchavati and then to his room, talking all the while with M. The disciple followed him, fascinated. At the Panchavati Sri Ramakrishna touched with his forehead the raised platform around the banyan-tree. This was the place of his intense spiritual discipline, where he had wept bitterly for the vision of the Divine Mother, where he had held intimate communion with Her, and where he had seen many divine forms.

The Master and M. passed the cluster of bakul-trees and came to the nahabat. Hazra was there. The Master said to him: "Don't eat too much, and give up this craze for outer cleanliness. People with a craze do not attain Knowledge. Follow conventions only as much as necessary. Don't go to excess." The Master entered his room and sat on the couch.

Sri Ramakrishna was resting after his midday meal when Surendra, Ram, and other devotees arrived from Calcutta. It was about one o'clock. While M. was strolling alone under the pine-trees, Harish came there and told him that the Master wanted him in his room. Someone was going to read from the Śiva Samhitā, a book containing instructions about yoga and the six centres.

M. entered the room and saluted the Master. The devotees were seated on the floor, but no one was reading the book. Sri Ramakrishna was talking to the devotees.

MASTER: "The gopis cherished ecstatic love for Krishna. There are two elements in such love: 'I-ness' and 'my-ness'. 'I-ness' is the feeling that Krishna will be ill if 'I' do not serve Him. In this attitude the devotee does not look upon his Ideal as God.

" 'My-ness' is to feel that the Beloved is 'my' own. The gopis had such a feeling of 'my-ness' toward Krishna that they would place their subtle bodies under His feet lest His soles should get hurt.

"Yaśodā remarked: 'I don't understand your Chintāmani Krishna. To me He is simply Gopāla.' The gopis also said: 'Oh, where is Krishna, our Beloved? Where is Krishna, our Sweetheart?' They were not conscious of His being God.

"It is like a small child saying 'my daddy'. If someone says to the child, 'No, he is not your daddy', the child says, 'Yes, he is my daddy.'

"God, incarnating Himself as man, behaves exactly like a man. That is why it is difficult to recognize an Incarnation. When God becomes man, He is exactly like man. He has the same hunger, thirst, disease, grief, and sometimes even fear. Rāma was stricken with grief for Sītā. Krishna carried on His head the shoes and wooden stool of His father Nanda.

"In the theatre, when an actor comes on the stage in the role of a holy man, he behaves like one, and not like the actor who is taking the part of the king. He plays his own role.

"Once an impersonator dressed himself as a world-renouncing monk. Pleased with the correctness of his disguise, some rich people offered him a rupee. He did not accept the money but went away shaking his head. Afterwards he removed his disguise and appeared in his usual dress. Then he said to the rich people, 'Please give me the rupee.' They replied: 'Why, you went away refusing our present. Why do you ask for it now?' The man said: 'But then I was in the role of a holy man. I could not accept money.' Likewise, when God becomes man He behaves exactly like a man.

"At Vrindāvan one sees many places associated with Krishna's life."

SURENDRA: "We were there during the holidays. Visitors were continually pestered for money. The priests and others asked for it continually. We told them that we were going to leave for Calcutta the next day, but we fled from Vrindāvan that very night."

MASTER: "What is that? Shame! You said you would leave the place the next day and ran away that very day. What a shame!"

SURENDRA (embarrassed): "Here and there we saw the bābājis in the woods practising spiritual discipline in solitude."

MASTER: "Did you give them anything?"

SURENDRA: "No, sir."

MASTER: "That was not proper of you. One should give something to monks and devotees. Those who have the means should help such persons when they meet them.

"I went to Vrindāvan with Mathur Babu. The moment I came to the Dhruva Ghāt[5] at Mathurā, in a flash I saw Vasudeva crossing the Jamunā with Krishna in his arms.

"One evening I was taking a stroll on the beach of the river. There were small thatched huts on the beach and big plum-trees. It was the 'cow-dust' hour. The cows were returning from the pasture, raising dust with their

[5] A bathing-place in the Jamunā, where, according to tradition, Vasudeva, the father of Krishna, crossed the river carrying the new-born child through a stormy night.

hoofs. I saw them fording the river. Then came some cowherd boys crossing the river with their cows. No sooner did I behold this scene than I cried out, 'O Krishna, where are You?' and became unconscious.

"I wanted to visit Śyāmakunda and Rādhākunda; so Mathur Babu sent me there in a palanquin. We had a long way to go. Food was put in the palanquin. While going over the meadow I was overpowered with emotion and wept: 'O Krishna, I find everything the same; only You are not here. This is the very meadow where You tended the cows.' Hriday followed me on foot. I was bathed in tears. I couldn't ask the bearers to stop the palanquin.

"At Śyāmakunda and Rādhākunda I saw the holy men living in small mud huts. Facing away from the road lest their eyes should fall on men, they were engaged in spiritual discipline. One should visit the 'Twelve Grove'.

"I went into samādhi at the sight of the image of Bankuvihāri. In that state I wanted to touch it. I did not want to visit Govindaji twice. At Mathurā I dreamt of Krishna as the cowherd boy. Hriday and Mathur Babu had the same dream.

(To Surendra) "You have both—yoga and bhoga. There are different classes of sages: the brahmarshi, the devarshi, and the rājarshi. Śukadeva is an example of the brahmarshi. He didn't keep even one book with him. An example of the devarshi is Nārada. Janaka was a rājarshi, devoted to selfless work.

"The devotee of the Divine Mother attains dharma and moksha. He enjoys artha and kāma as well. Once I saw you in a vision as the child of the Divine Mother. You have both—yoga and bhoga; otherwise your countenance would look dry.

"The man who renounces all looks dry. Once I saw a devotee of the Divine Mother at the bathing-ghāt on the Ganges. He was eating his meal and at the same time worshipping the Mother. He looked on himself as the Mother's child.

"But it isn't good to have much money. I find that Jadu Mallick is drowned in worldliness. It is because he has too much money. Nabin Niyogi, too, has both yoga and bhoga. I saw him and his son waving the fan before the image of the Divine Mother at the time of the Durgā Pujā."

SURENDRA: "Sir, why can't I meditate?"

MASTER: "You remember God and think of Him, don't you?"

SURENDRA: "Yes, sir. I go to sleep repeating the word 'Mother'."

MASTER: "That is very good. It will be enough if you remember God and think of Him."

Sri Ramakrishna had taken Surendra's responsibilities on himself. Why should Surendra worry about anything?

It was evening. The Master was sitting on the floor of his room with the devotees. He was talking to them about yoga and the six centres. These are described in the Śiva Samhitā.

MASTER: "Idā, Pingalā, and Sushumnā are the three principal nerves. All the lotuses are located in the Sushumnā. They are formed of Consciousness, like a tree made of wax—the branches, twigs, fruits, and so forth all of wax. The Kundalini lies in the lotus of the Mulādhāra. That lotus has fourteen petals. The Primordial Energy resides in all bodies as the Kundalini. She is like a sleeping snake coiled up—'of the form of a sleeping snake, having the Mulādhāra for Her abode'. (To M.) The Kundalini is speedily awakened if one follows the path of bhakti. God cannot be seen unless She is awakened. Sing earnestly and secretly in solitude:

> Waken, O Mother! O Kundalini, whose nature is Bliss Eternal!
> Thou art the serpent coiled in sleep, in the lotus of the Mulādhāra.

"Rāmprasād achieved perfection through singing. One obtains the vision of God if one sings with yearning heart."

M: "Grief and distress of mind disappear if one has these experiences but once."

MASTER: "That is true. Distress of mind disappears for ever. I shall tell you a few things about yoga. But you see, the mother bird doesn't break the shell until the chick inside the egg is matured. The egg is hatched in the fullness of time. It is necessary to practise some spiritual discipline. The guru no doubt does everything for the disciple; but at the end he makes the disciple work a little himself. When cutting down a big tree, a man cuts almost through the trunk; then he stands aside for a moment, and the tree falls down with a crash.

"The farmer brings water to his field through a canal from the river. He stands aside when only a little digging remains to be done to connect the field with the water. Then the earth becomes soaked and falls of itself, and the water of the river pours into the canal in torrents.

"A man is able to see God as soon as he gets rid of ego and other limitations. He sees God as soon as he is free from such feelings as 'I am a scholar', 'I am the son of such and such a person', 'I am wealthy', 'I am honourable', and so forth.

" 'God alone is real and all else unreal; the world is illusory'—that is discrimination. One cannot assimilate spiritual instruction without discrimination.

"Through the practice of spiritual discipline one attains perfection, by the grace of God. But one must also labour a little. Then one sees God and enjoys bliss. If a man hears that a jar filled with gold is buried at a certain place, he rushes there and begins to dig. He sweats as he goes on digging. After much digging he feels the spade strike something. Then he throws away the spade and looks for the jar. At the sight of the jar he dances for joy. Then he takes up the jar and pours out the gold coins. He takes them into his hand, counts them, and feels the ecstasy of joy. Vision—touch—enjoyment. Isn't it so?"

M: "Yes, sir."

The Master was silent a moment and then went on.

MASTER: "Those who are my own will come here even if I scold them. Look at Narendra's nature! At first he used to abuse my Mother Kāli very much. One day I said to him sharply, 'Rascal! Don't come here any more.'

He slowly left the room and prepared a smoke. He who is one's own will not be angry even if scolded. What do you say?"

M: "That is true, sir."

MASTER: "Narendra is perfect from his very birth. He is devoted to the ideal of the formless God."

M. (smiling): "Whenever he comes here he brings along great excitement."

Sri Ramakrishna smiled and said, "Yes, excitement indeed."

The following day was Tuesday, the ekādaśi day of the lunar fortnight. It was eleven o'clock in the morning and the Master had not yet taken his meal. M., Rakhal, and other devotees were sitting in the Master's room.

MASTER (to M.): "One should fast on the eleventh day of the lunar fortnight. That purifies the mind and helps one to develop love of God. Isn't that so?"

M: "Yes, sir."

MASTER: "But you may take milk and puffed rice. Don't you think so?"

M. AT DAKSHINESWAR (II)

SRI RAMAKRISHNA, accompanied by Manilal Mallick, M., and several other devotees, was in a carriage on his way to Ram's new garden. The garden, which Ram had recently purchased, was next to Surendra's. Ram adored the Master as an Incarnation of God. He visited Sri Ramakrishna frequently at Dakshineswar. Manilal Mallick was a member of the Brāhmo Samāj. The Brāhmos do not believe in Divine Incarnations.

MASTER (*to Manilal*): "In order to meditate on God, one should try at first to think of Him as free from upādhis, limitations. God is beyond upādhis. He is beyond speech and mind. But it is very difficult to achieve perfection in this form of meditation.

"But it is easy to meditate on an Incarnation—God born as man. Yes, God in man. The body is a mere covering. It is like a lantern with a light burning inside, or like a glass case in which one sees precious things."

Arriving at the garden, the Master got out of the carriage and accompanied Ram and the other devotees to the sacred tulsi-grove. Standing near it, he said: "How nice! It is a fine place. You can easily meditate on God here."

Sri Ramakrishna sat down in the house, which stood to the south of the lake. Ram offered him a plate of fruit and sweets which he enjoyed with the devotees. After a short time he went around the garden.

Next Sri Ramakrishna proceeded toward Surendra's garden. He walked on foot a little distance and saw a sādhu sitting on a couch under a tree. At once he went up to the holy man and joyfully began a conversation with him.

MASTER: "To which order of monks do you belong? Have you any title—Giri, Puri, or the like?"

SĀDHU: "People call me a paramahamsa."

MASTER: "That is good. 'I am Śiva'—that is a good attitude. But I must tell you something else. The process of creation, preservation, and destruction that is going on day and night is due to Śakti, the Power of God. This Primal Power and Brahman are one and the same. Śakti cannot exist without Brahman, just as waves cannot exist without water. There cannot be any instrumental music without an instrument.

"As long as God keeps us in His relative world, so long we feel that there are two. If one accepts Śakti, one accepts Brahman as well. If one is aware of night, one is also aware of day. If one is aware of knowledge, one is also aware of ignorance.

"But there is another state in which God reveals to His devotee that Brahman is beyond both knowledge and ignorance. It cannot be described in words. What exists, exists."

After a pleasant conversation with the sādhu, the Master returned to the carriage, the holy man walking with him. Sri Ramakrishna looked upon him as a friend of long acquaintance, and they walked arm in arm.

The Master arrived at Surendra's garden. The very first thing he talked about was the sādhu.

MASTER: "He is a very nice man. (*To Ram*) Bring him to Dakshineswar when you come. He is really a good man. There is a line in a song to the effect that a man cannot recognize a holy person unless he is holy himself.

"The sādhu believes in God without form. That is good. God is both formless and endowed with form. He is many things more. The Absolute and the Relative belong to one and the same Reality. What is beyond speech and mind is born in the flesh, assuming various forms and engaging in various activities. From that one Om have sprung 'Om Śiva', 'Om Kāli', and 'Om Krishna'. Suppose the master of a house has sent out a small boy of the family to invite people to a feast. All look on the boy with great fondness and affection because he is the son or grandson of a prominent man."

The Master took refreshments at Surendra's garden house and then set out for Dakshineswar with the devotees.

Thursday, December 27, 1883

The temple garden was filled with the sweet music of the dawn service, which mingled with the morning melody from the nahabat. Leaving his bed, Sri Ramakrishna chanted the names of God in sweet tones. Then he bowed before the pictures of the different deities in his room and went to the west porch to salute the Ganges.

Some of the devotees who had spent the night at the temple garden came to the Master's room and bowed before him. Rakhal was staying with the Master, and Baburam had come the previous evening. M. had been staying there two weeks.

Sri Ramakrishna said to M.: "I have been invited to Ishan's this morning. Baburam will accompany me, and you too." M. made ready to go with the Master.

At eight o'clock the carriage hired for the Master stood waiting in front of the nahabat. On all sides plants and trees were in flower, and the river sparkled in the sunlight of the bright winter's day. The Master bowed once more before the pictures. Then, still chanting the name of the Divine Mother, he got into the carriage, followed by M. and Baburam. The devotees took with them Sri Ramakrishna's woolen shawl, woolen cap, and small bag of spices.

Sri Ramakrishna was very happy during the trip and enjoyed it like a child. About nine o'clock the carriage stopped at the door of Ishan's house.

Ishan and his relatives greeted the Master and led him to the parlour on the first floor. Shrish, Ishan's son, was introduced to Sri Ramakrishna. The young man practised law at Alipur. He had been a brilliant student, having stood first in two of the university examinations, but he was extremely modest.

MASTER (to Shrish): "What is your profession?"

SHRISH: "I am practising law at Alipur."

MASTER (to M.): "For such a man to be a lawyer! (To Shrish) Well, have you any questions to ask? Perhaps you want to know how to live un- attached in the world. Isn't that so?"

SHRISH: "Under the pressure of duties people do many unrighteous things in the world. Further, some are engaged in good work, and some in evil. Is this due to their actions in previous births? Is that why they act this way?"

MASTER: "How long should a man perform his duties? As long as he has not attained God. Duties drop away after the realization of God. Then one goes beyond good and evil. The flower drops off as soon as the fruit appears. The flower serves the purpose of begetting the fruit.

"How long should a devotee perform daily devotions such as the sandhyā? As long as his hair does not stand on end and his eyes do not shed tears at the name of God. These things indicate that the devotee has realized God. From these one knows that he has attained pure love of God. Realizing God one goes beyond virtue and vice.

I bow my head, says Prasād, before desire and liberation;
Knowing the secret that Kāli is one with the highest Brahman,
I have discarded, once for all, both righteousness and sin.

"The more you advance toward God, the less He will give you worldly duties to perform."

SHRISH: "It is extremely difficult to proceed toward God while leading the life of a householder."

MASTER: "Why so? What about the yoga of practice? At Kāmārpukur I have seen the women of the carpenter families selling flattened rice. Let me tell you how alert they are while doing their business. The pestle of the husking-machine that flattens the paddy constantly falls into the hole of the mortar. The woman turns the paddy in the hole with one hand and with the other holds her baby on her lap as she nurses it. In the mean time cus- tomers arrive. The machine goes on pounding the paddy, and she carries on her bargains with the customers. She says to them, 'Pay the few pennies you owe me before you take anything more.' You see, she has all these things to do at the same time—nurse the baby, turn the paddy as the pestle pounds it, take the flattened rice out of the hole, and talk to the buyers. This is called the yoga of practice. Fifteen parts of her mind out of sixteen are fixed on the pestle of the husking-machine, lest it should pound her hand. With only one part of her mind she nurses the baby and talks to the buyers. Like- wise, he who leads the life of a householder should devote fifteen parts of his mind to God; otherwise he will face ruin and fall into the clutches of

Death. He should perform the duties of the world with only one part of his mind.

"A man may lead the life of a householder after attaining Knowledge. But he must attain Knowledge first. If the milk of the mind is kept in the water of the world, they get mixed. Therefore he should turn the milk into curd and extract butter from it by churning it in solitude; then he may keep the butter in the water of the world. Therefore, you see, spiritual discipline is necessary. When the aśwattha tree is a mere sapling, it must be enclosed by a fence; otherwise the cattle will eat it. But the fence may be taken away when the trunk grows thick and strong. Then even an elephant tied to the tree cannot harm it.

"Therefore at the beginning the aspirant should go into solitude now and then. Spiritual discipline is necessary. You want to eat rice; suppose you sit down somewhere and say, 'Wood contains fire and fire cooks rice.' Can saying it cook the rice? You must get two pieces of wood and by rubbing them together bring out the fire.

"By eating siddhi one becomes intoxicated and feels happy. But suppose you haven't eaten the stuff or done anything else with it; you simply sit down somewhere and mutter, 'Siddhi! siddhi!' Will that intoxicate you or make you happy?

"You may learn a great deal from books; but it is all futile if you have no love for God and no desire to realize Him. A mere pundit, without discrimination and renunciation, has his attention fixed on 'woman and gold'. The vulture soars very high but its eyes are fixed on the charnel-pit.

"That alone is Knowledge through which one is able to know God. All else is futile. Well, what is your idea about God?"

SHRISH: "Sir, I feel that there is an All-knowing Person. We get an indication of His Knowledge by looking at His creation. Let me give an illustration. God has made devices to keep fish and other aquatic animals alive in cold regions. As water grows colder, it gradually shrinks. But the amazing thing is that, just before turning into ice, the water becomes light and expands. In the freezing cold, fish can easily live in the water of a lake: the surface of the lake may be frozen, but the water below is all liquid. If a very cold breeze blows, it is obstructed by the ice. The water below remains warm."

MASTER: "That God exists may be known by looking at the universe. But it is one thing to hear of God, another thing to see God, and still another thing to talk to God. Some have heard of milk, some have seen it, and some, again, have tasted it. You feel happy when you see milk; you are nourished and strengthened when you drink it. You will get peace of mind only when you have seen God. You will enjoy bliss and gain strength only when you have talked to Him."

SHRISH: "We do not have time to pray to God."

MASTER (with a smile): "That is true. Nothing comes to pass except at the right time. Going to bed, a child said to his mother, 'Mother, please wake me up when I feel the call of nature.' 'My son,' said the mother, 'that urge itself will wake you up. I don't have to wake you.'

"It is all decided beforehand by God what each one shall receive. A mother-in-law used to measure rice with a dish for her daughters-in-law. But it was not enough for them. One day the dish was broken and that made the girls happy. But the mother-in-law said to them, 'Children, you may shout and dance, but I can measure the rice with the palm of my hand.'

(To Shrish): "Surrender everything at the feet of God. What else can you do? Give Him the power of attorney. Let Him do whatever He thinks best. If you rely on a great man, he will never injure you.

"It is no doubt necessary to practise spiritual discipline; but there are two kinds of aspirants. The nature of the one kind is like that of the young monkey, and the nature of the other kind is like that of the kitten. The young monkey, with great exertion, somehow clings to its mother. Likewise, there are some aspirants who think that in order to realize God they must repeat His name a certain number of times, meditate on Him for a certain period, and practise a certain amount of austerity. An aspirant of this kind makes his own efforts to catch hold of God. But the kitten, of itself, cannot cling to its mother. It lies on the ground and cries, 'Mew, mew!' It leaves everything to its mother. The mother cat sometimes puts it on a bed, sometimes on the roof behind a pile of wood. She carries the kitten in her mouth hither and thither. The kitten doesn't know how to cling to the mother. Likewise, there are some aspirants who cannot practise spiritual discipline by calculating about japa or the period of meditation. All that they do is cry to God with yearning hearts. God hears their cry and cannot keep Himself away. He reveals Himself to them."

At noon the host wished to feed the Master and the devotees. Sri Rama-krishna was smilingly pacing the room. Now and then he exchanged a few words with the musician.

MUSICIAN: "It is God alone who is both the 'instrument' and the 'cause'. Duryodhana said to Krishna: 'O Lord, Thou art seated in my heart. I act as Thou makest me act.'"

MASTER (with a smile): "Yes, that is true. It is God alone who acts through us. He is the Doer, undoubtedly, and man is His instrument. But it is also true that an action cannot fail to produce its result. Your stomach will certainly burn if you eat hot chilli. It is God who has ordained that chilli will burn your stomach. If you commit a sin, you must bear its fruit. But one who has attained perfection, realized God, cannot commit sin. An expert singer cannot sing a false note. A man with a trained voice sings the notes correctly: sā, re, gā, mā, pā, dhā, ni."

The meal was ready. The Master and the devotees went to the inner court, where they were treated to a generous feast.

About three o'clock in the afternoon the Master was seated again in Ishan's drawing-room with M. and Shrish. He resumed his conversation with Shrish.

MASTER: "What is your attitude toward God? 'I am He', or 'Master and servant'? For the householder it is very good to look on God as the Master. The householder is conscious of doing the duties of life himself. Under such conditions how can he say, 'I am He'? To him who says, 'I am He' the world appears to be a dream. His mind, his body, even his ego, are dreams to him. Therefore he cannot perform worldly duties. So it is very good for the householder to look on himself as the servant and on God as the Master.

"Hanumān had the attitude of a servant. He said to Rāma: 'O Rāma, sometimes I meditate on You as the whole and on inyself as the part. Sometimes I feel that You are the Master and I am the servant. But when I have the Knowledge of Reality, I see that I am You and You are I.'

"In the state of Perfect Knowledge one may feel, 'I am He'; but that is far beyond the ordinary man's experience."

SHRISH: "That is true, sir. The attitude of a servant relieves a man of all his worries. The servant depends entirely upon his master. A dog is devoted to its master. It depends upon him and is at peace."

MASTER: "Well, what suits your taste—God with form or the formless. Reality? But to tell you the truth, He who is formless is also endowed with form. To His bhaktas He reveals Himself as having a form. It is like a great ocean, an infinite expanse of water, without any trace of shore. Here and there some of the water has been frozen. Intense cold has turned it into ice. Just so, under the cooling influence, so to speak, of the bhakta's love, the Infinite appears to take a form. Again, the ice melts when the sun rises; it becomes water as before. Just so, one who follows the path of knowledge —the path of discrimination—does not see the form of God any more. To him everything is formless. The ice melts into formless water with the rise of the Sun of Knowledge. But mark this: form and formlessness belong to one and the same Reality."

At dusk the Master was ready to start for Dakshineswar. He stood on the south porch of the drawing-room, talking to Ishan. Someone remarked that the chanting of God's holy name did not always produce results. Ishan said: "How can you say that? The seeds of an aśwattha tree are no doubt tiny, but in them lie the germs of big trees. It may take a very long time for them to grow."

"Yes, yes!" said the Master. "It takes a long time to see the effect."

Next to Ishan's was his father-in-law's house. Sri Ramakrishna stood at the door of this house, ready to get into the carriage. Ishan and his friends stood around to bid him adieu. Sri Ramakrishna said to Ishan: "You are living in the world as a mudfish lives in the mud. It lives in the mud but its body is not stained.

"There are both vidyā and avidyā in this world of māyā. Who may be called a paramahamsa? He who, like a swan, can take the milk from a mixture of milk and water, leaving aside the water. He who, like an ant, can take the sugar from a mixture of sugar and sand, leaving aside the sand."

It was evening. The Master stopped at Ram's house on his way to Dakshineswar. He was taken to the drawing-room and there he engaged in conversation with Mahendra Goswami. Mahendra belonged to the Vaishnava sect and was Ram's neighbour. Sri Ramakrishna was fond of him.

MASTER: "The worshippers of Vishnu and the worshippers of Śakti will all ultimately reach one and the same goal; the ways may be different. The true Vaishnavas do not criticize the Śāktas."

GOSWAMI (*smiling*): "Śiva and Pārvati are our Father and Mother."

Sri Ramakrishna, out of his stock of a dozen English words, said sweetly, "Thank you!" Then he added, "Yes, Father and Mother!"

GOSWAMI: "Besides, it is a sin to criticize anyone, especially a devotee of God. All sins may be forgiven, but not the sin of criticizing a devotee."

MASTER: "But this idea of sin does not by any means affect all. For instance, the Iśvarakotis, such as Incarnations of God, are above sin. Sri Chaitanya is an example.

"A child, walking on a narrow ridge and holding to his father, may slip into the ditch. But that can never happen if the father holds the child by the hand.

"Listen. I prayed to the Divine Mother for pure love. I said to Her: 'Here is Thy righteousness, here is Thy unrighteousness. Take them both and give me pure love for Thee. Here is Thy purity, here is Thy impurity. Take them both and give me pure love for Thee. O Mother, here is Thy virtue, here is Thy vice. Take them both and give me pure love for Thee.'"

GOSWAMI: "Yes, sir. That is right."

MASTER: "You should undoubtedly bow before all views. But there is a thing called unswerving devotion to one ideal. True, you should salute everyone. But you must love one ideal with your whole soul. That is unswerving devotion.

"Hanumān could not take delight in any other form than that of Rāma. The gopis had such single-minded love for the cowherd Krishna of Vrindāvan that they did not care to see the turbaned Krishna of Dwārakā.

"A wife may serve her husband's brothers by fetching water, or in other ways, but she cannot serve them in the way she does her husband. With him she has a special relationship."

Ram treated the Master to sweets. Sri Ramakrishna was ready to start for Dakshineswar. He put on his woolen shawl and cap, and got into the carriage with M. and the other devotees. Ram and his friends saluted the Master.

Saturday, December 29, 1883

It was the day of the new moon, auspicious for the worship of the Divine Mother. At one o'clock in the afternoon Sri Ramakrishna got into a carriage to visit the temple of Kāli at Kālighāt. He intended to stop at Adhar's house on the way, since Adhar was to accompany him to the temple. While the carriage was waiting near the north porch of the Master's room, M. went to the Master and said, "Sir, may I also go with you?"

MASTER: "Why?"

M: "I should like to visit my home in Calcutta."

Sri Ramakrishna reflected a moment and said: "Must you go home? Why? You are quite all right here."

M. wanted to see his people a few hours, but evidently the Master did not approve.

Sunday, December 30, 1883

At three o'clock in the afternoon, while M. was walking up and down under a tree, a devotee came to him and said that the Master had sent for him. M. went to Sri Ramakrishna's room and found a number of devotees there. He saluted the Master.

Ram, Kedar, and others had arrived from Calcutta. Ram had brought with him the Vedāntist monk whom the Master had visited near his garden a few days earlier. On that occasion Sri Ramakrishna had asked him to bring the sādhu to Dakshineswar.

The monk was sitting on the small couch with the Master. They were talking happily in Hindusthāni.

MASTER: "What do you feel about all this?"

MONK: "It is all like a dream."

MASTER: "Brahman alone is real and the world illusory. Well, sir, what is Brahman?"

MONK: "Brahman is the Sound. It is Om."

MASTER: "But there must be something indicated by the sound. Isn't that so?"

MONK: "That Itself is the thing indicated as well as the indicator."

At these words Sri Ramakrishna went into samādhi and sat motionless. The monk and the devotees looked wonderingly at him in his ecstatic condition. Kedar said to the monk: "Look at him, sir. This is samādhi."

The monk had read of samādhi but had never seen it before. After a few minutes the Master began gradually to come down to the normal plane of consciousness. He said to the Divine Mother: "Mother, I want to be normal. Please don't make me unconscious. I should like to talk to the sādhu about Satchidānanda. Mother, I want to be merry talking about Satchidānanda."

The monk was amazed to see the Master's condition and to hear these words. Sri Ramakrishna said to him: "Please do away with your 'I am He'. Let us now keep 'I' and 'Thou' to enjoy the fun."

A little later the Master was walking in the Panchavati with Ram, Kedar, M., and the other devotees.

MASTER (to Kedar, with a smile): "What did you think of the sādhu?"

KEDAR: "It is all dry knowledge. The pot has just been put on the fire, but as yet there is no rice in it."

MASTER: "That may be true. But he has renounced everything. He who has renounced the world has already made great progress. The sādhu belongs to the stage of the beginner. Nothing can be achieved without the realization of God. When a man is intoxicated with ecstatic love of God, he doesn't take delight in anything else. Then—

> Cherish my precious Mother Śyāmā
> Tenderly within, O mind;
> May you and I alone behold Her,
> Letting no one else intrude."

Kedar repeated the words of a song in keeping with the Master's feeling:

> How shall I open my heart, O friend?
> It is forbidden me to speak.
> I am about to die, for lack of a kindred soul
> To understand my misery. . . .

Sri Ramakrishna returned to his room. About four o'clock the door of the Kāli temple was opened, and the Master walked to the temple with the monk; M. accompanied them. Entering the inner chamber, the Master prostrated himself reverently before the image. The monk, with folded hands, also bowed his head repeatedly before Kāli.

MASTER: "What do you think of Kāli?"

MONK (with devotion): "Kāli is supreme."

MASTER: "Kāli and Brahman are identical. Is that not so?"

MONK: "As long as one's mind is turned to the outer world, one must accept Kāli. As long as a man sees the outer world, and discriminates between good and evil, he must accept good and reject evil. To be sure, all names and forms are illusory; but as long as the mind sees the outer world, the aspirant must give up woman. The ideas of good and evil are applied to one who is still a student on the path; otherwise he will stray from the path of righteousness."

Thus conversing, the Master and the monk returned from the temple.

MASTER (to M.): "Did you notice that the sādhu bowed before Kāli?"

M: "Yes, sir."

Monday, December 31, 1883

At four o'clock in the afternoon the Master was sitting in his room with M., Rakhal, Latu, Harish, and other devotees.

Addressing M. and Balaram, the Master said: "Haladhari followed the path of knowledge. Day and night he used to study the Upanishads, the Adhyātma Rāmāyana, and similar books on Vedānta. He would turn up his nose at the mention of the forms of God. Once I ate from the leaf-plates of the beggars. At this Haladhari said to me, 'How will you be able to marry your children?' I said: 'You rascal! Shall I ever have children? May your mouth that repeats words from the Gītā and the Vedānta be blighted!' Just fancy! He declared that the world was illusory and, again, would meditate in the temple of Vishnu with turned-up nose."

In the evening Balaram and the other devotees returned to Calcutta. The Master remained in his room, absorbed in contemplation of the Divine Mother. After a while the sweet music of the evening worship in the temples was heard.

A little later the Master began to talk to the Mother in a tender voice that touched the heart of M., who was seated on the floor. After repeating, "Hari Om! Hari Om! Om!", the Master said: "Mother, don't make me unconscious with the Knowledge of Brahman. Mother, I don't want Brahmajnāna. I want to be merry. I want to play." Again he said: "Mother, I don't know the Vedānta; and Mother, I don't even care to know. The Vedas and the Vedānta remain so far below when Thou art realized, O Divine Mother!" Then he said: "O Krishna, I shall say to Thee, 'Eat, my Child! Take this, my Child!' O Krishna, I shall say to Thee, 'My Child, Thou hast assumed this body for my sake.'"

Wednesday, January 2, 1884

Rakhal, Latu, Harish, Ramlal, and M. had been staying with Sri Rama-krishna at the temple garden. About three o'clock in the afternoon M. found the Master on the west porch of his room engaged in conversation with a Tāntrik devotee. The Tāntrik was wearing an ochre cloth. Sri Ramakrishna asked M. to sit by his side. Perhaps the Master intended to instruct him through his talk with the Tāntrik devotee. Mahima Chakravarty had sent the latter to the Master.

MASTER (to the Tāntrik): "It is a part of the Tāntrik discipline to drink wine from a human skull. This wine is called 'kārana'. Isn't that so?"

TĀNTRIK: "Yes, sir."

MASTER: "But I cannot touch wine at all."

TĀNTRIK: "You have spontaneous Divine Bliss. One who enjoys that Bliss wants nothing else."

MASTER: "I don't care for japa and austerity. But I have constant remem-brance and consciousness of God.

"Tell me, when they speak of the six centres, what do they mean?"

TĀNTRIK: "These are like different holy places. In each of the centres dwell Śiva and Śakti. One cannot see them with the physical eyes. One cannot take them out by cutting open the body."

M. listened silently to the conversation. Looking at him, the Master asked the Tāntrik devotee, "Can a man attain perfection without the help of a vija mantra, a sacred word from the guru?"

TĀNTRIK: "Yes, he can if he has faith—faith in the words of the guru."

The Master turned to M. and said, drawing his attention, "Faith!"

After the Tāntrik devotee had taken his leave, Jaygopal Sen, a member of the Brāhmo Samāj, arrived. The Master talked with him.

MASTER (to Jaygopal): "One should not harbour malice toward any per-son or any opinion. The believers in the formless God and the worshippers of God with form are all, without exception, going toward God alone. The jnāni, the yogi, the bhakta—all, without exception, are seeking Him alone. The follower of the path of knowledge calls Him 'Brahman'. The yogi calls Him 'Ātman' or 'Paramātman'. The bhakta calls Him 'Bhagavān'. Further, it is said that there is the Eternal Lord and His Eternal Servant."

JAYGOPAL: "How can we know that all paths are true?"

MASTER: "A man can reach God if he follows one path rightly. Then he can learn about all the other paths. It is like reaching the roof by some means or other. Then one is able to climb down by the wooden or stone stairs, by a bamboo pole, or even by a rope.

"A devotee can know everything when God's grace descends on him. If you but realize Him, you will be able to know all about Him. You should somehow meet the master of a house and become acquainted with him; then he himself will tell you how many houses he owns and all about his gardens and government securities."

JAYGOPAL: "How does one receive the grace of God?"

MASTER: "Constantly you have to chant the name and glories of God and give up worldly thoughts as much as you can. With the greatest effort you may try to bring water into your field for your crops, but it may all leak out through holes in the ridges. Then all your efforts to bring the water by digging a canal will be futile.

"You will feel restless for God when your heart becomes pure and your mind free from attachment to the things of the world. Then alone will your prayer reach God. A telegraph wire cannot carry messages if it has a break or some other defect.

"I used to cry for God all alone, with a longing heart. I used to weep, 'O God, where art Thou?' Weeping thus, I would lose all consciousness of the world. My mind would merge in the Mahāvāyu.

"How can one attain yoga? By completely renouncing attachment to worldly things. The mind must be pure and without blemish, like the telegraph wire that has no defect.

"One must not cherish any desire whatever. The devotion of a man who has any desire is selfish. But desireless devotion is love for its own sake. You may love me or not, but I love you: this is love for its own sake.

"The thing is that one must love God. Through intense love one attains the vision of Him. The attraction of the husband for the chaste wife, the attraction of the child for its mother, the attraction of worldly possessions for the worldly man—when a man can blend these three into one, and direct it all to God, then he gets the vision of God."

Jaygopal was a man of the world. Was this why the Master gave instruction suited to him?

At eight o'clock that evening the Master was sitting in his room with Rakhal and M. It was the twenty-first day of M.'s stay with Sri Ramakrishna. The Master had forbidden him to indulge in reasoning.

MASTER (to Rakhal): "It is not good to reason too much. First comes God, and then the world. Realize God first; then you will know all about His world. (To M. and Rakhal) If first one is introduced to Jadu Mallick, then one can know everything about him—the number of his houses, gardens, government securities, and so on. For this reason the rishi Nārada advised Vālmiki[1] to repeat the word 'marā'. 'Ma' means God, and 'rā' the world. First comes God, and then the world. Krishnakishore said that the word 'marā' is a holy mantra because it was given to Vālmiki by the rishi. 'Ma' means God, and 'rā' the world.

[1] The author of the Rāmāyaṇa. It is said that this sage had lived the life of a highwayman. Coming in contact with Nārada, he became eager to lead a spiritual life. Nārada asked him to chant the holy name of Rāma as a spiritual discipline; but on account of the sinful tendency of his mind, Vālmiki could not utter the holy word. He was then advised to repeat the word 'marā', the reverse of 'Rāma'. Through yearning and earnestness the heart of the robber became purified, and it was then possible for him to chant Rāma's name. As a result he attained perfection.

"Therefore, like Vālmiki, one should at first renounce everything and cry to God in solitude with a longing heart. The first thing necessary is the vision of God; then comes reasoning—about the scriptures and the world.

(*To M.*) "That is why I have been telling you not to reason any more. I came from the pine-grove to say that to you. Through too much reasoning your spiritual life will be injured; you will at last become like Hazra. I used to roam at night in the streets, all alone, and cry to the Divine Mother, 'O Mother, blight with Thy thunderbolt my desire to reason!' Tell me that you won't reason any more."

M: "Yes, sir. I won't reason any more."

MASTER: "Everything can be achieved through bhakti alone. Those who want the Knowledge of Brahman will certainly achieve that also by following the trail of bhakti.

"Can a man blessed with the grace of God ever lack Knowledge? At Kāmārpukur I have seen grain-dealers measuring paddy. As one heap is measured away another heap is pushed forward to be measured. The Mother supplies the devotees with the 'heap' of Knowledge.

"After attaining God, one looks on a pundit as mere straw and dust. Padmalochan said to me: 'What does it matter if I accompany you to a meeting at the house of a fisherman?[2] With you I can dine even at the house of a pariah.'

"Everything can be realized simply through love of God. If one is able to love God, one does not lack anything. Kārtika and Ganeśa[3] were seated near Bhagavati, who had a necklace of gems around Her neck. The Divine Mother said to them, 'I will present this necklace to him who is the first to go around the universe.' Thereupon Kārtika, without losing a moment, set out on the peacock, his carrier. Ganeśa, on the other hand, in a leisurely fashion went around the Divine Mother and prostrated himself before Her. He knew that She contained within Herself the entire universe. The Divine Mother was pleased with him and put the necklace around his neck. After a long while Kārtika returned and found his brother seated there with the necklace on.

"Weeping, I prayed to the Mother: 'O Mother, reveal to me what is contained in the Vedas and the Vedānta. Reveal to me what is in the Purāna and the Tantra.' One by one She has revealed all these to me.

"Yes, She has taught me everything. Oh, how many things She has shown me! One day She showed me Śiva and Śakti everywhere. Everywhere I saw the communion of Śiva and Śakti. Śiva and Śakti existing in all living things—men, animals, trees, plants. I saw Them in the communion of all male and female elements.

"Another day I was shown heaps of human heads, mountain high. Nothing else existed, and I was seated alone in their midst.

"Still another day She showed me an ocean. Taking the form of a salt doll, I was going to measure its depth. While doing this, through the grace of the guru I was turned to stone. Then I saw a ship and at once got into it.

[2] A reference to Mathur Babu, who belonged to the fisherman caste. The orthodox brāhmin refuses to set foot in the house of a fisherman, who belongs to a low caste.
[3] The two sons of Bhagavati, the Divine Mother.

The helmsman was the guru. I hope you pray every day to Satchidānanda, who is the Guru. Do you?"

M: "Yes, sir."

MASTER: "The guru was the helmsman in that boat. I saw that 'I' and 'you' were two different things. Again I jumped into the ocean, and was changed into a fish. I found myself swimming joyfully in the Ocean of Satchidānanda.

"These are all deep mysteries. What can you understand through reasoning? You will realize everything when God Himself teaches you. Then you will not lack any knowledge."

Friday, January 4, 1884

Sri Ramakrishna was sitting in his room. M. was still staying with the Master, devoting his time to the practice of spiritual discipline. He had been spending a great part of each day in prayer and meditation under the bel-tree, where the Master had performed great austerities and had seen many wonderful visions of God.

MASTER (*to M.*): "Don't reason any more. In the end, reasoning only injures the aspirant. One should assume a particular attitude toward God while praying to Him—the attitude of friend or servant or son or 'hero'.

"I assume the attitude of a child. To me every woman is my mother. The divine Māyā, seeing this attitude in an aspirant, moves away from his path out of sheer shame.

"The attitude of 'hero' is extremely difficult. The Śāktas and the Bāuls among the Vaishnavas follow it, but it is very hard to keep one's spiritual life pure in that attitude. One can assume other attitudes toward God as well—the attitude in which the devotee serenely contemplates God as the Creator, the attitude of service to Him, the attitude of friendship, the attitude of motherly affection, or the attitude of conjugal love. The conjugal relationship, the attitude of a woman to her husband or sweetheart, contains all the rest —serenity, service, friendship, and motherly affection. (*To M.*) Which one of these appeals to your mind?"

M: "I like them all."

MASTER: "When one attains perfection one takes delight in all these relationships. In that state a devotee has not the slightest trace of lust. The holy books of the Vaishnavas speak of Chandidās and the washerwoman. Their love was entirely free from lust.

"In that state a devotee looks on himself as a woman. He does not regard himself as a man. Sanātana Goswāmi refused to see Mirābāi because she was a woman. Mirā informed him that at Vrindāvan the only man was Krishna and that all others were His handmaids. 'Was it right of Sanātana to think of himself as a man?' Mirā inquired."

At dusk M. was sitting at the Master's feet. Sri Ramakrishna had been told that Keshab's illness had taken a turn for the worse. He was talking about Keshab and incidentally about the Brāhmo Samāj.

MASTER (*to M.*): "Do they only give lectures in the Brāhmo Samāj? Or do they also meditate? I understand that they call their service in the temple upāsana.

"Keshab at one time thought a great deal of Christianity and the Christian views. At that time, and even before, he belonged to Devendranath Tagore's organization."

M: "Had Keshab Babu come here from the very beginning, he would not have been so preoccupied with social reform. He would not have been so busy with the abolition of the caste system, widow remarriage, inter-caste marriage, women's education, and such social activities."

MASTER: "Keshab now believes in Kāli as the Embodiment of Spirit and Consciousness, the Primal Energy. Besides, he repeats the holy name of the Mother and chants Her glories.

"Do. you think the Brāhmo Samāj will develop in the future into a sort of social-reform organization?"

M: "The soil of this country is different. Only what is true survives here."

MASTER: "Yes, that is so. The Sanātana Dharma, the Eternal Religion declared by the rishis, will alone endure. But there will also remain some sects like the Brāhmo Samāj. Everything appears and disappears through the will of God."

Earlier in the afternoon several devotees from Calcutta had visited the Master and had sung many songs. One of the songs contained the following idea: "O Mother, You have cajoled us with red toys. You will certainly come running to us when we throw them away and cry ourselves hoarse for You."

MASTER (to M.): "How well they sang about the red toys!"

M: "Yes, sir. You once told Keshab about the red toys."

MASTER: "Yes. I also told him about the Chidākāśa, the Inner Consciousness, and about many other things. Oh, how happy we were! We used to sing and dance together."

Saturday, January 5, 1884

It was the twenty-third day of M.'s stay with Sri Ramakrishna. M. had finished his midday meal about one o'clock and was resting in the nahabat when suddenly he heard someone call his name three or four times. Coming out, he saw Sri Ramakrishna calling to him from the verandah north of his room.

M. saluted the Master and they conversed on the south verandah.

MASTER: "I want to know how you meditate. When I meditated under the bel-tree I used to see various visions clearly. One day I saw in front of me money, a shawl, a tray of sandesh, and two women. I asked my mind, 'Mind, do you want any of these?' I saw the sandesh to be mere filth. One of the women had a big ring in her nose. I could see both their inside and outside—entrails, filth, bone, flesh, and blood. The mind did not want any of these—money, shawl, sweets, or women. It remained fixed at the Lotus Feet of God.

"A small balance has two needles, the upper and the lower. The mind is the lower needle. I was always afraid lest the mind should move away from the upper needle—God. Further, I would see a man always sitting by me with a trident in his hand. He threatened to strike me with it if the lower needle. moved away from the upper one.

"But no spiritual progress is possible without the renunciation of 'woman and gold'. I renounced these three: land, wife, and wealth. Once I went to the Registry Office to register some land, the title of which was in the name of Raghuvir. The officer asked me to sign my name; but I didn't do it, because I couldn't feel that it was 'my' land. I was shown much respect as the guru of Keshab Sen. They presented me with mangoes, but I couldn't carry them home. A sannyāsi cannot lay things up.

"How can one expect to attain God without renunciation? Suppose one thing is placed upon another; how can you get the second without removing the first?

"One must pray to God without any selfish desire. But selfish worship, if practised with perseverance, is gradually turned into selfless worship. Dhruva practised tapasyā to obtain his kingdom, but at last he realized God. He said, 'Why should a man give up gold if he gets it while searching for glass beads?'

"God can be realized when a man acquires sattva. Householders engage in philanthropic work, such as charity, mostly with a motive. That is not good. But actions without motives are good. Yet it is very difficult to leave motives out of one's actions.

"When you realize God, will you pray to Him, 'O God, please grant that I may dig reservoirs, build roads, and found hospitals and dispensaries'? After the realization of God all such desires are left behind.

"Then mustn't one perform acts of compassion, such as charity to the poor? I do not forbid it. If a man has money, he should give it to remove the sorrows and sufferings that come to his notice. In such an event the wise man says, 'Give the poor something.' But inwardly he feels: 'What can I do? God alone is the Doer. I am nothing.'

"The great souls, deeply affected by the sufferings of men, show them the way to God. Śankarāchārya kept the 'ego of Knowledge' in order to teach mankind. The gift of knowledge and devotion is far superior to the gift of food. Therefore Chaitanyadeva distributed bhakti to all, including the out-caste. Happiness and suffering are the inevitable characteristics of the body. You have come to eat mangoes. Fulfil that desire. The one thing needful is jnāna and bhakti. God alone is Substance; all else is illusory.

"It is God alone who does everything. You may say that in that case man may commit sin. But that is not true. If a man is firmly convinced that God alone is the Doer and that he himself is nothing, then he will never make a false step.

"It is God alone who has planted in man's mind what the 'Englishman'[4] calls free will. People who have not realized God would become engaged in more and more sinful actions if God had not planted in them the notion of free will. Sin would have increased if God had not made the sinner feel that he alone was responsible for his sin.

"Those who have realized God are aware that free will is a mere appear-

[4] Sri Ramakrishna used this word to denote Europeans in general, and also those whose ways and thoughts were largely influenced by Western ideas.

ance. In reality man is the machine and God its Operator, man is the carriage and God its Driver."

It was about four o'clock. Rakhal and several other devotees were listening to a kirtan by M. in the hut at the Panchavati. Rakhal went into a spiritual mood while listening to the devotional song. After a while the Master came to the Panchavati accompanied by Baburam and Harish. Other devotees followed.

RAKHAL: "How well he [referring to M.] sang kirtan for us! He made us all very happy."

The Master sang in an ecstatic mood:

> O friends, how great is my relief
> To hear you chanting Krishna's name! . . .

To the devotees he said, "Always sing devotional songs." Continuing, he said: "To love God and live in the company of the devotees: that is all. What more is there?" He said, again: "When Krishna went to Mathurā, Yaśodā came to Rādhā, who was absorbed in meditation. Afterwards Rādhā said to Yaśodā: 'I am the Primordial Energy. Ask a boon of Me.' 'What other boon shall I ask of You?' said Yaśodā. 'Only bless me that I may serve God with my body, mind, and tongue; that I may behold His devotees with these eyes, that I may meditate on Him with this mind, and that I may chant His name and glories with this tongue.'

"But those who are firmly established in God may do as well without the devotees. This is true of those who feel the presence of God both within and without. Sometimes they don't enjoy the devotees' company. You don't whitewash a wall inlaid with mother of pearl—the lime won't stick."

The Master returned presently from the Panchavati, talking to M.

MASTER: "You have the voice of a woman. Can't you practise a song such as this?—

> Tell me, friend, how far is the grove
> Where Krishna, my Beloved, dwells?

(To M., pointing to Baburam) "You see, my own people have become strangers; Ramlal and my other relatives seem to be foreigners. And strangers have become my own. Don't you notice how I tell Baburam to go and wash his face? The devotees have become relatives.

(Looking at the Panchavati) "I used to sit there. In course of time I became mad. That phase also passed away. Kāla, Śiva, is Brahman. That which sports with Kāla is Kāli, the Primal Energy. Kāli moves even the Immutable."

Saying this, the Master sang:

> My mind is overwhelmed with wonder,
> Pondering the Mother's mystery;
> Her very name removes
> The fear of Kāla, Death himself;
> Beneath Her feet lies Mahā-Kāla. . . .

Then he said to M.: "Today is Saturday.[5] Go to the temple of Kāli."

[5] Saturday and Tuesday are regarded as auspicious days for the worship of the Divine Mother.

As the Master came to the bakul-tree he spoke to M. again: "Chidātmā and Chitśakti. The Purusha is the Chidātmā and Prakriti is the Chitśakti. Sri Krishna is the Chidātmā and Sri Rādhā the Chitśakti. The devotees are so many forms of the Chitśakti. They should think of themselves as companions or handmaids of the Chitśakti, Sri Rādhā. This is the whole gist of the thing."

After dusk Sri Ramakrishna went to the Kāli temple and was pleased to see M. meditating there.

The evening worship was over in the temples. The Master returned to his room and sat on the couch, absorbed in meditation on the Divine Mother. M. sat on the floor. There was no one else in the room.

The Master was in samādhi. He began to come gradually down to the normal plane. His mind was still filled with the consciousness of the Divine Mother. In that state he was speaking to Her like a small child making importunate demands on his mother. He said in a piteous voice: "Mother, why haven't You revealed to me that form of Yours, the form that bewitches the world? I pleaded with You so much for it. But You wouldn't listen to me. You act as You please."

The voice in which these words were uttered was very touching.

He went on: "Mother, one needs faith. Away with this wretched reasoning! Let it be blighted! One needs faith—faith in the words of the guru, childlike faith. The mother says to her child, 'A ghost lives there', and the child is firmly convinced that the ghost is there. Again, the mother says to the child, 'A bogy man is there', and the child is sure of it. Further, the mother says, pointing to a man, 'He is your elder brother', and the child believes that the man is one hundred and twenty-five per cent his brother. One needs faith. But why should I blame them, Mother? What can they do? It is necessary to go through reasoning once. Didn't You see how much I told him about it the other day? But it all proved useless."

The Master was weeping and praying to the Mother in a voice choked with emotion. He prayed to Her with tearful eyes for the welfare of the devotees: "Mother, may those who come to You have all their desires fulfilled! But please don't make them give up everything at once, Mother. Well, You may do whatever You like in the end. If You keep them in the world, Mother, then please reveal Yourself to them now and then. Otherwise, how will they live? How will they be encouraged if they don't see You once in a while? But You may do whatever You like in the end."

The Master was still in the ecstatic mood. Suddenly he said to M: "Look here, you have had enough of reasoning. No more of it. Promise that you won't reason any more."

M. (with folded hands): "Yes, sir. I won't."

MASTER: "You have had enough of it. When you came to me the first time, I told you your spiritual Ideal. I know everything about you, do I not?"

M. (with folded hands): "Yes, sir."

MASTER: "Yes, I know everything: what your Ideal is, who you are, your inside and outside, the events of your past lives, and your future. Do I not?"

M. (*with folded hands*): "Yes, sir."

MASTER: "I scolded you on learning that you had a son. Now go home and live there. Let them know that you belong to them. But you must remember in your heart of hearts that you do not belong to them nor they to you."

M. sat in silence. The Master went on instructing him.

MASTER: "You have now learnt to fly. But keep your loving relationship with your father. Can't you prostrate yourself before him?"

M. (*with folded hands*): "Yes, sir. I can."

MASTER: "What more shall I say to you? You know everything. You understand, don't you?"

M. sat there without uttering a word.

MASTER: "You have understood, haven't you?"

M: "Yes, sir, I now understand a little."

MASTER: "No, you understand a great deal. Rakhal's father is pleased about his staying here."

M. remained with folded hands.

MASTER: "Yes, what you are thinking will also come to pass."

Sri Ramakrishna now came down to the normal state of mind. Rakhal and Ramlal entered the room. At the Master's bidding Ramlal sang:

> Who is the Woman yonder who lights the field of battle?
> Darker Her body gleams even than the darkest storm-cloud
> And from Her teeth there flash the lightning's blinding flames! . . .

He sang again:

> Who is this terrible Woman, dark as the sky at midnight?
> Who is this Woman dancing over the field of battle? . . .

MASTER: "The Divine Mother and the earthly mother. It is the Divine Mother who exists in the form of the universe and pervades everything as Consciousness. The earthly mother gives birth to this body. I used to go into samādhi uttering the word 'Mā'. While repeating the word I would draw the Mother of the Universe to me, as it were, like the fishermen casting their net and after a while drawing it in. When they draw in the net they find big fish inside it.

"Gauri once said that one attains true Knowledge when one realizes the identity of Kālī and Gaurānga.[6] That which is Brahman is also Śakti, Kālī. It is That, again, which, assuming the human form, has become Gaurānga."

At the Master's request, Ramlal sang again, this time about Gaurānga.

MASTER (*to M.*): "The Nitya and the Līlā are the two aspects of the Reality. God plays in the world as man for the sake of His devotees. They can love God only if they see Him in a human form; only then can they show their affection for Him as their Brother, Sister, Father, Mother, or Child.

"It is just for this love of the devotees that God contracts Himself into a human form and descends on earth to play His līlā."

[6] An uncompromising hostility exists between the devotees of Kālī and the devotees of Gaurānga.

THE MASTER AND HIS INJURED ARM

Saturday, February 2, 1884

IT WAS THREE O'CLOCK in the afternoon. Sri Ramakrishna had been conversing with Rakhal, Mahimacharan, Hazra, and other devotees, when M. entered the room and saluted him. He brought with him splint, pad, and lint to bandage the Master's injured arm.

One day, while going toward the pine-grove, Sri Ramakrishna had fallen near the railing and dislocated a bone in his left arm. He had been in an ecstatic mood at the time and no one had been with him.

MASTER (to M.): "Hello! What was ailing you? Are you quite well now?"

M: "Yes, sir, I am all right now."

MASTER (to Mahima): "Well, if I am the machine and God is its Operator, then why should this have happened to me?"

The Master was sitting on the couch, listening to the story of Mahimacharan's pilgrimage. Mahima had visited several holy places twelve years before.

MAHIMA: "I found a brahmachāri in a garden at Sicrole in Benares. He said he had been living there for twenty years but did not know its owner. He asked me if I worked in an office. On my answering in the negative, he said, 'Then are you a wandering holy man?' I saw a sādhu on the bank of the Narmadā. He repeated the Gāyatri mentally. It so thrilled him that the hair on his body stood on end. And when he repeated the Gāyatri and Om aloud, it thrilled those who sat near him and caused their hair to stand on end."

The Master was in the mood of a child. Being hungry he said to M., "What have you brought for me?" Looking at Rakhal he went into samādhi.

He was gradually coming down to the normal plane. To bring his mind back to the consciousness of the body, he said: "I shall eat some jilipi. I shall drink some water."

Weeping like a child, he said to the Divine Mother: "O Brahmamayi! O Mother! Why hast Thou done this to me? My arm is badly hurt. (To the devotees) Will I be all right again?" They consoled him, as one would a child, and said: "Surely. You will be quite well again."

MASTER (to Rakhal): "You aren't to blame for it, though you are living here to look after me; for even if you had accompanied me, you certainly wouldn't have gone up to the railing."

The Master again went into a spiritual mood and said: "Om! Om! Om! Mother, what is this that I am saying? Don't make me unconscious, Mother, with the Knowledge of Brahman. Don't give me Brahmajñāna. I am but Thy child. I am easily worried and frightened. I want a Mother. A million salutations to the Knowledge of Brahman! Give it to those who seek it. O Ānandamayi! O Blissful Mother!"

Uttering loudly the word "Ānandamayi", he burst into tears and said:

> Mother, this is the grief that sorely grieves my heart,
> That even with Thee for Mother, and though I am wide awake,
> There should be robbery in my house.

Again he said to the Divine Mother: "What wrong have I done, Mother? Do I ever do anything? It is Thou, Mother, who doest everything. I am the machine and Thou art its Operator.

(To Rakhal, smiling) "See that you don't fall! Don't be piqued and cheat yourself."

Again addressing the Mother, Sri Ramakrishna said: "Do I weep because I am hurt? Not at all.

> Mother, this is the grief that sorely grieves my heart,
> That even with Thee for Mother, and though I am wide awake,
> There should be robbery in my house."

The Master was again talking and laughing, like a child who, though ailing, sometimes forgets his illness and laughs and plays about.

MASTER (to the devotees): "It will avail you nothing unless you realize Satchidānanda. There is nothing like discrimination and renunciation. The worldly man's devotion to God is momentary—like a drop of water on a red-hot frying-pan. Perchance he looks at a flower and exclaims, 'Ah, what a wonderful creation of God!'

"One must be restless for God. If a son clamours persistently for his share of the property, his parents consult with each other and give it to him eve though he is a minor. God will certainly listen to your prayers if you feel restless for Him. Since He has begotten us, surely we can claim our inheritance from Him. He is our own Father, our own Mother. We can force our demand on Him. We can say to Him, 'Reveal Thyself to me or I shall cut my throat with a knife!' "

Sri Ramakrishna taught the devotees how to call on the Divine Mother.

MASTER: "I used to pray to Her in this way: 'O Mother! O Blissful One! Reveal Thyself to me. Thou must!' Again, I would say to Her: 'O Lord of the lowly! O Lord of the universe! Surely I am not outside Thy universe. I am bereft of knowledge. I am without discipline. I have no devotion. I know nothing. Thou must be gracious and reveal Thyself to me.' "

Thus the Master taught the devotees how to pray. They were deeply touched. Tears filled Mahimacharan's eyes.

Sri Ramakrishna looked at him and sang:

> Cry to your Mother Śyāmā with a real cry, O mind!
> And how can She hold Herself from you?
> How can Śyāmā stay away? . . .

Several devotees arrived from Shibpur. Since they had come from a great distance the Master could not disappoint them. He told them some of the essentials of spiritual life.

MASTER: "God alone is real, and all else illusory. The garden and its owner. God and His splendour. But people look at the garden only. How few seek out the owner!"

A DEVOTEE: "Sir, what is the way?"

MASTER: "Discrimination between the Real and the unreal. One should always discriminate to the effect that God alone is real and the world unreal. And one should pray with sincere longing."

DEVOTEE: "But, sir, where is our leisure for these things?"

MASTER: "Those who have the time must meditate and worship. But those who cannot possibly do so must bow down whole-heartedly to God twice a day. He abides in the hearts of all; He knows that worldly people have many things to do. What else is possible for them? You don't have time to pray to God; therefore give Him the power of attorney. But all is in vain unless you attain God and see Him."

ANOTHER DEVOTEE: "Sir, to see you is the same as to see God."

MASTER: "Don't ever say that again. The waves belong to the Ganges, not the Ganges to the waves. A man cannot realize God unless he gets rid of all such egotistic ideas as 'I am such an important man' or 'I am so and so'. Level the mound of 'I' to the ground by dissolving it with tears of devotion."

DEVOTEE: "Why has God put us in the world?"

MASTER: "To perpetuate His creation. It is His will, His māyā. He has deluded man with 'woman and gold'."

DEVOTEE: "Why has He deluded us? Why has He so willed?"

MASTER: "If but once He should give man a taste of divine joy, then man would not care to lead a worldly life. The creation would come to an end.

"The grain-dealer stores rice in huge bags in his warehouse. Near them he puts some puffed rice in a tray. This is to keep the rats away. The puffed rice tastes sweet to the rats and they nibble at it all night; they do not seek the rice itself. But just think! One seer of rice yields fourteen seers of puffed rice. How infinitely superior is the joy of God to the pleasure of 'woman and gold'! To one who thinks of the beauty of God, the beauty of even Rambhā and Tilottamā[1] appears as but the ashes of a funeral pyre."

DEVOTEE: "Why do we not feel intense restlessness to realize Him?"

MASTER: "A man does not feel restless for God until all his worldly desires are satisfied. He does not remember the Mother of the Universe until his share of the enjoyment of 'woman and gold' is completed. A child absorbed in play does not seek his mother. But after his play is over, he says, 'Mother! I must go to my mother.' Hriday's son was playing with the pigeons, calling

[1] Two celestial dancing-girls of exquisite beauty.

27

to them, 'Come! Ti, ti!' When he had had enough of play he began to cry. Then a stranger came and said: 'Come with me. I will take you to your mother.' Unhesitatingly he climbed on the man's shoulders and was off.

"Those who are eternally free do not have to enter worldly life. Their desire for enjoyment has been satisfied with their very birth."

At five o'clock in the afternoon Dr. Madhusudan arrived. While he prepared the bandage for the Master's arm, Sri Ramakrishna laughed like a child and said, "You are the Madhusudan[2] of both this world and the next!"

DR. MADHUSUDAN (smiling): "I only labour under the weight of my name."

MASTER (smiling): 'Why, is the name a trifling thing? God is not different from His name. Satyabhāmā tried to balance Krishna with gold and precious stones, but could not do it. Then Rukmini put a tulsi-leaf with the name of Krishna on the scales. That balanced the Lord."

The doctor was ready to bandage the Master's arm. A bed was spread on the floor and the Master, laughing, lay down upon it. He said, intoning the words: "Ah! This is Rādhā's final stage. But Brindē says, 'Who knows what is yet to be?'"

The devotees were sitting around the Master. He sang:

The gopis all were gathered about the shore of the lake.

Sri Ramakrishna laughed and the devotees laughed with him.

After his arm was bandaged he said: "I haven't very much faith in your Calcutta physicians. When Sambhu became delirious, Dr. Sarvadhikari said: 'Oh, it is nothing. It is just grogginess from the medicine. And a little while after, Sambhu[3] breathed his last."

It was evening and the worship in the temples was over. A few minutes later Adhar arrived from Calcutta to see the Master. Mahimacharan, Rakhal, and M. were in the room.

ADHAR: "How are you?"

MASTER (affectionately): "Look here. How my arm hurts! (Smiling) You don't have to ask how I am!"

Adhar sat on the floor with the devotees. The Master said to him, "Please stroke here gently." Adhar sat on the end of the couch and gently stroked Sri Ramakrishna's feet.

The Master conversed with Mahimacharan.

MASTER: "It will be very good if you can practise unselfish love for God. A man who has such love says: 'O Lord, I do not seek salvation, fame, wealth, or cure of disease. None of these do I seek. I want only Thee.' Many are the people who come to a rich man with various desires. But if someone comes to him simply out of love, not wanting any favour, then the rich man feels attracted to him. Prahlāda had this unselfish love, this pure love for God without any worldly end."

Mahimacharan sat silent. The Master turned to him.

---

[2] Also a name of Krishna.
[3] Sambhu Mallick died in 1877.

MASTER: "Now let me tell you something that will agree with your mood. According to the Vedānta one has to know the real nature of one's own Self. But such knowledge is impossible without the renunciation of ego. The ego is like a stick that seems to divide the water in two. It makes you feel that you are one and I am another. When the ego disappears in samādhi, then one knows Brahman to be one's own inner consciousness.

"One must renounce the 'I' that makes one feel, 'I am Mahima Chakravarty', 'I am a learned man', and so on. But the 'ego of Knowledge' does not injure one. Śankarāchārya retained the 'ego of Knowledge' in order to teach mankind.

"One cannot obtain the Knowledge of Brahman unless one is extremely cautious about women. Therefore it is very difficult for those who live in the world to get such Knowledge. However clever you may be, you will stain your body if you live in a sooty room. The company of a young woman evokes lust even in a lustless man.

"But it is not so harmful for a householder who follows the path of knowledge to enjoy conjugal happiness with his own wife now and then. He may satisfy his sexual impulse like any other natural impulse. Yes, you may enjoy a sweetmeat once in a while. (*Mahimacharan laughs.*) It is not so harmful for a householder.

"But it is extremely harmful for a sannyāsi. He must not look even at the portrait of a woman. A monk enjoying a woman is like a man swallowing the spittle he has already spat out. A sannyāsi must not sit near a woman and talk to her, even if she is intensely pious. No, he must not talk to a woman even though he may have controlled his passion.

"A sannyāsi must renounce both 'woman' and 'gold'. As he must not look even at the portrait of a woman, so also he must not touch gold, that is to say, money. It is bad for him even to keep money near him, for it brings in its train calculation, worry, insolence, anger, and such evils. There is an instance in the sun: it shines brightly; suddenly a cloud appears and hides it.

"That is why I didn't agree to the Mārwāri's depositing money for me with Hriday. I said: 'No, I won't allow even that. If I keep money near me, it will certainly raise clouds.'

"Why all these strict rules for a sannyāsi? It is for the welfare of mankind as well as for his own good. A sannyāsi may himself lead an unattached life and may have controlled his passion, but he must renounce 'woman and gold' to set an example to the world.

"A man will have the courage to practise renunciation if he sees one hundred per cent renunciation in a sannyāsi. Then only will he try to give up 'woman and gold'. If a sannyāsi does not set this example, then who will?

"One may lead a householder's life after realizing God. It is like churning butter from milk and then keeping the butter in water. Janaka led the life of a householder after attaining Brahmajnāna.

"Janaka fenced with two swords, the one of jnāna and the other of karma. The sannyāsi renounces action; therefore he fences with one sword only, that of knowledge. A householder, endowed with knowledge like

Janaka's, can enjoy fruit both from the tree and from the ground. He can serve holy men, entertain guests, and do other things like that. I said to the Divine Mother, 'O Mother, I don't want to be a dry sādhu.'

"After attaining Brahmajnāna one does not have to discriminate even about food. The rishis of olden times, endowed with the Knowledge of Brahman and having experienced divine bliss, ate everything, even pork.

(To Mahima) "Generally speaking there are two kinds of yoga: karma-yoga and manoyoga, that is to say, union with God through work and through the mind.

"There are four stages of life: brahmacharya, gārhasthya, vānaprastha, and sannyās. During the first three stages a man has to perform his worldly duties. The sannyāsi carries only his staff, water-pot, and begging-bowl. He too may perform certain nityakarma, but his mind is not attached to it; he is not conscious of doing such work. Some sannyāsis perform nityakarma to set an example to the world. If a householder or a man belonging to the other stages of life performs action without attachment, then he is united with God through such action.

"In the case of a paramahamsa, like Śukadeva, all karmas—all pujā, japa, tarpan, sandhyā, and so forth—drop away. In this state a man communes with God through the mind alone. Sometimes he may be pleased to perform outward activities for the welfare of mankind. But his recollection and contemplation of God remain uninterrupted."

It was about eight o'clock in the evening. Sri Ramakrishna asked Mahima-charan to recite a few hymns from the scriptures. Mahima read the first verse of the Uttara Gītā, describing the nature of the Supreme Brahman:

> He, Brahman, is one, partless, stainless, and beyond the ether;
> Without beginning or end, unknowable by mind or intelligence.

Finally he came to the seventh verse of the third chapter, which reads:

> The twice-born[4] worships the Deity in fire,
> The munis contemplate Him in the heart,
> Men of limited wisdom see Him in the image,
> And the yogis who have attained samesightedness
> Behold Him everywhere.

No sooner did the Master hear the words "the yogis who have attained samesightedness" than he stood up and went into samādhi, his arm supported by the splint and bandage. Speechless, the devotees looked at this yogi who had himself attained the state of samesightedness.

After a long time the Master regained consciousness of the outer world and took his seat. He asked Mahima to recite verses describing the love of God. The latter recited from the Nārada Pancharātra:

> What need is there of penance if God is worshipped with love?
> What is the use of penance if God is not worshipped with love?

---

[4] A man belonging to the brāhmin, kshatriya, or vaiśya caste, who has his second or spiritual birth at the time of his investiture with the sacred thread.

What need is there of penance if God is seen within and without?
What is the use of penance if God is not seen within and without?

O Brahman! O my child! Cease from practising further penances.
Hasten to Śankara, the Ocean of Heavenly Wisdom;
Obtain from Him the love of God, the pure love praised by devotees,
Which snaps in twain the shackles that bind you to the world.

MASTER: "Ah! Ah!"

On hearing these verses the Master was about to go again into an ecstatic mood, but he restrained himself with effort.

Mahima read from the *Yatipanchaka*:

I am She, the Divine Mother, in whom the illusion of the universe of animate and inanimate things is seen, as in magic, and in whom the universe shines, being the play of Her mind. I am She, the Embodiment of Consciousness, who is the Self of the universe, the only Existence, Knowledge, and Bliss.

When the Master heard the line, "I am She, the Embodiment of Consciousness", he said with a smile, "Whatever is in the microcosm is also in the macrocosm."

Next Mahima read the Six Stanzas on Nirvāna:

Om. I am neither mind, intelligence, ego, nor chitta,
Neither ears nor tongue nor the senses of smell and sight;
Nor am I ether, earth, fire, water, or air:
I am Pure Knowledge and Bliss: I am Śiva! I am Śiva!

I am neither the prāna, nor the five vital breaths,
Neither the seven elements of the body nor its five sheaths,
Nor hands nor feet nor tongue, nor the organs of sex and voiding:
I am Pure Knowledge and Bliss: I am Śiva! I am Śiva!

Neither loathing nor liking have I, neither greed nor delusion;
No sense have I of ego or pride, neither dharma nor moksha;
Neither desire of the mind nor object for its desiring:
I am Pure Knowledge and Bliss: I am Śiva! I am Śiva!

Neither right nor wrongdoing am I, neither pleasure nor pain,
Nor the mantra, the sacred place, the Vedas, the sacrifice;
Neither the act of eating, the eater, nor the food:
I am Pure Knowledge and Bliss: I am Śiva! I am Śiva!

Death or fear I have none, nor any distinction of caste;
Neither father nor mother nor even a birth have I;
Neither friend nor comrade, neither disciple nor guru:
I am Pure Knowledge and Bliss: I am Śiva! I am Śiva!

I have no form or fancy; the All-pervading am I;
Everywhere I exist, yet I am beyond the senses;
Neither salvation am I, nor anything that may be known:
I am Pure Knowledge and Bliss: I am Śiva! I am Śiva!

Each time Mahima repeated: "I am Śiva! I am Śiva!", the Master rejoined with a smile: "Not I! Not I! Thou art Knowledge Absolute."

Mahima read a few more verses and also a description of the six psychic centres of the body. He said that in Benares he had witnessed the death of a yogi in the state of yoga.

MAHIMA: "There are fine passages in the *Rāma Gītā*."

MASTER: "You are speaking of the *Rāma Gītā*. Then you must be a staunch Vedāntist. How many books of that kind the sādhus used to read here!"

Mahima recited the description of Om:

It is like the unceasing flow of oil. like the long peal of a bell.

About the characteristics of samādhi he read: "The man established in samādhi sees the upper region filled with Ātman, the nether region filled with Ātman, the middle region filled with Ātman. He sees all filled with Ātman."

Adhar and Mahima saluted the Master and departed.

At noon the following day, after his midday meal, Sri Ramakrishna was sitting on the small couch, when Ram, Surendra, and a few other devotees arrived from Calcutta. They were worried about the Master's injured arm. The arm was bandaged. M. was present.

MASTER (*to the devotees*): "The Mother has put me in such a state of mind that I cannot hide anything from anyone. Mine is the condition of a child. Rakhal doesn't understand it. He covers my injured arm, wrapping my body with a cloth lest others should see my injury and criticize me. He took Dr. Madhu aside and reported my illness. But I shouted and said: 'Hello! Where are you, Madhusudan? Come and see. My arm is broken!'

"I used to sleep in the same room with Mathur and his wife. They took care of me as if I were their own child. I was then passing through a state of divine madness. Mathur would ask me, 'Father, do you hear our conversation?' 'Yes', I would reply.

"Once Mathur's wife became suspicious of his movements and said to him, 'If you go anywhere, he[5] must accompany you.' One day Mathur went to a certain place and asked me to wait downstairs. He returned after half an hour and said to me: 'Come, father, let us go now. The carriage is waiting.' When Mathur's wife asked me about it, I reported the thing correctly. I said to her: 'We went to a certain house. He told me to stay downstairs and himself went upstairs. He came down after half an hour and we left the place.' Of course she understood the thing in her own way.

"A partner of Mathur's estate used to take fruits and vegetables stealthily from the temple garden. When the other partners asked me about it, I told them the exact truth."

Sunday, February 24, 1884

Sri Ramakrishna was resting in his room after his midday meal, and Mani Mallick was sitting on the floor beside him, when M. arrived. M. saluted

[5] The Master.

the Master and sat down beside Mani. The Master's injured arm was bandaged.

MASTER (*to M.*): "How did you come?"

M: "I came as far as Ālambāzār in a carriage and from there I walked."

MANILAL: "Oh, he is so hot!"

MASTER (*with a smile*): "This makes me think that all these are not mere fancies of my brain. Otherwise why should these 'Englishmen' take so much trouble to come here?"

Sri Ramakrishna began to talk to them about his health and his injured arm.

MASTER: "Now and then I become impatient about my arm. I show it to this or that man and ask him whether I shall get well again. That makes Rakhal angry. He doesn't understand my mood. Now and then I say to myself, 'Let him go away.' Again I say to the Mother: 'Mother, where will he go? Why should he burn himself in the frying-pan of the world?'

"This childlike impatience of mine is nothing new. I used to ask Mathur Babu to feel my pulse and tell me whether I was ill.

"Well, where then is my faith in God? Once I was going to Kāmārpukur in a bullock-cart, when several persons came up to the cart with clubs in their hands. They looked like highwaymen. I began to chant the names of the gods. Sometimes I repeated the names of Rāma and Durgā, and sometimes 'Om Tat Sat', so that in case one failed another would work.

(*To M.*) "Can you tell me why I am so impatient?"

M: "Your mind, sir, is always absorbed in samādhi. You have kept a fraction of it on your body for the welfare of the devotees. Therefore you feel impatient now and then for your body's safety."

MASTER: "That is true. A little of the mind is attached to the body. It wants to enjoy the love of God and the company of the devotees."

Mani Mallick told the Master about an exhibition that was being held in Calcutta. He described a beautiful image of Yaśodā with the Baby Krishna on her lap. Sri Ramakrishna's eyes filled with tears. On hearing about Yaśodā, the embodiment of maternal love, his spiritual consciousness was kindled and he wept.

MANILAL: "If you were not unwell, you could visit the exhibition in the Maidān."

MASTER (*to M. and the others*): "I shan't be able to see everything even if I go. Perhaps my eyes will fall on some certain thing and I shall become unconscious. Then I shall not be able to see the rest. I was taken to the Zoological Garden. I went into samādhi at the sight of the lion, for the carrier[6] of the Mother awakened in my mind the consciousness of the Mother Herself. In that state who could see the other animals? I had to return home after seeing only the lion. Hence Jadu Mallick's mother first suggested that I should go to the exhibition and then said I should not."

Mani Mallick, about sixty-five years old, had been a member of the Brāhmo Samāj for many years, and Sri Ramakrishna gave him instruction that would agree with his mood.

[6] In Hindu mythology the lion is the carrier of Durgā, the Divine Mother.

MASTER: "Pundit Jaynarayan had very liberal views. I visited him once and liked his attitude. But his sons wore high boots. He told me he intended to go to Benares and live there, and at last he carried out his intention; for later on he did live in Benares and die there. When one grows old one should retire, like Jaynarayan, and devote oneself to the thought of God. What do you say?"

MANILAL: "True, sir. I don't relish the worries and troubles of the world."

MASTER: "Gauri used to worship his wife with offerings of flowers. All women are manifestations of the Divine Mother. (To Manilal) Please tell them that little story of yours."

MANILAL (smiling): "Once several men were crossing the Ganges in a boat. One of them, a pundit, was making a great display of his erudition, saying that he had studied various books—the Vedas, the Vedānta, and the six systems of philosophy. He asked a fellow passenger, 'Do you know the Vedānta?' 'No, revered sir.' 'The Sāmkhya and the Pātanjala?' 'No, revered sir.' 'Have you read no philosophy whatsoever?' 'No, revered sir.' The pundit was talking in this vain way and the passenger sitting in silence, when a great storm arose and the boat was about to sink. The passenger said to the pundit, 'Sir, can you swim?' 'No', replied the pundit. The passenger said, 'I don't know the Sāmkhya or the Pātanjala, but I can swim.' "

MASTER (smiling): "What will a man gain by knowing many scriptures? The one thing needful is to know how to cross the river of the world. God alone is real, and all else illusory.

"While Arjuna was aiming his arrow at the eye of the bird, Drona asked him: 'What do you see? Do you see these kings?' 'No, sir', replied Arjuna. 'Do you see me?' 'No.' 'The tree?' 'No.' 'The bird on the tree?' 'No.' 'What do you see then?' 'Only the eye of the bird.'

"He who sees only the eye of the bird can hit the mark. He alone is clever who sees that God is real and all else is illusory. What need have I of other information? Hanumān once remarked: 'I don't know anything about the phase of the moon or the position of the stars. I only contemplate Rāma.'

(To M.) "Please buy a few fans for our use here.

(To Manilal) "Look here, pay a visit to his [meaning M.'s] father. The sight of a devotee will inspire you.

(To M.) "Since my arm was injured a deep change has come over me. I now delight only in the Naralīlā, the human manifestation of God. Nitya and Līlā. The Nitya is the Indivisible Satchidānanda, and the Līlā, or Sport, takes various forms, such as the Līlā as God, the Līlā as the deities, the Līlā as man, and the Līlā as the universe.

"Vaishnavcharan used to say that one has attained Perfect Knowledge if one believes in God sporting as man. I wouldn't admit it then. But now I realize that he was right. Vaishnavcharan liked pictures of man expressing tenderness and love.

(To Manilal) "It is God Himself who is sporting in the form of man. It is He alone who has become Mani Mallick. The Sikhs teach: 'Thou art Satchidānanda.'

"Now and then man catches a glimpse of his real Self and becomes speechless with wonder. At such times he swims in an ocean of joy. It is like suddenly meeting a dear relative. (*To M.*) The other day as I was coming here in a carriage, I felt like that at the sight of Baburam. When Śiva realizes His own Self, He dances about in joy exclaiming, 'What am I! What am I!'

"The same thing has been described in the *Adhyātma Rāmāyana*. Nārada said, 'O Rāma, all men are Thy forms, and it is Sītā who has become all women.' On looking at the actors in the Rāmlīlā, I felt that Nārāyana Himself had taken these human forms. The genuine and the imitation appeared to be the same.

"Why do people worship virgins? All women are so many forms of the Divine Mother. But Her manifestation is greatest in pure-souled virgins.

(*To M.*) "Why do I become impatient when I am ill? Because the Mother has placed me in the state of a child. The child depends entirely on its mother. The child of the maidservant, when he quarrels with the child of the master, says, 'I shall tell my mother.'

"I was taken to Rādhābāzār to be photographed. It had been arranged that I should go to Rajendra Mitra's house that day. I heard that Keshab would be there. I planned to tell them certain things, but I forgot it all when I went to Rādhābāzār. I said: 'O Mother, Thou wilt speak. What shall I say?'

"I have not the nature of a jnāni. He considers himself great. He says, 'What? How can I be ill?'

"Koar Singh once said to me, 'You still worry about your body.' But it is my nature to believe that my Mother knows everything. It was She who would speak at Rajendra Mitra's house. Hers are the only effective words. One ray of light from the Goddess of Wisdom stuns a thousand scholars.

"The Mother has kept me in the state of a bhakta, a vijnāni. That is why I joke with Rakhal and the others. Had I been in the condition of a jnāni I couldn't do that.

"In this state I realize that it is the Mother alone who has become everything. I see Her everywhere. In the Kāli temple I found that the Mother Herself had become everything—even the wicked, even the brother of Bhagavat Pundit.

"Once I was about to scold Ramlal's mother, but I had to restrain myself. I saw her to be a form of the Divine Mother. I worship virgins because I see in them the Divine Mother. My wife strokes my feet, but I salute her afterwards.

"You salute me by touching my feet. But had Hriday been here, who would have dared to touch them? He wouldn't have allowed anyone to do it. I have to return your salutes because the Mother has placed me in a state in which I see God in everything.

"You see, one cannot exclude even a wicked person. A tulsi-leaf, however dry or small, can be used for worship in the temple."

Sunday, March 2, 1884

Sri Ramakrishna was sitting on the small couch in his room, listening to devotional music by Trailokya Sannyal of the Brāhmo Samāj. He had not yet recovered from the effects of the injury to his arm, which was still supported by a splint. Many devotees, including Narendra, Surendra, and M., were sitting on the floor.

Narendra's father, a lawyer of the High Court of Calcutta, had passed away suddenly. He had not been able to make provision for the family, which consequently faced grave financial difficulties. The members of the family sometimes had to go without food. Narendra was therefore passing his days in great anxiety.

Trailokya sang about the Divine Mother:

> O Mother, I hide myself in Thy loving bosom;
> I gaze at Thy face and cry out, "Mother! Mother!"
> I sink in the Sea of Bliss and am lost to sense
> In yoga-sleep; I gaze with unwinking eyes
> Upon Thy face, powerless to turn away.
> O Mother, I am terrified by this world;
> My spirit trembles and cries out in fear.
> Keep me, sweet Mother, in Thy loving bosom;
> Cover me with the spreading skirt of Thy love.

The Master shed tears of love and cried out, "Ah me! Ah me!"

Trailokya sang again:

> O Lord, Destroyer of my shame! Who but Thyself can save
> The honour of Thy devotee?
> Thou art the Ruler of my soul, my very life's Support,
> And I am Thy slave for evermore. . . .

He continued:

> Seeking a shelter at Thy feet,
> I have for ever set aside
> My pride of caste and race, O Lord,
> And turned my back on fear and shame.
> A lonely pilgrim on life's way,
> Where shall I go for succour now?
> For Thy sake, Lord, I bear men's blame;
> They rail at me with bitter words
> And hate me for my love of Thee.
> Both friends and strangers use me ill.
>
> Thou art the Guardian of my name;
> Thou mayest save or slay me, Lord!
> Upon the honour of Thy servant
> Rests, O Lord, Thy name as well;
> Thou art the Ruler of my soul,
> The glow of love within my heart;
> Do with me as it pleases Thee!

Once more he sang:

> Lord, Thou hast taken me from home and made me captive with
> Thy love;
> Shield me for ever at Thy feet, O Thou Beloved One!
> Upon the Nectar of Thy love, feed me both day and night,
> And save Premdās, who is Thy slave.

The Master again shed tears of joy. He sang some lines from a song of Rāmprasād:

> Glory and shame, bitter and sweet, are Thine alone;
> This world is nothing but Thy play.
> Then why, O Blissful One, dost Thou cause a rift in it?

Addressing Trailokya, the Master said: "Ah! How touching your songs are! They are genuine. Only he who has gone to the ocean can fetch its water."

Trailokya sang again:

> Thou it is that dancest, Lord, and Thou that singest the song;
> Thou it is that clappest Thy hands in time with the music's beat;
> But man, who is an onlooker merely, foolishly thinks it is he.

> Though but a puppet, man becomes a god if he moves with Thee;
> Thou art the Mover of the machine, the Driver of the car;
> But man is weighted down with woe, dreaming that he is free.

> Thou art the Root of everything, Thou the Soul of our souls;
> Thou art the Master of our hearts; through Thine unbounded grace
> Thou turnest even the meanest sinner into the mightiest saint.

The singing came to an end. The Master engaged in conversation with the devotees.

MASTER: "God alone is the Master, and again, He is the Servant. This attitude indicates Perfect Knowledge. At first one discriminates, 'Not this, not this', and feels that God alone is real and all else is illusory. Afterwards the same person finds that it is God Himself who has become all this—the universe, māyā, and the living beings. First negation and then affirmation. This is the view held by the Purānas. A vilwa-fruit, for instance, includes flesh, seeds, and shell. You get the flesh by discarding the shell and seeds. But if you want to know the weight of the fruit, you cannot find it if you discard the shell and seeds. Just so, one should attain Satchidānanda by negating the universe and its living beings. But after the attainment of Satchidānanda one finds that Satchidānanda Itself has become the universe and the living beings. It is of one substance that the flesh and the shell and seeds are made, just like butter and buttermilk.

"It may be asked, 'How has Satchidānanda become so hard?' This earth does indeed feel very hard to the touch. The answer is that blood and semen are thin liquids, and yet out of them comes such a big creature as man. Everything is possible for God. First of all reach the indivisible Satchidānanda, and then, coming down, look at the universe. You will then find that everything is Its manifestation. It is God alone who has become everything. The world by no means exists apart from Him.

"All elements finally merge in ākāśa. Again, at the time of creation, ākāśa evolves into mahat and mahat into ahamkāra. In this way the whole world-system is evolved. It is the process of involution and evolution. A devotee of God accepts everything. He accepts the universe and its created beings as well as the indivisible Satchidānanda.

"But the yogi's path is different. He does not come back after reaching the Paramātman, the Supreme Soul. He becomes united with It.

"The 'partial knower' limits God to one object only. He thinks that God cannot exist in anything beyond that.

"There are three classes of devotees. The lowest one says, 'God is up there.' That is, he points to heaven. The mediocre devotee says that God dwells in the heart as the 'Inner Controller'. But the highest devotee says: 'God alone has become everything. All that we perceive is so many forms of God.' Narendra used to make fun of me and say: 'Yes, God has become all! Then a pot is God, a cup is God!' (Laughter.)

"All doubts disappear when one sees God. It is one thing to hear of God, but quite a different thing to see Him. A man cannot have one hundred per cent conviction through mere hearing. But if he beholds God face to face, then he is wholly convinced.

"Formal worship drops away after the vision of God. It was thus that my worship in the temple came to an end. I used to worship the Deity in the Kāli temple. It was suddenly revealed to me that everything is Pure Spirit. The utensils of worship, the altar, the door-frame—all Pure Spirit. Men, animals, and other living beings—all Pure Spirit. Then like a madman I began to shower flowers in all directions. Whatever I saw I worshipped.

"One day, while worshipping Śiva, I was about to offer a bel-leaf on the head of the image, when it was revealed to me that this Virāt, this Universe, itself is Śiva. After that my worship of Śiva through the image came to an end. Another day I had been plucking flowers, when it was revealed to me that the flowering plants were so many bouquets."

TRAILOKYA: "Ah! How beautiful is God's creation!"

MASTER: "Oh no, it is not that. It was revealed to me in a flash. I didn't calculate about it. It was shown to me that each plant was a bouquet adorning the Universal Form of God. That was the end of my plucking flowers. I look on man in just the same way. When I see a man, I see that it is God Himself who walks on earth, as it were, rocking to and fro, like a pillow floating on the waves. The pillow moves with the waves. It bobs up and down.

"The body has, indeed, only a momentary existence. God alone is real. Now the body exists, and now it does not. Years ago, when I had been suffering terribly from indigestion, Hriday said to me, 'Do ask the Mother to cure you.' I felt ashamed to speak to Her about my illness. I said to Her: 'Mother, I saw a skeleton in the Asiatic Society Museum. It was pieced together with wires into a human form. O Mother, please keep my body together a little, like that, so that I may sing Thy name and glories.'

"Why this desire to live? After Rāvana's death Rāma and Lakshmana entered his capital and saw Nikashā, his old mother, running away. Lakshmana was surprised at this and said to Rāma, 'All her children are dead, but still life attracts her so much!' Rāma called Nikashā to His side and said: 'Don't be afraid. Why are you running away?' She replied: 'Rāma, it was not fear that made me flee from You. I have been able to see

all these wondrous actions of Yours simply because I am alive. I shall see
many more things like these if I continue to live. Hence I desire to live.'
    "Without desires the body cannot live. (Smiling) I had one or two desires.
I prayed to the Mother, 'O Mother, give me the company of those who have
renounced "woman and gold".' I said further: 'I should like to enjoy the
society of Thy jnānis and bhaktas. So give me a little strength that I may
walk hither and thither and visit those people.' But She did not give me the
strength to walk."
    TRAILOKYA (smiling): "Have all the desires been fulfilled?"
    MASTER (smiling): "No, there are still a few left. (All laugh.)
    "The body is really impermanent. When my arm was broken I said to
the Mother, 'Mother, it hurts me very much.' At once She revealed to me a
carriage and its driver. Here and there a few screws were loose. The carriage
moved as the driver directed it. It had no power of its own.
    "Why then do I take care of the body? It is to enjoy God, to sing His
name and glories, and to go about visiting His jnānis and bhaktas."
    Narendra was sitting on the floor in front of the Master.
    MASTER (to Trailokya and the other devotees): "The joys and sorrows
of the body are inevitable. Look at Narendra. His father is dead, and his
people have been put to extreme suffering. He can't find any way out of it.
God places one sometimes in happiness and sometimes in misery."
    TRAILOKYA: "Revered sir, God will be gracious to Narendra."
    MASTER (with a smile): "But when? It is true that no one starves at the
temple of Annapurnā in Benares; but some must wait for food till evening.
    "Once Hriday asked Sambhu Mallick for some money. Sambhu held the
views of 'Englishmen' on such matters. He said to Hriday: 'Why should I
give you money? You can earn your livelihood by working. Even now you
are earning something. The case of a very poor person is different. The
purpose of charity is fulfilled if one gives money to the blind or the lame.'
Thereupon Hriday said: 'Sir, please don't say that. I don't need your money.
May God help me not to become blind or deaf or extremely poor! I don't
want you to give, and I don't want to receive.'"
    The Master spoke as if piqued because God had not yet shown His kind-
ness to Narendra. Now and then he cast an affectionate glance at his
beloved disciple.
    NARENDRA: "I am now studying the views of the atheists."
    MASTER: "There are two doctrines: the existence and the non-existence
of God. Why don't you accept the first?"
    SURENDRA: "God is just. He must look after His devotees."
    MASTER: "It is said in the scriptures that only those who have been
charitable in their former births get money in this life. But to tell you the
truth, this world is God's māyā. And there are many confusing things in
this realm of māyā. One cannot comprehend them.
    "The ways of God are inscrutable indeed. Bhishma lay on his bed of
arrows. The Pāndava brothers visited him in Krishna's company. Presently
Bhishma burst into tears. The Pāndavas said to Krishna: 'Krishna, how
amazing this is! Our grandsire Bhishma is one of the eight Vasus. Another

man as wise as he is not to be found. Yet even he is bewildered by māyā and weeps at death.' 'But', said Krishna, 'Bhishma isn't weeping on that account. You may ask him about it.' When asked, Bhishma said: 'O Krishna, I am unable to understand anything of the ways of God. God Himself is the constant companion of the Pāndavas, and still they have no end of trouble. That is why I weep. When I reflect on this, I realize that one cannot understand anything of God's ways.'

"God has revealed to me that only the Paramātman, whom the Vedas describe as the Pure Soul, is as immutable as Mount Sumeru, unattached, and beyond pain and pleasure. There is much confusion in this world of His māyā. One can by no means say that 'this' will come after 'that' or 'this' will produce 'that'."

SURENDRA (smiling): "If by giving away money in a previous birth one gets wealth in this life, then we should all give away money now."

MASTER: "Those who have money should give it to the poor and needy. (To Trailokya) Jaygopal Sen is well-to-do. He should be charitable. That he is not so is to his discredit. There are some who are miserly even though they have money. There is no knowing who will enjoy their money afterwards.

"Jaygopal came here the other day. He drove over here in a carriage. The lamps were broken, the horse seemed to have been returned from the charnel-house, and the coachman looked as if he had just been discharged from the Medical College Hospital. And he brought me two rotten pomegranates!" (All laugh.)

SURENDRA: "Jaygopal Babu belongs to the Brāhmo Samāj. I understand that now there is not one worth-while man in Keshab's organization. Vijay Goswami, Shivanath, and other notables have organized the Sādhāran Brāhmo Samāj."

MASTER (smiling): "Govinda Adhikari, it is said, would not keep good actors in his theatre lest they should claim a share of the profit. (All laugh.)

"The other day I saw a disciple of Keshab. A theatrical performance was being given in Keshab's house, and I saw the disciple dancing on the stage with a child in his arms. I understand that this man delivers 'lectures'. He had better lecture to himself."

Trailokya sang:

> Upon the Sea of Blissful Awareness waves of ecstatic love arise:
> Rapture divine! Play of God's Bliss!
> Oh, how enthralling!
> Wondrous waves of the sweetness of God, ever new and ever
>   enchanting,
> Rise on the surface, ever assuming
> Forms ever fresh.
> Then once more in the Great Communion all are merged, as the
>   barrier walls
> Of time and space dissolve and vanish:
> Dance then, O mind!
> Dance in delight, with hands upraised, chanting Lord Hari's holy
>   name.

Sri Ramakrishna requested Trailokya to sing the song beginning, "O Mother, make me mad with Thy love".

Trailokya sang:

O Mother, make me mad with Thy love!
What need have I of knowledge or reason?
Make me drunk with Thy love's Wine;
O Thou who stealest Thy bhaktas' hearts,
Drown me deep in the Sea of Thy love!
Here in this world, this madhouse of Thine
Some laugh, some weep, some dance for joy:
Jesus, Buddha, Moses, Gaurānga,
All are drunk with the Wine of Thy love.
O Mother, when shall I be blessed
By joining their blissful company?

RULES FOR HOUSEHOLDERS AND MONKS

Sunday, March 9, 1884

SRI RAMAKRISHNA was sitting in his room at Dakshineswar with many devotees. Among them were Mani Mallick, Mahendra Kavirāj, Balaram, M., Bhavanath, Rakhal, Latu, and Harish. The Master's injured arm was in a splint. In spite of the injury he was constantly absorbed in samādhi or instructing the devotees.

Mani Mallick and Bhavanath referred to the exhibition which was then being held near the Asiatic Museum. They said: "Many mahārājās have sent precious articles to the exhibition—gold couches and the like. It is worth seeing."

MASTER (*to the devotees, with a smile*): "Yes, you gain much by visiting those things. You realize that those articles of gold and the other things sent by mahārājās are mere trash. That is a great gain in itself. When I used to go to Calcutta with Hriday, he would show me the Viceroy's palace and say: 'Look, uncle! There is the Viceroy's palace with the big columns.' The Mother revealed to me that they were merely clay bricks laid one on top of another.

"God and His splendour. God alone is real; the splendour has but a two-days existence. The magician and his magic. All become speechless with wonder at the magic, but it is all unreal. The magician alone is real. The rich man and his garden. People see only the garden; they should look for its rich owner."

MANI MALLICK (*to the Master*): "What a big electric light they have at the exhibition! It makes us think how great He must be who has made such an electric light."

MASTER (*to Mani*): "But according to one view it is He Himself who has become everything. Even those who say that are He. It is Satchidānanda Itself that has become all—the Creator, māyā, the universe, and living beings."

The conversation turned to the museum.

MASTER (*to the devotees*): "I visited the museum once. I was shown fossils. A whole animal has become stone! Just see what an effect has been

400

produced by company! Likewise, by constantly living in the company of a holy man one verily becomes holy."

MANI (*smiling*): "Had you visited the exhibition only once, we could receive instruction for ten or fifteen years."

MASTER (*with a smile*): "How so? You mean illustrations?"

BALARAM: "No, you shouldn't go. Your arm won't heal if you go here and there."

MASTER: "I should like to have two pictures. One of a yogi seated before a lighted log, and another of a yogi smoking hemp and the charcoal blazing up as he pulls. Such pictures kindle my spiritual consciousness, as an imitation fruit awakens the idea of a real one.

"The obstacle to yoga is 'woman and gold'. Yoga is possible when the mind becomes pure. The seat of the mind is between the eyebrows; but its look is fixed on the navel and the organs of generation and evacuation, that is to say, on 'woman and gold'. But through spiritual discipline the same mind looks upward.

"What are the spiritual disciplines that give the mind its upward direction? One learns all this by constantly living in holy company. The rishis of olden times lived either in solitude or in the company of holy persons; therefore they could easily renounce 'woman and gold' and fix their minds on God. They had no fear nor did they mind the criticism of others.

"In order to be able to renounce, one must pray to God for the will-power to do so. One must immediately renounce what one feels to be unreal. The rishis had this will-power. Through it they controlled the sense-organs. If the tortoise once tucks in its limbs, you cannot make it bring them out even by cutting it into four pieces.

"The worldly man is a hypocrite. He cannot be guileless. He professes to love God, but he is attracted by worldly objects. He doesn't give God even a very small part of the love he feels for 'woman and gold'. But he says that he loves God. (*To Mani Mallick*) Give up hypocrisy."

MANI: "Regarding whom, God or man?"

MASTER: "Regarding everything—man as well as God. One must not be a hypocrite.

"How guileless Bhavanath is! After his marriage he came to me and asked, 'Why do I feel so much love for my wife?' Alas, he is so guileless!

"Isn't it natural for a man to love his wife? This is due to the world-bewitching māyā of the Divine Mother of the Universe. A man feels about his wife that he has no one else in the world so near and dear; that she is his very own in life and death, here and hereafter.

"Again, how much a man suffers for his wife! Still he believes that there is no other relative so near. Look at the sad plight of a husband. Perhaps he earns twenty rupees a month and is the father of three children. He hasn't the means to feed them well. His roof leaks, but he hasn't the wherewithal to repair it. He cannot afford to buy new books for his son. He cannot invest his son with the sacred thread. He begs a few pennies from his different friends.

"But a wife endowed with spiritual wisdom is a real partner in life. She greatly helps her husband to follow the religious path. After the birth of one or two children they live like brother and sister. Both of them are devotees of God—His servant and His handmaid. Their family is a spiritual family. They are always happy with God and His devotees. They know that God alone is their own, from everlasting to everlasting. They are like the Pāndava brothers; they do not forget God in happiness or in sorrow.

"The longing of the worldly-minded for God is momentary, like a drop of water on a red-hot frying-pan. The water hisses and dries up in an instant. The attention of the worldly-minded is directed to the enjoyment of worldly pleasure. Therefore they do not feel yearning and restlessness for God.

"People may observe the ekādaśi in three ways. First, the 'waterless' ekādaśi—they are not permitted to drink even a drop of water. Likewise, an all-renouncing religious mendicant completely gives up all forms of enjoyment. Second, while observing the ekādaśi they take milk and sandesh. Likewise, a householder devotee keeps in his house simple objects of enjoyment. Third, while observing the ekādaśi they eat luchi and chakkā. They eat their fill. They keep a couple of loaves soaking in milk, which they will eat later on.[1]

"A man practises spiritual discipline, but his mind is on 'woman and gold'—it is turned toward enjoyment. Therefore, in his case, the spiritual discipline does not produce the right result.

"Hazra used to practise much japa and austerity here. But in the country he has his wife, children, and land. Therefore along with his spiritual discipline he carried on the business of a broker. Such people cannot be true to their word. One moment they say they will give up fish, but the next moment they break their vow.

"Is there anything that a man will not do for money? He will even compel a brāhmin or a holy man to carry a load.

"In my room sweets would turn bad; still I could not give them away to the worldly-minded. I could accept dirty water from others, but not even touch the jar of a worldly person.

"At the sight of rich people Hazra would call them to him. He would give them long lectures. He would say to them: 'You see Rakhal and the other youngsters. They do not practise any spiritual discipline. They simply wander about merrily.'

"A man may live in a mountain cave, smear his body with ashes, observe fasts, and practise austere discipline; but if his mind dwells on worldly objects, on 'woman and gold', I say, 'Shame on him!' But I say that a man is blessed indeed who eats, drinks, and roams about, but who keeps his mind free from 'woman and gold'.

(*Pointing to Mani Mallick*) "There is no picture of a holy man at his house. Divine feeling is awakened through such pictures."

MANILAL: "Yes, there is. In one room there is a picture of a pious Christian woman engaged in prayer. There is another picture in which a man holds

---

[1] This observance is an ekādaśi in name only, since the observer fills his stomach with delicious food. By avoiding rice and a few cooked articles, he keeps to the letter of the law.

to the Hill of Faith; below is an ocean of immeasurable depth. If he gives up his hold on faith, he will drop into the bottomless water. There is still a third picture. Several virgins are keeping vigil, feeding their lamps with oil in expectation of the Bridegroom. A sleeping virgin is by their side. She will not behold the Bridegroom when He arrives. God is described here as the Bridegroom."

MASTER (smiling): "That's very nice."

MANILAL: "I have other pictures too—one of the 'Tree of Faith' and another of 'Sin and Virtue'."

MASTER (to Bhavanath): "Those are good pictures. Go to his house and see them."

The Master remained silent a few minutes.

MASTER: "Now and then I reflect on these ideas and find that I do not like them. In the beginning of spiritual life a man should think about sin and how to get rid of it. But when, through the grace of God, devotion and ecstatic love are awakened in his heart, then he altogether forgets virtue and sin. Then he leaves the scriptures and their injunctions far behind. Thoughts of repentance and penance do not bother him at all.

"It is like going to your destination along a winding river. This requires great effort and a long time. But when there is a flood all around, then you can go straight to your destination in a short time. Then you find the land lying under water deep as a bamboo pole.

"In the beginning of spiritual life one goes by a roundabout way. One has to suffer a great deal. But the path becomes very easy when ecstatic love is awakened in the heart. It is like going over the paddy-field after the harvest is over. You may then walk in any direction. Before the harvest you had to go along the winding balk, but now you can walk in any direction. There may be stubble in the field, but you will not be hurt by it if you walk with your shoes on. Just so, an aspirant does not suffer if he has discrimination, dispassion, and faith in the guru's words."

MANILAL (to the Master): "Well, what is the rule for concentration? Where should one concentrate?"

MASTER: "The heart is a splendid place. One can meditate there or in the Sahasrāra. These are rules for meditation given in the scriptures. But you may meditate wherever you like. Every place is filled with Brahman-Consciousness. Is there any place where It does not exist? Nārāyana, in Vali's presence, covered with two steps the heavens, the earth, and the interspaces.[2] Is there then any place left uncovered by God? A dirty place is as holy as the bank of the Ganges. It is said that the whole creation is the Virāt, the Universal Form of God.

"There are two kinds of meditation, one on the formless God and the other on God with form. But meditation on the formless God is extremely

---

[2] A reference to a story in the *Bhāgavata*. King Vali was proud of his charity. God appeared before him in the form of a dwarf and asked him for the space that He could cover with three steps. Vali granted the boon. With two steps the Lord covered the earth, the heavens, and the interspaces. Vali was forced to place his own head before the Lord for the third step. This curbed his pride.

difficult. In that meditation you must wipe out all that you see or hear. You contemplate only the nature of your Inner Self. Meditating on His Inner Self, Śiva dances about. He exclaims, 'What am I! What am I!' This is called the 'Śiva yoga'. While practising this form of meditation, one directs one's look to the forehead. It is meditation on the nature of one's Inner Self after negating the world, following the Vedāntic method of 'Neti, neti'.

"There is another form of meditation known as the 'Vishnu yoga'. The eyes are fixed on the tip of the nose. Half the look is directed inward and the other half outward. This is how one meditates on God with form. Sometimes Śiva meditates on God with form, and dances. At that time he exclaims, 'Rāma! Rāma!' and dances about."

Sri Ramakrishna then explained the sacred Word "Om" and the true Knowledge of Brahman and the state of mind after the attainment of Brahmajnāna.

MASTER: "The sound Om is Brahman. The rishis and sages practised austerity to realize that Sound-Brahman. After attaining perfection one hears the sound of this eternal Word rising spontaneously from the navel.

"'What will you gain', some sages ask, 'by merely hearing this sound?' You hear the roar of the ocean from a distance. By following the roar you can reach the ocean. As long as there is the roar, there must also be the ocean. By following the trail of Om you attain Brahman, of which the Word is the symbol. That Brahman has been described by the Vedas as the ultimate goal. But such vision is not possible as long as you are conscious of your ego. A man realizes Brahman only when he feels neither 'I' nor 'you', neither 'one' nor 'many'.

"Think of the sun and of ten jars filled with water. The sun is reflected in each jar. At first you see one real sun and ten reflected ones. If you break nine of the jars, there will remain only the real sun and one reflection. Each jar represents a jīva. Following the reflection one can find the real sun. Through the individual soul one can reach the Supreme Soul. Through spiritual discipline the individual soul can get the vision of the Supreme Soul. What remains when the last jar is broken cannot be described.

"The jīva at first remains in a state of ignorance. He is not conscious of God, but of the multiplicity. He sees many things around him. On attaining Knowledge he becomes conscious that God dwells in all beings. Suppose a man has a thorn in the sole of his foot. He gets another thorn and takes out the first one. In other words, he removes the thorn of ajnāna, ignorance, by means of the thorn of jnāna, knowledge. But on attaining vijnāna, he discards both thorns, knowledge and ignorance. Then he talks intimately with God day and night. It is no mere vision of God.

"He who has merely heard of milk is 'ignorant'. He who has seen milk has 'knowledge'. But he who has drunk milk and been strengthened by it has attained vijnāna."

Thus the Master described his own state of mind to the devotees. He was indeed a vijnāni.

MASTER (to the devotees): "There is a difference between a sādhu endowed with jnāna and one endowed with vijnāna. The jnāni sādhu has a certain way of sitting. He twirls his moustache and asks the visitor, 'Well, sir! Have you any question to ask?' But the man who always sees God and talks to Him intimately has an altogether different nature. He is sometimes like an inert thing, sometimes like a ghoul, sometimes like a child, and sometimes like a madman.

"When he is in samādhi, he becomes unconscious of the outer world and appears inert. He sees everything to be full of Brahman-Consciousness; therefore he behaves like a ghoul. He is not conscious of the holy and the unholy. He does not observe any formal purity. To him everything is Brahman. He is not aware of filth as such. Even rice and other cooked food after a few days become like filth.

"Again, he is like a madman. People notice his ways and actions and think of him as insane. Or sometimes he is like a child—no bondage, no shame, no hatred, no hesitation, or the like.

"One reaches this state of mind after having the vision of God. When a boat passes by a magnetic hill, its screws and nails become loose and drop out. Lust, anger, and the other passions cannot exist after the vision of God.

"Once a thunderbolt struck the Kāli temple. I noticed that it flattened the points of the screws.

"It is no longer possible for the man who has seen God to beget children and perpetuate the creation. When a grain of paddy is sown it grows into a plant; but a grain of boiled paddy does not germinate.

"He who has seen God retains his 'I' only in name. No evil can be done by that 'I'. It is a mere appearance, like the mark left on the coconut tree by its branch. The branch has fallen off. Only the mark remains.

"I said to Keshab Sen, 'Give up the ego that makes you feel, "I am the doer; I am teaching people."' Keshab said to me, 'Sir, then I cannot keep the organization.' Thereupon I said to him, 'Give up the "wicked ego".' One doesn't have to renounce the ego that makes one feel, 'I am the servant of God; I am His devotee.' One doesn't develop the 'divine ego' as long as one retains the 'wicked ego'. If a man is in charge of the store-room, the master of the house doesn't feel responsible for it.

(*To the devotees*) "You see, my nature is changing on account of this injury to my arm. It is being revealed to me that there is a greater manifestation of God in man than in other created beings. God is telling me, as it were: 'I dwell in men. Be merry with men.'. Among men God manifests Himself in a still greater degree in pure-souled devotees. That is why I feel great longing for Narendra, Rakhal, and other such youngsters.

"One often sees small holes along the edge of a lake. Fish and crabs accumulate there. Just so, there is a greater accumulation of divinity in man. It is said that man is greater than the śālagrām. Man is Nārāyana Himself. If God can manifest Himself through an image, then why not through man also?

"God is born as man for the purpose of sporting as man. Rāma, Krishna, and Chaitanya are examples. By meditating on an Incarnation of God one meditates on God Himself."

Bhagavan Das, a Brāhmo devotee, arrived.

MASTER (to Bhagavan Das): "The Eternal Religion, the religion of the rishis, has been in existence from time out of mind and will exist eternally. There exist in this Sanātana Dharma all forms of worship—worship of God with form and worship of the Impersonal Deity as well. It contains all paths—the path of knowledge, the path of devotion, and so on. Other forms of religion, the modern cults, will remain for a few days and then disappear."

March 23, 1884

Sri Ramakrishna was sitting in his room after his midday meal, with Rakhal, Ram, and some other devotees. He was not quite well. The injured arm was still bandaged.

But in spite of his illness, his room was a veritable mart of joy and he the centre of it. Devotees thronged there daily to see the Master. Spiritual talk went on incessantly, and the very air of the room vibrated with bliss. Sometimes the Master would sing the name and glories of God, and sometimes he would go into samādhi, the devotees being amazed at the ease with which the Master freed himself from the consciousness of the body.

RAM: "There is talk of Narendra's marrying Mr. R. Mitra's daughter. Narendra has been offered a large dowry."

MASTER (smiling): "Yes, Narendra may thus become a leader of society or something like that. He will be an outstanding man, whatever career he follows."

The Master did not much encourage the conversation about Narendra.

MASTER (to Ram): "Well, can you tell me why I become so impatient when I am ill? Sometimes I ask this man and sometimes that man how I may be cured. You see, one must either believe everyone or no one at all.

"It is God Himself who has become the physicians. Therefore one must believe all of them. But one cannot have faith in them if one thinks of them as mere men.

"Sambhu was fearfully delirious. Dr. Sarvadhikari said that the delirium was due to the strong medicine. Haladhari asked the doctor to feel his pulse. The doctor said: 'Let me see your eyes. Oh, it is an enlargement of the spleen!' Haladhari said he had nothing of the sort. But Dr. Madhu gives good medicine."

RAM: "The medicine by itself does no good, though it greatly helps nature."

MASTER: "If that is so, why does opium cause constipation?"

Ram referred to Keshab Sen's death.

RAM: "You were quite right. You said that a gardener uncovers the roots of a good rose-plant so that it may absorb the dew and grow stronger and healthier. The words of a holy man have been fulfilled."

MASTER: "I don't know about that. I wasn't calculating when I said it. It is you who say that."

RAM: "The Brāhmos have published something about you in their magazine."

MASTER: "Published about me? Why? Why should they write now? I eat and drink and make merry. I don't know anything else.

"I once asked Keshab, 'Why have you written about me?' He said that it would bring people here. But man cannot teach by his own power. One cannot conquer ignorance without the power of God.

"At one time two men were engaged to wrestle. One of them was Hanumān Singh and the other a Mussalmān from the Punjab. The Mussalmān was a strong, stout man. He had eaten lustily of butter and meat for fifteen days before the day of the wrestling-match, and even on that day. All thought he would be the victor. Hanumān Singh, on the other hand, clad in a dirty cloth, had eaten sparingly for some days before the day of the match and devoted himself to repeating the holy name of Mahāvir.[3] On the day of the match he observed a complete fast. All thought that he would surely be defeated. But it was he who won, while the man who had feasted for fifteen days lost the fight.

"What is the use of printing and advertising? He who teaches men gets his power from God. None but a man of renunciation can teach others. I am the greatest of all fools!" (All laugh.)

A DEVOTEE: "Then how is it that the Vedas and the Vedānta, and many things besides, come out of your mouth?"

MASTER (smiling): "During my boyhood I could understand what the sādhus read at the Lahas' house at Kāmārpukur, although I would miss a little here and there. If a pundit speaks to me in Sanskrit I can follow him, but I cannot speak it myself.

"To realize God is the one goal of life. While aiming his arrow at the mark, Arjuna said, 'I see only the eye of the bird and nothing else—not the kings, not the trees, not even the bird itself.'

"The realization of God is enough for me. What does it matter if I don't know Sanskrit?

"The grace of God falls alike on all His children, learned and illiterate—whoever longs for Him. The father has the same love for all his children. Suppose a father has five children. One calls him 'Bābā', some 'Bā', and some 'Pā'. These last cannot pronounce the whole word. Does the father love those who address him as 'Bābā' more than those who call him 'Pā'? The father knows that these last are simply too young to say 'Bābā' correctly.

"Since this injury to my arm a change has been coming over my mind. I have been feeling much inclined to the Naralīlā. It is God Himself who plays about as human beings. If God can be worshipped through a clay image, then why not through a man?

"Once a merchant was shipwrecked. He floated to the shore of Ceylon, where Bibhishana was the king of the monsters. Bibhishana ordered his servants to bring the merchant to him. At the sight of him Bibhishana was overwhelmed with joy and said: 'Ah! He looks like my Rāma. The same human form!' He adorned the merchant with robes and jewels, and worshipped him. When I first heard this story, I felt such joy that I cannot describe it.

[3] Mahāvir, or Hanumān, is the patron deity of wrestlers.

"Vaishnavcharan said to me, 'If a person looks on his beloved as his Ishta, he finds it very easy to direct his mind to God.' The men and women of a particular sect[4] at Śyāmbāzār, near Kāmārpukur, say to each other, 'Whom do you love?' 'I love so-and-so.' 'Then know him to be your God.' When I heard this, I said to them: 'That is not my way. I look on all women as my mother.' I found out that they talked big but led immoral lives. The women then asked me if they would have salvation. 'Yes,' I said, 'if you are absolutely faithful to one man and look on him as your God. But you cannot be liberated if you live with five men.'"

RAM: "I understand that Kedar Babu has recently visited the Kartābhajās' place."

MASTER: "He gathers honey from various flowers. (*To Ram, Nityagopal, and the others*) If a devotee believes one hundred per cent that his Chosen Ideal is God, then he attains God and sees Him.

"People of bygone generations had tremendous faith. What faith Haladhari's father had! Once he was on the way to his daughter's house when he noticed some beautiful flowers and vilwa-leaves. He gathered them for the worship of the Family Deity and walked back five or six miles to his own house.

"Once a theatrical troupe in the village was enacting the life of Rāma. When Kaikeyi asked Rāma to go into exile in the forest, Haladhari's father, who had been watching the performance, sprang up. He went to the actor who played Kaikeyi, crying out, 'You wretch!', and was about to burn the actor's face with a torch. He was a very pious man. After finishing his ablutions he would stand in the water and meditate on the Deity, reciting the invocation: 'I meditate on Thee, of red hue and four faces', while tears streamed down his cheeks.

"When my father walked along the lanes of the village wearing his wooden sandals, the shopkeepers would stand up out of respect and say, 'There he comes!' When he bathed in the Hāldārpukur, the villagers would not have the courage to get into the water. Before bathing they would inquire if he had finished his bath.

"When my father chanted the name of Raghuvir, his chest would turn crimson. This also happened to me. When I saw the cows at Vrindāvan returning from the pasture, I was transported into a divine mood and my body became red.

"Very strong was the faith of the people in those days. One hears that God used to dance then, taking the form of Kāli, while the devotee clapped his hands keeping time."

A hathayogi was staying in the hut at the Panchavati. Ramprasanna, the son of Krishnakishore of Āriādaha, and several other men had become his devotees. The yogi needed twenty-five rupees a month for his milk and

---

[4] The reference is to certain minor sects of Vaishnavism, such as the Kartābhajā and the Navarasika, which teach that men and women should live together in the relationship of love. Gradually they should idealize their love by looking upon each other as divine, eventually realizing that their physical love is also the love of God. This is very difficult to realize.

opium; so Ramprasanna had requested Sri Ramakrishna to speak to his
devotees about the yogi and get some money. The Master said to several
devotees: "A hathayogi has come to the Panchavati. Go and visit him. See
what sort of man he is."

A young man of twenty-seven or twenty-eight, known as Thākur Dādā,
entered the room with a few friends and saluted the Master. He lived at
Barānagore and was the son of a brāhmin pundit. He was practising the
kathakatā[5] in order to earn money to meet his family's expenses. At one
time he had been seized with the spirit of renunciation and had gone away
from his family. Even now he practised spiritual discipline at home.

MASTER: "Have you come on foot? Where do you live?"

DĀDĀ: "Yes, sir, I have walked from home. I live at Barānagore."

MASTER: "Have you come here for any particular purpose?"

DĀDĀ: "I have come here to visit you. I pray to God. But why do I suffer
now and then from worries? For a few days I feel very happy. Why do I feel
restless afterwards?"

MASTER: "I see. Things have not been fitted quite exactly. The machine
works smoothly if the mechanic fits the cogs of the wheels correctly. In
your case there is an obstruction somewhere."

DĀDĀ: "Yes, sir. That must be so."

MASTER: "Are you initiated?"

DĀDĀ: "Yes, sir."

MASTER: "Do you have faith in your mantra?"

A friend of Thākur Dādā said that the latter could sing well. The Master
asked him to sing.

Thākur Dādā sang:

> I shall become a yogi and dwell in Love's mountain cave;
> I shall be lost in yoga beside the Fountain-head of Bliss.
> I shall appease my hunger for Knowledge with the fruit of Truth;
> I shall worship the feet of God with the flower of Dispassion.
>
> I shall not seek a well to slake the burning thirst of my heart,
> But I shall draw the water of Peace into the jar of my soul.
> Drinking the glorious Nectar of Thy blessed Lotus Feet,
> I shall both laugh and dance and weep and sing on the heights of Joy.

MASTER: "Ah, what a nice song! 'Fountain-head of Bliss'! 'Fruit of Truth'!
'Laugh and dance and weep and sing'! Your song tastes very sweet to me.
Why should you worry?

"Pleasure and pain are inevitable in the life of the world. One suffers now
and then from a little worry and trouble. A man living in a room full of
soot cannot avoid being a little stained."

DĀDĀ: "Please tell me what I should do now."

MASTER: "Chant the name of Hari morning and evening, clapping your
hands. Come once more when my arm is healed a bit."

Mahimacharan entered the room and saluted the Master. Sri Ramakrishna

[5] The recital of stories from religious books, with appropriate music.

said to him: "Ah! He has sung a nice song. Please sing it again." Thākur Dādā repeated the song.

MASTER (to Mahima): "Please recite that verse, the one about devotion to Hari."

Mahimacharan recited, quoting from the Nārada Pancharātra:

> What need is there of penance if God is worshipped with love?
> What is the use of penance if God is not worshipped with love?
> What need is there of penance if God is seen within and without?
> What is the use of penance if God is not seen within and without?

MASTER: "Recite that part also—'Obtain from Him the love of God'."

Mahima recited:

> O Brahman! O my child! Cease from practising further penances.
> Hasten to Śankara, the Ocean of Heavenly Wisdom;
> Obtain from Him the love of God, the pure love praised by devotees,
> Which snaps in twain the shackles that bind you to the world.

MASTER: "Yes, Śankara will bestow the love of God."

MAHIMA: "One who is free from bondage is the eternal Śiva."

MASTER: "Shame, hatred, fear, hesitation—these are the shackles. What do you say?"

MAHIMA: "Yes, sir. And also the desire to conceal, and shrinking before praise."

MASTER: "There are two signs of knowledge. First, an unshakable buddhi. No matter how many sorrows, afflictions, dangers, and obstacles one may be faced with, one's mind does not undergo any change. It is like the blacksmith's anvil, which receives constant blows from the hammer and still remains unshaken. And second, manliness—very strong grit. If lust and anger injure a man, he must renounce them once for all. If a tortoise once tucks in its limbs, it won't put them out again though you may cut it into four pieces. (To Thākur Dādā and the others) There are two kinds of renunciation: intense and feeble. Feeble renunciation is a slow process; one moves in a slow rhythm. Intense renunciation is like the sharp edge of a razor. It cuts the bondage of māyā easily and at once.

"One farmer labours for days to bring water from the lake to his field. But his efforts are futile because he has no grit. Another farmer, after labouring for two or three days, takes a vow and says, 'I will bring water into my field today, and not till then will I go home.' He puts aside all thought of his bath or his meal. He labours the whole day and feels great joy when in the evening he finds water entering his field with a murmuring sound. Then he goes home and says to his wife: 'Now give me some oil. I shall take my bath.' After finishing his bath and his meal he lies down to sleep with a peaceful mind.

"A certain woman said to her husband: 'So-and-so has developed a spirit of great dispassion for the world, but I don't see anything of the sort in you. He has sixteen wives. He is giving them up one by one.' The husband, with a towel on his shoulder, was going to the lake for his bath. He said to his wife: 'You are crazy! He won't be able to give up the world. Is it ever possible to renounce bit by bit? I can renounce. Look! Here I go.' He didn't stop even to settle his household affairs. He left home just as he was, the towel on his shoulder, and went away. That is intense renunciation.

"There is another kind of renunciation, called 'markatavairāgya', 'monkey renunciation'. A man, harrowed by distress at home, puts on an ochre robe and goes away to Benares. For many days he does not send home any news of himself. Then he writes to his people: 'Don't be worried about me. I have got a job here.'

"There is always trouble in family life. The wife may be disobedient. Perhaps the husband earns only twenty rupees a month. He hasn't the means to perform the 'rice-eating ceremony' for his baby. He cannot educate his son. The house is dilapidated. The roof leaks and he hasn't the money to repair it.

"Therefore when the youngsters come here I ask them whether they have anyone at home. (*To Mahima*) Why should householders renounce the world? What great troubles the wandering monks pass through! The wife of a certain man said to him: 'You want to renounce the world? Why? You will have to beg morsels from eight different homes. But here you get all your food at once place. Isn't that nice?'

"Wandering monks, while searching for a sadāvrata,[6] may have to go six miles out of their way. I have seen them travelling along the regular road after their pilgrimage to Puri and making a detour to find an eating-place.

"You are leading a householder's life. That is very good. It is like fighting from a fort. There are many disadvantages in fighting in an open field. So many dangers, too. Bullets may hit you.

"But one should spend some time in solitude and attain Knowledge. Then one can lead the life of a householder. Janaka lived in the world after attaining Knowledge. When you have gained it, you may live anywhere. Then nothing matters."

MAHIMA: "Sir, why does a man become deluded by worldly objects?"

MASTER: "It is because he lives in their midst without having realized God. Man never succumbs to delusion after he has realized God. The moth no longer enjoys darkness if it has once seen the light.

"To be able to realize God, one must practise absolute continence. Sages like Śukadeva are examples of an urdharetā.[7] Their chastity was absolutely unbroken. There is another class, who previously have had discharges of semen but who later on have controlled them. A man controlling the seminal fluid for twelve years develops a special power. He grows a new inner nerve called the nerve of memory. Through that nerve he remembers all, he understands all.

"Loss of semen impairs the strength. But it does not injure one if one loses it in a dream. That semen one gets from food. What remains after nocturnal discharge is enough. But one must not know a woman.

[6] An eating-place where food is supplied free to monks and beggars.
[7] A man of unbroken and complete continence.

"The semen that remains after nocturnal discharge is very 'refined'. The Lahas kept jars of molasses in their house. Every jar had a hole in it. After a year they found that the molasses had crystallized like sugar candy. The unnecessary watery part had leaked out through the hole.

"A sannyāsi must absolutely renounce woman. You are already involved; but that doesn't matter.

"A sannyāsi must not look even at the picture of a woman. But this is too difficult for an ordinary man. Sā, re, gā, mā, pā, dhā, ni are the seven notes of the scale. It is not possible to keep your voice on 'ni' a long time.

"To lose semen is extremely harmful for a sannyāsi. Therefore he must live so carefully that he will not have to see the form of a woman. He must keep himself away from a woman even if she is a devotee of God. It is injurious for him to look even at the picture of a woman. He will lose semen in a dream, if not in the waking state.

"A sannyāsi may have control over his senses, but to set an example to mankind he should not talk with women. He must not talk to one very long, even if she is a devotee of God.

"Living as a sannyāsi is like observing the ekādaśi without drinking even a drop of water. There are two other ways of observing the day. You may eat fruit or take luchi and curry. With the luchi and curry you may also take slices of bread soaked in milk. (All laugh.)

(Smiling) "Absolute fasting is not possible for you.

"Once I saw Krishnakishore eating luchi and curry on an ekādaśi day. I said to Hriday, 'Hridu, I want to observe Krishnakishore's ekādaśi!' (All laugh.) And so I did one day. I ate my fill. The next day I had to fast." (Laughter.)

The devotees who had gone to the Panchavati to visit the hathayogi came back.

MASTER (addressing them): "Well, what do you think of him? I dare say you have measured him with your own tape."

Sri Ramakrishna saw that very few of the devotees were willing to give money to the hathayogi.

MASTER: "You don't like a sādhu if you have to give him money. Rajendra Mitra draws a salary of eight hundred rupees a month. He had been to Allāhābād to see the kumbhamelā. I asked him, 'Well, what kind of sādhus did you see at the fair?' Rajendra said: 'I didn't find any very great sādhu there. I noticed one, it is true. But even he accepted money.'

"I say to myself, 'If no one gives money to a sādhu, then how will he feed himself?' There is no collection plate here; therefore all come. And I say to myself: 'Alas! They love their money. Let them have it.'"

The Master rested awhile. A devotee sat on the end of the small couch and gently stroked his feet. The Master said to him softly: "That which is formless again has form. One should believe in the forms of God also. By meditating on Kāli the aspirant realizes God as Kāli. Next he finds that the form merges in the Indivisible Absolute. That which is the Indivisible Satchidānanda is verily Kāli."

Sri Ramakrishna was sitting on the semicircular porch west of his room,

talking with Mahima and other devotees about the hathayogi. The talk
drifted to Ramprasanna, the son of Krishnakishore. The Master was fond
of the young man.

MASTER: "Ramprasanna roams about aimlessly. The other day he came
here and sat in the room, but he did not speak a word. He pressed his
nostrils with his fingers, practising prānāyāma. I offered him something to
eat, but he wouldn't take it. On another occasion I had asked him to sit by
me. He squatted on the floor placing one leg upon the other. He was rather
discourteous to Captain. I weep at his mother's suffering.

(To Mahima) "Ramprasanna asked me to speak to you about the hathayogi. The yogi's daily expenses are six and a half ānnās. But he won't tell
you about it himself."

MAHIMA: "Who will listen to him even if he does?"

Mani Sen of Pānihāti entered the room with several friends, one of whom
was a physician. Mani asked the Master about his injured arm. The doctor
did not approve of the medicine prescribed by Pratap Mazumdar. The Master said to him: "Why should you say that? Pratap is no fool."

Suddenly Latu cried out, "Oh! The medicine bottle has dropped and
broken."

It was not yet dusk. The Master, seated on the couch, was talking to M.
Mahimacharan was on the semicircular porch engaged in a loud discussion
of the scriptures with the physician friend of Mani Sen. Sri Ramakrishna
heard it and with a smile said to M.: "There! He is delivering himself.
That is the characteristic of rajas. It stimulates the desire to 'lecture' and
to show off one's scholarship. But sattva makes one introspective. It makes
one hide one's virtues. But I must say that Mahima is a grand person. He
takes such delight in spiritual talk."

Adhar entered the room, saluted the Master, and sat by M.'s side. He had
not come for the past few days.

MASTER: "Hello! Why haven't you come all these days?"

ADHAR: "Sir, I have been busy with so many things. I had to attend a
conference of the school committee and various other meetings."

MASTER: "So you completely lost yourself in schools and meetings and
forgot everything else?"

ADHAR: "Everything else was hidden away in a corner of my mind. How
is your arm?"

MASTER: "Just look. It is not yet healed. I have been taking medicine
prescribed by Pratap."

After a time the Master suddenly said to Adhar: "Look here. All these
are unreal—meetings, school, office, and everything else. God alone is the
Substance, and all else is illusory. One should worship God with one's whole
mind."

Adhar sat without speaking a word.

MASTER: "All else is illusory. This moment the body is and the next
moment it is not. One must make haste to worship God.[8]

"But you don't have to renounce everything. Live in the world the way

[8] A few months after this conversation Adhar died.

the tortoise does. The tortoise roams about in the water but keeps its eggs on land. Its whole mind is on the eggs.

"What a nice state of mind Captain has developed! He looks like a rishi when he is seated to perform worship. He performs the ārati with lighted camphor and recites beautiful hymns. When he rises from his seat after finishing the worship, his eyes are swollen from emotion, as if bitten by ants. Besides, he always devotes himself to the study of the sacred books, such as the Gītā and the Bhāgavata. Once I used one or two English words before him, and that made him angry. He said, 'English-educated people are profane.'"

After a while Adhar said humbly to the Master: "Sir, you haven't been to our place for a long time. The drawing-room smells worldly and everything else appears to be steeped in darkness."

The Master was deeply touched by these words of his devotee. He suddenly stood up and blessed M. and Adhar in an ecstatic mood, touching their heads and hearts. In a voice choked with love the Master said: "I look upon you as Nārāyana Himself. You are indeed my own."

Mahimacharan entered the room.

MASTER (to Mahima): "What I said about aspirants practising continence is true. Without chastity one cannot assimilate these teachings.

"Once a man said to Chaitanya: 'You give the devotees so much instruction. Why don't they make much progress?' Chaitanya said: 'They dissipate their powers in the company of women. That is why they cannot assimilate spiritual instruction. If one keeps water in a leaky jar, the water escapes little by little through the leak.'"

Mahima and the other devotees remained silent. After a time Mahima said, "Please pray to God for us that we may acquire the necessary strength."

MASTER: "Be on your guard even now. It is difficult, no doubt, to check the torrent in the rainy season. But a great deal of water has gone out. If you build the embankment now it will stand."

21

A DAY AT DAKSHINESWAR

Saturday, April 5, 1884

IT WAS ABOUT EIGHT O'CLOCK in the morning when M. arrived at the temple garden and found Sri Ramakrishna seated on the small couch in his room. A few devotees were sitting on the floor. The Master was talking to them. Prankrishna Mukherji was there.

Prankrishna belonged to an aristocratic family and lived in the northern part of Calcutta. He held a high post in an English business firm. He was very much devoted to Sri Ramakrishna and, though a householder, derived great pleasure from the study of Vedānta philosophy. He was a frequent visitor at the temple garden. Once he invited the Master to his house in Calcutta and held a religious festival. Every day, early in the morning, he bathed in the holy water of the Ganges. Whenever it was convenient, he would come to Dakshineswar in a hired country boat.

That morning he had hired a boat and invited M. to accompany him to Dakshineswar. The boat had hardly left shore when the river became choppy. M. had become frightened and begged Prankrishna to put him back on land. In spite of assurances, M. had kept saying: "You must put me ashore. I shall walk to Dakshineswar." And so M. came on foot and found Sri Ramakrishna talking to Prankrishna and the others.

MASTER (to Prankrishna): "But there is a greater manifestation of God in man. You may ask, 'How is it possible for God to be incarnated as a man who suffers from hunger, thirst, and the other traits of an embodied being, and perhaps also from disease and grief?' The reply is, 'Even Brahman weeps, entrapped in the snare of the five elements.'

"Don't you know how Rāma had to weep, stricken with grief for Sītā? Further, it is said that the Lord incarnated Himself as a sow in order to kill the demon Hiranyāksha. Hiranyāksha was eventually killed, but God would not go back to His abode in heaven. He enjoyed His sow's life. He had given birth to several young ones and was rather happy with them. The gods said among themselves: 'What does this mean? The Lord doesn't care to return to heaven!' They all went to Śiva and laid the matter before him. Śiva came down and urged the Lord to leave the sow body and return to heaven. But the sow only suckled her young ones. (Laughter.) Then Śiva destroyed the sow body with his trident, and the Lord came out laughing aloud and went back to His own abode."

PRANKRISHNA (to the Master): "Sir, what is the Anāhata sound?"

MASTER: "It is a spontaneous sound constantly going on by itself. It is the sound of the Pranava, Om. It originates in the Supreme Brahman and is heard by yogis. People immersed in worldliness do not hear it. A yogi alone knows that this sound originates both from his navel and from the Supreme Brahman resting on the Ocean of Milk."[1]

PRANKRISHNA: "Sir, what is the nature of the life after death?"

MASTER: "Keshab Sen also asked that question. As long as a man remains ignorant, that is to say, as long as he has not realized God, so long will he be born. But after attaining Knowledge he will not have to come back to this earth or to any other plane of existence.

"The potter puts his pots in the sun to dry. Haven't you noticed that among them there are both baked and unbaked ones? When a cow happens to walk over them, some of the pots get broken to pieces. The broken pots that are already baked, the potter throws away, since they are of no more use to him. But the soft ones, though broken, he gathers up. He makes them into a lump and out of this forms new pots. In the same way, so long as a man has not realized God, he will have to come back to the Potter's hand, that is, he will have to be born again and again.

"What is the use of sowing a boiled paddy grain? It will never bring forth a shoot. Likewise, if a man is boiled in the fire of Knowledge, he will not be used for new creation. He is liberated.

"According to the Purānas, the bhakta and the Bhagavān are two separate entities. 'I' am one and 'You' are another. The body is a plate, as it were, containing the water of mind, intelligence, and ego. Brahman is like the sun. It is reflected in the water. Therefore the devotee sees the divine form.

"According to the Vedānta, Brahman alone is real and all else is māyā, dreamlike and unsubstantial. The ego, like a stick, lies across the Ocean of Satchidānanda. (To M.) Listen to what I am saying. When this ego is taken away, there remains only one undivided Ocean of Satchidānanda. But as long as the stick of ego remains, there is an appearance of two: here is one part of the water and there another part. Attaining the Knowledge of Brahman one is established in samādhi. Then the ego is effaced.

"But Sankarāchārya retained the 'ego of Knowledge'[2] in order to teach

---

[1] According to Hindu mythology, after the dissolution of the universe and before the next creation, the Supreme Lord rests on the Ocean of the Great Cause, also called the "Ocean of Milk".

[2] The ego illumined and purified by the Knowledge of God. Following the method of discrimination, the jnāni, in samādhi, merges his ego in Brahman. Thereafter he may come down to the relative plane with an appearance of individuality, but even then he is always conscious of his identity with Brahman. This apparent ego is called the "ego of Knowledge". A bhakta, following the path of love, realizes his eternal relationship with God. He too keeps an appearance of individuality on the relative plane. This ego has none of the characteristics of the worldly ego and is called the "ego of Devotion". The two egos here described refer to the same state of realization.

men. (*To Prankrishna*) But there are signs that distinguish the man of Knowledge. Some people think they have Knowledge. What are the characteristics of Knowledge? A jnāni cannot injure anybody. He becomes like a child. If a steel sword touches the philosopher's stone, it is transformed into gold. Gold can never cut. It may seem·from the outside that a jnāni also has anger or egotism, but in reality he has no such thing.

"From a distance a burnt string lying on the ground may look like a real one; but if you come near and blow at it, it disappears altogether. The anger and egotism of a jnāni are mere appearances; they are not real.

"A child has no attachment. He makes a play house, and if anyone touches it, he will jump about and cry. The next moment he himself will break it. This moment he may be very attached to his cloth. He says: 'My daddy has given it to me. I won't part with it.' But the next moment you can cajole him away from it with a toy. He will go away with you, leaving the cloth behind.

"These are the characteristics of a jnāni. Perhaps he has many luxuries at home—couch, chairs, paintings, and equipage. But any day he may leave all these and go off to Benares.

"According to Vedānta the waking state, too, is unreal. Once a wood-cutter lay dreaming, when someone woke him up. Greatly annoyed, he said: 'Why have you disturbed my sleep? I was dreaming that I was a king and the father of seven children. The princes were becoming well versed in letters and military arts. I was secure on my throne and ruled over my subjects. Why have you demolished my world of joy?' 'But that was a mere dream', said the other man. 'Why should that bother you?' 'Fool!' said the wood-cutter. 'You don't understand. My becoming a king in the dream was just as real as is my being a wood-cutter. If being a wood-cutter is real, then being a king in a dream is real also.' "

Prankrishna always talked about jnāna. Was this why the Master described the state of the jnāni? Now he proceeded to describe the state of the vijnāni.

MASTER: "Jnāna is the realization of Self through the process of 'Neti, neti', 'Not this, not this'. One goes into samādhi through this process of elimination and realizes the Ātman.

"But vijnāna means Knowledge with a greater fullness. Some have heard of milk, some have seen milk, and some have drunk milk. He who has merely heard of it is 'ignorant'. He who has seen it is a jnāni. But he who has drunk it has vijnāna, that is to say, a fuller knowledge of it. After having the vision of God one talks to Him as if He were an intimate relative. That is vijnāna.

"First of all you must discriminate, following the method of 'Neti, neti': 'He is not the five elements, nor the sense-organs, nor the mind, nor the intelligence, nor the ego. He is beyond all these cosmic principles.' You want to climb to the roof; then you must eliminate and leave behind all the steps, one by one. The steps are by no means the roof. But after reaching the roof you find that the steps are made of the same materials—brick, lime, and brick-dust—as the roof. It is the Supreme Brahman that has become the universe and its living beings and the twenty-four cosmic principles. That which is Ātman has become the five elements. You may ask why the earth is so hard, if it has come out of Ātman? All is possible through the will of God. Don't you see that bone and flesh are made from blood and semen? How hard 'sea-foam'[3] becomes!

"After attaining vijnāna one can live in the world as well. Then one clearly realizes that God Himself has become the universe and all living beings, that He is not outside the world.

(To Prankrishna) "The fact is that one must have the 'spiritual eye'. You will develop that eye as soon as your mind becomes pure. Take for instance the Kumāri Pujā. I worshipped a virgin. The girl, to be sure, had all her human imperfections; still I regarded her as the Divine Mother Herself.

"On one side is the wife and on the other the son. Love is bestowed on both, but in different ways. Therefore it comes to this, that everything depends upon the mind. The pure mind acquires a new attitude. Through that mind one sees God in this world. Therefore one needs spiritual discipline.

"Yes, spiritual discipline is necessary. You should know that a man becomes easily attached to a woman. A woman naturally loves a man, and a man also naturally loves a woman. Therefore both fall speedily from their spiritual ideal. But it also must be said that there is a great advantage in leading the life of a householder. In case of urgent necessity a man may live with his wife.

(Smiling) "Well, M., why are you smiling?"

M. (to himself): "The Master makes this much allowance for householders since they cannot renounce everything. Is complete and absolute continence impossible for a householder?"

The hathayogi who had been living in the Panchavati entered the room. He was in the habit of taking milk and opium. He did not eat rice or other food and had no money to buy the milk and opium. The Master had talked with him in the Panchavati. The hathayogi had told Rakhal to ask the Master to make some provision for him, and Sri Ramakrishna had promised ,to speak about it to the visitors from Calcutta.

HATHAYOGI (to the Master): "What did you say to Rakhal about me?"

MASTER: "I said that I would ask some rich visitors to help you. But— (to Prankrishna) you, perhaps, do not like these yogis?"

Prankrishna remained silent. The hathayogi left the room and the conversation went on.

MASTER (to Prankrishna and the others): "If a man leads a householder's life he must have unflagging devotion to truth. God can be realized through truth alone. Formerly I was very particular about telling the truth, though now my zeal has abated a little. If I said, 'I shall bathe', then I would get into the water of the Ganges, recite the mantra, and sprinkle a little water over my head. But still there would remain some doubt in me as to whether my bath was complete. Once I went to Ram's house in Calcutta. I hap-

[3] The Master perhaps referred to the cuttle-bone found on the seashore. The popular belief is that it is hardened foam.

pened to say, 'I shall not take any luchi.' When I sat down for the meal I felt hungry. But I had said I would not eat the luchi; so I had to fill my stomach with sweets. (*All laugh.*)

"But my zeal for truthfulness has abated a little now. Once I said I would go to the pine-grove, but then I felt I had no particular urge to go. What was to be done? I asked Ram[4] about it. He said I didn't have to go. Then I reasoned to myself: 'Well, everyone is Nārāyana. So Ram, too, is Nārāyana. Why shouldn't I listen to him? The elephant is Nārāyana no doubt, but the māhut is Nārāyana too. Since the māhut asked me not to go near the elephant, then why shouldn't I obey him?' Through reasoning like this my zeal for truthfulness is slightly less strong now than before.

"I find a change coming over me. Years ago Vaishnavcharan said to me, 'One attains Perfect Knowledge when one sees God in man.' Now I see that it is God alone who is moving about in various forms: as a holy man, as a cheat, as a villain. Therefore I say, 'Nārāyana in the guise of the sādhu, Nārāyana in the guise of the cheat, Nārāyana in the guise of the villain, Nārāyana in the guise of the lecher.'

"Now my problem is how I can feed all of you. I want to feed everyone. So I keep one at a time with me and feed him."

Prankrishna (*looking at M. and smiling*): "A fine man, indeed! (*To the Master*) He would not let us go till we put him ashore."

MASTER (*smiling*): "Why? What happened?"

PRANKRISHNA: "He was in our boat. Seeing that the river was slightly rough, he insisted on being put ashore. (*To M.*) How did you come?"

M. (*smiling*): "On foot."

Sri Ramakrishna laughed.

PRANKRISHNA (*to the Master*): "Sir, I am thinking now of giving up my work. One who is involved in activity cannot accomplish anything. (*Pointing to his companion*) I am training him to do my work. After I resign, he will relieve me. Work has become intolerable."

MASTER: "Yes, work is very troublesome. It is now good for you to meditate on God for a few days in solitude. No doubt you say that you would like to give up your work. Captain said the same thing. Worldly people talk that way; but they don't succeed in carrying out their intention.

"There are many pundits who speak words of wisdom. But they merely talk; they don't live up to them. They are like vultures, which soar very high but keep their gaze fixed on the charnel-pit. What I mean is that these pundits are attached to the world, to 'woman and gold'. If I hear that pundits are practising discrimination and dispassion, then I fear them. Otherwise I look upon them as mere goats and dogs."

Prankrishna saluted the Master and took his leave. He said to M., "Will you come with us?"

M: "No, sir! Catch me going with you again! Good-bye."

Prankrishna laughed and said, "I see you won't come in the boat."

M. took a little stroll near the Panchavati and bathed in the river. Then he went to the temples of Rādhākānta and Kāli and prostrated himself be-

4 Ram Chatterji, the priest in the Rādhākānta temple.

fore the images. He said to himself: "I have heard that God has no form. Then why do I bow before these images? Is it because Sri Ramakrishna believes in gods and goddesses with form? I don't know anything about God, nor do I understand Him. The Master believes in images; then why shouldn't I too, who am so insignificant a creature, accept them?"

M. looked at the image of Kāli. He saw that the Divine Mother holds in Her two left hands a man's severed head and a sword. With Her two right hands She offers boons and reassurance to Her devotees. In one aspect She is terrible, and in another She is the ever affectionate Mother of Her devotees. The two ideals are harmonized in Her. She is compassionate and affectionate to Her devotees, to those who are submissive and helpless. It is also true that She is terrible, the "Consort of Death". She alone knows why She assumes two aspects at the same time.

M. remembered this interpretation of Kāli given by the Master. He said to himself, "I have heard that Keshab accepted Kāli in Sri Ramakrishna's presence. Is this, as Keshab used to say, the Goddess, all Spirit and Consciousness, manifesting Herself through a clay image?"

M. returned to the Master's room and sat on the floor. Sri Ramakrishna offered him some fruit and sweets to eat. On account of trouble in the family, M. had recently rented a house in another section of Calcutta near his school, his father and brothers continuing to live in the ancestral home. But Sri Ramakrishna wanted him to return to his own home, since a joint family affords many advantages to one leading a religious life. Once or twice the Master had spoken to M. to this effect, but unfortunately he had not yet returned to his family. Sri Ramakrishna referred to the matter again.

MASTER: "Tell me that you are going to your ancestral home."

M: "I can never persuade myself to enter that place."

MASTER: "Why? Your father is making over the whole house."

M: "I have suffered too much there. I can by no means make up my mind to go there."

MASTER: "Whom do you fear?"

M: "All of them."

MASTER (seriously): "Isn't that like your being afraid to get into the boat?"

The midday worship and the offering of food in the temples were over. The bells, gongs, and cymbals of the ārati were being played, and the temple garden was filled with joyful activity. Beggars, sādhus, and guests hurried to the guest-house for the noonday meal, carrying leaf or metal plates in their hands. M. also took some of the prasād from the Kāli temple.

Sri Ramakrishna had been resting awhile after his meal when several devotees, including Ram and Girindra, arrived. They sat down after saluting the Master. The conversation turned to the New Dispensation Church of Keshab Chandra Sen.

RAM (to the Master): "Sir, I don't think the Navavidhān has done people any good. If Keshab Babu himself was a genuine man, why are his disciples left in such a plight? I don't think there is anything at all in the New Dispensation. It is like rattling some potsherds in a room and then

A Day at Dakshineswar

locking it up. People may take it to be the jingling of coins, but inside there is nothing but potsherds. Outsiders don't know what is inside."

MASTER: "There must be some substance in it. Otherwise, why should so many people respect Keshab? Why isn't Shivanath honoured as much as Keshab? Such a thing cannot happen without the will of God.

"But a man cannot act as an āchārya without renouncing the world. People won't respect him. They will say: 'Oh, he is a worldly man. He secretly enjoys "woman and gold" himself but tells us that God alone is real and the world unsubstantial, like a dream.' Unless a man renounces everything his teachings cannot be accepted by all. Some worldly people may follow him. Keshab led the life of a householder; hence his mind was directed to the world also. He had to safeguard his family interests. That is why he left his affairs in such good order though he delivered so many religious lectures. What an aristocratic man he married his daughter to! Inside Keshab's inner apartments I saw many big bedsteads. All these things gradually come to one who leads a householder's life. The world is indeed a place for enjoyment."

RAM: "Keshab Sen inherited those bedsteads when his ancestral property was divided. And for Keshab to take part in the division of property! Whatever you may say, sir, Vijay Babu told me that Keshab had said to him, 'I am a partial manifestation of Christ and Gaurānga. I suggest that you declare yourself as Advaita.'[5] Do you know what else he said? He said that you too were a follower of the New Dispensation." (All laugh.)

MASTER (laughing): "Who knows? But as for myself, I don't even know what the term 'New Dispensation' means." (Laughter.)

RAM: "Keshab's disciples say that he was the first to harmonize jnāna and bhakti."

MASTER (in surprise): "How is that? What then of the Adhyātma Rāmāyana? It is written there that, while praying to Rāma, Nārada said: 'O Rāma, Thou art the Supreme Brahman described in the Vedas. Thou dwellest with us as a man; Thou appearest as a man. In reality Thou art not a man; Thou art that Supreme Brahman.' Rāma said: 'Nārada, I am very much pleased with you. Accept a boon from Me.' Nārada replied: 'What boon shall I ask of Thee? Grant me pure love for Thy Lotus Feet, and may I never be deluded by Thy world-bewitching māyā!' The Adhyātma Rāmāyana is full of such statements regarding jnāna and bhakti."

The conversation turned to Amrita, a disciple of Keshab.

RAM: "Amrita Babu seems to be in very bad shape."

MASTER: "Yes, he looked very ill when I saw him the other day."

RAM: "Sir, let me tell you about the lectures of the New Dispensation. While the drum is being played, the members cry out, 'Victory unto Keshab!' You say that 'dal'[6] grows only in a stagnant pool. So Amrita said one day in the course of his sermon: 'The holy man[7] has no doubt said that

complete---

[5] An intimate companion of Gaurānga.
[6] The word has the double meaning of "sedge" and "sect".
[7] Referring to Sri Ramakrishna.

'dal' grows in a stagnant pool. But, brothers, we want 'dal', we want a sect. Really and truly, I tell you that we want a sect.' "

MASTER: "What nonsense! Shame on him! What kind of sermon is that?" The conversation drifted to the desire of some people for praise.

MASTER: "They took me to Keshab's house to see a performance of the Nimāi-sannyās. I heard, that day, someone speaking of Keshab and Pratap as Chaitanya and Nityānanda. Prasanna asked me, 'Who are you then?' Keshab looked at me to see what I would say. I said to him, 'I am the servant of your servant, the dust of the dust of your feet.' Keshab said with a smile, 'You can't catch him!' "

RAM: "Sometimes Keshab used to say you were John the Baptist."

A DEVOTEE: "But Keshab also said you were the Chaitanya of the nineteenth century [said in English]."

MASTER: "What does that mean?"

DEVOTEE: "That Chaitanya has been incarnated again in the present century of the Christian era, and that you are he."

MASTER (absent-mindedly): "What of it? Can you tell me now how my arm can be cured? This arm is worrying me so much."

They talked about Trailokya's music. Trailokya sang devotional songs in Keshab's Brāhmo Samāj.

MASTER: "Ah! How nice his songs are!"

RAM: "Do you think they are genuine?"

MASTER: "Yes, they are. Otherwise, why should I be so drawn to them?"

RAM: "He has composed his songs by borrowing your ideas. While conducting the worship Keshab Sen described your feelings and realizations, and Trailokya Babu composed songs accordingly. Take this song, for instance:

> There is an overflow of Joy in the market-place of Love;
> See how the Lord sports with His own in the ecstasy of Bliss!

He saw you enjoying divine bliss in the company of devotees and wrote songs like this."

MASTER (with a smile): "Stop! Don't torment me any more. Why should I be involved in all this?" (All laugh.)

GIRINDRA: "The Brāhmos say that the Paramahamsadeva has no faculty for organization [said in English]."

MASTER: "What does that mean?"

M: "That you don't know how to lead a sect; that your intellect is rather dull. They say things like that." (All laugh.)

MASTER (to Ram): "Now tell me why my arm was hurt. Stand up and deliver a lecture on that. (Laughter.)

"The Brāhmos insist that God is formless. Suppose they do. It is enough to call on Him with sincerity of heart. If the devotee is sincere, then God, who is the Inner Guide of all, will certainly reveal to the devotee His true nature.

"But it is not good to say that what we ourselves think of God is the only truth and what others think is false; that because we think of God as formless, therefore He is formless and cannot have any form; that because we think of God as having form, therefore He has form and cannot be formless. Can a man really fathom God's nature?

"This kind of friction exists between the Vaishnavas and the Śāktas. The Vaishnava says, 'My Keśava is the only Saviour', whereas the Śākta insists, 'My Bhagavati is the only Saviour.'

"Once I took Vaishnavcharan to Mathur Babu. Now, Vaishnavcharan was a very learned Vaishnava and an orthodox devotee of his sect. Mathur, on the other hand, was a devotee of the Divine Mother. They were engaged in a friendly discussion when suddenly Vaishnavcharan said, 'Keśava is the only Saviour.' No sooner did Mathur hear this than his ‚face became red with anger and he blurted out, 'You rascal!' (All laugh.) He was a Śākta. Wasn't it natural for him to say that? I gave Vaishnavcharan a nudge.

"I see people who talk about religion constantly quarrelling with one another. Hindus, Mussalmāns, Brāhmos, Śāktas, Vaishnavas, Śaivas, all quarrel with one another. They haven't the intelligence to understand that He who is called Krishna is also Śiva and the Primal Śakti, and that it is He, again, who is called Jesus and Āllāh. 'There is only one Rāma and He has a thousand names.'

"Truth is one; only It is called by different names. All people are seeking the same Truth; the variance is due to climate, temperament, and name. A lake has many ghāts. From one ghāt the Hindus take water in jars and call it 'jal'. From another ghāt the Mussalmāns take water in leather bags and call it 'pāni'. From a third the Christians take the same thing and call it 'water'. (All laugh.) Suppose someone says that the thing is not 'jal' but 'pāni', or that it is not 'pāni' but 'water', or that it is not 'water' but 'jal'. It would indeed be ridiculous. But this very thing is at the root of the friction among sects, their misunderstandings and quarrels. This is why people injure and kill one another, and shed blood, in the name of religion. But this is not good. Everyone is going toward God. They will all realize Him if they have sincerity and longing of heart.

(To M.) "This is for you. All scriptures—the Vedas, the Purānas, the Tantras—seek Him alone and no one else, only that one Satchidānanda. That which is called Satchidānanda Brahman in the Vedas is called Satchidānanda Śiva in the Tantra. Again it is He alone who is called Satchidānanda Krishna in the Purānas."

The Master was told that now and then Ram cooked his own food at home.

MASTER (to M.): "Do you too cook your own meals?"

M: "No, sir."

MASTER: "You may try it. With your meals take a little clarified butter made from cow's milk. That will purify your body and mind."

A long conversation ensued about Ram's household affairs. Ram's father was a devout Vaishnava and worshipped Krishna daily at home. He had married a second time when Ram was quite young. Both the father and the stepmother lived with Ram at Ram's house. But Ram was never happy with his stepmother, and this sometimes created a misunderstanding between himself and his father.

They were talking about this when Ram said, "My father has gone to the dogs!"

MASTER (to the devotees): "Did you hear that? The father has gone to the dogs and the son is all right!"

RAM: "There is no peace when my stepmother comes home. There is always some trouble or other. Our family is about to break up. So I say, let her live with her father."

GIRINDRA (to Ram): "Why don't you too keep your wife at her father's home?" (Laughter.)

MASTER (smiling): "Are husband and wife like earthen pots or jars, that you may keep the pot in one place and the lid in another? Siva in one place and Sakti in another?"

RAM: "Sir, we are quite happy. But when she comes the family is broken up. If such is the case—"

MASTER: "Then build them a separate home. That will be a different thing. You will defray their monthly expenses. How worthy of worship one's parents are! Rakhal asked me if he could take the food left on his father's plate. 'What do you mean?' I said. 'What have you become that you cannot?' But it is also true that good people won't give anyone, even a dog, the food from their plates."

GIRINDRA: "Sir, suppose one's parents are guilty of a terrible crime, a heinous sin?"

MASTER: "What if they are? You must not renounce your mother even if she commits adultery. The woman guru of a certain family became corrupt. The members of the family said that they would like to make the son of the guru their spiritual guide. But I said: 'How is that? Will you accept the shoot and give up the yam? Suppose she is corrupt; still you must regard her as your Ishta. "Though my guru visits the tavern, still to me he is the holy Nityānanda." '

"Are father and mother mere trifles? No spiritual practice will bear fruit unless they are pleased. Chaitanya was intoxicated with the love of God. Still, before taking to the monastic life, for how many days did he try to persuade his mother to give him her permission to become a monk! He said to her: 'Mother, don't worry. I shall visit you every now and then.'

(To M., reproachfully) "And let me say this to you. Your father and mother brought you up. You yourself are the father of several children. Yet you have left home with your wife. You have cheated your parents. You have come away with your wife and children, and you feel you have become a holy man. Your father doesn't need any money from you; otherwise I should have cried, 'Shame on you!' "

Everybody in the room became grave and remained silent.

MASTER: "A man has certain debts to pay: his debts to the gods and rishis, and his debts to mother, father, and wife. He cannot achieve anything without paying the debt he owes to his parents. A man is indebted to his wife as well. Harish has renounced his wife and is living here. If he had left her unprovided for, then I should have called him an abominable wretch.

"After attaining Knowledge you will regard that very wife as the manifestation of the Divine Mother Herself. It is written in the *Chandi*, 'The Goddess dwells in all beings as the Mother.' It is She who has become your mother.

"All the women you see are only She, the Divine Mother. That is why I cannot rebuke even Brindē, the maidservant. There are people who spout verses from the scriptures and talk big, but in their conduct they are quite different. Ramprasanna is constantly busy procuring opium and milk for the hathayogi. He says that Manu enjoins it upon man to serve the sādhu. But his old mother hasn't enough to eat. She walks to the market to buy her own groceries. It makes me very angry.

"But here you have to consider another thing. When a man is intoxicated with ecstatic love of God, then who is his father or mother or wife? His love of God is so intense that he becomes mad with it. Then he has no duty to perform. He is free from all debts. What is this divine intoxication? In this state a man forgets the world. He also forgets his own body, which is so dear to all. Chaitanya had this intoxication. He plunged into the ocean not knowing that it was the ocean. He dashed himself again and again on the ground. He was not aware of hunger, of thirst, or of sleep. He was not at all conscious of any such thing as his body."

All at once Sri Ramakrishna exclaimed, "Ah, Chaitanya!" and stood up.

MASTER (*to the devotees*): "Chaitanya means 'Undivided Consciousness'. Vaishnavcharan used to say that Gaurānga was like a bubble in the Ocean of Undivided Consciousness.

(*To the elder Gopal[8]*) "Do you intend to go on a pilgrimage now?"

GOPAL: "Yes, sir. I should like to wander about a little."

RAM (*to Gopal*): "He [meaning the Master] says that one becomes a kutichaka after being a vahudaka. The sādhu that visits many holy places is called a vahudaka. He whose craving for travel has been satiated and who sits down in one place is called a kutichaka.

"He also tells us a parable. Once a bird sat on the mast of a ship. When the ship sailed through the mouth of the Ganges into the 'black waters' of the ocean, the bird failed to notice the fact. When it finally became aware of the ocean, it left the mast and flew north in search of land. But it found no limit to the water and so returned. After resting awhile it flew south. There too it found no limit to the water. Panting for breath the bird returned to the mast. Again, after resting awhile, it flew east and then west. Finding no limit to the water in any direction, at last it settled down on the mast of the ship."

MASTER (*to the elder Gopal and the other devotees*): "As long as a man feels that God is 'there', he is ignorant. But he attains Knowledge when he feels that God is 'here'.

"A man wanted a smoke. He went to a neighbour's house to light his charcoal. It was the dead of night and the household was asleep. After he

[8] A monastic disciple of the Master, known later as Swami Advaitananda.

had knocked a great deal, someone came down to open the door. At sight of the man he asked, 'Hello! What's the matter?' The man replied: 'Can't you guess? You know how fond I am of smoking. I have come here to light my charcoal.' The neighbour said: 'Ha! Ha! You are a fine man indeed! You took the trouble to come and do all this knocking at the door! Why, you have a lighted lantern in your hand!' (*All laugh.*)

"What a man seeks is very near him. Still he wanders about from place to place."

RAM: "Sir, I now realize why a guru asks some of his disciples to visit the four principal holy places of the country. Once having wandered about, the disciple discovers that it is the same here as there. Then he returns to the guru. All this wandering is only to create faith in the guru's words."

After this conversation had come to an end, Sri Ramakrishna extolled Ram's virtues.

MASTER (*to the devotees*): "How many fine qualities Ram possesses! How many devotees he serves and looks after! (*To Ram*) Adhar told me that you showed him great kindness."

Adhar, a beloved householder devotee of the Master, had recently arranged some religious music at his house. The Master and many devotees had been present. But Adhar had forgotten to invite Ram, who was a very proud man and had complained about it to his friends. So Adhar had gone to Ram's house to express his regret for the mistake.

RAM: "It wasn't really Adhar's mistake. I have come to know that Rakhal is to blame. Rakhal was given charge—"

MASTER: "You mustn't find fault with Rakhal. He's a mere child. Even now you can bring out his mother's milk by squeezing his throat."

RAM: "Sir, why should you speak that way? It was such an occasion!"

MASTER: (*interrupting*): "Adhar simply didn't remember to invite you. He is absent-minded. The other day he went with me to Jadu Mallick's house. As we took our leave, I said to him, 'You haven't offered anything to the Goddess in the chapel.' 'Sir,' he said, 'I didn't know one should.'

(*To Ram*) "Suppose he didn't invite you to his house. Why such a fuss about going to a place where the name of the Lord was sung? One may go unasked to participate in religious music. One doesn't have to be invited."

ADVICE TO AN ACTOR

Saturday, May 24, 1884

SRI RAMAKRISHNA was sitting on the small couch in his room. Rakhal, M., and several other devotees were present. A special worship of Kāli had been performed in the temple the previous night. In connexion with the worship a theatrical performance of the *Vidyāsundar* had been staged in the nātmandir. The Master had watched a part of it that morning. The actors came to his room to pay him their respects. The Master, in a happy mood, became engaged in conversation with a fair-complexioned young man who had taken the part of Vidyā and played his part very well.

MASTER (*to the actor*): "Your acting was very good. If a person excels in singing, music, dancing, or any other art, he can also quickly realize God provided he strives sincerely.

"Just as you practise much in order to sing, dance, and play on instruments, so one should practise the art of fixing the mind on God. One should practise regularly such disciplines as worship, japa, and meditation.

"Are you married? Any children?"

ACTOR: "Yes, sir. I had a girl who died. Another child has been born."

MASTER: "Ah! A death and a birth, and all so quickly! You are so young! There is a saying: 'My husband died just after our marriage. There are so many nights for me to weep!' You are no doubt realizing the nature of worldly happiness. The world is like a hog plum. The hog plum has only pit and skin, and after eating it you suffer from colic.

"You are an actor in the theatre. That's fine. But it is a very painful profession. You are young now; so you have a full, round face. Afterwards there will be hollows in your cheeks. Almost all actors become like that; they get hollow cheeks and big bellies. (*Laughter.*)

"Why did I stay to watch your performance? I found the rhythm, the music, and the melody all correct. Then the Divine Mother showed me that it was God alone who acted in the performance in the roles of the players."

ACTOR: "Sir, what is the difference between lust and desire?"

MASTER: "Lust is like the root of the tree, and desires are branches and twigs.

427

"One cannot completely get rid of the six passions: lust, anger, greed, and the like. Therefore one should direct them to God. If you must have desire and greed, then you should desire love of God and be greedy to attain Him. If you must be conceited and egotistic, then feel conceited and egotistic thinking that you are the servant of God, the child of God.

"A man cannot see God unless he gives his whole mind to Him. The mind is wasted on 'woman and gold'. Take your own case. You have children and are occupied with the theatre. The mind cannot be united with God on account of these different activities.

"As long as there is bhoga, there will be less of yoga. Furthermore, bhoga begets suffering. It is said in the *Bhāgavata* that the Avadhuta chose a kite as one of his twenty-four gurus. The kite had a fish in its beak; so it was surrounded by a thousand crows. Whichever way it flew with the fish, the crows pursued it crying, 'Caw! Caw!' When all of a sudden the fish dropped from its beak, the crows flew after the fish, leaving the kite alone.

"The 'fish' is the object of enjoyment. The 'crows' are worries and anxiety. Worries and anxiety are inevitable with enjoyment. No sooner does one give up enjoyment than one finds peace.

"What is more, money itself becomes a source of trouble. Brothers may live happily, but they get into trouble when the property is divided. Dogs lick one another's bodies; they are perfectly friendly. But when the householder throws them a little food, they get into a scrap.

"Come here now and then. (*Pointing to M. and the others*) They come here on Sundays and other holidays."

ACTOR: "We have holidays for three months, during the rainy and harvest seasons. It is our good fortune to be able to visit you. On our way to Dakshineswar we heard of two persons—yourself and Jnanarnava."

MASTER: "Be on friendly terms with your brothers. It looks well. You must have noticed in your theatrical performance that if four singers sing each in a different way, the play is spoiled."

ACTOR: "Yes, sir. Many birds are trapped in a net; if they all fly together and drag the net in one direction, then many of them may be saved. But that doesn't happen if they try to fly in different directions.

"One also sees in a theatrical performance a person keeping a pitcher of water on his head and at the same time dancing about."

MASTER: "Live in the world but keep the pitcher steady on your head; that is to say, keep the mind firmly on God.

"I once said to the sepoys from the barracks: 'Do your duty in the world but remember that the "pestle of death" will some time smash your hand. Be alert about it.'

"In Kāmārpukur I have seen the women of carpenter families making flattened rice with a husking-machine. One woman kicks the end of the wooden beam, and another woman, while nursing her baby, turns the paddy in the mortar dug in the earth. The second woman is always alert lest the pestle of the machine should fall on her hand. With the other hand she fries the soaked paddy in a pan. Besides, she is talking with customers; she says: 'You owe us so much money. Please pay it before you go.' Likewise, do your different duties in the world, fixing your mind on God. But practice is necessary, and one should also be alert. Only in this way can one safeguard both—God and the world."

ACTOR: "Sir, what is the proof that the soul is separate from the body?"

MASTER: "Proof? God can be seen. By practising spiritual discipline one sees God, through His grace. The rishis directly realized the Self. One cannot know the truth about God through science. Science gives us information only about things perceived by the senses, as for instance: this material mixed with that material gives such and such a result, and that material mixed with this material gives such and such a result.

"For this reason a man cannot comprehend spiritual things with his ordinary intelligence. To understand them he must live in the company of holy persons. You learn to feel the pulse by living with a physician."

ACTOR: "Yes, sir. Now I understand."

MASTER: "You must practise tapasyā. Only then can you attain the goal. It will avail you nothing even if you learn the texts of the scriptures by heart. You cannot become intoxicated by merely saying 'siddhi' over and over. You must swallow some.

"One cannot explain the vision of God to others. One cannot explain conjugal happiness to a child five years old."

ACTOR: "How does one realize the Ātman?"

Just then Rakhal was about to take his meal in the Master's room. He hesitated at the sight of so many people. During those days the Master looked on Rakhal as Gopāla and on himself as Mother Yaśodā.

MASTER (to Rakhal): "Why don't you eat? Let the people stand aside if you wish it. (To a devotee) Keep some ice for Rakhal. (To Rakhal) Do you intend to go to Vanhooghly? Don't go in this sun."

Rakhal sat down to his meal. Sri Ramakrishna again spoke to the actor.

MASTER: "Why didn't all of you take your meal from the kitchen of the Kāli temple? That would have been nice."

ACTOR: "All of us don't have the same opinion about food; so our food is cooked separately. All don't like to eat in the guest-house."

While Rakhal was taking his meal, the Master and the devotees sat on the porch and continued their conversation.

MASTER (to the actor): "You asked me about Self-realization. Longing is the means of realizing Ātman. A man must strive to attain God with all his body, with all his mind, and with all his speech. Because of an excess of bile one gets jaundice. Then one sees everything as yellow; one perceives no colour but yellow. Among you actors, those who take only the roles of women acquire the nature of a woman; by thinking of woman your ways and thoughts become womanly. Just so, by thinking day and night of God one acquires the nature of God.

"The mind is like white linen just returned from the laundry. It takes on the colour you dip it in."

ACTOR: "But it must first be sent to the laundry."

MASTER: "Yes. First is the purification of the mind. Afterwards, if you direct the mind to the contemplation of God, it will be coloured by God-

Consciousness. Again, if you direct the mind to worldly duties, such as the acting of a play, it will be coloured by worldliness."

Sri Ramakrishna had rested on his bed only a few minutes when Hari,[1] Narayan, Narendra Bannerji, and other devotees arrived from Calcutta and saluted him. Narendra Bannerji was the son of the professor of Sanskrit at the Presidency College of Calcutta. Because of friction with other members of the family, he had rented a separate house where he lived with his wife and children. Narendra was a very simple and guileless man. He practised spiritual discipline and, at the time of meditation, heard various sounds— the sound of a gong, and so on. He had travelled in different parts of India and he visited the Master now and then.

Narayan was a schoolboy sixteen or seventeen years old. He often visited the Master, who was very fond of him.

Hari lived with his brothers at their Bāghbāzār house. He had studied up to the matriculation class in the General Assembly Institution. Then he had given up his studies and devoted his time at home to the contemplation of God, the reading of the scriptures, and the practice of yoga. He also visited the Master now and then. Sri Ramakrishna often sent for Hari when he went to Balaram's house in Bāghbāzār.

MASTER (to the devotees): "I have heard a great deal about Buddha. He is one of the ten Incarnations of God.[2] Brahman is immovable, immutable, inactive, and of the nature of Consciousness. When a man merges his buddhi, his intelligence, in Bodha, Consciousness, then he attains the Knowledge of Brahman; he becomes buddha, enlightened.

"Nangtā used to say that the mind merges in the buddhi, and the buddhi in Bodha, Consciousness.

"The aspirant does not attain the Knowledge of Brahman as long as he is conscious of his ego. The ego comes under one's control after one has obtained the Knowledge of Brahman and seen God. Otherwise the ego cannot be controlled. It is difficult to catch one's own shadow. But when the sun is overhead, the shadow is within a few inches of the body."

A DEVOTEE: "What is the vision of God like?"

MASTER: "Haven't you seen a theatrical performance? The people are engaged in conversation, when suddenly the curtain goes up. Then the entire mind of the audience is directed to the play. The people don't look at other things any longer. Samādhi is to go within oneself like that. When the curtain is rung down, people look around again. Just so, when the curtain of māyā falls, the mind becomes externalized.

(To Narendra Bannerji) "You have travelled a great deal. Tell us something about the sādhus."

Narendra told the story of two yogis in Bhutān who used to drink daily a pound of the bitter juice of neem-leaves. He had also visited the hermitage of a holy man on the bank of the Narmadā. At the sight of the Bengali

---

[1] A monastic disciple of the Master, later known as Swami Turiyananda.
[2] Hindu mythology speaks of ten Incarnations of God.

Babu dressed in European clothes, the sādhu had remarked, "He has a knife hidden under his clothes, next to his belly."

MASTER: "One should keep pictures of holy men in one's room. That constantly quickens divine ideas."

BANNERJI: "I have your picture in my room; also the picture of a sādhu living in the mountains, blowing on a piece of lighted charcoal in a bowl of hemp."[3]

MASTER: "It is true that one's spiritual feelings are awakened by looking at the picture of a sādhu. It is like being reminded of the custard-apple by looking at an imitation one, or like stimulating the desire for enjoyment by looking at a young woman. Therefore I tell you that you should constantly live in the company of holy men.

(To Bannerji) "You know very well the suffering of the world. You suffer whenever you accept enjoyment. As long as the kite kept the fish in its beak, it was tormented by the flock of crows.

"One finds peace of mind in the company of holy men. The alligator remains under water a long time. But every now and then it rises to the surface and breathes with a deep wheezing noise. Then it gives a sigh of relief."

ACTOR: "Revered sir, what you have just said about enjoyment is very true. One ultimately courts disaster if one prays to God for enjoyment. Various desires come to the mind and by no means all of them are good. God is the Kalpataru, the Wish-fulfilling Tree. A man gets whatever he asks of God. Suppose it comes to his mind: 'God is the Kalpataru. Well, let me see if a tiger will appear before me.' Because he thinks of the tiger, it really appears and devours him."

MASTER: "Yes, you must remember that the tiger comes. What more shall I tell you? Keep your mind on God. Don't forget Him. God will certainly reveal Himself to you if you pray to Him with sincerity. Another thing. Sing the name of God at the end of each performance.. Then the actors, the singers, and the audience will go home with the thought of God in their minds."

The actors saluted the Master and took their leave.

Two ladies, devotees of Sri Ramakrishna, entered the room and saluted the Master. They had been fasting in preparation for this visit. They were sisters-in-law, the wives of two brothers, and were twenty-two or twenty-three years old. They were mothers of children. Both of them had their faces covered with veils.

MASTER (to the ladies): "Worship Śiva. This worship is described in a book called the Nityakarma. Learn the rituals from it. In order to perform the worship of God you will be preoccupied for a long time with such religious duties as plucking flowers, making sandal-paste, polishing the utensils of worship, and arranging offerings. As you perform these duties your mind will naturally be directed to God. You will get rid of meanness, anger, jealousy, and so forth. When you two sisters talk to each other, always talk about spiritual matters.

[3] Many wandering monks smoke Indian hemp.

"The thing is somehow to unite the mind with God. You must not forget Him, not even once. Your thought of Him should be like the flow of oil, without any interruption. If you worship with love even a brick or stone as God, then through His grace you can see Him.

"Remember what I have just said to you. One should perform such worship as the Śiva Pujā. Once the mind has become mature, one doesn't have to continue formal worship for long. The mind then always remains united with God; meditation and contemplation become a constant habit of mind."

ELDER SISTER-IN-LAW: "Will you please give us some instruction?"

MASTER (affectionately): "I don't give initiation. If a guru gives initiation he must assume responsibility for the disciple's sin and suffering. The Divine Mother has placed me in the state of a child. Perform the Śiva Pujā as I told you. Come here now and then. We shall see what happens later on through the will of God. I asked you to chant the name of Hari at home. Are you doing that?"

ELDER SISTER-IN-LAW: "Yes."

MASTER: "Why have you fasted? You should take your meal before you come here. Women are but so many forms of my Divine Mother. I cannot bear to see them suffer. You are all images of the Mother of the Universe. Come here after you have eaten, and you will feel happy."

Saying this, Sri Ramakrishna asked Ramlal to give the ladies some food. They were given fruit, sweets, drinks, and other offerings from the temple.

The Master said: "You have eaten something. Now my mind is at peace. I cannot bear to see women fast."

It was about five o'clock in the afternoon. Sri Ramakrishna was sitting on the steps of the Śiva temples. Adhar, Dr. Nitai, M., and several other devotees were with him.

MASTER (to the devotees): "I want to tell you something. A change has been coming over my nature."

The Master came down a step and sat near the devotees. It seemed that he intended to communicate some of his deeper experiences to them.

MASTER: "You are devotees. I have no hesitation in telling you this. Nowadays I don't see the Spirit-form of God. He is revealed to me in human form. It is my nature to see the form of God, to touch and embrace Him. God is saying to me, 'You have assumed a body; therefore enjoy God through His human forms.'

"God no doubt dwells in all, but He manifests Himself more through man than through other beings. Is man an insignificant thing? He can think of God, he can think of the Infinite, while other living beings cannot. God exists in other living beings—animals, plants, nay, in all beings—, but He manifests Himself more through man than through these others. Fire exists in all beings, in all things; but its presence is felt more in wood. Rāma said to Lakshmana: 'Look at the elephant, brother. He is such a big animal, but he cannot think of God.'

"But in the Incarnation there is a greater manifestation of God than in other men. Rāma said to Lakshmana, 'Brother, if you see in a man ecstatic love of God, if he laughs, weeps, and dances in divine ecstasy, then know for certain that I dwell in him.'

The Master remained silent. After a few minutes he resumed the conversation.

MASTER: "Keshab Sen used to come here frequently. As a result he changed a great deal. Of late he became quite a remarkable man. Many a time he came here with his party; but he also wanted to come alone. In the earlier years of his life Keshab didn't have much opportunity to live in the company of holy men.

"I visited him at his house in Coolootola Street. Hriday was with me. We were shown into the room where Keshab was working. He was writing something. After a long while he put aside his pen, got off his chair, and sat on the floor with us. But he didn't salute us or show us respect in any other way.

"He used to come here now and then. One day in a spiritual mood I said to him: 'One should not sit before a sādhu with one leg over the other. That increases one's rajas.' As soon as he and his friends would arrive, I would salute them before they bowed to me. Thus they gradually learnt to salute a holy man, touching the ground with their foreheads.

"I said to Keshab: 'Chant the name of Hari. In the Kaliyuga one should sing the name and glories of God.' After that they began to sing the name of God with drums and cymbals.[4]

"Do you know how my faith in the name of Hari was all the more strengthened? Holy men, as you know, frequently visit the temple garden. Once a sādhu from Multan arrived. He was waiting for a party going to Gangāsāgar. (*Pointing to M.*) The sādhu was of his age. It was he who said to me, 'The way to realize God in the Kaliyuga is the path of bhakti as prescribed by Nārada.'

"One day Keshab came here with his followers. They stayed till ten at night. We were all seated in the Panchavati. Pratap and several others said they would like to spend the night here. Keshab said: 'No, I must go. I have some work to do.' I laughed and said: 'Can't you sleep without the smell of your fish-basket? Once a fishwife was a guest in the house of a gardener who raised flowers. She came there with her empty basket, after selling fish in the market, and was asked to sleep in a room where flowers were kept. But, because of the fragrance of the flowers, she couldn't get to sleep for a long time. Her hostess saw her condition and said, "Hello! Why are you tossing from side to side so restlessly?" The fishwife said: "I don't know, friend. Perhaps the smell of the flowers has been disturbing my sleep. Can you give me my fish-basket? Perhaps that will put me to sleep."

[4] For some years before meeting the Master, Keshab and his followers had been singing the name of "Brahma" to the accompaniment of drums and cymbals. After meeting Sri Ramakrishna in 1875, Keshab showed particular devotion to the singing of the names of Hari and the Divine Mother. [Foot-note by M. in the Bengali *Gospel of Sri Ramakrishna*, vol. v, p. 113.]

The basket was brought to her. She sprinkled water on it and set it near her nose. Then she fell sound asleep and snored all night.'

"At this story the followers of Keshab burst into loud laughter.

"Keshab conducted the prayer that evening at the bathing-ghāt on the river. After the worship I said to him: 'It is God who manifests Himself, in one aspect, as the scriptures; therefore one should worship the sacred books, such as the Vedas, the Purānas, and the Tantras. In another aspect He has become the devotee. The heart of the devotee is God's drawing-room. One can easily find one's master in the drawing-room. Therefore, by worshipping His devotee, one worships God Himself.'

"Keshab and his followers listened to my words with great attention. It was a full-moon night. The sky was flooded with light. We were seated in the open court at the top of the stairs leading to the river. I said, 'Now let us all chant, "Bhāgavata—Bhakta—Bhagavān." ' All chanted in unison, 'Bhāgavata—Bhakta—Bhagavān.' Next I said to them, 'Say, "Brahman is verily Śakti; Śakti is verily Brahman." ' Again they chanted in unison, 'Brahman is verily Śakti; Śakti is verily Brahman.' I said to them: 'He whom you address as Brahma is none other than She whom I call Mother. Mother is a very sweet name.'

"Then I said to them, 'Say, "Guru—Krishna—Vaishnava." '[5] At this Keshab said: 'We must not go so far, sir. If we do that, then all will take us for orthodox Vaishnavas.'

"I used to tell Keshab now and then: 'He whom you address as Brahma is none other than She whom I call Śakti, the Primal Energy. It is called Brahman in the Vedas when It transcends speech and thought and is without attributes and action. I call It Śakti, Ādyāśakti, and so forth, when I find It creating, preserving, and destroying the universe.'

"I said to Keshab: 'It is extremely difficult to realize God while leading a worldly life. How can a typhoid patient be cured if he is kept in a room where tamarind, pickle, and jars of water are kept? Therefore one should go into solitude now and then to practise spiritual discipline. When the trunk of a tree becomes thick and strong, an elephant can be tied to it; but a young sapling is eaten by cattle.' That is why Keshab would say in his lectures, 'Live in the world after being strengthened in spiritual life.'

(To the devotees) "You see, Keshab was a great scholar. He lectured in English. Many people honoured him. Queen Victoria herself talked to him. But when Keshab came here he would be bare-bodied and bring some fruit, as one should when visiting a holy man. He was totally free from egotism.

(To Adhar) "You are a scholar and a deputy magistrate, but with all that you are hen-pecked. Go forward. Beyond the forest of sandal-wood there are many more valuable things: silver-mines, gold-mines, diamonds, and other gems. The wood-cutter was chopping wood in the forest; the brahma-chāri said to him, 'Go forward.' "

Sri Ramakrishna came down from the steps of the Śiva temples and went

---

[5] The Master meant that the guru, Krishna, and the Vaishnava were to be equally revered. One should honour the Vaishnava because God dwells in his heart.

to his own room through the courtyard. The devotees were with him. Just then Ram Chatterji came and said that the Holy Mother's attendant had had an attack of cholera.

RAM (*to the Master*): "I told you about it at ten o'clock this morning, but you didn't pay any attention to me."

MASTER: "What could I do?"

RAM: "Yes, what could you do! But there were Rakhal, Ramlal, and others. Even they didn't pay any attention."

M: "Kishori has gone to Ālambāzār to get medicine."

MASTER: "Alone? Where will he get medicine?"

M: "Yes, alone. He will get it at Ālambāzār."

MASTER (*to M.*): "Tell the nurse what to do if the illness takes a turn for the worse or if the patient feels better."

M: "Yes, sir."

The ladies mentioned before saluted the Master and were about to take their leave. Sri Ramakrishna again said to them: "Perform the Śiva Pujā according to my instruction. And have something to eat before you come here. Otherwise I shall feel unhappy. Come another day."

Sri Ramakrishna sat down on the porch west of his room. Narendra Bannerji, Hari, M., and others sat by his side. The Master knew about Narendra's family difficulties.

MASTER: "You see, all these sufferings are 'because of a piece of loin-cloth'.[6] A man takes a wife and begets children; therefore he must secure a job. The sādhu is worried about his loin-cloth, and the householder about his wife. Further, the householder may not live on good terms with his relatives; so he must live separately with his wife. (*With a laugh*) Chaitanya once said to Nityānanda: 'Listen to me, brother. A man entangled in worldliness can never be free.'"

M. (*to himself*): "Perhaps the Master is referring to the world of avidyā. It is the world of avidyā that entangles a householder."

M. was still living in a separate house with his wife, on account of a misunderstanding with the other members of his family.

MASTER (*to Bannerji, pointing to M.*): "He also lives in a separate house. You two will get along very well. Once two men happened to meet. One said to the other, 'Who are you?' 'Oh, I am away from my country', was the other's reply. The second man then asked the first, 'And who are you,

---

[6] A reference to the following story, which Sri Ramakrishna often told his devotees: There was a sannyāsi whose only possession was two pairs of loin-cloths. One day a mouse nibbled at one piece. So the holy man kept a cat to protect his loin-cloths from the mouse. Then he had to keep a cow to supply milk for the cat. Later he had to engage a servant to look after the cow. Gradually the number of his cows multiplied. He acquired pastures and farm land. He had to engage a number of servants. Thus he became, in course of time, a sort of landlord. And, last of all, he had to take a wife to look after his big household. One day, one of his friends, another monk, happened to visit him and was surprised to see his altered circumstances. When asked the reason, the holy man said, "It is all for the sake of a piece of loin-cloth!"

pray?' 'Oh, I am away from my beloved', was the answer. Both were in the same plight; so they got along very well. (*All laugh.*)

"But one need not have any fear if one takes refuge in God. God protects His devotee."

HARI: "Well, why does it take many people such a long time to realize Him?"

MASTER: "The truth is that a man doesn't feel restless for God unless he is finished with his enjoyments and duties. The physician says, referring to the patient: 'Let a few days pass first. Then a little medicine will do him good.'

"Nārada said to Rāma: 'Rāma, You are passing Your time in Ayodhyā. How will Rāvana be killed? You have taken this human body for that purpose alone.' Rāma replied: 'Nārada, let the right time come. Let Rāvana's past actions begin to bear fruit. Then everything will be made ready for his death.'"

HARI: "Why is there so much suffering in the world?"

MASTER: "This world is the līlā of God. It is like a game. In this game there are joy and sorrow, virtue and vice, knowledge and ignorance, good and evil. The game cannot continue if sin and suffering are altogether eliminated from the creation.

"In the game of hide-and-seek one must touch the 'granny' in order to be free. But the 'granny' is never pleased if she is touched at the very outset. It is God's wish that the play should continue for some time. Then—

> Out of a hundred thousand kites, at best but one or two break free;
> And Thou dost laugh and clap Thy hands, O Mother, watching them!

In other words, after the practice of hard spiritual discipline, one or two have the vision of God, through His grace, and are liberated. Then the Divine Mother claps Her hands in joy and exclaims, 'Bravo! There they go!'"

HARI: "But this play of God is our death."

MASTER (*smiling*): "Please tell me who *you* are. God alone has become all this—māyā, the universe, living beings, and the twenty-four cosmic principles. 'As the snake I bite, and as the charmer I cure.' It is God Himself who has become both vidyā and avidyā. He remains deluded by the māyā of avidyā, ignorance. Again, with the help of the guru, He is cured by the māyā of vidyā, Knowledge.

"Ignorance, Knowledge, and Perfect Wisdom. The jnāni sees that God alone exists and is the Doer, that He creates, preserves, and destroys. The vijnāni sees that it is God who has become all this.

"After attaining mahābhāva and prema one realizes that nothing exists but God. Bhakti pales before bhāva. Bhāva ripens into mahābhāva and prema.

(*To Bannerji*) "Do you still hear that gong-like sound at the time of meditation?"

BANNERJI: "Yes, sir. Every day. Besides, I have visions of God's form. Do such things stop after the mind has once experienced them?"

MASTER: "True. Once the wood catches fire, it cannot be put out. (*To the devotees*) He knows many things about faith."

BANNERJI: "I have too much faith."

MASTER: "Bring the women of your family with those of Balaram's."

BANNERJI: "Who is Balaram?"

MASTER: "Don't you know Balaram? He lives at Bosepārā."

Sri Ramakrishna loved guileless people. Narendra Bannerji was absolutely guileless. The Master loved Niranjan[7] because he, too, was without guile.

MASTER (*to M.*): "Why do I ask you to see Niranjan? It is to find out if he is truly guileless."

Sunday, May 25, 1884

Sri Ramakrishna was sitting on the cement platform that encircled the trunk of the old banyan-tree in the Panchavati. Vijay, Surendra, Bhavanath, Rakhal, and other devotees were present, a few of them sitting with the Master on the platform, the rest on the ground below. The devotees had thought of celebrating the Master's birthday, which had had to be put off because of his illness. Since Sri Ramakrishna now felt much better, the devotees wanted to have the celebration that day. A woman musician, a famous singer of kirtan, was going to entertain them with devotional songs.

It was one o'clock in the afternoon. M. had been looking for Sri Ramakrishna in the Master's room. When he did not find him there, he went to the Panchavati and eagerly asked the devotees, "Where is he?" He was standing right in front of the Master but in his excitement did not notice him. The devotees laughed loudly. A moment later M. saw Sri Ramakrishna and felt very much embarrassed. He prostrated himself before the Master, who sat there facing the south and smiling happily. Kedar and Vijay were sitting at his left. These two devotees had had a misunderstanding recently when Kedar had cut off his connexion with the Brāhmo Samāj.

MASTER (*to M., with a smile*): "You see how I have united them?"

The Master had brought a mādhavi creeper from Vrindāvan in the year 1868 and had planted it in the Panchavati. The creeper had grown big and strong. Some children were jumping and swinging from it. The Master observed them and laughed. He said: "They are like young monkeys. They will not give up swinging even though they sometimes fall to the ground." Noticing that Surendra was standing before him, the Master said to him affectionately: "Come up and sit with us on the platform. Then you can dangle your feet comfortably." Surendra went up and took his seat. Bhavanath had his coat on. Surendra said to him, "Are you going to England?"

MASTER (*smiling*): "God is our England. Now and then I used to leave off my clothes and joyfully roam about naked. Once Sambhu said to me: 'It is very comfortable to walk about naked. That is why you do it. Once I did it myself.'"

[7] A young disciple of the Master, who later became a monk under the name of Swami Niranjanananda.

SURENDRA: "On returning from the office, as I put away my coat and trousers, I say to the Divine Mother, 'O Mother, how tightly You have bound me to the world!' "

MASTER: "There are eight fetters with which man is bound: shame, hatred, fear, pride of caste, hesitation, the desire to conceal, and so forth."

Sri Ramakrishna sang:

> Mother, this is the grief that sorely grieves my heart,
> That even with Thee for Mother, and though I am wide awake,
> There should be robbery in my house. . . .

He continued:

> In the world's busy market-place, O Śyāmā, Thou art flying kites;
> High up they soar on the wind of hope, held fast by māyā's string.
> Their frames are human skeletons, their sails of the three gunas made;
> But all their curious workmanship is merely for ornament.
>
> Upon the kite-strings Thou hast rubbed the mānjā-paste of worldliness,
> So as to make each straining strand all the more sharp and strong.
> Out of a hundred thousand kites, at best but one or two break free;
> And Thou dost laugh and clap Thy hands, O Mother, watching them!
>
> On favouring winds, says Rāmprasād, the kites set loose will speedily
> Be borne away to the Infinite, across the sea of the world.

MASTER: " 'Māyā's string' means wife and children.

> Upon the kite-strings Thou hast rubbed the mānjā-paste of worldliness.

'Worldliness' means 'woman and gold'.

"The three gunas—sattva, rajas, and tamas—have men under their control. They are like three brothers. As long as sattva exists, it calls on rajas for help; and rajas can get help from tamas. The three gunas are so many robbers. Tamas kills and rajas binds. Sattva no doubt releases man from his bondage, but it cannot take him to God."

VIJAY (smiling): "It is because sattva, too, is a robber."

MASTER (smiling): "True. Sattva cannot take man to God, but it shows him the way."

BHAVANATH: "These are wonderful words indeed."

MASTER: "Yes, this is a lofty thought."

Listening to these words of the Master, the devotees felt very happy.

MASTER: " 'Woman and gold' is the cause of bondage. 'Woman and gold' alone constitutes samsāra, the world. It is 'woman and gold' that keeps one from seeing God. (Holding the towel in front of his face) Do you see my face any more? Of course not. The towel hides it. No sooner is the covering of 'woman and gold' removed than one attains Chidānanda, Consciousness and Bliss.

"Let me tell you something. He who has renounced the pleasure of a wife has verily renounced the pleasure of the world. God is very near to such a person."

The devotees listened to these words in silence.

MASTER (*to Kedar, Vijay, and the other devotees*): "He who has renounced the pleasure of a wife has verily renounced the pleasure of the world. It is 'woman and gold' that hides God. You people have such imposing moustaches, and yet you too are involved in 'woman and gold'. Tell me if it isn't true. Search your heart and answer me."

VIJAY: "Yes, it is true."

Kedar remained silent.

MASTER: "I see that all are under the control of woman. One day I went to Captain's house. From there I was to go to Ram's house. So I said to Captain, 'Please give me my carriage hire.' He asked his wife about it. She too held back and said: 'What's the matter? What's the matter?' At last Captain said, 'Ram will take care of it.' You see, the *Gītā*, the *Bhāgavata*, and the Vedānta all bow before a woman! (*All laugh.*)

"A man leaves his money, his property, and everything in the hands of his wife. But he says with affected simplicity, 'I have such a nature that I cannot keep even two rupees with me.'

"A man went to an office in search of a job. There were many vacancies, but the manager did not grant his request. A friend said to the applicant, 'Appeal to Golapi, and you will get the job.' Golapi was the manager's mistress.

"Men do not realize how far they are dragged down by women. Once I went to the Fort in a carriage, feeling all the while that I was going along a level road. At last I found that I had gone four storeys down. It was a sloping road.

"A man possessed by a ghost does not know he is under the ghost's control. He thinks he is quite normal."

VIJAY (*smiling*): "But he can be cured by an exorcist if he finds one."

In answer to Vijay Sri Ramakrishna only said, "That depends on the will of God." Then he went on with his talk about women.

MASTER: "Everyone I talk to says, 'Yes, sir, my wife is good.' Nobody says that his wife is bad. (*All laugh.*) Those who constantly live with 'woman and gold' are so infatuated with it that they don't see things properly. Chess-players oftentimes cannot see the right move for their pieces on the board. But those who watch the game from a distance can understand the moves more accurately.

"Woman is the embodiment of māyā. In the course of his hymn to Rāma, Nārada said: 'O Rāma, all men are parts of Thee. All women are parts of Sītā, the personification of Thy māyā. Please deign to grant that I may have pure love for Thy Lotus Feet and that I may not be deluded by Thy world-bewitching māyā. I do not want any other favour than that.'"

Surendra's younger brother and his nephews were present. The brother worked in an office and one of the nephews was studying law.

MASTER (*to Surendra's relatives*): "My advice to you is not to become attached to the world. You see, Rakhal now understands what is knowledge and what is ignorance. He can discriminate between the Real and the unreal. So I say to him: 'Go home. You may come here once in a while and spend a day or two with me.'

"Have a friendly relationship with one another. That will be for your good and make you all happy. In a theatre the performance goes well only if the musicians sing with one voice. And that also gladdens the hearts of the audience.

"Do your worldly duties with a part of your mind and direct most of it to God. A sādhu should think of God with three quarters of his mind and with one quarter should do his other duties. He should be very alert about spiritual things. The snake is very sensitive in its tail. Its whole body reacts when it is hurt there. Similarly, the whole life of a sādhu is affected when his spirituality is touched."

Sri Ramakrishna was going to the pine-grove and asked Gopal of Sinthi to take his umbrella to his room. Arrangements had been made in the Panchavati for the kirtan. When the Master had returned and taken his seat again among the devotees, the musician began her song. Suddenly there came a rain-storm. The Master went back to his room with the devotees, the musician accompanying them to continue her songs there.

MASTER (*to Gopal*): "Have you brought the umbrella?"

GOPAL: "No, sir. I forgot all about it while listening to the music."

The umbrella had been left in the Panchavati and Gopal hurried to fetch it.

MASTER: "I am generally careless, but not to that extent. Rakhal also is very careless. Referring to the date of an invitation, he says 'the eleventh' instead of 'the thirteenth'. And Gopal—he belongs in a herd of cows!"[8]

The musician sang a song about the monastic life of Chaitanya. Now and then she improvised lines: "He will not look upon a woman; for that is against the sannyāsi's duty." "Eager to take away men's sorrows, he will not look upon a woman." "For the Lord's birth as Sri Chaitanya otherwise would be in vain."

The Master stood up, as he heard about Chaitanya's renunciation, and went into samādhi. The devotees put garlands of flowers around his neck. Bhavanath and Rakhal supported his body lest he should fall on the ground. Vijay, Kedar, Ram, M., Latu, and the other devotees stood around him in a circle, recalling one of the scenes of Chaitanya's kirtan.

The Master gradually came down to the sense plane. He was talking to Krishna, now and then uttering the word "Krishna". He could not say it very distinctly because of the intensity of his spiritual emotion. He said: "Krishna! Krishna! Krishna! Krishna Satchidānanda! Nowadays I do not see Your form. Now I see You both inside me and outside. I see that it is You who have become the universe, all living beings, the twenty-four cosmic principles, and everything else. You alone have become mind, intelligence, everything. It is said in the 'Hymn of Salutation to the Guru': 'I bow down

[8] There is a pun on the word "Gopal", which means also "herd of cows".

to the Guru by whose grace I have realized Him who pervades the indivisible universe of the animate and the inanimate.'

"You alone are the Indivisible. Again, it is You who pervade the universe of the animate and the inanimate. You are verily the manifold universe; again, You alone are its basis. O Krishna! You are my life. O Krishna! You are my mind. O Krishna! You are my intelligence. O Krishna! You are my soul. O Govinda! You are my life-breath. You are my life itself."

Vijay was also in an ecstatic mood. The Master asked him, "My dear sir, have you too become unconscious?" "No, sir", said Vijay humbly.

The music went on. The musician was singing about the blinding love of God. As she improvised the lines:

> O Beloved of my soul! Within the chamber of my heart
> I would have kept You day and night!

the Master again went into samádhi. His injured arm rested on Bhavanath's shoulder.

Sri Ramakrishna partly regained outer consciousness. The musician improvised:

> Why should one who, for Thy sake, has given up everything
> Endure so much of suffering?

The Master bowed to the musician and sat down to listen to the music. Now and then he became abstracted. When the musician stopped singing, Sri Ramakrishna began to talk to the devotees.

MASTER (to Vijay and the others): "What is prema? He who feels it, this intense and ecstatic love of God, not only forgets the world but forgets even the body, which is so dear to all. Chaitanya experienced it."

The Master explained this to the devotees by singing a song describing the ecstatic state of prema:

> Oh, when will dawn the blessed day
> When tears of joy will flow from my eyes
> As I repeat Lord Hari's name? . . .

The Master began to dance, and the devotees joined him. He caught M. by the arm and dragged him into the circle. Thus dancing, Sri Ramakrishna again went into samádhi. Standing transfixed, he looked like a picture on canvas. Kedar repeated the following hymn to bring his mind down from the plane of samádhi:

> We worship the Brahman-Consciousness in the Lotus of the Heart,
> The Undifferentiated, who is adored by Hari, Hara, and Brahmá;
> Who is attained by yogis in the depths of their meditation;
> The Scatterer of the fear of birth and death,
> The Essence of Knowledge and Truth, the Primal Seed of the world.

Sri Ramakrishna gradually came back to the plane of normal consciousness. He took his seat and chanted the names of God: "Om Satchidánanda! Govinda! Govinda! Govinda! Yogamáyá! Bhágavata—Bhakta—Bhagaván!"

The Master took dust from the place where the kirtan had been sung and touched it to his forehead.

A little later Sri Ramakrishna was sitting on the semicircular porch facing the Ganges, the devotees sitting by his side. Now and then the Master would exclaim, "Ah, Krishnachaitanya!"[9]

MASTER (to Vijay and the others): "There has been much chanting of the Lord's name in the room. That is why the atmosphere has become so intense."

BHAVANATH: "Words of renunciation, too."

The Master said, "Ah, how thrilling!" Then he sang about Gaurānga and Nityānanda:

> Gorā bestows the Nectar of prema;
> Jar after jar he pours it out,
> And still there is no end!
> Sweetest Nitāi is summoning all;
> Beloved Gorā bids them come;
> Shāntipur is almost drowned,
> And Nadiā[10] is flooded with prema!

MASTER (to Vijay and the others): "The musician sang rightly: 'A sannyāsi must not look at a woman.' This is the sannyāsi's dharma. What a lofty ideal!"

VIJAY: "Yes indeed, sir."

MASTER: "Others learn from the sannyāsi's example. That is why such strict rules are prescribed for him. A sannyāsi must not look even at the portrait of a woman. What a strict rule! The slaughtering of a black goat is prescribed for the worship of the Divine Mother; but a goat with even a slight wound cannot be offered. A sannyāsi must not only not have intercourse with woman; he must not even talk to her."

VIJAY: "Young Haridās talked with a pious woman. For that reason Chaitanya banished him from his presence."

MASTER: "A sannyāsi associated with 'woman and gold' is like a beautiful damsel with a bad odour. The odour makes her beauty useless.

"Once a Mārwāri devotee wanted to give me some money. Mathur wanted to deed me some land. But I couldn't accept either.

"The rules for the life of a sannyāsi are very strict indeed. If a man takes the garb of a sannyāsi, he must act exactly like one. Haven't you noticed in the theatre that the man who takes the part of the king acts like a king, and the man who takes the part of a minister acts like a minister?

"But on attaining the state of the paramahamsa one becomes like a child. A child five years old doesn't know the difference between a man and a woman. But even a paramahamsa must be careful, so as not to set a bad example to others."

Referring to Keshab's association with "woman and gold", which had hin-

---

[9] One of the names of Gaurānga.
[10] Shāntipur and Nadiā are places associated with Chaitanya.

dered his work as a spiritual teacher, Sri Ramakrishna said to Vijay, "He—do you understand?"

VIJAY: "Yes, sir."

MASTER: "He couldn't achieve very much because he wanted to satisfy both God and the world."

VIJAY: "Chaitanya said to Nityānanda: 'Nitāi, I shall not be able to do the people any good unless I renounce the world. All will imitate me and want to lead the life of a householder. No one will try to direct his whole mind to the Lotus Feet of God, renouncing "woman and gold".'"

MASTER: "Yes. Chaitanyadeva renounced the world to set an example to mankind.

"The sannyāsi must renounce 'woman and gold' for his own welfare. Even if he is unattached, and consequently not in danger, still, in order to set an example to others, he must not keep 'woman and gold' near him. The sannyāsi, the man of renunciation, is a world teacher. It is his example that awakens the spiritual consciousness of men."

It was nearly dusk. The devotees saluted the Master and took their leave.

FESTIVAL AT SURENDRA'S HOUSE

Sunday, June 15, 1884

SRI RAMAKRISHNA arrived in the morning at the garden house of Surendra, one of his beloved householder disciples, in the village of Kānkurgāchi near Calcutta. Surendra had invited him and a large number of the devotees to a religious festival.

Occasions like this were a source of great happiness and rejoicing to the Master's devotees. He was then seen at his best. He joined with the others in devotional music and in chanting the names of God, frequently going into ecstasy. He poured out his entire soul in inspired talk, explaining the various phases of God-Consciousness. The impressions of such a festival lingered in the minds of all for many days.

The devotees stood in rows inside the big hall of the garden house to hear the music sung by the professional singers. The floor of the room was covered with a carpet over which was spread a white sheet; a few bolsters, pillows, and cushions lay here and there.

The musicians were singing of the episodes in the life of Sri Krishna especially associated with His divine love for the gopis of Vrindāvan. This was a theme which always appealed to the Master and would throw him into ecstatic moods.

Krishna, God Incarnate, lived the years of His boyhood in Vrindāvan as a cowherd. He tended His cows on the green meadows along the bank of the Jamunā and played His flute. The milkmaids could not resist the force of His divine attraction. At the sound of His flute they would leave their household duties and go to the bank of the sacred river. Their love for Krishna destroyed their attachment to worldly things. Neither the threats of their relatives nor the criticism of others could make them desist from seeking the company of Krishna. In the love of the gopis for Krishna there was not the slightest trace of worldliness. It was the innate attraction of God for pure souls, as of the magnet for iron. The author of the *Bhāgavata* has compared this love to the all-consuming love of a woman for her beloved. Before the onrush of that love all barriers between man and God are swept away. The devotee surrenders himself completely to his Divine Beloved and in the end becomes one with Him.

Rādhā was the foremost of the gopis, and Krishna's chief playmate. She felt an indescribable longing for union with Him. A moment's separation from Krishna would rend her heart and soul. During many a moonlit night Krishna would dance with Rādhā and the gopis in the sacred groves of Vrindāvan, and on such occasions the gopis would experience the highest religious ecstasy. At the age of eleven Krishna was called to be the king of Mathurā. He left the gopis, promising them, however, His divine vision whenever they concentrated on Him in their hearts.

For centuries and centuries the lovers of God in India have been worshipping the Divine by recreating in themselves the yearning of the gopis for Krishna. Many of the folk-songs of India have as their theme this sweet episode of Krishna's life. Sri Chaitanya revived this phase of Hindu religious life by his spiritual practice and his divine visions. In his ecstatic music Chaitanya assumed the role of Rādhā and manifested the longing to be united with Krishna. For a long period Sri Ramakrishna also worshipped God as his beloved Krishna, looking on himself as one of the gopis or as God's handmaid.

At Surendra's garden house the kirtan had begun early in the morning. The musicians were singing about the love of Krishna and Rādhā for each other. The Master was frequently in samādhi. The room was crowded with devotees, among them Bhavanath, Niranjan, Rakhal, Surendra, Ram, and M., and many members of the Brāhmo Samāj.

In accordance with the custom, the kirtan had begun with an introductory song about Gaurānga. Gaurānga embraces monastic life. He is being consumed with longing for a vision of Krishna. He leaves Navadvip and goes away as a wandering monk to seek out his Beloved. His devotees, unable to bear the pangs of separation, weep bitterly and beg Gaurānga to return.

The musician sang:

O Gaur, come back to Nadiā!

Next the musician sang about the anguish of Rādhā at her separation from Krishna. When Sri Ramakrishna heard the song he suddenly stood up. Assuming the mood of Rādhā, he sang in a voice laden with sorrow, improvising the words: "O friend, either bring my beloved Krishna here or take me to Him." Thus singing, he completely lost himself in Rādhā and could not continue the song. He became speechless, his body motionless, his eyes half closed, his mind totally unconscious of the outer world. He was in deep samādhi.

After a long time he regained normal consciousness and said in the same heart-rending voice: "O friend, take me to my beloved Krishna and make me your bondslave. I shall be your handmaid for ever. O friend, it was you who taught me how to love Krishna. O Krishna! O Beloved of my soul!"

The professional musicians continued their song. They took the part of Rādhā and sang as if she were talking to her friend: "O friend, I shall not go again to the Jamunā to draw water. Once I beheld my beloved Friend under the kadamba tree. Whenever I pass it I am overwhelmed."

The Master again became abstracted. Heaving a deep sigh he said, "Ah me! Ah me!"

The song went on. Rādhā says:

> Even the desire for Krishna's presence
> Has cooled and refreshed my feverish body.

Now and then the musicians improvised lines to the music, continuing in the attitude of Rādhā: "O friends, you can wait. Show me Krishna, my Beloved." Again: "Do not bother about my ornaments. I have lost my most precious Ornament." And again: "Alas! I have fallen on evil days. My happy days are over." And finally: "This unhappy time lingers so long!"

Sri Ramakrishna improvised a line himself: "Are not better times yet in sight for me?" The musicians then improvised: "Such a long time has passed! Are not better times yet in sight for me?"

The musicians sang Rādhā's words to a friend:

> O friend, I am dying! Surely I die.
> The anguish of being kept apart
> From Krishna is more than I can bear.
> Alas! to whom then shall I leave
> My priceless Treasure?[1] When I am dead,
> I beg you, do not burn my body;
> Do not cast it into the river.
> See that it is not given to the flames;
> Do not cast it into the water.
> In this body I played with Krishna.
>
> Bind my lifeless form, I beg you,
> To the black tamāla's branches;
> Tie it to the tamāla tree.
> Touching tamāla it touches black.
> Krishna is black, and black is tamāla;
> Black is the colour that I love.
> From earliest childhood I have loved it.
> To the black Krishna my body belongs;
> Let it not lie apart from black!

Rādhā reaches her last extremity. She faints away.

> Rādhā has fallen to the·ground;
> She lies there lost to outward sense,
> Repeating her precious Krishna's name,
> And straightway closes both her eyes.
> Ah, has the drama reached its end?
> What ails you, O delight of Krishna?
> Only a moment ago you spoke.
>
> Her friends, anointing Rādhā's form
> With cool and soothing sandal-paste,
> Attempt to bring her back to earth.
> Some of them weep in bitter grief;
> They cannot bear to see her die.
> Some sprinkle water on her face;

[1] Krishna.

Perhaps she will revive again!
But, oh, can water give back life
To one who dies of Krishna's love?

Rādhā's friends chant Krishna's sweet name in her ears. This brings her
back to partial consciousness. She looks at the black tamāla tree and thinks
that Krishna stands before her.

Krishna's name restores her life;
Once more her two eyes gaze around,
But Krishna's face she cannot see.
Alas, how bitterly she weeps!
"Where is my Krishna? Where is He
Whose name you chanted in my ears?
Bring Him but once before me here!"

Seeing the black tamāla tree,
She stares at it and cries aloud:
"There is His crest! I see it clearly!
There is my Krishna's lovely crest!"
But only a peacock did she see,
Whose glistening feathers she mistook
For the gay feather on Krishna's crest.

Krishna has gone to Mathurā to assume His royal duties. He has discarded
His cowherd's dress and flute and put on the royal regalia. Rādhā's friends,
after a hurried consultation, send a gopi to Mathurā as messenger. She meets
a woman of that city, of her own age, who asks her where she comes from.

Rādhā's friend says: "I don't have to call Krishna. He Himself will come
to me." But none the less she follows the woman of Mathurā and goes to
Krishna's palace. In the street she weeps, overcome with grief, and prays to
Krishna: "O Hari, where are You? O Life of the gopis! O Enchanter of our
hearts! O Beloved of Rādhā! O Hari, Remover of Your devotees' shame!
Come to us once more! With great pride I said to the people of Mathurā
that You Yourself would come to me. Please do not humiliate me."

In scorn says the woman of Mathurā:
"Oh, you are only a simple milkmaid!
How can you go to see our King,
Our Krishna, in your beggar's rags?
Behind seven doors His chamber stands.
You cannot enter. How can you go?
I die of shame to see your boldness.
Tell me, how will you manage to enter?"

Says the gopi: "Krishna! Beloved!
Soul of the gopis! Oh, where are You?
Come to me here and save my life.
Where are You, adorable Soul of the gopis?
Come to me, Lord of Mathurā!
And save the life of Your sorrowing handmaid.
Ah, where are You, Beloved of Rādhā?
Lord of our hearts and Friend of our souls!

> O Hari, Destroyer of our shame!
> O priceless Treasure of the gopis!
> Come to Your handmaid and save her honour."

Thus the messenger weeps and cries out for Krishna.

When the musicians sang, "Where are You, adorable Soul of the gopis?" the Master went into samādhi. As the music neared its end the musicians sang louder. Sri Ramakrishna was on his feet, again in deep samādhi. Regaining partial consciousness, he said in a half articulate voice, "Kitna! Kitna!" He was too much overwhelmed to utter Krishna's name distinctly.

The kirtan was coming to a close. At the reunion of Rādhā and Krishna the Master sang with the musicians, composing the lines himself:

> Behold, there Rādhā stands by Krishna;
> On His bosom she reclines.
> Behold her standing at His left,
> Like a golden creeper twining
> Round a black tamāla tree!

As the music came to a close the Master led the chorus. All chanted together to the accompaniment of drums and cymbals: "Victory to Rādhā and Krishna! Hallowed be the names of Rādhā and Krishna!" The devotees felt a. surge of divine emotion and danced around the Master. He too danced in an ecstasy of joy. The names of God echoed and re-echoed in the house and garden.

After the music the Master sat with the devotees. Just then Niranjan arrived and prostrated himself before him. At the very sight of this beloved disciple the Master stood up, with beaming eyes and smiling face, and said: "You have come too! (*To M.*) You see, this boy is absolutely guileless. One cannot be guileless without a great deal of spiritual discipline in previous births. A hypocritical and calculating mind can never attain God.

"Don't you see that God incarnates Himself only in a family where innocence exists? How guileless Daśaratha was! So was Nanda, Krishna's father. There is a saying: 'Ah, how innocent a man he is! He is just like Nanda.'

(*To Niranjan*) "I feel as if a dark veil has covered your face. It is because you have accepted a job in an office. One must keep accounts there. Besides, one must attend to many other things, and that always keeps the mind in a state of worry. You are serving in an office like other worldly people; but there is a slight difference, in that you are earning money for the sake of your mother. One must show the highest respect to one's mother, for she is the very embodiment of the Blissful Mother of the Universe. If you had accepted the job for the sake of wife and children, I should have said: 'Fie upon you! Shame! A thousand shames!'

(*To Mani Mallick, pointing to Niranjan*) "Look at this boy. He is absolutely guileless. But he has one fault: he is slightly untruthful nowadays. The other day he said that he would visit me again very soon, but he didn't come. (*To Niranjan*) That is why Rakhal asked you why you didn't come to see me while you were at Āriādaha, so near Dakshineswar."

NIRANJAN: "I was there only a couple of days."

MASTER (*to Niranjan, pointing to M.*) "He is the headmaster of a school. At my bidding he went to see you. (*To M.*) Did you send Baburam to me the other day?"

The Master went to an adjoining room and began to talk with some devotees there.

MASTER (*to M.*): "Ah! How wonderful was the yearning of the gopis for Krishna! They were seized with divine madness at the very sight of the black tamāla tree. Separation from Krishna created such a fire of anguish in Rādhā's heart that it dried up even the tears in her eyes! Her tears would disappear in steam. There were other times when nobody could notice the depth of her feeling. People do not notice the plunge of an elephant in a big lake."

M: "Yes, sir, that is true. Chaitanya, too, experienced a similar feeling. He mistook a forest for the sacred grove of Vrindāvan, and the dark water of the ocean for the blue Jamunā."

MASTER: "Ah! If anyone has but a particle of such prema! What yearning! What love! Rādhā possessed not only one hundred per cent of divine love, but one hundred and twenty-five per cent. This is what it means to be intoxicated with ecstatic love of God. The sum and substance of the whole matter is that a man must love God, must be restless for Him. It doesn't matter whether you believe in God with form or in God without form. You may or may not believe that God incarnates Himself as man. But you will realize Him if you have that yearning. Then He Himself will let you know what He is like. If you must be mad, why should you be mad for the things of the world? If you must be mad, be mad for God alone."

Presently Sri Ramakrishna returned to the main hall of the house. A big pillow was placed near him for his use. Before touching it he said, "Om Tat Sat."[2] Perhaps the pillow had been used by many worldly people, and that was why he purified it in this way. Bhavanath, M., and other devotees sat near him. It was getting late, but there was no indication that the meal was going to be served. The Master became impatient, like a child, and said: "I don't see any sign of food. What's the matter? Where is Narendra?"

A DEVOTEE (*with a smile*): "Sir, Ram Babu is the manager of the feast. He is superintending everything."

MASTER (*laughing*): "Oh, Ram is the manager! Then we know what to expect."

A DEVOTEE: "Things like this always happen when he is the supervisor." (*All laugh.*)

MASTER (*to the devotees*): "Where is Surendra? What a nice disposition he has now! He is very outspoken; he isn't afraid to speak the truth. He is unstinting in his liberality. No one that goes to him for help comes away empty-handed. (*To M.*) You went to Bhagavan Das.[3] What sort of man is he?"

---

[2] A sacred formula of the Hindu religion, meaning, "The Lord is the only Reality."

[3] A great Vaishnava devotee.

M: "He is very old now. I saw him at Kālnā. It was night. He lay on a carpet and a devotee fed him with food that had been offered to God. He can hear only if one speaks loudly into his ear. Hearing me mention your name he said, 'You have nothing to worry about.'"

BHAVANATH (to M.): "You haven't been to Dakshineswar for a long time. The Master asked me about you and said one day, 'Has M. lost all taste for this place?'"

Bhavanath laughed as he said these words. The Master heard their conversation and said to M. in a loving voice: "Yes, that is true. Why haven't you been to Dakshineswar for such a long time?" M. could only stammer some lame excuses.

Just then Mahimacharan arrived. He lived at Cossipore near Calcutta. Mahimacharan held the Master in great respect and was a frequent visitor at the temple garden. He was a man of independent means, having inherited some ancestral property. He devoted his time to religious thought and to the study of the scriptures. He was a man of some scholarship, having studied many books, both Sanskrit and English.

MASTER (to Mahima): "What is this? I see a steamship here. (All laugh.) We expect here a small boat at the most, but a real steamship has arrived. But then I know. It's the rainy season!" (Laughter.)

The Master was conversing with Mahimacharan. He asked him: "Isn't feeding people a kind of service to God? God exists in all beings as fire. To feed people is to offer oblations to that Indwelling Spirit. But then one shouldn't feed the wicked, I mean people who are entangled in gross worldliness or who have committed heinous crimes like adultery. Even the ground where such people sit becomes impure to a depth of seven cubits. Once Hriday fed a number of people at his native place. A good many of them were wicked. I said to Hriday: 'Look here. If you feed such people I shall leave your house at once.' (To Mahima) I hear that you used to feed people; but now you don't give any such feasts. Is it because your expenses have gone up?" (Laughter.)

The meal was to be served on the south verandah of the house. Leaf-plates were being placed on the floor. The Master said to Mahimacharan: "Please go there and see what they are doing. You may help them a little in serving the food. But I shouldn't ask you." Mahimacharan said: "Let them bring in the food. I shall see." Hemming and hawing, he went toward the kitchen, but presently he came back.

Sri Ramakrishna and the devotees enjoyed the meal greatly. Afterwards he rested awhile. About two o'clock in the afternoon Pratap Chandra Mazumdar of the Brāhmo Samāj arrived. He was a co-worker of Keshab Chandra Sen and had been to Europe and America in connection with the Brāhmo missionary work. He greeted Sri Ramakrishna, and the Master, too, bowed before him with his usual modesty. They were soon engaged in conversation.

PRATAP: "I have been to Darjeeling recently for a change of air."

MASTER: "But your health hasn't much improved. What are you suffering from?"

PRATAP: "The same illness that Keshab died of."

They began to talk about Keshab. Pratap said: "Even in boyhood he showed non-attachment to worldly things, seldom making merry with other boys. He was a student in the Hindu College. At that time he became friendly with Satyendra and through him made the acquaintance of his father, Devendranath Tagore. Keshab cultivated bhakti and at the same time practised meditation. At times he would be so much overcome with divine love that he would become unconscious. The main purpose of his life was to introduce religion among householders."

The conversation next turned to a certain Mārhāttā lady.

PRATAP: "Some women of our country have been to England. This Mārhāttā lady, who is very scholarly, also visited England. Later she embraced Christianity. Have you heard her name, sir?"

MASTER: "No. But from what you say it seems to me that she has a desire for name and fame. That kind of egotism is not good. The feeling 'I am the doer' is the outcome of ignorance. But the feeling that God does everything is due to knowledge. God alone is the Doer; all others are mere instruments in His hands.

"The misfortune that befalls a man on account of his egotism can be realized if you only think of the condition of the calf. The calf says, 'Hāmmā! Hāmmā!', that is, 'I! I!' And just look at its misfortune! At times it is yoked to the plough and made to work in the field from sunup to sundown, rain or shine. Again, it may be slaughtered by the butcher. In that case the flesh is eaten and the skin tanned into hide. From the hide shoes are made. People put on these shoes and walk on the rough ground. Still that is not the end of its misfortunes. Drums are made from its skin and mercilessly beaten with sticks. At last its entrails are made into strings for the bow used in carding cotton. When used by the carder the string gives the sound 'Tuhu! Tuhu!', 'Thou! Thou!'—that is, 'It is Thou, O Lord! It is Thou!' It no longer says, 'Hāmmā! Hāmmā!', 'I! I!' Only then does the calf's trouble come to an end, and it is liberated. It doesn't return to the world of action.

"Likewise, when the embodied soul says: 'O God, I am not the doer; Thou art the Doer. I am the machine and Thou art its Operator', only then does its suffering of worldly life come to an end; only then does it obtain liberation. It no longer has to be reborn in this world of action."

A DEVOTEE: "How can a man get rid of his ego?"

MASTER: "You cannot get rid of it until you have realized God. If you find a person free from ego, then know for certain that he has seen God."

DEVOTEE: "What, sir, are the signs of God-vision?"

MASTER: "Yes, there are such signs. It is said in the Bhāgavata that a man who has seen God behaves sometimes like a child, sometimes like a ghoul, sometimes like an inert thing, and sometimes like a madman.

"The man who has seen God becomes like a child. He is beyond the three gunas; he is unattached to any of them. He behaves like a ghoul, for he maintains the same attitude toward things holy and unholy. Again, like a madman, he sometimes laughs and sometimes weeps. Now he dresses himself like a dandy and the next moment he goes entirely naked and roams about with his cloth under his arm. Therefore he seems to be a lunatic. Again, at times he sits motionless like an inert thing."

DEVOTEE: "Does the ego disappear altogether after the realization of God?"

MASTER: "Yes, sometimes God totally effaces the ego of His devotee, as in the state of samādhi. But in many cases He keeps a trace of ego. But that doesn't injure anybody. It is like the ego of a child. A five-year-old child no doubt says 'I', but that ego doesn't harm anybody. At the touch of the philosopher's stone, steel is turned into gold; the steel sword becomes a sword of gold. The gold sword has the form of a sword, no doubt, but it cannot injure anybody. One cannot cut anything with a gold sword.

(To Pratap) "You have been to England. Tell us what you saw there."

PRATAP: "The English people worship what you call 'gold'. Of course, there are also some good people in England, those who live an unattached life. But generally one finds there a great display of rajas in everything. I saw the same thing in America."

MASTER (to Pratap): "It is not in England alone that one sees attachment to worldly things. You see it everywhere. But remember that work is only the first step in spiritual life. God cannot be realized without sattva—love, discrimination, kindness, and so on. It is the very nature of rajas to involve a man in many worldly activities. That is why rajas degenerates into tamas. If a man is entangled in too many activities he surely forgets God. He becomes more and more attached to 'woman and gold'.

"But it is not possible for you to give up work altogether. Your very nature will lead you to it whether you like it or not. Therefore the scriptures ask you to work in a detached spirit, that is to say, not to crave the work's results. For example, you may perform devotions and worship, and practise austerities, but your aim is not to earn people's recognition or to increase your merit.

"To work in such a spirit of detachment is known as karmayoga. But it is very difficult. We are living in the Kaliyuga, when one easily becomes attached to one's actions. You may think you are working in a detached spirit, but attachment creeps into the mind from nobody knows where. You may worship in the temple or arrange a grand religious festival or feed many poor and starving people. You may think you have done all this without hankering after the results. But unknown to yourself the desire for name and fame has somehow crept into your mind. Complete detachment from the results of action is possible only for one who has seen God."

A DEVOTEE: "Then what is the way for those who have not seen God? Must they give up all the duties of the world?"

MASTER: "The best path for this age is bhaktiyoga, the path of bhakti prescribed by Nārada: to sing the name and glories of God and pray to Him with a longing heart, 'O God, give me knowledge, give me devotion, and reveal Thyself to me!' The path of karma is extremely difficult. Therefore one should pray: 'O God, make my duties fewer and fewer; and may I, through Thy grace, do the few duties that Thou givest me without any attachment to their results! May I have no desire to be involved in many activities!'

"It is not possible to give up work altogether. Even to think or to meditate is a kind of work. As you develop love for God, your worldly activities become fewer and fewer of themselves. And you lose all interest in them. Can one who has tasted a drink made of sugar candy enjoy a drink made of ordinary molasses?"

A DEVOTEE: "The English people always exhort us to be active. Isn't action the aim of life then?"

MASTER: "The aim of life is the attainment of God. Work is only a preliminary step; it can never be the end. Even unselfish work is only a means; it is not the end.

"Sambhu Mallick once said to me, 'Please bless me, sir, that I may spend all my money for good purposes, such as building hospitals and dispensaries, making roads, and digging wells.' I said to him: 'It will be good if you can do these things in a spirit of detachment. But that is very difficult. Whatever you may do, you must always remember that the aim of this life of yours is the attainment of God and not the building of hospitals and dispensaries. Suppose God appeared before you and said to you, "Accept a boon from Me." Would you then ask Him, "O God, build me some hospitals and dispensaries"? Or would you not rather pray to Him: "O God, may I have pure love at Your Lotus Feet! May I have Your uninterrupted vision!"? Hospitals, dispensaries, and all such things are unreal. God alone is real and all else unreal. Furthermore, after realizing God one feels that He alone is the Doer and we are but His instruments. Then why should we forget Him and destroy ourselves by being involved in too many activities? After realizing Him, one may, through His grace, become His instrument in building many hospitals and dispensaries.'

"Therefore I say again that work is only the first step. It can never be the goal of life. Devote yourself to spiritual practice and go forward. Through practice you will advance more and more in the path of God. At last you will come to know that God alone is real and all else is illusory, and that the goal of life is the attainment of God.

"Once upon a time a wood-cutter went into a forest to chop wood. There suddenly he met a brahmachāri. The holy man said to him, 'My good man, go forward.' On returning home the wood-cutter asked himself, 'Why did the brahmachāri tell me to go forward?' Some time passed. One day he remembered the brahmachāri's words. He said to himself, 'Today I shall go deeper into the forest.' Going deep into the forest, he discovered innumerable sandal-wood trees. He was very happy and returned with cart-loads of sandal-wood. He sold them in the market and became very rich.

"A few days later he again remembered the words of the holy man to go forward. He went deeper into the forest and discovered a silver-mine near a river. This was even beyond his dreams. He dug out silver from the mine and sold it in the market. He got so much money that he didn't even know how much he had.

"A few more days passed. One day he thought: 'The brahmachāri didn't ask me to stop at the silver-mine; he told me to go forward.' This time he went to the other side of the river and found a gold-mine. Then he exclaimed: 'Ah, just see! This is why he asked me to go forward.'

"Again, a few days afterwards, he went still deeper into the forest and found heaps of diamonds and other precious gems. He took these also and became as rich as the god of wealth himself.

"Therefore I say that, whatever you may do, you will find better and better things if only you go forward. You may feel a little ecstasy as the result of japa, but don't conclude from this that you have achieved everything in spiritual life. Work is by no means the goal of life. Go forward, and then you will be able to perform unselfish work. But again I say that it is most difficult to perform unselfish work. Therefore with love and longing in your heart pray to God: 'O God, grant me devotion at Thy Lotus Feet and reduce my worldly duties. Please grant me the boon that the few duties I must do may be done in a detached spirit.' If you go still farther you will realize God. You will see Him. In time you will converse with Him."

Next the conversation turned to the quarrels among the members of the Brāhmo Samāj. They had had a misunderstanding about the right to preach in the temple after Keshab's death.

MASTER (to Pratap): "I hear that some members of the Samāj have quarrelled with you about the altar. But they are most insignificant persons—mere nobodies.

(To the devotees): "People like Pratap and Amrita are like good conchshells, which give out a loud sound. And the rest, about whom you hear so much, don't give out any sound at all." (All laugh.)

PRATAP: "Speaking of sounds, even such a worthless thing as a mango-stone makes a sound!"[4]

MASTER (to Pratap): "One can very well understand the inner feeling of a teacher of your Brāhmo Samāj by hearing his preaching. Once I went to a meeting of a Hari Sabhā. The preacher of the day was a pundit named Samadhyayi. And can you imagine what he said? He said in the course of his sermon: 'God is dry. We must make Him sweet and fresh with our love and devotion.' I was stunned to hear these words. Then I was reminded of a story. A boy once said: 'At my uncle's house there are many horses. Oh, yes! His whole cow-shed is full of them.' Now if it was really a cow-shed, then horses could not be kept there. Possibly he had only cows. What did people think on hearing such an incoherent statement? They believed that there were surely no such animals as horses in the shed." (Laughter.)

A DEVOTEE: "True, sir, there were not only no horses, but possibly there were also no cows!" (Laughter.)

MASTER: "Just fancy, to describe God, who is of the very nature of Love and Bliss, as dry! It only proves that the man has never experienced what God is like.

(To Pratap) "Let me tell you something. You are a learned and intelligent and serious-minded soul. Keshab and you were like the two brothers, Gaur and Nitāi. You have had enough of lectures, arguments, quarrels,

---

[4] The split stone of a mango, about to sprout, makes a sound when one blows through it.

discussions, and dissensions. Can such things interest you any more? Now gather your whole mind and direct it to God. Plunge deep into God."

PRATAP: "Yes, sir, you are right. That is surely my only duty now. But I am doing all these things only to perpetuate Keshab's name."

MASTER (*with a smile*): "No doubt you say now that you are doing all this to keep his name alive; but in a few days you won't feel that way. Listen to a story. A man had built a house on a hill. It was only a mud hut, but he had built it with great labour. A few days after, there came a violent storm and the hut began to rock. The man became very anxious to save it and prayed to the god of the winds, 'O god of the winds, please don't wreck the house!' But the god of the winds paid no heed to his prayer. The house was about to crash. Then he thought of a trick. He remembered that Hanumān was the son of the god of the winds. At once he cried out with great earnestness: 'O revered sir, please don't pull down the house. It belongs to Hanumān. I beseech you to protect it.' But still the house continued to shake violently. Nobody seemed to listen to his prayer. He repeated many times, 'Oh, this house belongs to Hanumān!' But the fury of the wind did not abate. Then he remembered that Hanumān was the devoted servant of Rāma, whose younger brother was Lakshmana. Desperately the man prayed, crying aloud, 'Oh, this house belongs to Lakshmana!' But that also failed to help matters. So the man cried out as a last resort: 'This is Rāma's house. Don't break it down, O god of the winds! I beseech you most humbly.' But this too proved futile, and the house began to crash down. Whereupon the man, who now had to save his own life, rushed out of it with the curse: 'Let it go! This is the devil's own hut!'

(*To Pratap*): "You don't have to perpetuate Keshab's name. Remember that he achieved all his success through the will of God. Through the divine will his work was established, and through the divine will it is disintegrating. What can you do about it? Now it is your bounden duty to give your entire mind to God, to plunge deep into the Ocean of His Love."

Saying these words the Master sang in his sweet voice:

> Dive deep, O mind, dive deep in the Ocean of God's Beauty;
> If you descend to the uttermost depths,
> There you will find the gem of Love.
>
> Go seek, O mind, go seek Vrindāvan in your heart,
> Where with His loving devotees
> Sri Krishna sports eternally.
>
> Light up, O mind, light up true wisdom's shining lamp,
> And let it burn with steady flame
> Unceasingly within your heart.
>
> Who is it that steers your boat across the solid earth?
> It is your guru, says Kubir;
> Meditate on his holy feet.

The Master continued, addressing Pratap: "Did you listen to the song? You have had enough of lectures and quarrels. Now dive deep into the Ocean of God. There is no fear of death from plunging into this Ocean, for this is the Ocean of Immortality. Don't think that this will make you lose your head. Never for a moment harbour the idea that by thinking too much of God one becomes insane. Once I said to Narendra—"

PRATAP: "Who is Narendra, sir?"

MASTER: "Oh, never mind. There is a young man of that name. I said to Narendra: 'Look here, my boy. God is the Ocean of Bliss. Don't you want to plunge into this Ocean? Suppose there is a cup of syrup and you are a fly. Where will you sit to sip the syrup?' Narendra said, 'I will sit on the edge of the cup and stick my head out to drink it.' 'Why?' said I. 'Why should you sit on the edge?' He replied, 'If I go far into the syrup, I shall be drowned and lose my life.' Then I said to him: 'But, my child, there is no such fear in the Ocean of Satchidānanda. It is the Ocean of Immortality. By plunging into It a man does not die; he becomes immortal. Man does not lose his consciousness by being mad about God.

(To the devotees) "The feeling of 'I' and 'mine' is ignorance. People say that Rāni Rasmani built the Kāli temple; but nobody says it was the work of God. They say that such and such a person established the Brāhmo Samāj; but nobody says it was founded through the will of God. This feeling, 'I am the doer', is ignorance. On the contrary, the idea, 'O God, Thou art the Doer and I am only an instrument; Thou art the Operator and I am the machine', is Knowledge. After attaining Knowledge a man says: 'O God, nothing belongs to me—neither this house of worship nor this Kāli temple nor this Brāhmo Samāj. These are all Thine. Wife, son, and family do not belong to me. They are all Thine.'

"To love these objects, regarding them as one's own, is māyā. But to love all things is dayā, compassion. To love only the members of the Brāhmo Samāj or of one's own family is māyā; to love one's own countrymen is māyā. But to love the people of all countries, to love the members of all religions, is dayā. Such love comes from love of God, from dayā.

"Māyā entangles a man and turns him away from God. But through dayā one realizes God. Sages like Śukadeva and Nārada always cherished dayā in their hearts."

PRATAP: "Revered sir, are those who live with you making progress in spiritual life?"

MASTER: "I tell people that there is nothing wrong in the life of the world. But they must live in the world as a maidservant lives in her master's house. Referring to her master's house, she says, 'That is our house.' But her real home is perhaps in a far-away village. Pointing out her master's house to others, she says, no doubt, 'This is our house', but in her heart she knows very well that it doesn't belong to her and that her own house is in a far-away village. She brings up her master's son and says, 'My Hari has grown very naughty', or 'My Hari doesn't like sweets.' Though she repeats, 'My Hari' with her lips, yet she knows in her heart that Hari doesn't belong to her, that he is her master's son.

"Thus I say to those who visit me: 'Why don't you live in the world? There is no harm in that. But always keep your mind on God. Know for certain that house, family, and property are not yours. They are God's. Your real home is in God.' Also I ask them to pray always with a longing heart for love of God's Lotus Feet."

Again the conversation turned to the English people. A devotee said, "Sir, I understand that nowadays the pundits of England do not believe in the existence of God."

PRATAP: "However they may talk, I don't believe that any of them is a real atheist. Many of them have had to admit that there is a great power behind the activities of the universe."

MASTER: "Well, that is enough. They believe in Śakti, don't they? Then why should they be atheists?"

PRATAP: "They also believe in the moral government of the universe."

Pratap was now about to take leave of the Master.

MASTER (to Pratap): "What more shall I say to you? My only request is that you do not involve yourself in quarrels and dissensions any more. Another thing. It is 'woman and gold' that keeps men away from God. That is the barrier. Don't you find that everyone has nothing but praise for his own wife? (All laugh.) A wife may be good or bad; but if you ask her husband about her he will always say, 'Oh, she is very good—' "

At this point Pratap bade the Master good-bye. He did not wait to hear the end of Sri Ramakrishna's words about the renunciation of "woman and gold". Those burning words touched the hearts of the devotees and were carried away on the wind through the gently rustling leaves in the garden.

A few minutes later Mani Mallick said to Sri Ramakrishna: "Sir, it is time for you to leave for Dakshineswar. Today Keshab's mother and the other ladies of his family are going to the temple garden to visit you. They will be hurt if they do not find you there."

Keshab had passed away only a few months before. His old mother and his other relatives wanted to visit the Master.

MASTER (to Mani Mallick): "Don't hurry me, please. I didn't sleep well. I can't rush. They are going to Dakshineswar. What am I to do about it? They will stroll in the garden and enjoy it thoroughly."

After resting a little the Master was ready to leave for Dakshineswar. He was thinking of Surendra's welfare. He visited the different rooms, softly chanting the holy name of God. Suddenly he stood still and said: "I didn't eat any luchi at meal-time. Bring me a little now." He ate only a crumb and said: "There is much meaning in my asking for the luchi. If I should remember that I hadn't eaten any at Surendra's house, then I should want to come back for it." (All laugh.)

MANI MALLICK: "That would have been nice. Then we too should have come with you."

The devotees laughed.

Friday, June 20, 1884

It was dusk. Sri Ramakrishna was sitting in his room, absorbed in contemplation of the Divine Mother. Now and then he was chanting Her name. Rakhal, Adhar, M., and several other devotees were with him.

After a while the evening worship began in the temples. Adhar left the room to see the worship. Sri Ramakrishna and M. conversed.

MASTER: "Tell me, does Baburam intend to continue his studies? I said to him, 'Continue your studies to set an example to others.' After Sītā had been set free, Bibhishana refused to become king of Ceylon. Rāma said to him: 'You should become king to open the eyes of the ignorant. Otherwise they will ask you what you have gained as a result of serving Me. They will be pleased to see you acquire the kingdom.'

"I noticed the other day that Baburam, Bhavanath, and Harish have a feminine nature. In a vision I saw Baburam as a goddess with a necklace around her neck and with woman companions about her. He has received something in a dream. His body is pure. Only a very little effort will awaken his spiritual consciousness.

"You see, I am having some difficulty about my physical needs. It will be nice if Baburam lives with me. The nature of these attendants of mine is undergoing a change. Latu is always tense with spiritual emotion. He is about to merge himself in God. Rakhal is getting into such a spiritual mood that he can't do anything even for himself. I have to get water for him. He isn't of much service to me.

"Among the youngsters Baburam and Niranjan are rather exceptional. If other boys come in the future, they will, it seems to me, receive instruction and then go away.

"But I don't want Baburam to tear himself away from his family. It may make trouble at home. (Smiling) When I ask him, 'Why don't you come?', he says, 'Why not make me come?'. He looks at Rakhal and weeps. He says, 'Rakhal is very happy here.'

"Rakhal now lives here as one of the family. I know that he will never again be attached to the world. He says that worldly enjoyments have become tasteless to him. His wife came here on her way to Konnagar. She is fourteen. He too was asked to go to Konnagar, but he didn't go. He said, 'I don't like merriment and gaiety.'

"What do you think of Niranjan?"

M: "He is very handsome."

MASTER: "No, I am not asking about his looks. He is guileless. One can easily realize God if one is free from guile. Spiritual instruction produces quick results in a guileless heart. Such a heart is like well cultivated land from which all the stones have been removed. No sooner is the seed sown than it germinates. The fruit also appears quickly.

"Niranjan will not marry. It is 'woman and gold' that causes entanglement. Isn't that so?"

M: "Yes, sir."

MASTER: "What will one gain by renouncing betel-leaf and tobacco? The real renunciation is the renunciation of 'woman and gold'.

"I came to know in an ecstatic mood that, though Niranjan had accepted a job in an office, he would not be stained by it. He is earning money for his mother. There is no harm in that.

"The work you are doing won't injure you either. What you are doing is good. Suppose a clerk is sent to jail; he is shut up there and chained, and at last he is released. Does he cut capers after his release? Of course not. He works again as a clerk. It is not your intention to accumulate money. You only want to support your family. Otherwise, where will they go?"

M: "I shall be relieved if someone takes charge of them."

MASTER: "That is true. But now do 'this' as well as 'that'."[5]

M: "It is great luck to be able to renounce everything."

MASTER: "That is true. But people act according to their inherent tendencies. You have a few more duties to perform. After these are over you will have peace. Then you will be released. A man cannot easily get out of the hospital once his name is registered there. He is discharged only when he is completely cured.

"The devotees who come here may be divided into two groups. One group says, 'O God, give me liberation.' Another group, belonging to the inner circle, doesn't talk that way. They are satisfied if they can know two things: first, who I[6] am; second, who they are and what their relationship to me is. You belong to this second group; otherwise . . .

"Bhavanath, Baburam, and a few others have a feminine nature. Harish sleeps in a woman's cloth. Baburam says that he too likes the womanly attitude. So I am right. Bhavanath also is like that. But Narendra, Rakhal, and Niranjan have a masculine nature.

"Please tell me one thing. What is the significance of my having hurt my arm? Once my teeth were broken while I was in a state of ecstasy. It is the arm this time."

Seeing M. silent, the Master himself continued the conversation.

MASTER: "My arm was broken in order to destroy my ego to its very root. Now I cannot find my ego within myself any more. When I search for it I see God alone. One can never attain God without completely getting rid of the ego. You must have noticed that the chātak bird has its nest on the ground but soars up very high.

"Captain says I haven't acquired any occult powers because I eat fish. I tremble with fear lest I should acquire those powers. If I should have them, then this place would be turned into a hospital or a dispensary. People would flock here and ask me to cure their illness. Is it good to have occult powers?"

M: "No, sir. You have said to us that a man cannot realize God if he possesses even one of the eight occult powers."

MASTER: "Right you are. Only the small-minded seek them. If one asks something of a rich man, one no longer receives any favour from him. The rich man doesn't allow such a person to ride in the same carriage with him. Even if he does, he doesn't allow the man to sit near him. Therefore love without any selfish motive is best.

"God with form and the formless God are both equally true. What do you say? One cannot keep one's mind on the formless God a long time. That is why God assumes form for His devotees.

"Captain makes a nice remark in this connexion. He says that when a

[5] That is to say, both worldly duty and spiritual practice.
[6] Referring to himself.

bird gets tired of soaring very high it perches on a tree and rests. First is the formless God, and then comes God with form.

"I shall have to go to your house once. I saw in a vision that the houses of Adhar, Balaram, and Surendra were so many places for our forgathering. But it makes no difference to me whether they come here or not."

M: "That's right. Why shouldn't it be so? One must feel misery if one feels happiness. But you are beyond both."

MASTER: "Yes. Further, I think of the magician and his magic. The magician alone is real. His magic is illusory, like a dream. I realized this when I heard the *Chandi* recited. Sumbha and Nisumbha[7] were scarcely born when I learnt that they both were dead."

M: "Yes, sir. Once I was going to Kālnā with Gangadhar in a steamer. A country boat struck our ship and sank with twenty or twenty-five passengers. They all disappeared in the water, like foam churned up by the steamer.

"May I ask you one thing? Does a man watching magic really feel compassion when he sees suffering in the performance? Does he feel, at that time, any sense of responsibility? One thinks of compassion only when one feels responsibility. Isn't that so?"

MASTER: "A jnāni sees everything at once—God, māyā, the universe, and living beings. He sees that vidyāmāyā, avidyāmāyā, the universe, and all living beings exist and at the same time do not exist. As long as he is conscious of 'I,' he is conscious of 'others' too. Nothing whatsoever exists after he cuts through the whole thing with the sword of jnāna. Then even his 'I' becomes as unreal as the magic of the magician."

M. was reflecting on these words, when the Master said: "Do you know what it is like? It is as if there were a flower with twenty-five layers of petals, and you cut them all with one stroke.

"The idea of responsibility! Goodness gracious! Men like Sankarāchārya and Sukadeva kept the 'ego of Knowledge'. It is not for man to show compassion, but for God. One feels compassion as long as one has the 'ego of Knowledge'. And it is God Himself who has become the 'ego of Knowledge'.

"You may feel a thousand times that it is all magic; but you are still under the control of the Divine Mother. You cannot escape Her. You are not free. You must do what She makes you do. A man attains Brahmajnāna only when it is given to him by the Ādyāsakti, the Divine Mother. Then alone does he see the whole thing as magic; otherwise not.

"As long as the slightest trace of ego remains, one lives within the jurisdiction of the Ādyāsakti. One is under Her sway. One cannot go beyond Her.

"With the help of the Ādyāsakti, God sports as an Incarnation. God, through His Sakti, incarnates Himself as man. Then alone does it become possible for the Incarnation to carry on His work. Everything is due to the Sakti of the Divine Mother.

"When anyone asked the former manager of the temple garden a great favour, the manager would say, 'Come after two or three days.' He must ask the proprietor's permission.

---

[7] Two demons mentioned in the *Chandi*, who were killed by the Divine Mother.

"God will incarnate Himself as Kalki at the end of the Kaliyuga. He will be born as the son of a brāhmin. Suddenly and unexpectedly a sword and horse will come to him. . . ."

Adhar returned to the Master's room after watching the evening worship in the temples.

MASTER (to Adhar and the others): "Bhuvan was here and brought me twenty-five Bombay mangoes and some sweets. She said to me, 'Will you eat a mango?' I said, 'My stomach is heavy today.' And to tell you the truth, I am feeling uncomfortable after eating a few of the sweets."

Bhuvanmohini was a nurse who used to visit Sri Ramakrishna now and then. The Master could not eat the food offerings of everyone, especially of physicians and nurses. It was because they accepted money from the sick in spite of the suffering of these people.

MASTER: "Keshab Sen's mother, sisters, and other relatives came here; so I had to dance a little. I had to entertain them. What else could I do? They were so grief-stricken!"

PUNDIT SHASHADHAR

Wednesday, June 25, 1884

IT WAS THE DAY of the Rathayātrā, the Car Festival of the Hindus. At Ishan's invitation Sri Ramakrishna went to his house in Calcutta. For some time the Master had had a desire to meet Pundit Shashadhar Tarkachudāmani, who had been staying with one of Ishan's neighbours. So it was decided that he would visit the pundit in the afternoon.

A few devotees, including Hazra, accompanied the Master to Ishan's house. Ishan had invited one or two brāhmin scholars and a devotee who followed the Tāntrik method of worship. Shrish and Ishan's other sons were also present.

The Master noticed that the Tāntrik worshipper had a vermilion mark on his forehead, and smilingly said, "I see he is branded."

After a while M. and Narendra arrived and bowed before Sri Ramakrishna. The Master had previously informed M. that he would be at Ishan's house.

The Master joked about the delay in serving their meal. One of the scholars quoted a Sanskrit verse about the anxiety created in people's minds by the pangs of hunger. Proceeding to explain the verse he said: "The study of philosophy is indeed edifying, but poetry is more fascinating than philosophy. People listening to good poems think of the study of philosophy —Vedānta, Nyāya, Sāmkhya, and so forth—as dry and insipid. Again, music is more attractive than poetry. Music melts even a heart of stone. But a beautiful woman has an even greater attraction for a man's heart than music. Such a woman, passing by, diverts a man's attention from both poetry and music. But when a man feels the pangs of hunger, everything else—poetry, music, and woman—appears as of no consequence. Thus hunger is the most arresting thing."

The Master remarked with a smile, "The pundit is witty."

Soon Narendra began to sing. A few moments later the Master went upstairs for a little rest. M. and Shrish accompanied him. M. introduced Shrish to the Master, saying: "He is a scholar and a man of peaceful nature. We were fellow students in our boyhood. Now he is a lawyer."

MASTER: "It is a pity that such a man should practise law."

M: "Yes, sir. It was a mistake on his part."

MASTER: "I know a few lawyers. One of them shows me great respect. He is a straightforward man. (To Shrish) What is your idea about the most essential thing in life?"

SHRISH: "God exists and He alone does everything. But the attributes we ascribe to Him are not the right ones. How can a man conceive of Him? His nature is infinite."

MASTER: "What need is there of your counting the number of trees and branches in an orchard? You have come to the orchard to eat mangoes. Do that and be happy. The aim of human birth is to love God. Realize that love and be at peace.

"Suppose you have entered a tavern for a drink. Is it necessary for you to know how many gallons of wine there are in the tavern? One glass is enough for you. What need is there of your knowing the infinite qualities of God? You may discriminate for millions of years about God's attributes and still you will not know them."

The Master remained silent a few minutes. A brāhmin pundit came into the room.

MASTER (to M.): "There is no substance whatsoever in the worldly life. The members of Ishan's family are good; so he has some peace here. Suppose his sons had been lewd, disobedient, and addicted to drink and other vices. Then there would have been no end to his troubles. One very seldom comes across such a religious family, in which all the members are devoted to God. I have seen only two or three such families. Generally one finds quarrels, misunderstanding, jealousy, and friction. Besides, there are disease, grief, and poverty in the world. Seeing this condition, I prayed to the Divine Mother, 'O Mother, turn my mind at once from the world to God.'

"Look at Narendra's troubles. His father is dead and the members of his family are starving. He has been trying his utmost to secure a position, but he has not yet found one. Just see how unsettled his mind is!

(To M.) "You used to come to Dakshineswar very frequently. But why have you become such a rare visitor? Perhaps you have become particularly friendly with your wife. Is it true? Why should I blame you? The influence of 'woman and gold' is everywhere. Therefore I pray, 'O Divine Mother, please don't make me a worldly man if I am to be born again in a human body.'"

BRĀHMIN SCHOLAR: "Why should you say that, sir? The scriptures extol the life of a householder."

MASTER: "Yes, that is true. But it is very difficult to lead the true life of a householder. (To M.) How wrong of us! They are singing, especially Narendra, and we have left the room."

About four o'clock in the afternoon the Master left in a carriage for the house where Pundit Shashadhar was staying. As soon as Sri Ramakrishna got into the carriage he went into samādhi. His physical frame was very tender as a result of the austerities he had undergone during the long years of his spiritual discipline and his constant absorption in God-Consciousness. The Master would suffer from the slightest physical discomfort and even from the vibration of worldly thoughts around him. Once Keshab Chandra Sen had said that Sri Ramakrishna, Christ, and Sri Chaitanya belonged to a delicate species of humanity that should be kept in a glass case and protected from the vulgar contact of the world.

It was the rainy season, and a fine drizzle of rain had made the road muddy. The sky was overcast. The devotees followed the carriage on foot. As the carriage stopped in front of the house, the host and his relatives welcomed the Master and took him upstairs to the drawing-room. There the Master met the pundit.

Pundit Shashadhar, a man of fair complexion and no longer young, had a string of rudrāksha beads around his neck. He was one of the renowned Sanskrit scholars of his time—a pillar of orthodox Hinduism, which had reasserted itself after the first wave of Christianity and Western culture had passed over Hindu society. His clear exposition of the Hindu scriptures, his ringing sincerity, and his stirring eloquence had brought back a large number of the educated young Hindus of Bengal to the religion of their forefathers.

The pundit saluted the Master with reverence. Narendra, Rakhal, Ram, Hazra, and M., who had come with the Master, seated themselves in the room as near the Master as they could, anxious not to miss one of his words.

At the sight of the pundit the Master again went into samādhi. After a while, still remaining in that state, he looked at the pundit and said with a smile, "Very well, very well." Then, addressing the pundit, the Master said, "Tell me how you give lectures."

PUNDIT: "Sir, I try to explain the teachings of the Hindu scriptures."

MASTER: "For the Kaliyuga the path of devotion described by Nārada is best. Where can people find time now to perform their duties according to the scriptural injunctions? Nowadays the decoctions of roots and herbs of the orthodox Hindu physicians cannot be given to a fever patient. By the time that kind of medicine begins its slow process of curing, the patient is done for. Therefore only a drastic medicine like the allopathic 'fever mixture' is effective now. You may ask people to practise scriptural rites and rituals; but, when prescribing the rituals, remove the 'head and tail'.[1] I tell people not to bother about the elaborate rituals of the sandhyā as enjoined in the scriptures. I say that it will be enough for them to repeat the Gāyatri alone. If you must give instruction about scriptural ceremonies, do so only to a very few, like Ishan.

"You may deliver thousands of lectures, but they won't make the slightest impression on worldly people. Can one drive a nail into a stone wall? The point of the nail will sooner break than make a dent in the stone. What will you gain by striking the tough skin of the crocodile with a sword? The sādhu's water-bowl, made from the shell of a bitter gourd, may visit the four principal holy places of India with its owner, but it will still remain as bitter as ever. Your lectures are not helping worldly people very much; and

[1] The non-essential parts. The allusion is to the head and tail of fish, which are non-essential.

you will realize this by and by. The calf cannot stand on its legs all at once. Now it drops to the ground and now it stands up. So it learns to stand firmly on its legs and walk.

"You cannot distinguish a lover of God from a worldly person. It isn't your fault, of course. When the first onrush of the gale shakes the trees, it is impossible to distinguish one tree from another—the mango from the tamarind, for instance.

"Without having realized God one cannot give up rituals altogether. How long should one practise the sandhyā and other forms of ritualistic worship? As long as one does not shed tears of joy at the name of God and feel a thrill in one's body. You will know that your ritualistic worship has come to an end when your eyes become filled with tears as you repeat 'Om Rāma'. Then you do not have to continue your sandhyā or other rituals.

"When the fruit appears the blossom drops off. Love of God is the fruit, and rituals are the blossom. When the daughter-in-law of the house becomes pregnant, she cannot do much work. Her mother-in-law gradually lessens her duties in the house. When her time arrives she does practically nothing. And after the child is born her only work is to play with it. She doesn't do any household duties at all. The sandhyā merges in the Gāyatri, the Gāyatri in Om, and Om in samādhi. It is like the sound of a bell: t—a—m. The yogi, by following in the trail of the sound Om, gradually merges himself in the Supreme Brahman. His sandhyā and other ritualistic duties disappear in samādhi. Thus the duties of the jnāni come to an end."

As the Master talked of samādhi, he himself went into that state. His face radiated a heavenly light. Bereft of outer consciousness, he could not utter another word. His gaze was indrawn and transfixed in communion with the Self. After a long time the Master began to recognize the world around him and said, like a child, "I shall have a drink of water." Whenever after samādhi the Master asked for a drink of water, his devotees knew that he was gradually becoming conscious of the outer world.

Still lingering in the state of ecstasy, he said to the Divine Mother: "O Mother, the other day You showed me Pundit Iswar Chandra Vidyāsāgar. Then I told You that I should like to see another pundit, and so You have brought me here."

Looking at the pundit, he said: "My child, add a little more to your strength. Practise spiritual discipline a few days more. You have hardly set your foot on the tree, yet you expect to lay hold of a big cluster of fruit. But, of course, you are doing all this for the welfare of others." With these words he bowed his head before the pundit.

The Master continued: "When I first heard about you, I inquired whether you were merely erudite or whether you had discrimination and renunciation. A pundit who doesn't know how to discriminate between the Real and the unreal is no pundit at all.

"There is no harm in teaching others if the preacher has a commission from the Lord. Nobody can confound a preacher who teaches people after having received the command of God. Getting a ray of light from the goddess of learning, a man becomes so powerful that before him big scholars seem mere earthworms.

"When the lamp is lighted the moths come in swarms. They don't have to be invited. In the same way, the preacher who has a commission from God need not invite people to hear him. He doesn't have to announce the time of his lectures. He possesses such irresistible attraction that people come to him of their own accord. People of all classes, even kings and aristocrats, gather around him. They say to him: 'Revered sir, what can we offer you? Here are mangoes, sweets, money, shawls, and other things. What will you be pleased to accept?' In that case I say to them: 'Go away. I don't care for these. I don't want anything.'

"Does the magnet say to the iron, 'Come near me?' That is not necessary. Because of the attraction of the magnet, the iron rushes to it.

"Such a preacher may not be a scholarly person, but don't conclude from that that he has any lack of wisdom. Does book-learning make one wise? He who has a commission from God never runs short of wisdom. That wisdom comes from God; it is inexhaustible. At Kāmārpukur I have seen people measuring grain. It lies in a heap. One man keeps pushing grain from the heap toward another man, who weighs it on a scales. So the man who weighs doesn't run short of grain. It is the same with the preacher who has received a commission from God. As he teaches people, the Divine Mother Herself supplies him with fresh knowledge from behind. That knowledge never comes to an end.

"Can a preacher ever lack knowledge if but once he is favoured with a benign glance from the Divine Mother? Therefore I ask you whether you have received any commission from God."

HAZRA: "Oh yes, he must have it. (To the pundit) Isn't it true, sir?"

PUNDIT: "Commission? No, sir, I am afraid I haven't received any such thing."

HOST: "He may not have received the commission, but he preaches from a sense of duty."

MASTER: "What will a man accomplish by mere lectures without the commission from God? Once a Brāhmo preacher said in the course of his sermon, 'Friends, how much I used to drink!' and so on. Hearing this the people began to whisper among themselves: 'What is this fool saying? He used to drink!' Now these words produced a very unfavourable effect. This shows that preaching cannot bring a good result unless it comes from a good man.

"A high government official from Barisāl once said to me, 'Sir, if you begin the work of preaching, I too shall gird my loins.' I told him the story of people's dirtying the bank of the Hāldārpukur and of its being stopped only when a constable, armed with authority from the government, put up a notice prohibiting it.

"So I say, a worthless man may talk his head off preaching, and yet he will produce no effect. But people will listen to him if he is armed with a badge of authority from God. One cannot teach others without the commission from God. A teacher of men must have great power. There's many a

Hanumanpuri[2] in Calcutta. It is with them that you will have to wrestle. (*Pointing to the people assembled there*) These are mere sheep!

"Chaitanyadeva was an Incarnation of God. How little is left of what he accomplished—not to speak of a lecturer who preaches without authority from God! What good will a lecturer do?

"Therefore I say to you, dive deep in God-Consciousness."

Saying this, the Master began to sing in an ecstasy of love for God:

> Dive deep, O mind, dive deep in the Ocean of God's Beauty;
> If you descend to the uttermost depths,
> There you will find the gem of Love. . . .

The Master continued: "One does not die if one sinks in this Ocean. This is the Ocean of Immortality. Once I said to Narendra: 'God is the Ocean of Bliss. Tell me if you want to plunge into It. Just imagine there is some syrup in a cup and that you have become a fly. Now tell me where you will sit to sip the syrup.' Narendra answered: 'I will sit on the edge of the cup and stretch out my neck to drink, because I am sure to die if I go far into the cup.' Then I said to him: 'But my child, this is the Ocean of Satchidānanda. There is no fear of death in It. This is the Ocean of Immortality. Only ignorant people say that one should not have an excess of devotion and divine love. How foolish! Can there be any excess of divine love?'

(*To the pundit*) "Therefore I say to you, dive into the Ocean of Satchidānanda. Nothing will ever worry you if you but realize God. Then you will get His commission to teach people.

"There are innumerable pathways leading to the Ocean of Immortality. The essential thing is to reach the Ocean. It doesn't matter which path you follow. Imagine that there is a reservoir containing the Elixir of Immortality. You will be immortal if a few drops of the Elixir somehow get into your mouth. You may get into the reservoir either by jumping into it, or by being pushed into it from behind, or by slowly walking down the steps. The effect is one and the same. You will become immortal by tasting a drop of that Elixir.

"Innumerable are the ways that lead to God. There are the paths of jnāna, of karma, and of bhakti. If you are sincere, you will attain God in the end, whichever path you follow. Roughly speaking, there are three kinds of yoga: jnānayoga, karmayoga, and bhaktiyoga.

"What is jnānayoga? The jnāni seeks to realize Brahman. He discriminates, saying, 'Not this, not this'. He discriminates, saying, 'Brahman is real and the universe illusory.' He discriminates between the Real and the unreal. As he comes to the end of discrimination, he goes into samādhi and attains the Knowledge of Brahman.

"What is karmayoga? Its aim is to fix one's mind on God by means of work. That is what you are teaching. It consists of breath-control,[3] concentration, meditation, and so on, done in a spirit of detachment. If a householder performs his duties in the world in a spirit of detachment, surrender-

---

[2] A noted wrestler of the time.
[3] Breathing exercises as prescribed in rājayoga.

ing the results to God and with devotion to God in his heart, he too may be said to practise karmayoga. Further, if a person performs worship, japa, and other forms of devotion, surrendering the results to God, he may be said to practise karmayoga. Attainment of God alone is the aim of karmayoga.

"What is bhaktiyoga? It is to keep the mind on God by chanting His name and glories. For the Kaliyuga the path of devotion is easiest. This is indeed the path for this age.

"The path of karma is very difficult. First of all, as I have just said, where will one find the time for it nowadays? Where is the time for a man to perform his duties as enjoined in the scriptures? Man's life is short in this age. Further, it is extremely difficult to perform one's duties in a spirit of detachment, without craving the result. One cannot work in such a spirit without first having realized God. Attachment to the result somehow enters the mind, though you may not be aware of it.

"To follow jnānayoga in this age is also very difficult. First, a man's life depends entirely on food. Second, he has a short span of life. Third, he can by no means get rid of body-consciousness; and the Knowledge of Brahman is impossible without the destruction of body-consciousness. The jnāni says: 'I am Brahman; I am not the body. I am beyond hunger and thirst, disease and grief, birth and death, pleasure and pain.' How can you be a jnāni if you are conscious of disease, grief, pain, pleasure, and the like? A thorn enters your flesh, blood flows from the wound, and you suffer very badly from the pain; but nevertheless if you are a jnāni you must be able to say: 'Why, there is no thorn in my flesh at all. Nothing is the matter with me.'

"Therefore bhaktiyoga is prescribed for this age. By following this path one comes to God more easily than by following the others. One can undoubtedly reach God by following the paths of jnāna and karma, but they are very difficult paths.

"Bhaktiyoga is the religion for this age. But that does not mean that the lover of God will reach one goal and the philosopher and worker another. It means that if a person seeks the Knowledge of Brahman he can attain It by following the path of bhakti, too. God, who loves His devotee, can give him the Knowledge of Brahman if He so desires.

"But the bhakta wants to realize the Personal God endowed with form and talk to Him. He seldom seeks the Knowledge of Brahman. But God, who does everything at His pleasure, can make His devotee the heir to His infinite glories if it pleases Him. He gives His devotee both the Love of God and the Knowledge of Brahman. If one is able somehow to reach Calcutta, one can see the Maidān and the museum and other places too. The thing is how to reach Calcutta.

"By realizing the Divine Mother of the Universe, you will get Knowledge as well as Devotion. You will get both. In bhāva samādhi you will see the form of God, and in nirvikalpa samādhi you will realize Brahman, the Absolute Existence-Knowledge-Bliss. In nirvikalpa samādhi ego, name, and form do not exist.

"A lover of God prays to the Divine Mother: 'O Mother, I am very much afraid of selfish actions. Such actions have desires behind them, and if I perform them I shall have to reap their fruit. But it is very difficult to work in a detached spirit. I shall certainly forget Thee, O Mother, if I involve myself in selfish actions. Therefore I have no use for them. May my actions, O Divine Mother, be fewer every day till I attain Thee. May I perform, without attachment to the results, only what action is absolutely necessary for me. May I have great love for Thee as I go on with my few duties. May I not entangle myself in new work so long as I do not realize Thee. But I shall perform it if I receive Thy command. Otherwise not.'"

PUNDIT: "How far did you go in visiting the sacred places?"

MASTER: "Oh, I visited a few places. (*With a smile*) But Hazra went farther and also climbed higher. He visited Hrishikesh, but I didn't go so far or so high.

"You must have noticed kites and vultures soaring very high in the sky; but their eyes are always fixed on the charnel-pits. Do you know the meaning of 'charnel-pits'? It is 'woman and gold'.

"What is the use of making pilgrimages if you can attain love of God remaining where you are? I have been to Benares and noticed the same trees there as here. The same green tamarind-leaves!

"Pilgrimage becomes futile if it does not enable you to attain love of God. Love of God is the one essential and necessary thing. Do you know the meaning of 'kites and vultures'? There are many people who talk big and who say that they have performed most of the duties enjoined in the scriptures. But with all that their minds are engrossed in worldliness and deeply preoccupied with money, riches, name, fame, creature comforts, and such things."

PUNDIT: "It is true, sir. Going on a pilgrimage is like seeking diamonds and gems, while discarding the precious stone that is worn by Nārāyana Himself on His breast."

MASTER: "I want you to remember this. You may impart thousands of instructions to people, but they will not bear fruit except in proper time. On going to bed, a child said to his mother, 'Mother, please wake me up when I feel the call of nature.' The mother said: 'Don't worry about it, my child. That call will wake you up itself.' (*All laugh.*) One feels yearning for God at the proper time.

"There are three classes of physicians. The physicians of one class feel the patient's pulse and go away, merely prescribing medicine. As they leave the room they simply ask the patient to take the medicine. They are the poorest class of physicians. Likewise, there are teachers who only give instruction, but do not stop to see whether their teachings have produced a good or bad effect. They do not think at all about the disciple.

"There are physicians of another class, who prescribe medicine and ask the patient to take it. If the patient is unwilling to follow their directions, they reason with him. They are the mediocre physicians. Likewise, there are mediocre teachers. They give instruction to the student and, further, try to persuade him in various ways to follow the instruction.

"Lastly, there are the physicians of the highest class. If the patient does not respond to their gentle persuasion, they even exert force upon him. If necessary, they press their knees on the patient's chest and force the medicine down his throat. Likewise, there are teachers of the highest class, who even exert force to direct the mind of the pupil toward God."

PUNDIT: "Sir, if there are such superior teachers as you have described, then why should you say that one does not get the Knowledge of God until the right time comes?"

MASTER: "You are right. But what will the physician do if the medicine runs out of the patient's mouth and doesn't reach his stomach? In such a case even the best physician can't do anything.

"The teacher should judge the fitness of the student before giving him instruction. But you don't discriminate in your instruction. When a young man comes to me for instruction, first of all I ask him about his relatives at home. Suppose he has lost his father; suppose his father has left some debts for him. How can such a person direct his mind to God? Are you listening to me?"

PUNDIT: "Yes, sir. I am paying attention to every word."

MASTER: "One day some Sikh soldiers came to the temple garden at Dakshineswar. I met them in front of the Kāli temple. One of them referred to God as very compassionate. 'Indeed!' I said. 'Is that true? But how do you know?' He answered, 'Because, sir, God gives us food and takes every care of us.' I said: 'Why should that surprise you? God is the Father of us all. Who will look after the child if the father doesn't? Do you mean to say that the people of the neighbouring village should look after the child?'"

NARENDRA: "Then shouldn't we call God kind?"

MASTER: "Have I forbidden you to? What I mean is that God is our very own. He is not a stranger to us."

PUNDIT: "Priceless words!"

MASTER (to Narendra): "I listened to your singing, but I didn't enjoy it. So I left the room. Your mind is now set on seeking a job, and therefore your song sounded dull."

Narendra flushed. He felt ashamed of himself and remained silent.

The Master asked for a drink of water. A glass of water had been placed 'near him, but he could not take it. He asked for some fresh water. Later it was found that a man of immoral character had touched the first glass.

PUNDIT (to Hazra): "You live in his company day and night. You must be very happy."

MASTER (with a smile): "This is indeed a great occasion for me. Today I have seen the crescent moon of the second day of the bright fortnight. (All laugh.) Do you know why I referred to the moon of the second day? Sītā once said to Rāvana, 'You are the full moon and Rāma is the crescent moon of the second day of the bright fortnight.' Rāvana did not understand the meaning of these words. He thought Sītā was flattering him and became exceedingly happy. But Sītā meant that Rāvana had reached the fullest limit of his power and prosperity, and that thenceforth he would wane like the full moon. Rāma, on the other hand, was like the moon of the second day. He would wax day by day."

The Master was about to take his leave. The pundit and his friends bowed low before him.

It was not yet dusk, and Sri Ramakrishna returned to Ishan's house with the devotees. The Master took his seat in the drawing-room with Ishan and his sons, a pundit, and a few devotees.

MASTER (*smiling, to Ishan*): "I said to Pundit Shashadhar: 'You have hardly set your foot on the tree, and yet you aspire to lay hold of a big bunch of fruit. First of all practise some spiritual discipline. Then you may teach others.'"

ISHAN: "Every preacher thinks that he enlightens others. The glow-worm also may think that it illumines the world. Imagining this to be the glow-worm's feeling, someone said to it: 'O glow-worm, how can you bring light to the world? You only reveal the intensity of the darkness.'"

MASTER (*with a smile*): "But Shashadhar is not just a scholar. He also has a little discrimination and dispassion."

A pundit who was present said to Sri Ramakrishna, "You are indeed a great soul."

MASTER: "You may say that about sages like Nārada, Prahlāda, or Śukadeva. I am like your son.

"Of course, in one sense your words are true. It is said that in one respect the devotee of God is greater than God Himself, because he carries God in his heart. (*All rejoice.*) It is said in the Vaishnava books: 'A devotee regards himself as a higher, and God as a lower, being.' Yaśodā, the mother of Krishna, was about to fetter Krishna, who was God Incarnate, with chains! She believed that no one but herself could take care of Krishna.

"Sometimes God acts as the magnet and the devotee as the needle. God attracts the devotee to Himself. Again, sometimes the devotee acts as the magnet and God as the needle. Such is the attraction of the devotee that God comes to him, unable to resist his love."

The Master was about to leave for Dakshineswar. Ishan and the other devotees stood around him while he gave Ishan various words of advice.

MASTER: "A devotee who can call on God while living a householder's life is a hero indeed. God thinks: 'He who has renounced the world for My sake will surely pray to Me. He must serve Me. Is there anything very remarkable about it? People will cry shame on him if he fails to do so. But he is blessed indeed who prays to Me in the midst of his worldly duties. He is trying to find Me, overcoming a great obstacle—pushing away, as it were, a huge block of stone weighing a ton. Such a man is a real hero.'"

PUNDIT: "You are right, sir. The scripture says the same thing. There is in the *Mahābhārata* the story of the 'pious hunter' and the 'chaste woman'. Once a hermit was disturbed in his meditation by a crow. When he cast an angry glance at the bird, it was reduced to ashes. The hermit said to himself: 'I have destroyed the crow by a mere glance. I must have made great progress in spiritual life.' One day he went to a woman's house to beg his food. She was devoted to her husband and served him day and night; she provided him with water to wash his feet and even dried them with her hair. When the hermit knocked at her door for alms, she was serving her husband

and could not open the door at once. The hermit, in a fit of anger, began to curse her. The chaste woman answered from the inner apartments: 'I am not your crow. Wait a few minutes, sir. After finishing my service to my husband I shall give you my attention.' The hermit was very much surprised to find that this simple woman was aware of his having burnt the crow to ashes. He wanted her to give him spiritual instruction. At her bidding he went to the 'pious hunter' at Benares. This hunter sold meat, but he also served his parents day and night as embodiments of God. The hermit said to himself in utter amazement: 'Why, he is a butcher and a worldly man! How can he give me the Knowledge of Brahman?' But the hunter was a knower of Brahman and had acquired divine knowledge through the performance of his worldly duties. The hermit was illumined by the instruction of the 'pious hunter'."

The Master was about to take his leave. He was standing at the door of the next house, where Ishan's father-in-law lived. Ishan and the other devotees stood by the Master. They were waiting to bid him good-bye. Sri Ramakrishna said to Ishan: "Live in the world like an ant. The world contains a mixture of truth and untruth, sugar and sand. Be an ant and take the sugar.

"Again, the world is a mixture of milk and water, the bliss of God-Consciousness and the pleasure of sense-enjoyment. Be a swan and drink the milk, leaving the water aside.

"Live in the world like a waterfowl. The water clings to the bird, but the bird shakes it off. Live in the world like a mudfish. The fish lives in the mud, but its skin is always bright and shiny.

"The world is indeed a mixture of truth and make-believe. Discard the make-believe and take the truth."

Sri Ramakrishna got into the carriage and left for Dakshineswar.

25

ADVICE TO PUNDIT SHASHADHAR

Monday, June 30, 1884

SRI RAMAKRISHNA was in his room, sitting on a mat spread on the floor. Pundit Shashadhar and a few devotees were with him on the mat, and the rest sat on the bare floor. Surendra, Baburam, M., Harish, Latu, Hazra, and others were present. It was about four o'clock in the afternoon.

Sri Ramakrishna had met Pundit Shashadhar six days before in Calcutta, and now the pundit had come to Dakshineswar to visit the Master. Bhudar Chattopadhyaya and his elder brother, the pundit's hosts, were with him.

The pundit was a follower of the path of jnāna. The Master was explaining this path to him. He said: "Nityā and Līlā are the two aspects of one and the same Reality. He who is the Indivisible Satchidānanda has assumed different forms for the sake of His Līlā." As he described the nature of the Ultimate Reality the Master every now and then became unconscious in samādhi. While he talked he was intoxicated with spiritual fervour. He said to the pundit: "My dear sir, Brahman is immutable and immovable, like Mount Sumeru. But He who is 'immovable' can also 'move'."

The Master was in ecstasy. He began to sing in his melodious voice:

> Who is there that can understand what Mother Kālī is?
> Even the six darśanas are powerless to reveal Her. . . .

He went on:

> Is Mother merely a simple woman, born as others are born?
> Only by chanting Her holy name
> Does Śiva survive the deadly poison.[1]

> She it is who creates the worlds, She who preserves and destroys,
> With a mere wink of Her wondrous eyes;
> She holds the universe in Her womb.

> Seeking a shelter at Her feet, the gods themselves feel safe;
> And Mahādeva, God of Gods,
> Lies prostrate underneath Her feet.

[1] An allusion to the poison that appeared when the ocean was churned by the gods and demons. Śiva drank it out of kindness to others, and the poison remained in His throat, giving it a blue colour. Therefore Śiva is known as the "god with a blue throat".

473

Again he sang:

> Is Mother only Śiva's wife? To Her must needs bow down
> The all-destroying King of Death!
> Naked She roams about the world, slaying Her demon foes,
> Or stands erect on Śiva's breast.
> Her feet upon Her Husband's form! What a strange wife She makes!
> My Mother's play, declares Prasād, shatters all rules and laws:
> Strive hard for purity, O mind,
> And understand my Mother's ways.

And again:

> I drink no ordinary wine, but Wine of Everlasting Bliss,
> As I repeat my Mother Kāli's name;
> It so intoxicates my mind that people take me to be drunk! . . .

And again:

> Can everyone have the vision of Śyāmā? Is Kāli's treasure for
>   everyone?
> Oh, what a pity my foolish mind will not see what is true!
> Even with all His penances, rarely does Śiva Himself behold
> The mind-bewitching sight of Mother Śyāmā's crimson feet.

> To him who meditates on Her the riches of heaven are poor indeed;
> If Śyāmā casts Her glance on him, he swims in Eternal Bliss.
> The prince of yogis, the king of the gods, meditate on Her feet in
>   vain;
> Yet worthless Kamalākānta yearns for the Mother's blessed feet!

The Master's ecstatic mood gradually relaxed. He stopped singing and sat in silence. After a while he got up and sat on the small couch.

Pundit Shashadhar was charmed with his singing. Very humbly he said to Sri Ramakrishna, "Are you going to sing any more?"

A little later the Master sang again:

> High in the heaven of the Mother's feet, my mind was soaring like
>   a kite,
> When came a blast of sin's rough wind that drove it swiftly toward
>   the earth. . . .

Then he sang:

> Once for all, this time, I have thoroughly understood;
> From One[2] who knows it well, I have learnt the secret of bhāva.
> A man has come to me from a country where there is no night,
> And now I cannot distinguish day from night any longer;
> Rituals and devotions have all grown profitless for me.

> My sleep is broken; how can I slumber any more?
> For now I am wide awake in the sleeplessness of yoga.
> O Divine Mother, made one with Thee in yoga-sleep[3] at last,
> My slumber I have lulled asleep for evermore.

[2] God, whom the poet worshipped as the Divine Mother.
[3] Samādhi, which makes one appear asleep.

I bow my head, says Prasād, before desire and liberation;
Knowing the secret that Kāli is one with the highest Brahman,
I have discarded, once for all, both righteousness and sin.

Sri Ramakrishna continued:

I have surrendered my soul at the fearless feet of the Mother;
Am I afraid of Death any more?
Unto the tuft of hair on my head
Is tied the almighty mantra, Mother Kāli's name.
My body I have sold in the market-place of the world
And with it have bought Sri Durgā's name.

As Sri Ramakrishna sang the line, "And with it have bought Sri Durgā's
name", the tears flowed from Pundit Shashadhar's eyes. The Master went on
with the song:

Deep within my heart I have planted the name of Kāli,
The Wish-fulfilling Tree of heaven;
When Yama, King of Death, appears,
To him I shall open my heart and show it growing there.
I have cast out from me my six unflagging foes;[4]
Ready am I to sail life's sea,
Crying, "To Durgā, victory!"

Again he sang:

Dwell, O mind, within yourself;
Enter no other's home.
If you but seek there, you will find
All you are searching for. . . .

And again:

Though I[5] am never loath to grant salvation,
I hesitate indeed to grant pure love.
Whoever wins pure love surpasses all;
He is adored by men;
He triumphs over the three worlds. . . .

The pundit had studied the Vedas and the other scriptures. He loved to
discuss philosophy. The Master, seated on the couch, cast his benign look
on the pundit and gave him counsel through parables.

MASTER (to the pundit): "There are many scriptures like the Vedas. But
one cannot realize God without austerity and spiritual discipline. 'God
cannot be found in the six systems, the Vedas, or the Tantra.'

"But one should learn the contents of the scriptures and then act according
to their injunctions. A man lost a letter. He couldn't remember where he
had left it. He began to search for it with a lamp. After two or three people
had searched, the letter was at last found. The message in the letter was:
'Please send us five seers of sandesh and a piece of wearing-cloth.' The man

---

[4] The six passions.
[5] The song represents Sri Krishna's words.

read it and then threw the letter away. There was no further need of it; now all he had to do was to buy the five seers of sandesh and the piece of cloth.

"Better than reading is hearing, and better than hearing is seeing. One understands the scriptures better by hearing them from the lips of the guru or of a holy man. Then one doesn't have to think about their non-essential part. Hanumān said: 'Brother, I don't know much about the phase of the moon or the position of the stars. I just contemplate Rāma.'

"But seeing is far better than hearing. Then all doubts disappear. It is true that many things are recorded in the scriptures; but all these are useless without the direct realization of God, without devotion to His Lotus Feet, without purity of heart. The almanac forecasts the rainfall of the year. But not a drop of water will you get by squeezing the almanac. No, not even cne drop.

"How long should one reason about the texts of the scriptures? So long as one does not have direct realization of God. How long does the bee buzz about? As long as it is not sitting on a flower. No sooner does it light on a flower and begin to sip honey than it keeps quiet.

"But you must remember another thing. One may talk even after the realization of God. But then one talks only of God and of Divine Bliss. It is like a drunkard's crying, 'Victory to the Divine Mother!' He can hardly say anything else on account of his drunkenness. You can notice, too, that a bee makes an indistinct humming sound after having sipped the honey from a flower.

"The jnāni reasons about the world through the process of 'Neti, neti', 'Not this, not this'. Reasoning in this way, he at last comes to a state of Bliss, and that is Brahman. What is the nature of a jnāni? He behaves according to scriptural injunctions.

"Once I was taken to Chānak and saw some sādhus there. Several of them were sewing. (All laugh.) At the sight of us they threw aside their sewing. They sat straight, crossing their legs, and conversed with us. (All laugh.)

"But jnānis will not talk about spiritual things without being asked. They will inquire, at first, about such things as your health and your family.

"But the nature of the vijnāni is different. He is unconcerned about anything. Perhaps he carries his wearing-cloth loose under his arm, like a child; or perhaps the cloth has dropped from his body altogether.

"The man who knows that God exists is called a jnāni. A jnāni is like one who knows beyond a doubt that a log of wood contains fire. But a vijnāni is he who lights the log, cooks over the fire, and is nourished by the food. The eight fetters have fallen from the vijnāni. He may keep merely the appearance of lust, anger, and the rest."

PUNDIT: " 'The knots of his heart are cut asunder; all his doubts are destroyed.' "

MASTER: "Yes. Once a ship sailed into the ocean. Suddenly its iron joints, nails, and screws fell out. The ship was passing a magnetic hill, and so all its iron was loosened.

"I used to go to Krishnakishore's house. Once, when I was there, he said to me, 'Why do you chew betel-leaf?' I said: 'It is my sweet pleasure. I shall chew betel-leaf, look at my face in the mirror, and dance naked among a thousand girls.'[6] Krishnakishore's wife scolded him and said: 'What have you said to Ramakrishna? You don't know how to talk to people.'

"In this state, passions like lust and anger are burnt up, though nothing happens to the physical body. It looks just like any other body; but the inside is all hollow and pure."

A DEVOTEE: "Does the body remain even after the realization of God?"

MASTER: "The body survives with some so that they may work out their prārabdha karma or work for the welfare of others. By bathing in the Ganges a man gets rid of his sin and attains liberation. But if he happens to be blind, he doesn't get rid of his blindness. Of course, he escapes future births, which would otherwise be necessary for reaping the results of his past sinful karma. His present body remains alive as long as its momentum[7] is not exhausted; but future births are no longer possible. The wheel moves as long as the impulse that has set it in motion lasts. Then it comes to a stop. In the case of such a person, passions like lust and anger are burnt up. Only the body remains alive to perform a few actions."

PUNDIT: "That is called samskāra."

MASTER: "The vijnāni always sees God. That is why he is so indifferent about the world. He sees God even with his eyes open. Sometimes he comes down to the Līlā from the Nitya, and sometimes he goes up to the Nitya from the Līlā."

PUNDIT: "I don't understand that."

MASTER: "The jnāni reasons about the world through the process of 'Neti, neti', and at last reaches the Eternal and Indivisible Satchidānanda. He reasons in this manner: 'Brahman is not the living beings; It is neither the universe nor the twenty-four cosmic principles.' As a result of such reasoning he attains the Absolute. Then he realizes that it is the Absolute that has become all this—the universe, its living beings, and the twenty-four cosmic principles.

"Milk sets into curd, and the curd is churned into butter. After extracting the butter one realizes that butter is not essentially different from buttermilk and buttermilk not essentially different from butter. The bark of a tree goes with the pith and the pith goes with the bark."

PUNDIT (smiling, to Bhudar): "Did you understand that? It is very difficult."

MASTER: "If there is butter, there must be buttermilk also. If you think of butter, you must also think of buttermilk along with it; for there cannot be any butter without buttermilk. Just so, if you accept the Nitya, you must also accept the Līlā. It is the process of negation and affirmation. You realize the Nitya by negating the Līlā. Then you affirm the Līlā, seeing in it the manifestation of the Nitya. One attains this state after realizing Reality in

---

[6] Because the Master was a vijnāni.

[7] The momentum of the actions of his previous birth, which has given rise to his present body.

both aspects: Personal and Impersonal. The Personal is the embodiment of Chit, Consciousness; and the Impersonal is the Indivisible Satchidānanda.

"Brahman alone has become everything. Therefore to the vijnāni this world is a 'mansion of mirth'. But to the jnāni it is a 'framework of illusion'. Rāmprasād described the world as a 'framework of illusion'. Another man said to him by way of retort:

> This very world is a mansion of mirth;
> Here I can eat, here drink and make merry.
> O physician,[8] you are a fool!
> You see only the surface of things.
> Janaka's might was unsurpassed;
> What did he lack of the world or the Spirit?
> Holding to one as well as the other,
> He drank his milk from a brimming cup!

"The vijnāni enjoys the Bliss of God in a richer way. Some have heard of milk, some have seen it, and some have drunk it. The vijnāni has drunk milk, enjoyed it, and been nourished by it."

The Master remained silent a few moments and then asked Pundit Shashadhar to have a smoke. The pundit went to the southeast verandah to smoke. Soon he came back to the room and sat on the floor with the devotees. Seated on the small couch, the Master continued the conversation.

MASTER (to the pundit): "Let me tell you something. There are three kinds of ānanda, joy: the joy of worldly enjoyment, the joy of worship, and the Joy of Brahman. The joy of worldly enjoyment is the joy of 'woman and gold', which people always enjoy. The joy of worship one enjoys while chanting the name and glories of God. And the Joy of Brahman is the joy of God-vision. After experiencing the joy of God-vision the rishis of olden times went beyond all rules and conventions.

"Chaitanyadeva used to experience three spiritual states: the inmost, the semi-conscious, and the conscious. In the inmost state he would see God and go into samādhi. He would be in the state of jaḍa samādhi. In the semi-conscious state he would be partially conscious of the outer world. In the conscious state he could sing the name and glories of God."

HAZRA (to the pundit): "So your doubts are now solved."

MASTER (to the pundit): "What is samādhi? It is the complete merging of the mind in God-Consciousness. The jnāni experiences jaḍa samādhi, in which no trace of 'I' is left. The samādhi attained through the path of bhakti is called 'chetana samādhi'. In this samādhi there remains the consciousness of 'I'—the 'I' of the servant-and-Master relationship, of the lover-and-Beloved relationship, of the enjoyer-and-Food relationship. God is the Master; the devotee is the servant. God is the Beloved; the devotee is the lover. God is the Food, and the devotee is the enjoyer. 'I don't want to be sugar. I want to eat it.'"

PUNDIT: "What will happen if God dissolves all of the 'I', if He changes the enjoyer himself into sugar?"

MASTER (smiling): "Come, come! Tell me what is in your mind. But

[8] Rāmprasād belonged to the physician caste.

don't the scriptures mention Nārada, Sanaka, Sanātana, Sananda, and Sanatkumāra?"

PUNDIT: "Yes, sir. They do."

MASTER: "Though they were jnānis, yet they kept the 'I' of the bhakta. Haven't you read the *Bhāgavata*?"

PUNDIT: "I have read only part of it, not the whole."

MASTER: "Pray to God. He is full of compassion. Will He not listen to the words of His devotee? He is the Kalpataru. You will get whatever you desire from Him."

PUNDIT: "I haven't thought deeply about these things before. But now I understand."

MASTER: "God keeps a little of 'I' in His devotee even after giving him the Knowledge of Brahman. That 'I' is the 'I of the devotee', the 'I of the jnāni'. Through that 'I' the devotee enjoys the infinite play of God.

"The pestle⁹ was almost worn out with rubbing. Only a little was left. That fell into the underbrush and brought about the destruction of the lunar race, the race of the Yadus. The vijnāni retains the 'I of the devotee', the 'I of the jnāni', in order to taste the Bliss of God and teach people.

"The rishis of old had timid natures. They were easily frightened. Do you know their attitude? It was this: 'Let me somehow get my own salvation; who cares for others?' A hollow piece of drift-wood somehow manages to float; but it sinks if even a bird sits on it. But Nārada and sages of his kind are like a huge log that not only can float across to the other shore but can carry many animals and other creatures as well. A steamship itself crosses the ocean and also carries people across.

"Teachers like Nārada belong to the class of the vijnāni. They were much more courageous than the other rishis. They are like an expert satrancha-player. You must have noticed how he shouts, as he throws the dice: 'What do I want? Six? No, five! Here is five!' And every time he throws the dice he gets the number he wants. He is such a clever player! And while playing he even twirls his moustaches.

"A mere jnāni trembles with fear. He is like an amateur satrancha-player. He is anxious to move his pieces somehow to the safety zone, where they won't be overtaken by his opponent. But a vijnāni isn't afraid of anything. He has realized both aspects of God: Personal and Impersonal. He has talked with God. He has enjoyed the Bliss of God.

"It is a joy to merge the mind in the Indivisible Brahman through contemplation. And it is also a joy to keep the mind on the Līlā, the Relative, without dissolving it in the Absolute.

"A mere jnāni is a monotonous person. He always analyses, saying: 'It is not this, not this. The world is like a dream.' But I have 'raised both my hands'. Therefore I accept everything.

"Listen to a story. Once a woman went to see her weaver friend. The weaver, who had been spinning different kinds of silk thread, was very

⁹ The story is told in the *Mahābhārata* of how the relatives of Krishna quarrelled over a fragment of a pestle and exterminated themselves by fighting with one another.

happy to see her friend and said to her: 'Friend, I can't tell you how happy I am to see you. Let me get you some refreshments.' She left the room. The woman looked at the threads of different colours and was tempted. She hid a bundle of thread under one arm. The weaver returned presently with the refreshments and began to feed her guest with great enthusiasm. But, looking at the thread, she realized that her friend had taken a bundle. Hitting upon a plan to get it back, she said: 'Friend, it is so long since I have seen you. This is a day of great joy for me. I feel very much like asking you to dance with me.' The friend said, 'Sister, I am feeling very happy too.' So the two friends began to dance together. When the weaver saw that her friend danced without raising her hands, she said: 'Friend, let us dance with both hands raised. This is a day of great joy.' But the guest pressed one arm to her side and danced raising only the other. The weaver said: 'How is this, friend? Why should you dance with only one hand raised? Dance with me raising both hands. Look at me. See how I dance with both hands raised.' But the guest still pressed one arm to her side. She danced with the other hand raised and said with a smile, 'This is all I know of dancing.' "

The Master continued: "I don't press my arm to my side. Both my hands are free. I am not afraid of anything. I accept both the Nitya and the Līlā, both the Absolute and the Relative.

"I said to Keshab Sen that he would not be able to realize God without renouncing the ego. He said, 'Sir, in that case I should not be able to keep my organization together.' Thereupon I said to him: 'I am asking you to give up the "unripe ego", the "wicked ego". But there is no harm in the "ripe ego", the "child ego", the "servant ego", the "ego of Knowledge".'

"The worldly man's ego, the 'ignorant ego', the 'unripe ego', is like a thick stick. It divides, as it were, the water of the Ocean of Satchidānanda. But the 'servant ego', the 'child ego', the 'ego of Knowledge', is like a line on the water. One clearly sees that there is only one expanse of water. The dividing line makes it appear that the water has two parts, but one clearly sees that in reality there is only one expanse of water.

"Śankarāchārya kept the 'ego of Knowledge' in order to teach people. God keeps in many people the 'ego of a jnāni' or the 'ego of a bhakta' even after they have attained Brahmajnāna. Hanumān, after realizing God in both His Personal and His Impersonal aspect, cherished toward God the attitude of a servant, a devotee. He said to Rāma: 'O Rāma, sometimes I think that You are the whole and I am a part of You. Sometimes I think that You are the Master and I am Your servant. And sometimes, Rāma, when I contemplate the Absolute, I see that I am You and You are I.'

"Yaśodā became grief-stricken at being separated from Krishna, and called on Rādhā. Rādhā saw Yaśodā's suffering and revealed herself to her as the divine Śakti, which was her real nature. She said to Yaśodā: 'Krishna is Chidātmā, Absolute Consciousness, and I am Chitśakti, the Primal Power. Ask a boon of Me.' Yaśodā said: 'I don't want Brahmajnāna. Please grant me only this: that I may see the form of Gopāla in my meditation; that I may always have the company of Krishna's devotees; that I may always serve the devotees of God; that I may always chant God's name and glories.'

"Once the gopis felt a great desire to see the forms of the Lord. So Krishna asked them to dive into the water of the Jamunā. No sooner did they dive into the water than they all arrived at Vaikuntha. There they saw the form of the Lord endowed with His six celestial splendours. But they did not like it. They said to Krishna: 'We want to see Gopāla and serve Him. Please grant us that boon alone. We don't want anything else.'

"Before His departure for Mathurā, Krishna wanted to give the Knowledge of Brahman to the gopis. He said to them: 'I dwell both inside and outside all beings. Why should you see only one form of Mine?' The gopis cried in chorus: 'O Krishna, do You want to go away from us? Is that why You are instructing us in Brahmajnāna?'

"Do you know the attitude of the gopis? It is this: 'We are Rādhā's and Rādhā is ours.' "[10]

A DEVOTEE: "Does this 'I' of the devotee never disappear altogether?"

MASTER: "Yes, it disappears at times. Then one attains the Knowledge of Brahman and goes into samādhi. I too lose it, but not for all the time. In the musical scale there are seven notes: sā, re, gā, mā, pā, dhā, and ni. But one cannot keep one's voice on 'ni' a long time. One must bring it down again to the lower notes. I pray to the Divine Mother, 'O Mother, do not give me Brahmajnāna.' Formerly believers in God with form used to visit me a great deal. Then the modern Brahmajnānis[11] began to arrive. During that period I used to remain unconscious in samādhi most of the time. Whenever I regained consciousness, I would say to the Divine Mother, 'O Mother, please don't give me Brahmajnāna.' "

PUNDIT: "Does God listen to our prayers?"

MASTER: "God is the Kalpataru, the Wish-fulfilling Tree. You will certainly get whatever you ask of Him. But you must pray standing near the Kalpataru. Only then will your prayer be fulfilled. But you must remember another thing. God knows our inner feeling. A man gets the fulfilment of the desire he cherishes while practising sādhanā. As one thinks, so one receives. A magician was showing his tricks before a king. Now and then he exclaimed: 'Come confusion! Come delusion! O King, give me money! Give me clothes!' Suddenly his tongue turned upward and clove to the roof of his mouth. He experienced kumbhaka. He could utter neither word nor sound, and became motionless. People thought he was dead. They built a vault of bricks and buried him there in that posture. After a thousand years someone dug into the vault. Inside it people found a man seated in samādhi. They took him for a holy man and worshipped him. When they shook him his tongue was loosened and regained its normal position. The magician became conscious of the outer world and cried, as he had a thousand years

---

[10] The ideal of the gopis was not to merge themselves in God-Consciousness, but to keep their individuality in order to enjoy the communion of Rādhā and Krishna. They regarded themselves as the companions of Rādhā.

[11] The members of the Brāhmo Samāj, who believed in the formless Brahman.

before: 'Come confusion! Come delusion! O King, give me money! Give me clothes!'

"I used to weep, praying to the Divine Mother, 'O Mother, destroy with Thy thunderbolt my inclination to reason.'"

PUNDIT: "Then you too had an inclination to reason?"

MASTER: "Yes, once."

PUNDIT: "Then please assure us that we shall get rid of that inclination too. How did you get rid of yours?"

MASTER: "Oh, somehow or other."

Sri Ramakrishna was silent awhile. Then he went on with his conversation.

MASTER: "God is the Kalpataru. One should pray standing near It. Then one will get whatever one desires.

"How many things God has created! Infinite is His universe. But what need have I to know about His infinite splendours? If I must know these, let me first realize Him. Then God Himself will tell me all about them. What need have I to know how many houses and how many government securities Jadu Mallick possesses? All that I need is somehow to converse with Jadu Mallick. I may succeed in seeing him by jumping over a ditch or through a petition or after being pushed about by his gate-keeper. Once I get a chance to talk to him, then he himself will tell me all about his possessions if I ask him. If one becomes acquainted with the master, then one is respected by his officers too. (All laugh.)

"There are some who do not care to know the splendours of God. What do I care about knowing how many gallons of wine there are in the tavern? One bottle is enough for me. Why should I desire the knowledge of God's splendours? I am intoxicated with the little wine I have swallowed.

"Both bhaktiyoga and jnanayoga are paths by which you can realize God. Whatever path you may follow, you will certainly realize Him. The path of bhakti is an easy one. The path of knowledge and discrimination is very difficult. Why should one reason so much to know which path is the best? I talked about this with Vijay for many days. Once I told him about a man who used to pray, 'O God, reveal to me who and what You are.'

"The path of knowledge and discrimination is difficult indeed. Pārvati, the Divine Mother, revealed Her various forms to Her father and said, 'Father, if you want Brahmajnāna, then live in the company of holy men.'

"Brahman cannot be described in words. It is said in the Rāma Gitā that Brahman has only been indirectly hinted at by the scriptures. When one speaks about the 'cowherd village on the Ganges', one indirectly states that the village is situated on the bank of the Ganges.

"Why shouldn't a man be able to realize the formless Brahman? But it is extremely difficult. He cannot if he has even the slightest trace of worldliness. He can be directly aware of Brahman in his inmost consciousness only when he renounces all sense-objects—form, taste, smell, touch, and sound—and only when his mind completely stops functioning. And then, too, he knows only this much of Brahman—that It exists."

Quoting from an Upanishad, the pundit said, "It is to be experienced only as Existence."

MASTER: "In order to realize God a devotee should make use of a particular attitude—the attitude of a 'hero' or a friend or a handmaid or a child."

MANI MALLICK: "Only then can one feel attached to God."

MASTER: "For many days I cherished the feeling that I was a companion of the Divine Mother. I used to say: 'I am the handmaid of Brahmamayi, the Blissful Mother. O companions of the Divine Mother, make me the Mother's handmaid! I shall go about proudly, saying, "I am Brahmamayi's handmaid!"'

"Some souls realize God without practising any spiritual discipline. They are called nityasiddha, *eternally* perfect. Those who have realized God through austerity, japa, and the like, are called sādhanasiddha, perfect through *spiritual discipline*. Again, there are those called kripāsiddha, perfect through *divine grace*. These last may be compared to a room kept dark a thousand years, which becomes light the moment a lamp is brought in.

"There is also a class of devotees, the hathātsiddha, that is to say, those who have *suddenly* attained God-vision. Their case is like that of a poor boy who has suddenly found favour with a rich man. The rich man marries his daughter to the boy and along with her gives him land, house, carriage, servants, and so forth.

"There is still another class of devotees, the svapnasiddha, who have had the vision of God in a *dream*."

SURENDRA (*smiling*): "Let us go to sleep then. We shall wake and find ourselves babus, aristocrats."

MASTER (*tenderly*): "You are already a babu. When the letter 'ā' is joined to the letter 'ka', 'ka' becomes 'kā'. It is futile to add another 'ā'. If you add it, you will still have the same 'kā'. (*All laugh.*)

"The nityasiddha is in a class apart. He is like arani wood.[12] A little rubbing produces fire. You can get fire from it even without rubbing. The nityasiddha realizes God by practising slight spiritual discipline and sometimes without practising any at all. But he does practise spiritual discipline after realizing God. He is like the gourd or pumpkin vine—first fruit, then flower."

The pundit smiled at this illustration.

MASTER: "There is the instance of Prahlāda. He was a nityasiddha. While writing the letter 'ka' he shed a stream of tears."[13]

The Master was pleased with the pundit's humility. He praised him to the devotees.

MASTER: "He has such a nice nature. You find no difficulty in driving a nail into a mud wall. But its point breaks if you try to drive it against a stone; and still it will not pierce it. There are people whose spiritual consciousness is not at all awakened even though they hear about God a thou-

[12] A piece of wood used for kindling the sacred fire by friction.
[13] Because the latter "ka" reminded Prahlāda of Krishna, his Ideal Deity.

sand times. They are like a crocodile, on whose hide you cannot make any impression with a sword."

PUNDIT: "But one can hurt a crocodile by throwing a spear into its belly." (*All laugh.*)

MASTER (*smiling*): "What good is there in reading a whole lot of scriptures? What good is there in the study of philosophy? What is the use of talking big? In order to learn archery one should first aim at a banana tree, then at a reed, then at a wick, and last at a flying bird. At the beginning one should concentrate on God with form.

"Then there are devotees who are beyond the three gunas. They are eternally devoted to God, like Nārada. These devotees behold Krishna as Chinmaya, all Spirit, His Abode as Chinmaya, His devotee as Chinmaya. To them God is eternal, His Abode is eternal, His devotee is eternal.

"Those who reason and speculate following the process of 'Neti, neti' do not accept the Incarnation of God. Hazra says well that Divine Incarnation is only for the bhakta, and not for the jnāni, because the jnāni is quite contented with his ideal, 'I am He'."

Sri Ramakrishna and the devotees remained silent awhile. The pundit resumed the conversation.

PUNDIT: "Sir, how does one get rid of callousness? Laughter makes me think of muscles and nerves. Grief makes me think of the nervous system."

MASTER (*smiling*): "That is why Narayan Shastri used to say, 'The harmful effect of the study of the scriptures is that it encourages reasoning and arguing.'"

PUNDIT: "Is there no way for us then?"

MASTER: "Yes, there is the path of discrimination. In a song occurs the line: 'Ask her son Discrimination about the Truth.'

"The way lies through discrimination, renunciation, and passionate yearning for God. Unless a man practises discrimination, he cannot utter the right words. One time, after expounding religion at great length, Pundit Samadhyayi said, 'God is dry.' He reminded me of the man who once said, 'My uncle's cow-shed is full of horses.' Now, does anyone keep horses in a cow-shed? (*With a smile*) You have become like a chānābarā[14] fried in butter. Now it will be good for you, and for others as well, if you are soaked in syrup a few days. Just a few days."

PUNDIT (*smiling*): "The sweetmeat is over-fried. It has become charred."

MASTER (*with a laugh*): "No! No! It is brown as a cockroach. Just the right colour."

HAZRA: "The sweetmeat is well cooked. It has become spongy. Now it will soak up the syrup nicely."

MASTER: "You see, there is no need to read too much of the scriptures. If you read too much you will be inclined to reason and argue. Nangtā used to teach me thus: What you get by repeating the word 'Gītā' ten times is the essence of the book. In other words, if you repeat 'Gītā' ten times it is reversed into 'tāgi', which indicates renunciation.

[14] A Bengali sweetmeat made from cheese, first fried in butter and then soaked in syrup.

"Yes, the way to realize God is through discrimination, renunciation, and yearning for Him. What kind of yearning? One should yearn for God as the cow, with yearning heart, runs after its calf."

PUNDIT: "The same thing is said in the Vedas: 'O God, we call on Thee as the cow lows for the calf.'"

MASTER: "Add your tears to your yearning. And if you can renounce everything through discrimination and dispassion, then you will be able to see God. That yearning brings about God-intoxication, whether you follow the path of knowledge or the path of devotion. The sage Durvāsā was mad with the Knowledge of God.

"There is a great deal of difference between the knowledge of a house-holder and that of an all-renouncing sannyāsi. The householder's knowledge is like the light of a lamp, which illumines only the inside of a room. He cannot see anything, with the help of such knowledge, except his own body and his immediate family. But the knowledge of the all-renouncing monk is like the light of the sun. Through that light he can see both inside and outside the room. Chaitanyadeva's knowledge had the brilliance of the sun —the sun of Knowledge. Further, he radiated the soothing light of the moon of Devotion. He was endowed with both—the Knowledge of Brahman and ecstatic love of God.

(To the pundit) "One can attain spiritual consciousness through both affirmation and negation. There is the positive path of love and devotion, and there is the negative path of knowledge and discrimination. You are preaching the path of knowledge. But that creates a very difficult situation: there the guru and the disciple do not see each other. Śukadeva went to Janaka for instruction about the Knowledge of Brahman. Janaka said to him: 'You must pay me the guru's fee beforehand. When you attain the Knowledge of Brahman you won't pay me the fee, because the knower of Brahman sees no difference between the guru and the disciple.'

"Both negation and affirmation are ways to realize one and the same goal. Infinite are the opinions and infinite are the ways. But you must remember one thing. The injunction is that the path of devotion described by Nārada is best suited to the Kaliyuga. According to this path, first comes bhakti; then bhāva, when bhakti is mature. Higher than bhāva are mahābhāva and prema. An ordinary mortal does not attain mahābhāva and prema. He who has achieved these has realized the goal, that is to say, has attained God."

PUNDIT: "In expounding religion one has to use a great many words."

MASTER: "While preaching, eliminate the 'head and tail', that is to say, emphasize only the essentials."

The pundit and Mani Mallick became engaged in conversation. Mani was a member of the Brāhmo Samāj. The pundit argued vehemently about the good and bad sides of the Samāj. Sri Ramakrishna was seated on the small couch and looked on, smiling. Presently he remarked: "This is the tāmasic aspect of sattva, the attitude of a hero. This is necessary. One should not hold one's tongue at the sight of injustice and untruth. Suppose a bad woman wants to drag you from the path of righteousness. You must then assume the heroic attitude and say: 'What? You witch! You dare injure my spiritual life? I shall cut your body in two right now.' "

With a smile Sri Ramakrishna said to the pundit: "Mani Mallick has been following the tenets of the Brāhmo Samāj a long time. You can't convert him to your views. Is it an easy thing to destroy old tendencies? Once there lived a very pious Hindu who always worshipped the Divine Mother and chanted Her name. When the Mussalmāns conquered the country, they forced him to embrace Islām. They said to him: 'You are now a Mussalmān. Say "Allāh". From now on you must repeat only the name of Allāh.' With great difficulty he repeated the word 'Allāh', but every now and then blurted out 'Jagadambā'.[15] At that the Mussalmāns were about to beat him. Thereupon he said to them: 'I beseech you! Please do not kill me. I have been trying my utmost to repeat the name of Allāh, but our Jagadambā has filled me up to the throat. She pushes out your Allāh.' (All laugh.)

(To the pundit) "Please don't say anything to Mani Mallick. You must know that there are different tastes. There are also different powers of digestion. God has made different religions and creeds to suit different aspirants. By no means all are fit for the Knowledge of Brahman. Therefore the worship of God with form has been provided.

"The mother brings home a fish for her children. She curries part of the fish, part she fries, and with another part she makes pilau. By no means all can digest the pilau. So she makes fish soup for those who have weak stomachs. Further, some want pickled or fried fish. There are different temperaments. There are differences in the capacity to comprehend."

All sat in silence. Sri Ramakrishna said to the pundit, "Go and visit the temples and take a stroll in the garden." It was about half past five in the afternoon. The pundit left the room with his friends and several of the devotees.

After a while the Master went with M. toward the bathing-ghāt on the Ganges. He said to M., "Baburam now says, 'What shall I gain by study?' " On the bank of the river he met the pundit and said to him, "Aren't you going to the Kāli temple?" The pundit said: "Yes, sir. Let us go together."

With a smiling face Sri Ramakrishna proceeded to the temple through the courtyard. He said to the pundit, "Listen to a song."

He sang:

> Is Kāli, my Mother, really black?
> The Naked One, of blackest hue,
> Lights the Lotus of the Heart. . . .

As he was going through the courtyard, he quoted to the pundit from a song:

> Lighting the lamp of Knowledge in the chamber of your heart,
> Behold the face of the Mother, Brahman's Embodiment.

They came to the temple. Sri Ramakrishna saluted the Divine Mother, touching the ground with his forehead.

[15] "The Mother of the Universe", a name of the Divine Mother.

Red hibiscus flowers and vilwa-leaves adorned the Mother's feet. Her three eyes radiated love for Her devotees. Two of Her hands were raised as if to give them boons and reassurance; the other two hands held symbols of death. She was clothed in a sāri of Benares silk and was decked with ornaments.

Referring to the image, one of the party remarked, "I heard it was made by the sculptor Nabin." The Master answered: "Yes, I know. But to me She is the Embodiment of Spirit."

As Sri Ramakrishna was coming back to his room with the devotees, he said to Baburam, "Come with us." M. also joined them.

It was dusk. The Master was sitting on the semicircular porch west of his room. Baburam and M. sat near him. He was in a mood of partial ecstasy.

Rakhal was not then living with Sri Ramakrishna, and therefore the Master was having difficulties about his personal service. Several devotees lived with him, but he could not bear the touch of everyone during his spiritual moods. He hinted to Baburam: "Do stay with me. It will be very nice. In this mood I cannot allow others to touch me."

The pundit entered the Master's room after visiting the temples. The Master said to him from the porch, "Take some refreshments." The pundit said that he had not yet performed his evening devotions. At once Sri Ramakrishna stood up and sang in an exalted mood:

Why should I go to Gangā or Gayā, to Kāśi, Kānchi, or Prabhās,
So long as I can breathe my last with Kāli's name upon my lips?
What need of rituals has a man, what need of devotions any more,
If he repeats the Mother's name at the three holy hours? . . .

Intoxicated with ecstatic love, the Master said: "How long should one perform devotions? So long as one's mind does not merge in God while repeating Om."

PUNDIT: "Then let me eat the refreshments. I shall perform the devotions later on."

MASTER: "No, I don't want to obstruct the current of your life. It is not good to renounce anything before the proper time arrives. When the fruit ripens, the flower drops off of itself. One shouldn't forcibly tear off the green branch of a coconut tree. That injures the tree."

Surendra was about to leave. He invited his friends into his carriage. The Master, still in an ecstatic mood, said, "Don't take more people than your horse can draw." Surendra took leave of Sri Ramakrishna. The pundit left the room to perform his worship. M. and Baburam saluted the Master. They were about to leave for Calcutta. Sri Ramakrishna was still in an ecstatic mood.

MASTER (to M.): "I cannot utter a word now. Stay a few minutes."

M. again took his seat and waited for the Master's command. Sri Ramakrishna motioned to Baburam to take a seat and asked him to fan him a little. M. also took part in rendering this personal service to the Master.

MASTER (to M., tenderly): "Why don't you come here so frequently now?"

M: "Not for any special reason. I have been rather busy at home."

MASTER: "Yesterday I came to know Baburam's inner nature. That is why I have been trying so hard to persuade him to live with me. The mother bird hatches the egg in proper time. Boys like Baburam are pure in heart. They have not yet fallen into the clutches of 'woman and gold'. Isn't that so?"

M: "It is true, sir. They are still stainless."

MASTER: "They are like a new pot. Milk kept in it will not turn sour."

M: "Yes, sir."

MASTER: "I need Baburam here. I pass through certain spiritual states when I need someone like him. He says he must not, all at once, live with me permanently, for it will create difficulties. His relatives will make trouble. I am asking him to come here Saturdays and Sundays."

The pundit entered the room with his friends. He had finished his devotions and was ready to eat the refreshments. One of his companions asked the Master: "Shall we succeed in spiritual life? Please tell us what our way is."

MASTER: "You all have the yearning for liberation. If an aspirant has yearning, that is enough for him to realize God. Don't eat any food of the śrāddha ceremony.[16] Live in the world like an unchaste woman. She performs her household duties with great attention, but her mind dwells day and night on her paramour. Perform your duties in the world but keep your mind always fixed on God."

The pundit finished eating his refreshments.

MASTER (to the pundit): "You have read the Gītā, no doubt. It says that there is a special power of God in the man who is honoured and respected by all."

The pundit quoted the verse from the Gītā.

MASTER: "You surely possess divine power."

PUNDIT: "Shall I labour with perseverance to finish the task that I have accepted?"

Sri Ramakrishna forced himself, as it were, to say, "Yes." He soon changed the conversation.

MASTER: "One cannot but admit the manifestation of power. Vidyāsāgar once asked me, 'Has God given more power to some than to others?' I said to him: 'Certainly. Otherwise, how can one man kill a hundred? If there is no special manifestation of power, then why is Queen Victoria so much honoured and respected? Don't you admit it?' He agreed with me."

The pundit and his friends saluted the Master and were about to take their leave. Sri Ramakrishna said to the pundit: "Come again. One hemp-smoker rejoices in the company of another hemp-smoker. They even embrace each other. But they hide at the sight of people not of their own kind. A cow licks the body of her calf; but she threatens a strange cow with her horns." (All laugh.)

The pundit left the room. With a smile the Master said: "He has become 'diluted' even in one day. Did you notice how modest he was? And he accepted everything I said."

[16] Offering of food and drink to deceased relatives, especially ancestors.

Moonlight flooded the semicircular porch. Sri Ramakrishna was still seated there. M. was about to leave.

MASTER (*tenderly*): "Must you go now?"

M: "Yes, sir. Let me say good-bye."

MASTER: "I have been thinking of visiting the houses of the devotees. I want to visit yours also. What do you say?"

M: "That will be very fine."

Thursday, July 3, 1884

Sri Ramakrishna was sitting in Balaram Bose's house in Calcutta. It was the day of the "Return Car Festival". The Lord of the Universe was worshipped in Balaram's house as Jagannāth. There was a small car in the house for use during the Car Festival.

Balaram's father was a pious Vaishnava who devoted most of his time to prayer and meditation in his garden house at Vrindāvan. He also studied devotional books and enjoyed the company of devotees. Balaram had brought his father to Calcutta to meet the Master.

Sri Ramakrishna was in a very happy mood. Seated near him were Ram, Balaram, Balaram's father, M., Manomohan, and several young devotees. He was conversing with them.

MASTER (*to Balaram's father and the others*): "The *Bhaktamāla* is one of the Vaishnava books. It is a fine book. It describes the lives of the various Vaishnava devotees. But it is one-sided. At one place the author found peace of mind only after compelling Bhagavati, the Divine Mother, to take Her initiation according to the Vaishnava discipline.

"Once I spoke highly of Vaishnavcharan to Mathur and persuaded him to invite Vaishnavcharan to his house. Mathur welcomed him with great courtesy. He fed his guest from silver plates. Then do you know what happened? Vaishnav said in front of Mathur, 'You will achieve nothing whatsoever in spiritual life unless you accept Krishna as your Ideal.' Mathur was a follower of the Śākta cult and a worshipper of the Divine Mother. At once his face became crimson. I nudged Vaishnavcharan.

"I understand that the *Bhāgavata* also contains some statements like that. I hear that it is said there that trying to cross the ocean of the world without accepting Krishna as the Ideal Deity is like trying to cross a great sea by holding to the tail of a dog. Each sect magnifies its own view.

"The Śāktas, too, try to belittle the Vaishnavas. The Vaishnavas say that Krishna alone is the Helmsman to take one across the ocean of the world. The Śāktas retort: 'Oh, yes! We agree to that. Our Divine Mother is the Empress of the Universe. Why should She bother about a ferry-boat? Therefore She has engaged that fellow Krishna for the purpose.' (*All laugh.*)

"Besides, how vain people are about their own sects! There are weavers in the villages near Kāmārpukur. Many of them are Vaishnavas and like to talk big. They say: 'Which Vishnu does he worship? The Preserver? Oh, we wouldn't touch him!' Or: 'Which Siva are you talking about? We accept the Ātmārāma Śiva.' Or again, 'Please explain to us which Hari you worship.' They spin their yarn and indulge in talk like that.

"Rati's mother, Rāni Katyayani's favourite confidante, is a follower of Vaishnavcharan. She is a bigoted Vaishnava. She used to visit me very frequently, and none could outdo her in devotion. One day she noticed me eating the prasād from the Kāli temple. Since then I haven't seen even her shadow.

"He is indeed a real man who has harmonized everything. Most people are one-sided. But I find that all opinions point to the One. All views—the Śākta, the Vaishnava, the Vedānta—have that One for their centre. He who is formless is, again, endowed with form. It is He who appears in different forms. The attributeless Brahman is my Father. God with attributes is my Mother. Whom shall I blame? Whom shall I praise? The two pans of the scales are equally heavy.'

"He who is described in the Vedas is also described in the Tantras and the Purānas. All of them speak about the one Satchidānanda. The Nitya and the Līlā are the two aspects of the one Reality. It is described in the Vedas as 'Om Satchidānanda Brahman', in the Tantras as 'Om Satchidānanda Śiva', the ever-pure Śiva, and in the Purānas as 'Om Satchidānanda Krishna'. All the scriptures, the Vedas, the Purānas, and the Tantras, speak only of one Satchidānanda. It is stated in the Vaishnava scriptures that it is Krishna Himself who has become Kāli."

Sri Ramakrishna went to the porch for a few minutes and then returned. As he was going out, Vishvamvhar's daughter, six or seven years old, saluted him. On returning to the room, the Master began talking to the little girl and her companions, who were of the same age.

THE CHILD (to the Master): "I saluted you and you didn't even notice it."

MASTER (smiling): "Did you? I really didn't notice."

CHILD: "Then wait. I want to salute you again—the other foot too."

Sri Ramakrishna laughed and sat down. He returned the salute and bowed to the child, touching the ground with his forehead. He asked her to sing. The child said, "I swear I don't sing." When the Master pressed her again, she said, "Should you press me when I said 'I swear'?" The Master was very happy with the children and sang light and frivolous songs to entertain them. He sang:

> Come, let me braid your hair,
> Lest your husband should scold you
> When he beholds you!

The children and the devotees laughed.

MASTER (to the devotees): "The paramahamsa is like a five-year-old child. He sees everything filled with Consciousness. At one time I was staying at Kāmārpukur when Shivaram[17] was four or five years old. One day he was trying to catch grasshoppers near the pond. The leaves were moving. To stop their rustling he said to the leaves: 'Hush! Hush! I want to catch a grasshopper.' Another day it was stormy. It rained hard. Shivaram was with me inside the house. There were flashes of lightning. He wanted to open the door and go out. I scolded him and stopped him, but still he peeped out

[17] A nephew of the Master.

now and then. When he saw the lightning he exclaimed, 'There, uncle! They are striking matches again!'

"The paramahamsa is like a child. He cannot distinguish between a stranger and a relative. He isn't particular about worldly relationships. One day Shivaram said to me, 'Uncle, are you my father's brother or his brother-in-law?'

"The paramahamsa is like a child. He doesn't keep any track of his whereabouts. He sees everything as Brahman. He is indifferent to his own movements. Shivaram went to Hriday's house to see the Durgā Pujā. He slipped out of the house and wandered away. A passer-by saw the child, who was then only four years old, and asked, 'Where do you come from?' He couldn't say much. He only said the word 'hut'. He was speaking of the big hut in which the image of the Divine Mother was being worshipped. The stranger asked him further, 'Whom are you living with?' He only said the word 'brother'.

"Sometimes the paramahamsa behaves like a madman. When I experienced that divine madness I used to worship my own sexual organ as the Śiva-phallus. But I can't do that now. A few days after the dedication- of the temple at Dakshineswar, a madman came there who was really a sage endowed with the Knowledge of Brahman. He had a bamboo twig in one hand and a potted mango-plant in the other, and was wearing torn shoes. He didn't follow any social conventions. After bathing in the Ganges he didn't perform any religious rites. He ate something that he carried in a corner of his wearing-cloth. Then he entered the Kāli temple and chanted hymns to the Deity. The temple trembled. Haladhari was then in the shrine. The madman wasn't allowed to eat at the guest-house, but he paid no attention to this slight. He searched for food in the rubbish heap where the dogs were eating crumbs from the discarded leaf-plates. Now and then he pushed the dogs aside to get his crumbs. The dogs didn't mind either. Haladhari followed him and asked: 'Who are you? Are you a purnajnāni?'[18] The madman whispered, 'Sh! Yes, I am a purnajnāni.' My heart began to palpitate as Haladhari told me about it. I clung to Hriday. I said to the Divine Mother, 'Mother, shall I too have to pass through such a state?' We all went to see the man. He spoke words of great wisdom to us but behaved like a madman before others. Haladhari followed him a great way when he left the garden. After passing the gate he said to Haladhari: 'What else shall I say to you? When you no longer make any distinction between the water of this pool and the water of the Ganges, then you will know that you have Perfect Knowledge.' Saying this he walked rapidly away."

Sri Ramakrishna began to talk with M. Other devotees, too, were present.

MASTER (to M.): "How do you feel about Shashadhar?"

M: "He is very nice."

MASTER: "He is very intelligent, isn't he?"

M: "Yes, sir. He is very erudite."

MASTER: "According to the Gitā there is a power of God in one who is respected and honoured by many. But Shashadhar has still a few things to do.

[18] A perfect knower of Brahman.

What will he accomplish with mere scholarship? He needs to practise some austerity. It is necessary to practise some spiritual discipline.

"Gauri Pundit practised austerity. When he chanted a hymn to the Divine Mother, the other pundits would seem no more than earthworms.

"Narayan Shastri was not merely a scholar, either. He practised sādhanā as well. He studied for twenty-five years without a break. Nyāya alone, he studied for seven years. Still he would go into ecstasy while repeating the name of Śiva. The King of Jaipur wanted to make him his court pundit, but Narayan refused. He used to spend much time here. He had a great desire to go to the Vasishtha Āśrama to practise tapasyā. He often spoke to me about it, but I forbade him to go there. At that he said: 'Who knows when I shall die? When shall I practise sādhanā? Any day I may crack.' After much insistence on his part I let him go. Some say that he is dead, that he died while practising austerity. Others say that he is still alive and that they saw him off on a railway train.

"Before meeting Keshab, I asked Narayan Shastri to visit him and tell me what he thought of him. Narayan reported that Keshab was an adept in japa. He knew astrology and remarked that Keshab had been born under a good star. Then I went to visit Keshab in the garden house at Belgharia. Hriday was with me. The moment I saw Keshab, I said: 'Of all the people I see here, he alone has dropped his tail. He can now live on land as well as in water, like a frog.'

"Keshab sent three members of the Brāhmo Samāj to the temple garden at Dakshineswar to test me. Prasanna was one of them. They were commissioned to watch me day and night, and to report to Keshab. They were in my room and intended to spend the night there. They constantly uttered the word 'Dayāmaya'[19] and said to me: 'Follow Keshab Babu. That will do you good.' I said, 'I believe in God with form.' Still they went on with their exclamations of 'Dayāmaya!' Then a strange mood came over me. I said to them, 'Get out of here!' I didn't allow them to spend the night in my room. So they slept on the verandah. Captain also spent the night in the temple garden the first time he visited me.

"Michael[20] visited the temple garden when Narayan Shastri was living with me. Dwarika Babu, Mathur's eldest son, brought him here. The owners of the temple garden were about to get into a lawsuit with the English proprietors of the neighbouring powder magazine; so they wanted Michael's advice. I met him in the big room next to the manager's office. Narayan Shastri was with me. I asked Narayan to talk to him. Michael couldn't talk very well in Sanskrit. He made mistakes. Then they talked in the popular dialect. Narayan Shastri asked him his reason for giving up the Hindu religion. Pointing to his stomach, Michael said, 'It was for this.' Narayan said, 'What shall I say to a man who gives up his religion for his belly's sake?' Thereupon Michael asked me to say something. I said: 'I don't know

---

[19] "The Compassionate One." The Brāhmos are fond of using this name for God, whom they believe to be formless and yet personal and endowed with attributes.

[20] Michael Madhusudan Dutt, a lawyer, and one of the greatest of Bengali poets. He was a convert to Christianity.

why, but I don't feel like saying anything. Someone seems to be pressing my tongue.' "

MANOMOHAN: "Mr. Choudhury will not come. He said: 'That fellow Shashadhar from Faridpur will be there. I shall not go.' "

Mr. Choudhury had obtained his Master's degree from Calcutta University. He drew a salary of three or four hundred rupees. After the death of his first wife he had felt intense dispassion for the world, but after some time he had married again. He frequently visited the Master at the temple garden.

MASTER: "How mean of him! He is vain of his scholarship. Besides, he has married a second time. He looks on the world as a mere mud-puddle.

(*To the devotees*) "This attachment to 'woman and gold' makes a man small-minded. When I first saw Haramohan he had many good traits. I longed to see him. He was then seventeen or eighteen years old. I used to send for him every now and then, but he wouldn't come. He is now living away from the family with his wife. He had been living with his uncle before. That was very good. He had no worldly troubles. Now he has a separate home and does the marketing for his wife daily. The other day he came to Dakshineswar. I said to him: 'Go away. Leave this place. I don't even feel like touching you.' "

Sri Ramakrishna went to the inner apartments to see the Deity. He offered some flowers. The ladies of Balaram's family were pleased to see him.

The Master came back to the drawing-room and said: "The worldly-minded practise devotions, japa, and austerity only by fits and starts. But those who know nothing else but God repeat His name with every breath. Some always repeat mentally, 'Om Rāma'. Even the followers of the path of knowledge repeat, 'Soham', 'I am He'. There are others whose tongues are always moving, repeating the name of God. One should remember and think of God constantly."

Pundit Shashadhar entered the room with one or two friends and saluted the Master.

MASTER (*smiling*): "We are like the bridesmaids waiting near the bed for the arrival of the groom."

The pundit laughed. The room was filled with devotees, among them Dr. Pratap and Balaram's father. The Master continued his talk.

MASTER (*to Shashadhar*): "The first sign of knowledge is a peaceful nature, and the second is absence of egotism. You have both. There are other indications of a jnāni. He shows intense dispassion in the presence of a sādhu, is a lion when at work, for instance, when he lectures, and is full of wit before his wife. (*All laugh.*)

"But the nature of the vijnāni is quite different, as was the case with Chaitanyadeva. He acts like a child or a madman or an inert thing or a ghoul. While in the mood of a child, he sometimes shows childlike guileless-ness, sometimes the frivolity of adolescence, and sometimes, while instruct-ing others, the strength of a young man."

PUNDIT: "By what kind of bhakti does one realize God?"

MASTER: "Three kinds of bhakti are found, according to the nature of the man: sāttvic bhakti, rājasic bhakti, and tāmasic bhakti.

"Sāttvic bhakti is known to God alone. It makes no outward display. A man with such devotion loves privacy. Perhaps he meditates inside the mosquito net, where nobody sees him. When this kind of devotion is awakened, one hasn't long to wait for the vision of God. The appearance of the dawn in the east shows that the sun will rise before long.

"A man with rājasic bhakti feels like making a display of his devotion before others. He worships the Deity with 'sixteen ingredients',[21] enters the temple wearing a silk cloth, and puts around his neck a string of rudrāksha beads interspersed here and there with beads of gold and ruby.

"A man with tāmasic bhakti shows the courage and boisterousness of a highway robber. A highway robber goes on his expedition openly, shouting, 'Kill! Plunder!' He isn't afraid even of eight police inspectors. The devotee with tāmasic bhakti also shouts like a madman: 'Hara! Hara! Vyom! Vyom![22] Victory to Kāli!' He has great strength of mind and burning faith.

"A Śākta has such faith. He says: 'What? I have uttered once the name of Kāli and of Durgā! I have uttered once the name of Rāma! Can there be any sin in me?'

"The Vaishnavas have a very humble and lowly attitude. (Looking at Balaram's father) They tell their rosary and whine and whimper: 'O Krishna, be gracious to us! We are wretched! We are sinners!'

"A man should have such fiery faith as to be able to say, 'I have uttered the name of God; how can I be a sinner?' Imagine a man repeating the name of Hari day and night and at the same time saying that he is a sinner!"

So saying, Sri Ramakrishna became overwhelmed with divine ecstasy and sang:

> If only I can·pass away repeating Durgā's name,
> How canst Thou then, O Blessed One,
> Withhold from me deliverance,
> Wretched though I may be?
> I may have stolen a drink of wine, or killed a child unborn,
> Or slain a woman or a cow,
> Or even caused a brāhmin's death;
> But, though it all be true,
> Nothing of this can make me feel the least uneasiness;
> For through the power of Thy sweet name
> My wretched soul may still aspire
> Even to Brahmanhood.

He sang again:

> Behold my Mother playing with Śiva, lost in an ecstasy of joy!
> Drunk with a draught of celestial wine, She reels, and yet She
> does not fall.

[21] As prescribed in the books of Hindu ritual.
[22] By such loud exclamations a devotee of Śiva invokes his Ideal Deity.

Erect She stands on Śiva's bosom, and the earth trembles under
    Her tread;
She and Her Lord are mad with frenzy, casting aside all fear and
    shame!

Pundit Shashadhar was weeping. Vaishnavcharan, the musician, sang:

O tongue, always repeat the name of Mother Durgā!
Who but your Mother Durgā will save you in distress?
Thou art the heavens and the earth, and Thou the nether world;
From Thee have the twelve Gopālas and Hari and Śiva sprung.
The ten Embodiments of Divine Śakti art Thou,
And Thou the ten Avatārs: this time, save me Thou must!
The moving and the unmoving, the gross and the subtle, art Thou;
Creation and preservation art Thou, and the last dissolution.
Thou art the Primal Root of this manifold universe;
The Mother of the three worlds, their only Saviour, art Thou;
Thou art the Śakti of all, and Thou Thine own Śakti, too.

As the Master listened to the last few lines, he went into an ecstatic mood.
The Master himself sang:[23]

O Mother, for Yaśodā Thou wouldst dance, when she called Thee
    her precious "Blue Jewel":[24]
Where hast Thou hidden that lovely form, O terrible Śyāmā?
Dance that way once for me, O Mother! Throw down Thy sword
    and take the flute;
Cast off Thy garland of heads, and wear Thy wild-flower garland.
If without Śiva Thou canst not dance, then let Balarāma be Thy
    Śiva.
Dance, O Śyāmā, as Thou didst dance when Thou wast Krishna!

Mother, play on Thy flute again, once so full of delight for the
    gopis;
Play again on Thy magic flute, which called the cattle in from the
    pasture,
Stopping the Jamunā's murmuring flow and turning it backward.

Hot in the sky the sun would burn, when Yaśodā, restless for her
    Krishna,
Fondly would call: "Here, my Gopāla! Cream and butter—eat
    them, my Darling!"
And she would comb His long black hair and carefully braid it.

Bending Thy supple body, Mother, both at the neck, the waist,
    and the knee,
Thou didst dance with Thy friend Śridāma, while Thy two anklets
    played the music:
Tā-thaiā! Tā-thaiā! Tā-tā! Thaiā-thaiā!
Hearing their captivating sound, the gopis would rush there.

Again Pundit Shashadhar shed tears of love.
Sri Ramakrishna came down to consciousness of the world. Pointing to
[23] This song signifies the oneness of Krishna and Kāli.
[24] A pet name of the Baby Krishna.

Shashadhar, he said to M., "Why don't you prod him?" He wanted M. or
some other devotee to ask Shashadhar a question.

RAMDAYAL (to Shashadhar): "The scriptures speak of Brahman's form as a
projection of mind. Who is it that projects?"

SHASHADHAR: "It is Brahman Itself that does so. It is no projection of a
man's mind."

PRATAP: "Why does Brahman project the form?"

MASTER: "You ask why? Brahman doesn't act in consultation with others.
It is Brahman's pleasure. Brahman is self-willed. Why should we try to
know the reason for Brahman's acting this way or that? You have come to
the orchard to eat mangoes. Eat the mangoes. What is the good of calculating
how many trees there are in the orchard, how many thousands of branches,
and how many millions of leaves? One cannot realize Truth by futile arguments and reasoning."

PRATAP: "Shouldn't we reason any more then?"

MASTER: "I am asking you not to indulge in futile reasoning. But reason,
by all means, about the Real and the unreal, about what is permanent and
what is transitory. You must reason when you are overcome by lust, anger,
or grief."

SHASHADHAR: "That is different. It is called reasoning based on discrimination."

MASTER: "Yes, discrimination between the Real and the unreal."

All sat in silence. Again the Master spoke, addressing the pundit.

MASTER: "Formerly many great men used to come here."

SHASHADHAR: "You mean rich people?"

MASTER: "No. Great scholars."

In the mean time the small car of Jagannāth had been brought to the
verandah. Inside the car were the images of Krishna, Balarāma, and Subha-
drā. They were adorned with flowers, garlands, jewelry, and yellow apparel.
Balaram was a sāttvic worshipper: there was no outward grandeur in his
worship. Outsiders did not even know of this Car Festival at his house. The
Master and the devotees went to the verandah. Sri Ramakrishna pulled the
car by the rope. Then he began to sing:

> See how all Nadiā is shaking
> Under the waves of Gaurānga's love. . . .

He sang again:

> Behold, the two brothers[25] have come, who weep while chanting
>   Hari's name,
> The brothers who, in return for blows, offer to sinners Hari's
>   love. . . .

Sri Ramakrishna danced with the devotees. The musician and his party
joined the Master in the music and dancing. Soon the whole verandah was
filled with people. The ladies witnessed this scene of joy from an adjoining

<hr>

[25] Gaurānga and Nityānanda.

room. It appeared as if Chaitanya himself were dancing with his devotees, intoxicated with divine love.

It was not yet dusk. Sri Ramakrishna returned to the drawing-room with the devotees.

MASTER (to Shashadhar): "This is called bhajanānanda, the bliss of devotees in the worship of God. Worldly people keep themselves engrossed in the joy of sensuous objects, of 'woman and gold'. Through worship devotees receive the grace of God, and then His vision. Then they enjoy Brahmānanda, the Bliss of Brahman."

Shashadhar and the devotees listened to these words with rapt attention.

SHASHADHAR (humbly): "Sir, please tell us what kind of yearning gives one this blissful state of mind."

MASTER: "One feels restless for God when one's soul longs for His vision. The guru said to the disciple: 'Come with me. I shall show you what kind of longing will enable you to see God.' Saying this, he took the disciple to a pond and pressed his head under the water. After a few moments he released the disciple and asked, 'How did you feel?' The disciple answered: 'Oh, I felt as if I were dying! I was longing for a breath of air.' "

SHASHADHAR: "Yes! Yes! That's it. I understand it now."

MASTER: "To love God is the essence of the whole thing. Bhakti alone is the essence. Nārada said to Rāma, 'May I always have pure love for Your Lotus Feet; and may I not be deluded by Your world-bewitching māyā!' Rāma said to him, 'Ask for some other boon.' 'No,' said Nārada, 'I don't want anything else. May I have love for Your Lotus Feet. This is my only prayer.' "

Pundit Shashadhar was ready to leave. Sri Ramakrishna asked a devotee to bring a carriage for the pundit.

SHASHADHAR: "Don't trouble yourself. I shall walk."

MASTER (smiling): "Oh, how can that be? 'You are beyond the reach of even Brahmā's meditation.' "

SHASHADHAR: "There is no particular need of my going just now. The only thing is that I shall have to perform my sandhyā."

MASTER: "The Divine Mother has taken away my sandhyā and other devotions. The purpose of the sandhyā is to purify body and mind. I am no longer in that state."

The Master sang the following lines of a song:

> When will you learn to lie, O mind, in the abode of Blessedness,
> With Cleanliness and Defilement on either side of you?
> Only when you have found the way
> To keep these wives contentedly under a single roof,
> Will you behold the matchless form of Mother Śyāmā.

Pundit Shashadhar saluted the Master and went away.

RAM: "I visited Shashadhar yesterday. You asked me to."

MASTER: "Did I? I don't remember. But it is nice that you went."

RAM: "The editor of a newspaper[26] was abusing you."

---

[26] The Indian Empire.

MASTER: "Suppose he was. What does it matter?"

RAM: "Please listen. Then I began to talk to the editor about you. He wanted to hear more and wouldn't let me go."

It was dusk. Sri Ramakrishna began to chant the names of the Divine Mother, Krishna, Rāma, and Hari. The devotees sat in silence. The Master chanted the names in such sweet tones that the hearts of the devotees were deeply touched. That day Balaram's house was like Navadvip when Chaitanya lived there. On the verandah it was like Navadvip, and in the parlour it was like Vrindāvan.

That same night Sri Ramakrishna was to go to Dakshineswar. Balaram took him into the inner apartments and served him with refreshments. The ladies of the family saluted the Master.

The devotees were singing kirtan in the drawing-room, awaiting the Master's coming. Presently Sri Ramakrishna came and joined the singers.

The kirtan went on:

> Behold, my Gorā is dancing! With the devotees
> He dances in Śrivās's courtyard, singing the kirtan.
> Gorā says to all, "Repeat the name of Hari!"
> He looks at Gadādhar, and from his red eyes
> Are flowing tears of love over his golden body.

The Master improvised the lines:

> Gorā is dancing in the kirtan:
> There he dances, Sachi's darling!
> There he dances, my Gaurānga!
> There he dances, my soul's beloved!

FESTIVAL AT ADHAR'S HOUSE

S^{RI RAMAKRISHNA} was sitting in his room in the temple garden at Dakshineswar after his midday meal. A party of Bāuls from Shibpur, several devotees from Bhawānipur, Balaram, and M. were in the room. Rakhal, Latu, and Harish were then living with the Master. They too were present.

The Master began the conversation by addressing the Bāul musicians from Shibpur.

MASTER: "Yoga is not possible if the mind dwells on 'woman and gold'. The mind of a worldly man generally moves among the three lower centres: those at the navel, at the sexual organ, and at the organ of evacuation. After great effort and spiritual practice the Kundalini is awakened. According to the yogis there are three nerves in the spinal column: Idā, Pingalā, and Sushumnā. Along the Sushumnā are six lotuses, or centres, the lowest being known as the Mulādhāra. Then come successively Svādhisthāna, Manipura, Anāhata, Viśuddha, and Ājnā. These are the six centres. The Kundalini, when awakened, passes through the lower centres and comes to the Anāhata, which is at the heart. It stays there. At that time the mind of the aspirant is withdrawn from the three lower centres. He feels the awakening of Divine Consciousness and sees Light. In mute wonder he sees that radiance and cries out: 'What is this? What is this?'

"After passing through the six centres, the Kundalini reaches the thousand-petalled lotus known as the Sahasrāra, and the aspirant goes into samādhi.

"According to the Vedas these centres are called 'bhumi', 'planes'. There are seven such planes. The centre at the heart corresponds to the fourth plane of the Vedas. According to the Tantra there is in this centre a lotus called Anāhata, with twelve petals.

"The centre known as Viśuddha is the fifth plane. This centre is at the throat and has a lotus with sixteen petals. When the Kundalini reaches this plane, the devotee longs to talk and hear only about God. Conversation on worldly subjects, on 'woman and gold', causes him great pain. He leaves a place where people talk of these matters.

"Then comes the sixth plane, corresponding to the centre known as Ājnā. This centre is located between the eyebrows and it has a lotus with two petals. When the Kundalini reaches it, the aspirant sees the form of God. But still there remains a slight barrier between the devotee and God. It is like a light inside a lantern. You may think you have touched the light, but in reality you cannot because of the barrier of glass.

"And last of all is the seventh plane, which, according to Tantra, is the centre of the thousand-petalled lotus. When the Kundalini arrives there, the aspirant goes into samādhi. In that lotus dwells Satchidānanda Śiva, the Absolute. There Kundalini, the awakened Power, unites with Śiva. This is known as the union of Śiva and Śakti.

"When the Kundalini rises to the Sahasrāra and the mind goes into samādhi, the aspirant loses all consciousness of the outer world. He can no longer retain his physical body. If milk is poured into his mouth, it runs out again. In that state the life-breath lingers for twenty-one days and then passes out. Entering the 'black waters' of the ocean, the ship never comes back. But the Iśvarakotis, such as the Incarnations of God, can come down from this state of samādhi. They can descend from this exalted state because they like to live in the company of devotees and enjoy the love of God. God retains in them the 'ego of Knowledge' or the 'ego of Devotion' so that they may teach men. Their minds move between the sixth and the seventh planes. They run a boat-race back and forth, as it were, between these two planes.

"After attaining samādhi some souls of their own accord keep the 'ego of Knowledge'. But that ego does not create any attachment. It is like a line drawn on the water.

"Hanumān kept the 'servant ego' after realizing God in both His Personal and His Impersonal aspects. He thought of himself as the servant of God. The great sages, such as Nārada, Sanaka, Sananda, Sanātana, and Sanat-kumāra, after attaining the Knowledge of Brahman, kept the 'servant ego' and the 'ego of Devotion'. They are like big steamships, which not only cross the ocean themselves but carry many passengers to the other shore.

"There are two classes of paramahamsas, one affirming the formless Reality and the other affirming God with form. Trailanga Swami believed in the formless Reality. Paramahamsas like him care for their own good alone; they feel satisfied if they themselves attain the goal.

"But those paramahamsas who believe in God with form keep the love of God even after attaining the Knowledge of Brahman, so that they may teach spiritual truth to others. They are like a pitcher brimful of water. Part of the water may be poured into another pitcher. These perfected souls describe to others the various spiritual disciplines by which they have realized God. They do this only to teach others and to help them in spiritual life. With great effort men dig a well for drinking-water, using spades and baskets for the purpose. After the digging is over, some throw the spades and other implements into the well, not needing them any more. But some put them away near the well, so that others may use them.

"Some eat mangoes secretly and remove all trace of them by wiping their mouths with a towel. But some share the fruit with others. There are sages who, even after attaining Knowledge, work to help others and also to enjoy the Bliss of God in the company of devotees. 'I want to eat sugar. I don't want to be sugar.'

"The gopis of Vrindāvan, too, attained the Knowledge of Brahman; but they were not seeking It. They wanted to enjoy God, looking on themselves as His mother, His friend, His handmaid, or His lover."

The Bāuls from Shibpur began to sing to the accompaniment of a stringed instrument. A line in the first song was:

We are sinners: redeem us, O merciful Lord!

MASTER (to the devotees): "It is the attitude of a beginner to worship God out of fear. Please sing about God-realization—songs expressing divine joy.

(To Rakhal) "How well they sang that song the other day at Nabin Niyogi's house: 'Be drunk, O mind, be drunk with the Wine of Heavenly Bliss'! While singing religious songs one should not constantly refer to one's worries. One should rather feel joyous and ecstatic as one chants God's name."

A DEVOTEE: "Sir, won't you sing?"

MASTER: "What shall I sing? Well, I may sing when the spirit moves me."

After a few minutes the Master began to sing. His eyes were turned upward. He sang.

Lehold the waves of Gorā's ecstatic love;
Under them all the universe lies submerged!
And in his love I, too, long to be drowned.
O friend, Gaurānga's love has swallowed me;
Who else feels for our misery like Gaurānga,
Dragging us from the mire of worldliness?

He sang again:

Dive deep, O mind, dive deep in the Ocean of God's·Beauty;
If you descend to the uttermost depths,
There you will find the gem of Love. . . .

Then he sang about the Divine·Mother:

Can everyone have the vision of Śyāmā? Is Kāli's treasure for
    everyone?
Oh, what a pity my foolish mind will not see what is true! . . .

He continued:

The black bee of my mind is drawn in sheer delight
To the blue lotus flower of Mother Śyāmā's feet. . . .

And again:

O Mother, what a machine[1] is this that Thou hast made!
What pranks Thou playest with this toy
Three and a half cubits high! . . .

[1] The human body.

As Sri Ramakrishna sang the last song he went into samādhi. The devotees sat speechless, gazing at his radiant figure. After some time he regained partial consciousness of the world and began to talk to the Divine Mother.

The Master said, "Mother, please come down from up there." Did he feel his mind still lingering in the seventh plane of consciousness, the thousand-petalled lotus of the Sahasrāra?

"Please do come down", he said. "Don't torment me that way. Be still, Mother, and sit down.

"O Mother, everybody's future is determined by the tendencies of his previous births. What shall I say to these people? Nothing can be achieved without discrimination and renunciation."

Sri Ramakrishna had now regained full consciousness of the world, and he continued: "There are many kinds of renunciation. One of them may be called 'markatavairāgya', 'monkey renunciation'. It is a false renunciation stimulated by the afflictions of the world. That renunciation doesn't last long. Then there is real renunciation. A man with everything in the world, lacking nothing, feels all to be unreal.

"It is not possible to acquire renunciation all at once. The time factor must be taken into account. But it is also true that a man should hear about it. When the right time comes, he will say to himself, 'Oh yes, I heard about this.'

"You must also remember another thing. By constantly hearing about renunciation one's desire for worldly objects gradually wears away. One should take rice-water in small doses to get rid of the intoxication of liquor. Then one gradually becomes normal.

"An aspirant entitled to the Knowledge of God is very rare. It is said in the Gītā that one in thousands desires to know God, and again, that among thousands who have such a desire, only one is able to know Him."

A devotee quoted the text from the Gītā.

MASTER: "As your attachment to the world diminishes, your spiritual knowledge will increase. Attachment to the world means attachment to 'woman and gold'.

"It is not given to everybody to feel prema, ecstatic love of God. Chaitanya experienced it. An ordinary man can at the most experience bhāva. Only the Iśvarakotis, such as Divine Incarnations, experience prema. When prema is awakened the devotee not only feels the world to be unreal, but forgets even the body, which everyone loves so intensely.

"In a Persian book it is said that inside the skin is the flesh, inside the flesh the bone, inside the bone the marrow, and so on, but that prema is the innermost of all. One becomes soft and tender through prema. On account of this prema, Krishna became tribhanga.[2]

"Prema is the rope by which you can tether God, as it were. Whenever you want to see Him you have merely to pull the rope. Whenever you call Him, He will appear before you.

"The mature stage of bhakti is bhāva. When one attains it one remains

---

[2] Literally, "bent in three places". The usual standing figure of Krishna is bent in three places, namely, the neck, the waist, and the knees.

speechless, thinking of Satchidānanda. The feeling of an ordinary man can go only that far. When bhāva ripens it becomes mahābhāva. Prema is the last. You know the difference between a green mango and a ripe one. Unalloyed love of God is the essential thing. All else is unreal.

"Once Rāma was pleased with the prayer of Nārada and told him to ask for a boon. Nārada prayed for pure love and said further, 'O Rāma, please grant that I may not be deluded by Thy world-bewitching māyā.' Rāma said: 'That is all right. But ask for something else.' Nārada replied: 'I don't want anything else. I pray only for pure love.'

"How can a devotee attain such love? First, the company of holy men. That awakens śraddhā, faith in God. Then comes nishthā, single-minded devotion to the Ideal. In that stage the devotee does not like to hear anything but talk about God. He performs only those acts that please God. After nishthā comes bhakti, devotion to God; then comes bhāva. Next mahābhāva, then prema, and last of all the attainment of God Himself. Only for Iśvarakotis, such as the Incarnations, is it possible to have mahābhāva or prema.

"The knowledge of a worldly person, the knowledge of a devotee, and the Knowledge of an Incarnation are by no means of the same degree. The knowledge of a worldly person is like the light of an oil lamp, which shows only the inside of a room. Through such knowledge he eats and drinks, attends to household duties, protects his body, brings up his children, and so on.

"The knowledge of a devotee is like the light of the moon, which illumines objects both inside and outside a room. But such light does not enable him to see a distant or a very minute object.

"The Knowledge of an Incarnation of God is like the light of the sun. Through that light the Incarnation sees everything, inside and outside, big and small.

"The mind of a worldly person is, no doubt, like muddy water; but it can be made clear by a purifying agent. Discrimination and renunciation are the purifying agent."

The Master spoke to the devotees from Shibpur.

MASTER: "Have you any questions to ask?"

A DEVOTEE: "We have listened to your words."

MASTER: "Yes, it is good to listen to these things. But nothing will happen except at the right time. What can quinine do for a fever patient when he runs a high temperature? Only when his temperature comes down through the use of 'fever mixture' or a purgative should quinine be prescribed. There are patients who get rid of their fever even without quinine. A child said to his mother, when he was put to bed, 'Mother, please wake me up when I feel the call of nature.' The mother said: 'My child, I shall not have to wake you. The urge itself will wake you.'

"Different kinds of people come here. Some come by boat with the devotees. But they do not enjoy spiritual talk. They keep nudging their friends and whispering: 'When shall we leave here? When are we going?' If the friends show no sign of getting up, they say, 'We would rather wait for you in the boat.'

"Those who have a human body for the first time need the experience of sense enjoyments. Spiritual consciousness is not awakened unless certain duties have been performed."

The Master was going to the pine-grove. With a smile he said to M., on the semicircular porch, "Well, what do you think of my state of mind?"

M. (*smiling*): "On the surface you are very simple, but inwardly very deep. It is extremely difficult to understand you."

MASTER (*smiling*): "True. It is like the cement floor of a house. People see only the outer surface and do not know how many materials there are under it."

It was about four o'clock in the afternoon. Balaram and several other devotees got into a country boat to return to Calcutta. It was ebb-tide in the Ganges. A gentle breeze was blowing from the south, covering the bosom of the sacred river with ripples. M. looked at the scene a long time. As the boat disappeared in the direction of Calcutta, he came back to the Master.

Sri Ramakrishna was going to the pine-grove. A beautiful, dark rain-cloud was to be seen in the northwest. The Master asked M.: "Do you think it will rain? Please bring my umbrella." M. brought the umbrella. Reaching the Panchavati, the Master said to Latu, who also accompanied him, "Why do you look so sickly?"

LATU: "I can hardly eat anything."

MASTER: "Is that the only reason? It is also a bad time of the year. Are you meditating too much? (*To M.*) I have a request to make of you. Please tell Baburam to stay with me a day or two during Rakhal's absence. Otherwise I shall feel very unhappy."

M: "Yes, sir. I shall tell him."

Sri Ramakrishna asked M. whether he thought that Baburam was guileless.

Presently the Master left them, going in the direction of the pine-trees. After a few minutes M. and Latu, standing in the Panchavati, saw the Master coming back toward them. Behind him the sky was black with the rain-cloud. Its reflection in the Ganges made the water darker. The disciples felt that the Master was God Incarnate, a Divine Child five years old, radiant with the smile of innocence and purity. Around him were the sacred trees of the Panchavati under which he had practised spiritual discipline and had beheld visions of God. At his feet flowed the sacred river Ganges, the destroyer of man's sins. The presence of this God-man charged the trees, shrubs, flowers, plants, and temples with spiritual fervour and divine joy.

Sri Ramakrishna returned to his room and sat on the small couch. He began to praise a medicine that a certain brahmachāri had prepared for him. Referring to this man, Hazra said: "He is now entangled in many worldly anxieties. What a shame! Look at Nabai Chaitanya of Konnagar. Though a householder, he has put on a red cloth."

MASTER: "What shall I say? I clearly see that it is God Himself who has assumed all these human forms. Therefore I cannot take anybody to task."

HAZRA: "Narendra is again involved in a lawsuit."

MASTER: "He doesn't believe in Śakti, the Divine Mother. If one assumes a human body, one must recognize Her."

HAZRA: "Narendra says: 'If I believed in Śakti, all would follow me. Therefore I cannot.'"

MASTER: "But it is not good for him to go to the extreme of denying the Divine Mother. He is now under Śakti's jurisdiction. Even a judge, while giving evidence in a case, comes down and stands in the witness-box.

(To M.) "Have you seen Narendra lately?"

M: "Not during the last few days."

MASTER: "See him and bring him here in a carriage.

(To Hazra) "Well, what is his relation to this [meaning himself]?"

HAZRA: "He expects help from you."

MASTER: "And what about Bhavanath? Would he come here so frequently if he didn't have good tendencies? What about Harish and Latu? They always meditate. Why is that?"

HAZRA: "That's right. Why should they devote all their time to meditation? It is quite a different thing for them to stay here to attend to your personal needs."

MASTER: "Possibly you are right. Perhaps others may take their place now."

Hazra left the room, leaving the Master alone with M.

MASTER: "Does what I say in the state of ecstasy attract people?"

M: "Oh, yes. Very much."

MASTER: "What do people think of me? Do they think anything in particular about me when they see me in that condition?"

M: "We feel in you a wonderful synthesis of knowledge, love, and renunciation, and on the surface a natural spontaneity. Many divine experiences have passed, like huge steamboats, through the deep of your inner consciousness; still you maintain outwardly this utter simplicity. Many cannot understand it, but a few are attracted by this state alone."

MASTER: "There is a sect of Vaishnavas known as the Ghoshpārā, who describe God as the 'Sahaja', the 'Simple One'. They say further that a man cannot recognize this 'Simple One' unless he too is simple. (To M.) Have I any ego?"

M: "Yes, sir. A little. You have kept it to preserve your body, and to enjoy divine love in the company of the devotees and impart spiritual knowledge to them. Further, you have kept this trace of ego by praying to the Divine Mother for it."

MASTER: "No. I have not kept it. It is God Himself who has left it in me. Can you tell me how I appear in the state of samādhi?"

M: "As you said a little while ago, you see the form of God when your mind rises to the 'sixth plane'. When you speak after that, your mind comes down to the 'fifth plane'."

MASTER: "It is God who does all these things. I do not know anything."

M: "That is why you attract people so much. Sir, I have a question to ask. There are two opinions in the scriptures. According to one Purāna, Krishna is Chidātmā, the Absolute, and Rādhā is Chitśakti, Its Divine Power; but according to another, Krishna Himself is Kāli, the Primordial Energy."

MASTER: "This second view is held in the *Devi Purāna*. According to it,

Kāli Herself has become Krishna. But what difference does it make? God is infinite, and infinite are the ways to reach Him."

M. remained speechless with wonder for a few moments and then said: "Oh, now I understand. As you say, the important thing is to climb to the roof. Our goal will be achieved if we can accomplish it by following any of the means—a rope or a pole."

MASTER: "It is through the grace of God that you have understood that. Without His grace doubt is never cleared up.

"The important thing is somehow to cultivate devotion to God and love for Him. What is the use of knowing many things? It is enough to cultivate love of God by following any of the paths. When you have this love, you are sure to attain God. Afterwards, if it is necessary, God will explain everything to you and tell you about the other paths as well. It is enough for you to develop love of God. You have no need of many opinions and discussions. You have come to the orchard to eat mangoes. Enjoy them to your heart's content. You don't need to count the branches and leaves on the trees. It is wise to follow the attitude of Hanumān: 'I do not know the day of the week, the phase of the moon, or the position of the stars; I only contemplate Rāma.' "

M: "I now desire that my activities may be much reduced and that I may devote myself greatly to God."

MASTER: "Ah! Certainly your desire will be fulfilled. But a jnāni can live unattached in the world."

M: "True, sir. But one needs special power to lead an unattached life."

MASTER: "That is also true. But perhaps you wanted the worldly life. Krishna had been enshrined in Rādhā's heart; but Rādhā wanted to sport with Him in human form. Hence all the episodes of Vrindāvan. Now you should pray to God that your worldly duties may be reduced. And you will achieve the goal if you renounce mentally."

M: "But mental renunciation is prescribed for those who cannot give up the world outwardly. For superior devotees total renunciation is enjoined —both outer and inner."

Sri Ramakrishna was silent a few minutes and then resumed the conversation.

MASTER: "How did you like what I said about renunciation a little while ago?"

M: "Very much, sir."

MASTER: "Tell me, what is the meaning of renunciation?"

M: "Renunciation does not mean simply dispassion for the world. It means dispassion for the world and also longing for God."

MASTER: "You are right. You no doubt need money for your worldly life; but don't worry too much about it. The wise course is to accept what comes of its own accord. Don't take too much trouble to save money. Those who surrender their hearts and souls to God, those who are devoted to Him and have taken refuge in Him, do not worry much about money. As they earn, so they spend. The money comes in one way and goes out the other. This is what the Gītā describes as 'accepting what comes of its own accord'."

The Master referred to Haripada and said, "He came here the other day."

M: "He knows how to sing the stories of the Purāna. He sings melodiously about the life of Prahlāda and the nativity of Sri Krishna."

MASTER: "Is that so? That day I looked into his eyes. They had an inward look. I asked him whether he meditated a great deal, but he sat with his eyes cast down and didn't answer. Then I said to him, 'Look here, don't strain yourself too much.'"

It was now dusk. Sri Ramakrishna, as was usual with him during this part of the day, chanted the names of God and turned his mind to contemplation. Soon the moon rose in the sky. The temples, courtyards, and trees were bathed in its silvery light, and millions of broken moons played on the rippling surface of the Ganges. Rakhal and M. were with the Master in his room.

MASTER (to M.): "Baburam says, 'Oh, the worldly life! God forbid!'"

M: "His opinion is based on mere hearsay. What does he know of the world? He is a mere child."

MASTER: "Yes, that is true. Have you noticed Niranjan? He is utterly artless."

M: "Yes, sir. His very appearance attracts people. How expressive his eyes are!"

MASTER: "Not only his eyes, but his entire person. His relatives proposed that he marry. At this he said, 'Why are you going to drown me?' (With a smile) Tell me this. People say that a man finds great pleasure in the company of his wife after the hard work of the day."

M: "That is no doubt true of those who think that way. (To Rakhal, with a smile) We are now being examined. This is a leading question."

Both Rakhal and M. were married.

MASTER (with a smile): "A mother says, 'I shall heave a sigh of relief if I can procure a "shade-tree"[3] for my son. He will rest in its shade when scorched by the heat of the world.'"

M: "True, sir. But there are parents and parents. A father who is spiritually illumined doesn't give his children in marriage. If he does, his is a fine spirituality!"

Adhar Sen arrived from Calcutta and saluted the Master. After a few minutes he went to the temple of Kāli, where M. followed him.

A little later M. was sitting at the bathing-ghat on the Ganges. The flood-tide had just set in. As he listened to the waters lapping against the bank, many pictures of Sri Ramakrishna's divine life flitted before his mind: the Master's deep samādhi, his constant ecstasy, his joy in the love of God, his untiring discourse on spiritual life, his genuine love for the devotees, and, above all, his childlike simplicity. Who was this man? Was it God who had embodied Himself on earth for the sake of His devotees?

Adhar and M. returned to the Master's room. Adhar had been to Chittagong, in East Bengal, on official duty. He was telling the Master about his visit to the Chandranāth Hills and Sītākunda, sacred places of Chittagong.

[3] The word means "wife".

ADHAR: "Near Sītākunda I visited a well where I saw fire in the water. It is always burning on the water with leaping tongues."

MASTER: "How is that possible?"

ADHAR: "The water contains phosphorous."

Presently Ram Chatterji entered the room. The Master said some kind words about him to Adhar.

MASTER: "Ram's presence in the temple garden has relieved us of many anxieties. He searches out Harish, Latu, and the others at meal-time. Very often they are absorbed in meditation in some corner of the temple garden. It is Ram who sees that they eat at the proper time."

Saturday, September 6, 1884

About three o'clock in the afternoon Sri Ramakrishna was seated in Adhar's parlour on the second floor. Narendra, the Mukherji brothers, Bhavanath, M., Hazra, and other devotees were with the Master.

Arrangements were being made for Narendra to sing. While he was tuning the tānpurā, one of the strings snapped, and the Master exclaimed, "Oh! What have you done?" Narendra then tuned the drums. The Master said to him, "You are beating that drum, and I feel as if someone were slapping my cheek."

Referring to the kirtan, Narendra said: "There is not much rhythm in the kirtan. That's why it is so popular and people love it so much."

MASTER: "How silly! People like it because it is so tender and full of pathos."

Narendra sang:

> Sweet is Thy name, O Refuge of the humble!
> It falls like sweetest nectar on our ears
> And comforts us, Beloved of our souls! . . .

He sang again:

> O Lord, must all my days pass by so utterly in vain?
> Down the path of hope I gaze with longing, day and night.
> Thou art the Lord of all the worlds, and I but a beggar here;
> How can I ask of Thee to come and dwell within my heart?
> My poor heart's humble cottage door is standing open wide;
> Be gracious, Lord, and enter there but once, and quench its thirst!

MASTER (to Hazra, smiling): "That was the first song he sang for me."

Narendra sang one or two more songs. Then Vaishnavcharan sang, describing the grief of the gopis at the sight of Krishna as king of Mathurā:

> O Hari, how shall we know You now?
> In Mathurā's royal splendour You have forgotten us. . . .

MASTER: "Won't you sing that one—'O vīnā, sing Lord Hari's name'?"

Vaishnavcharan sang:

> O vīnā, sing Lord Hari's name!
> Without the blessing of His feet

> You cannot know the final Truth.
> The name of Hari slays all grief:
> Sing Hari's name! Sing Krishna's name!
> If only Hari shows His grace,
> Then I shall never be distressed.
> O vīnā, sing His name but once;
> No earthly gem is half so rare.
> Govinda says: In vain my days
> Have passed. No longer may I float
> Here in life's trackless ocean waste!

While listening to the song, the Master became abstracted. Saying "Ah me! Ah me!", he went into samādhi. The devotees were sitting around him, their eyes riveted on him. The room was filled with people.

The musician sang again. As he improvised new lines describing ecstatic love of God, the Master stood up and danced. He himself improvised lines and sang them with outstretched arms. Soon he went into samādhi and sat down, with his head resting on the bolster in front of him. The musician was also carried away with emotion and sang new songs. Sri Ramakrishna again stood up and began to dance. The devotees could not control themselves. They too danced with the Master. While dancing, Sri Ramakrishna every now and then went into deep samādhi. When he was in the deepest samādhi he could not utter a word and his whole body remained transfixed. The devotees danced encircling him. After a while, regaining partial consciousness, he danced with the strength of a lion, intoxicated with ecstatic love. But even then he could not utter a word. Finally, regaining more of the consciousness of the world, he sang again, improvising the lines. An intense spiritual atmosphere was created in Adhar's parlour. At the sound of the loud music a large crowd had gathered in the street.

Sri Ramakrishna danced a long time in the company of the devotees. When he resumed his seat, still tinged with the lingering glow of divine fervour, he asked Narendra to sing "O Mother, make me mad with Thy love".

Narendra sang:

> O Mother, make me mad with Thy love!
> What need have I of knowledge or reason? . . .

MASTER: "And that one—'Upon the Sea of Blissful Awareness'."

Narendra sang:

> Upon the Sea of Blissful Awareness waves of ecstatic love arise:
> Rapture divine! Play of God's Bliss!
> Oh, how enthralling! . . .

MASTER: "And that one too—'In Wisdom's firmament'. Perhaps it is too long. Do you think so? All right, sing it slowly."

Narendra sang:

> In Wisdom's firmament the moon of Love is rising full,
> And Love's flood-tide, in surging waves, is flowing everywhere.
> O Lord, how full of bliss Thou art! Victory unto Thee! . . .

MASTER: "And won't you sing that one—'The Wine of Heavenly Bliss'?"
Narendra sang:

> Be drunk, O mind, be drunk with the Wine of Heavenly Bliss!
> Roll on the ground and weep, chanting Hari's sweet name!
> Fill the arching heavens with your deep lion roar,
> Singing Hari's sweet name! With both your arms upraised,
> Dance in the name of Hari and give His name to all.
> Swim by day and by night in the bliss of Hari's love;
> Slay desire with His name, and blessed be your life!

The Master improvised, "Be drunk with prema and weep, chanting Hari's
sweet name." And, "Be mad with divine fervour and weep, chanting His
name."

Sri Ramakrishna and the devotees rested awhile. Narendra said to the
Master in a low voice, "Will you kindly sing that one?"

MASTER: "My voice has become a little hoarse."

After a few minutes he asked Narendra, "Which one?"

NARENDRA: "'Gaur, whose beauty delights the world.'"

Sri Ramakrishna sang, describing the beauty of Sri Chaitanya:

> Who has brought Gaur to Nadiā—
> Gaur, whose beauty delights the world?
> His face, covered with ringlets of hair,
> Shines like lightning against a dark cloud. . . .

Again he sang, this time about the grief of a gopi at her separation from
Sri Krishna:

> I have not found my Krishna, O friend! How cheerless my home
>   without Him!
> Ah, if Krishna could only be the hair upon my head,
> Carefully I should braid it then, and deck it with bakul-flowers;
> Carefully I should fashion the braids out of my Krishna-hair.
> Krishna is black, and black is my hair; black would be one with
>   black.
>
> Ah, if Krishna could only be the ring I wear in my nose,
> Always from my nose He would hang, and my two lips could
>   touch Him.
> But it can never be, alas! Why should I idly dream?
> Why should Krishna care at all to be the ring in my nose?
>
> Ah, if Krishna could only be the bracelets on my arms,
> Always He would cling to my wrists, and proudly I should walk,
> Shaking my bracelets to make them sound, shaking my arms to
>   show them;
> Down the king's highway I should walk, wearing my Krishna-
>   bracelets.

The music was over. The Master began to talk with the devotees.

MASTER (smiling): "Hazra danced."

NARENDRA: "Yes, a little."

MASTER: "A little?"

NARENDRA: "Yes. His belly danced too." (*All laugh.*)

Pundit Shashadhar's host had been thinking of inviting the Master for dinner.

MASTER: "I have heard that his host is not an honest man. He is immoral."

NARENDRA: "That is why you didn't drink the water he touched. It happened the first day you met Shashadhar at his house. How did you come to know he was immoral?"

MASTER (*smiling*): "Hazra knows of another instance. It happened at Sihore in Hriday's house."

HAZRA: "The man was a .Vaishnava. He came with me to see you [meaning Sri Ramakrishna]. As soon as he sat in front of you, you turned your back on him."

MASTER: "We learnt later that he led an immoral life. (*To Narendra*) You used to say, at first, that these were all hallucinations."

NARENDRA: "How was I to know? Now I see that you are always right."

Adhar had prepared a feast for the Master and the devotees, and now he invited them to the meal. The Master said to the Mukherji brothers: "What? Won't you eat?" They said humbly, "Please excuse us."

MASTER: "But why? You are doing everything else. Why this hesitation only about eating the meal?"

Adhar was a low-caste Hindu. Therefore some of the Master's brāhmin devotees hesitated to eat at his house. They came to their senses at last when they saw Sri Ramakrishna himself eating.

It was about nine o'clock. The Master was resting in the drawing-room with the devotees. He would soon leave for Dakshineswar.

The Mukherji brothers had arranged with a singer of kirtan to entertain the Master the following day. Ram was taking singing-lessons from this musician. Sri Ramakrishna asked Narendra to come to Dakshineswar to hear the kirtan.

MASTER (*to Narendra*): "Come tomorrow, won't you?"

NARENDRA: "I shall try, sir."

MASTER: "You can bathe there and also take your meal. (*Pointing to M.*) He may dine there too. (*To M.*) Are you quite well now? I hope you are not on a diet."

M: "No, sir. I shall come."

Nityagopal was living at Vrindāvan. Chunilal had returned from Vrindāvan only a few days before, and the Master inquired about Nityagopal.

As Sri Ramakrishna was about to leave, M. saluted him, touching the Master's feet with his forehead. The Master said to him tenderly: "Then I shall see you tomorrow. Narendra! Bhavanath! Please come tomorrow." Then with several devotees he set out for Dakshineswar.

The other devotees returned home in the moonlit night, cherishing in their hearts the Master's ecstatic music and dancing.

AT DAKSHINESWAR

IT WAS ABOUT ELEVEN O'CLOCK. The Master was sitting in his room at Dakshineswar. He had not yet taken his midday meal.

Arrangements had been made with the musician Shyamdas to entertain the Master and the devotees with his kirtan. Baburam, M., Manomohan, Bhavanath, Kishori, Chunilal, Haripada, the Mukherji brothers, Ram, Surendra, Tarak, Niranjan, and others arrived at the temple garden. Latu, Harish, and Hazra were staying with the Master.

When M. saluted Sri Ramakrishna, the Master asked: "Where is Narendra? Isn't he coming?" M. told him that Narendra could not come.

A brāhmin devotee was reading to the Master from a book of devotional songs by Rāmprasād. Sri Ramakrishna asked him to continue. The brāhmin read a song, the first line of which was: "O Mother, put on Thy clothes."

MASTER: "Stop, please! These ideas are outlandish and bizarre. Read something that will awaken bhakti."

The brāhmin read:

> Who is there that can understand what Mother Kāli is?
> Even the six darśanas are powerless to reveal Her. . . .

MASTER (to M.): "I got a pain because I lay too long on one side while in samādhi yesterday at Adhar's house; so now I'll take Baburam with me when I visit the houses of the devotees. He is a sympathetic soul."

With these words the Master sang:

> How shall I open my heart, O friend?
> It is forbidden me to speak.
> I am about to die, for lack of a kindred soul
> To understand my misery.
>
> Simply by looking in his eyes,
> I find the beloved of my heart;
> But rare is such a soul, who swims in ecstatic bliss
> On the high tide of heavenly love.

MASTER: "The Bāuls sing songs like that. They also sing another kind of song:

Stay your steps, O wandering monk!
Stand there with begging-bowl in hand,
And let me behold your radiant face.

"According to the Śakti cult the siddha is called a koul, and according to
the Vedānta, a paramahamsa. The Bāuls call him a sāi. They say, 'No one is
greater than a sāi.' The sāi is a man of supreme perfection. He doesn't see
any differentiation in the world. He wears a necklace, one half made of
cow bones and the other of the sacred tulsi-plant. He calls the Ultimate
Truth 'Ālekh', the 'Incomprehensible One'. The Vedas call It 'Brahman'.
About the jīvas the Bāuls say, 'They come from Ālekh and they go unto
Ālekh.' That is to say, the individual soul has come from the Unmanifest
and goes back to the Unmanifest. The Bāuls will ask you, 'Do you know
about the wind?' The 'wind' means the great current that one feels in the
subtle nerves, Iḍā, Pingalā, and Sushumnā, when the Kundalini is awakened. They will ask you further, 'In which station are you dwelling?' According to them there are six 'stations', corresponding to the six psychic centres
of Yoga. If they say that a man dwells in the 'fifth station', it means that his
mind has climbed to the fifth centre, known as the Viśuddha chakra. (To
M.) At that time he sees the Formless."

Saying this the Master sang:

Within the petals of this flower there lies concealed a subtle space,
Transcending which, one sees at length the universe in Space
dissolve.

"Once a Bāul came here. I asked him, 'Have you finished the task of
"refining the syrup"? Have you taken the pot off the stove?' The more you
boil the juice of sugar-cane, the more it is refined. In the first stage of boiling
it is simply the juice of the sugar-cane. Next it is molasses, then sugar, then
sugar candy, and so on. As it goes on boiling, the substances you get are
more and more refined.

"When does a man take the pot off the stove? That is, when does a man
come to the end of his sādhanā? He comes to the end when he has acquired
complete mastery over his sense-organs. His sense-organs become loosened
and powerless, as the leech is loosened from the body when you put lime
on its mouth. In that state a man may live with a woman, but he does not
feel any lust for her.

"Many of the Bāuls follow a 'dirty' method of spiritual discipline. It is like
entering a house through the back door by which the scavengers come.

"One day I was taking my meal when a Bāul devotee arrived. He asked
me, 'Are you yourself eating, or are you feeding someone else?' The meaning
of his words was that the siddha sees God dwelling within a man. The
siddhas among the Bāuls will not talk to persons of another sect; they call
them 'strangers'.

"The Bāuls designate the state of perfection as the 'sahaja', the 'natural'
state. There are two signs of this state. First, a perfect man will not 'smell of
Krishna'. Second, he is like the bee that lights on the lotus but does not sip
the honey. The first means that he keeps all his spiritual feelings within

himself. He doesn't show outwardly any sign of spirituality. He doesn't even utter the name of Hari. The second means that he is not attached to woman. He has completely mastered his senses.

"The Bāuls do not like the worship of an image. They want a living man. That is why one of their sects is called the Kartābhajā. They worship the kartā, that is to say, the guru, as God.

"You see how many opinions there are about God. Each opinion is a path. There are innumerable opinions and innumerable paths leading to God."

BHAVANATH: "Then what should we do?"

MASTER: "You must stick to one path with all your strength. A man can reach the roof of a house by stone stairs or a ladder or a rope-ladder or a rope or even by a bamboo pole. But he cannot reach the roof if he sets foot now on one and now on another. He should firmly follow one path. Likewise, in order to realize God a man must follow one path with all his strength.

"But you must regard other views as so many paths leading to God. You should not feel that your path is the only right path and that other paths are wrong. You mustn't bear malice toward others.

"Well, to what path do I belong? Keshab Sen used to say to me: 'You belong to our path. You are gradually accepting the ideal of the formless God.' Shashadhar says that I belong to his path. Vijay, too, says that I belong to his—Vijay's—path."

Sri Ramakrishna walked toward the Panchavati with M. and a few other devotees. It was midday and time for the flood-tide in the Ganges.

They waited in the Panchavati to see the bore of the tide.

MASTER (to the devotees): "The ebb-tide and flood-tide are indeed amazing. But notice one thing. Near the sea you see ebb-tide and flood-tide in a river, but far away from the sea the river flows in one direction only. What does this mean? Try to apply its significance to your spiritual life. Those who live very near God feel within them the currents of bhakti, bhāva, and the like. In the case of a few—the Iśvarakotis, for instance—one sees even mahābhāva and prema.

(To M.) "What is the explanation of the ebb-tide and flood-tide?"

M: "According to Western astronomy, they are due to the attraction of the sun and the moon."

In order to explain it, M. drew figures on the earth and began to show the Master the movement of the earth, the sun, and the moon. The Master looked at the figures for a minute and said: "Stop, please! It gives me a headache."

Presently the tide came up the Ganges. They heard the sound of the rushing water. The tide struck the bank of the river and flowed toward the north. Sri Ramakrishna looked at it intently and exclaimed like a child: "Look at that boat! I wonder what is going to happen to it."

The Master and M. sat down for a while in the Panchavati, Sri Ramakrishna placing his umbrella on the cement platform. The conversation turned to Narayan. The boy was a student Sri Ramakrishna looked upon him as Nārāyana, God Himself, and was very fond of him.

MASTER: "Have you noticed Naran's[1] nature? He can mix with all, old and young. One cannot do this without a special power. Besides, all love him. Is he really artless?"

M: "I think so."

MASTER: "I understand that he goes to your place. Is that so?"

M: "Yes, sir. He has visited me once or twice."

MASTER: "Will you give him a rupee? Or shall I ask Kali[2] about it?"

M: "Very well, sir. I shall give him the money."

MASTER: "That's fine. It is good to help those who yearn for God. Thus one makes good use of one's money. What will you gain by spending everything on your family?"

Kishori had several children. His salary was too small to support his family. Sri Ramakrishna said to M.: "Naran said he would get a job for Kishori. Please remind him of it."

The Master walked away in the direction of the pine-grove. Returning to the Panchavati, he said to M.: "Please ask someone to spread a mat outside my room. I shall lie down a few minutes. I am coming presently."

When the Master returned to his room, he could not find his umbrella and exclaimed: "You have all forgotten the umbrella! The busybody doesn't see a thing even when it is very near him. A man went to a friend's house to light the charcoal for his smoke, though all the time he had a lighted lantern in his hand. Another man looked everywhere for his towel. Finally he discovered that it had been on his shoulder all the time."

It was about one o'clock in the afternoon. The Master ate the prasad from the Kāli temple. Then he wanted to rest awhile, but the devotees were still sitting in his room. They were asked to go out, and then the Master lay down. He said to Baburam, "Come here; sit near me." Baburam answered, "I am preparing betel-leaf." The Master said, "Put your betel-leaf aside."

The devotees sat under the bakul-tree in the Panchavati. Tarak, who had just returned from Vrindāvan, told them stories of his visit.

A little later Sri Ramakrishna was seated again on his couch, the devotees sitting on the floor. Shyamdas was singing with his party. He sang of the gopis' grief at their separation from Sri Krishna:

> Dry as a desert seemed the happy lake to them:
> The chātak died of thirst, gazing toward the clouds.

The Master became somewhat abstracted, but the musician could not create a spiritual atmosphere. Sri Ramakrishna asked Nabai of Konnagar to sing a kirtan. Nabai was Manomohan's uncle. He lived on the bank of the Ganges, devoting his time to prayer and meditation, and was a frequent visitor of Sri Ramakrishna at Dakshineswar.

Nabai began the kirtan in a loud voice. The Master left the couch and began to dance. Immediately Nabai and other devotees began to dance around him. The atmosphere became intense with spiritual fervour.

[1] Short for Narayan, a young disciple of the Master.
[2] A devotee of the Master.

After the kirtan, Sri Ramakrishna resumed his seat. With great feeling he began to sing of the Divine Mother, his eyes turned upward:

> O Mother, ever blissful as Thou art,
> Do not deprive Thy worthless child of bliss!
> My mind knows nothing but Thy Lotus Feet.
> The King of Death scowls at me terribly;
> Tell me, Mother, what shall I say to him? . . .

He sang again:

> As is a man's meditation, so is his feeling of love;
> As is a man's feeling of love, so is his gain;
> And faith is the root of all. . . .

He continued:

> This world, O Mother, is Thy madhouse! What can I say of all
>   Thy virtues?
> Setting aside Thine elephant, Thou roamest about on foot;
> Putting off Thy gems and pearls, O Self-willed Mother,
> Thou dost adorn Thy comely neck with a garland of human heads.
> Now Thou must rescue Rāmprasād out of the forest of this world.

Again he sang:

> Why should I go to Gangā or Gayā, to Kāśi, Kānchi, or Prabhās,
> So long as I can breathe my last with Kāli's name upon my
>   lips? . . .

And again:

> Dwell, O mind, within yourself;
> Enter no other's home.
> If you but seek there, you will find
> All you are searching for. . . .

And then:

> The black bee of my mind is drawn in sheer delight
> To the blue lotus flower of Mother Śyāmā's feet. . . .

And then:

> Cherish my precious Mother Śyāmā
> Tenderly within, O mind;
> May you and I alone behold Her,
> Letting no one else intrude. . . .

As the Master sang this last song he stood up. He was almost intoxicated with divine love. Again and again he said to the devotees, "Cherish my precious Mother Śyāmā tenderly within." Then he danced and sang:

> Is Kāli, my Mother, really black?
> The Naked One, of blackest hue,
> Lights the Lotus of the Heart. . . .

The Master reeled as he sang. Niranjan came forward to hold him. The Master said to him softly, "Don't touch me, you rascal!" Seeing the Master dance, the devotees stood up. He caught hold of M.'s hand and said: "Don't be foolish! Dance!"

Sri Ramakrishna resumed his seat, still charged with divine ecstasy. Coming down a little to the normal state, he said: "Om! Om! Om! Om! Om! Om Kāli!" Again he said, "Let me have a smoke." Many of the devotees stood around. Mahimacharan was fanning him. The Master asked him to sit down and recite from the scriptures. Mahimacharan recited from the *Mahānirvāna Tantra*:

> Om. I bow to Thee, the Everlasting Cause of the world;
> I bow to Thee, Pure Consciousness, the Soul that sustains the whole universe.
> I bow to Thee, who art One without duality, who dost bestow liberation;
> I bow to Thee, Brahman, the all-pervading Attributeless Reality.
>
> Thou alone art the Refuge, the only Object of adoration;
> Thou art the only Cause of the universe, the Soul of everything that is;
> Thou alone art the world's Creator, Thou its Preserver and Destroyer;
> Thou art the immutable Supreme Lord, the Absolute; Thou art unchanging Consciousness.
>
> Dread of the dreadful! Terror of the terrible!
> Refuge of all beings! Purity of purifiers!
> Thou alone dost rule over those in the high places,
> Supreme over the supreme, the Protector of protectors.
>
> Almighty Lord, who art made manifest as the Form of all, yet art Thyself unmanifest and indestructible;
> Thou who art imperceptible to the senses, yet art the very Truth;
> Incomprehensible, imperishable, all-pervading, hidden, and without form;
> O Lord! O Light of the Universe! Protect us from harm.
>
> On that One alone we meditate; that One is the sole object of our worship;
> To That alone, the non-dual Witness of the Universe, we bow.
> In that One who alone exists and who is our sole eternal Support, we seek refuge,
> The self-dependent Lord, the Vessel of Safety in the ocean of existence.

Sri Ramakrishna listened to the hymn with folded hands. After it was sung he saluted Brahman. The devotees did likewise.

Adhar arrived from Calcutta and bowed down before the Master.

MASTER (to M.): "We have had such joy today! How much joy Hari's name creates! Is it not so?"

M: "Yes, sir."

Mahimacharan was a student of philosophy. That day he too had chanted the name of Hari and danced during the kirtan. This made the Master very happy.

It was about dusk. Many of the devotees took their leave. A lamp was lighted in Sri Ramakrishna's room and incense was burnt. After some time the moon came out, flooding the sky with its light.

Sri Ramakrishna was sitting on his couch. He was in a spiritual mood, absorbed in contemplation of the Divine Mother. Now and then he chanted Her hallowed name. Adhar was sitting on the floor. M. and Niranjan, too, were there. Sri Ramakrishna began to talk to Adhar.

MASTER: "What! You have come just now! We have had so much kirtan and dancing. Shyamdas began the kirtan. He is Ram's music teacher. But I didn't enjoy his singing very much; I didn't feel like dancing. Later I heard about his character. I was told that he had as many mistresses as there are hairs on a man's head.

"Didn't you get the job?"

Adhar held the post of deputy magistrate, a government post that carried with it great prestige. He earned three hundred rupees a month. He had applied for the office of vice-chairman of the Calcutta Municipality. The salary attached to this office was one thousand rupees. In order to secure it, Adhar had interviewed many influential people in Calcutta.

MASTER (to M. and Niranjan): "Hazra said to me, 'Please pray to the Divine Mother for Adhar, that he may secure the job.' Adhar made the same request to me. I said to the Mother: 'O Mother, Adhar has been visiting You. May he get the job if it pleases You.' But at the same time I said to Her: 'How small-minded he is! He is praying to You for things like that and not for Knowledge and Devotion.'

(To Adhar) "Why did you dance attendance on all those small-minded people? You have seen so much; you have heard so much! 'After reading the entire Rāmāyana, to ask whose wife Sītā is!'"

ADHAR: "A man cannot but do these things if he wants to lead a house-holder's life. You haven't forbidden us to, have you?"

MASTER: "Nivritti alone is good, and not pravritti.[3] Once, when I was in a God-intoxicated state, I was asked to go to the manager of the Kāli temple to sign the receipt for my salary.[4] They all do it here. But I said to the manager: 'I cannot do that. I am not asking for any salary. You may give it to someone else if you want.' I am the servant of God alone. Whom else shall I serve? Mallick noticed the late hours of my meals and arranged for a cook. He gave me one rupee for a month's expenses. That embarrassed me. I had to run to him whenever he sent for me. It would have been quite a different thing if I had gone to him of my own accord.

"In leading the worldly life one has to humour mean-minded people and do many such things. After the attainment of my exalted state, I noticed how things were around me and said to the Divine Mother, 'O Mother,

[3] Nivritti and pravritti mean, respectively, inwardness of the mind and its inclination to outer enjoyment.

[4] Sri Ramakrishna was then acting as the salaried priest of the Kāli temple.

please change the direction of my mind right now, so that I may not have
to flatter rich people.'

(*To Adhar*) "Be satisfied with the job you have. People hanker after a
post paying fifty or a hundred rupees, and you are earning three hundred
rupees! You are a deputy magistrate. I saw a deputy magistrate at Kāmārpukur. His name was Ishwar Ghoshal. He had a turban on his head. Men's
very bones trembled before him. I remember having seen him during my
boyhood. Is a deputy magistrate a person to be trifled with?

"Serve him whom you are already serving. The mind becomes soiled by
serving but one master. And to serve five masters!

"Once a woman became attached to a Mussalmān and invited him to her
room. But he was a righteous person; he said to her that he wanted to use
the toilet and must go home to get his water-jar for water. The woman
offered him her own, but he said: 'No, that will not do. I shall use the jar
to which I have already exposed myself. I cannot expose myself before a
new one.' With these words he went away. That brought the woman to
her senses. She understood that a new water-jar, in her case, signified a
paramour."

Narendra was in straitened circumstances on account of his father's
unexpected death. He had been seeking a job to maintain his mother,
brothers, and sisters. He had served a few days as headmaster of the
Vidyāsāgar School at Bowbāzār.

ADHAR: "May I ask if Narendra would accept a job?"

MASTER: "Yes, he would. He has his mother, brothers, and sisters to
support."

ADHAR: "Well, Narendra can support his family with fifty or with a
hundred rupees. Will he try for a hundred?"

MASTER: "Worldly people think highly of their wealth. They feel that
there is nothing like it. Sambhu said, 'It is my desire to leave all my property
at the Lotus Feet of God.' But does God care for money? He wants from
His devotees knowledge, devotion, discrimination, and renunciation.

"After the theft of the jewelry from the temple of Rādhākānta, Mathur
Babu said: 'O God, You could not protect Your own jewelry! What a shame!'
Once he wanted to give me an estate and consulted Hriday about it. I overheard the whole thing from the Kāli temple and said to him: 'Please don't
harbour any such thought. It will injure me greatly.'"

ADHAR: "I can tell you truthfully, sir, that not more than six or seven
persons like you have been born since the creation of the world."

MASTER: "How so? There certainly are people who have given up everything for God. As soon as a man gives up his wealth, people come to know
about him. But it is also true that there are others unknown to people. Are
there not such holy men in upper India?"

ADHAR: "I know of at least one such person in Calcutta. He is Devendranath Tagore."

MASTER: "What did you say? Who has enjoyed the world as much as he?
Once I visited him at his house with Mathur Babu. I saw that he had many
young children. The family physician was there writing out prescriptions.

If, after having eight children, a man doesn't think of God, then who will? If, after enjoying so much wealth, Devendranath hadn't thought of God, then people would have cried shame upon him."

NIRANJAN: "But he paid off all his father's debts."

MASTER: "Keep quiet! Don't torment me any more. Do you call anyone a man who doesn't pay off his father's debts if he is able to? But I admit that Devendranath is infinitely greater than other worldly men, who are sunk in their worldliness. They can learn much from him.

"There is an ocean of difference between a real all-renouncing devotee of God and a householder devotee. A real sannyāsi, a real devotee who has renounced the world, is like a bee. The bee will not light on anything but a flower. It will not drink anything but honey. But a devotee leading the worldly life is like a fly. The fly sits on a festering sore as well as on a sweetmeat. One moment he enjoys a spiritual mood, and the next moment he is beside himself with the pleasure of 'woman and gold'.

"A devotee who has really and truly renounced all for God is like the chātak bird. It will drink only the rain-water that falls when the star Svāti is in the ascendant. It will rather die of thirst than touch any other water, though all around there may lie seven oceans and rivers full to the brim with water. An all-renouncing devotee will not touch 'woman and gold'. He will not keep 'woman and gold' near him lest he should feel attached."

ADHAR: "But Chaitanya, too, enjoyed the world."

MASTER (amazed): "What? What did he enjoy in the world?"

ADHAR: "Scholarship! Honour!"

MASTER: "It was honour in the sight of others, but nothing to him. Whether you—a deputy magistrate—or this youngster Niranjan honours me, it is all the same to me. And I tell you this truthfully: the idea of controlling a wealthy man never enters my mind. Surendra once said, rather condescendingly, that Rakhal's father could sue me for letting Rakhal[5] stay with me. When I heard this from Manomohan, I said: 'Who is this Surendra? How does he dare make a remark like that? He keeps a carpet and pillow here and gives me some money. Is that his excuse for daring to make such an impudent remark?'"

ADHAR: "I understand that he gives ten rupees a month. Isn't that so?"

MASTER: "That covers two months' expenses. The devotees stay here and he gives the money for their service. It is he who earns the merit. What is that to me? Is it for my personal gain that I love Narendra, Rakhal, and the others?"

M: "Your love for them is like a mother's for her children."

MASTER: "But even behind the mother's love lies her hope that the children will support her later on. But I love these youngsters because I see in them Nārāyana Himself. These are not mere words.

(To Adhar) "Listen. There is no scarcity of moths when the lamp is lighted. When God is realized, He Himself provides everything for His devotees. He sees that they do not lack anything. When God is enshrined in the heart, many people come forward to offer their services.

[5] Rakhal was then a minor.

"Once a young sannyāsi went to a householder to beg his food. He had lived as a monk from his very birth; he knew nothing of worldly matters. A young daughter of the householder came out to give him alms. He turned to her mother and said, 'Mother, has this girl abscesses on her chest?' The mother said: 'No, my child. God has given her breasts to nurse her child when she becomes a mother.' Thereupon the sannyāsi said: 'Then why should I worry about myself? Why should I beg my food? He who has created me will certainly feed me.'

"Listen. If a woman renounces everything for her paramour, she can say to him, if need be, 'You wretch! I shall sit on your chest and devour you.'

"Nangtā told me of a certain king who gave a feast to the sādhus, using plates and tumblers of gold. I noticed in the monasteries at Benares with what great respect the abbots were treated. Many wealthy up-country people stood before them with folded hands, ready to obey their commands. But a true sādhu, a man who has really renounced everything, seeks neither a gold plate nor honour. God sees that he lacks nothing. God gives the devotee everything that is needed for realizing Him.

(*To Adhar*) "You are an executive officer. What shall I say to you? Do whatever you think best. I am an illiterate person."

Adhar (*smiling, to the devotees*): "Now he is examining me."

MASTER (*smiling*): "Dispassion alone is good. Don't you see, I didn't sign the receipt for my salary? God alone is real and all else is illusory."

Hazra entered the room and sat with the devotees on the floor. Hazra repeated now and then, "Soham! Soham!", "I am He! I am He!" To Latu and other devotees he often said: "What does one gain by worshipping God with offerings? That is merely giving Him things that are His already." He had said this once to Narendra.

The Master spoke to him.

MASTER: "I explained to Latu who the object of the devotee's worship is."

HAZRA: "The devotee really prays to his own Self."

MASTER: "What you say is a very lofty thought. The aim of spiritual discipline, of chanting God's name and glories, is to realize just that. A man attains everything when he discovers his true Self in himself. The object of sādhanā is to realize that. That also is the purpose of assuming a human body. One needs the clay mould as long as the gold image has not been cast; but when the image is made, the mould is thrown away. The body may be given up after the realization of God.

"God is not only inside us; He is both inside and outside. The Divine Mother showed me in the Kāli temple that everything is Chinmaya, the Embodiment of Spirit; that it is She who has become all this—the image, myself, the utensils of worship, the door-sill, the marble floor. Everything is indeed Chinmaya.

"The aim of prayer, of spiritual discipline, of chanting the name and glories of God, is to realize just that. For that alone a devotee loves God. These youngsters[6] are on a lower level; they haven't yet reached a high

[6] Referring to Latu and the others.

spiritual state. They are following the path of bhakti. Please don't tell them such things as 'I am He'."

Like the mother bird brooding over her chicks, Sri Ramakrishna was alert to protect his devotees.

Adhar and Niranjan went out on the porch to take refreshments. Presently they returned to the room.

ADHAR (smiling): "We talked about so many things. (Pointing to M.) But he didn't utter a word."

MASTER: "In Keshab's organization there was a young man with four university degrees. He laughed when he saw people arguing with me. He said: 'To argue with him! How silly!' I saw him again, later on, at one of Keshab's meetings. But then he did not have the same bright complexion."

Sri Ramakrishna sat on the floor for his supper. It was a light meal of a little farina pudding and one or two luchis that had been offered in the Kāli temple. M. and Latu were in the room. The devotees had brought various sweets for the Master. He touched a sandesh and asked Latu, "Who is the rascal that brought this?" He took it out of the cup and left it on the ground. He said to Latu and M.: "I know all about him. He is immoral."

LATU: "Shall I give you this sweet?"

MASTER: "Kishori brought it."

LATU: "Will it suit you?"

MASTER (smiling): "Yes."

M. had received an English education. Sri Ramakrishna said to him: "It is not possible for me to eat things offered by anyone and everyone. Do you believe this?"

M: "Gradually I shall have to believe all these things."

MASTER: "Yes, that is so."

After finishing the meal Sri Ramakrishna washed his mouth. He said to M., "Then will you give the rupee to Naran?" "Yes," said M., "certainly I will."

The moon rose in the clear autumn sky and was reflected in the river. It was ebb-tide in the Ganges and the river flowed south toward the sea.

Sunday, September 14, 1884

Sri Ramakrishna was sitting in his room with Narendra, Bhavanath, the Mukherji brothers, and other devotees. Rakhal was staying with Balaram at Vrindāvan and was laid up with an attack of fever. Narendra was preparing himself for his coming law examination.

About eleven o'clock Jnan Babu arrived. He was a government official and had received four university degrees.

MASTER (at the sight of Jnan Babu): "Well! Well! This sudden awakening of 'knowledge'!"[7]

JNAN (smiling): "You must admit, sir, that one sees the awakening of knowledge as a result of very good fortune."

MASTER (smiling): "You are Jnan. Then why should you have ajnan,

---

[7] "Jnān" means "knowledge".

ignorance? Oh, I understand. Where there is knowledge there is also ignorance. The sage Vaśishtha was endowed with great knowledge and still he wept at the death of his sons. Therefore I ask you to go beyond both knowledge and ignorance. The thorn of ignorance has pierced the sole of a man's foot. He needs the thorn of knowledge to take it out. Afterwards he throws away both thorns. The jnāni says, 'This world is a "framework of illusion".' But he who is beyond both knowledge and ignorance describes it as a 'mansion of mirth'. He sees that it is God Himself who has become the universe, all living beings, and the twenty-four cosmic principles.

"A man can live in the world after attaining God. Then he can lead the life of detachment. In the country I have seen the women of the carpenter families making flattened rice with a husking-machine. With one hand one of them turns the paddy in the hole and with the other she holds a nursing child. At the same time she talks with the buyer. She says to him: 'You owe me two ānnās. Pay it before you go.' But seventy-five per cent of the woman's mind is on her hand lest it should be crushed by the pestle of the husking-machine.

"A man should do his worldly duties with only twenty-five per cent of his mind, devoting the rest to God."

Referring to Pundit Shashadhar, the Master said to the devotees, "I found him monotonous—engaged in the dry discussion of philosophy.

"He alone who, after reaching the Nitya, the Absolute, can dwell in the Līlā, the Relative, and again climb from the Līlā to the Nitya, has ripe knowledge and devotion. Sages like Nārada cherished love of God after attaining the Knowledge of Brahman. This is called vijnāna.

"Mere dry knowledge is like an ordinary rocket: it bursts into a few sparks and then dies out. But the Knowledge of sages like Nārada and Śukadeva is like a good rocket: for a while it showers balls of different colours, and then it stops; again it throws out new balls, and again it stops; and thus it goes on. Those sages had prema for God. Prema is the rope by which one can reach Satchidānanda."

The Master finished his midday meal and rested a few minutes. Bhavanath, M., the Mukherji brothers, Hazra, and several other devotees sat down under the bakul-tree and began to converse. The Master stopped there awhile on his way to the pine-grove.

HAZRA (to the younger Gopal): "Please prepare a smoke for him [meaning the Master]."

MASTER (smiling): "Why don't you admit that you want it?" (All laugh.)

MUKHERJI (to Hazra): "You must have learnt much wisdom from him [meaning the Master]."

MASTER (smiling): "No, he has been wise like this from his boyhood." (All laugh.)

Presently Sri Ramakrishna returned from the pine-grove. The devotees noticed that he was in an ecstatic mood and was reeling like a drunkard. After reaching his room he regained the normal state.

Many devotees gathered in the room. Among them was a new-comer, a sādhaka from Konnagar, who looked over fifty years of age and seemed to have great vanity of scholarship.

The Master stood in the middle of the room and suddenly said to M., "He came here—Naran."

Narendra was engaged in a discussion with Hazra and a few others on the verandah. They could be heard from the room.

MASTER (*referring to Narendra*): "The chatterbox! But he is now much worried about his family."

M: "Yes, sir, it is true."

MASTER: "Once he said that he would look upon adversity as his good fortune. Isn't that so?"

M: "He has great strength of mind."

A DEVOTEE: "Does he lack strength in anything?"

Pointing to the sādhaka from Konnagar, a devotee said to the Master: "Sir, he has come to visit you. He has some questions to ask." The sādhaka was seated erect, his chin up.

SĀDHAKA: "Sir, what is the way?"

MASTER: "Faith in the guru's words. One attains God by following the guru's instructions step by step. It is like reaching an object by following the trail of a thread."

SĀDHAKA: "Is it possible to see God?"

MASTER: "He is unknowable by the mind engrossed in worldliness. One cannot attain God if one has even a trace of attachment to 'woman and gold'. But He is knowable by the pure mind and the pure intelligence—the mind and intelligence that have not the slightest trace of attachment. Pure Mind, Pure Intelligence, Pure Ātman, are one and the same thing."

SĀDHAKA: "But the scriptures say, 'From Him words and mind return baffled.' He is unknowable by mind and words."

MASTER: "Oh, stop! One cannot understand the meaning of the scriptures without practising spiritual discipline. What will you gain by merely uttering the word siddhi?[8] The pundits glibly quote the scriptures; but what will that accomplish? A man does not become intoxicated even by rubbing siddhi on his body; he must swallow it. What is the use of merely repeating, 'There is butter in the milk'? Turn the milk into curd and churn it. Only then will you get butter."

SĀDHAKA: "You talk about churning butter. But you too are quoting the scriptures."

MASTER: "What will one gain by merely quoting or hearing the scriptures? One must assimilate them. The almanac makes a forecast of the rainfall for the year, but you won't get a drop by squeezing its pages."

SĀDHAKA: "You talk about churning butter. Have you done it yourself?"

MASTER: "You don't have to bother about what I have or haven't done. Besides, it is very difficult to explain these things to others. Suppose someone asks you, 'What does ghee taste like?' Your answer will be, 'Ghee tastes like ghee.'

"To understand these things one needs to live with holy men, just as to

[8] Indian hemp.

understand the pulse of bile,[9] of phlegm, and so on, one needs to live with a physician."

SĀDHAKA: "There are some people who are irritated by others' company."

MASTER: "That happens only after the attainment of Knowledge, after the realization of God. Shouldn't a beginner live in the company of holy men?"

The sādhaka sat in silence a few moments. Then he said with some irritation: "Please tell me whether you have realized God either directly or intuitively. You may answer me if you are able, or you may keep silent if you wish." The Master said with a smile: "What shall I say? One can only give a hint."

SĀDHAKA: "Then tell us that much."

Narendra was going to sing. He said, "No one has brought a pākhoāj."

THE YOUNGER GOPAL: "Mahimacharan has one."

MASTER (interrupting): "No, we don't want anything of his here."

A devotee from Konnagar sang a song. Every now and then Sri Ramakrishna glanced at the sādhaka. The singer and Narendra became engaged in a furious discussion about musical technique. The sādhaka said to the singer, "What is the use of such discussions?" Referring to another man who had joined in the discussion, Sri Ramakrishna said to the sādhaka, "Why didn't you scold him, too?" It could be seen that the sādhaka was not on friendly terms with his companions from Konnagar.

Narendra sang:

O Lord, must all my days pass by so utterly in vain?
Down the path of hope I gaze with longing, day and night. . . .

The sādhaka closed his eyes in meditation as he listened to the song. It was four o'clock in the afternoon. The rays of the setting sun fell on his body. Sri Ramakrishna quickly opened an umbrella and placed it near the door so that the sun might not disturb the sādhaka.

Narendra sang again:

How shall I call on Thee, O Lord, with such a stained and worldly
    mind?
Can a straw remain unharmed, cast in a pit of flaming coals?
Thou, all goodness, art the fire, and I, all sin, am but a straw:
How shall I ever worship Thee?

The glory of Thy name, they say, redeems those even past
    redeeming;
Yet, when I chant Thy sacred name, alas! my poor heart quakes
    with fright.
I spend my life a slave to sin; how can I find a refuge, then,
O Lord, within Thy holy way?

In Thine abounding kindliness, rescue Thou this sinful wretch;
Drag me off by the hair of my head and give me shelter at Thy
    feet.

[9] According to orthodox Hindu medicine, phlegm, bile, and wind are the three humours that control physical health. A physician can determine their condition by feeling the patient's pulse.

Again he sang:

> Sweet is Thy name, O Refuge of the humble!
> It falls like sweetest nectar on our ears
> And comforts us, Beloved of our souls!
> The priceless treasure of Thy name alone
> Is the abode of Immortality,
> And he who chants Thy name becomes immortal.
> Falling upon our ears, Thy holy name
> Instantly slays the anguish of our hearts,
> Thou Soul of our souls, and fills our hearts with bliss!

As Narendra sang the line, "And he who chants Thy name becomes immortal", the Master went into samādhi. At first his fingers, especially the thumbs, began to tremble. The devotees from Konnagar had never seen the Master in samādhi. Seeing him silent, they were about to leave the room. Bhavanath said to them: "Why are you going away? This is his samādhi." The devotees resumed their places.

Narendra sang:

> I have laboured day and night
> To make Thy seat within my heart;
> Wilt Thou not be kind to me,
> O Lord of the World, and enter there?

Sri Ramakrishna, still in the ecstatic mood, came down from his couch to the floor and sat by Narendra. The beloved disciple sang again:

> In Wisdom's firmament the moon of Love is rising full,
> And Love's flood-tide, in surging waves, is flowing everywhere.
> O Lord, how full of bliss Thou art! Victory unto Thee! . . .

As Narendra sang the last line, Sri Ramakrishna stood up, still absorbed in samādhi.

After a long time the Master regained partial consciousness of the world and sat down on the mat. Narendra finished his singing, and the tānpurā was put back in its place. The Master was still in a spiritual mood and said: "Mother, tell me what this is. They want someone to extract the butter for them and hold it to their mouths. They won't throw the spiced bait into the lake. They won't even hold the fishing-rod. Someone must catch the fish and put it into their hands! How troublesome! Mother, I won't listen to any more argument. The rogues force it on me. What a bother! I shall shake it off. God is beyond the Vedas and their injunctions. Can one realize Him by studying the scriptures, the Vedas, and the Vedānta? (To Narendra) Do you understand this? The Vedas give only a hint."

Narendra wanted the tānpurā again. The Master said, "I want to sing." He was still in an ecstatic mood and sang:

> Mother, this is the grief that sorely grieves my heart,
> That even with Thee for Mother, and though I am wide awake,
> There should be robbery in my house. . . .

The Master said, "Mother, why do You make me argue?" He sang again:

> Once for all, this time, I have thoroughly understood;
> From One who knows it well, I have learnt the secret of
> bhāva. . . .

The Master said, "I am quite conscious." But he was still groggy with divine fervour. He sang once more:

> I drink no ordinary wine, but Wine of Everlasting Bliss,
> As I repeat my Mother Kāli's name;
> It so intoxicates my mind that people take me to be drunk! . . .

Sri Ramakrishna had said, "Mother, I won't listen to any more argument." Narendra sang:

> O Mother, make me mad with Thy love!
> What need have I of knowledge or reason? . . .

Sri Ramakrishna said with a smile: "O Mother, make me mad! God cannot be realized through knowledge and reasoning, through the arguments in the scriptures." He had been pleased with the singing of the musician from Konnagar and said to him humbly: "Please sing about the Divine Mother. Please—one song."

MUSICIAN: "You must excuse me, sir."

MASTER (bowing with folded hands): "No, sir. I can enforce this demand." Saying this, Sri Ramakrishna sang a few lines from a kirtan, assuming the attitude of a gopi:

> Rādhā has every right to say it;
> She has kept awake for Krishna.
> She has stayed awake all night,
> And she has every right to be piqued.

Then he said to the musician: "My dear sir, you are a child of the Divine Mother. She dwells in all beings. Therefore I have every right to enforce my demand. A farmer said to his guru, 'I shall get my mantra from you by beating you, if I have to.'"

MUSICIAN (smiling): "By a shoe-beating?"

MASTER (smiling): "No! I won't go that far."

Again in an abstracted mood Sri Ramakrishna said: "The beginner, the struggling, the perfect, and the supremely perfect. Which are you—perfect or supremely perfect? Come along! Sing for us."

The musician complied. He sang just a melody.

MASTER: "My dear sir, that too makes me happy."

The musician then sang a song. When the music was over, the devotees from Konnagar saluted the Master and took their leave. The sādhaka bowed before him with folded hands and said, "Holy man, let me say good-bye."

Sri Ramakrishna, still in an ecstatic mood, was talking to the Divine Mother.

MASTER: "Mother, is it You or I? Do I do anything? No. no! It is You.

Was it You who heard the arguments all this time, or was it I? No, not I. It was You."

Sri Ramakrishna became conscious of the outer world and began to converse with Narendra, Bhavanath, and the other devotees. They were talking about the sādhaka.

BHAVANATH (smiling): "What kind of man is he?"

MASTER: "He is a tāmasic devotee."

BHAVANATH: "He can certainly recite Sanskrit verses."

MASTER: "Once I said to a man about a sādhu: 'He is a rājasic sādhu. Why should one give him food and other presents?' At this another sādhu taught me a lesson by saying to me: 'Don't say that. There are three classes of holy men: sāttvic, rājasic, and tāmasic.' Since that day I have respected holy men of all classes."

NARENDRA (smiling): "What? Is it like the 'elephant God'? All, indeed, are God."

MASTER (smiling): "It is God Himself who sports in the world as both vidyā and avidyā. Therefore I salute both. It is written in the Chandi: 'The Divine Mother is the good fortune of the blessed and the ill fortune of the unlucky.' (To Bhavanath) Is that mentioned in the Vishnu Purāna?"

BHAVANATH (smiling): "I don't know, sir. The devotees from Konnagar did not understand your samādhi and were about to leave the room."

MASTER: "Who was it that asked them to remain?"

BHAVANATH (smiling): "It was I."

MASTER: "My child, you are equally good in bringing people here and in driving them away."

The conversation turned to the argument that Narendra had had with the musician from Konnagar.

MUKHERJI: "Narendra didn't spare him."

MASTER: "That's right. One needs such grit. This is called the influence of tamas on sattva. Must a man listen to everything another man says? Should one say to a prostitute, 'All right, you may do whatever you like'? Must one listen to her? At one time Rādhā was piqued. A friend said, 'Her ego has been roused.' Brindē, another friend, said: 'Whose is this ego? Her ego belongs to Krishna alone. She is proud in the pride of Krishna.'"

The conversation turned to the glory of God's name.

BHAVANATH: "I feel such relief while chanting the name of Hari."

MASTER: "He who relieves us of sin is Hari. He relieves us of our three afflictions in the world. Chaitanya preached the glory of Hari's name; so it must be good. You see, he was such a great scholar, and an Incarnation too. Since he preached that name, it must be good. (Smiling) Once some peasants were invited to a feast. They were asked if they would eat a preparation of hog plum. They answered: 'You may give it to us if the gentlemen have eaten it. If they enjoyed it, then it must be good.' (All laugh.)

(To the Mukherji brothers) "I should like to visit Shivanath. I won't have to hire a carriage if you take me in yours."

MUKHERJI: "All right, sir, we shall set a day."

MASTER (*to the devotees*): "Do you think the Brāhmos will like me? They criticize those who believe in God with form."

Mahendra Mukherji wanted to go on a pilgrimage. He told Sri Rama-krishna so.

MASTER (*smiling*): "How is that? Do you want to go when the sprout of divine love has hardly come up? First comes the sprout, then the tree, then the fruit. We are so happy to have you here to talk to."

MAHENDRA: "I feel like visiting the holy places a little. I shall return soon."

It was about five o'clock in the afternoon. Sri Ramakrishna left his room. The devotees were walking in the garden. Many of them were about to leave.

The Master was conversing with Hazra on the north verandah. They were talking of Narendra's frequent visits to Annada, the eldest son of the Guhas.

HAZRA: "I hear that Annada is now practising austerity. He lives on very little food and eats rice once every four days."

MASTER: "Is that so? 'Who knows? One may realize God even by means of a religious garb.'"

HAZRA: "Narendra sang the āgamani."[10]

MASTER (*eagerly*): "How did he sing it?"

Kishori stood close by. The Master said to him, "Are you well?"

A little later the Master was standing on the west porch. Since it was autumn, he had put on a flannel shirt dyed with ochre. He asked Narendra, "Is it true that you[11] sang the āgamani?"

Accompanied by Narendra and M., Sri Ramakrishna walked to the em-bankment of the Ganges.

Narendra sang the āgamani:

> Tell me, my Umā, how have you fared, alone in the Stranger's[12] house?
> People speak so much ill of us! Alas, I die of shame!
> My Son-in-law smears His body with ashes from the funeral pyre
> And roams about in great delight;
> You too, along with Him, cover with ash your golden skin.
> He begs the food that He eats! How can I bear it, being your mother?
> This time, when He returns to claim you, I shall say to Him,
> "My daughter Umā is not at home."

[10] A class of songs invoking Durgā, the Divine Mother. According to Hindu mythology Durgā, or Umā, is the daughter of King Himālaya. She was married, against the will of Her parents, to Śiva, who roams in the cremation ground in the company of ghosts, smearing His body with ashes and living on alms. According to the terms of the marriage, Durgā was allowed to stay with Her parents three days each year. The Hindu women of Bengal look on Durgā as their own daughter. On the first day of the Durgā Pūjā they sing the āgamani to welcome the Divine Mother. The song is full of the tenderness and affection of a mother for her daugh-ter who is returning home from her husband's house after a long time.

[11] As a member of the Brāhmo Samāj, Narendra at that time did not believe in the gods and goddesses of the Hindu religion.

[12] Śiva, Umā's Husband.

Sri Ramakrishna stood listening to the song and went into samādhi. The sun was still above the horizon as the Master stood on the embankment in the ecstatic mood. On one side of him was the Ganges, flowing north with the flood-tide. Behind him was the flower garden. To his right one could see the nahabat and the Panchavati. Narendra stood by his side and sang. Gradually the darkness of evening fell upon the earth.

After Narendra and several other devotees had saluted the Master and left for Calcutta, Sri Ramakrishna returned to his room. He was absorbed in meditation on the Divine Mother and was chanting Her holy name.

Jadu Mallick had arrived at his garden house next to the Kāli temple. He sent for the Master. Adhar, too, had arrived from Calcutta, and he saluted Sri Ramakrishna. The Master asked Latu to light the lantern and accompany him to Jadu's garden.

MASTER (to M.): "Why didn't you bring Naran with you?"

M: "Shall I come with you?"

MASTER: "Do you want to come? Adhar and the others are here. All right, you may come. Will the Mukherjis also come with us? (To the Mukherjis) Come along. Then we can leave Jadu Mallick quickly."

The Master went to Jadu's drawing-room. It was a well furnished room, with everything spick and span. The lamps were lighted. Jadu was sitting with his friends and was playing with the children. Servants were in attendance. Smiling, Jadu welcomed Sri Ramakrishna, but he did not get up. He treated the Master as a friend of long acquaintance.

Jadu was a devotee of Gaurānga. He had just seen a performance of Gaurānga's life at the Star Theatre and told the Master about it. The Master listened to his account joyfully and played with the children. M. and the Mukherji brothers sat near him. In the course of the conversation Sri Ramakrishna told Jadu that Adhar had not been able to secure the post of vice-chairman of the Calcutta Municipality. Jadu said that Adhar was still young and could try for it again. At his request the Master sang a few songs about Gaurānga.

After the music was over, the Mukherjis were about to take their leave. The Master, too, was ready to go, but he was in an ecstatic mood. On coming to the porch he went into samādhi. The gate-keeper of the garden house was a pious man. Now and then he invited the Master to his house and fed him. Sri Ramakrishna stood there in samādhi, and the gate-keeper fanned him with a large fan. Ratan, the manager of the garden house, saluted the Master, and Sri Ramakrishna, returning to the consciousness of the relative world, greeted the manager and the gate-keeper, saying, "Nārāyana". Then, accompanied by the devotees, he went back to the temple garden through the main gate.

MASTER (to the Mukherjis, pointing to M.): "Please visit him often."

MUKHERJI (smiling): "Yes, henceforth he will be our teacher."

MASTER: "It is the nature of the hemp-smoker to make merry in the company of another hemp-smoker. He will not talk even to an āmir, but he will embrace a wretched hemp-smoker if he happens to meet one." (All laugh.)

It was about nine o'clock. The Mukherji brothers saluted the Master and went away. Adhar and M. sat on the floor in the Master's room while he talked to Adhar about Rakhal.

Rakhal was staying in Vrindāvan with Balaram. The Master had learnt from a letter about Rakhal's illness. He was so worried about him that two or three days earlier he had wept before Hazra like a child. Adhar had sent a registered letter to Rakhal but had received no reply.

MASTER (to Adhar): "Naran has received a letter from Vrindāvan. Why haven't you received a reply to yours?"

ADHAR: "I haven't yet heard from Vrindāvan."

MASTER: "M. has also received a letter from Vrindāvan."

They began to talk of Sri Ramakrishna's seeing a play, at the Star Theatre, about the life of Gaurānga.

MASTER (smiling): "Jadu told me that one could see the play very well from a one-rupee seat.[13] Very cheap! Once we were talking about going to Pānihāti. Jadu wanted me to go in a country boat with a whole crowd of passengers. (All laugh.)

"Formerly he liked to hear a little about God. But I don't see Jadu much nowadays. He is always surrounded by flatterers. They have spoiled him. He is a man of a very calculating nature. I would no sooner set foot in his house than he would ask me, 'How much is the carriage hire?'[14] I would say: 'You don't have to bother about it. You may give two and a half rupees.' That would keep him quiet." (All laugh.)

It was late. Adhar was about to depart. The Master asked M. to bring Naran with him.

[13] In spite of his great wealth, Jadu Mallick was very miserly.
[14] It is customary for a householder in India to pay the carriage hire of a holy man when the latter visits his house.